DICTIONARY OF MEDICAL ETHICS

DICTIONARY OF MEDICAL ETHICS

REVISED AND ENLARGED EDITION

[2nd edition]

Edited by A. S. Duncan
G. R. Dunstan and R. B. Welbourn

DARTON, LONGMAN & TODD
LONDON

First published in Great Britain in 1977
by Darton, Longman & Todd Ltd
89 Lillie Road, London SW6 1UD

© Darton, Longman & Todd 1977 and 1981

Revised and enlarged edition 1981

British Library Cataloguing in Publication Data

Dictionary of medical ethics. – 2nd ed.
1. Medical ethics – Dictionaries
I. Duncan, Archibald Sutherland
II. Dunstan, Gordon Reginald
III. Welbourn, Richard Burkewood
174'.2'03   R724

ISBN 0–232–51492–5

Phototypeset by Input Typesetting Ltd, London SW19 8DR
Printed in Great Britain by The Anchor Press Ltd
and bound by Wm. Brendon & Son Ltd,
both of Tiptree, Essex

Preface

The first edition of the Dictionary was well received and reviewed and we have been encouraged not to delay in offering a second edition. Helpful comments and suggestions reached us through various channels. Nearly all the entries have been revised, some extensively, and a significant number of new entries and cross-references have been added.

The objectives of the work have not changed and we therefore reproduce the Introduction from the first edition. On the other hand we feel that although happily there is increasing and more widespread debate on many of the moral dilemmas, we have been able as a result of our earlier experience to offer now a more definitive volume. This is because in large measure each contributor is recognized in his own field of interest and has given time to review his entry or entries in order to present up to date thinking on the subject. While the Dictionary is intended primarily for readers in the UK, an attempt has been made to cater for an international readership.

An important change is the introduction of two essays which form the basis of our thinking on the evolution of Medical Science and of Medical Ethics. In the first edition we simply started with the letter A. We now feel it would be helpful to the reader of whatever category to have these extended introductions to what is otherwise a book of reference. The references to the entries have been arranged in accordance with the 'Vancouver style'. All numbered references refer back directly to the text; those without numbers are suggestions for related reading.

Once more while thanking the contributors we should like to express our particular appreciation of the help given by our advisers. Sir Cyril Clarke and Professor Desmond Pond have again guided us in relation to entries in the field of genetics and psychiatry respectively. Dr Alastair Donald has for this edition not only contributed a number of short addenda on issues as they affect general practice but has also reviewed other entries and made helpful suggestions from the viewpoint of primary care. We gratefully acknowledge his help and also pay tribute to Mr John Rivers who was Executive Editor of the first edition and remains a contributor to this one. Our publisher, Mr John Todd, has taken a great personal interest in the work and has contributed to our discussions and thinking. The help of his assistant, Mrs Deborah Andrews, has been invaluable in the final preparation of the entries and Mrs Eileen Clark has also given devoted and very helpful service.

A. S. Duncan
G. R. Dunstan
R. B. Welbourn

Introduction
to the First Edition

A Dictionary may be simply 'a book dealing with the words of a language'* or it may be 'a book of information or reference on any subject or branch of knowledge'.* We hope that the present work will fulfil both of these functions. Members of the medical and allied professions and students in these disciplines require rapid access to a brief but authoritative statement on this or that subject which has moral or ethical implications. Sometimes they also require key references in the literature for deeper study of the subject and for the sources of research and philosophical thinking in relation to the particular topic. The entries and bibliographies are designed to supply this need.

Increasingly, however, there are other members of the community who need information about matters which are of widespread public concern but about which they cannot be expected to have knowledge or understanding without access to a source of information. Medical, biological and scientific progress has been so great and so rapid over the last quarter of a century that remedies and procedures undreamt of two or three decades ago are now available and even commonplace. With these new procedures have come new moral dilemmas and ethical problems. In some cases the progress has been so rapid that the innovators themselves have not had time to examine all the implications of the advances. An interdisciplinary approach to the problems generated is therefore timely.

Even more important is the fact that a much wider public than formerly is concerned and involved in these problems. Very many members of society in all countries now play their part in making decisions or recommendations which call for accurate background knowledge of issues which until recently were considered to be the business of the specialist rather than of the layman. Ministers of religion, teachers, social workers and counsellors of all types are expected to have knowledge of complex medical problems as they affect decisions by the individual. They may be required or feel constrained to enter the debate and to do so must start from a recognized data base of facts and arguments.

The general public are made aware of the problems through the press and other media but often lack a concise description of the issues involved.

The interest of an individual may stem from personal involvement of

* Shorter Oxford English Dictionary.

himself or his family. If he has read a brief account of the matter couched in lay terms he is better able to ask relevant questions of his medical adviser and to understand the answers given and their implications for his individual problem. Or he may not be involved personally; he may be an elected or appointed representative of the people, in a legislative assembly, in a regional or district council, on a health authority or a community or local health council, or a lay member of an ethical committee which considers medical research projects.

The health of the people is now the concern of the people as well as of the health professional. There are few health problems without ethical or moral implications. The problems range from the use of highly technical procedures which only the expert can fully understand to the everyday, but just as difficult, matter of allocation of resources. How much of the gross national product should be devoted to health? What are the relative priorities between health education and the care of the fit on the one hand and the services for the acutely ill or the disabled on the other? What is the cost-effectiveness of different types of research and indeed of different diagnostic or curative procedures? How can health and life itself be valued in monetary terms? The issues discussed in this book concern the whole community and it is the duty of every responsible member of society to have some knowledge and appreciation of the ethical problems related to health and health care in the widest sense. Some of these are socio-medical issues, and once the social dimension is admitted at all it is impossible to draw a clear line between topics that are admissible and those that are not. We believe that the ethics of medical practice cannot be kept within technical and professional limits and have therefore included consideration of the more important issues that involve both medicine and society as a whole.

Similarly it has not always been possible to draw a distinction between ethics in the general sense and the 'etiquette' of the medical profession which its rules and customs require. Matters of etiquette usually have a firm ethical basis which alone would justify their inclusion here, while variations in practice in different parts of the world are of increasing interest and relevance.

Often there is no clear single answer to a problem and we have endeavoured to ensure that biased views are not expressed or, if they are, to place before the reader alternative views expressed by either the same or a different contributor. This has entailed difficult decisions in the case of some entries.

This book is intended to provide a ready source of summary information and a guide to the best and most authoritative literature on different aspects and views of each of the items listed. The references quoted are, where possible, to books and papers which themselves contain extensive bibliographies.

A. S. Duncan
G. R. Dunstan
R. B. Welbourn

List of Contributors

*Page numbers of contributions appear in **bold** type at the end of each entry.*

List of Contributors

J. S. Calnan, FRCSE, FRCPE. Professor of Plastic and Reconstructive Surgery, Royal Postgraduate Medical School and Hammersmith Hospital, London. 121–3

R. Y. Calne, MA, MS, FRCS, FRS. Professor of Surgery, University of Cambridge. 435–9

The Revd A. V. Campbell, MA, BD, ThD. Department of Christian Ethics and Practical Theology, University of Edinburgh. 298–9

C. O. Carter, DM, FRCP. Professor of Clinical Genetics and Director, MRC Clinical Genetics Unit, Institute of Child Health, London. 181–6, 190

R. D. Catterall, FRCPE, FRCP. Director, Department of Venereology, The Middlesex Hospital, London. 396–7

Maurice Cranston, MA, BLitt, FSL. Professor of Political Science, London School of Economics and Political Science. 236–7

Sir John Crofton, MD, FRCP (Edin and Lond). Professor (Emeritus) of Respiratory Diseases, University of Edinburgh. 252–5, 439–41

Sir John Halliday Croom, FRCPE. Past President, Royal College of Physicians of Edinburgh. 77–80, 243

Sidney Crown, PhD, FRCP, FRCPsych. Consultant Psychiatrist, The London Hospital, London. 213–8, 364–8

James Cyriax, MD, MRCP. Formerly Orthopaedic Physician, St Thomas's Hospital, London. Visiting Professor of Orthopaedic Medicine, Rochester University, New York. 65, 315–7

D. Russell Davis, MD, FRCPsych. Professor (Emeritus) of Mental Health, University of Bristol. 104–9, 167–8, 291–3, 408–9

J. Duncan M. Derrett, DCL, LLD, PhD. Professor of Oriental Laws, School of Oriental and African Studies, University of London. 207–10

Hugh E. de Wardener, MBE, MD, FRCP. Professor of Medicine, Charing Cross Hospital Medical School, University of London. 193–4

Sir John Dewhurst, MB, FRCSE, FRCOG. Professor of Obstetrics and Gynaecology, Institute of Obstetrics and Gynaecology, Queen Charlotte's Hospital, London. 255–7

D. H. Dick, MA, MB, MRCPsych, DPM. Director, Health Advisory Service. 196–8

George Dick, MD, FRCP, FRCPath. Professor of Pathology, University of London. Honorary Consultant, Institute of Child Health; Assistant Director, British Postgraduate Medical Federation; Regional Postgraduate Dean, South West Thames Regional Health Authority. 243–6

James A. S. Dickson, FRCSE, FRCS. Consultant Paediatric Surgeon, Children's Hospital, Western Bank, Sheffield. 405–8

J. Dominian, MD, FRCPEd, FRCPsych, DSc (Hon). Consultant Psychiatrist, Central Middlesex Hospital, London. 273–9

Alastair G. Donald, MA, MB, ChB, FRCGP. Regional Adviser in

General Practice (South East Scotland). **81, 109, 205, 255, 429–33, 450– 1**

Sir John Donne. Chairman, South East Thames Regional Health Authority. **227–9**

A. S. Duncan, DSC, FRCPE, FRCSE, FRCOG. Professor (Emeritus) of Medical Education, University of Edinburgh. **75–6, 81, 279–81, 369–70, 428–33**

John W. Dundee, PhD, MD, FFARCS, MRCP. Professor of Anaesthetics, Queen's University of Belfast. **318–20**

Sir Derrick Dunlop, MD, FRCP, FACP. Formerly Professor (Emeritus) of Therapeutics and Clinical Medicine, University of Edinburgh. **326– 9**

J. F. Dunne, BSc, MB, PhD. Secretary, Committee on Research Involving Human Subjects, World Health Organization, Geneva. **458– 9**

J. Englebert Dunphy, MD. Professor (Emeritus) of Surgery, University of California School of Medicine, San Francisco, California. **144–5, 270–3**

The Revd Canon G. R. Dunstan, MA, Hon DD, FSA. Professor of Moral and Social Theology, King's College, London. **xxviii–xxxi, 6– 8, 27–30, 145, 154–5, 257–8, 266–8, 347, 384–5, 452–3**

The Rt Hon Lord Justice Edmund-Davies, PC, LLD. A Lord Justice of Appeal. **443–5**

J. H. Edwards, FRCP, FRS. Professor of Genetics, University of Oxford. **19–22, 297–8, 380–1**

R. G. Edwards, PhD, DSc. Physiological Laboratory, University of Cambridge. **152–3**

Kenneth T. Evans, FRCP, FRCR. Professor of Diagnostic Radiology, Welsh National School of Medicine, Cardiff. **141–2**

M. D. Arwyn Evans, MD, FRCS, FRCOG. Formerly Obstetrician and Gynaecologist, United Cardiff Hospitals and Welsh National School of Medicine. **240–2**

R. M. Fagley. Formerly Consultant to the Christian Medical Commission, World Council of Churches, and the International Planned Parenthood Federation, New York. **120–1**

C. M. Fletcher, CBE, MD, FRCP, FFCM. Professor (Emeritus) of Clinical Epidemiology, University of London (Royal Postgraduate Medical School). **87–93**

A. P. M. Forrest, MD, ChM, FRCS. Regius Professor of Clinical Surgery, University of Edinburgh. **47–9**

Richard Fox, MB, BS, MRCP, FRCPsych, DPM. Formerly Consultant Psychiatrist, Severalls Hospital, Colchester, Essex; Honorary Psychiatric Consultant to the Samaritans; UK Representative and First Vice-President, International Association for Suicide Prevention and Crisis Intervention. **31–2, 424–7**

List of Contributors

John Fry, OBE, MD, FRCS, FRCGP. General Practitioner, Beckenham, Kent. **178–81, 194–6**

C. S. B. Galasko, ChM, FRCS. Professor of Orthopaedic Surgery, University of Manchester. **94–6**

Charles F. George, BSc, MD, FRCP. Professor of Clinical Pharmacology, University of Southampton. **81–6, 329–31**

Ronald H. Girdwood, PhD, MD, FRCP, FRCPE, FRCPath, FRSE. Professor of Therapeutics and Clinical Pharmacology, University of Edinburgh. **286–8**

M. M. Glatt, MD, DSc, FRCP, FRCPsych, DPM. Honorary Consultant Physician, Department of Psychological Medicine, University College Hospital, London. **14–19**

Colin Godber, MPhil, BM, BCh, MRCP, MRCPsych. Consultant Psychiatrist (Psychogeriatrics), Southampton University Group Hospitals. **351–3**

Sir George Godber, GCB, DM, FRCP, DPH. Formerly Chief Medical Officer, Department of Health and Social Security. **202–5, 399–402, 412–7**

E. Grey-Turner, CBE, MC, TD, MD. Secretary, British Medical Association, 1976–9. **459**

John Gunn, MD, AcadDPM, FRCPsych. Professor of Forensic Psychiatry, Institute of Psychiatry, London. **172–5**

The Rt Revd John Habgood, MA, PhD, DD. Bishop of Durham. **66–71**

D. G. Harnden, PhD, MRCPath, FIBiol. Professor and Head of the Department of Cancer Studies, University of Birmingham. **71–3**

Peter Hebblethwaite, MA. Rome Correspondent, *The National Catholic Reporter*. **237–40**

Andrew Herxheimer, FRCP, MB, BS. Senior Lecturer in Clinical Pharmacology and Therapeutics, Charing Cross Hospital Medical School, London. **457–8**

Seitaro Higuchi, Associate, Teachers' Training School for Postgraduates, Chiba Prefecture, Japan. **397–9**

Walter W. Holland, MD, FRCP, FFCM. Professor of Clinical Epidemiology and Community Medicine, St Thomas's Hospital Medical School, London. **385–6**

Louis Jacobs. Rabbi of the New London Synagogue; Chairman, Academic Committee, Leo Baeck Training College for Rabbis. **263–4**

Bryan Jennett, MD, FRCS. Professor of Neurosurgery, Institute of Neurological Sciences, University of Glasgow. **128–30**

Sir Francis Avery Jones, CBE, MD, FRCP. Consulting Physician, Department of Gastroenterology, Central Middlesex Hospital; Consulting Gastroenterologist, St Mark's Hospital, and to the Royal Navy; Honorary Consulting Physician, St Bartholomew's Hospital, London. **86–7, 301–3, 343–6**

C. R. B. Joyce, PhD. Ciba-Geigy Ltd, Basle, Switzerland. **359–61**

I. M. Kennedy, LLM. Reader in English Law, King's College, London; Visiting Professor, School of Law, University of California, San Diego. **446–50**

François Lafitte. Professor of Social Policy and Administration, University of Birmingham. **334–6**

John G. McK. Laws, MA. Barrister-at-Law of the Inner Temple, London. **96–9**

Ian C. Lodge Patch, MD, FRCP, FRCPsych, DPM. Honorary Consultant in Psychological Medicine, Hammersmith Hospital, London. **151–2**

John A. Loraine, DSc, MB, PhD, FRCPEd, FRSE. Senior Lecturer, Department of Community Medicine, University of Edinburgh; Executive Director, Centre for Human Ecology, University of Edinburgh; formerly Director, MRC Clinical Endocrinology Unit, Edinburgh. **331–3**

John Lorber, MD, FRCP. Professor and Head of Department, Department of Paediatrics, University of Sheffield. **109–13**

Nancy B. Loudon, MB, ChB. Medical Co-ordinator, Lothian Health Board Family Planning and Well Woman Services. **117–19**

W. Lutz, MSc. Director, Medical Computing and Statistics Unit, University of Edinburgh. **103–4**

L. B. McCullough, PhD. Associate Director, Division of Health and Humanities, Department of Community and Family Medicine, School of Medicine, Georgetown University, Washington, D.C., and Senior Research Scholar, Center for Bioethics, Kennedy Institute of Ethics, Georgetown University, Washington, D.C. **246–8**

P. J. M. McEwan, MA, PhD. Editor-in-Chief, *Ethics in Science and Medicine*. **156–7**

The Revd T. Stewart McGregor, MA, BD. Former Chairman, Edinburgh District Local Health Council; Chaplain, Royal Infirmary, Edinburgh; Part-time Lecturer, Department of Christian Ethics and Practical Theology, University of Edinburgh. **199–202**

Donald McIntosh, MD, FRCS. Lately Consultant Surgeon, Royal Infirmary, Edinburgh. **282–5**

Dougal Mackay, BA, MSc, ABPsS. Principal Psychologist, St Mary's Hospital (Harrow Road), London. **33–6**

Ronald C. MacKeith, DM, FRCP, DCH. Formerly Physician, Children's Department and Director, Paediatric Teaching Department, Guy's Hospital, London. **51–5, 74–5**

Gordon McLachlan, CBE, BCom, FCA, LLD (Hon), FRCGP (Hon). Secretary, Nuffield Provincial Hospitals Trust, London. **307–8**

Una Maclean, MD, PhD, DPH, FFCM. Reader in Community Medicine, University of Edinburgh. **12–14**

List of Contributors

Ronald W. McNeur, PhD. Executive Director, Society for Health and Human Values, Philadelphia. **404–5**

Bertram Mandelbrote, FRCP, FRCPsych, DPM. Consultant Psychiatrist, Littlemore Hospital, Oxford. **293–5**

J. N. Mansbridge, PhD, FDS. Professor (Emeritus) of Preventive Dentistry, University of Edinburgh. **171–2**

J. K. Mason, CBE, MD, FRCPath, DMJ. Professor of Forensic Medicine, University of Edinburgh. **38–42, 125–7**

Major-General J. M. Matheson, OBE, TD, FRCSEd and Eng, FRCPEd. Postgraduate Dean, Faculty of Medicine, University of Edinburgh. **295–7**

Harold Merskey, DM, FRCP(C), FRCPsych. Director of Education and Research, London Psychiatric Hospital, London, Ontario; Professor of Psychiatry, University of Western Ontario, Canada. **347–51**

Surgeon Rear-Admiral Stanley Miles, CB, MSc, MD, FRCP, FRCS, MFCM, MFOM, DTM and H. Chairman, National Trauma Foundation; formerly Dean of Postgraduate Medical Studies, University of Manchester. **155–6**

David Mitchell, MA, MD, FRCP, FRCPI. President, The Medical Council, Dublin; Member of the Conférence Internationale des Ordres. **160–4**

Martin C. Mitcheson, MB, BChir, DPM. Consultant-in-Charge, Drug Dependence Clinic, University College Hospital, London. **146–50**

D. A. D. Montgomery, MBE, MD, DSc (hc NUI), FRCP, FRCPI. Chairman, Northern Ireland Council for Postgraduate Medical Education. Formerly Professor of Endocrinology, Queen's University of Belfast. **249–50**

The Revd E. Garth Moore, Fellow of Corpus Christi College, Cambridge; of Gray's Inn Barrister-at-Law; Chancellor of the Dioceses of Durham, Southwark and Gloucester; Chairman of the Legal Advisory Commission of the Church of England. **303–4, 346–7**

David C. F. Muir, MD, PhD, FRCP. Director, Occupational Health Program, McMaster University, Ontario, Canada. **313–4**

William W. Mushin, CBE, MA, FRCS, FFARCS. Professor (Emeritus) of Anaesthetics, Welsh National School of Medicine, Cardiff. **22–4**

P. R. Myerscough, FRCSE, FRCOG. Consultant Obstetrician and Gynaecologist, Royal Infirmary and Simpson Memorial Maternity Pavilion, Edinburgh. **55–9, 417–21**

Vivian Nutton, MA, PhD. Historian to the Wellcome Institute for the History of Medicine. **210–2**

Teizo Ogawa. Professor of Medical History, Juntendo University School of Medicine, Tokyo. **397–9**

S. G. Owen, CBE, MD, FRCP. Second Secretary, Medical Research Council, London. **374–7**

Colin Murray Parkes, MD, FRCPsych, DPM. Senior Lecturer, The

London Hospital Medical College; Honorary Consultant Psychiatrist to St Christopher's Hospice, London. **36–8**

Sir John Peel, KCVO, FRCP, FRCS, FRCOG. Past President, Royal College of Obstetricians and Gynaecologists. **169–71**

The Revd John Perryman, MA. Assistant Chaplain, St George's Hospital, London. **223–5**

G. E. Phalp, CBE, TD. Secretary, King Edward's Hospital Fund for London. **265**

Raymond Plant, BA, PhD. Professor of Politics, University of Southampton. **234–6**

A. R. W. Porter, MA. Secretary and Registrar, Royal College of Veterinary Surgeons, London. **24–6**

K. R. D. Porter, MBE, FRCP, LDSRCS, DPH. Formerly Regional Medical Officer, South East Thames Regional Health Authority. **252–5**

Ruth Porter, FRCP, MRCPsych. Deputy Director, The CIBA Foundation, London. **73–4**

Sir Idwal Pugh. Formerly Parliamentary Commissioner for Administration and Health Services. **205–7**

Donald D. Reid, MD, DSc, FRCP. Formerly Professor and Director, Department of Epidemiology, London School of Hygiene and Tropical Medicine. **103–9**

Philip Rhodes, MA, MB, BChir, FRCS (Eng), FRCOG, FACMA. Postgraduate Dean of Medical Studies, University of Southampton. **421–4**

The Rt Hon Lord Richardson, MVO, MD, FRCP. Past President, General Medical Council, London. **142–4, 176–8**

D. A. Ritchie, PhD, FIBiol, FRSE. Professor of Genetics, University of Liverpool. **186–90**

John Rivers. Formerly Managing Director, J. & A. Churchill Ltd, Medical Publishers. Executive Editor of the First Edition of the *Dictionary of Medical Ethics*. **44–6, 198–9, 250, 279**

D. F. Roberts, ScD. Professor of Human Genetics, University of Newcastle upon Tyne. **86, 157–60**

D. H. H. Robertson, MB, FRCP, DTM and H. Consultant Venereologist, Royal Infirmary, Edinburgh; Senior Lecturer, Department of Venereal Diseases, University of Edinburgh. **101–3**

John S. Robinson, MD, FFARCS. Professor of Anaesthetics, University of Birmingham. **250–2**

Richard Robinson, MA. District Manager, Christian Science Committees on Publication for Great Britain and Ireland, London. **65–6**

J. G. Robson, CBE, FFARCS. Professor of Anaesthetics, Royal Postgraduate Medical School, University of London. **8–10**

Joseph Rotblat, CBE, DSc, PhD, FInstP. Professor (Emeritus) of Physics, University of London. **258–60**

List of Contributors

Dame Cicely Saunders, DBE, MD, FRCP. Medical Director, St Christopher's Hospice, London. 218–23

P. D. Scott, CBE, MD, FRCP, FRCPsych. Formerly Consultant in Forensic Psychiatry, The Maudsley Hospital, London, and to the Home Office. 339–43

Alexander Shapiro, CBE, MD, FRCPsych. Formerly Consultant Psychiatrist to Harperbury Hospital, Consultant Psychiatrist in Mental Handicap to the Middlesex Hospital and the Royal Free Hospital, and Senior Lecturer in Mental Handicap at the Middlesex Hospital Medical School, London. 288–91

The Revd Prebendary E. F. Shotter, BA. Director of Studies, Society for the Study of Medical Ethics, London. 263, 405

Tony Smith, MD, BM, BCh. Medical Correspondent of *The Times*. 33, 212–3, 281–2, 381–2

Ronald Smither, BSc, CPA. Group Patents and Trademarks Controller, Beecham Group Ltd, Brentford, Middlesex. 321–3

Jean M. Snelling, MA, Cert Social Admin (LSE), Cert Inst Almoners (Lond). Head of Department of Applied Social Studies, Polytechnic of North London. 402–4

Faith Spicer, OBE, MD, MB, BS. Medical Director, London Youth Advisory Centre. 387–9

Patrick C. Steptoe, FRCSE, FRCOG. Formerly Consultant Obstetrician and Gynaecologist, Oldham Area Health Authority. 154

J. Leahy Taylor, MB, BS, DMJ, MRCGP. Secretary, The Medical Protection Society Ltd, London. 10–12, 30–1, 140–1, 304–7

William T. Thom, OBE, MBChB, DTM and H, FFCM. Director, Scottish Hospital Advisory Service. 196–8

Lt-Col Michael John Glyn Thomas, MA, MB, DTM and H. Chairman, Central Ethical Committee, British Medical Association. 44

W. W. Thomson, BSc, RGN, SCM, ONC, Dip Nursing Admin. Reg Nurse Tutor; Nursing Officer (Education), Scottish Office. 311–2

Ronald C. Tress, CBE, DSc, LLD, DSc (Soc Sci), DUniv. Director, The Leverhulme Trust, London. 266

R. G. Twycross, MA, DM, MRCP. Consultant Physician, Sir Michael Sobell House, The Churchill Hospital, Headington, Oxford. 164–7

Peter Tyrer, MD, MRCP, FRCPsych. Consultant Psychiatrist, Mapperley Hospital, Nottingham. 441–2

Paul U. Unschuld, PhD, MPH. Associate Professor, School of Hygiene and Public Health, Johns Hopkins University, Baltimore, Md., USA, and Lecturer at the University of Marburg, Germany. 59–65

Owen Lyndon Wade, MA, MD, FRCP, FRCPI (Hon). Dean of the Faculty of Medicine and Dentistry; Professor of Therapeutics and Clinical Pharmacology, University of Birmingham. 229–34, 336–8, 371–4

John Wallace, BSc, MD, FRCP (Glasgow), FRCPath. Clinical Scientist,

Medical Research Council Common Cold Unit, Harvard Hospital, Salisbury; formerly Regional Director, Glasgow and West of Scotland Blood Transfusion Service. **42–4**

Mary Warnock, MA. Talbot Research Fellow, Lady Margaret Hall, Oxford. **323–5**

The Revd Frederick Burkewood Welbourn, MA. Formerly Senior Lecturer in Religious Studies, University of Bristol. **167–8, 408–9**

R. B. Welbourn, MA, MD, Hon MD (Karolinska), FRCS, FCS (West Africa), Hon MRCS (Denmark). Professor of Surgical Endocrinology, Royal Postgraduate Medical School, University of London, and Hammersmith Hospital, London. **xviii–xxvii, 49–51, 285–6, 299–300, 320–1, 382–3, 408–9, 429–33, 442–3**

Rachel M. Welbourn, BDS. Member: International Association for Volunteer Education; Association pour le Volontariat à l'acte gratuit en Europe; Voluntary Braille teacher. **453–6**

Thomas S. West, OBE, MD. Deputy Medical Director, St Christopher's Hospice, London. **124–5, 433–5**

A. W. Wilkinson, ChM, FRCSE. Professor (Emeritus) of Paediatric Surgery, Institute of Child Health, University of London. **113–7**

F. D. K. Williams, CBE, MA. Director, The Linacre Centre, London. **268–9**

Michael Wilson, MD, MRCP, DTM and H. Senior Lecturer in Pastoral Studies, Theology Department, University of Birmingham. **225–7**

Medical Science
The scientific basis of medical practice

For many centuries practitioners of medicine, at least in the Western world, have accepted a moral obligation to serve their patients to the best of their ability (see *Hippocratic Oath; Hippocratic Tradition*) and in recent years the medical profession throughout the world has affirmed this principle repeatedly (see *Declarations*). Sympathy and the desire to heal and comfort those in physical or mental distress have always characterized the good physician, but worthy motives are not enough. The doctor must have knowledge of people in health and disease, practical skill in dealing with patients and judgement to enable him to use those resources of medicine which are most appropriate to the needs of each individual. He must, in fact, practise good medicine and today this requires him to have a thorough knowledge of medical science.

Until recent times two separate elements influenced medical practice. One consisted of ideas about life and death, the structure and function of the body, the nature of disease and the effectiveness of therapeutic procedures. Often these ideas were derived from primitive religion, superstition and magic, but sometimes, as in ancient Greece, they resulted from abstract thought of a high order. They contained such beliefs as that disease was a punishment for sin (see *Christianity; Hindu Medicine*), the result of evil spells (see *Exorcism*) or a derangement of hypothetical 'humours'. Treatment of illnesses, which included purging, starvation, bleeding, the application of leeches and the prescription of alcohol, often did more harm than good.

The second element was observation and description of the patterns of diseases and of the results of therapeutic procedures which had been found by experience to be effective. Two physicians, renowned for their clear descriptions of accurate observations, were the Greek, Hippocrates, who practised in the 5th century, B.C., and the 17th-century Englishman, Thomas Sydenham. Effective therapeutic measures, developed empirically, included opium for relieving pain (discovered 5,000 years ago in China), iron for anaemia, quinine for malaria, mercury for syphilis, digitalis for heart failure, surgical drainage of abscesses, mechanical reductions of fractures and dislocations, and cutting to remove stones from the bladder.

Both these elements are defective. The first suffers from the assumption that ideas do not require validation by experience, the second from a failure to recognize that observation, however extensive, does not lead to understanding, unless accompanied by ideas. Nevertheless, both can still be recognized in many quarters today.

Modern Western medicine as a whole, however, is distinguished by being based on science, that is on knowledge obtained by observation *combined with* ideas and reason. Observation is needed to find the facts of nature, while ideas and reason are required to discover what they mean. The scientist attempts, from observation of particular objects or events, to make abstract generalizations about them. Thus, the medical scientist may notice in the course of his work, and record carefully, certain features common to several individual patients, and conclude that they all suffer from some disease which has not been described before. Burkitt, Colles, Hodgkin and Parkinson are a few of the hundreds of well-known examples. The patients with their distinctive features are concrete facts, while the concept of the new disease is the abstraction which, if true, advances knowledge and assists in the diagnosis and treatment of other individual patients.

The scientific method of research, by which the truth of generalizations is tested, is a powerful intellectual tool and science's most distinctive feature. When facts have been discovered by observation, a hypothesis is proposed to explain them or to describe how they are related to other facts. A hypothesis is an idea or imaginative leap into the unknown. Its validity is tested by deducing, by formal logic, all the facts which must follow if it is true. Further observations are then planned and undertaken to discover whether or not they do. If any of the logical consequences do not follow, the hypothesis must be rejected and a modified or new one proposed. This in turn must be tested in the same way. Hypotheses can be proved false, but never true, even if the obvious logical consequences are confirmed, for several reasons. These are: (1) 'factual' observations are subject to error and often (as will be discussed later) describe statistical probabilities, not certainties, (2) new facts may come to light in the future which cause the hypotheses to be rejected, and (3) new ones may be proposed which provide better descriptions of the relationships between the facts. In scientific terms, therefore, truth is relative, not absolute, but the more often a hypothesis stands up to rigorous testing, the longer it can be retained and used as a basis for future work. Hypotheses which describe and unify large fields of knowledge are known as theories, e.g. the atomic theory, the theory of evolution, the theory of relativity and, in medicine, the germ theory of disease. When sufficient confidence is felt in the truth of a hypothesis, it may be used as a basis for action in, for instance, engineering, space travel or medical practice.

Observations are sometimes qualitative (that is of kind) and sometimes quantitative (of number). The latter are usually more accurate and informative, and scientists generally search in their material for things which they can measure. Measurements are then subjected to calculations, which form the basis of reasoning for the formulation of abstract generalizations. Mathematics is the most abstract form of science attainable, and often the most fruitful method of making progress in scientific generalization is to convert a problem into mathematical terms.

Frequently simple observation of a complex matter fails to provide the facts that are needed. Instead the observer must take a hand himself and create new situations by experiment. This means that he isolates factors, manipulates them one at a time and observes what then happens. Measurement and experiment are the scientist's most fruitful sources of knowledge and often demand elaborate equipment and sophisticated statistics and computing. These, however, do not make medical or any other research work scientific unless they are used to test hypotheses or to provide the bases of new ones. Indeed, at the other extreme, anyone who makes an observation, however simple, perhaps of a symptom or clinical sign, ponders on its meaning and then tests the truth of his ideas by further careful observations, is practising science and advancing knowledge.

Three creative concepts have been central to science at different stages in its development. These are the ideas of Order, Cause and Probability. They have not always followed each other in a regular fashion (and different branches of science have matured at different times), but each successive concept has embodied, modified and extended what preceded it.

The idea of Order, with Greek, Roman and Jewish origins, was developed to a high degree in the Middle Ages. It is based on the belief that the world is rational, uniform, reliable and predictable. An observation made by one person can be repeated and confirmed by another. In an ordered world things can be classified into groups, based on similarities and differences: men, women and children; infections, dyspepsias and tumours. Classification has been used extensively in medicine and probably always will be, because it is useful. It is, however, a primitive activity of science. It may employ irrelevant distinguishing characteristics, it emphasises qualitative rather than quantitative differences, and it creates artificial distinctions between normality and disease.

Medieval medicine, based on the idea of order, contained many errors and was wedded to an unquestioning reverence for authority, especially that of the Church. Scholars were concerned more with preserving the concepts of order that the old masters had taught than with discovery and new ideas. Galen, a Greek physician, who practised in Rome in the 2nd century A.D., dominated medicine through his writings for 15 centuries. He was authoritarian and, although ignorant of much, had a ready answer to every question. His prestige was such that men looked only for things which he had taught them and, when they could not see them because they were not there, thought that they themselves were at fault. This is an attitude of mind which most people consciously repudiate today but one which many still embrace. Late medieval speculation and the Renaissance of learning of the 16th and 17th centuries broke this authoritarian view. In medicine one of the first in the scientific revolution was Vesalius of Padua who, in the middle of the 16th century, dissected the human body for himself, described and drew what he saw and provided for the first time an accurate account of the anatomy of the human body.

The idea of Cause was explored philosophically by Aristotle 500 years B.C., but it was not until the Renaissance that much progress was made in elucidating causes and their effects. Pre-eminent in this field was William Harvey, an English physician of the early 17th century, who discovered the circulation of the blood. Previously it had been thought to ebb and flow separately in two main compartments, the arteries and the veins. The original observation, which had been made by others, was that the heart and the veins contained valves. Harvey had the idea that they allowed blood to flow in one direction only and formed the hypothesis that the heart was a pump, which forced the blood into the vessels, and that the valves allowed it to flow in one direction only. To test his hypothesis he collected evidence from animals and men. He observed directly, by experiment, the action of the valves in the veins and calculated from measurements that the amount of blood which passed through the heart in a short time was greater than that which the whole body contained. It seemed that these observations could be explained only if the blood circulated round the body in a continuous stream. Harvey's work was a milestone in the development of the scientific method, for never before had ideas, observation, reason, experiment, measurement and calculation been brought together so elegantly to elucidate causes and their effects.

Harvey's work accelerated understanding of the normal function of the body, but major advances in knowledge of the causes of disease remained dormant for 200 years when, in the middle of the 19th century, the French chemist, Louis Pasteur, and others discovered the causative role of bacteria in many diseases. For instance the British surgeon, Lord Lister, impressed by Pasteur's work, used an antiseptic agent to prevent the infection which usually complicated wounds and often proved fatal, and thereby made surgical operations safe. An example of the rigorous methods which were then used for the elucidation of cause and effect is the set of postulates which the German, Robert Koch, one of the founders of bacteriology, proposed for establishing the specificity of a particular organism as the aetiological agent in a disease. These are: (1) the organism should always be associated with the disease, (2) it must be isolated in a pure form from those suffering from the disease, (3) it should reproduce the disease when administered to a healthy, susceptible animal, and (4) it must be isolated in pure form from the animal so infected.

In therapeutics the same principles of establishing cause and effect combined with rational methods of combating disease have met with remarkable success. Scientists have learned how to make disciplined attacks upon one problem after another in bridging the gaps between existing scientific knowledge and their ultimate goals. In the present century Banting's and Best's successful search for insulin and its use in the treatment of diabetes, Fleming's casual but inspired discovery of penicillin, the subsequent development of other antibiotics and their use in many infectious diseases, the introduction of cardiac surgery and the transplanting of organs, and many other advances have changed the face of medicine. At the same time physics, chemistry, biology, engineering and other branches of science have grown up and reached maturity. So successful, in fact, have these ideas been in so many fields that some people have come to think that in time scientists will understand, predict and control everything completely.

Scientists themselves do not believe this today, because they have a new creative concept, that of Probability. Mathematicians started to develop probability theory in relation to games of chance in the 17th century, but it had little impact in biology and medicine until Gregor Mendel, the Austrian abbot, discovered 200 years later that, when he crossed tall and dwarf peas, he could predict the outcome only in statistical terms, namely that the chances of one particular offspring being tall or dwarf were 75 per cent and 25 per cent respectively. These statistical laws of probability were the same as those which governed the throw of dice. One of the recent discoveries of science is that the smallest units in any organized system – quanta, electrons, atoms, molecules, cells, individual animals and people – behave in a random or chance manner, and that it is only when they are observed in the mass that they exhibit the relationship of cause and effect.

This concept is a direct extension of the role of measurement in observation and has important implications for medicine. For example the blood pressures of people who are apparently normal show considerable random or chance variations, both in the same person at different times and in different people at the same time. Moreover, the blood pressure increases with age and is higher in women than in men. Some people, however, are hypertensive, that is their pressures are appreciably greater than normal and, if they are not treated effectively, may suffer serious consequences such as blindness, strokes and death. The old ideas of order, classification and measurement suggested that the normal blood pressure was constant and that anything higher constituted hypertension. It is now recognized that the ranges of pressure in normal and hypertensive individuals, which can be expressed in statistical terms, overlap considerably and that, when account is taken of all known influences, it is only possible to define the *probability* that a particular person is normotensive or hypertensive. Similar considerations apply to many other diseases, such as diabetes, in which there is a steady gradation and overlap between the chemical changes observed in normal people and in those who are frankly diabetic.

Human bodies are highly complex organisms, composed of many interacting chemical, physical and cellular systems, all governed by chance. External factors, such as weather, epidemics and hazards on the road vary in similar ways and chance plays a large part in deciding when and how people fall ill and whether or not they will recover. The aim of the medical scientist is not to discover causes and inevitable effects but, by the study of many people, to define as precisely as possible the probable course of events in each individual patient.

It is possible, for instance, to define from past experience the statistical probability that any one person will develop cancer of the lung within the next year. It is known that the chances are higher for men than for women and that they are greater for urban than for rural dwellers. They are highest for those who smoke cigarettes and the more cigarettes people smoke the greater are their chances of developing cancer. Moreover, if they stop smoking, the chances are quickly reduced. The precise causative roles of some of these factors may be established, and others may be found which influence the probability, but it will never be possible to eliminate the element of chance.

When a patient with hypertension, diabetes, cancer of the lung or any other form of disease is treated with drugs, a surgical operation, radiotherapy, or some other therapeutic measure, analysis of past experience will define the probable outcome – whether or not he will respond favourably, what complications may ensue, whether or not he will be cured or receive temporary amelioration only, how long he is likely to survive, and so on. But the outcome for the individual can never be predicted precisely.

Medical science today comprises a large body of knowledge derived from the ideas of order, cause and probability, won by the application of scientific method, and an incalculable amount remains to be learned in the future. Medical science is rooted firmly in biological science and draws freely on chemistry, physics, engineering and mathematics. Although it owes much to the study of other animals (see *Animal Experiment*), it concerns ultimately man in health and disease, so that human observation and experiment, rigorously controlled by scientific method, are vital to progress (see *Human Experiment*). The structure and function of the body have been clarified to a great extent down to the cellular, molecular and ionic levels. The causes, mechanisms and manifestations of many diseases have been elucidated and clues to the understanding of others are emerging. Mental illness (q.v.), which in the past has been regarded as different in kind from physical disease, is now recognized as susceptible to scientific study, and several forms (e.g. those caused by endocrine disease) have been found to have reversible organic causes. It is generally accepted that prevention is better than cure and, if aetiological factors in the environment or in the individual can be defined, appropriate measures at the administrative or at the personal level may be taken (see *Alcoholism; Drug Dependence; Fluoridation; Health Education; Tobacco Smoking*).

Therapeutic measures are not based on the primitive belief that every 'disease' has a 'cure' and every 'poison' an 'antidote', but on the analysis of disease processes – predisposing causes, aetiological agents and bodily reactions – and the rational application of measures to prevent, destroy or augment them respectively, in such a way that they predispose towards cure or the relief of distress. The effective available measures include drugs, surgical operations, radiotherapy, physiotherapy, manipulations, psychotherapy (q.v.) and various other procedures, many of which have been evaluated scientifically and all of which are susceptible to such assessment (see *Clinical Trials*). They require practical skills which must be learned and kept efficient by frequent use.

The clinician who is consulted by a sick patient has a different task from that of the medical scientist (see *Clinical Practice; Patients*). The latter's main purpose is to increase knowledge by making generalizations from the study of individual cases. The clinician's is to draw on his general knowledge to solve the problems of individual patients. There are, however, many clinical scientists who combine both roles and organize their work for patients in such a way that they provide care of the highest order and at the same time undertake research.

The clinician's first task is analytical and is based on his knowledge of medical science. Using skills which he has learned and acquired through practice, he gleans information from the patient and examines him physically. From his findings he forms ideas or hypotheses about the diagnosis and tests them by further questions and examination, by the use of special investigations in the laboratory, by X-rays and so forth. Often the diagnosis is made rapidly, sometimes it involves a large number of tests and a long period of observation, and occasionally no firm diagnosis can be made. It is important to appreciate that the word 'diagnosis' means much more than the naming of a disease or the attachment of a label. It implies, as its Greek roots suggest, a 'thorough knowledge' of the patient, his antecedents and his circumstances, the whole process of injury to the body and mind, the patient's response and the probable outcome in terms of health and life. The clinician's knowledge is almost certainly incomplete and possibly quite erroneous and, because of his scientific education, he should appreciate this. But many patients expect their doctors to be omniscient and to advise them accordingly. If doctors admit to uncertainty, their patients may lose confidence and consult others who pretend to know more, even if they actually know less. Doctors are well aware of the necessity to compromise between their understanding of the truth and what their patients need and want to know. There are times, therefore, when they quite ethically profess to more knowledge than they possess and when it would be unethical to tell the truth (q.v.) as they know it. At the same time they must retain their patients' confidence, accept full responsibility and be prepared to tell what they believe to be the full truth at the appropriate time.

The clinician's second task, which is imperative, whether he has made a diagnosis or not, is therapeutic. He must assess the patient's needs and the probable outcome of the various therapeutic measures available to him. He must decide, by the balancing of probabilities based on statistical knowledge and his sympathetic assessment of the individual patient, whether he can be cured of his disease. If he cannot, the doctor must assess his prospects of symptomatic relief from procedures of varying magnitude (see *Palliative Surgical Operations*). He must then exercise judgement in deciding what therapeutic measures to advise in the patient's best interests. The possibilities of therapy based on scientific knowledge are now so great that they run the risk of outstripping judgement. Often doctors are embarrassed, and people in general are affronted, by the achievements of modern medicine. Those whose lives have really run their course can be resuscitated, nearly half the body can be removed (see *Mutilation*), children with serious congenital deformities can be kept alive or half alive (see *Congenital Malformations; Spina Bifida*), and so on. The fact that such things are possible does not mean that they should be undertaken whenever they are feasible, either for the benefit of the individual or in the interests of society as a whole. Survival is not enough; what matters is a life worth living (see *Life, Prolongation of; Ordinary and Extraordinary Means*).

Who is to take decisions about these matters? In the past doctors tended to take them on their own, because they thought that they knew best. They must still play the major role because their patients trust them and they usually know best the probable results of alternative courses of action. But patients who are rational and responsible must be involved in making decisions about such important issues as major surgical operations (see *Clinical Autonomy; Communication; Consent*), because it is their lives which are at stake, and their families and others close to them must often be implicated also (see *Confidentiality*). Society as a whole is also involved in many ways. For instance, economic factors and lack of resources (q.v.) may prohibit the use of life-saving procedures which medical science has made possible. Different countries have different laws, and different groups of people, often for religious reasons, hold diverse views on such issues as abortion (q.v.), sterilization (q.v.), blood transfusion (q.v.), brain death (see *Death, Determination of*), transplantation (see *Tissue Transplant*) and artificial insemination (q.v.). In all such matters the doctor must exercise fine judgement in balancing the scientific resources with the needs and wishes of his patient and the freedom or constraints determined by society.

When the doctor decides that active curative measures are no longer in the patient's best interests, he must institute terminal care (q.v. and see *Hospices*). Scientific research, directed towards helping patients to die in a dignified way, in peace and free from pain, is at least as valuable as that which is intended to cure diseases. It is a neglected field of work but one in which some important contributions have been made in recent years.

While individual doctors must exercise judgement in using the resources of medicine most appropriate to each patient, governments and other organizations must often select those which are most suitable for particular countries or populations. Many developing countries are striving to introduce Western scientific medicine as an alternative to the primitive systems which have held sway for hundreds of years. Often public health measures and the establishment of a widespread simple form of primary medical care meet the basic needs of a large population more effectively than concentration on the provision of hospitals with highly specialized services (see *Chinese Medicine; Health Care Services; Resources*). In whatever way the resources are allocated, medical science is vital to all these forms of medical care and no one of them is necessarily more scientific than the others.

Many of the ethical aspects of medical science have been touched on already, particularly in the context of the doctor's relationship with his patients. Indeed it is impossible to discuss one without reference to the other. There are, however, some other general principles which must be considered. Medical science provides the surest basis of knowledge which man has developed for the practice of medicine, and the scientific method allows the advance of knowledge by the introduction and rigorous testing of radically new ideas. It is, therefore, the standard by which other systems of medicine must be judged. For instance, osteopathy (q.v.), chiropractic (q.v.), homoeopathy (q.v.), Christian Science (q.v.), acupuncture (q.v.) and other forms of 'fringe' medicine (q.v.) are based on principles which, although susceptible to scientific scrutiny, are not so tested by their proponents, as are the hypotheses of scientific medicine. Their practitioners, who are full of confidence, often help patients greatly, sometimes when orthodox (scientific) doctors have failed, but they do so by using skills whose success is based on empiricism. These systems cannot make progress, except in small details, because they are closed and their advocates are not receptive to new ideas.

Medical science provides much of the framework of modern medicine. Doctors must therefore be thoroughly grounded in it if, as they are morally obliged to do, they are to serve their patients to the best of their ability. People in general are entitled to know the possibilities and the limitations of medical practice and they will appreciate these best if they understand the principles of its scientific basis. Any discussion of medical ethics, either in general or in relation to specific issues, must start with full knowledge of the scientific aspects of the matter under consideration.

Further Reading

Bernard C. *An introduction to the study of experimental medicine*. New York: Dover, 1957. (First published 1865).

Bronowski J. *The common sense of science*. Harmondsworth: Penguin Books, 1960.

Butterfield H. *The origins of modern science: 1300–1800*. London: Bell, 1968.

Dollery C. *The end of an age of optimism: medical science in retrospect and prospect*. London: Nuffield Provincial Hospitals Trust, 1978.

Dudley HAF. The clinical task. *Lancet* 1970; 2: 1352–4.

Garrison FH. *An introduction to the history of medicine*. Philadelphia: Saunders, 1929.

Medawar PB. Two conceptions of science. In: *The art of the soluble.* London: Methuen, 1967: 113–28.

Medawar PB. Hypothesis and imagination. In: *The art of the soluble.* London: Methuen, 1967: 131–55.

Paton W. Ends, means and achievement in medical research. *Lancet* 1979; 2: 512–6.

Pickering G. Physician and scientist. *Br Med J* 1964; 2: 1615–9.

Popper KR. *The logic of scientific discovery.* London: Hutchinson, 1972.

Thomas DP. Experiment versus authority: James Lind and Benjamin Rush. *N Engl J Med* 1969; 281: 932–4.

Wangensteen OH, Wangensteen SD. *The rise of surgery: from empiric craft to scientific discipline.* Folkestone, Kent: Dawson, 1978.

Welbourn RB. Science and surgery. *Aust N Z J Surg* 1979; 49: 179–86.

Whitehead AN. *Science and the modern world.* Cambridge: University Press, 1943.

Wightman WPD. *The growth of scientific ideas.* Edinburgh: Oliver and Boyd, 1951.

Woodruff M. *On science and surgery.* Edinburgh: University Press, 1977.

R. B. Welbourn

Medical Ethics

By medical ethics we mean the obligations of a moral nature which govern the practice of medicine. They are the common possession of the medical profession, and members are expected, both by fellow-doctors and by the society in which their patients are found, to adhere to them. Indeed, the possession of a corporate ethics, or standard of practice, is one of the essential marks of a profession as we know it. R. K. Merton listed three 'social values' in his concept of a profession:

> First, the value placed upon systematic knowledge and the intellect: knowing. Second, the value placed upon technical skill and trained capacity: doing. And third, the value placed upon putting this conjoint knowledge and skill to work in the service of others: helping. It is these three values as fused in the concept of a profession that enlist the respect of men.[1]

Professional ethics subordinate the 'knowing' and the 'doing' to the 'helping'; they govern the relationship between practitioner and client. Their purpose is to create and maintain trust: the client's trust in the practitioner, practitioners' trust in one another, and the trust of society as a whole in the profession corporately. It is the responsibility of the profession to develop its ethics to accommodate new demands and circumstances not encountered before; to transmit its ethics to each new generation of practitioners; to help and sustain its members in the practice of their profession; and to discipline them when, by unethical conduct, they deny to their clients the standard of service they may properly expect, or violate trust, and so damage public confidence in the profession as a whole.

These general statements about a profession are readily applicable to the profession of medicine (see *Clinical Practice*). The knowledge characteristic of the profession is medical science (q.v.); the skills and trained capacities derive from the application of that knowledge to human beings vulnerable in their physical, mental and emotional nature; the manner of help given is conditioned by a fundamental belief that the respect due to human beings is not diminished by their dependency, their 'client' status, their human need.

The ethics of medicine, then, are a corporate possession exercised by each member personally. The ethics are as old as the profession itself. In

Western civilization the history goes back to the Hippocratic tradition (q.v.), itself eclectic. The philosophical and practical tradition was incorporated into the main religious cultures of the West, notably Judaism, Christianity and Islam, on each of which entries appear in this Dictionary by name. In other cultures medicine took different courses: see for instance, the entries on African medicine, Buddhism, Chinese medicine, Hinduism and Shinto. The spread of Western medicine, however, both as science and as practical skill, carried with it ethical values as well – which, because they are essentially human values, were readily absorbed into the medical ethics of other cultures. There are differences of detail, of course, as readers of the relevant entries will perceive; but little difference in principle: medicine is now largely 'Hippocratic' in its ethics all the world over.

It is for this reason that it has been possible to draw up and to promulgate Declarations on various aspects of medical practice which doctors all over the world can subscribe, and which can be appealed to as authoritative by a public which needs to know what it may properly expect of their doctors. They are all loosely derived from and extensions of the so-called Hippocratic Oath (q.v.). The impulse to their formulation was given by the Nuremberg Tribunal, which set down the ethical standards which Nazi doctors had notoriously transgressed. Their promulgation has been the work of international professional associations, like the World Medical Association or the World Psychiatric Association. These documents are quoted, under Declarations, in chronological order. National Medical Associations, bodies corporate of specialists within the profession, like the Royal Colleges (q.v.) in Britain, and particular councils like the Medical Research Council (q.v.), also issue codes of practice for the guidance of their own constituencies.

Declarations and codes are necessarily general statements of principle. They are not rules, applicable in all circumstances, for infringement of which a practitioner is liable to penalty. They embody the standards by which each practitioner should inform his conscience, his capacity for moral reasoning, and so govern himself in his practice. Some principles are given legal embodiment in the form of laws – in statute law, for instance, or legal codes of practice, or terms of contractual relationship. These are sanctioned at law by penalty or legal enforcement (see *Disciplinary Procedures*). Some are embodied in what are more properly called rules of etiquette, internal rules by which the profession, in its various constituencies, regulates its own internal life (see, e.g., *Advertising*). Most, however, are carried in the practitioner's own professional consciousness: they become as 'natural' to him as morality is to man. (The motto which William of Wykeham gave to his twin foundations, Winchester College and New College Oxford, *Manners makyth man*, means precisely this, that man is constituted by his moral capacity – not by what we now call 'good manners'). This does not mean that medical practice can always be by rule of thumb, by an habituated routine: some occasions call for fine decision, and the practitioner's professional training and experience should prepare him for them.

Most of these 'occasions' are the subjects of entries in this *Dictionary*. They are never divorced from the empirical features of the particular case: from, in short (to take the three 'values' set out above as the mark of a profession) the actual state of 'knowledge', the range of available 'skill', and what is calculated to be of 'help' to the patient. So there may be a calculation of risk against benefit – and this can sometimes involve a demanding statistical exercise, involving knowledge and reasonable prediction across a wide range of body systems: the more invasive and far-reaching is the intervention, the more widely must risk and benefit be calculated. There may well be a choice between administering a remedy known to be specific to a particular ill or withholding it because not appropriate to a particular patient. There may well be conflicts of claims, as between a patient's wishes and his interests as the doctor sees them; or between duty to patient and duty to society (see, e.g. *Confidentiality; Notification*); or between what a patient asks for and what a doctor's conscience may forbid him to provide (see, e.g. *Abortion; Contraception*); or between an established procedure indicated by the patient's condition and a refusal of it indicated by the patient's religious belief (see, e.g., *Blood Transfusion; Jehovah's Witnesses*). In these and other cases the doctor, as the responsible and capable moral agent, has to make up his mind and act as he thinks right, taking into account any relevant law, the general guidance of the Declarations and other professional codes and, no doubt, the good advice of his colleagues.

Conscience is a tricky concept in such matters. The doctor has his own conscience to keep – and it were well for patients to be more aware of this sometimes. There is a corporate conscience, of a sort, in his profession, of which he is custodian. The society in which he works forms its own conscience – even more roughly – and changes it with embarrassing impetus, though never without controversy and division: witness the highly emotive debates on abortion in Western Europe and North America in recent decades. The patient, finally, has a conscience and may choose to follow it in rejecting a proffered medical procedure. His right to do so, even though he might die as a result, is recognized in ethics and in law under the principle of consent (q.v.). Even on the allowance due to consent, however, different strains within the moral tradition lay different emphases. Orthodox Judaism, because of its belief that every moment of human life is infinitely precious, limits very strictly a Jewish patient's right to refuse a procedure which would prolong his life, until the process of dying has clearly and irreversibly begun. In the Roman Catholic and general Hippocratic traditions, however, consent is paramount because of the respect due to every human being in his own moral autonomy; so, in this tradition, the patient's conscience rules, provided that the consequences are for him alone, without threat to the interests of others.

Decisions would sometimes be easier for the doctor if he had only one principle to be applied at a time; he might read off from it a course of action with relative ease. But that luxury is not always allowed him. A cluster of principles may be relevant to a particular decision. It might be easier to decide between conflicting interests, between, say, that of a patient in having his confidence kept and that of society in the doing of justice, if either or both of them were not complicated by matters of principle. But the doctor is bound *qua* doctor to the principle of keeping confidences and *qua* citizen to the principle that justice should be done. He may therefore be stretched between two conflicting principles, from which, whether he likes it or not, the process of law may insist on delivering him. Sometimes his action may be misconstrued by attachment to the wrong principle. If, for instance, a prisoner goes on hunger strike, the prison doctor is forbidden to feed him forcibly, even though the prisoner might die. This restraint comes from a recognition, not of a supposed right of suicide (for suicide is a mere liberty, not a right) but of a genuine right not to be treated medically without consent: forcible feeding without consent is an assault. It is in the social interest, as well as the doctor's, to keep the relation of rules or actions to principles, so far as possible, unconfused. And since ethics represent *mutual* expectations, what rational people may reasonably expect of one another in common situations, the ethics of medical practice must be matched by an ethics of patient practice: the lay public has obligations to its doctors which are not, perhaps, sufficiently brought to mind.

It is not to be thought that a doctor's life, from moment to moment, is thus burdened with decision. Normally, because of the commitment of his personality to his profession, his ethics are 'part of him': he makes what he calls medical judgments without isolating or reflecting on the ethical ingredient inherent in them. He would probably say that his aim is 'to do his best for the patient'. But that simple avowal has a basic, perhaps *the* basic, principle hidden within it. It means that the doctor, for all his attachment to medical science ('knowledge'), for all the possibilities opened to him by medical technology and pharmacology ('skill'), knows that these must be subordinated to 'help' – to offering his patient a management specific to him in his present condition and particularity, and not specific to a medical condition irrespective of the human being in whom it is found. The proper concern of ethics is with man. That is axiomatic, whether or not one goes further and adds that the ultimate concern of man is with God.

1. Merton RK. Some thoughts on the professions in American society. *Brown University Papers* XXXVII: 9. Quoted, without date, in Emmet D. *Rules, roles and relations*. London: Macmillan, 1966: 162n.

G. R. Dunstan

A

Abortion. The termination of a pregnancy, either spontaneously or by intervention before the fetus reaches viability. In the UK a fetus is legally viable at the age of 28 weeks from the first day of the last monthly period, but in keeping with the practice in other countries, steps are now being taken to reduce the accepted age of viability to a lower level. A child born alive at any age is counted as live born and an attempt to kill it would constitute murder or manslaughter.

Spontaneous abortion of an intrauterine pregnancy is common and occurs in at least 20 per cent of all pregnancies. In lay parlance the word miscarriage has been preferred, the term abortion generally being thought to indicate a deliberate act. Medical usage does not normally include this distinction and abortion is the usual term used to cover both accidental and intentional interruption of pregnancy, although the word termination is often used for the intentional act. The causes of abortion are many and sometimes no cause can be established. Studies in recent years have shown that in many cases pregnancy occurs without the development of an embryo, the so-called 'blighted ovum'; in these cases abortion of the fruitless pregnancy will occur in due course. Studies of chromosomes in cases of spontaneous abortion have shown gross abnormalities in a significant proportion. The normal human number is 46 but in spontaneously aborted material there may be 69 (triploidy) or 92 (tetraploidy). These abnormalities are incompatible with the birth of a normal child.

Induced abortion may be criminal or therapeutic. It has a long history and was almost certainly practised by prehistoric peoples. In most civilizations it has been an offence; in Western Europe it has been a criminal act under the laws of both Church and State. It first became a statutory crime in England and Wales in 1803 (after a long history as an offence against Canon Law) but was not controlled in Scotland until the Abortion Act of 1967 came into force. The Offences Against the Person Act, 1861, laid down that an abortion however and whenever induced (by the woman herself or by another) is a felony punishable by life imprisonment.

Criminal abortion has been attempted or achieved by various means, all of them dangerous. Drugs of several types were formerly sold, often as 'female pills', but to be effective they had to be taken in near fatal doses; local interference by means of household implements

1

inserted into the uterus was commonly practised, but these might perforate the uterus or vagina with disastrous results. Douching under pressure with solutions of soap or antiseptics was employed; these, or air, might enter the blood stream with fatal results. 'Back street' abortions were often done by women with little or no training; often their financial gain was insignificant and their motive seemed to be to help their fellow women in distress. Various assessments of the number of criminal abortions in Great Britain before the Abortion Act, 1967 (which does not apply to Northern Ireland) ranged from 20,000 to 100,000 annually. The best indices are the number of women admitted to hospitals suffering from incomplete or septic abortions, some illegally induced, and the mortality from abortion.

In the latest Report on Confidential Enquiries into Maternal Deaths in England and Wales (1979)[1] dealing with the years 1973 – 1975 it is noted that for the first time since 1955 abortion was not the most frequent cause of maternal death. This reflects not only the decline in criminal abortion but also the fact that with experience legal abortions are being performed more skilfully and under better conditions.

Therapeutic abortion is artificial termination of pregnancy in the interest of the mother's life or health. Doctors have not hesitated to terminate pregnancy when there was a risk to maternal life. In the Bourne case (1938) the judge held that it was not unlawful to terminate the pregnancy of a 15-year-old girl pregnant as the result of rape by several soldiers in that her life, in the sense of her mental well-being, was at risk if this were not done, a *ratio* brought into the law of abortion from the Infant Life Preservation Act of 1929. This defined the offence of child destruction.

Up to the 12th or 13th week of pregnancy, termination is most often performed by dilating the cervix and removing the products of conception with a curette, or preferably with an apparatus which sucks them out of the uterus. After 13 weeks termination is more difficult, more dangerous and more distasteful for all concerned. Abortion may be induced with drugs and prostaglandins are those most often used; injections of solutions of saline or urea or glucose into the amniotic sac (the fluid surrounding the fetus) are also used in some hospitals. After induction of abortion curettage is usually necessary to ensure that the uterus is empty. Another method for terminating relatively late pregnancies is to perform hysterotomy; this is a miniature Caesarean operation when the uterus is opened and the products of conception removed; this has been shown to carry a greater risk than the other methods described.

The Abortion Act of 1967 (in fact the sixth such Bill to be introduced into the British parliament) arose from disquiet at the problems of the maternal death rate and long-standing ill-health following recourse to 'back-street' abortions, particularly when it was contrasted with the ease with which the rich could obtain abortion in safer circumstances if they could engage a co-operative operator and an accommodating psychiatrist. There was also justifiable anxiety at the squalor and hardship in which unwanted children were brought up by poverty-stricken women in ill-health. The questions of the impregnation of young girls and of the victims of rape and incest were also raised. Additional factors in the increasing demand for abortion are: public concern about overpopulation; greater frankness on sexual matters; weakening of traditional religious, moral and ethical beliefs; permissiveness among the young leading to an increased pregnancy rate among teenagers; higher expectations (especially among young married couples) of material welfare and possessions which have made large families unacceptable to the majority; scientific advances in the antenatal diagnosis of congenital abnormalities; improved and safer techniques of operations for termination of pregnancy. Since 1971 family planning and sterilization have been, at least in theory, freely available to all. The result has been a fall in the birth rate which has been most notable in Social Classes IV and V (partly skilled and unskilled manual workers) but less marked in Social Classes I and II (professional and executive workers).

The Act declares abortion to be no offence when two registered medical practitioners certify in good faith that the continuance of the pregnancy would constitute a risk to the life or health of the pregnant woman or to the health of her existing children greater than if the pregnancy were terminated. Termination may also be carried out if there is a risk that the child if born would suffer serious physical or mental handicap. Termination of pregnancy under the Act must be notified to the Chief Medical Officer by the operating doctor. In reaching a decision the practitioners may take into account the woman's total environment, actual or reasonably foreseeable. The Act became operative in 1968 and the immediate effect was the notification of very large numbers of legal abortions but a significant decrease in abortion mortality. Numbers of private clinics were set up which led to some scandals on account of the high fees charged, the commercial exploitation, the number of foreign women coming to Britain for abortion and the touting for custom by taxi drivers and by doubtful referral agencies. On the other hand the charities, the Pregnancy Advisory Service (q.v.) and the British Pregnancy Advisory Service, sought to care for women seeking abortion for a reasonable fixed fee and in satisfactory clinical conditions. They also provided a much-needed counselling service and relieved the pressure on the already strained National Health Service. Many, including the author, believe that legalized abortion as provided for in the Act has benefited thousands of women and prevented many illegal, squalid, 'back street' abortions.

However, the Act in operation has seemed to others to be too liberal and abortion too easy to obtain and this has caused considerable disquiet among anti-abortionists as shown by the support for groups such as the Society for the Protection of the Unborn Child (SPUC) and Life. There have been several attempts to bring in amending legislation, the most recent being the Corrie Bill, which was withdrawn (1980).

RELIGIOUS OPINIONS. The Roman Catholic Church is opposed to abortion. The papal encyclical *Humanae Vitae* (q.v.) re-asserted the prohibition of all interference with procreation and directly-willed abortion, even for therapeutic reasons. The Church of England Board for Social Responsibility[2] concluded that abortion should not be refused in all circumstances though the intention of the moral tradition was to uphold the inviolability of human life and the burden of proof lay with those who would terminate it. The Methodist Church expressed broadly the same view.

Judaism (q.v.) although generally against abortion does not preclude it when there are strong medical and social indications. In Islamic Law (q.v.) abortion is less strictly prohibited.

There is evidence that religion, at least in Britain, is not always a strong factor in the woman's decision to seek abortion and that Roman Catholics are not much less likely to do so than others. The decision may lead to a crisis of conscience in the individual.

LEGAL, SOCIAL AND MEDICAL CONSIDERATIONS. Although the Abortion Act (1967) provides legal abortion under certain well-defined conditions in Britain, it has been pointed out by Tunkel (1979)[3], a lawyer, that the total legal position is far from clear. He pointed out that the position regarding menstrual extraction (when the contents of the uterus are aspirated at or shortly after the time when a period is due), the post-coital insertion of an intrauterine contraceptive or the position when an aborted fetus lives have not been satisfactorily resolved from the legal viewpoint. Legal abortion has undoubtedly contributed to the decline in the birth rate in Britain which in 1978 reached its lowest level in modern times, but the wider use of contraception, especially the pill, and sterilization have also contributed. The number of legal abortions notified in resident women has remained fairly constant at about 100,000 per year. The numbers of foreign women coming here for abortion has tended to decline as other countries have introduced more liberal abortion laws. In 1978, these women came mainly from Italy, Spain and the Republic of Ireland.

Abortion has been legal in Eastern Europe for many years and in some countries, e.g. Hungary, the number of legal abortions has exceeded the number of live births. This is partly because contraceptives have been less readily available and abortion has come to be used as a method of family limitation and of population control. Most countries in Western Europe, including Great Britain, and some of the United States, have introduced relatively liberal abortion laws; France has had legal abortion for several years and an abortion law was recently passed in Italy.

It is disappointing that, in spite of freely available contraception and sterilization, the number of legal abortions notified in Britain remains static. The effects of the operation both physical and psychological may be deleterious and may be too lightly discounted when decisions to proceed to abortion are taken. It is generally agreed that abortion should not be used as an alternative to a responsible attitude to sexual matters or to the proper use of contraception or, when indicated, male or female sterilization.

There are differences of opinion on the factors which should influence a decision for abortion. Those who favour abortion on demand believe that only the woman herself should decide, but this was rejected for Britain by the Lane Committee [4] on the grounds that it would reduce abortion to a mere commercial transaction and that women with unplanned or unwanted pregnancies would not receive the help or counselling they need. Panels and referees were also rejected in Britain (but not in some other countries) because women appearing before them might seem to be on trial, while those who did not appear might not accept the findings of enquiries made in their absence. The decision whether or not to perform the operation lies in the event with the operating doctor and the Lane Committee recommended that abortion should remain a medical matter and that doctors should continue to make the decisions. They may be assisted by others familiar with the woman's condition. The medical team should not fail in their duty to give careful help and advice. The danger must be realised of pressure being put on the woman, especially by her near kin who may see themselves disadvantaged by the pregnancy or simply because facilities exist, particularly in the private sector where commercial considerations may also apply. There the advice given is almost invariably in favour of abortion. The fact that abortion can now be procured with relative ease may influence a woman to seek abortion when she would not otherwise have done so. There are particular problems of confidentiality (q.v) when girls under the age of 16 seek termination of pregnancy.

The Abortion Act, (1967), provides that no one who objects on the grounds of conscience has to take part in operations to terminate pregnancy; this may apply to terminations in all circumstances or to individual cases. When the Act first became law doctors were divided on this issue. Surveys have shown that general practitioners tended to take a more liberal view than gynaecologists. Some nurses and other hospital staff expressed disquiet at abortions taking place in NHS hospitals.

After more than ten years, many of the problems appear to have eased. Anxieties about deprivation of other gynaecological services have been lessened by the fact that many early abortions are done as day cases and by the fact that, for other reasons, duration of hospital stay in general gynaecology has been reduced. Many of the hospital staff who had strong feelings about abortion have left or gone to other work. There may be problems with medical staff in smaller hospitals and there have been complaints that gynaecologists were not appointed to senior posts because of their objection to abortion.

A more serious complaint is the difficulty that women may find in obtaining abortions in the National Health Service because of a lack of local facilities; statistics of notification have shown that in some regions women have often been forced to travel many miles to get an abortion.

At present over 50 per cent of all legal abortions notified in Britain are performed outside the National Health Service, mainly by the charities. In view of the present constraints on the Service they may be held to have performed a useful service at low cost (necessitous women receive treatment free) and they do provide a service of counselling and after-care.

A new dimension to the abortion problem has arisen in recent years since it has become possible to study the unborn fetus and to detect certain serious abnormalities likely to lead to handicap in the child. One example is rubella (German measles) long known, if contracted early in pregnancy, to lead to disabilities of sight and hearing, to heart disease and mental handicap. Infection with rubella can now be detected and the mother, if appropriate, offered termination of her pregnancy. Congenital defects of the central nervous system may be detected, though not before the 16th week, by estimation of alpha-fetoprotein (see *Amniocentesis*) and by ultrasound scan. The diagnosis of Down's syndrome (*Mongolism*, q.v.) and certain other abnormalities can be made by amniocentesis and culture of fetal cells. Some units offer this for all mothers over the age of 35. These tests carry a small risk of abortion and the results may not be clear cut. But the public is coming to insist that where possible a handicapped child is not born. This raises important ethical and legal questions. Certainly amniocentesis to detect a fetal abnormality should not be done without adequate explanation to the parents or without their agreement that if such an abnormality is found, termination of pregnancy will be performed albeit at a relatively late stage of pregnancy, 18 to 20 weeks, or even later.

Josephine Barnes

GENERAL ETHICAL CONSIDERATIONS. Recent controversy and attempts to legislate in several countries have polarized the debate into two extreme positions, neither of which carries universal consent in the medical profession, or in the general view. In one the fetus is regarded as physically a part of a woman's body which she is free to excise at will; her 'right' to decide whether or not to bear a child conceived in her is absolute, so that it can override all rights incompatible with it; this view is prominent in 'women's liberation' propaganda. At the other extreme the fetus is invested with an absolute right to life, so that no consideration could prevail to secure its termination. Roman Catholic teaching comes near to this position, in that it forbids any *direct* killing of the fetus, even to safeguard the life of the mother. It does not, however, condemn an unavoidable death of a fetus indirectly occasioned by a surgical operation necessarily directed towards another end, e.g. the removal of a cancerous uterus or of a Fallopian tube containing an ectopic pregnancy (the principle of double effect (q.v.)).

In between is a position which seems more consistent with the tradition of medical ethics, and with the law and ethics on the safe-guarding of life in general. It may be named the ethics of 'justifiable feticide', by analogy with 'justifiable homicide'. The Western ethical tradition does not place an *absolute* value on human life – for that would imply that no life might ever be taken, and that every life must be prolonged so far as possible by every available means. It places a *very high* value on human life, with a presumptive right to protection so strong that anyone who violates that right, or fails to protect it, has to justify his action or non-action before appropriate legal tribunals. Self-defence is a sufficient justification or defence to a charge of homicide, when no less drastic remedy was available, and when no more force was used than was necessary to deter the aggressor. The defence remains good whether the aggressor be 'guilty' or 'innocent' – incapable, for instance, of forming a guilty intent because of diminished mental incapacity. An ethics of 'justifiable feticide' would, by analogy, permit the killing of a fetus as an aggressor (albeit innocent) against a vital interest of the mother in her life and health (if seriously imperilled), no less drastic remedy being available.

Such a defence would not cover abortion to avert inconvenience, social or economic, because, in all but the poorest and most over-populated of countries, less drastic remedies should be available. The plea that abortion be offered as a remedy when the family's cohesion and survival as a unit are at risk comes into this category. Such a family may need social or economic support, a new environment, or all three. Abortion should not be relied on to relieve us of the effort of providing the proper remedy. Neither would the formula of 'justifiable feticide' cover abortion for the avoidance of congenital handicap, for this is undertaken, presumably, in the interest of the child itself on the supposition that it were better for it not to live than to live grossly malformed. For this, however, another defence is entertained, again in relation to an established ethical practice, namely the recognition that a doctor is not under duty to intervene, e.g. surgically, to prolong the life of a grossly handicapped newborn child for whom no assured long-term alleviation is foreseeable, but only increasing and distressing dependency on surgical intervention. (He owes it a duty of care, discharged by ordinary medical and nursing attention while it lives; but this does not imply a duty of active intervention; neither does it permit the negligent killing of the child.) It would seem morally odd, therefore, to shrink from the abortion of a fetus for which there was such an assured adverse prognosis that, if born, it would not be encouraged to live. Practitioners are not impressed by the view that the argument for selective abortion for congential handicap would lead to selective infanticide on the same grounds. They feel as morally bound to perform the one as they are morally restrained from performing the other. (See also *Amniocentesis; Child; Chromosome Disorders; Congenital Malformations; Contraception; Fetus, Research on; Genetic Disorders; Infanticide; Sterilization; Unborn Child, Rights of.*)

G. R. Dunstan

1. DHSS. Report on Confidential Enquiries into Maternal Deaths in England and Wales 1973–1975. London: HMSO, 1979.
2. Church of England Board for Social Responsibility. *Abortion: an ethical discussion.* London: CIO, 1965.
3. Tunkel V. Abortion: how early, how late, how legal? *Br Med J* 1979; 2:253–6.
4. The Committee on the Working of the Abortion Act (Lane Committee). *Report.* London: HMSO, 1974, Cmnd 5538.
Baird D. Induced abortion: epidemiological aspect. *J Med Ethics* 1975; 1:122–6.
Dunstan GR. *The artifice of ethics.* 2nd ed. London: SCM Press, 1978.
Gardner RFR. *Abortion: the personal dilemma.* Exeter: The Paternoster Press, 1972.
Harris H. *Genetic screening and selective abortion.* London: Nuffield Provincial Hospitals Trust, 1974.
Hordern A. *Legal abortion: the English experience.* Oxford: Pergamon Press, 1971.
Potts M, Diggory P, Peel J. *Abortion.* Cambridge: University Press, 1977.

Acupuncture. Acupuncture is the technique of inserting very fine sharp needles into precise points on the body surface. The sites of insertion are determined by reference to charts of these points based on 'meridians' which have no discovered anatomical basis, but which originated some thousands of years ago in China.

The needles vary from about 2 cm to 15 cm in length and have wire wound hubs which are twirled by hand or stimulated electrically to produce the desired effects.

The practice of acupuncture is associated with diagnostic processes which are incomprehensible to those trained in Western medicine, and which have no basis other than that of faith or intuition, for most of the conditions which its practitioners purport to diagnose.

There is, however, no reason to suppose that acupuncturists do not derive as much information from feeling the pulses, one of their main diagnostic methods, as would conventional medical practitioners, but the use of the needling technique has not been proved to have any therapeutic effect on any of the organic disease processes discoverable by this method.

This is in no way a criticism of the practice of acupuncture in China, where only a very small fraction of the huge population has access to modern medical diagnostic methods or to adequate surgical treatment.

The therapeutic effect is sometimes augmented in traditional Chinese medicine by burning a pledgelet of the herb 'Moxa' on the end of the needle once it is in place, and this may add heat to the local stimulus of needling.

Acupuncture provides pain relief by mechanisms which are well understood by Western scientists. By exhortation of the late Chairman Mao Tse Tung the technique was developed by Chinese doctors to provide pain relief during surgical operations, a unique Chinese contribution to medicine. The mechanisms as we now understand them depend upon:

1. *Cultural and environmental factors.* Faith that it will be effective. Acupuncture is not used in those too young to comprehend and believe, or in those with mental disturbance or in the unbeliever. It has however a long history of acceptance in China and is taught to children in schools at a very young age.

2. *Suggestion.* There is a strong conditioning process for those about to be operated upon under Acupuncture and only those adequately suggestible are accepted for operation under this technique.

3. *Distraction.* It is undoubted that adequate distraction will relieve pain and the stimulus of Acupuncture at selected sites provides a very adequate and very powerful distraction.

4. *Relief of anxiety.* Acupuncturists preparing patients for operation induce tranquillity, a practice which might well be adopted more widely in the West.

5. *Confidence.* This is part of the conditioning process and is consciously fostered in the Chinese sense of a brotherhood developing between the patient and the Acupuncturist.

6. *Drugs.* During operations there is no hesitation in augmenting the technique by narcotic drugs and by local anaesthetic injection.

Acupuncture therefore clearly differs from hypnotic suggestion. There is no trance-like state, but it is effective through psycho-physical mechanisms, and would be usable in about the same proportion of the population as hypnotism.

It has become fashionable with the recent work on the encephalins to assume that the stimulation of tissues by Acupuncture releases endogenous morphine-like substances in the brain which produce the analgesic state, but there is no hard evidence for this explanation.

Acupuncture for anaesthesia is only used in selected major centres in China in about 6% of surgical patients (1974) and these patients are carefully screened and undergo prolonged conditioning. It has been used for the surgery of thyroid tumours, the heart, neurosurgery and Caesarean section, etc., but it appears to be ineffective in other abdominal surgery or surgery of the hand.

The therapeutic effectiveness of Acupuncture in conditions such as arthritis, diabetes, etc., is not known, because there are no properly controlled trials for reference, although it is undoubted that in some conditions symptomatic palliation may be achieved.

The ethical dangers of Acupuncture in the West lie in its undoubted effectiveness in pain relief in subjects prepared to believe in it. It may mask the warning sign of pain which signifies that serious pathological processes exist. The danger is related to the diagnostic processes used by professional acupuncturists and by the adoption of acupuncture by otherwise untrained people. In addition, considerable damage may be done to nerves, vessels and other structures through lack of anatomical knowledge, and pneumothorax has been reported. (See also *Chinese Medicine*.)

Mann RF. *Acupuncture – the ancient Chinese art of healing.* London: Heinemann Medical, 1972.
Wall PD. Acupuncture revisited. *New Sci* 1974; 64: 31–4.

J. G. Robson

Addiction to Drugs. The state of dependence ultimately produced by the habitual taking of certain drugs, e.g. barbiturates, amphetamines, and also alcohol and nicotine. Treatment is designed to achieve withdrawal and subsequent total abstention. For consideration of the ethical aspects see *Alcoholism; Drug Dependence; Tobacco Smoking.*

Advertising.

(1) BY MEDICAL PRACTITIONERS. Advertising is considered unethical on the grounds that patients would be unable to evaluate claims made. It would not therefore assist patients to make the best choice of doctor and might give false hopes of cure. Further, it could lead to competing claims between doctors and tacit or overt depreciation of one doctor by another, itself unethical.

Such notice to the public as is traditionally given by nameplates, letter headings, etc., is not considered as advertising, although size and wording should not be such as to appear to induce members of the public to consult that particular doctor.

Newspaper announcements of practice arrangements, holidays, locums, etc., are in general considered unethical in the UK. In some countries they are acceptable as being the most efficient method of giving patients necessary information.

It is accepted that the public have a right to be informed of advances in medicine and advised on matters of general health interest and therefore that doctors should write books and articles for the public and take part in TV and radio programmes. Depending on the subject matter, the public may further require to know something of the status of the doctor, so that they may evaluate the opinion expressed. In considering whether any publication amounts to advertising, regard is had to the primary purpose of the communication. If this is considered to have been the professional or financial benefit or advancement of the doctor, his actions would be considered unethical. Were the primary purpose the informing of the public on a matter of general interest, and any professional or financial advantage incidental and unavoidable, no offence would have been committed. Publication of scientific information in professional books and journals is, of course, a different matter, and *failure* to disseminate information would be unethical. When general practitioners are invited to take part in public meetings on medical matters, they must take care, especially when speaking within their own communities, to avoid suggesting that they provide services within their practices which may contrast with those provided by local colleagues, e.g. well woman clinics, child surveillance clinics.

Canvassing in person or through an agent for the purpose of gaining patients is also unethical, the objections being the same as for advertising. As with advertising, the offence would be committed by a doctor who knowingly acquiesced in the actions of others which drew attention to his services or skills with a view to his professional or financial advantage.

Of recent years screening, health check, pregnancy advisory and sterilization clinics have come into being. Some are owned wholly or in part by doctors, some are under entirely lay management. Some employ doctors whole or part time, some refer their clients to selected doctors. Recommendations recently made by the General Medical Council distinguish between organizations which advertise to the public and those which advertise only to the medical profession.

Where the organization advertises to the public, a doctor who is an owner or shareholder should not also undertake clinical work for it. The usual prohibitions regarding personal involvement and the use of a doctor's qualifications in advertising apply and, moreover, the doctor should ensure that the organization's advertising maintains proper professional standards. Doctors who undertake clinical or managerial work for such organizations should be paid on a sessional basis irrespective of the number of patients attending.

Where the organization advertises only to the medical profession, the doctor, owner or shareholder should ensure that advertisements, in detailing the services provided, and in reference to other organizations, do not infringe the normal ethical rules. (See *Communication; General Medical Council.* See also *Abortion; Medical Journalism; Pregnancy Advisory Services.*)

(2) BY PHARMACEUTICAL MANUFACTURERS. While the ethics of

11

advertising are not in dispute, the manner in which pharmaceutical companies advertise the medicines they produce is often criticised as wasteful of resources and lacking in objectivity, and in the UK fiscal measures have been introduced which effectively limit the amount of advertising expenditure. (See *Pharmaceutical Industry; Prescribing.*)

British Medical Association. *Handbook of medical ethics.* London: BMA, 1980.
Burton AW. *Medical ethics and the law.* Sydney: Australasian Medical Publishing Company, 1971.
General Medical Council. *Professional conduct and discipline.* London: GMC, 1979.
Knight B. *Legal aspects of medical practice.* Edinburgh and London: Churchill Livingstone, 1972.
Taylor JL. *Doctor and the law.* London: Pitman Medical, 1970.

J. Leahy Taylor

African Medicine. Because of the immense size of the continent and the innumerable cultures which it contains generalizations about trad-itional medical systems and practices in Africa are hazardous. But the subject has received a great deal of detailed attention, from both anthropologists and doctors.

American applied anthropologists now designate a whole sub-spe-cialty of ethno-medicine, within which they include ideas about the nature and causes of illness, the categories and functions of indigenous healers and the strengths and weaknesses of various traditional sys-tems. The field has been commended for further study by the World Health Organization, in its optimistic efforts to promote medical care for everyone by the year 2000[1].

However modern medical practice may grow it is always liable to be in relatively short supply and concentrated in urban areas, leaving the great mass of African people still dependent upon beliefs and treatments which have served their ancestors for countless generations. Moreover, African patients and their kin are essentially pragmatists, who are likely to combine patronage of modern and traditional med-icine, using their experience of both modes of therapy to judge which they consider best for particular conditions or stages of illness. It therefore behoves anyone in clinical practice in Africa to become acquainted with the nature of the local indigenous system which is almost certainly existing in parallel to Western medicine.

A comprehensive source book of specialist papers has been edited by Ayoade *et al.*[2] Foster and Anderson have written a general, well annotated work on social anthropology[3]. African examples are only a part of their concern but their work is useful on account of the numerous correspondences in human responses to disease, disability and death throughout the world. For case studies in several different

African societies readers could refer to Imperato's authoritative work on the Bambara of Mali[4], to Janzen's account of how serious disease is confronted in Lower Zaire, emphasising the existence of an extensive lay therapy management group which is formed to act on the patient's behalf[5], and to the present author's writings on the Yoruba of Nigeria[6].

It is important to bear in mind that medical systems are an integral part of any society's beliefs about the universe. African patients and their practitioners operate at several different levels, depending on their assessment of the nature and seriousness of an affliction. There are, for instance, thousands upon thousands of herbal remedies for commonplace symptoms. Only a minute proportion of these have been compiled, far less tested. There are concoctions which depend for their effectiveness on symbolic rather than pharmacological components. Home remedies are universal. In Africa these often involve an explicit element of sympathetic magic and may be obtained in the market place or from a traditional herbalist who has spent a lifetime in their study.

Whilst many simple conditions are attributed to natural causes, if symptoms fail to respond a whole range of supernatural or malevolent human agencies may be suspected. In this case help is sought from a superior diagnostician with the skills to divine what has gone wrong in the sufferer's life. Such specialists are concerned to answer the patient's insistent question, 'Why should this happen to me?' Western doctors are uneasy with such philosophical considerations, preferring to concentrate on how a disease state has come about. The African diviner priest focusses on disturbances of social, interpersonal relationships. The way in which the proceedings are conducted, the explanations offered and the regimens prescribed vary from one cultural setting to another, but patient and therapist will share the same fundamental preconceptions about life and fate.

African medical systems may deal more effectively than Western ones with life crises. Birth and death have not become institutionalized, they are part of everyone's experience, familiar to children as well as adults and they are accompanied by supportive rituals. Although Western medicine has many clear areas of superiority to African systems the latter still have much to teach us about the dependence of health on harmonious social functioning.

1. WHO. *The promotion and development of traditional medicine.* Technical Report Series No 622. Geneva: World Health Organization, 1978.
2. Ayoade AA, Warren M, Ademawegun ZA, Harrison E eds. *African therapeutic systems.* Brandeis University: Crossroads Press, 1978.
3. Foster M, Anderson G. *Medical anthropology.* New York: Wiley, 1978.

13

4. Imperato PJ. *African folk medicine: practices and beliefs of the Bambara and other peoples.* Baltimore: York Press, 1977.
5. Janzen JM. *The quest for therapy in Lower Zaire.* University of California Press: 1978.
6. Maclean U. *Magical medicine: A Nigerian case study,* London: Allen Lane, 1971.

Una Maclean

Alcoholism. The most widely quoted definition of alcoholism is that of the World Health Organization:[1] 'Alcoholics are those excessive drinkers whose dependence upon alcohol has attained such a degree that it shows a noticeable mental disturbance or an interference with their bodily and mental health, their interpersonal relations, and their smooth social and economic functioning; or who show the prodromal signs of such developments. They therefore require treatment.' For practical purposes, however, perhaps the brief statement may suffice, that 'alcoholics are people whose excessive drinking has led to a state of (psychological and/or physical) dependence upon alcohol, and/or to complications in the mental, physical or social spheres'.

For many years, 'the man in the street has usually regarded alcoholism as a weakness of character; the moralist sees it as a vice; the law representative as a crime; the psychiatrist as a symptom of underlying personality difficulties; the sociologist as a social problem; and possibly many clergymen as a sin'.[2] Recently some have described alcoholism as a 'learnt' behavioural disorder. Alcoholics Anonymous (AA) approaches it as a disease, a concept which has gained increasing acceptance in recent years, mainly because of the practical successes of AA and the theoretical formulations and researches of Jellinek,[3] though it has recently come in for some criticism, arising to some extent from the difficulty of clearly defining the terms 'alcoholism' and 'disease'.[4] Jellinek regarded only two types of alcoholism as diseases because they involved definite physiopathological changes. These are (1) the 'Loss of control' or gamma type – said to be more common in mainly spirit-drinking, e.g. Anglo-Saxon countries – and (2) the 'Inability to abstain' or delta types, relatively more common in predominantly wine-drinking countries such as France.

'Loss of control alcoholism'[3,1] – in Jellinek's view – involves an increased tissue tolerance to alcohol, adaptation of cell metabolism, withdrawal symptoms and loss of control over alcohol intake on a given occasion once the person has taken one or two drinks (although he can abstain for days, weeks, or even months).[2] However, 'loss of control' (upon which the disease concept is largely based) is not an absolute loss, but, rather, a relative lack of control: i.e. it does not mean that such a drinker has always to continue drinking once, on a given occasion, he has taken a drink or two; rather that he can never be certain that he will be able to stop drinking at will once, on a given occasion, he has had a drink or two![5,2] (Apart from physical and biochemical, psychosocial factors also enter into the loss of control phenomenon and might on occasion function as relative 'brakes', helping such a drinker to stop drinking. Thus many alcoholics can occasionally, or frequently, stop after one or two drinks only to relapse into uncontrolled drinking sooner or later, and no one can know at present which alcoholic would be among the small minority who could possibly learn to drink in moderation.)[5] 'Inability to abstain alcoholism' involves acquired increased tissue tolerance to alcohol, adaptation of cell metabolism, withdrawal symptoms and inability to abstain, so that the drinker has to take alcoholic drink intermittently throughout the day without necessarily getting drunk, but without being able to abstain from alcohol for shorter or longer periods. 'Loss of control alcoholism' is probably the most prevalent type in the UK, USA and many other countries, although in practice the gamma and delta types often co-exist in the same drinker.

The acceptance of the disease concept of alcoholism by no means eliminates the possible involvement of ethical factors. According to Clinebell,[6] in whose view 'to moralize with an alcoholic is the ultimate in counselling futility', alcoholism is not a simple moral problem but certainly has ethical implications. In a survey among Protestant ministers who had attended the Yale Summer School of Alcohol Studies, the most commonly held view was that alcoholism begins as a personal sin and ends as a sickness.[6] The alcoholic 'is responsible for having caught the compulsion or illness'. Clinebell, however, feels that the alcoholic is 'a compulsive person even before he becomes a compulsive drinker', his early drinking being 'part of a total behavioural pattern . . . strongly influenced by his damaged personality as well as by cultural pressures. He is not a completely free agent.' Other clergymen regarded alcoholism as 'a sickness which involved the sin of abuse' (the Roman Catholic view), or 'a sickness . . . caused by a combination of factors both sin and sickness', or 'a social sin' in the sense that society has failed to bring about a world free from tensions and conflicts.

The assumption 'that certain aspects of alcoholism have the natures of diseases' implies that the act which results in intoxication is outside the volitional sphere of the alcoholic.[3] However, 'the question of impaired volition does not arise' in the period preceding the onset of loss of control, so that 'the acquisition of the "disease" (i.e. uncontrolled drinking) is in a limited way voluntary, but . . . once the disease form is reached it is no different from other disease, i.e. . . . not any more in the sphere of volition to terminate it.' As in some cultures drinking 'comes very near to being an institution' (in a sociological sense), and as the changes from the socially normal towards pathological drinking are so insidious, to define alcoholism as self-inflicted becomes more and more questionable.

Many laymen and professional people probably still regard

alcoholism as wilful misconduct to be condemned or punished, but at what stage is it wilful? Alcoholism is, of course, not synonymous with deliberate acute intoxication for which a drinker is generally held responsible. It can hardly be regarded as wilful at those stages where psychological or physical dependence* have occurred – which drive the individual towards further drinking – even though in most aspects of alcoholism pharmacological factors are not solely in command but interact with social, psychological and possibly physiological factors. Ethical questions are obviously involved in self-indulgent heavy drinking, and possibly (or probably) in the heavy drinking of psychopaths, and in 'symptomatic excessive drinking' arising from underlying emotional states such as depression and anxiety. In all these conditions, inadequacy of personality or other problems may have greatly affected the individual's control of, and responsibility for, his heavy drinking.

Yet even in the 'average' alcoholic – initially free from serious personality problems – it may be difficult to defend the view that alcoholism is a sin or a crime or even weakness of character. With a few important exceptions, religious and national laws do not condemn or prohibit moderate drinking and the average person may feel somewhat of an outsider if he refuses to partake in social drinking. Thus at an initial stage when he could cut down on his drinking, the future alcoholic sees no need to do so; in later stages, when he ought to drink less, his drinking has become compulsive and he cannot reduce it without outside help because of the superimposed loss of control, even though social and psychological factors may be involved in loss of control as well as physical ones.[2,3,4] Even after the onset of loss of control, the alcoholic would bear some responsibility for accepting and co-operating with treatment offered to him.

Ethical and moral questions are certainly involved in the attitude of society towards alcoholism. It has failed to educate the general public, and in particular the young and members of exposed, especially vulnerable occupational groups, about the risks involved in heavy drinking, such as the dangers of dependence and other (physical or psychosocial) complications. It has also failed to interfere with indiscriminate, unscrupulous advertising, either intentional or subliminal. In fact, it has recently been stressed that alcoholism is not only a social and medical but also a political problem.[7] For example, there exists a definite co-relation between the per capita consumption in a given population and the incidence of alcohol induced complications, and it has been suggested that prevention of alcohol related problems may be largely a task of the politician, for instance by raising taxation as well as by pressing for wider lay and professional education. How-

---

* Psychological dependence – a condition in which a drug produces 'a feeling of satisfaction and a psychic drive that require periodic or continuous administration of the drug to produce pleasure or to avoid discomfort'. Physical dependence – 'an adaptive state that manifests itself by intense physical disturbance when the administration of the drug is suspended'.

ever, politicians obviously cannot move too far ahead of popular acceptance, and it should be the task of the medical profession to contribute in this sphere to the education of the politicians as well as of the general public.

THE DOCTOR'S RESPONSIBILITY. The failure of society to educate the young about the risks involved in heavy drinking also extends to the field of medical education, so that there is a widespread lack of interest and understanding among doctors of the problems of alcoholism. Little notice has been taken of the disease concept of the subject and partly because of this doctors and alcoholics have tended to keep out of each other's way. This indifference of the medical profession has also helped to perpetuate the stigma attached to alcoholism. A first task, therefore, is to get doctors interested and informed about the subject by adequate undergraduate training so that they come to accept alcoholism as an illness (rather than as a crime or sin) – a socio-medical disorder (with important psychosocial as well as physiological facets) that legitimately belongs to the medical sphere. Only when doctors approach the alcoholic as a sick man will they be prepared to listen to him and to help him and also his long-suffering family. The lack of undergraduate medical information in this field is also reflected in the relatively high proportion of doctors who themselves become victims of alcoholism.[2]

The question of treatment goals has recently become a matter of some controversy: can alcoholics learn to drink safely in moderation? The majority view would still be 'no', i. e. there is only one way for an alcoholic to lead a happy, healthy and useful life and that is by means of total abstinence. There is, however, a body of opinion that believes that, as alcoholism is a learnt disorder, what can be learnt can also be unlearnt, so that some alcoholics could become moderate drinkers. An ethical question might thus be involved as to whether an individual doctor might feel that, in spite of the majority view, he would leave it to the patient which path to choose, having explained to him that the matter is as yet unresolved and controversial. Or, as the recent Royal College of Psychiatrists' report puts it:[7] 'It is best to admit that the "return to normal drinking" argument is at present not fully resolved, while meanwhile acknowledging that individual judgement as to what constitutes the most responsible and caring advice for a patient (after discussion with that patient) remains the only touchstone.' However, the doctor should also keep in mind the likelihood that the alcoholic's long-suffering family might be much less enthusiastic about the prospect of the drinker being given yet another chance to attempt controlled drinking, which very likely he has tried so often in the past and failed.

Alcoholism is, of course, a family disorder:[2] the alcoholic's spouse and children often suffer a great deal in silence and anonymity, and the doctor can bring much help to the family members by an understanding approach even at a time when the drinker is not prepared to co-operate. An ethical question which commonly arises is posed by patients or their relatives who directly approach a consultant and ask for his help. When asked for an introductory letter from their general practitioner, they frequently assert, rightly or wrongly: 'There is no point in asking our GP because he does not want to know.' While each case has to be dealt with on its merits, the alcoholic's condition is often so serious as to warrant some active intervention. The consultant may himself telephone the GP and tactfully suggest that some form of treatment may be indicated and may even be urgent. The doctor's responsibility in such cases extends not only to his patient but also to society, which may be endangered by, for example, the risks of habitual alcohol-affected driving.[2,5] The risks to society also affect the difficult question of how to deal with an alcoholic medical colleague, and how to assess his competence (q.v.) to practise medicine. In the interests of the doctor himself and of society, a realistic view should be taken and the doctor advised not to resume medical practice until after he has accepted, and benefited from, treatment. On the other hand, the alcoholic doctor who has satisfactorily co-operated with treatment and benfited from it, should be given all possible help when attempting to resume his (former) specialty.

A doctor may know or suspect that one of his patients is an alcoholic although he has not consulted him. This may arise from the wife deciding at last to confide in the doctor, while pleading with him not to tell her husband who had revealed his condition. Again the guiding consideration should probably be that the patient himself is likely to suffer if his alcoholism is allowed to proceed unchecked. While a direct 'frontal assault' by the practitioner is likely to lead to angry, indignant denials, it will often be possible by sympathetic probing to establish a helping relationship which in the long run will assist the patient to talk about his problems; meanwhile the family could be helped by their learning to see the drinking relative's unpredictable behaviour as indicative of an illness rather than of wishful, self-indulgent, hedonistic 'acting-out'. This process often takes time but the doctor must remember that alcoholism is all too often a relapsing disorder and patience and tolerance are required. Many alcoholics have ultimately recovered only after a number of relapses. However, the knowledge that the majority of alcoholics can, at least, greatly improve if they are approached with understanding and acceptance should be the doctor's main consideration. Sometimes this may raise the controversial issue whether it may be in the interests not only of the family but also of the alcoholic to apply a temporary Hospital Order if, owing to his compulsion to continue excessive drinking, he is seriously damaging his health to a life-threatening degree. While his behaviour is dictated by physical or strong psychological dependency, such an individual is not really a free agent. Care should, however, be taken in such cases to refer such a patient to a hospital or unit properly equipped to deal constructively with alcoholics, and staffed by professionals experienced in looking after them.

Contrary to an often heard criticism, the disease concept of alcoholism does not imply freeing the patient from all responsibilities. Just as a patient with pneumonia or diabetes is expected to keep to his doctor's prescriptions, it is also the alcoholic's responsibility to co-operate with his doctor's attempts to help him towards recovery from his illness, and to follow advice as to life style, drinking (or rather non-drinking) habits, etc., to the best of his ability. (See also *Drug Dependence.*)

1. World Health Organization. Committee on Mental Health, Alcoholism Subcommittee, Second Report. World Health Organization Technical Report Series 1952; 48:16.
2. Glatt MM. *Alcoholism: a social disease.* London: Teach Yourself Books, 1975:1,4.
3. Jellinek EM. *The disease concept of alcoholism.* Connecticut: Hillhouse Press, 1960: 45–52.
4. Glatt MM. Alcoholism disease concept, and loss of control revisited. *Br J Addict* 1976; 71: 135–44.
5. Glatt MM. *A guide to addiction and its treatments: drugs, society and man.* Lancaster: Medical and Technical Publishing, 1974.
6. Clinebell HJ Jr. *Understanding and counselling the alcoholic through religion and psychology.* Nashville: Abingdon Press, 1956: 157–69.
7. Special Committee Royal College of Psychiatrists. Alcohol and Alcoholism. *Report.* London: Tavistock Publications, 1979: 128, 134.

Kendall RE. Alcoholism: a medical or a political problem. *Br Med J* 1979; 1: 367–71.

World Health Organization. Expert Committee on Drug Dependence. 20th Report. Geneva: WHO, 1974:14.

M. M. Glatt

Amniocentesis. Amniocentesis describes the act of tapping the amniotic fluid or liquor. This fluid is contained within the fetal membranes, and is entirely fetal in origin. It consists primarily of fetal urine, and is continuously circulated by fetal swallowing, and, to a lesser extent, by absorption through other surfaces, including the lining of the lungs. These many surfaces continuously shed cells: most are dead or dying, and are little more than fetal dandruff, but a small minority, whose origin is unknown, have the ability to divide.

Tapping the fluid may be done in late pregnancy to relieve both mother and child from the effects of excess; a rare but potentially lifesaving procedure for both parties. This is usually, but not always, associated with a failure to swallow, either from absence of the brain or obstruction of the gullet: the latter is now usually amenable to curative surgery. In mid-pregnancy tapping may be done to test for fetal jaundice, a predictable consequence of rhesus disease in which the fetal red cells are destroyed, the red haemoglobin becoming degraded to the yellow bilirubin which causes jaundice. Since the father is frequently of a blood group which gives each fetus a fifty per cent chance of normality, and this cannot always be inferred from studying antibodies in maternal blood, and since severe cases benefit from direct fetal transfusion, and mild cases from induced premature delivery, this test provides an important guide for the treatment of the sick fetus, and for the protection of the normal or mildly affected from the dangers of transfusion or untimely birth. Since the baby is of substantial size and usually surrounded by a sufficient volume of fluid to allow for fetal movement, the tapping itself is usually safe and simple except in the very fat mother, or in the presence of twinning.

Until recently rhesus disease and the rare excess of fluid sometimes found (hydramnios) provided the main indications for amniocentesis: it was always done directly by a needle through the abdominal wall. The 'breaking of the waters' to induce labour, which is done from below, although technically 'amniocentesis', is rarely implied by this word.

The possibility of fetal diagnosis with a view to elimination by abortion, rather than to therapy, has been discussed for many years, but the absence of any ethical situation in which such fluid could be obtained in early pregnancy, or of an adequate technique for obtaining it, as well as a reluctance to introduce elimination into medical practice, made development slow. The increase in the abortion rate in the 1960s, and the use of a tapping procedure to introduce fluids into the amniotic cavity to terminate pregnancy, provided the basis for the development of these techniques.

These procedures can now be used with safety by experienced operators with adequate ultrasound equipment in the absence of twinning, gross obesity, unusual placentation, or other problems, to sample the fetal fluid with its included cells. The acquisition of experience requires a rather costly apprenticeship and this can no longer be acquired by inducing abortion since injection methods are now obsolete. In practice the fetal mortality in regular practice is probably at least 1%; non-fatal injuries are extremely rare.

There is general agreement that the best compromise between safety for the fetus and the maternal anxieties of delay, together with the hazards and unpleasantness of late termination, is to do the test at 16 weeks. In practice sexing takes a day, tests for spina bifida a week (since batching is necessary for both economy and reliability), chromosomal analysis up to a month, and enzyme studies 3–6 weeks. Different abnormalities require the use of one or other of these various tests. Sexing by examining the uncultured cells is occasionally difficult, and may need chromosomal confirmation in rare cases or in inexperienced laboratories.

The indications are, obviously, the detection of conditions sufficiently common to justify the risks of the procedure, and sufficiently unpleasant for a correctly informed woman to prefer elimination of the fetus to its crippled survival or certain death.

High risk groups can be defined by age, experience, or by direct diagnosis of the carrier state. Women aged 40 have a 1% risk of mongolism (Down's syndrome), rising to 4% at 45. Women who have experienced birth of a child with mongolism of the regular type have a 1% risk of recurrence. Common malformations usually have a 3% recurrence risk: the only common form capable of early diagnosis, spina bifida, has this risk, but also carries a 2% risk of a similar but invariably fatal disorder which prevents the brain forming (anencephaly). Anencephaly also implies a 2% risk of spina bifida.

Recessive disorders are individually rare, except for thalassaemia and sickle cell disease, which are restricted to Old World racial groups recently exposed to malaria in Italy, Greece, Africa or the Far East. In most Northern Caucasians cystic fibrosis is the commonest recessive (1 in 2000). Tay-Sachs disease* has a similar incidence in Ashkenazi Jews (the numerically dominant group). All other recessives are rarer. Only a minority are expressed in the cells available for amniocentesis, and only in a minority can the carrier be diagnosed. About 15% of cases are second affected children: elimination of the first affected requires screening. Exact methods are available in sickle cell and probabilistic methods in Tay-Sachs disease and thalassaemia, but technically better methods can be expected. Tests on fetal blood, which would be necessary for detecting blood disorders such as sickling, are restricted by the difficulty in obtaining it and separating it from maternal blood.

ETHICAL PROBLEMS. Amniocentesis involves serious ethical problems since it is not without risk to the unborn child, and is only indicated if the tests performed will lead to a result in which termination would be acceptable. To undertake the procedure on a woman who would not tolerate abortion would be unsuited to most societies, as would its performance for an indication, such as sexing or consistency with some tests for paternity, in which most obstetricians would consider abortion as a response to the result to be unjustifiable feticide.

Various justifications for the operation have been made, including maternal anxiety, or the 'preparation' of parents for tragedy or the reception of a crippled child, or for 'getting ready for treatment', but none of these seems to stand up to informed and humane criticism.

The simplest example is when affliction is certain and the conse-

---

* Tay-Sachs disease, a serious genetic disorder, has its onset shortly after birth and is characterised by progressive mental deterioration, blindness and paralysis and is usually fatal by the age of 2 or 3. There is no effective treatment.

quences inevitably distressing to both the child and the parents, as in spina bifida, a condition in which survivors will be subjected to repeated hospitalization and surgery. More difficult problems arise in Duchenne's disease, when half the boys will have a tragic and protracted death, the other half being completely free from disease, or in mongolism (Down's syndrome) when the patient seldom suffers, the burden being with the parents.

At the other end of the spectrum are those who wish to abort for the presence of such normal variants as those defining sex, legitimacy, race, or those related to correctable, or easily avoidable, metabolic disorders such as one deficiency on the pathway of sugar metabolism, whose victims need merely to avoid broad beans and a few varieties of pills.

The long-term consequences of elimination on the incidence of inherited diseases at conception are slight, and not necessarily beneficial, since the overall fitness of carriers may be increased. The incidence of diseases at birth by elimination of those capable of accurate diagnosis is, in principle, capable of indefinite reduction. However, it is clear from their low recurrence risk that the majority of malformations and mental deficiencies do not have any simple determinants, and the overall demands for the support of this group will continue to be large and, in most societies, insufficient resources will be provided to meet them. (See *Abortion; Chromosome Disorders; Congenital Malformations; Genetic Conditions.*)

Fairweather DVI, Eskes TKAB. *Amniotic fluid: research and clinical application.* Amsterdam: Excerpta Medica, 1973.

Galjaard H. European experience with prenatal diagnosis of congenital disease: a survey of 6121 cases. *Cytogenet Cell Genet* 1976; 16: 453–67.

MRC. Report on an assessment of hazards in amniocentesis. *Br J Obstet Gynaecol* 1978; 85: Supplement No 2.

Simpson NE *et al.* Prenatal diagnosis of genetic disease in Canada: report of a collaborative study. *Can Med Assoc J* 1976; 115: 739–48.

J. H. Edwards

Anaesthesia. The administration of an anaesthetic is a serious matter and is never to be undertaken lightly; in no other circumstances is a patient deliberately brought so near to death for therapeutic purposes. During general anaesthesia the patient is unconscious, and is therefore unaware of, and is incapable of consciously participating in, the procedure performed on him. He is therefore entirely dependent on his anaesthetist and surgeon for his safety and health.

Leaving aside such fundamental moral and legal obligations as consent, confidentiality, and the exercise of care, common to all doctors, the anaesthetist has particular ethical responsibilities both to the patient and to the surgeon.

1. *To the patient.* The anaesthetist is responsible for the general well-being of the patient who has placed his life in his hands. Before even agreeing to administer anaesthesia, the anaesthetist must reassure himself that no illegal or improper operation is to be performed. He must know the nature and purpose of the operation, and these are normally readily available in everyday hospital practice. If surgical or anaesthetic research or experiment is involved, the usual ethical concern should be resolved by discussion, and by the knowledge that the consent of the appropriate ethical committees has been obtained.

2. *To the surgeon.* The anaesthetist is a partner with the surgeon in a therapeutic team, and while each has his well-defined area of skill and responsibility, neither can entirely dissociate himself from what the other does. Thus the anaesthetist also should not use methods which are of an experimental nature or are widely regarded as unsafe, without informing his surgical colleague. A harmonious relationship between the two, born of mutual trust, is the best guarantee that the maximum benefit will be derived by the patient from the operation.

The anaesthetist's moral as well as medical responsibility continues until full recovery from the anaesthetic. His concern will therefore also be directed to other workers such as junior doctors, nurses, operating department assistants, porters, and others, who may at some time during the recovery period be virtually in sole charge of the patient. The anaesthetist must assure himself that they too have been made aware of their ethical responsibilities to the patient – not very different from his own in respect of confidentiality and care – before he permits use to be made of their services in this connection.

Several of the drugs used by the anaesthetist are known to be addictive and everyone who handles these drugs, particularly those who are responsible for supervising their security, should be aware of this possibility. Cases of addiction have occurred among anaesthetists, although very rarely. More often it has been other workers, in the places where anaesthetic drugs are kept and used, that have been involved. This is not only tragic from the point of view of the individual concerned, but carries serious risks for the patient, who might suffer as a result of diminished judgement and responsibility on the part of those looking after him.

Of the inhalational anaesthetics, nitrous oxide, trichloroethylene (Trilene), chloroform, and ether, are all known to be addictive and the probability is that the others are too. The anaesthetist should be vigilant that no drug within his sphere of practice is misused or stolen. Any evidence that this has occurred should alert him, and his suspicion shared with senior colleagues. He should be particularly on the look-out for such things as surreptitious 'sniffing' of anaesthetic vapours of gases by anybody in the operating department environs. (See also

Clinical Practice; Competence to Practise; Drug Dependence; Human Experiment; Interprofessional Relationships; Teamwork.)

William W. Mushin

Analgesia. See *Anaesthesia; Pain.*

Animal Experiment. The use of live animals for research purposes. The term 'vivisection' is also widely used but is less accurate since it should strictly be applied only to surgical procedures on living animals. Experiments with animals may also involve medical procedures, test feeding or the external or internal application of particular substances.

Experiments may be carried out for (1) the testing of new medical products and implants intended for ultimate use on animals or human beings, (2) the assessment of any likely danger in products which although not designed to be used medically by human beings will be used by them for other purposes and may prove to have harmful side effects, and (3) the furtherance of knowledge of a physiological nature which will provide a basis for advances in medical and surgical knowledge.

Some believe that man has no moral right to use animals for research purposes since animals are as much God's creatures as man and should not be used for man's selfish ends and personal benefit. However, most consider that the use of animals can be justified on moral and ethical grounds provided man's dominant position in relation to animals is not abused. The considerations which it is generally felt should apply to the use of animals for research purposes include: (a) the use of as few animals as possible; (b) the maximum possible avoidance of pain; (c) the use of animals only for research with justifiable ends; (d) control of the types of animals used; and (e) effective legal and administrative safeguards against any breach of the foregoing. Any worker wishing to conduct an animal experiment must first obtain a Home Office licence for the procedure.

The use of as few animals as possible not only involves the avoidance of wasteful numbers of animals in any experiment and the avoidance of repetitious experiments, but also raises the issue of the use of alternative methods, e.g. the use of chemical methods in assaying compounds with biological effect and the use of organ, tissue and cell culture. In certain cases, what are known as *in vitro** methods can produce quicker results, with greater accuracy and at less cost, than if animals are used, and research workers are resentful of the allegation that they will not look for other methods of research so long a animals are available. They point out that experiments *in vitro* and on the living animal are normally complementary and *not* alternative.

There is general agreement that pain should be avoided wherever

---

* *in vitro* – literally 'in the test tube'. Commonly used to describe an experiment which is to be distinguished from one carried out on a living organism.

possible. It will normally be countered by anaesthetizing the animal, unless anaesthesia would nullify the purposes of the experiment, and by the destruction of the animal at the conclusion of the experiment (if possible while still under anaesthesia) in order to avoid subsequent pain. Pain is, nevertheless, an unfortunate concomitant in some experiments.

For some people, views on the ethics and morality of the infliction of pain – and of such experiments – depend on the purposes for which the research is being carried out. Research carried out with a view to eliminating disease or alleviating suffering in animals or man is considered acceptable by the majority of people. There has, however, been considerable criticism of research into the dangers of cigarette smoking (involving the inhaling of cigarette smoke by dogs and other animals), and research relating to the safe preparation of cosmetics. It is contended that man need not smoke and his wife need not use cosmetics, so that it is morally and ethically indefensible to use animals in order to protect human beings against their own folly. Against that, there are thousands of cases referred annually to the National Poisons Information Service in which the appeal for help arises as the result of the ingestion (frequently by children) of products such as cosmetics, household cleansers and gardening aids.

The greatest revulsion to the use of animals in research occurs in relation to companion animals such as dogs, cats and horses, and also monkeys. Experiments carried out on rats and mice appear to arouse less strong emotions – but the distinction is based more on man's relative affection for different species than on assessment of different thresholds of pain. This is reflected also in differing attitudes to the use of animals bred specifically for research purposes, animals which are strays and are therefore destined for euthanasia, and animals which are alleged to be stolen and sold to research centres. Research workers often prefer animals specifically bred for research purposes (as these can, for example, then be SPF* animals), but in some countries stray dogs from dog pounds are looked upon as acceptable material for research as they will in any event have to be put down. To steal animals for research purposes is, of course, not only ethically, morally and emotionally unacceptable, but also illegal. Notwithstanding these distinctions, animals of the same species whether bred, acquired or misappropriated for research will be sensitive to pain to the same degree.

Where scientific and medical objectives are complicated by a desire to act justly towards animals, a compromise is almost inevitable. This involves the acceptance of certain legal and administrative controls and awareness that the governing bodies of the professions most

---

* SPF – 'specific pathogen-free'; a term used to describe animals removed from the uterus at birth in a sterile manner and reared in isolation premises to preserve a disease-free state.

involved in research exercise ethical restraints (often not specifically expressed) upon their members. Unfortunately in a number of countries the restraints and controls upon researchers are few, with consequent lack of protection for the animals concerned.

In this connection, however, it is hoped that it may be possible, within the next few years, to arrive at a common understanding throughout the continent of Europe, as to the safeguards which should be enshrined in national laws relating to animal experiments. Representatives of those countries which are members of the Council of Europe are currently working on the preparation of a Convention designed to protect the interests of experimental animals. If this can be agreed, signatory countries will then seek to ensure that the provisions of the Convention are observed in their national legislation (See also *Human Experiment.*)

De Boer J, Archibald J, Downie HG, eds. *An introduction to experimental surgery. A guide to experimenting with laboratory animals.* Amsterdam and New York: Excerpta Medica, 1975.

Departmental Committee on Experiments in Animals. Report. London: HMSO, 1965, Cmnd 2641.

Lane-Potter W. The ethics of animal experimentation. *J Med Ethics* 1976; 2: 118–26.

Michon JP. *Le problème de l'expérimentation sur les animaux. Etude comparée des législations françaises et étrangères.* Alfort. Thesis, 1970.

Ryder RD. *Victims of science. The use of animals in research.* London: David-Poynter, 1975.

Singer P. *Animal liberation.* London: Jonathan Cape, 1976.

Smyth DH. *Alternatives to animal experiments.* London: Scolar Press in association with the Research Defence Society, 1978.

Universities Federation for Animal Welfare. *The rational use of living systems in bio-medical research.* Potters Bar: UFAW, 1972.

A. R. W. Porter

Antenatal Diagnosis. While, strictly speaking, antenatal diagnosis may refer to any diagnostic procedure undertaken on a pregnant woman, the term is now specifically used to describe investigations designed to discover abnormalities, genetic or otherwise, of the fetus, and/or its sex. Such investigations may be by radiography (X-rays), by scanning with ultrasound or thermography, or by chemical or chromosomal analysis of a sample of the amniotic fluid obtained by amniocentesis (q.v.). Radiography and amniocentesis carry risks to mother and/or fetus and should not be undertaken without good cause. If results indicate that the fetus is likely, or certain, to be born malformed, the possibility of abortion (q.v.) is discussed by the medical team and with the parents, with whom the risks of future preg nancies are also considered. (See also *Amniocentesis; Chromosome Disorders; Congenital Malformations; Genetic Conditions; Unborn Child, Rights of.*)

Artificial Insemination. The insemination of a woman by a medical practitioner with semen collected from her husband (AIH) or from another donor (AID). An essential prerequisite is a complete investigation of *the couple* in order to establish a correct diagnosis of the cause of the infertility.[1] The indications for AI are thus stated by Foss[2]: 1. Gross male subfertility – (a) oligo- or azoospermia; (b) gross hypomotility, possibly with plasma-enzyme deficiency; (c) morphological defects; (d) genetic defects of vasa or epididymes; (e) testicular atrophy, from mumps or torsion, or trauma at breech presentation; (f) undescended testes; (g) hypogonadism; (h) chromosomal defects, e.g. Klinefelter syndrome. 2. Hereditary and familial disease, e.g. cystic fibrosis or neurological disease. 3. Lesser indications are impotence in the male, or vasectomy after a previously fertile marriage.

The semen used may be fresh or, now more commonly, frozen with glycerol as a cryo-protective agent. The speed of freezing and of thawing is found to affect motility. The insemination is performed once, twice or even three times in the middle of the woman's cycle at dates established by temperature change and bio-chemical test. Some think it unfair to patients to continue for more than nine to twelve months if no positive results are achieved, but a decision will depend on the individual patient.

The ethics of AIH are uncomplicated – except for persons with residual objections to masturbation *per se* – and are those normal to such medical investigation and intervention.

The ethics of AID are more complicated: for the spouses, in relation to their perception of marriage; for the donor, in respect of his responsibility for his procreative powers; for the practitioner in his part in a transaction still, in most jurisdictions, unrecognized by law and which results in a child of uncertain identity and status. Social recognition and legal provision lag behind the mounting acceptance of the practice by doctors and by couples seeking the benefit.[3,4]

For the spouses the choice, in liberal societies, is an open one. If they believe that there is a nexus between marriage and begetting so strong and exclusive that any invasion of it from without is wrong, even though extra-marital conception can be achieved without adulterous sexual union, they will not ask for AID. If one of them (say the husband) believes this while the other does not, there can be a serious strain on the marriage; the practitioner must look out for this, and assure full consent from the husband, out of respect for him and for the marriage, and for the child who might otherwise be born into a divided home. If, on the other hand, both see the bond between husband and wife as excluding no more than physical congress, and the seed of a third party as no more than a fertilizing agent whose part and product in conception imports nothing alien into their marriage relationship, then they are free to accept AID if it is clinically indicated. This freedom is now recognized in the UK in that AID is available under the National Health Service. Some practitioners keep private records of the subsequent history of marriages with AID children; the incidence of breakdown is said to be low[5].

For the donor the ethical questions seem to be (1) should he divorce his procreative power from the responsibilities of parenthood – i.e., should he allow his seed to be used to create a child of whose existence he must remain ignorant and for whose well-being he can take no care? and (2) should he accept payment for what nature has given him freely and in plenty; should he, indeed, donate with payment as his motive? Practitioners say that they would rather pay donors than accept 'cranky volunteers', a preference at variance with the analogous practice of blood donation, in which it is established that a voluntary system yields better blood than a payments system, because payment induces the indigent to conceal or falsify adverse factors in their medical history[6] (see *Blood Transfusion*). While practitioners commonly rely for medical and genetic history on interview with semen donors, without further test, veracity is of the highest importance; and this a money payment may put at risk.

For the practitioner the ethics of AID are complicated by the ambiguity of social attitudes and the obsolete state of the law. The practice has developed in the face of moralistic, religious and legal disapproval[7,8,9,10]. In the UK a Departmental Committee (the Feversham Committee), rejecting pressure to recommend that the practice be made a statutory crime, declared it a mere 'liberty', an act, permitted but socially disapproved, which 'while not prohibited by law will receive no kind of support or encouragement from the law'[9]. In English law the AID child is undoubtedly illegitimate. (American jurisdictions vary in according or denying him legitimate status.) Knowingly to enter the husband's name in the Reigster of Births as the child's father is to commit an offence. The husband and wife may take out a shortened birth certificate for the child, thus concealing the bastardy from casual inspection but not cancelling it; or they may formally adopt the child. In any event, the child will not know his genetic identity, and this may turn to his disadvantage should he come for genetic counselling before his own marriage later. It is common practice to conceal from AID children knowledge of that fact – though for reasons surmised rather than established, and, again, at variance with the settled practice with adopted children, who are commonly told of their status early in life, and without generally observed harm. In the UK, since November 1976 adopted children, at majority, may require the Registrar General to disclose their natural parentage as recorded in the Adoption Register. It may be that, before long, potential donors will have to face the possibility of similar disclosure to AID children also; it is hard to sustain a convincing argument why knowledge of their true identity should be denied them.

The Law Commission considered the paternity of children conceived by AID in its Working Paper on *Family Law: Illegitimacy*.[11] It suggests 'a statutory deeming provision' to enact a 'policy that the law should recognize social reality at the expense of genetic truth and treat the mother's husband (provided that he has consented) as the legal father of an AID child'. It sees fewer objections to this than to other solutions proposed.

The secrecy of the proceeding, undertaken as an ethical obligation to the receiving parents and to the donor, has hitherto hindered the development of a good scientific base to the practice. There has been no common protocol, e.g. for the selection of patients or of donors, or for the recording and publishing of data for objective assessment of results. An initiative to break with this tradition has been taken in Nottingham, England[12], and is likely to be followed elsewhere. Donations and inseminations are coded and recorded in such a way that, while confidence is preserved, normal research and assessment will be possible. The mixing of semen – in itself clinically suspect – will stop because it is adverse to good science.

A good ethics of the practice, then, requires adjustments in social and legal attitudes to enable the practitioner to serve a patient's interest without being a party to what may amount to a legal offence (the falsifying of the register of births), a deceit upon society, and an act of injustice to a disadvantaged child. He will then be free to attend more closely to the ethics of his relationship with the parties concerned: the spouses, the child to be born to them, and the donor. To the spouses he owes a duty of diagnostic vigilance, both as to their physical and psychological state and as to the stability of their relationship. This vigilance is in the interest of the child whom they may bring up as much as in their own. To the child he owes a duty of the utmost care in the selection of a donor, in order to exclude the excludable risks of genetic handicap, including an adverse Rh factor. To the donor he owes a duty of personal consideration, not to exploit or spoil a man, not to impose on a dependent or client relationship; one of the most neglected areas of the practice is the psychology of the donor[13].

The practice of AID will undoubtedly grow. Its establishment within the most reputable and public sectors of the medical profession will enable the nation to deal more prudently with contingent social issues of ethical importance as they arise. Sperm banks, in which frozen semen is stored for future use, whether personal to the donor or unrelated to him, can serve a legitimate interest, or they can be exploited commercially with resultant social harm. A code of ethical practice is necessary. Control may be either by professional regulation and convention, or, in default, imposed by legislation. The quality of the public debate, when it opens, will depend very much on the established integrity of the practice.

1. Newton JR. In: Brudenell M, McLaren A, Short R, Symonds M. *Artificial insemination.* London: Royal College of Obstetricians and Gynaecologists, 1977.
2. Foss GL. In: Brudenell M, McLaren A, Short R, Symonds M. *Artificial insemination,* op. cit.
3. Dunstan GR. In: Wolstenhome GEW, Fitzsimons DW, eds. *Law and ethics of AID and embryo transfer.* Ciba Foundation Symposium No 17 (NS). Amsterdam: Elsevier, 1973.
4. Dunstan GR. In: Brudenell M, McLaren A, Short R, Symonds M. *Artificial insemination,* op. cit.
5. Jackson MCN. In: Brudenell M, McLaren A, Short R, Symonds M. *Artificial insemination,* op. cit.
6. Titmuss RM. *The gift relationship.* London: Allen and Unwin, 1971.
7. Church Information Office. *Artificial insemination by donor: two contributions to a Christian judgement.* Evidence submitted on behalf of the Church of England to the Feversham Committee. London CIO, 1960.
8. Catholic Truth Society. *Artificial insemination. Evidence on behalf of the Catholic body in England and Wales* (submitted to the Feversham Committee). London: CTS, 1960.
9. Feversham Departmental Committee on Human Artificial Insemination. *Report.* London: HMSO, 1960. Cmnd 1105.
10. Archbishop of Canterbury's Commission. *Artificial human insemination.* London: SPCK, 1948.
11. Law Commission. *Family law: illegitimacy.* London: HMSO, 1979, Working Paper No 74.
12. Ledward RS, Crich J, Sharp P, Cotton RE, Symonds EM. A programme on AID within the National Health Service. *Br J Obstet Gynaecol* 1976; 83:719.
13. Symonds EM. In: Brudenell M, McLaren A, Short R, Symonds M. *Artificial insemination,* op. cit.

G. R. Dunstan

Assault. Both a crime and a civil wrong. Any examination involving touching the body, investigation or operation without consent constitutes an assault. Consent forms seek to protect the doctor against actions for assault, not against actions for negligence. Where consent is unobtainable owing to unconsciousness, mental incapacity or patient being under age of 16, the doctor may act as an agent of necessity in emergency but should limit his treatment to that which is essential to save life or prevent serious deterioration in the patient's health. The problem of assault hinges on the adequacy of the patient's understanding which determines the validity of his consent. (See *Consent*.)

J. Leahy Taylor

Attempted Suicide. A poor term in that it may cover a range of self-injuring behaviour, from for example the 12 (out of about 700) survivors of leaps from the Golden Gate Bridge in San Francisco to the girl who scratches her wrists in an overt attempt to gain the sympathy of a boyfriend. For this reason the term 'parasuicide' for deliberate, non-fatal self-injury, is increasingly used. The 12 survivors were apparently all glad to be alive and support the suicide barrier proposal; this gives the lie to those who say that those determined on suicide will eventually succeed and that intervention is therefore pointless. Some twenty years ago about 10% of parasuicides repeated within a year and 1% succeeded. Life expectancy of a suicidal ending was about 10%. The continuing rise of parasuicides (over 90% of which are, in Britain, by overdose) and reduction of suicide itself renders these figures obsolete and the point remains that the overwhelming majority of self-injured die eventually from natural causes. Overdosing is now the major cause of emergency admissions to medical wards (about 200,000 per year in England and Wales) and the repetitive cases, who usually want to 'escape' into the safety of a psychiatric ward, are one of the biggest worries to the medical and social services. No special rehabilitation programme has so far been shown to reduce the rate of repeat. Motives are immensely varied, from the true failed suicide *via* 'cries for help', impulsive acts for which the victim cannot account, conscious and unconscious manipulations, gestures punitive to others, or simply the desire to 'opt out' into a period of oblivion. It is rare for such people, on recovery, to regret being alive. The typical overdoser is female, young, harassed and neurotic, but the typical suicide male, old and lonely; there has been a converging tendency in rates as to both age and sex. Generalizations are dangerous. Overdosing, as a particularly dramatic form of non-verbal communication, can have a constructive outcome if appropriate help can be speedily brought in. 'Crisis intervention' is now a discipline in its own right.

Patients admitted with an overdose need a proper assessment of the psychosocial situation preceding it and of mental state on recovery. Comparatively simple questions can adequately pick out those at low and high risk for subsequent attempts, and a psychiatric interview at this stage is not necessarily required for all, provided psychiatric service is available and monitors the situation. Ways of reducing the present epidemic of attempted suicide by overdose have not so far been devised. The 'reward' of medical and psychosocial care assures the popularity of this pseudo solution to crises. Society has not yet found means of expressing disapproval of such behaviour. (See also *Suicide*.)

Richard Fox

Audit, Medical. See *Quality Assurance*.

Autism. A mental condition of unknown origin found in children, in which there is a marked tendency to become self-centred and to be withdrawn from the world around. Such children may need care in special centres, raising problems of resources (q.v.) and duties to the handicapped (q.v.).

Autonomy. See *Clinical Autonomy; Moral Autonomy*.

Aversion Therapy. Treatment by medicines or by psychotherapy causing intense dislike or painful stimulation, and hence rejection by the recipient of the addiction or abnormal or undesirable behaviour for which the treatment is designed. Examples are to be found in the treatment of alcoholism (q.v.) and of some sexual deviations or variations (q.v.). The ethical principles involved are those of *Behaviour Therapy* (q.v.) and *Psychotherapy* (q.v.).

B

Barefoot Doctor. A category of personnel working in the People's Republic of China who combine part-time medical practice with their normal occupation. They are trained to diagnose and treat the diseases prevalent in the regions where they work (see *Chinese Medicine*).

Battered Babies. See *Child Abuse*.

Battered Wives. Seeing a woman who has been repeatedly beaten by her husband, a doctor's instinct may be to urge her to complain to the police. Almost always that is a mistake, unless she has decided to leave home. Court proceedings are seldom possible while the husband and wife cohabit, for the threat of further violence is more powerful than legal sanctions. Even if a case is taken to court, either a fine or imprisonment is likely to cause further financial hardship to the woman and her children and to give the man a further grudge against his wife. In these circumstances medical intervention should be judged on its likely benefits to the woman rather than any obligations to society. What is needed is a place of sanctuary to which she and her children can go while there is a risk of continued violence. So long as the woman wishes to try to preserve her marriage no action should be taken that might make that more difficult. The case should be referred to a social worker or to the probation service only with the genuine consent of the woman. Ideally some form of psychological and practical longterm support should be arranged so that the woman knows she can get help when she needs it.

Tony Smith

Behaviour Control. See *Behaviour Therapy; Psychopharmacology; Psychotherapy*.

Behaviour Therapy. A psychological approach to treatment, based on the principles of learning which have emerged from the experimental work of the academic school of behaviourism.[1]

Neurotic and personality disorders are regarded as maladaptive patterns of behaviour which have developed through traumatic or

33

inappropriate learning experiences. Proponents of this approach reject the notion that symptoms are mere indications of either underlying organic pathology or deep-seated conflicts. These external signs constitute the disorder. The behaviourist approach to treatment therefore involves eliminating unwanted behaviour and replacing it with more appropriate response sequences.

The most widely used techniques are as follows:–

Phobias are treated by *systematic desensitization* (presentation of successive approximations to feared stimuli under anxiety-free conditions), *flooding* (prolonged exposure to the phobic object), or *anxiety management training* (development of skills to control tension). *Aversion therapy* (the pairing of a hitherto attractive object with a noxious stimulus) is used in the treatment of sexual deviants and alcoholics. Rehabilitation of psychogeriatric and chronic schizophrenic patients takes place in *token economy régimes* (reward-based, ward management schemes).

Of all the schools of psychotherapy, the behavioural approach is the one which has most often been criticized from an ethical standpoint. It has been argued[2] that the main reason for this is that behaviourists have traditionally used such emotive words as 'control', 'conditioning', and 'modification' when describing their work. However, the issue cannot be so lightly dismissed. Many critics[3] fear that advances in behavioural research could lead to more powerful interventions by the State and a corresponding decline in the freedom of the individual. They point to the fact that, until recently, aversion therapy was used with homosexuals who were referred by the courts for 'treatment'.[4] Events such as this have given rise to the common belief that behavioural methods are inextricably bound up with the politics of the Right. Kazdin,[5] however, challenges the logic underlying this view: 'Behaviour technology, like any other technology, is ethically neutral in that it has the potential for use and misuse. Thus objections lie not with the techniques *per se* but rather with the potential abuses'.

Thus behaviourists do not deny that their techniques could be used to the disadvantage of certain members of society. However, they would claim that all treatment methods in psychiatry set out to change attitudes and behaviour and are therefore equally open to this charge. At least in behaviour therapy, the patient is made fully aware of the goals and methods of treatment and can therefore choose not to comply if he is unhappy about any aspect of the programme. In those psychotherapies where the contrast is less explicit, so it is argued, he is much more open to subtle manipulation.

Leaving ideological issues aside, certain behavioural techniques have been criticised on the grounds that they involve inflicting unnecessary hardships on patients. Aversion therapy is an obvious example here. Those who apply this method claim that the distress caused is considerably less than the guilt and anguish that would be experienced were treatment to be withheld. What is clear is that it is quite unethical to make patients suffer to a degree which cannot be justified on grounds of efficacy. Extremely painful shocks are often used, yet they are no more effective than stimuli of moderate intensity.[1] Similarly there is no evidence to show that massed practice (treatment sessions given with short intervals between them) is superior to distributed practice (treatment sessions spread out over days or weeks). Nevertheless, despite the fact that it is more traumatic for the patient, many clinicians do use massed practice schedules regularly.

More recently, many behaviour therapists have preferred to carry out *covert sensitization* (aversion therapy in fantasy) than to administer electric shocks, mainly because they themselves find it less distressing. However, although patients can find this at least as unpleasant as faradic aversion therapy, its efficacy has not yet been properly established. Thus although aversion therapy itself can be justified, it is the practitioner's responsibility to ensure that the patient experiences as little hardship as possible.

Another technique which has been the source of some controversy is the token economy régime, i.e. the patient is rewarded for desired behaviour with tokens which he can exchange for a variety of privileges, actual goods, etc. It has been argued that this method of behavioural control is used more for the benefit of the nurses and family members than the patient. Behaviourists[5] reply that the targets they employ are those considered desirable by society as a whole (e.g. increased capacity for self-help; improved social skills). Furthermore, the reason why these people have been admitted to an institution in the first place is presumably because they are deficient in these respects. Nevertheless, the therapist should always obtain the full consent of the patient before starting treatment. However, since many of these patients have been involuntarily confined or are incapable of understanding what is involved, not a great deal of reliance can be placed on verbal agreement.

Another difficulty concerning token economy régimes is the choice of reinforcers. In order to provide the patient with a powerful incentive to change, the therapist has to impose moderately severe restrictions on his behaviour. However, since it is now considered unethical to deprive a patient of food, water, shelter, toilet amenities, privacy and human contact,[5] there are few possibilities open to the therapist.

Behaviour therapists have recently become very concerned to ensure that their techniques are used in the best interests of the individual patient. In 1975, for example, the Association for the Advancement of Behavior Therapy set up a committee to consider ethical issues concerning clinical practice. In its report[6], the committee produced the following list of questions:

Have the goals of treatment been adequately considered?

Has the choice of treatment methods been adequately considered?

Is the client's participation voluntary?

When another person or an agency is empowered to arrange for therapy, have the interests of the subordinated client been sufficiently considered?

Has the adequacy of treatment been evaluated?

Does the therapist refer the clients to other therapists when necessary?

Is the therapist qualified to provide treatment?

If followed, these guidelines should go a considerable way towards safeguarding the interests of those individuals who undergo behavioural programmes. (See also *Consent; Psychotherapy; Sex Therapy.*)

1. Bandura A. *Principles of behaviour modification.* New York: Holt, Rinehart & Winston, 1969.
2. Woolfolk AE, Woolfolk RL, Wilson GT. A rose by any other name – labeling bias and attitude toward behaviour modification. *J Consult Clin Psychol* 1977; 45(2):184–91.
3. London P, Hunt WA, eds. *Human behaviour and its controls.* Cambridge, Mass.: Schenkman, 1971: 128.
4. Feldman MP, MacCulloch MJ. *Homosexual behaviour – therapy and assessment.* Oxford: Pergamon Press, 1971.
5. Kazdin AE. *History of behaviour modification.* Baltimore: University Park, 1978.
6. Association for the Advancement of Behavior Therapy. Newsletter, 1977.

Dougal Mackay

Bereavement. Loss of a loved person (sometimes widened to include loss of other attachment objects).

In recent years evidence for the potentially damaging effects of bereavement on physical and mental health has accumulated and it is sometimes possible to identify individuals who are at special risk before, or at the time of, bereavement. Preventive intervention programmes aimed at reducing the incidence of social, psychological and health problems in the bereaved have been set up but there are a number of ethical problems which must be solved if the work is to bear fruit.

1. *Death Education.* The notion that we may be able to prepare people, including young children, for bereavements later in life by planned programmes of education at school or university or via the mass media raises problems similar to those raised by sex education (q.v.). There is the possibility that such programmes may inflict pain, distress or harm on some who take part in them, and questions arise

regarding the rights of parents or guardians to protect their dependents from exposure to such programmes. Teachers and other 'educators' must take responsibility for carrying out death education programmes and for the establishment of standards by which programmes can be judged and the qualifications of 'death educators' be established. It is also questionable to what extent the news media should provide live coverage of public deaths, bereavements, disasters, assassinations, etc. Some assert that open and realistic reporting of such events prepares people for losses in their own lives by exposing them to 'facts of death' which tend to be denied or avoided in many countries today. Opponents suggest that repeated exposure to the manifestations of grief and distress in others may blunt tender feelings, create excessive anxiety or evoke an appetite for sado-masochistic gratification. There may also be dangers in the exploitation of dying or bereaved individuals who, wittingly or unwittingly, take part in programmes of this type. (For further discussion of related issues, see *Death, Attitudes to*.)

2. *Anticipatory Guidance.* There is evidence that sudden, unexpected, and untimely bereavements are a greater hazard to later health and adjustment than bereavements which are expected. Doctors and others who are aware that illness or injury may be fatal can reduce the risk to family members and others likely to be affected by bereavement by warning them in advance. Ethical issues arise concerning the extent to which doctors and others covered by codes of confidentiality (q.v.) are at liberty to disclose information to such people without the patient's specific permission. This is particularly likely to arise if the doctor thinks that the information which he feels obliged to communicate to the family would harm the patient if communicated to him (see *Terminal Care; Truth*).

3. *Post-bereavement Counselling.* Several studies have demonstrated that support given to certain categories of bereaved persons may reduce the risk of subsequent ill health, but this also raises some thorny ethical problems.

There is some evidence that those most in need of help after bereavement are not necessarily the ones most likely to ask for it. However, doctors and nurses are often aware that a particular person is 'at risk', and the systematic assessment of risk could become a routine activity. To avoid suggesting to bereaved people that they become sick, such assessments are likely to be made without their knowledge. In so doing we are creating a category of confidential information which is capable of being misused. The very fact that some are selected for support, and others not, raises the possibility of stigma once the rationale of bereavement visiting becomes widely known.

Many programmes make use of non-professional or voluntary counsellors, the selection and supervision of whom raises special difficulties as does the extent to which they should be made privy to confidential information about the bereaved people whom they visit.

Unsolicited visiting of the bereaved runs the risk of being seen as intrusion upon private grief. The proponents of this approach argue that more harm is done by ignoring evident needs for help than by running the risk that an offer of help may be intrusive. The risk would seem to be minimized if the visitor is someone already known to and accepted by the bereaved. In the past this was often a local clergyman and the clergy still have an important role to play, but members of other caring professions are now the principal source of professional support to the bereaved.

Mourning rituals are carried out by all societies to sanction, articulate and support the passage of the survivors from one social state to another. Initially social sanction is provided for the expression of sorrow, anger and even self-punitive acts (making restitution for past errors and countering survival guilt). In many societies a second ceremony marks the end of mourning and provides sanction for the resumption of normal pleasures and activities. Mourning rituals have become attenuated in 'advanced' societies leaving the bereaved uncertain of their place in the world, their right to grieve and their right, after a period of time has elapsed, to stop grieving.

1. Parkes CM. *Bereavement: studies of grief in adult life*. London: Tavistock; New York: International Universities Press; Swedish Edn., Stockholm: Wahlström and Widstrand; German Edn., Hamburg: Rowohlt. Paperback edition Harmondsworth: Penguin Books, 1975.

C. Murray Parkes

Bioethics, Bibliography of. An annual volume which attempts to identify the central issues in bioethics, to develop standardized index terminology, and to provide a comprehensive guide to materials on bioethical topics. It is compiled by the Director of the Center for Bioethics, Kennedy Institute, Georgetown University, USA. Available from Gale Research Co., Book Tower, Detroit, Michigan 48226, USA.

Blood Donors. See *Blood Transfusion*.

Blood Grouping for Paternity Purposes. Very occasionally, an allegation may be made that a child has been wrongly identified in the maternity ward; both maternity and paternity will then be in doubt. Bizarre cases of child stealing have been reported. Otherwise, the use of blood groups as genetic markers is, in practice, confined to problems of paternity; these may arise in divorce proceedings and in the adjudication of affiliation orders or, rarely, in deciding legitimacy.

The principles of paternity testing are:

a) Save in conditions of extreme rarity such as the deletion of genes, blood group genes and antigens are passed on 'true' by a parent to its offspring. No proven case of a blood group mutating between two generations has ever been found. A blood group antigen cannot, therefore, be present in a child unless it is also present in at least one parent.

b) One gene of an allelic pair* is derived from each parent. Each parent has one of two genes to donate at random.

c) If one parent possesses a homozygous allelic gene pair then that gene must be conferred on all his or her offspring.

Blood group antigens are contained in a number of independent 'systems', each system containing one or more allelic pairs or triplets. In addition, some serum proteins and red cell enzymes exist as alleles and are inherited in the same way as are red cell antigens. The 'value' of these systems in paternity testing depends, amongst other things, on the number of allelic combinations contained and the relative distribution of the genes in the population.

Paternity testing will only be required if the putative father is denying a liability. He will, in effect, seek to be excluded from fatherhood and it will be seen from the principles given above that this is the only thing which can be deduced with certainty. Confirmation of paternity, to be discussed later, can never be more than a probability. It will be seen that the man has everything to gain from paternity testing and very much less to lose; by contrast, the mother, except when there are two or three admitted candidates for paternity, has relatively little expectation of advantage.

The chances of excluding a man wrongly accused of parenthood depend upon the number of systems analysed. If only the ABO, MNS and Rhesus systems are tested, some 60% of such men can be eliminated. This rises to 89% if six red cell antigens, three serum proteins and six red cell enzyme systems are used. These are *average* figures; the more precise chances that an individual set of results would have of showing non-paternity can be calculated.

The legal basis for paternity testing varies between England and Wales, where the Family Law Reform Act of 1969 operates, and Scotland, where it does not apply.

This 1969 Act gives the Court power to make a direction for blood grouping tests at the request of one or other concerned party. The age of consent is 16 and the Court may draw appropriate conclusions from a refusal to comply with a direction. There is, of course, nothing to prevent a privately agreed arrangement for investigation and this is the most common practice. The Act lays down that blood group investigations may only be undertaken by a blood grouping specialist

---

* For definition of terms in general see *Genetic Conditions*. An allele is one of the two or more genes which may be situated at the same locus in a chromosome.

appointed and authorised by the Home Office. The actual specimens are likely to be taken by the general practitioner.

The important features in the collection of specimens include:

a) Specimens should be taken from the mother, child and any putative fathers with their consent (the person in charge of a child under sixteen can give consent on his or her behalf).

b) The parties must be adequately identified. A passport photograph is desirable and, in the case of a Court direction, a certified photograph must be available to the doctor taking the specimen.

c) Labelling should be done in the view of, and attested by, the donor.

d) Declarations should be obtained that there has been no blood transfusion within the last three months. Children should not be younger than two months and preferably aged more than six months.

e) These conditions are obligatory when the Court has directed the examinations and a comprehensive Direction Form, supplied by the Court and running to seven parts, must be completed by the sampler. A statutory sampling fee is payable and the doctor will not be called to give evidence in person.

Part 1 of the report that the tester must supply requires comments on the value of the result in determining whether any person tested is the father of the child in question. The general method is to consider the proportion of men in the community that cannot be shown not to possess all the genes shown by the test to have been received by the child from the father; the smaller the proportion satisfying the criteria, the greater is the likelihood of paternity. Alternatively, one can work out how much more often an accused man is likely to produce a gene pattern in a child than would men in general. In either case, a factor of 100 goes some way to making paternity probable. The probabilities are, of course, greatly increased if a very uncommon factor is present in both man and child.

Blood tests have been relied upon far less frequently in Scotland, possibly because Scottish Courts will not compel a party to provide evidence to support the opponent's case and also because of the innate reluctance to rebut a presumption to the disadvantage of a child; this is particularly so when a child cannot give consent to a step which the law would not compel.

Nevertheless, there is widespread support for Mr Justice Ormrod's view that 'there is nothing more shocking than that injustice should be done on the basis of a legal presumption when justice could be done on the basis of fact'.

Brownlie AR. Blood and the blood groups – a developing field for expert evidence. *J Forensic Sci Soc* 1965; 5: 124–74.

Dodd BE, Lincoln PJ. Blood groups in problems of doubtful paternity. In: *Blood group topics*. London: Arnold, 1975: Ch 12.

Grant A, Bradbook ID. Newer techniques in paternity blood group ing. In Mant AK, ed. *Modern trends in forensic medicine – 3*. London: Butterworths, 1973: Ch 3.

J. K. Mason

Blood Testing, Random. Research into such subjects as the geographic or ethnic distribution of body chemicals or genes, the epidemiology of drug abuse or the distribution of pathogenic organisms is clearly desirable and can be facilitated by the routine use of blood specimens collected for quite unassociated reasons. The donor will have no knowledge of this and therefore cannot consent. Are such procedures ethical?

Following the method of 'consequentialist' ethics[1], the governing factor would seem to be the practical effect on the individuals concerned. Studies in which there is absolute anonymity and inability to trace the abnormal are of limited value; some means of retrieval is almost always needed. The problem then seems to resolve itself as to what action is indicated in the event of discovery of an abnormal subject.

At its simplest, if it is unethical to withhold a result – say, the random discovery of sero-positive syphilis – then it must be unethical to conduct the survey without consent; blood donors consent to such tests by implication and are informed of the positive result while being recommended to consult their practitioner. It is more difficult if the result is of potential or dubious significance. What is to be done, for instance, if a survey of abnormal haemoglobins throws up a recessive gene which could be combined to form a homozygous child? The answer would lie in the precise circumstances of the survey but, as regards this particular case, it is doubtful if hidden surveys incorporating ethnic overtones would ever be entirely immune to criticism. At the other end of the spectrum, there are circumstances in which a survey might be directly detrimental to the subject. As an extreme example, the police cannot obtain a blood alcohol result without the consent of the subject; it would be quite improper, therefore, to conduct a personal survey on the alcohol content of routine specimens intended for blood grouping and to record the results in such a way as to be available for subsequent litigation.

It might be argued that such a situation could never arise. But it must be remembered that the whole case notes are available to civil litigants at an early stage in proceedings concerned with personal injury and that this is not now confined to a doctor/doctor exchange[2]. It appears to be proper to cover up any irrelevant part of a document that is subject to disclosure. This practice should therefore be followed as regards test results which have no bearing on the treatment or clinical investigation of a patient; better still, they should never be included in the notes. (See *Confidentiality; Consent; Human Experiment; Medical Records.*)

Blood Transfusion

1. Brody H. *Ethical decisions in medicine*. Boston: Little, Brown, 1976.
2. Legal Correspondent. Disclosure of medical records. *Br Med J* 1978; 2: 135.

J. K. Mason

Blood Transfusion. Blood transfusion is essentially a form of replacement therapy, in that a patient who has a deficiency in one or more components of normal blood is given donor blood from a healthy volunteer. Whole blood, so called because it contains all the blood components, is transfused to patients who have suddenly lost large volumes of blood as the result of e.g. a serious accident, the complications of childbirth, a surgical operation or internal bleeding. Alternatively, a donation of whole blood may be separated into constituent parts, and each derivative then used to treat a patient whose blood is deficient in that particular component. This is called blood component therapy and ensures the optimal use of a valuable and scarce commodity, human blood. Major hospitals maintain banks of stored whole blood and of the various components, so that life-saving blood products of the correct group for the individual patient are quickly available.

The practice of blood transfusion involves donors, donations and recipients, and great care is taken to ensure that no harm results. In the UK any healthy person between the ages of 18 and 65 years may become a blood donor. The selection of donors is based on medical history, simple medical examination and laboratory tests. In this way only fit persons are accepted as donors and the recipient is safeguarded, particularly in respect of infectious diseases such as hepatitis which may be transmitted from donor to recipient by transfusion.

Blood transfusion is often life-saving but a patient may die from complications of transfusion therapy. Before transfusing a patient, a practitioner has to weigh the inherent dangers of transfusion therapy against the risk to life of withholding it. The hazards of transfusion can be reduced by appropriate laboratory, clinical and administrative measures but a transfusion, like any other injection, cannot be guaranteed as free from risk.

Practitioners may encounter adult patients or parents, such as Jehovah's Witnesses, whose religious persuasion forbids blood transfusion. These adult patients who refuse to receive blood products should sign a form accepting full responsibility for their action. Some surgeons and anaesthetists are prepared to perform major operations using synthetic plasma volume expanders, but in a life threatening emergency may after due consultation decide to use blood products and risk litigation. Parents who refuse permission for the transfusion of their child may prejudice his survival. Such an attitude has been successfully challenged in a Court of Law and infants may legally be taken into the care of the local authority or made wards of court until treatment is complete. In any event, the common law defence of necessity would doubtless be available.

In some countries donors are paid for their services, but gradually more and more countries are adopting the recommendation of the World Health Organization to use unpaid volunteers. Because of financial inducement some donors may damage their health by giving blood too frequently, and payment may cause volunteers to hide certain aspects of their medical history lest disclosure result in their rejection. It has been established that viral hepatitis occurs more frequently in patients given blood from paid than from unpaid donors. Payments may attract chronic alcoholics, drug addicts and those suffering from sexually transmitted disease.

Tropical diseases such as malaria can be transmitted by blood transfusion. White donors who have visited the tropics recently are just as liable to transmit tropical disease by transfusion as coloured donors now living in temperate zones.

With careful selection of donors, it is most unusual for volunteers to suffer ill effects, although bruising at the site of collection from a vein in front of the elbow and fainting occur occasionally. There is a danger that the fainting donor may suffer injury as he falls. If, by mischance, a donor suffers injury causing absence from work, claims for loss of wages should be considered sympathetically by the transfusion service.

1. Blood transfusion and blood products. In: Cash JD, ed. *Clinics in hematology.* Philadelphia and London: Saunders, 1976, Vol 5, No 1: 1–226.
2. Mollison PL. *Blood transfusion in clinical medicine.* 6th edn. Oxford: Blackwell Scientific, 1979.
3. Titmuss RM. *The gift relationship: from human blood to social policy.* London: Allen & Unwin, 1971.
4. Wallace J. *Blood transfusion for clinicians.* 1st edn. Edinburgh and London: Churchill Livingstone, 1977.
5. Wallace J. Blood and blood products. In: Alstead S, Girdwood RH, eds. *Textbook of medical treatment.* 14th edn. Edinburgh and London: Churchill Livingstone, 1978: Ch 8: 120–34.

John Wallace

Bone Marrow Transfusion. Bone marrow taken from unrelated donors has been successfully grafted to patients with blood diseases. The removal of bone marrow involves giving the donor a general anaesthetic while the marrow is aspirated from the pelvic bones by needle. Although the risk to a healthy person is small, the volunteer should be fully informed of the risks involved, and his fitness checked thoroughly. The operation should be performed by skilled practition-

ers in a well equipped hospital. Even when a bone marrow donor has consented in writing to donate, he should be free to withdraw at any time. Arrangements should be made to ensure that a volunteer suffers no financial loss as a result of giving bone marrow.
(For references see *Blood Transfusion*.)

John Wallace

Brain Death. See *Death, Determination of*.

British Medical Association. The primary objects for which the British Medical Association is established are to promote the medical and allied sciences and to maintain the honour and interests of the medical profession.

The Central Ethical Committee (CEC) is a Committee of Council which has the task of considering the ethical implications of all matters concerning the relationship between the medical profession, the public and the State and of giving appropriate advice to the Council. Since 1979 the terms of reference of the CEC reflect the change in emphasis in the work of the committee from concern with professional etiquette and organizational regulations to patient–oriented ethics.

Consideration of ethics as a bargain struck between one group in society and the remainder of the community has led the committee to consider, over the past two years, such topics as the doctor and state, medical confidentiality, the role of the doctor in immigration control, co-operation between the doctor and the police, and patient participation groups. The Committee has discussed these and other subjects, and has met with interested lay groups. It has advised the Association to press for legislation in some instances, or sought to persuade organizations to modify their views in others.

The new edition of the *Handbook of Medical Ethics* (1980), which is drafted by the Committee, is based on the profession's commitments to the ethics of practice. It includes a chapter on ethical dilemmas, which is intended to inform and provoke debate among the profession as a whole.

The address of the BMA and of its CEC is: BMA House, Tavistock Square, London WC1H 9JP.

Michael J.G. Thomas

Buddhism. The principles governing Buddhism and the practice of medicine have much in common. The Buddhist Path of Life offers prescriptions for the ethico-spiritual well-being of every individual, and the compassion for all creatures without discrimination which it teaches is a necessary part of the physician's attitude towards his patients. Buddhism and medicine are both, in their own ways, concerned with the alleviation, control, and ultimate removal of human suffering.

As a result, Buddhism has been closely allied with medicine since its earliest days. The Buddha himself is said to have exercised a ministry of healing and many legends exist of the skills of his personal physician, Jivaka. As early as the time of the Emperor Asoka, who reigned in India in the third century B.C., hospitals were set up both for humans and for animals, and Buddhism inspired the setting up of many institutions for the sick in India and Ceylon and subsequently in other Southeast Asian countries.

Buddhism devotes itself to the purification of the mind – to mental culture – as the predominant means of attaining the state of Supreme Enlightenment, the ultimate goal of man. It seeks to enable persons to meet both present and changing circumstances with serenity of mind.

The approach of Buddhism to medicine is therefore very much along psychosomatic lines, although the socio-economic condition of people is not ignored, since this needs to be right and wholesome if the behaviour of the individual is to be correct. 'Mind is the forerunner of all evil and good conditions; it is the chief; mind-made are all things.'

It is not suggested, however, that physical disease does not exist. Disease and suffering are a part of the life of all men until suffering is eventually eliminated when Supreme Deliverance is achieved. The Buddhist emphasis on medical care derives from the fact that physical health is a necessary basis for mental culture, and the medical profession has an important part to play in curing physical diseases in order that the mind may develop. Buddhism encourages a flow of intelligent faith, and trust in the doctor will help in recovery from systemic disease, as will the patient's serenity – the calm and relaxation which derives from cultivation of the mind. By converse, while the ethical good is proclaimed, each man is free to act according to his own desires, but must take the consequences of his actions. These will show themselves in the differing results obtained in the treatment of different individuals; and resistance to treatment may be due to evil actions committed by the patient in previous existences.

All Buddhists are expected to take reasonable care of their own health, since disease and the resulting mental suffering are a hindrance to the march towards enlightenment. This correlation between bodily health and the higher life adds a spiritual dimension to medical ethics through the ideal of selfless service.

One of the eight steps in the Path of Life – or Middle Way (because in general it stipulates a life of moderation) – is 'right conduct'. In Buddhism morality and intellectual enlightenment are inseparable. Included in 'right conduct' are the obligations to abstain from killing any living creature (even the breaking of an egg, a potential life, is condemned), and from unlawful sexual intercourse. To the strict Buddhist, therefore, it would be unacceptable to perform abortion, and countries in which Buddhism has retained much of its original purity, such as Burma, have opposed contraception until recent times.

Buddhism

Bentley-Taylor D. Buddhism. In: Anderson JND, ed. *The world's religions*. 2nd edn. London: IVF, 1951.

Soni RL. Buddhism in relation to the profession of medicine. In: Millard DW, ed. *Religion and Medicine 3*. London: SCM Press, 1976.

John Rivers

C

Cancer. A group of diseases, characterized by the uncontrolled growth of cells. To the layman, cancer is a 'growth' developing within an organ or tissue which it progressively invades to 'burst out' throughout the body and cause pain, misery and inevitable death. To the doctor it is a tumour or 'neoplasm' consisting of cells which no longer respond to normal controlling mechanisms but continue progressively to divide and grow. Endowed with unusual invasive powers, they enter the blood and lymphatic channels, by which they become widely disseminated to remote sites where they form secondary tumours or metastases. Death may occur from complications of the primary growth or by destruction of organ function by secondary deposits.

Traditionally the treatment of cancer is by the surgical removal of the primary tumour or its destruction by radiotherapy. The development of more and more radical operations (for example, amputations) was based on the belief that cancer remained localized to its organ of origin and the glands of the lymphatic system draining it for a considerable period of time, during which the best chance of cure was by the eradication of every last cancer cell. It is now recognized that dissemination of a cancer takes place early and that, in many instances, systemic treatment, e.g. by chemotherapy, is a necessary part of its control. The chronic progressive course, and frequently incurable nature of the disease, raise particular ethical problems.

Should the patient know? Normally a patient with incurable cancer is not told the true nature of his disease unless he asks. Some believe that patients with early disease should also be shielded from this stark reality and not told the truth, but others are frank about the diagnosis and describe the steps which will be taken to treat the disease. They believe that provided the information, suitably edited, is given in an unhurried way, doubts can be dispelled and the patient is better equipped to face the future. To many it is fear of the unknown which is most terrifying. But has the doctor the right to decide and has not the patient the right to know? (See *Truth, Telling the.*)

How intensive should be the treatment? Some question if expensive and scarce resources should be used to treat a disease where the benefit to the patient is likely to be doubtful. Doctors are taught to balance the intensity of their endeavours against the likely outcome but moral dilemmas can occur particularly when the disease is known to be advanced. Should it be treated aggressively or should one await the onset of troublesome symptons which may be relieved by the simplest of measures? If an acute and possibly remediable disease develops, should effective treatment be instituted or should it be allowed to run its natural course, even if this should prove fatal? Who should make these decisions? (See *Resources*.)

Who should treat? The freedom to choose one's doctor and the freedom of the doctor to practise as he considers best are essential rights of a free society. However, the doctor is ethically responsible to be competent and is expected to use new methods of treatment while discarding the old. The cancer patient is vulnerable and may require to be protected against the 'quack' whose competence may be in doubt (see *Competence to Practise*).

Even the competent doctor may not have the specialized training to handle some new and complex forms of treatment. He should refer the patient to another but this is not always easy as he may feel it an abdication of his responsibility to his patient.

Co-ordinated Cancer Centres, as have developed in the USA, are now being planned in Britain where those with special expertise, e.g. of radiation therapy (radiation oncologists) or chemotherapy (medical oncologists) are collaborating closely with others to form multidisciplinary groups who manage the patient with cancer. As part of this co-ordinated activity, clinical trial centres are also being set up. Such organized specialization may improve the care of the patient, but group pressure can impinge on personal and professional freedom. Patients cannot be looked after by a committee, yet preservation of the one doctor/one patient relationship poses problems.

The role of the nurse. Certain operations for cancer have serious psychological effects over and above those caused by the fear of cancer. For example, removal of the female breast can cause serious anxiety, depression, and upset family and sexual relationships. It has been shown by scientific studies that a 'nurse-counsellor' can do much to counteract these effects. Other roles have been defined for 'nurse-practitioners', e.g. the giving of chemotherapeutic drugs. These roles even include the *physical examination* of patients attending early diagnosis or follow-up clinics. These are duties which traditionally have been performed by medically trained personnel and the ethos of the doctor/patient and doctor/nurse relationships can be disturbed. (See *Teamwork*.)

Screening programmes. Screening (q.v.) is the application of diagnostic measures to apparently well persons in the hope of uncovering cancer before it causes symptons. It is usually applied to the discovery of cancer of the uterine cervix, and experimental programmes have been instituted for the early detection of breast cancer and cancer of the digestive system. Some believe that this causes more anxiety to the public than benefit. All such measures must be scientifically assessed before being put into general practice. Such assessments should rightly include their psychological effects.

Incurable cases. More than 100,000 persons die from cancer in England and Wales each year. Society does not allow them to decide when this should be. Legally, a doctor cannot induce death but he is not expected to prolong dying and must control pain and discomfort even if life is thereby shortened.

Many patients die at home surrounded by family and community. Others die in an acute hospital where the emphasis is on recovery and the caring professions may lack time to give to dying patients and their relatives the support, trust and encouragement which they require. Others spend their remaining time in a 'terminal care home' where they are tended by sympathetic and understanding staff and gain considerable corporate support from other patients, but are shut off from their own family and friends.

As patients are often unaware of the imminence of death, they have little choice in which of these places they will die. Their family, their doctors and the community choose for them and thus may deny them their right to die peaceably in familiar surroundings (see *Death, Attitudes to; Euthanasia; Hospices; Terminal Care*).

Health education (q.v.). Most of these problems stem from the public's fear of cancer and the reluctance on the part of doctors and relatives to discuss with the patient what could lie ahead. There is need for education of the public so that they can accept that cancer is a disease which may be cured or may be associated with long periods of normal living, and not a sentence of death. It should not be regarded differently from other diseases which may carry a similar prognosis but not a similar image in the patient's mind. Then the doctor will be able to discuss each situation frankly with the patient and act in accordance with his wishes.

Programmes of public education must be very carefully planned and controlled so that they do not cause anxiety.

Bennette G. *People and cancer.* London: British Cancer Council, 1969.

Bennette G. *The problem of relevance in cancer research.* London: British Cancer Council, 1969.

Bennette G. *Cancer priorities.* London: British Cancer Council, 1971.

A. P. M. Forrest

Care, Terminal; (Care of the Dying). See *Hospices; Terminal Care.*

Casti Connubii. See *Contraception.*

Castration. Removal of *both* of the gonads (testicles or ovaries). The term is sometimes also used to describe destruction of the gonads by ionizing irradiation.

Removal of one gonad has little effect, but castration causes irreversible sterility. It also results, before puberty, in failure of the development of secondary sex characters and, after puberty, in some regression of those characters which have developed already. No effects are discernible in women past the menopause. A male, castrated before puberty, is called a eunuch. Secondary sex characters, but not fertility, can be induced or restored by the administration of male or female sex hormones respectively. Plastic or metal prostheses, which may be inserted into the scrotum, resemble normal testes.

Deliberate castration, to degrade men, to provide attendants for harems or to perpetuate treble voices in choristers, is generally regarded as unethical and is no longer tolerated in civilized communities.

Castration may, very seldom, be caused by accidental trauma, especially in the male, or by accidental irradiation. More often it is undertaken surgically for the treatment of disease of the gonads themselves (especially the ovaries) or of diseases which are influenced by the hormonal secretions of the gonads (cancer of the breast in women or of the prostate in men). When the uterus is being removed surgically (hysterectomy) on account of disease or displacement, the ovaries may be removed also or conserved. The decision depends sometimes on the nature of the disease and sometimes on other factors, including the age of the patient and the likelihood that disease will develop in the ovaries later. Very rarely both testicles are removed to facilitate the repair of bilateral hernias.

Castration is occasionally undertaken therapeutically in intersexual individuals (those with anomalous primary and/or secondary sexual characters) as part of the process of making all their organs conform, as far as possible, to the appropriate assigned sex (see *Intersex*). The decision may be difficult, but it is made on medical grounds and raises no special ethical problems. Castration is also undertaken in transsexuals (those who consider themselves to belong to the opposite sex), especially men, and is then usually combined with the administration of sex hormones, plastic procedures on the external genital organs and (in women) removal of the breasts. Castration in these circumstances raises more difficult issues and many surgeons and physicians regard such 'sex changes' as unethical (see *Cosmetic Surgery; Sexual Deviations or Variations*).

It is generally agreed that, if therapeutic castration is proposed, its effects should be explained to both patient and spouse. Written consent should be obtained from both, as for any form of sterilization (q.v.). It is also generally held that, because it is irreversible and impairs the secondary sex characters, castration is not admissible for sterilization alone.

Montgomery DAD, Welbourn RB. *Medical and surgical endocrinology*. London: Arnold, 1975.

R. B. Welbourn

Certification of Death. See *Death, Certification of.*

Certification of Mental Illness. See *Mental Illness, Certification of.*

Chaplains. See *Hospital Chaplains.*

Child. A child is no longer considered a chattel or property of his parents or other legal guardian. He is to be treated as a person with rights, albeit of less experience and knowledge than an adult.

Ethical problems arise at many stages of a child's life. In giving advice, the professional must assess the child for his potentialities as well as for what he is, while not forgetting his rights as an individual. He must have regard for the present situation and how it might develop if no action were taken; whether medical intervention would lead to a more rewarding life for the child or to one of misery; what would be the impact on the family of, for example, a handicapped child, with the possibilities of disruption of a marriage and harm to other children; and what would be the effect on society if the medical, social and educational care required by one individual were to absorb an undue proportion of the community's resources.

Parents may desire that their newly born child with severe spina bifida should not be operated upon and question whether doctors have the right to insist that the operation be done, and a patched up, severely handicapped, child returned to its parents (see *Congenital Malformations; Spina Bifida*). By contrast, it was recently decided that a girl aged 12, suffering from disease of obscure origin which produced mental retardation – and in whom the risk of an unwanted pregnancy was therefore thought to be high – should not be sterilized, although the parents and social workers were in favour of the operation being performed. It was argued that it was wrong to take away the basic human right of being able to bear a child (see *Sterilization*).

Issues arise in the use of behaviour therapy and the pain inflicted during aversion therapy. These are dealt with under *Behaviour Therapy*.

Problems arise even before birth and the unborn child is now achieving a status previously unconsidered. There are some, even, who ask whether a fetus has a right not to be born, or a newborn baby the right not to be helped to survive (see *Unborn Child, Rights of*).

Usually, a child's parents act and speak for him, but this must not be assumed; a child may need an advocate other than his parents. In general, parents give good care to their children but there are occasions when the parents' desires and the welfare of the child come into opposition. The courts and many social workers give great weight to the rights of parents. The parents are present in court and may be represented. The welfare of the child is often said to be paramount, but if his needs and rights are not put forward by a knowledgeable person, a court's decisions may not be in the best interests of the child. It has been suggested that there should be 'children's advocates' to act for them, but none exist as yet. A children's doctor, a social worker or a teacher may take this duty upon himself, and if he does so, he must prepare himself to speak effectively on the child's behalf. The special problems of child abuse are dealt with under this heading (see also *Risk Registers*).

Under UK law a child is a person under the age of 18 years. He may give his own consent (q.v.) for medical treatment, surgical operations and other procedures at the age of 16. Surprisingly, a circular from the Department of Health on the ethics of clinical research (HSC(5) 153) says that children of 12 (14 in Scotland) can give consent, yet there are those who, from mental or emotional handicap or delay, are still maturing at the age of 18. However, this circular has no legal status. The Family Law Reform Act gives a minor authority to give his consent to treatment (without any other consent), but this is understood not to cover research procedures, although the issue has never been tested in the courts. Likewise it is generally accepted that a parent or guardian has no right to give his consent to the performance of a non-therapeutic procedure in a child, however much this may be to the public interest, but again this has not been tested in the courts.

In the UK the 'age of consent', at which girls may legally have sexual intercourse, remains at 16 despite current attempts to have it lowered. Girls below this age frequently come to their doctors today to ask for the contraceptive pill because they are sleeping with their boy friends. The doctor's problem is twofold: firstly, should he inform the parents without the girl's permission and, secondly, should he give her the pill without telling them (and ignoring the legal situation) on the grounds that it is better to avoid an unwanted pregnancy in an immature woman with all the added problems this would entail? If the girl is already pregnant, additional problems arise. (See *Abortion; Confidentiality; Contraception.*)

A group of paediatricians in California[1] have considered critical issues in intensive care (q.v.) of the newborn. They concluded that there were situations in which they would not resuscitate, others in which they would not use all possible medical resources and others where they would agree to active measures to terminate life. They instanced the case of a newborn baby with Down's syndrome, perhaps basing their argument on the problem of the expense of maintaining a mentally handicapped person or merely on the value judgement of educated professionals being prepared to write off a person whose IQ would be 50 or less. However, many doctors would say that, although such babies would grow into adults with a varying degree of mental defect, they would not be unhappy people. And while it might be a reasonable decision not to resuscitate such a baby who had not started breathing, active termination of its life would be unacceptable both legally and ethically. The group also thought that all infants with chromosome abnormality should be allowed to die, but again this would not be generally acceptable. For example, children with Turner's syndrome who reach adult life are of normal or mildly low intelligence, able to work although sterile (see *Chromosome Disorders*).

Fifty years ago a family doctor, faced with a baby with severe spina bifida at a home delivery, would report a stillbirth. Delivery today is a public affair and resuscitation is embarked on for fear of criticism. It would be better if the management of all eventualities could be discussed beforehand by *all* involved and agreement reached on what to do – agreement based on 'those rational principles of our living without which constructive human association would be impossible' – as ethics has been defined by Hemming.[2]

It used to be thought that the doctor was bound to do all he could for the person who came to consult him. The claims of the family and of society are now admitted, so that the doctor (or other professional) must consider whether he has an ethical responsibility to give some of his time and thought to, for example, the excess of illness in children of unskilled workers and the lower paid, and whether he and his colleagues should agree to the wishes of some parents in performing medically useless procedures such as the majority of tonsillectomies at the expense of other more obvious needs. Is he only bound when society has set restraints – as for example on heart transplants in England and Wales?

1. Jonsen AR, Phibbs RH, Tooley WH, Garland MJ. Critical issues in newborn intensive care. *Paediatrics* 1975; 55: 75b.
2. Hemming J. Teaching them right. *New Humanist* 1975; 91: 102.
Fried C. Rights and health care . . . beyond quality and efficiency. *N Engl J Med* 1975; 293: 241.
Hiatt HH. Protecting the medical commons; who is responsible? *N Engl J Med* 1975; 293: 235.
Jonsen AR. Scientific medicine and therapeutic choice. *N Engl J Med* 1975; 293: 1126.

The late Ronald C. MacKeith

Child Abuse. Child abuse includes physical injury (baby battering) and other forms of neglect or injury such as emotional deprivation and starvation. If the diagnosis is evident or suspected, the child should be removed to a 'place of safety' – usually a children's ward in the first place – and an immediate case conference held, attended by the paediatrician, general practitioner, social worker, police and, often, an officer of the National Society for Prevention of Cruelty to Children. This will go better if good relations have already been built between these professionals. Each can usually contribute information on the background but each has different aims and may have different ideas on how to achieve what is best for the child. A doctor might consider it ethical, though illegal, not to tell the police, if he thought that unilateral action by the police would imperil the best management of the problem. A social worker may put greater emphasis on keeping children with their families; a doctor may think the risk so great that that would be medically and ethically wrong. Some will emphasize prevention of further injury, others the possibility of rehabilitation of the family in question.

There is great danger that injury to some children may be overlooked or concealed. The mother may not be at home when the health visitor calls, or may not allow the child to be undressed for physical examination.

There are abusing parents who are so sick that they are unfit to have the care of their children. There are others who, with good support by health visitor and/or social worker, will be able to cope with the stresses under which they have injured the child. Society is rightly intolerant of child abuse, but most parents can remember times when they could have injured their children but did not. Abusing parents are often under social and emotional stress with little support; they have often had a deprived childhood. Often the babies who are injured have been separated from their mothers – because of prematurity or other medical reasons – in the early days after birth during which mothers in general fall in love with their babies. Doctors are not entirely free of some responsibility for creating the abusing family.

Ethical aspects of the management of these problems are discussed by Arthur[1] and Hall[2]. The immediate and long-term welfare of the child and *his* rights (the child is no longer to be considered a chattel or property of his parents) are the principal guide. Rehabilitation rather than retribution for the parents may enable the child to grow up in a true home instead of in a hostel for children, and prison is unlikely to make anyone a better parent. Society may have to learn that these parents are often in need of medical and social help, perhaps protection from their own impulses and, sometimes, the opportunity to mature.

Neither doctor, police nor social worker can alone provide all the services needed for the child, his sibs and parents. None should act without first informing his colleagues. The best services are based on full trust and exchange of information between top-level professionals each of whom can act or waive rules as is jointly decided by them in discussion. The parents need someone they can ask for help at any time and people whom they can trust to be helpful. Some senior person must hold prime responsibility, not only to take the correct legal decisions but also the correct ethical ones. Each professional has a responsibility to the child, his parents, the family as a whole and his professional colleagues, as well as to the local community and to society at large.

We may recall that violence against children is, in our society, sometimes condoned as part of discipline in the home or, occasionally, at school. Whether or not we accept this as ethical will depend on our individual viewpoint. We may also recall that emotional deprivation can be as cruel and as lastingly harmful as physical injury and we may therefore act against all deprivation as well as against battering.

Any neglect of preventive measures would be unethical. It is often possible to identify parents at risk – young adults, who were themselves deprived in childhood, who in the maternity ward appear not to respond normally to their new babies – and to give them extra support in the way of counselling, advice, family planning and other services, money, housing, and maybe just listening. Those who try to help such families must be aware that the mortality of battered children is about one in ten.

On the other hand, proposals to establish registers of families at risk (see *Risk Registers*) raise other ethical issues – of confidentiality, of appearing to stigmatize families for all time, and of the uses to which such information might be put. Doctors involved need to ensure that proper safeguards are provided and maintained. (See also *Battered Wives*.)

1. Arthur LJ, Moncrieff WM, Milburn W *et al.* Non-accidental injury in children; what we do in Derby. *Br Med J* 1976; I: 1363–6.
2. Hall MH, A view from the emergency and accident department. In: Franklin AW, ed. *Concerning child abuse.* Edinburgh and London: Churchill Livingstone, 1975.
Franklin AW, ed. *The challenge of child abuse.* London: Academic Press, 1977.

The late Ronald C. MacKeith

Childbirth, Intervention in. The traditional conservatism of obstetric care has been changing a great deal in recent years. The ability and readiness of obstetricians to intervene in childbirth have been influenced by several developments. These can be briefly summarized, as follows:–

During the last decade, more effective methods of stimulating uterine contractions to induce or accelerate labour have been developed.[1] These at first involve amniotomy (rupture of the membranes) and administration of an oxytocic drug, usually by an intravenous 'drip', but sometimes by mouth. If successful these techniques allow labour to be induced at a chosen time, and delivery accomplished in almost all cases within about 12 hours. But in a small proportion of cases labour may not progress satisfactorily and therefore delivery has to be effected by Caesarean section. This inevitably increases the risk for the mother, both immediately and in all subsequent deliveries. Sophisticated forms of electronic controller are in use, by which the drip rate is automatically modulated using a feed-back signal from an intra-uterine pressure-recording catheter, which remains in the uterus throughout labour, and is a potential source of infection. The risks involved are increased if labour is accelerated too much, and the infant may then be in less good condition at birth. On the other hand, prolonged labour with its serious dangers is eliminated.[2]

More recent methods of induction involve insertion into the vagina of pessaries or jelly containing prostaglandin (a newer agent which stimulates uterine contractions). This simple technique appears much more acceptable to patients than amniotomy and a 'drip'.

The average duration of pregnancy is 280 days from the date of the last menstrual period. As in all other biological measurements, there is a range of variation, and sometimes there is no reliable date from which to calculate. It has been recognized for some years that, when pregnancy is unduly prolonged, the risk to the baby tends to increase. This hazard of 'postmaturity' mainly affects the babies of women pregnant for the first time, and of older women.[3] It has therefore become a general policy to set some limit to the duration of pregnancy, and to induce labour at that point. As more reliable techniques for inducing labour have been developed, the tendency has been to set this time-limit closer and closer to 40 weeks, sometimes involving induction of labour in up to half of all confinements. If an error is made in estimating the correct date, the well-being of the infant is threatened by the untimely premature birth which follows induction. Apart from those cases in which there appear to be medical reasons for inducing labour, induction may also be performed to suit the personal circumstances of the mother, or to enable labour and delivery to be conducted during the daytime, when the staffing resources of the hospital are likely to be fully available. The number and quality of medical and midwifery staff on duty during the night is likely to be smaller than by day, and access to laboratory facilities, X-rays, or skilled anaesthesia may only be obtainable with difficulty or delay, if at all.

Another changing trend has been the more widespread use of epidural nerve block for the relief of pain during labour.[4] This technique, first popularized during the 1940s in the USA and later in Britain, usually provides excellent analgesia, but necessitates more frequent recourse to forceps delivery, because it diminishes the mother's ability to expel the child by her own muscular efforts. Epidural block may cause a fall in blood pressure, which can reduce the amount of oxygen reaching the baby (asphyxia).

It is also relevant to refer to the adoption of new and sophisticated techniques of fetal monitoring during labour – the application of electronics and microchemistry to obstetrics.[5] External and internal sensing devices link the mother and infant to a recording unit throughout labour, to permit continuuous observation of uterine activity and of the fetal heart-rate. This information assists in the early detection of fetal asphyxia. An electrode clip may be attached to the infant's scalp throughout labour to pick up, without interference from other sources, the voltage signal from the infant's heartbeat. To confirm possible asphyxial changes, micro-samples of the infant's blood may be taken from time to time during labour, by making a small puncture of the scalp.[6] This is a relatively safe procedure although untoward bleeding occasionally occurs and one or two fatalities have been reported.

When epidural analgesia is used, the mother must lie all the time on her side to minimize adverse effects upon the circulation. In this position it is difficult to obtain a satisfactory recording of the fetal heartrate from an external detector, and therefore an internal scalp electrode has to be employed, which involves a slightly greater risk of infection.

To some extent, therefore, these changing practices are interrelated and sequential. The decision to induce labour may call for an oxytocic drip infusion, which must be continued throughout labour to maintain momentum, and so to curtail the time-interval between amniotomy and delivery and prevent an increased risk of infection. The more frequent and strong contractions may intensify the pain of labour, and call for epidural nerve block. To detect undue stresses on the infant in this situation, continuous monitoring is then indicated. If instrumental delivery is required, the baby will usually be kept under close observation for the first day of life apart from the mother. This separation, there is evidence to show, may impair the establishment of a normal emotional bond between mother and infant; it often causes the mother anxious concern. Such a chain of possible events raises doubts about the ethics of inducing labour solely to suit the personal convenience of the mother or the attendants.

Collectively, these changes can profoundly modify childbirth as an individual experience. The mother's role is more passive and less self-reliant, and so her sense of achievement may be diminished or entirely lost. The event tends to become technical and impersonal, so that its significance as the coming into being of a new individual is obscured.

In all cultures, the personal uniqueness of the day and time of birth is specially acknowledged. 'Monday's child is fair of face. . . .' In the Roman Catholic tradition, the infant may be named after the appropriate Saint, on whose day it is born. In the Orient, an astrologer is consulted to select a fitting name for the child, and this astrological 'identity', based on the exact moment of birth, will remain of the greatest importance throughout the individual's life influencing, for example, the eventual choice of a marriage partner. In our own computerized society, the combination of name and date of birth provides an almost unique identification code for indexing personal records, computer files, etc.

It is perhaps not surprising, therefore, that reactions against intervention in childbirth have occurred. Various movements advocating more sensitive approaches to childbirth have gained much support. In the USA, 'alternative childbirth centres' have sprung up, supported by those most averse to present day institutional methods. In Europe, the pattern of gentle, hushed delivery in dim light promoted by Leboyer has attracted much interest.

Apart from these consumer reactions, professional opinion also is now generally more conservative in its approach to intervention. But while induction of labour has become less common, Caesarean deliveries continue to increase.

It is possible then to identify certain areas of ethical concern related to these patterns of obstetric practice.

CONSENT. The obstetric patient's consent is generally obtained as a single 'blanket' statement covering all possible interventions (apart from sterilization). The extent to which this consent can be regarded as informed is crucially dependent upon continuing communication and explanation by the woman's attendants at all stages both before and during labour.

But some women would maintain that, in a matter in which individual emotions and personal fulfilment are so deeply involved, each mother should retain the greatest degree of freedom of choice and decision regarding the conduct of her confinement, in a manner different from the 'total' consent which might be given for (say) a surgical operation.

They hold that the types of intervention described above almost inevitably detract from the feeling of self-reliance on which a sense of achievement in childbirth is built. They would insist, therefore, that the woman's consent should be based upon informed discussion, be explicit for the use of particular drugs or procedures, and be free from pressure to conform to a particular 'policy', which may in some circumstances represent little more than an administrative convenience, or a clinical vogue.

IATROGENIC RISKS. It is generally accepted that the interventions employed in the induction or acceleration of labour, and the internal methods of fetal monitoring, involve elements of risk; but, overall, it is claimed that these are outweighed by the advantages. It is more debatable whether this is true for each individual mother or infant, particularly if intervention is adopted unselectively, as part of a general policy. Here again the issue turns on the degree to which all patients are expected to be dealt with according to a settled policy, or the extent to which it is practicable or desirable to treat each one individually according to her physical and emotional needs.

Since almost all confinements in Britain now take place in hospital, services for home delivery are difficult or impossible to arrange, and are likely to become more difficult to maintain in future, as fewer and fewer doctors and midwives possess the experience, skill and confidence necessary to conduct domiciliary delivery. This constriction of the woman's option, it may be argued, increases the obligation to offer the greatest degree of consumer choice within the hospital environment. (See also *Consent; Iatrogenic Disease; Patients; Patients' Association.*)

1. Turnbull A, Anderson ABM. Induction of labour. 3. Results with amniotomy and oxytocin 'titration'. *Journal of Obstetrics and Gynaecology of the British Commonwealth* 1968; 75:32–41.
2. O'Driscoll K, Jackson RJA, Gallaher JT. Prevention of prolonged labour. *Br Med J*, 1969; 2:4–77.
3. Butler NR, Alberman ED. *Perinatal problems. The second report of the 1958 British perinatal mortality survey under the auspices of the national birthday trust fund.* Edinburgh: Livingstone, 1958.
4. Crawford JS. *Principles and practice of obstetric anaesthesia.* 3rd edn. Oxford: Blackwell Scientific, 1972.
5. Hon EH. *An atlas of fetal heart rate patterns.* New Haven: Harty Press, 1968.
6. Saling E, Schneider D. Biochemical supervision of the fetus during labour. *Journal of Obstetrics and Gynaecology of the British Commonwealth* 1967; 74: 799.

P. R. Myerscough

Chinese Medicine. Since remote antiquity, the foundations of Chinese medicine have been intimately linked to the religious and socio-political aspects of Chinese society.

The oldest known system is 'ancestral medicine', in which the causes of disease and of all other significant occurrences on an individual level were thought to rest primarily with the intervention of ancestors. Diseases were prevented and treated, in the same way as other individual or social crises, by means of continual offerings and other attempts to satisfy or reconcile ancestors.

During the last 500 years B.C. the old stable order broke down; there was much fighting between rival groups and survival depended on the formation of alliances against opponents. Reflecting this situation, 'demonic medicine' emerged. Its basis was that man was surrounded by evil demons who constantly sought to overcome him and in the process inflicted diseases on him. Protection was guaranteed only by strengthening one's own inherent demons and by the formation of alliances with forces high in the demonic hierarchy. This tradition of medicine persisted into the 20th century.

It was followed by a system known as the 'medicine of systematic correspondence', which was supported by Confucian policy makers as the only orthodox medicine of their society. Confucianism was based on the view that the social order could only be maintained if everybody lived up to his social role, all roles in society being linked to one another. Only if every member observed the proper rules of behaviour and kept to the 'middle way' could social crises be averted. Confucianism was concerned with the ordering of the living society; the existence of gods or demons was not acknowledged. The 'medicine of systematic correspondence' reflected these concepts. Its practitioners asserted that diseases were caused by inappropriate exposure to the influences of outside sources such as heat, damp, wind, sun, heaven and earth, and by imbalances in the continuous exchange of influences in the various parts of the organism. If a man allowed outside influences to work upon him in the proper way and if he avoided excesses, he would remain free from diseases up to his timely death. It was in this system of medicine that acupuncture (q.v.) was established as the main method of treatment.

At about the same period, early Taoists developed the theory that a life free from crisis, both physical and social, could be achieved by acting in accordance with the law of nature. Individual life was believed to change from the corporeal to the spiritual and back to the corporeal state, and for this reason early Taoists ridiculed efforts to intervene medically in cases of disease or imminent death. Later, the proponents of a vulgar Tao sought to extend corporal life endlessly by, e.g., dietary measures, gymnastics, sexual practices and the intake of drugs. Out of this there developed a somewhat pragmatic system of medicine which was symptom-oriented and contained a rich *materia medica*. Both acupuncture and traditional drug remedies have their place in modern Chinese medical practice. Buddhism (q.v.) has also exerted a lasting influence on health care in some Chinese communities, particularly those outside the mainland. In the first half of the 20th century Chinese reformers and revolutionaries alike (including both Nationalists and Marxists) bitterly criticized traditional Chinese medical concepts and practices for their alleged inability to cope successfully with any major health problem, as well as for their obvious ties to the 'feudalistic society' of the Confucian past. Western scientific medicine, enthusiastically supported by all groups striving for a modernization of China, became the dominant factor, at least as far as medical training, public health politics and urban practice were concerned. In rural areas, though, traditional methods remained often the only ones available

In the People's Republic of China today, medicine has partly moved away from the Western style to an innovative and labour-intensive pattern specially adapted to the needs of a vast rural population and to the politico-economic goals of the Government. The opportunity for such a development arose from the magnitude of the health problems following years of war and the ability of Government to enforce its plans. As with most developing countries, such medical facilities as existed were concentrated in the cities and the profession had been trained to Western standards.

Guiding principles laid down in the 1950s were: (a) serve the workers, peasants and soldiers; (b) place the chief emphasis on prevention; (c) stress co-operation between western and traditional medicine; and (d) rely on mass movements to carry out health work. A new factor in this approach was to regard the maintenance of health not only from a humanitarian point of view but also as an essential part of the maintenance of production. This led to health services being taken to the people – to factories, farms and even into the fields – so that work should be hindered no more than necessary.

These early policies achieved some success, particularly in the area of preventive medicine, and the 'mass movement' principle was instrumental, through nationwide health campaigns, in helping to reduce the numbers of pests – flies, mosquitoes, sparrows – and the incidence of parasitic diseases. The same principle was extended to treatment and research: treatment was modified where possible so as to be suitable for 'mass' use, and research taken out of the highly scientific area and simplified so that lower grades of personnel could take part and applications be adopted for use by the 'many'.

Renewed encouragement was given to traditionally trained doctors, partly in an attempt to meet unfulfilled demands for medical care and partly to meet political and cultural aims. New schools were opened for their training and individual apprenticeship schemes re-introduced. There was mutual opposition between practitioners of the traditional and western styles of medicine, but traditional doctors made a significant contribution to health care in the 1960s and were undoubtedly better received in rural areas. In addition, their training was shorter and the herbal remedies they employed were much cheaper. It was later realized that the Western-style doctor was still needed and that the status of the traditional doctor had to be upgraded. A *modus vivendi* was achieved between the two groups; Western-style doctors were trained in traditional methods which were later also introduced into undergraduate courses. Methods from both traditions came to be employed together, e.g. acupuncture anaesthesia with modern surgery, and traditional remedies, largely herbal, were adopted widely, largely because the plants from which drugs were obtained could be grown locally as required. Research in this area produced a number of new and allegedly effective remedies.

However, the attempt to acclimatize urban doctors to rural conditions, coupled with the use of traditional physicians, still failed to meet the demand for medical care. It was also realized that university trained doctors were relatively ineffective in rural conditions where equipment and facilities for care were almost non-existent. In 1965 Mao Tse Tung issued a directive that the emphasis of health work should be shifted to the countryside. Two important developments have emerged from this: the training of barefoot doctors and the setting up of a locally financed co-operative health care system based on the commune. It was thought better to provide medical care competent for 90% of diseases, but resulting in a percentage of errors, than to provide highly efficient care for a small proportion of the population. The resources previously directed with little effect to the reorientation of the medical profession were devoted to the creation of a new medical work force, not determined by the profession but by political principles.

The extent to which these plans have been implemented cannot be ascertained but the Communist Party machine has been able to enforce acceptance of these principles and to overcome opposition from within the established medical profession. Until recently there was no licensing system for medical practice and roles were assigned more on the basis of demonstrated skills than on length of training or possession of credentials. This policy, however, was modified after the downfall in 1976 of the so-called 'gang of four', when professional training became once again regarded as decisive for a physician to acquire skills and competency.

The barefoot doctor is not a paramedical or a doctor's auxiliary working under supervision, but a part-time worker/part-time doctor trained to diagnose and treat without assistance the common or recurrent diseases peculiar to the region in which he or she lives. Selected and trained locally – the training is spread over three years but the content may vary from place to place – they are part of the local labour force in agriculture or industry, exercising their medical skills as required. When fully trained they are said to be able to treat about 100 diseases, apply 30 clinical techniques such as blood transfusion and acupuncture, and prescribe 80–90 kinds of traditional and Western-type medicines. They are responsible not only for curative medicine but also for vaccinations, sanitation and public health and for organizing the growing of medicinal herbs by the local community. The barefoot doctor may train a health worker to assist him. It is believed that some barefoot doctors may be accepted for further medical training after some time spent in practice.

Important shifts in emphasis took place in Chinese health care between 1973 and 1976 as a result of the politically dominant influence of the radically leftist Shanghai faction of the Communist Party, later called the 'gang of four'. In previous years, especially during the late fifties and early sixties, criticism of Western medical practice in China had remained limited to such superficialities as the alleged unwillingness of modern physicians to devote themselves to the health problems of the masses and to allegations of a 'capitalistic, imperialistic and colonialistic' context. During the early seventies, though, analyses appeared applying, for the first time, a critique from a Marxist-Maoist perspective in sociology of knowledge to the core of Western medicine, that is, to its concepts.

In his well known essay 'On Contradiction', Mao Tse Tung in

1937, following similar statements by Marx and Engels, had defined the theory of cognition of dialectic materialism mainly by contrasting it with the 'metaphysics of the bourgeoisie'. In this context he wrote: 'The metaphysical world outlook sees things as isolated, static and one-sided. . . . They ascribe the causes of social development to factors external to society, such as climate and geography. They search in an over-simplified way outside a thing for the causes of its development, and they deny the theory of materialistic dialectics which holds that development arises from the contradictions inside a thing.' In the early seventies these thoughts would be transferred from social to medical theory. Aspects of Western medicine were now invariably denounced as 'bourgeois' and 'metaphysical'; modern diagnosis which views the organs, their functional systems and diseases as isolated; modern etiology which for the most part only recognizes the impact of external pathological agents as the cause of disease, and drug, physical and surgical therapy which aim to induce changes in a passive patient.

A re-evaluation of traditional medicine occurred in a development parallel to the increasing separation of Marxist-Maoist dogmatists from Western medicine. There were surprising results. The ancient concepts of yinyang and of the Five Phases were discarded as Confucian machinations, but there remained in the practice of traditional medicine several elements which could be legitimized from a Marxist-Maoist perspective: for example, acupuncture which perfectly conforms to the demands of dialectic materialism in that it is only an external stimulus for change that must be worked out internally. This is especially evident with regard to so-called acupuncture anaesthesia which in contrast to drug based Western narcosis neither induces a passive patient to sleep nor introduces any substances into the organism which may exert pain killing functions.

The practice of traditional drug therapy emerged as another facet of traditional Chinese medicine worthy of support by Marxist-Maoist dogmatists. The fact that Western science so far had concentrated on an analysis of individual traditional drugs in search for their respective effective agents rather than to develop a pharmacological model to analyse conglomerates of effective agents in complex prescriptions made up from a variety of drugs was now denounced as a manifestation of 'bourgeois individualism'. Whereas, for a Western-style scientist the effects claimed traditionally for certain complex prescriptions remained at best questionable, if not absurd, the second law of dialectics as formulated by Engels, that is, the law of the transition of quantity into quality, offered a satisfactory explanation. Applied to drug therapy this law implies that the sum of the individual ingredients of a prescription formula exerts effects that are qualitatively different from those of the individual ingredients themselves.

In 1976 the Shanghai faction lost all its power and with the return of Teng Hsiao-p'ing into the centre of government, responsibility was once again resumed by those pragmatists who possibly are less interested in the realization of abstract social theories than in reserving for China a respectable political position in international diplomacy. Linked to this reorientation is a renewed enthusiastic support of the natural sciences and of science-based medicine; Chinese health planners have recently asked European firms to aid them in constructing a small number of science and technology-intensive hospitals that compare with the highest standards in the West and the basic sciences have been reintroduced into the curricula of medical students to a degree that seems exaggerated even in Western eyes. Accordingly, a more sober and less ideologically motivated attitude is increasingly adopted towards some of the highly propagated innovations of the recent past, e.g., acupuncture anaesthesia, the barefoot doctor system and traditional drug therapy.

Since 1976 a large number of high standard research results in modern medicine and pharmacology have been published, indicating that such work had been continued tacitly during previous years. The development of a male anti-fertility agent was an achievement attracting international attention. Realizing that low birth rates had been reported for several cotton producing provinces for centuries, Chinese scientists found that a concentrate produced from cotton oil (part of the daily diet in these regions) renders male sperm-cells non-viable. As early as in 1972 massive testing of the new contraceptive ('Gossypol') was conducted with 4000 human volunteers. Currently, about 10,000 males are reported to participate in a new series of trials. While Chinese scientists cite occasional side-effects (lack of appetite and gastric irritations) as a harmless problem but consider the unwillingness of Chinese males to accept such a contraceptive as a major obstacle to its general introduction, Western scientists have remained quite sceptical especially with regard to a possibility of long-term damage caused by this drug.

Although statistics and information are difficult to obtain, it is believed that the Chinese health system has been largely successful. It is practical and firmly directed to those areas where need is greatest. The acceptance of such priorities has been possible in China because of its highly organized political framework and the traditional communal life and culture of its people. Restriction of human rights and freedoms has been an essential part of this political system. The extent to which the Chinese pattern can be copied elsewhere depends on local factors; it remains as a source of ideas, but the ethical implications of the choices which these ideas present need careful consideration. (See also *Hospitals; Resources*.)

Unschuld PU. *Medical ethics in Imperial China. A study in historical anthropology.* Berkeley: University of California Press, 1979.
Unschuld PU. *Medizin in China. Eine ideengeschichte.* Munich: CH. Beck Verlag, 1980.

Wilensky P. *The delivery of health services in the People's Republic of China*. Ottawa: International Development Research Centre, 1976.

Paul U. Unschuld

Chiropractic. A system of treatment based on the view that disease is the result of abnormal function of the nervous system.

Many chiropractors give relief of symptoms by manipulation of the spinal column and this has led to demands in different countries for recognition of chiropractic as a specialty entitled to independent practice and to payment of fees from state insurance funds. The difference between chiropractic and osteopathy (q.v.) or manipulative treatment is that chiropractors believe that all diseases stem from abnormal function of the nervous system and are amenable to treatment by manipulation, usually of the spinal column.

Chiropractic was started by Palmer in 1898 after he had cured a friend of deafness by manipulating his neck. The school he founded still exists at Kirksville, USA. His theory was that all tissues contain nerves. This cannot be so, because cartilage has none. Chiropractors, though they intend to shift bones, in fact move fragments of disc, a cartilaginous tissue. According to them, treating the nerves can therefore cure everything. This is of course not so; but in any case they do not treat nerves at all but move the spinal joints.

In 1935 the chiropractors gave evidence at the enquiry in the House of Lords. They modestly described this craft as 'the science of palpating and adjusting the articulations of the human spinal column by hand only'. This is perfectly acceptable but by 1970 advertising broadsheets were distributed presenting an analysis of a quarter of a million cases. These included arthritis, diabetes, epilepsy, heart, kidney and liver disease. The lowest number of visits was 22 (for appendicitis!), the greatest 84 (for jaundice).

J. A. Cyriax

Christian Science. Christian Science (the Church of Christ, Scientist, founded in 1879) is a denomination best known for its reliance on spiritual power alone for the healing of disease. This practice it bases on the precedent of first-century Christianity. In its view, healing is an aspect of Christian regeneration, a natural effect of drawing closer to God in spirit and in the comprehension of the infinitude of His goodness and power.

Christian Scientists appreciate the humanitarian purpose of doctors but find that reliance on drug therapy cannot be effectively combined with their own method. However, they call in a doctor or qualified midwife in childbirth, and take their children to a doctor in accordance with child-care legislation. They do not object to a child receiving a blood transfusion if the medical authorities consider this necessary.

Legal requirements for immunization and quarantine are complied with, and it is fairly common for adherents to have a broken bone set by a doctor.

The Church's Committee on Publication at 108, Palace Gardens Terrace, London W8 4RT (Tel. 01–221 5650) is pleased to provide information and help with practical questions. (See also *Spiritual Healing*.)

A century of Christian Science healing. Boston: Christian Science Publishing Society, 1966.
John D. *The Christian Science way of life*. New Jersey: Prentice-Hall, 1962.

Richard Robinson

Christianity. In its origins Christianity shared with Judaism, and with most of the ancient world, a sense of the close relationship between religion and medicine. Salvation and healing, though not identical, were seen as different aspects of the same divine activity. Thus a cure for leprosy must have its ritual expression, and unforgiven sin might lie at the root of paralysis. Jesus told his followers to preach the gospel and heal the sick, and in his own ministry did both in such a way that the one illuminated and exemplified the other (e.g. Mark 2:17). Ethical problems, like whether or not it was permissible to heal on the Sabbath day (e.g. Mark 3:1–6), presupposed that healing was not an end in itself, but must be understood in the larger context of the religious meaning of life.

Though the emphasis on direct miraculous healing faded soon after the end of the New Testament period, Christianity never lost its broad concern with health. Care for the sick was institutionalized from the 4th century A.D. onwards in the development of Christian hospitals, almost invariably based on monastic foundations. Early scientific medicine, in the tradition of Hippocrates and Galen, was absorbed into mediaeval Christendom together with many other aspects of Graeco-Roman culture. But while the religious framework of life provided a support and justification for medicine, it also tended to inhibit discovery and innovation. The growth of modern medicine from the 17th century onwards demanded a sharp assertion of autonomy over against its former religious associations, and for a time there was widespread Christian opposition to new medical techniques. Anaesthesia, narcosis in childbirth, vaccination, contraception, sterilization and many other procedures have all been condemned by influential Christian bodies, and some still are. In more recent years, however, there has been a greater readiness from both sides to engage in rational and open discussion of the ethical implications of various kinds of scientific advance, and claims to strict autonomy, whether scientific, medical or religious, are being modified.

The classical Christian approach to general ethical questions has been through the concept of Natural Law, which dominated mediaeval moral theology, and still forms the basis of Roman Catholic thinking on these matters. The concept is usually justified in Christian terms on the basis of Romans 2:14–15, though its roots lie deeper in Stoic and Aristotelian ethics than in the Bible. It is assumed to be possible, in the light of reason, to discern the laws by which human beings should live in accordance with the given facts of human nature. These laws, it is claimed, are universal and apply to all men, though in practice they may need clarification through revelation, and reinforcement by the teaching authority of the Church.

So far as medicine is concerned, any deliberate interference with normal bodily functioning is, according to this view, a violation of Natural Law, but may be justified on one of two main grounds:

(a) The principle of totality, whereby any diseased part of the body may be removed or otherwise modified if its malfunctioning constitutes a serious threat to the whole.

(b) The principle of double effect (q.v.), whereby a good action is not forbidden, even if one of its unintended consequences is evil. A sterilization, for example, which would in other circumstances be condemned, might be permitted as an incidental result of the removal of ovaries for ovarian disease.

On the basis of very general principles of this kind, often applied with great refinement, the Roman Catholic Church has maintained a consistent tradition of medical ethics, particularly in areas affecting the integrity of human life and sexuality. Where possible Catholic hospitals have been established, within which the Church's distinctive ethical principles can be upheld. Directives containing precise and detailed instructions on a wide variety of medical issues have expounded the Natural Law traditions as interpreted in papal encyclicals and other pronouncements; the most famous recent example is the encyclical *Humanae Vitae* (q.v.) on the subject of contraception. A few modern Roman Catholic moral theologians, notably Bernard Häring, have recorded dissatisfaction with a tradition which, in their view, relies excessively on law, and presumes to dictate the limits of medical practice from some superior vantage point outside it. They have advocated a much more open and dialectical approach to medical ethics, in which theologians and medical workers share their respective insights and problems.

Outside the Roman tradition the approach to medical ethics has been less systematic, and prior to the mid-1950s it would have been difficult to find more than scattered references to a limited range of problems. In part this reflects Protestant suspicion of the Natural Law tradition and Roman Catholic methods of casuistry (the application of laws to particular cases). In part it also derives from the tendency of Reformed theologians to begin, not with abstract principles, but with the ethical problems raised from within medicine itself. Thus growth of interest in the subject has closely followed a period of major medical advance. Furthermore, a theology which emphasizes grace, to the virtual exclusion of law, is likely to content itself with general guidelines concerning Christian attitudes, rather than detailed instructions for Christian behaviour in specialist situations. This is part of the Protestant insistence that nothing must be allowed to stand between the believer and God, not even a system of ethics.

In its positive aspects Protestant ethical thinking has tended to concentrate on general questions about the nature of man, and the quality of a truly human life as made possible in those have responded to the grace of God. Love, freedom and forgiveness have been favourite themes, and earlier attempts to use the Bible as a source-book of answers to contemporary problems have largely been abandoned. Many now treat the Bible as a guide to the spirit in which problems must be tackled, an authority for the values which must be preserved, and an exploration of some of the basic issues, such as the ambiguity of human createdness and creativeness, which underlie the ethics of scientific advance.

One of the first modern attempts to provide a fairly comprehensive treatment of medical ethics within this tradition was made by Joseph Fletcher, who subsequently became well known for his advocacy of so called Situation Ethics. He described this as a person-centred rather than a principle-centred ethic, whose main thrust is to permit and encourage all that enhances personal life and freedom. In its developed form it admits of only one obligation – to love – whose implications must be worked out in an endless variety of unique situations. As a reminder that people are more important than ideas, and that circumstances alter cases, this approach has its value, but its main weakness is that it offers minimum guidance at the very times when guidance is most needed.

Unlike other Reformed Churches, Anglicanism never wholly abandoned the Catholic tradition of moral theology, but preserved a liberalized and less authoritarian version of it. The empiricism of the great eighteenth century moralist, Bishop Butler, enabled him to develop Natural Law tradition in a way which did justice to the actual complexities of human nature. This approach bore new fruit in the field of medical ethics in the mid-twentieth century, and a report, *The Family in Contemporary Society*, prepared by a widely representative group of experts in different disciplines for the 1958 Lambeth Conference of Anglican bishops, proved to be a landmark in moral thinking. It was the first report really to exploit the method of detailed empirical study, allied with interdisciplinary discussion, in such a way that theological insights were allowed to illuminate and articulate the moral claim inherent in the subject under study, without dictating prior conclusions. A notable series of similar reports, many of them on medical topics, e.g. abortion, sterilization, euthanasia, have followed the same method. It has clear affinities with the style now adopted by modern Roman Catholic moral theologians, which was referred to earlier; but it also stands well within the Protestant tradition of Biblically-inspired sensitivity and personal choice.

The use of theological insights, rather than the deduction of moral answers from unalterable moral principles, can be illustrated by some examples drawn from central Christian beliefs. Belief in creation, for instance, can act as a reminder of creatureliness, a permanent warning against the assumption of god-like powers over life and death, or against excessive interference with the actual conditions of human life as prescribed by the natural world. The doctrine has another side, though, in that it includes the notion that man himself shares in God's creative powers, and is called to act as a responsible steward towards the world of which he is a part, yet in a measure transcends. The application of such ideas to, say, the prospects of genetic engineering could be illuminating, but requires considerable subtlety in handling a delicately balanced argument.

The doctrines of the incarnation and of salvation are fundamental to Christianity and pervade most Christian thinking. One of their practical consequences is to encourage Christians to respect human potentialities even in the most unprepossessing people and the most unlikely circumstances. The belief that human nature is potentially capable of bearing the divine image has very widespread implications, which touch every aspect of the organization of social life. It might also have a quite specific and limited application, say, to questions concerning the treatment of sub-normal children.

Conversely, the doctrine of original sin, which asserts the existence of an evil bias in all human nature, acts as a corrective to naive optimism. One of its fruits may be a certain scepticism about the ability of human beings to plan successfully for their own future; there are numerous examples of its relevance to legislation in the frequency with which liberal intentions are exploited by the unscrupulous.

Attitudes towards death (q.v.) and suffering are of obvious concern to medical practice. The unconscious assumptions that death is the worst thing that can happen, and that suffering must at all costs be avoided, seem to underlie some excesses in modern medical treatment. Christian beliefs about life after death and the redemptive power of suffering may in the past have been used to justify unreasonable opposition to life-saving techniques, but there are valid questions to be asked from the Christian standpoint about the extent to which the pendulum has now swung too far the other way.

Contemporary discussions on the nature of health, and the social dimensions of medicine, open up interesting possibilities for the recovery of something like the Biblical perspective, in which health was seen as one part of a much larger quest for wholeness of personal and social life. In fact the open-ended character of the concept of health may provide one of the most fruitful new areas for mutual exploration

69

between doctors and some theologians. The very successes of medicine force it to take more seriously questions about its ultimate aims, while theologians, whose business is with ultimate questions, are being forced by conditions in the modern world to pay as much attention to physical as to spiritual realities.

These examples of the use of Christian theology imply that its characteristic contribution to the study of medical ethics is in the indicative rather than in the imperative mood. Granted a general benevolent concern for the well-being of individuals and society as a whole, different ethical choices are more likely to reflect differences of opinion, say, about the nature and destiny of man, than differences of ethical orientation. As the New Testament itself makes clear, it is easier to obtain agreement on the command to love one's neighbour than to answer the question about who precisely one's neighbour is (Luke 10:25–37). Few would disagree with the proposition that medicine is about love of one's neighbour. But what may be done to one's neighbour for his own well-being, or what constitutes his well-being, or how his claims are to be set against those of his fellows, depend upon the way in which his life is understood. And that is, at least in part, a matter of belief.

The final words, though, in a Christian account of ethics must be forgiveness and grace. This is not only because any workable ethic must make provision for failure, but mainly because part of the human predicament is the fact that many decisions entail choices between evils, and even the best actions leave many claims unmet. Finite human beings have to do the best they can. To live within the context of forgiveness and grace makes it possible to accept the inevitable ambiguities of human conduct, without relapsing into complacency or cynicism, or losing hold of the vision of some greater good.

Dunstan GR. *The artifice of ethics*. London: SCM Press, 1974:116.
Fletcher J. *Morals and medicine*. London: Gollancz, 1955:243.
Häring B. *Medical ethics*. Slough: St Paul Publications, 1972:233.
Kelly G. *Medico-moral problems*. St Louis: The Catholic Hospital Association, 1958:375.
Mackinnon DM. *Making moral decisions*, London: SPCK 1969:91.
Nelson JB. *Human medicine: ethical perspectives on new medical issues*, Minnesota: Augsburg Publishing House, 1973:207.
Wilson M. *Health is for people*. London: Darton, Longman & Todd, 1975:134.
See also:
The family in contemporary society. London: SPCK, 1958:229; and the following reports published by the Church Information Office, Westminster:
Artifical insemination by donor, 1960.
Sterilization: an ethical enquiry, 1962.
Decisions about life and death, 1965.

Abortion: an ethical discussion, 1968.
Vasectomy: a guide to personal decisions, 1973.
On dying well, 1975.

John Habgood

Chromosome Disorders. Chromosomes are small bodies found in the nucleus of the cell. They have specific staining characteristics and contain the chemical substance deoxyribonucleic acid (DNA) in which inherited information is encoded – the 'genetic code'. Chromosome disorders are developmental abnormalities known to be due to deviations from the normal number of 46 chromosomes, or to abnormal morphology of one or more chromosomes. Chromosomes are normally referred to by a system of numbers, while the sex chromosomes are labelled XY for males and XX for females.

The sex chromosomes are subject to various disorders. For example, in Klinefelter's syndrome there is an extra sex chromosome (47 XXY) leading to infertility and a tendency to mental retardation. The 47 XYY male has tall stature, and some abnormalities of behaviour have been described, although the majority are apparently normal males. The 47 XXX female has a tendency to mental retardation, with menstrual problems in some patients, although others are undetectable in the normal population except by chromosome analysis. Down's syndrome, formerly known as mongolism, is a condition caused by an additional chromosome 21 (trisomy 21). It is characterized by a variety of physical malformations and severe mental retardation. Chromosomal rearrangements may occur, either as exchanges between different chromosomes or parts of the same chromosomes. When balanced, i.e. with no change in total genetic material, they may occur in normal people. They may become unbalanced during the formation of the germ cells and cause severe mental or physical maldevelopment. About 25% of spontaneous abortions are chromosomally abnormal, and probably a much higher percentage of conceptuses that do not implant. Since about one in 100 live born babies has a chromosome abnormality, natural abortion is an efficient means of eliminating abnormal babies; yet when we strive to prevent miscarriage we cannot distinguish such rejection from failure to retain a normal baby because of an incompetent cervix or other factors. Some of the chromosomally abnormal babies will show a range of physical or mental defects, some will be apparently normal but develop problems later or pass the disorder on to their children; others will be unaware of their abnormal chromosomes.

Sexual abnormalities raise many problems, to doctors, parents and children. Where the subject is psychologically of one sex, but genetically of the opposite sex, as in males who, because of a chromosome exchange, appear to have two 'X' chromosomes, knowledge of the genetic sex could be profoundly disturbing. Equally, a patient with

Klinefelter's syndrome may find knowledge of his abnormal chromosomes more alarming than a non-chromosomal disorder. We should therefore consider whether a patient has a right to know his chromosome constitution regardless of the consequences. Prior consideration may avoid needlessly or fortuitously revealing facts which may be psychologically damaging. While some would agree to conceal from a young woman about to be married that she is a genetic male, the position of the husband-to-be ought to be considered. Routine screening of athletes for nuclear sex may occasionally reveal a sex discrepancy, but since blatant attempts to deceive can be discovered by simple physical examination, the value of such screening may be questioned, especially as disclosure of the results is not always in the best interests of the subject. The XXY and XYY male are reputed to have abnormalities of behaviour and in particular to exhibit antisocial tendencies. It has been argued that the possession of a chromosomal disorder renders the offender less culpable, morally and legally, but this ignores the possible social causes of deviant behaviour, and the position is complicated by the fact that only a small minority of XYY and XXY males have behavioural problems.

The frequency of chromosomal disorders is such that any large-scale screening may lead to the recognition of abnormalities. Detection of such abnormalities in apparently normal individuals raises problems of disclosure and subsequent handling. This is particularly acute where, in the course of a class exercise, a student discovers that he or she is chromosomally abnormal. Planned screening of newborns may reveal obvious developmental abnormalities and the ethical problems arising are relatively straightforward. However, patients with Down's syndrome may now live a long time since the advent of modern drug and other treatments, and decisions need to be taken whether or not to withhold antiobiotics, or the drug treatment of leukaemia or the surgery for heart defects to which these patients are subject. Such considerations apply particularly in societies which do not readily tolerate malformed children.

Even more urgent is a consideration of whether or not an abnormality of the chromosomes which does not lead to immediate developmental defects should be revealed to the parents. Some feel that it is a duty to reveal all available information while others believe that to reveal an abnormality which may not lead to problems until adulthood (the potent but infertile XXY) or which may never lead to problems at all (the majority of XYY males and some XXX females) could prejudice the relationship between parents and child. To avoid such dilemmas it has been suggested that such screening of newborns should not be carried out.

Since antenatal diagnosis of chromosome abnormalities is now possible, many of these arguments apply equally, but often with a different emphasis, to the fetus. In Western societies it is permissible to kill a trisomy 21 fetus but not a newborn trisomy 21 baby, when logic would seem to demand a consistent approach one way or the other. XXX female and XXY or XYY male fetuses appear normal at birth; some will indeed be normal, but others will be mentally retarded, sterile or criminal. The dilemma whether or not to terminate such pregnancies may soon be commonplace.

Chromosomal rearrangements also pose difficult problems. Mothers or fathers who are carriers of balanced rearrangements are usually recognized only after the birth of an abnormal baby but now the mother in such a family can be advised to become pregnant again in the knowledge that chromosomally unbalanced fetuses can be recognized and aborted. Fetuses with balanced rearrangements tend at present to be conserved since prior knowledge of the nature of the defect can, by antenatal diagnosis and selective termination, prevent the birth of malformed children.

The ability that we now have to diagnose sex accurately in early pregnancy is already posing problems. For some parents and in some societies a normal girl or a normal boy may be unwanted and selective termination requested for this reason. In most societies this will be totally unacceptable. (See also *Abortion; Amniocentesis; Antenatal Diagnosis; Congenital Malformations; Genetic Conditions.*)

Apgar V, Beck J. *Is my baby all right?* New York: Trident Press, 1972.

Etzioni A. *Genetic fix.* New York and London: Macmillan, 1973.

Fraser Roberts J A, Pambrey ME. *An introduction to medical genetics.* Oxford: University Press, 1978.

Ounstead C, Taylor DG. *Gender differences: their ontogeny and significance.* Edinburgh and London: Churchill Livingstone, 1972.

Packard V. *The people shapers.* London: Macdonald and Jane's, 1980.

D. G. Harnden

Ciba Foundation. The Ciba Foundation is a scientific and educational charity established in 1947 by the pharmaceutical company CIBA Ltd – now CIBA-GEIGY – of Basle. The Foundation is entirely financially supported by the Founder but operates independently in London and is registered as a charity under English trust law. The purpose of the Foundation is to advance and promote the study of research in all branches of the sciences of chemistry, medicine, surgery, and in particular to advance and promote international co-operation in medical, chemical, biological and pharmaceutical research.

The Ciba Foundation is best known for the arrangement of small, multidisciplinary, international symposia. Eight of these are held each year and the proceedings are published about nine months after the meeting. The subjects of these symposia cover many aspects of medical and chemical research and medical ethics may be part or, on a few occasions, the main subject of a meeting. Subjects in the past few years have included *Medical care of prisoners and detainees, The legal and ethical aspects of artificial insemination by donor (AID) and embryo transfer, Human rights in health, Outcome of severe CNS damage, Research and medical practice, Breast feeding and the mother, Health and disease in tribal societies, The cost of preventing major mental handicap, Genetics and human biology, Brain and mind.*

Since 1971 the Foundation has arranged five conferences for, and with, medical students. The subjects, chosen by the students, have all been related to medical ethics: *Normal and abnormal sex* (Newcastle), *Mental handicap: prevention and care* (Bristol), *The malformed child* (Oxford), *A critical look at unorthodox medicine* (Glasgow), *Trauma and after* (Sheffield).

The address of the Foundation is 41 Portland Place, London W1N 4BN.

Ruth Porter

Circumcision. Male circumcision is removal of the foreskin; female circumcision is removal of clitoris and labia minora and is sometimes accompanied by infibulation (fastening together of the labia majora with clasps or stitches), to prevent entry to the vagina. (Male infibulation is the insertion of wires through the foreskin to prevent the penis entering the vagina.)

Male circumcision is said to be the oldest and most widely spread surgical operation known and is practised by many tribes and races in Africa, Asia, South America and Australia. Frequently it is a part of the rite of initiation into male adult life and is done at or about the age of puberty. To the Jews, who perform it on the eighth day of life, it has a particular religious significance as a sign of their special relationship to God.[1]

In the USA most boy babies are circumcised; in Britain, Jewish boys and about one per cent of other boys, principally those of the wealthier classes. Male circumcision is said to be associated with a lower incidence of penile cancer and of cervical cancer in wives, probably because it makes personal cleanliness easier to achieve, but in certain races where these conditions are less often seen, the men are not circumcised.

Male circumcision is only rarely needed for medical reasons since the foreskin normally becomes retractable by the age of four years.[2] The operation takes time that could be more usefully spent, and to perform it so that the child can 'be like other boys' is an inadequate reason. Illingworth[3] wrote illuminatingly on the medical problem. He said that there were 16 deaths a year in Britain (but between 1939 and 1951 there was only one death among 566,483 boys circumcised in New York). Complications include infection, bleeding, meatal ulceration and, rarely, partial amputation of the glans penis.

Ethical considerations depend on the weight of medical, religious and other arguments for and against. If parents ask for circumcision of a male child, the doctor should not do it without explaining the risks involved. Female circumcision was recommended in Britain a hundred years ago as a treatment for masturbation and is practised in other parts of the world to reduce sexual desire, although it has been said[4] that circumcised women have a greater desire for sexual intercourse. It is a mutilating operation and, when performed only for the reasons given, an infringement of human rights.

1. *Jewish encyclopaedia.* New York and London: Funk & Wagnalls, 1971.
2. Gairdner D. The fate of the foreskin. In: *Chambers Encyclopaedia,* 1949.
3. Illingworth RS. *The normal child.* London: Churchill, 1968.
4. Edwardes A. *The jewel in the lotus: a historical survey of the sexual culture of the East.* London: Anthony Blond, 1961.
Editorial. The case against neonatal circumcision. *Br Med J* 1979; 2:1163–4.

The late Ronald C. MacKeith

Clinical Autonomy. The term 'clinical autonomy' is something of a sacred cow in medical practice. When the concept is analysed, it becomes clear that in some senses it remains a safeguard not only of the doctor's professional freedom but also of the patient's interest; from a different viewpoint and with a different connotation the concept may be becoming outmoded and no longer acceptable to society or indeed in the best interests of the patient. Important ethical issues are involved and are discussed under the headings shown below.

Basically the doctor feels that, since he has the ultimate responsibility for making clinical decisions affecting the management of his patient, no outside force must interfere with his 'clinical autonomy'. He will, of course, take many factors and the opinions of others into account before reaching his decision but the final judgement must be his. In the matter of consent (q.v.), for example, it is clearly not in the patient's interest to be told of every single adverse effect that has ever been reported in relation to the use of a therapeutic procedure. It is in the interest of the patient that the doctor should exercise his judgement in this respect when he is explaining the procedure and seeking informed, or true, consent (see also *Truth*).

The concept of clinical autonomy is questioned and may come to be eroded in three principal ways: (1) The patient may insist that the final decision is his. With the public better informed on health matters and technical advances some patients feel that they should be given all the evidence and then be left to make the decision. More often, save in questions like that of termination of pregnancy, the patient realizes that not having made a professional study of disease processes, he is better to participate in the discussions but to leave the ultimate decisions to the doctor. (2) Other members of the health team may feel that decisions should be made by consensus rather than by the doctor's autonomy (see *Teamwork*). Certainly the decisions may now involve so many complex and technical factors that the doctor with the final responsibility would be foolish not to seek the best advice or not to involve others in the decision-making process. (3) Society may feel that just as 'war is too important to be left to the generals', so health is too important to be left to the doctors. For example, every doctor has the right to prescribe whatever approved medicine he thinks fit for his patient. We know that enormous savings could be made if that freedom were restricted. Many believe that such restriction could be made without detriment to patients and that the savings should be put towards other aspects of health care. A very dangerous precedent would be set, however, if the State were to impose such restrictions. It would be a different matter if the profession were to impose them on itself (see *Resources*). When a Health Service Commissioner ('ombudsman') was first appointed in the UK in 1973, one of the matters excluded from investigation by him was 'action taken in connection with the diagnosis of illness or the care or treatment of the patient if, in the opinion of the commissioner, it was taken solely in consequence of the exercise of clinical judgement'. This exclusion was in order to preserve clinical autonomy. More recently Health Councils (q.v.) have sought the right to institute complaints procedures regarding the clinical judgements of doctors. The all-Party Select Committee on the Parliamentary Commissioner for Administration[1] supported this view and in 1979 the Secretary of State for Social Services accepted it in principle. Doctors have strongly opposed any such extension and will probably continue to do so. Certainly if doctors feel that their judgement is under such scrutiny, they may tend to play safe rather than to act with all the skill and experience at their command.

In defending the principle of clinical autonomy, doctors should take account of changing circumstances. In any attempt to reduce the clinical autonomy of doctors, society should beware of the adverse effect of such erosion on doctor/patient relationships, on the quality of persons entering the profession of medicine and on patient care in general. (See *Clinical Practice; Commercial Interests; Health Service Commissioners; Interprofessional Relationships; Moral Autonomy; Private Practice; Social Pressures; State Health Services*).

1. Select Committee on the Parliamentary Commissioner for Administration. *Independent review of hospital complaints on the NHS* (First Report). London: HMSO, 1977.

A. S. Duncan

Clinical Practice. When one searches for a word to epitomize the ethics of clinical practice, 'trust' comes to mind again and again; trust in the doctor by the patient; trust in the doctor by the other members of the health team, which is now really essential if the best service is to be provided for the patients; trust in the medical profession as a whole by the general public; and trust in the administration by the medical profession. If there is no trust, there will probably be inefficiency, and it is in the presence of inefficiency that unethical behaviour flourishes (see *Patients*).

What qualities in a doctor are likely to make a patient have trust in him?

Clearly, he must be a good doctor with a sound knowledge of basic science; he must have the ability to examine the human body, having analysed the clinical history: and his diagnoses and prognoses must be proved to be correct in a high proportion of cases. These attributes alone, however, will not necessarily engender the trust so essential for a good doctor/patient relationship. Most patients are frightened when they go to the doctor and confidence can only be established if doctors are willing to take time to explain the reasons for their decisions, the reasons for the particular treatment they are prescribing, and above all the course the illness is likely to take. (See *Communication*.) Patients are often ignorant as to how long they are likely to be incapacitated and grateful to learn the facts and lay their plans accordingly. Often the probabilities are more encouraging than they had imagined and a frank discussion at the outset can often prevent a person from being turned into a permanent invalid. The presence of the husband or wife at the discussion is particularly helpful in this respect. Explanations of this nature early in the course of an illness, once the diagnosis has been established, do much to cement a relationship between doctor and patient based on mutual trust.

If doctors are to maintain the trust of their patients they must continue their professional education. Medicine, in particular sophisticated aids to diagnosis and the therapeutic explosion of the last fifty years, is advancing so rapidly that the concept of the complete doctor emerging from our medical schools is no longer tenable, and continuing education is essential if doctors are to maintain their competence (q.v.) to practise. It is important to know which of the modern aids to diagnosis and additions to our therapeutic armamentarium are appropriate to any individual case. The mere application of blunderbuss methods of diagnosis or therapy, however modern, with batteries of tests and polypharmacy, soon engenders a feeling of mistrust in the patient and a sense of bewilderment at what is going on.

The question of what constitutes reasonable investigation of an individual patient has taken on a new importance. An immense investigative programme is available compared with even a few years ago. The temptation is to submit patients to a needless battery of tests, some uncomfortable, many expensive, some frightening and some not devoid of risk. In the hospital service junior staff are naturally anxious to anticipate their seniors' every possible wish. In hospital and in general practice the doctor may have lurking in the background the spectre of possible litigation for failure to take reasonable care (see *Defensive Medicine; Malpractice, Medical; Negligence*). The pressures must, however, be resisted and a balance struck between what is necessary and prudent and the performance of needless investigations initiated in an attempt to cover all possible eventualities, or to satisfy the natural scientific curiosity of the doctor.

Different people prefer to learn in different ways, but one way open to all is to develop the habit of discussion among friends and colleagues and to cultivate the ability to learn by one's own mistakes and from the successes of others. (See *Quality Assurance*.)

Apart from the patient's trust in a doctor because of his professional skill, and this applies to doctors practising in hospitals as well as to those in general practice, patients must have faith in the integrity of the doctor as a person. Perhaps rather too much emphasis is placed by the press on social misdemeanours when they report the work of the Disciplinary Committee of the General Medical Council (q.v.). Sex, alcoholism, drug abuse and assault are the subjects usually reported, but these are the exceptional cases and there are other problems which occur much more frequently in the average doctor's experience.

There is confidentiality (q.v.) of knowledge obtained in a professional capacity. This must be preserved absolutely. One word of gossip arising from a medical source could ruin a doctor/patient relationship. What is slightly more difficult is the revelation of a patient's medical history to insurance companies, employers and potential employers. With pension rights as a normal part of remuneration in industry and commerce – many of them financed through insurance schemes – examination of patients for this purpose has become a regular part of the doctor's daily task. The author has been concerned with this aspect of medicine as medical adviser to an assurance company, a bank and the civil service and knows how much value a well written private medical attendant's report can be to those responsible for the ultimate decision. As a consultant physician he also knows how essential it is to preserve that complete trust between patient and doctor outlined above. In the majority of cases the further information supplied by the family doctor, or occasionally by a specialist who has looked after the patient, will react in the patient's favour. In a minority it will not. This must be explained to the patient and his permission obtained before any information is given. In nearly every case the patient is willing but if, even after such explanation, he is not, his wishes must be observed absolutely without further pressure being put on him.

The question of disclosure of unpleasant facts to the patient, e.g. that he is suffering from a fatal illness, is another difficult problem. In the author's experience patients seldom press for a definite answer to this question, but if they do, and in the opinion of the doctor they are in good mental health, it is the doctor's duty to tell the truth (q.v.) and maintain the trust built up between them, often over many years. In any case the unpleasant task of informing near relatives must never be shirked so that they can give the patient the loving care and attention he requires and deserves. Whether or not to reveal a diagnosis of a condition with long periods of remission, such as disseminated sclerosis, is a different matter. On the whole it is probably best to be evasive here, unless by doing so the patient's trust is likely to be destroyed and with it the ability to be of most use to him in the future.

Continuity of care is something which must play an important part in the development of that trust which is essential for a good doctor/patient relationship. Too often nowadays one hears patients saying, 'I always see a different doctor', either at the health centre or hospital clinic. The author is the son of a single-handed practitioner and was brought up in an atmosphere where the doctor knew every patient in his practice, their close relatives and personal relationships and their personal problems as well as he knew his own. While well aware of the increasing movement within the population and the changing social scene, and well aware of the professional and educational advantages of the well run health centre, he still believes that each patient should feel that one person is his doctor. He believes also that the proliferation of hospital specialist and follow-up clinics does much to perpetuate the idea that no one person is responsible for any one patient and leads to confusion. A properly run appointments system with someone in charge with time to explain to patients that it is worth waiting to see their own doctor, and consultants prepared to refer patients back to their own doctors on completion of their treatment in hospital would do much to remedy the difficulty.

The wise and experienced practitioner will always see at the earliest possible moment a patient complaining of a symptom for the first time, partly because he may miss some serious condition which requires immediate action if he does not, but also because he may be able to reassure worried and anxious patients and relatives, which is one of the most rewarding and useful pieces of therapy at his disposal.

The imparting of useful ethical information to the inexperienced used to be confined largely to the major teaching hospitals where the consultants, mainly by example on ward rounds and in the outpatient departments, taught the principles of clinical medicine to undergraduate students and the techniques of specialized knowledge to postgraduates. Just as the hospital patient population has changed in the last twenty-five years, so has the opportunity of learning from example now spread to many district hospitals and teaching general practices. This can do nothing but good. The concept of the domiciliary consultation under the National Health Service was an admirable one providing an opportunity for a genuine consultation, with its educational value, between the consultant and the general practitioner, with or without his assistant or trainee. Alas, in many cases this has become a domiciliary visit with a written or telephonic report at the end.

It is now more than ever necessary for doctors to maintain good relationships with all branches of their profession and to trust and be trusted by their colleagues in the laboratory services and in community medicine. If there is a failure of communication between the branches of the profession, the best possible service to the patient will not be maintained. All are expanding, all can be subjected to needless over-work by demands on their time which could be avoided by adequate consultation and good communication. With the development of health centres and the social services, it is also essential for the doctor to maintain good personal relationships with the other members of the team concerned with the care of patients – nurses, members of the professions supplementary to medicine and social workers (See *Teamwork*). All these groups are at present seeking to improve their status in the team and demanding more autonomy. This is natural and desirable provided it does not lead to any attempt to treat by committee. The team based in the health centre or hospital ward with regular meetings and consultations is clearly the modern unit, and if properly managed probably the best unit of patient care there has ever been. The important word is management. No team has ever played well without a captain; no unit in any of the services has ever performed efficiently without a good commanding officer, and one of the skills of modern medicine is going to be leadership or management, not in a hectoring or authoritarian manner which would not be tolerated today, but in a genuine leadership role. In other words, the patient must feel that one individual is ultimately responsible for his health care.

If up and down the country doctors are trusted and respected by their individual patients, and if they are seen as leaders of happy, enthusiastic teams of health care professionals, the profession will be trusted by the general population. Similarly, if members of the profession know that they are receiving total support from the administration, that their views will be given adequate consideration, and that once decisions have been taken action will follow in a reasonable space of time, the profession will trust the administration. An attitude of mutual trust is the soil where ethics flourish and with continuing good communication between all concerned, and a genuine desire on all sides for continuing education, the present generation need not fear for the future of the profession. (See also *Medical Science* and *Clinical Autonomy; Clinical Teaching; Health (Hospital) Advisory Services; Health Service Commissioners; Hospitals; Iatrogenic Disease; Interprofessional Relationships; Medical Education; Medical Records; Patients*).

J. Halliday Croom

IN GENERAL PRACTICE. In primary care, trust between doctor and patient is the basis of good general practice which, when established, offers the patient the opportunity to discuss with his doctor any aspect from a whole spectrum of health. In general practice it is important therefore not to dismiss the patient who may test the doctor with an apparently trivial physical illness as the entry to discussing some deeper anxiety. Trust between doctor and patient will also allow the doctor to encourage and educate the patient in his own management of self-limiting illness. The organization of general practice is also an important aspect of developing trust so that the patient becomes confident he will obtain a speedy response in an urgent situation and that time will be set aside when required to discuss serious on-going problems. Modern group practice should not be incompatible with a good personal doctor/patient relationship which is the basis of sound clinical practice. (See *General Practice*.)

A. G. Donald

Clinical Teaching. The means by which ethical problems are brought before medical and other students are considered under *Teaching of Medical Ethics*, but the particular case of bedside teaching and teaching in the clinic or consulting room when the patient is present has implications not only for the teacher and student but for the doctor/patient relationship. The patient's permission should always be specifically sought in advance and care must be taken not to allow discussion of the case to be in such terms as might cause stress or anxiety in the patient's mind. Most patients find that teaching on their case is not only of interest but is actually enjoyable. The patient often has important comments to make and if allowed to be a full participant in the discussion will often illuminate not only the physical problems of the case but also the psychological and ethical aspects. Veiled terms intended to be incomprehensible or even misleading to the patient should be avoided. One of those present at the teaching session, preferably the teacher himself, should go back to the patient very soon afterwards to ask if there are any queries and to clear up any possible misunderstanding. (See also *Clinical Practice; Communication; Medical Education, Ethics of; Patients.*)

A. S. Duncan

Clinical Trials. DEFINITION: scientific studies in which the benefits of one or more medical treatments are assessed. These may be drugs and vaccines, surgical operations or physical treatments such as physiotherapy and radiotherapy.

BACKGROUND. The natural history of most human disease varies widely, and reactions to its treatments may be equally varied.

In the past many remedies were introduced on the basis of trial and error, and these commonly took little account of the natural history of disease. Some were long and widely used before falling into disrepute and vanishing. Greater emphasis is now placed on the value of objective measurements to assess the progress of illness and hence to distinguish the effects of treatment from the natural course of the disease. This has produced new observations on the natural history of many conditions, which have been of great value.

Although carefully designed clinical trials (in which patients are assigned at random to receive one of the treatments under examination – Controlled Trials or Randomized Controlled Trials) are more ethical than uncontrolled experiments with unproved products, new treatments are not without hazard and several disasters have occurred. These include congenital malformations associated with maternal consumption of thalidomide during pregnancy and the inoculation with live (non-attenuated) vaccines as well as the disintegration of the early surgical prostheses for arthritic hips. Many of these problems could probably have been recognized during preliminary investigations in laboratory animals and so avoided in man. However, animal studies can never have an absolute predictive value for adverse reactions in man, and the only way to find out whether a new therapy is safe and effective in man is to give it to man. Some risk is unavoidable if new treatments are to be developed, and medical progress will depend upon society acknowledging these risks and individual patients being prepared to contribute to the common good by voluntarily serving as experimental subjects. (See *Animal Experiment; Human Experiment*.)

However, no one should be coerced into 'volunteering' to participate in a clinical trial no matter how great may be the expected benefit for others. He must be able to make a free choice based upon valid information, clearly imparted and adequately understood. Volunteers have a right to a clear and detailed explanation of the nature and purposes of the proposed studies and must be free to withhold their consent (q.v.), even when they are receiving charity or are in prison. Patients with great trust in their doctor may accede to any request he may make and this trust should not be abused when consent is requested. The best account of the principles of consent are contained in the first of the ten clauses of the so-called Nuremberg Code (q.v.).

Although there is no medico-legal requirement or indeed benefit, informed consent should be obtained in writing whenever possible.

CHOICE OF HUMAN SUBJECTS FOR MEDICAL TRIALS. It is doubtful whether public appeal for volunteers to participate in experiments, even when the purposes and risks are plainly stated, will provide a sufficient number of public-spirited persons willing to accept the unpleasantness and dangers involved. Furthermore, to rely solely upon such persons might be disadvantageous because their strong psychological and spiritual motivation makes them unrepresentative of the population and may affect their response to treatment.

In the past, 'volunteers' for clinical trials of new drugs were frequently recruited either from within Federal Penitentiaries in the USA or from the pharmaceutical industry. However, prisoners participating in such projects have frequently enjoyed better living conditions, diet and health care than other inmates; they also enjoy the respect of their fellows. Similarly, doubts have been cast on whether employees of the pharmaceutical industry are truly volunteering to take part in studies on new drugs.

In view of the problems of obtaining 'normal volunteers' it has been argued that all clinical trials, including those of new remedies, should be performed on patients suffering from the disease for which the treatment is intended. No universally applicable guidelines have been defined, but society seeks to protect women and children (see *Child*) as well as the elderly from hazards; furthermore, it has been stated that the use of patients who are dying as subjects for experiments is shocking and wrong[1]. However, a rule forbidding experiments on any one class of person may discourage or prevent the conduct of research of value to that class; and to restrict clinical trials to young or middle-aged adults, frequently male, may unnecessarily inhibit research and deprive members of society of an opportunity to participate which they may welcome.

RESPONSIBILITIES OF THE INVESTIGATOR. Whether or not a clinical trial is justified depends on the following factors:–

1. Clinical trials must have the basic aim of testing a concept that could produce ultimate benefit to man.

2. In the case of a new treatment, the need for it in a particular disease should be assessed. Where such a trial appears justified, it may be appropriate for the new remedy to be compared with an inactive treatment known as a placebo (q.v.) provided that the risks of withholding treatment for a few days or weeks are not great. However, once benefits of newer or established treatments have been demonstrated they should only be compared with what is regarded as the standard therapy in subsequent clinical trials.

3. Where consideration has been given to a trial of a new remedy, the likelihood of the new treatment being an advance over existing ones should be carefully evaluated.

4. The likely risks involved should be assessed and should be explained to any volunteer/patient invited to participate.

5. It has been suggested that a trial is not ethical unless the physician could allow himself or a near relative to be included in it.

6. No clinical trial of a new drug should be undertaken unless the clinician is satisfied that the pre-trial information is adequate. Any doubts should be resolved by discussion with other scientists involved in the project and/or independent experts.

7. An outline of the proposed study must be submitted to the local ethical committee (see *Research Ethical Committee*) or their equivalent for clearance. No clinical trial can be regarded as ethical unless a well-designed protocol, which is capable of meeting the objectives of the

study, is followed. It would seem unethical to undertake such a study if an inadequate number of patients were available for study.

8. In the Federal Republic of Germany a new drug law came into force in 1978. In accordance with this, controlled trials are no longer demanded as a qualification for acceptance and registration of drugs. This decision appears to have resulted partly from legal pressure and partly because controlled clinical trials do not produce the truth automatically, but have to be evaluated. The extent to which the results of clinical trials are applicable to other patients has to be judged in the light of experience.

9. Even when there are no ethical problems apparent at the beginnning of a clinical trial, they can arise during its course. If a patient's condition appears to be deteriorating the ethical obligation must always entirely outweigh any experimental considerations. Thus, a physician must be free to treat the patient as he thinks appropriate even if by withdrawing the patient from the study he complicates the analysis of the data. Similarly, the development of unwanted effects relating to the treatment would normally necessitate withdrawal of the patient from the trial. If, in the course of a trial, it is becoming clear that one or other of the treatments is preferable, there may be ethical anxieties about continuing the trial to the stage of statistical significance. This difficulty is minimized by the use of 'blind' or 'double blind' trials in which the doctor and patient do not know in which category of treatment the patient falls. In 'double blind' trials it is important that an individual not concerned in the patient care should be aware of the categories so that in the event of very clear trends he may alert the research workers.

COMPENSATION. Patients recruited for entry into a clinical trial should be warned of any known adverse effects of the treatment and given some idea of their known or estimated incidence and severity. They should also be informed of the possibility of unknown effects. Nevertheless, in spite of careful planning and execution of clinical trials, unpredicted problems may sometimes be encountered. Although patients are at liberty to sue the physician in charge if the trial leads to pain or disability (either temporary or permanent) compensation is unlikely to be forthcoming unless negligence can be proved. However, it is important that society recognizes that subjects who allow themselves to be used for experimental purposes are making important contributions to medical progress and thus to the society. Means of compensating patients who suffer harm from drug therapy are being examined. According to a report of the Royal Commission on Civil Liability and Compensation for Personal Injury[2], the basis for compensation for prescribed drugs should be that of strict liability. In this it is necessary to prove cause and effect: negligence is not an issue. However, this recommendation is unacceptable to most members of the medical profession who would prefer to see a 'no-fault' scheme introduced: injuries due to drugs being compensated out of a fund financed perhaps by levies on drug sales.

PAYMENTS. It has been suggested that patients involved in clinical trials should be offered out-of-pocket expenses for additional out-patient attendances, and that non-patient volunteers should be treated similarly. However, there are differences of opinion as to whether or not a reasonable fee or equivalent reward should be paid for the time and trouble involved. Pappworth[1] has argued that if an experiment is innocuous, the offer of a reward to those who participate is unfair to those who have not had the chance. Payments are a particular problem when clinical trials carry some hazard: they should not provide an inducement to participate and if made should only cover out-of-pocket expenses such as loss of earnings and fares for additional out-patient attendances.

HANDLING OF RESULTS. Clinical trials sometimes fail to produce meaningful results because of inappropriate design. This can often be avoided by involving a statistician at the planning stage. The results of clinical trials belong to the investigator who must decide (often in consultation) when and where to publish his findings. Trials which produce negative results may be equally important to those with positive findings provided the assessment is sufficiently sensitive and an adequate number of patients are studied.

Guidelines for editors of journals are contained in a report from the Medico-Pharmaceutical Forum[3]. In addition to ethical considerations attention should be paid to the distinction between controlled and uncontrolled trials and the accuracy of summaries or abstracts.

1. Pappworth MH. *Human guinea-pigs.* London: Routledge and Kegan Paul, 1967.
2. Royal Commission on Civil Liability and Compensation for Personal Injury. *Report* (Pearson Report). London: HMSO, Cmnd 7054.
3. Medico-Pharmaceutical Forum. *A report of the Forum's working party on clinical trials.* Medico-Pharmaceutical Forum, London 1974.

Beecher HK. Consent in clinical experimentation: myth and reality. *JAMA*, 1966; 195:34.

Beecher HK. Ethics and clinical research. *N Eng J Med.* 1966; 274:1354.

Burkhardt R, Kienle G. Controlled clinical trials and medical ethics. *Lancet* 1978; 2:1356.

Council for International Organisations of Medical Science. *Controlled clinical trials.* Oxford: Blackwell, 1960.

Harris EL, Fitzgerald JD. *The principles and practice of clinical trials.* Edinburgh and London: Livingstone, 1970.

Proceedings of the First Deer Lodge Conference on Clinical Pharmacology. Clinical pharmacology and human volunteers. *Clin Pharmacol Ther* 1972; 13:769.

Welbourn RB. Controlled trials in surgery. In: McCredie JA, ed. *Basic surgery.* New York: Macmillan, 1977: 158–64.

Charles F. George

Cloning. Cloning is the process of asexual reproduction seen in bacteria, viruses and other unicellular microorganisms, which divide by simple fission. Hence the daughter cells are genetically identical to each other, and to the parent except where mutation occurs. As applied in genetic engineering (q.v.) in higher organisms, it refers to the process by which genetically identical individuals are produced. A somatic cell is taken from an embryo in an early stage of development, the nucleus transferred to an unfertilised egg from which the nucleus has been removed, and the product grown in culture; daughter cells from the earliest divisions are removed, and either encouraged to continue to grow in cell culture or implanted into host mothers; hence genetically identical offspring result. This very difficult procedure has so far been achieved only in amphibia and there has been no success in mammals. Its application *per se* to man is extremely unlikely even in the remote future, though one can envisage potential applications in animal rearing.

D. F. Roberts

Codes of Practice. See *Declarations; European Economic Community; Medical Research Council; Royal Colleges.*

Commercial Interests. There are situations where commercial interests might influence clinical judgment. Examples include: (1) the position of medically qualified employees in the pharmaceutical industry (q.v.) who may be under pressure to support exaggerated claims for medications; (2) the competitive claims of private practice (q.v.) versus the National Health Service (q.v.); (3) financial association with private clinics for abortion (q.v. and see *Pregnancy Advisory Services*); (4) meeting the public demand for what some may call non-essential cosmetic surgery (q.v.).

Apparent clashes of interest are seldom an important problem with professional people, because by their training and tradition they have a sense of responsibility towards society; furthermore, they have to conform to professional codes of ethical behaviour. Nevertheless, a minority of doctors, lawyers and politicians abuse their privileges and put financial considerations before the public interest. The majority of consultants meet the full claims of their sessional duties and undertake extra work when necessary; but there are a few who skimp their NHS work to provide more time for private practice. There are two approaches to this problem. First, restraints may be imposed on every member of the profession to prevent such abuses, but in practice these reduce the enthusiasm and morale of the majority. The other approach is to encourage those who are enthusiastic and to devise suitable restraints for those who are failing to pull their weight. Such restraints come much better from the professions than from the authorities. Unfortunately, the medical profession has not always done enough to deal with the problem of the minority, usually well known to their colleagues, who let the side down. Unhappily, professional organizations may have less concern with the needs of the public than of those whom they represent.

Hence, some built-in administrative protection is needed. Before the 1974 re-organization, the intervention of independent chairmen of Hospital Management Committees or Boards of Governors on the advice of their Chief Officers was of great help. Fortunately, their beneficial influence is likely to return under the new proposals for District Authorities in the 1980 re-re-organization.

F. Avery Jones

Committee on Safety of Medicines. See *Medicines, Safety of, Committee on.*

Communication.
1. WITH PATIENTS. The essential unit of medical practice is the consultation in which a doctor first elucidates his patient's problem and then advises him what is to be done. In hospitals the latter process may involve many other paramedical people who undertake special investigations and treatments. Skilful communication is necessary in all these complex activities. If communication fails, diagnosis and management may go astray. Thus, failure in this essential medical skill puts patients at risk of maltreatment or of needless anxiety and confusion and since it is usually the doctor's fault, it can reasonably be described as unethical. Failures of communication are often blamed on patients' stupidity, forgetfulness, ignorance or pig-headedness, but all patients have these characteristics to some degree and the doctor has to recognize and overcome them so far as possible. The importance of the problem is shown by the fact that nearly all complaints which reach the Health Service Commissioner (q.v.) originate in failures of communication, mostly with patients.

Few doctors are aware of how frequently they fail to communicate effectively. In both general and hospital practice poor communication is the commonest of patients' complaints[1,2]. When laymen are told that something is being done to improve the situation they show immediate concern and express their urgent hope that doctors may learn to communicate better with their patients.

Why should doctors so frequently fail in this essential part of medical practice? A number of reasons can be identified.

Lack of teaching. Few medical teachers seem to have read much of the modern work on this topic[1,3]. They regard it as something at which doctors are either naturally good or bad and erroneously believe that it cannot be taught. Questions of how much any patient knows about his illness, how much he needs to know, what his anxieties are and how much he understands about his treatment are not regularly discussed in clinical teaching. A few doctors appear to be, or admit that they are, interested chiefly in physiological disturbances in their patients' bodies and are not interested in or are even embarrassed by their patients' personal problems. This lack of interest is unethical for a doctor's calling is to help whole people, not just their bodies. Doctors who have this attitude might better retreat from clinical practice to laboratory or technical work where their lack of interest in their fellow men would do less harm.

Doctors' attitudes. Even if doctors express an interest in the whole man, some of them protect themselves from full involvement, often unconsciously, by adopting a dominant attitude to patients, regarding them as recipients of orders rather than as clients needing advice and counsel. They may show this dominant attitude by standing at the bedside, when talking to a patient who is supine and often unclothed, by discussing patients in the third person with others in their presence, by failing to give them a friendly greeting in the clinic and by many other subtle indications. Such doctors often believe that it is harmful for patients to know too much. They look on patients who ask too many questions as 'bad' and those who unquestionably accept all that is done to them as 'good'. This attitude can cause deep resentment especially in intelligent patients.

Lack of time. This is indeed a great problem, but can be overcome by much fuller use of written materials and audio-visual techniques for giving information.[3]

Jargon. Many doctors find it difficult to talk to their patients in language comprehensible to those who may not have even the most elementary knowledge of medical matters.

In view of the clinical and ethical importance of good communication, it is incumbent on every doctor to do his utmost to improve his skill and efficiency at it. For this an attitude of co-operation with rather than of dominance over patients is essential. It can be helpful for a doctor to monitor at least some of his own consultations on a simple audiotape recorder so that he discovers how he talks to patients. He can also arrange to have patients asked before they leave the clinic or ward how much of what they have been told they recall and understand. They should increase their efficiency by more use of written and audio-visual information. If they are teachers, they must acquaint themselves with the various modern means of teaching communication and consider this issue in all their clinical teaching[1,3]. In hospital practice they must ensure that patients are not confused by being given differing information by the various members of the clinical team.

A special problem arises when a patient has what is considered to be a fatal illness. Many doctors are embarrassed by the modern taboo on death and have not reconciled themselves to their own mortality. At one extreme some are forthright in telling the 'truth', while at the other many dissimulate. The harm that can be done by both these extreme policies has been well described as has the need of such patients to have their problems approached gradually in honesty clothed by optimism.[4] All clinicians should acquaint themselves with the excellent modern writing on this topic.[5] (See *Bereavement; Hospices; Truth, Telling the.*)

2. WITH THE PUBLIC. Since many doctors find difficulty in communicating with their patients it is not surprising that many believe it must be harmful, and thus unethical, to write for the press or to broadcast about clinical matters. How or when the profession's condemnation of public discussion of medical matters arose is uncertain. Until the 19th century, educated people were expected to have some knowledge of hygiene and the use of simple remedies but the illiterate public remained wholly ignorant. The great sanitary revolution of the Victorian era was accompanied by widening dissemination of knowledge about prevention of disease through what came to be known as 'Health Education' (q.v.)[6]; but at the same time it became generally accepted that the managing of illness was a matter which must be left to doctors and in which too much lay interest by laymen was improper. Victorian prudery may have contributed to the development of this attitude; for medicine was becoming based on knowledge of the working of the human body, open consideration of which was considered indecent and immoral. Perhaps doctors themselves fostered this idea, for virtually all their methods of treatment were wholly ineffective except for the confidence inspired by a man reputed to have been trained in the use of powerful remedies. To maintain this mystique, it was necessary that the facts should be concealed.

This did no harm when little benefit was to be gained from public knowledge of medical practice. But now that doctors have an ever-increasing number of specific and effective treatments for illnesses of all kinds, most of which demand some degree of understanding by patients if they are to be properly used, wide public education about treatment has become an essential part of efficient medical practice. Such public education can be achieved only if doctors are willing to make full use of modern means of public communication[7].

The benefits that can be conferred in this way may be briefly summarised:—

1. *Satisfaction of public interest.* General education of the public has led to an ever-increasing interest in the theory and practice of medical science which cannot be resisted and should be beneficially satisfied.

2. *Encouraging early diagnosis.* The earlier treatment is applied in

most illnesses the better the outcome. Early diagnosis can be encouraged by wider recognition of what medicine has to offer and about symptoms and signs which should be reported promptly to doctors and for which lay treatment is often ineffective or even harmful.

3. *Information about use of health service.* If people know more about the workings of the human body they could do more in the way of self-care and much unnecessary consultation of doctors on minor illnesses would be avoided. If they know more about the various services that are available for relief of disablement, about how to choose a doctor and how and when to ask for a second opinion, these Health Services would be more effectively used.

4. *Relief of false anxiety.* This is often caused by old wives' tales and by misconceptions about what doctors do, especially in hospitals, which better education could dispel.

5. *Promoting collaboration in the health service.* In the past, doctors have regarded running of health services as being their sole responsibility. Full lay participation is now increasing and must be based on intelligent appreciation of how doctors think and work.

6. *Guidance on social and moral aspects of medicine.* It is desirable that the voice of doctors should be heard in relation to the many social and ethical dilemmas which are increasingly encountered in modern medical practice. Such matters include the provision of services such as family planning (see *Contraception*) and abortion (q.v.), the handling of social ills such as battered wives (q.v.) and babies (see *Child Abuse*) and drug dependence (q.v.) including smoking (see *Tobacco Smoking*) and alcohol (q.v.) – and issues such as the maintenance of competence to practise (q.v.) and unnecessary prolongation of life (q.v.).

The desirability of public understanding of medical practice is now accepted by most doctors, but objections which are still raised and some problems encountered in its delivery have an ethical component.

A rule of anonymity for doctors who address the public about medicine has generally been accepted to ensure that they cannot be accused of advertising (q.v.) in order to gain patients[7,8]. Since this is the only reason for anonymity it need only be observed in public discussion of clinical practice, and is unnecessary in other branches of medicine. Even in clinical matters, anonymity, though desirable, is not essential so long as no suggestion of personal clinical prowess is given which might lead a reader, listener or viewer to wish to arrange a consultation. The profession has become less strict in its insistence on anonymity in writing for and broadcasting to the public; and reports and producers increasingly seek the help of doctors who do not insist on it.

It used to be supposed that public discussion of illnesses and their treatment might induce neurotic anxiety in laymen. Hypochondria is now recognised as a personality disorder which is not induced by sensible information about illness. There is, nevertheless, a real risk that if a common symptom or sign is mentioned in a press article or a broadcast, as being due to serious disease (such as tiredness being a symptom of cancer, or swelling of the ankles indicating heart failure), many quite healthy people may start worrying that they are seriously ill. This risk must be borne in mind and avoided by appropriate reassurance and explanation. Nevertheless the risk of causing anxiety through misunderstanding remains and must be balanced against the benefits which the article or broadcast is intended to confer. But, in general, the potential benefits of sensible and responsible publicity about the nature and management of illnesses greatly outweigh the risk of any anxiety which may occasionally result, particularly since those who are most anxious should be readily reassured if they consult their own doctors.

Communication about harmful side effects of medical and surgical treatment presents problems. So many people are now under treatment of one kind or another that large audiences can be obtained for articles or programmes on commonly used vaccines, drugs or operations. Recently, television producers have adopted a more critical attitude to doctors and have, in some programmes, stressed the damage done by drugs and vaccines so that alarm has been caused to both patients (who have discontinued or refused essential treatment) and the public (who have, for instance, stopped having their children immunized against pertussis, with serious increase in its frequency, morbidity and mortality). This change in policy may be because increasing numbers of intelligent people resent the dominant role assumed by many doctors (see above), and their unwillingness to give patients full information. The consequent conflict between doctors and the media still persists though better understanding is beginning to appear[9]. In fact, the media could all make useful contributions to getting better understanding of the balance of benefits and risks in modern therapy[10]. This could be done by simple expositions of the nature and use of common medical and surgical procedure and of any important risks they may bring. They should of course reassure patients about the rarity of all adverse effects, but give them some indication of those that they should report to their doctors. Such programmes might also encourage doctors to be more ready to inform their patients along similar lines. Simple written instructions to be issued with prescriptions of common drugs should be made available to facilitate this.[3] People may also be alarmed if a grave prognosis is given of a condition from which they know they are suffering but have not appreciated its gravity.

Objections have been raised about the 'dramatization' of medicine and surgery both in the press and in broadcasting – especially on television. But it has to be remembered that an article or broadcast is useless if it is not read or watched. It must therefore be made attractive and this can often best be done by some element of drama. There is no ethical objection to this so long as truth is maintained.

If the need for public information on medical matters is accepted, it follows that there will be many occasions when the initiative should come from doctors rather than be left to the media who often pick on curiosities which are trivial and may not distinguish between good and worthless evidence nor between the good and harm which may result from giving publicity to items of medical news. It would be helpful if more doctors considered the public's interest in and relevance of their work and were prepared either to submit articles to the press or invite reporters or broadcasters to discuss their findings in public. Better communication with the public about the prevention and treatment of common diseases might result if doctors themselves played a more active part, and learnt to write and speak on medical matters using language which is intelligible to laymen. (See *Medical Journalism*.)

3. WITHIN THE PROFESSION. *Communication in the practice of medicine*. Effective and efficient conduct of both preventive and therapeutic medicine depends on prompt and clear communication between doctors in relation to medical problems with which they are mutually concerned.

This is most often a matter of letters between general practitioners and consultants but may equally concern arrangements between community physicians and clinicians for preventive or after-care services. An inadequate and illegible letter from a general practitioner to a consultant or a long delay in a consultant's report to the practitioner may not be thought to involve any ethical issue but to be a mere matter of inevitable inefficiency in an under-staffed health service. But inefficiency where the welfare, or sometimes even the safety, of patients or members of the public are concerned, is undoubtedly a breach of the ethical standards demanded of doctors in whom patients or public have put their trust. This is not just a matter of immediate communication between consultant and general practitioner but is also important for the future care of patients, for this correspondence forms a part of patients' records which are important for later reference (see *Medical Records*).

Communication about the advance of medicine. Prompt and full communication at professional meetings or in professional journals of the results of clinical and laboratory research into medical matters is an ethical requirement for those engaged in such work in order that patients or public may benefit as soon as possible from advances in knowledge. There are two ethical requirements in relation to such communications.

First, truthfulness. Investigators occasionally obtain results in experiments or trials which conflict with other consistent results. If no experimental or computational error can be found to indicate that the aberrant results are false, but if they throw doubt on the conclusions which have been reached from the majority of concordant results, the investigator may be tempted to reject or conceal the awkward conflict of evidence. To do so is both scientifically and medically unethical for the discordant values may provide a clue to a different and more correct interpretation of the results from which benefit may be derived (See *Clinical Trials*).

Second, humility. The quest for priority in publication of new ideas or discoveries may be regarded as unethical by those who adopt the Christian view that pride is the first of the seven deadly sins but not by those who look on it as a cardinal virtue. It is certainly harmful if it results in premature publication of incomplete studies or in concealing important new findings lest others should develop them more speedily and thus obtain credit which the investigator wishes to retain for himself.

Both these ethical breaches are not infrequently encountered today. The contest for priority in medical research is sometimes described in academic circles as a 'rat-race comparable to the scramble up the consultant ladder' and there are academic departments where informal discussion of current research at professional meetings is forbidden lest ideas should be 'stolen' and published.

The ethical principles in this matter are clear and if they were generally accepted and acted upon, much unnecessary jealousy and delay in the spread of knowledge would be avoided.

1. Bennett EA, ed. *Communication between doctors and patients.* London: Oxford University Press for Nuffield Provincial Hospitals Trust.
2. Cartwright A. *Human relations and hospital care.* London: Routledge and Kegan Paul, 1964.
3. Fletcher CM. Towards better practice and teaching of communication between doctors and patients. In McLachlan G, ed. *Mixed communications.* Oxford University Press, 1979.
4. Brewin TB. The cancer patient: communication and morals. *Br Med J* 1977; 2:1623–7.
5. Fletcher CM. Annotated Bibliography. In: *Talking with patients: a teaching approach.* London: Oxford University Press with Nuffield Provincial Hospitals Trust, 1980.
6. Fletcher CM. *Communication in medicine.* London: The Rock Carling Fellowship, Nuffield Provincial Hospitals Trust, 1973.
7. Fletcher CM. *The profession and the mass media.* London: Royal College of Physicians, 1975.
8. Hadfield SJ. *The law and ethics for doctors* London: Eyre and Spottiswoode, 1958:78.
9. Swan M. Television medicine (letter). *Br Med J* 1978; 1:1274.
10. Fletcher CM. The media. In: Inman WHW, ed. *Monitoring for drug safety.* Lancaster: MTP Press, 1980.

Charles Fletcher

Community Health Councils. See *Health Councils.*

Compensation. The award of money (referred to as 'damages') made to a person injured, generally at work, in a road accident or as a result of criminal injury to compensate him for his injuries and for their effects. The exaggeration (not necessarily deliberate) or prolongation by a plaintiff in a claim for compensation for personal injuries of his condition so as to produce an inflation of the damages he is likely to receive, is sometimes called 'compensationitis'.

MEDICAL ASPECTS. The ethical problems facing a medical practitioner, when a patient presses a claim for compensation beyond what appears to be clinically justifiable, are extremely difficult. The majority of patients seen for medical reports have clear histories of trauma and have sustained injuries which are readily attributable to the accidents and whose course of recovery and subsequent complications (if any) can be anticipated from the injuries. On the other hand, very few patients are frank malingerers, in that their symptoms cannot be attributed to the injuries they sustained nor to the accident which they describe. However, some patients fall between these two categories and describe symptoms which are worse than those found in other patients who have sustained similar injuries. They are not malingerers, but often give the impression of exaggerating their symptoms. The main problem facing the medical practitioner is to determine whether the exaggeration is deliberate or psychoneurotic. There are three large groups of neurological symptoms which can complicate trauma. First, a genuine depressive illness or occasionally a frank anxiety. Secondly, the post-concussional syndrome which produces headache, postural dizziness, irritability, failure of concentration and an intolerance of noise, which suggests a structural or at least a pathophysiological basis and is organic in nature. Thirdly, the psychoneurotic accident neurosis[1]. The patient complains of continuous depression, restless sleep, hypochondriacal invalidism, disgruntlement and self-pity in varying proportions. Unlike the post-concussional syndrome these symptoms are frequently prolonged. He frequently complains of head pains or severe protracted and unrelenting pain at the site of injury. These symptoms occur only in injuries where the plaintiff feels that a third party is responsible and where there is a possibility of compensation. The symptoms usually settle rapidly once compensation has been settled, irrespective of the amount or whether the plaintiff was successful. It is for this reason that medical practitioners occasionally advise that litigation should be completed as soon as possible. Unfortunately, many cases tend to drag on for a long time, sometimes for years. If, during this period a vicious cycle of anxiety, muscle spasm, further pain and further anxiety is established it may be impossible to break and may explain why all patients with accident neurosis do not necessarily improve once litigation has been completed. The medical practitioner should inform his patient and the solicitor, with the patient's consent, what is happening and advise early settlement of the claim. However, his advice should not be misinterpreted by the court as an indication that the patient is deliberately exaggerating his symptoms. Although it is not possible to determine accurately whether the accident neurosis is at a conscious or sub-conscious level, in many patients it is probably at a sub-conscious level.

An associated problem is the correlation of symptoms with radiographic changes. There is no ethical or medical reason for obtaining X-rays of every injured region in every patient. X-rays need only be taken when there is a clinical suspicion of a bone injury. Ligamentous injuries may be painful for many months or even years, even when no bone injury is evident on the X-rays, and the movement of affected joints, particularly in the spine, may be limited. It is not ethical, therefore, to describe a patient as a malingerer where his signs and symptoms do not correlate with his X-rays.

The treatment of patients with anxiety and associated symptoms may be extremely difficult. When the doctor considers that there is a psychoneurotic element, he should explain it to the patient and, if necessary, seek neurological or psychiatric help. Sometimes symptoms respond to physiotherapy and this should be prescribed, when appropriate. The main difficulty arises when there is a question of surgical operation. On the one hand, some surgeons will not operate upon a patient until his claim has been settled, while the legal advisers may not want to settle until all the necessary operations have been done. Consequently, the patient may be left with his treatment incomplete and his claim unsettled. If the surgeon considers that most of the symptoms will subside when litigation is concluded, he should press for an early settlement and then re-assess the patient. If he is confident that there will be little improvement, he should proceed with the necessary operations. It is probably unethical to withhold operation from all patients until their claims for compensation are settled.

For several reasons, therefore, early settlement of the case would be to the patient's advantage. Even if it were not possible to determine the amount of compensation within six months of the injury early agreement as to liability would be an advantage.

The most important ethical principle is that the doctor's responsibility is to examine and investigate the patient and assess what symptoms and disability are directly attributable to the injuries, whether they are exaggerated as a result of associated anxiety, tension or other psychoneurotic states, whether the patient has a frank neurosis or whether the patient is malingering. When the symptoms are due to a soft tissue injury without radiographic changes it is the doctor's responsibility to indicate that they have a genuine pathological basis. When the symptoms are due to an accident neurosis it is his responsibility to inform the solicitor and advise early settlement of the claim as well as an early return to work.

1. Miller H. In: Lock S, Windle H, eds. *Remembering Henry.* London: British Medical Association, 1977: 101–32.

C. S. B. Galasko

LEGAL ASPECTS. In England and Wales, compensation is recoverable as damages only upon proof by the injured person of fault on the part of a person, company, or institution said to have caused the injury. The fault will either be negligence under the common law, or breach of a duty imposed by Act of Parliament. In either case it is open to the defendant to allege that the plaintiff is guilty of contributory negligence – has, by his own fault, contributed to his injuries; and such a plea, if successful, will diminish the damages by an appropriate proportion. The damages themselves are divided into (a) special damages: the plaintiff's actual financial loss, for example, his loss of earnings or medical expenses, and (b) general damages: a sum to compensate him for his injuries as such.

That is the 'common law' system, but a number of jurisdictions now operate what is known as a 'no-fault liability' system. It is in the considerations respectively advanced for and against the two systems that ethical questions primarily arise. On the 'no-fault' basis, the plaintiff is entitled to be compensated simply on proof of his injuries: the other motor-car driver, or the plaintiff's employer, will be liable to pay even if he is wholly blameless, although he may be allowed still to raise allegations of contributory negligence.

Ethically, the following propositions arise: (1) A civilized community will not permit the availability of resources necessary for the proper care – and indeed for the compensation – of an injured (particularly a seriously injured) person to depend wholly on the question of who was to blame for his injuries, when (a) no one may be to blame; (b) the blame, be it on plaintiff or defendant, may consist of no more than a momentary act or omission, and (c) its proof in court, often years after the event, may depend on the recollection of not necessarily reliable witnesses, and be, in general, fallible. On the other hand: (2) a legal liability to pay (or by insurance provide for the payment of) what may be large sums of money to injured persons should not be imposed on parties who are or may be entirely innocent of any act or omission causative of the injuries in question, since such an imposition (a) is contrary to canons of justice which many accept, (b) will require for the system's operation increased financial resources which may (if provided by compulsory state insurance) constitute a claim on the public purse not warranted by such advantages as the system may have, (c) will add by the necessarily increased insurance premiums to the already heavy costs of various activities, but most importantly those of industry, and (d) may tend to diminish the vigilance of at least some employers in the maintenance of high standards of safety procedures, since their liability to pay will not depend on proof by the plaintiff that such standards have not been complied with.

The report of the Royal Commission on Civil Liability and Compensation for Personal Injury, set up in 1973 under Lord Pearson, was published in 1978[1]. It recommends as changes in the English law (a) that a 'no-fault' compensation scheme for motor vehicle accidents should be established, (b) that there should be a revised system of awarding damages in accident cases, namely by the grant of periodical payments rather than a lump sum where there is serious and prolonged injury or dependency following death, (c) an improved industrial injuries scheme, and (d) certain new rights for severely handicapped children. There are of course many other recommendations, which cannot be reviewed here.[2] The report is certainly a document of the first importance in this field.

'No-fault' systems in relation to motor vehicle injuries are in existence in about half of the states in the United States, seven of the ten provinces of Canada, British Columbia, Manitoba, and Saskatchewan. There is a general 'no-fault' system in New Zealand.

In West Germany there have recently been introduced (6th May 1976) 'no-fault' provisions in respect only of damage or injury caused by pharmaceutical products: this change was the outcome of the cases in that country which came about as a result of the use there of the thalidomide drug. The thalidomide cases in the United Kingdom provide an important instance of the sort of circumstances to which those in favour of 'no-fault liability' have particular regard.

In June 1977 there was presented to Parliament the report of the Law Commission and the Scottish Law Commission on Liability for Defective Products[3]. It refers to an EEC draft directive proposing that producers should be liable without proof of fault to compensate people injured by their products, and to the Strasbourg Convention on Products Liability in regard to Personal Injury and Death. The report recommends the imposition of strict liability for injuries resulting from defects in products that are put into circulation in the course of a business, and that the liability should rest primarily on the producer.

The competing systems of compensation provide areas for the consideration of ethical questions from medical and jurisprudential, as well as from social and philosophical, points of view.

'*Compensationitis*'. In a claim for compensation the amount of damages depends on the seriousness of the plaintiff's condition in a number of respects: its likely duration, the extent to which it does, will, or may disable him from living a normal life, from earning his living, and so forth. Very frequently a plaintiff's condition may appear to be worse than, in purely pathological or physiological terms, it really is: sometimes because he exaggerates his ailments; more often because the very existence of his claim causes functional or psycho-neurotic states in which the plaintiff genuinely believes himself to be worse than is justified by purely objective clinical criteria as applied by the medical experts who examine, care for, and report on him – he suffers from what has become known as a 'functional overlay'.

If in a case of 'compensationitis' the functional nature of the plaintiff's condition is detected, it is very frequently predicted that his symptoms will (so far as attributable to these psychological factors) disappear with the disposal or settlement of his claim.

Ethically the situation of a plaintiff who deliberately exaggerates his claim poses no difficulty. The malingerer or 'lead-swinger' will not be thought entitled to any more by way of compensation than is war-ranted by the extent of his original, objectively provable, injuries. The position of the genuine plaintiff whose state is nevertheless attributable in whole or part to a 'functional overlay' is not so straightforward. If his psychological condition is as much a fact beyond his control as his broken leg, then (as the United Kingdom courts have recognized) he is as well entitled to compensation for one as for the other. But it is possible to distinguish the state of a plaintiff who, although entirely genuine, may nevertheless be capable of improving or remedying his condition by an effort of will. Such a plaintiff's precise future con-dition may depend upon his receiving a degree or type of encourage-ment or incentive effective to induce such an effort of will. In this area, ethical questions arise as to (a) the existence and extent of a duty upon those who have to do with such a plaintiff – including, perhaps, the doctor – to seek to promote his willpower; and here the psy-chiatrist treating the man should notice that the view he takes of his patient's disorders is or may be rootedly different from that taken by the lawyers (and in particular, of course, the judge) when a claim comes to be made; (b) the existence and extent of a duty upon the plaintiff *himself* to exercise his willpower; and (c) what difference, if any, should be made (for the purposes of the amount of compensation to be paid) between the plaintiff who is unable to improve his con-dition by willpower no matter how favourable the surrounding cir-cumstances, and the plaintiff for whom such improvement is possible but is not achieved. (See also *Immunization*.)

1. Royal Commission on Civil Liability and Compensation for Per-sonal Injury. *Report* (Pearson Report). London: HMSO, 1978, Cmnd 7054.
2. Marsh NS. The Pearson Report on Civil Liability and Compen-sation for Death or Personal Injury. *Law Quarterly Review.* 1979; 95.
3. Law Commission and the Scottish Law Commission. *Liability for defective products.* London: HMSO, 1977, Cmnd 6831.
4. Compensation for industrial injury. Memorandum of evidence submitted to the Royal Commission on Civil Liability and Com-

pensation for Personal Injuries by the Industrial Law Society. *Industrial Law Journal* 1975; 4:195–217.

5. Harrison RA, Mesher J. No-fault – private or social insurance? *Industrial Law Journal* 1975; 4:166–80.

6. Kennedy I, Edwards RG. A critique of the Law Commission Report on Injuries to Unborn Children and the proposed Congenital Disabilities (Civil Liability) Bill. *J Med Ethics* 1975; 1:116–21.

7. Law Commission. *Injuries to unborn children*. Working Paper 47. London: HMSO, 1973, Cmnd 5709.

8. Marks KH. A first national no-fault. *Australian Law Journal* 1973; 47:516–25.

9. McGregor H. *Damages* 14th edn. London: Sweet and Maxwell, 1980.

10. Munkman JH. *Damages for personal injuries and death*. 5th edn. London: Butterworths, 1973.

11. Parsons OH. A no-fault system? Not proven. *Industrial Law Journal* 1974; 3:128–37.

J. G. McK. Laws

Competence to Practise. The competent doctor is one who brings to his medical work a reasonable level of knowledge necessary and skills appropriate to his chosen branch of medicine. Competence is acquired through a process of education and training in which a basic core of knowledge forms the foundation for wider information and skills acquired in the process of further study and practice. This basic core embodies understanding of the scientific approach to information and its use in the context of man in health and disease, with respect also to his environment. It also inculcates the vocational sense which recognizes the need to continue learning.

Modern medicine is a tree of knowledge so branched and bearing such fruit that most individual doctors are wholly occupied within only a small part, or with a very limited concept of the whole, in the exercise of their profession. For the majority their work involves continuing or repeated contact with patients; in these an exchange of services for information takes place, so that the doctor continues learning from the source of his own practice. In this way, as well as from knowledge and skills derived from sharing with others, he extends his competence and becomes more effective in the service he provides.

How far the competence of an individual doctor can be judged depends upon the limits in assessing professional ability. As medical education and training evolve, assessment of the student is a changing process, tending towards continuing assessment so that the education process itself is subject to critical review. Since the completion of the training process must be marked by some act of approval to denote the fully competent doctor – one who is judged fit to exercise independent responsibility free of further supervision in any aspect of his chosen branch of medicine – registration is necessary, and in this way those who seek his services are also informed.

Medical education and training involve changing relationships between the basic syllabus, the nature and period of clinical instruction, and the length and content of vocational training; the overall aim being to ensure that the doctor in each field of practice has fulfilled the whole requirements of his training for that field according to the best current view of them, and has been assessed for his fitness for such independent practice by the most suitable methods. Thus in the UK the specialty of general practice, for example, now requires a longer period of vocational training and improved methods of assessment for those who enter it. Thereafter the registered practitioner is not further judged by his colleagues in respect of his competence; there are no satisfactory standards by which he can be wholly assessed in the educational sense as he acquires his individual character and particular kind of practice experience.

Nevertheless attempts are being made to assess the standards of practice and the content of their work of doctors engaged in practice in some other countries, especially the USA and Canada. Whether organizations set up to review professional standards and activity on a periodic or continuing basis, or the periodic re-licensure of doctors, will improve the quality or better distribution of medical care is not yet known, and although such systems may commend themselves to those who fund or use health services, acceptance of them by doctors must depend upon firm evidence to justify limiting or prohibiting their practice. Every doctor will, however, be expected to assess his own competence by such results of his work as he can discern, and he has some responsibility to share his experience with colleagues in the same field of work, for in this way his teachers derived their own knowledge on his behalf. He will also gain confidence from his colleagues from their assurance of parallel attitudes and practices in the course of this process of 'peer review'. He may in addition, or for preference, make use of more formal systems of confidential or self-assessment provided by educational bodies acting in authoritarian rather than 'peer' roles.

Apart from his colleagues, other professionals with whom he works and patients for whom he practises will form judgments of a doctor's competence which are based upon aspects of his effectiveness, his powers of communication and other qualities better defined as style rather than competence. The way in which he practises and the choice he makes of a particular field of work may well be decided by these qualities of style as well as his interests and inclinations; in general he will seek work where he is most effective.

The actions or omissions of a doctor, like those of any individual providing services to others, can be tested by legal processes or by forms of tribunal or other procedure set up by an authority which employs him for his professional services. Any outcome should depend upon the independent views of other doctors of what constitutes a reasonable level of care in the particular circumstance under review. Where the doctor has failed to meet the minimum so required of him he will be liable to penalty from his employer or for redress to his patient.

There are many fields of medical work in which doctors have no direct contact with patients but this detracts in no way from their need to exercise professional competence. In specialties of a wholly non-clinical or administrative kind, and especially in the growing field of community medicine, the doctor applies his knowledge and skills to interpret and facilitate the work of his colleagues in clinical practice; in so doing he has knowledge of their own work and its potential and he shares their objectives of better standards of individual patient care. In failing himself he diminishes the effectiveness of his colleagues.

Loss of competence results chiefly from sickness or ageing. Recognition of his limitations due to sickness and the need to seek medical care, will come naturally to a doctor on most occasions, although he may be careful in choosing colleagues for his own medical needs. But in some forms of illness, especially those concerning mental health or addiction, his loss of insight into causes and remedies can set up serious barriers against the help he needs, and in such circumstances his own sickness may endanger the welfare of his patients. It is to meet this type of problem that the Medical Act (1978) includes provision for the establishment by the General Medical Council (q.v.) of a Health Committee.

The process of ageing affects different doctors in varying degrees according to the changing nature of their field of work and the demands made upon them. In the past it has been common for doctors in acute or demand specialties to transfer to less exacting branches of medicine before retirement, while those in general practice may continue as long as their health allows. The increasingly sharp definition of the scope and training for each form of practice sets up barriers between them, and more systematic retraining or sheltered forms of practice will become the only alternative to retirement as accelerating changes in the nature of medicine confront the ageing doctor. (See *Medical Science* and *Disciplinary Procedures*; *Clinical Practice*; *European Economic Community*; *Quality Assurance*.)

1. *Competence to practise* (Alment Committee Report). London: Royal College of Obstetricians and Gynaecologists, 1976.

E. A. J. Alment

Compulsory Examination and Treatment. 'The only purpose for which power can rightfully be exercised over any member of a civilized community against his will is to prevent harm to others'[1] is the basic

Compulsory Examination and Treatment

argument which sets clear limits to the means of securing the examination and treatment of an individual. In the United Kingdom no one may be detained against his will for any investigation or treatment save under the provisions of an Act of Parliament, which relates to specific issues in mental illness, notifiable infectious disease or serious capacity in the aged.[2] In general, participation in treatment depends wholly on consent as coercion robs both doctor and patient of autonomy[3]. (See *Clinical Autonomy; Consent; Moral Autonomy*.) Compulsory isolation, say in the case of a serious infectious disease however, requires intervention of the courts, but this is seldom invoked as a patient may be properly warned of the impropriety of exposing others to infection, an action which may indeed be criminal.[2]

Under the Road Traffic Act it is an offence for a driver to refuse to provide a sample of blood or urine for analysis if requested to do so by the police when a driving offence has been committed.

In the case of children (see *Child*), parental rights are limited by the obligation to attend to their welfare. In the case of refusal of parental consent (q.v.), medical action is justifiable to save the life of a child or to prevent serious suffering (see also *Blood Transfusion*). In situations of lesser moment it may be necessary to seek help from the local children's authority.[2]

Diseases transmitted almost wholly by sexual intercourse, such as gonorrhoea and syphilis, although potentially dangerous, do not incapacitate the patient sufficiently to prevent their further dissemination. Frequently, but not always, it is the male who first presents to the doctor with an obvious symptom whereas the female is more commonly free from such an effect. This situation tends to give rise to a view that it is the latter who is responsible and that it is justified to use coercion to secure her medical examination and treatment and so protect the community. Experience of old Acts of Parliament (Contagious Diseases Acts, 1866, 1869; Defence of the Realm Act, 1918, Regulation 40D; Defence Regulation 1939, Regulation 33B) and the rejection of attempts at their renewal in bills presented by Mr Richard Marsh in 1962 and by Sir Myer Galpern in 1967 are in keeping with the fact that legal compulsion in this sensitive field is cumbersome, ineffective and discredited as a public health measure. Power to use compulsion in this way has a damaging effect in that it tends to lead to reliance on threats rather than on persuasion and on securing co-operation with patients. It is a matter for concern that provision for compulsory examinations is common in the legislation of many countries in Europe, and efforts are needed to examine this subject again. (See *Blood Testing, Random; Mental Illness, Certification of; Sexually Transmitted Disease*.)

1. Mill J. On liberty. See *On liberty, representative government and the subjection of women*. The World's Classics. Oxford: University Press, 1912:15

2. Speller SR. *Law of doctor and patient.* London: HK Lewis, 1973: 32, 94.

3. Moerloose J de, Rahm H. A survey of venereal disease legislation in Europe. *Acta Derm Venereol* 1964; 44:146–63.

Campbell AV. *Moral dilemmas in medicine.* Edinburgh: Churchill Livingstone, 1975:97.

Shannon NP. The compulsory treatment of venereal diseases under Regulation 33B. *Br J Vener Dis* 1943; 19:22–3; 67–77.

D. H. H. Robertson

Computers. The computer is a device into which data are fed together with a set of instructions or 'programs' and which, after manipulating the data in accordance with these instructions, prints out the results. As its name implies, the computer was originally designed for large scale calculation and is widely used in statistical work in medicine. Not only can the characteristics of groups of patients be rapidly and precisely computed, but derived functions of basic measurements can be readily acquired and added to the patient's record. The ease with which complex calculations can be performed has led to developments in diagnosis and prognosis where statistical techniques, such as linear discriminant analysis, are used to distinguish between patients suffering from different diseases. This form of analysis calculates the weighting that should be given to each item of diagnostic information in order to compute a score for each individual which will best discriminate between patients suffering from similar but different diseases.

The computer also affords a means of storing a large quantity of information, e.g. on hospital admissions, which can be rapidly produced. When individual patients can be easily and uniquely identified, as by a social security number, the computer can readily link various records for the same person. New information can be quickly added or test results kept up to date so that the monitoring of a patient's progress is feasible.

The ready accessibility of information on individuals and the possibility of linking files dealing with different aspects of their lives have led to some anxiety about the security of data held in computer systems. In practice, security of information stored in a computer is probably greater than in the conventional written records stored in a filing cabinet, and wider access to data which do not identify individuals allows epidemiological studies and regular statistical reports which are very much in the interest of the community.

Medical records are usually kept separately in different computer systems from other governmental (e.g. police or legal) information. Individual records are identified by number and not by name, and data can be stored or transmitted in some 'scrambled' form. Access can be allowed only when some key code is used by accredited operators. As the security systems of modern computers are becoming increasingly effective, the risks of accidental or malicious disclosure of medical information should become negligible.

It might well be regarded, however, as a basic right in a free and democratic society that all personal health data can be kept absolutely separately from other personal information so that they cannot be used for the prosecution or harassment of the subject. In the United Kingdom, for example, an official committee report[1] on Computers: Safeguards for Privacy, emphasizes the issues already discussed and the Government White Paper[2], in accepting the underlying principles, proposes the setting up of a statutory agency to supervise the use of computers that handle personal information of all kinds. (See also *Confidentiality: Medical Records.*)

Total separation of medical from all other official records, whilst ensuring confidentiality, does present other difficulties. The planning of state and local services aims to provide integrated health, economic and social support and such planning is difficult without access to all relevant information sources. Further, the Health Services and the Social Services aspire to serve the 'whole' individual and this is not possible without full knowledge of individual circumstances. Concern has also been expressed that total prohibition of access to medical data banks to everyone outwith the Health Service may inhibit independent enquiry into, and assessment of, the health and caring services.

1. Central Statistical Office. *Social Trends No 6.* London: HMSO, 1975.
2. Cabinet Office Central Policy Review Staff. *A joint framework for social policies.* London: HMSO, 1975.
Anonymous. Confidentiality, records and computers. *Br Med J* 1979; 1:698–9.
Barber B, Cohen RD, Kenny DJ, Rowson J, Scholes M. Some problems in confidentiality in medical computing. *J Med Ethics* 1976; 2:71–3.
Greisser G, ed. *Realization by data protection in health information systems.* Proceedings of the IFIP-WG Working Conference June 1976. North-Holland, 1977.

The late Donald Reid
revised by W. Lutz

Confidentiality. The principle of maintaining the security of information elicited from an individual in the privileged circumstances of a professional relationship.

The individual has a fundamental right to privacy; and this is of particular importance in the practice of medicine when the unauthorized disclosure of personal information may have personal, social or legal repercussions. On the other hand, information about him of a medical nature may have to be released to fulfil a statutory obligation such as the completion of a certificate of the causes of death, a document legally open to inspection by the public. The patient himself may release the doctor from the bond of secrecy by asking him in writing to report on his clinical condition to an employer, insurance company or solicitor.

Personal rights and public interest. Confidentiality is the rule, but the needs of the community sometimes take precedence over the risks to the individual inherent in disclosure. In a court of law the judge may rule that, despite the doctor's protest, the administration of justice demands that the seal of professional confidence must be broken. The statutory notification of infectious disease is perhaps the commonest example of the protection of the community, in this case from epidemic disease, overriding the individual's right to privacy. Another condition in which the rights of the individual may be overridden is when, in the doctor's opinion, he has ceased to be fully responsible by reason of mental disorder. If he appears to be a danger to himself or others, because of delusions, compulsions or dementia, sufficient information should be disclosed to ensure that proper steps are taken to protect him and others. These steps may include detention under the Mental Health Act (See *Mental Illness; Mental Illness, Certification of*).

Those who have committed crimes are entitled to expect strict observance of the rule of professional secrecy that the doctor does not disclose to others, without the patient's consent, anything learnt directly or indirectly in the professional relationship. Rarely, the immediacy and seriousness of the danger to persons may persuade the doctor that the public interest should override the rights of the patient. In such a case the doctor should first take advice from his defence organization or an experienced colleague, and be prepared to justify whatever he decides. He should give thought to what he should do in these worrying cases so that he is in a position to decide how to respond if the police make enquiries, at an accident department or psychiatric unit, for instance. However, he is under obligation to report the medical facts to the appropriate community physician if his examination of a child reveals injuries which he suspects to be 'non-accidental' (See *Child Abuse; Risk Registers*).

The duty to inform the licensing authority of a disability likely to cause the driver of a motor vehicle to be a source of danger to the public lies with the patient, and the doctor should so advise him. The doctor is under no obligation in law to disclose the information. Rarely, if the patient refuses to follow the advice, and the danger to the public warrants it, he may decide, after taking advice, that he ought to inform the licensing authority himself. Before doing so, he should tell the patient of his intention. Conflict between the rights of the patient and the safety of the public also arises sometimes when the patient suffers from a disability likely to be a source of danger to others if he continues in his job. The patient usually agrees that a report should be made to his employer's medical officer, and that he should be certified as fit to return to work only under conditions agreed with the medical officer.

Patient and family. In general, when a patient is rational and responsible, the doctor must take particular care not to give information to those closest to him – spouse, parents, other relatives, friends, colleagues or employer – without specific permission. To whom he may report, and within what limits, should be agreed between doctor and patient. He should make it clear to anyone who offers him information about the patient that he must retain the right to disclose its source; it is usually better to wait to receive it until he has the patient's permission to do so. He should stop the patient from disclosing, unnecessarily, sensitive information, such as the identity of sexual partners. A junior member of a clinical team should explain to a patient that he must share with the consultant and the other doctors the gist of what he is told.

In certain circumstances, especially when the patient is acutely and dangerously ill, e.g. immediately after a heart attack or emergency operation, or when he is thought or known to be suffering from a serious illness with a poor prognosis for health or life, e.g. incurable cancer or multiple sclerosis, it is often in his own best interests to be told only part of the truth and to have it put in the most favourable light. To do otherwise might seriously jeopardize his chances of recovery or induce unnecessary depression. At such times the patient's close associates usually ask for, and may need to know, more of the truth, so that they may help him in his recovery, support him in his illness or make practical arrangements for him. The doctor should always have a clear understanding with them about what he and they will disclose.

In most cases, when the patient has passed the acute stage of his illness, or when a serious diagnosis has been confirmed, the doctor should encourage openness and frank discussion. Families and friends whose relationships are close need mutual support and trust at such times, and secrecy about matters of life and death usually do more harm than good. Often relatives request, or even demand, that the patient should be kept in ignorance of the truth when, in the doctor's view, he is ready and has the right to learn it. The doctor should keep in mind that his professional relationship is with the patient and that he must act in accordance with his own view of what is best for him. In doing so he may have to overrule the relatives' requests, however well-intentioned they are, at the same time trying to make it easier for them and the patient to talk frankly together.

Particular problems arise with children. The doctor should be careful that any assurances about confidentiality he gives to a patient under 16 years of age do not stop him from insisting that the parents should be told if he feels that this is necessary (See *Child; Consent; Contraception*). It is usually sensible to give the patient the oppor-

tunity to tell his parents himself. When a girl under the age
seeks termination of pregnancy (see *Abortion*), the doctor has
ticularly difficult problem in that his proper wish that the pare
informed may be in conflict with his responsibilities to her as his
patient if she wishes to keep it secret from them. If the issues are
discussed with her with kindness, she is usually given the courage to
tell one of her parents, at least what has happened and what is being
proposed.

All the situations described above place a heavy burden of responsibility on the doctor and often demand careful thought, consultation
between colleagues (including consultant and general practitioner),
and fine judgement. He must be guided by sensible and sensitive
discretion rather than rigorous rules.

Security of documents. Since access to confidential records by an
unauthorized person may threaten the patient's health or welfare, the
physical security of documents is as much part of the doctor's duty
to his patient as is the conventional silence. Patients have the right to
expect that the information about them acquired in the course of
privileged consultation is kept in a secure cabinet or premises protected
against unauthorized entry. (See *Medical Records*.)

The instruction of secretarial and clerical staff in the importance of
confidentiality is essential; it is often useful to insist that they should
sign a statement that they have understood and agree to comply with
the instructions given.

Modern conditions demand informed co-operation between doctors
and other professional and ancillary workers, and this entails communication of information. Such extension of the bounds of confidentiality should be recognized by both patient and profession as
implicit in any request for medical care. Special problems arise when
suspicion of concealed family violence is to be reported with a view
to an entry in a risk register (*See Child Abuse: Risk Registers*). Also,
psychiatrists have expressed anxieties about the hazards from the
reporting to a government department of the specific diagnosis of
mental illness and other sensitive data on routine statistical returns
bearing the name of the patient and other facts, such as date of birth
and address, which could be used to identify him. The hazards are
largely removed if the coding of the forms is done in the hospital or
at the Regional Computer Centre. Those who supply the confidential
information should be able to monitor, perhaps through a representative of a medical committee, the precautions taken to ensure
confidentiality.

Others have emphasized the risks inherent in the capacity of the
computer to link records from different files if access were given, for
example, to both mental hospital records and police records of named
individuals. Such risks cannot be dismissed but they can be guarded
against by the legal prohibition of such linkage and the maintenance
of separate computer systems for each purpose. Anxiety is relieved

when advanced methods of storing information in computers (q.v.) are used, and when staff are of high calibre and well trained. Malicious removal of sensitive information from computer data banks appears to be less likely than with conventional methods of storing and filing medical records (q.v.).

Acceptance of the need for the transfer of information outside the immediate treatment team will depend on the benefit to the community. In the British National Health Service, all hospital records are the legal property of the Secretary of State and are thus at his disposal. However, the ethical principles involved are appreciated by the officials concerned, and standard codes of practice for the protection of the individual have been evolved, e.g. in Britain and the USA. Officially requested returns are thus handled with discretion, reinforced by legal sanctions. Published reports of official surveys give only a statistical summary with no information on any identifiable individual. Such accumulation of individual records can be justified by the expectation that they will lead to improvement in the efficiency of the health service.

Research. More in tune with public sympathies is research that can often only be pursued when the investigator has access to medical information about individuals for whom he has no clinical responsibility. The increasing degree of pollution of the environment, the advent of new and powerful but sometimes dangerous medicines, the changing habits of the population in regard to smoking, alcohol and other drugs of addiction present fresh threats to the public health which epidemiologists are engaged in detecting and assessing. To estimate relative risks, information on large numbers of cases has to be collected, and representative samples of apparently well populations interrogated or examined. Access to patients is usually only possible through hospital and similar records and then by courtesy of the attending physician. Transfer of information can take place because both investigator and physician are bound by the rules of professional secrecy, and mutual trust has been built up over the years. When a non-medically qualified collaborator such as sociologist or statistician is working as one of the investigating team, he can be regarded as being covered by the common professional ethics. Increasingly such investigators are working independently and codes of ethical practice have been drawn up by their own professions. The British Medical Research Council has published a code[1] outlining some of the problems and the ways in which they can be handled.

The code lays down the procedures to be followed by those in charge of collection of patients' records, e.g. in hospital. Advice is given on measures designed to maintain security, e.g. by identifying patients in computer records by number rather than name and using technical devices which ensure that access to records can be restricted to authorized staff who know confidential key codes. Publication of research results must never allow the identification of individuals.

Access should be given only with the agreement of a committee on which there is both medical and lay representation. All staff handling personal data must be instructed in the need for security. When cases of specific disease are discovered by reference to records, an approach to the patient can only be made through his personal doctor. The overriding consideration is the welfare of the patients involved and the Council has established a Standing Committee to which research proposals involving access to confidential information can be referred. Lay members represent the view of the public at large. The intention is that such committees should be established more widely so that the benefits to the community of epidemiological research can be gained while the patient's right to privacy is as securely guarded as possible. (See also *Computers; Interprofessional Relationships; Medical Records.*)

1. Medical Research Council. *Responsibility in the use of medical information for research.* London: Medical Research Council, 1972.

The late Donald Reid
revised by D. Russell Davis

IN GENERAL PRACTICE. Technically, the disclosure of information to a partner, without the patient's consent, represents a breach of confidentiality. This becomes even more important in regard to information given to practice nurses, health visitors, and secretaries since these members of the practice team are not governed by any strict ethical code even if their contracts of employment contain references to the need for strict confidentiality. It is increasingly common in general practice for patients to enquire whether specific items of information are being made available to health visitors and to request that their privacy in this respect is safeguarded. The changing societal norms make it less easy for a doctor to be sensitive to information a patient wishes to remain confidential. It may well be more important for a young executive to conceal information regarding chest pains or a consultation with a psychiatrist than to disclose an extra-marital affair, since the latter may increasingly be regarded as acceptable but the former may incur financial and promotional penalties. In practice, therefore, there is a conflict between strict interpretation of the code of privacy and the efficient functioning of medical teams whether in general practice or in hospital.

A. G. Donald

Confucianism. See *Chinese Medicine.*

Congenital Malformations. Congenital malformations are either of genetic origin, or result from maternal illness in pregnancy (e.g. rubella), or from the administration of drugs harmful to the fetus (e.g. thalidomide) or from abnormality of the uterus (e.g. oligohydramnios) or are due to other known or unknown causes, singly or in combination. Some common and gross malformations, such as anencephaly or open spina bifida, are considered by many to be due to such combination of genetic and environmental factors, though proof is lacking.

Some congenital malformations are readily recognizable at birth, such as open spina bifida, gross forms of congenital heart disease, exomphalos, tracheo-oesophageal fistula, etc., while others may not be apparent for hours, days (intestinal atresia) or even much longer, like the less obvious types of congenital heart disorders.

The incidence of congenital malformations is estimated to be about 5% of all live born babies. Many of these are trivial (accessory ear lobes or fingers, etc.), others are readily treatable and recovery is complete (pyloric stenosis, patent ductus arteriosis) and therefore ethical problems do not arise.

Major ethical problems arise when the malformation is severe (the worst cases of spina bifida) or if there is severe mental handicap (Down's syndrome) so that the quality of life of the individual and consequently of the family suffers. (See *Mongolism; Spina Bifida.*)

The ethical problems arise either at the preventive or therapeutic level.

True prevention of major malformations can only be achieved by avoidance of conception, but this is seldom practicable. However, it is possible to advise couples to avoid pregnancy if one or both partners are known to be carriers of disorders such as Duchenne's muscular dystrophy, haemophilia, cystic fibrosis or sickle cell disease.

Much more commonly and on an increasing scale prevention means termination of pregnancy, if the results of antenatal tests indicate that the fetus is affected by a serious disorder. The number of conditions which can now be readily and safely detected by antenatal tests is considerable and is rapidly increasing, though the number of individuals who can be saved from suffering are few. The ethical problem is that preventive abortion inevitably means the killing of the fetus. This is unacceptable to some individuals, or is forbidden by their religion and is illegal in several countries. However, in countries where termination is legal, the vast majority of parents consider that it is ethical and is in the interest of the fetus as well as the rest of the family. Couples at high risk and in whose country abortion is illegal often go abroad to obtain abortion, but only a few can afford to do this.

The ethical problems are of two different types. In one set of conditions of which mongolism (or Down's syndrome) is the commonest example, the affected child would be severely retarded, but, except for those with additional features, may lead a life without pain or discomfort and without being aware that he is even handicapped. In such cases it is the family and the community who suffer more than the individual. Nevertheless, most parents faced with such a risk prefer termination, if the diagnosis of the anomaly can be made with certainty, as is the case with chromosome disorders.

The second ethical problem is the termination of pregnancy when the fetus is known to be or could be severely handicapped. When the fetus is known to be severely affected, for example, with myelomeningocele, the overwhelming majority of parents, doctors and the community are in favour of termination, and this policy is generally applied in Britain. There are, nevertheless, a very few who consider that even in such circumstances termination is ethically unjustified, because it involves killing a human being.

More difficult is the decision when the fetus may be affected, either by a sex-linked genetically determined condition, such as Duchenne's muscular dystrophy or haemophilia or by other less common conditions. Only males will be affected, and only half of these. It is easy to diagnose the sex of the fetus. If it is male there is a 50% chance that he will be normal and cannot even be a carrier. In such a situation it is essential to discuss the issues fully with the parents and their views must be the final determinant regarding termination. Most will choose termination if the disorder is very severe (muscular dystrophy) but not necessarily if it is less severe, and especially if there is reasonable hope of effective treatment for the handicapped individual, either because it is already available, or may become available as a result of medical advances, as in the case of haemophilia.

Maternal rubella is another difficult example, because not all fetuses will be affected and not all will be affected to the same degree. If the mother gets rubella early in pregnancy the chances of severe malformations are much higher than if she contracts it in the second trimester. In the latter case the infant may be deaf but have no other handicap, or it may have no handicap at all. The dilemma is obvious. However, it is essential to remember that the risk of rubella will not recur and if a pregnancy is terminated, the couple can safely look forward to normal children in future pregnancies.

There are two other considerations to therapeutic abortion. One is the right of the unborn infant to live, or the alleged right to be spared a life of continued suffering because of failure to take appropriate action if he was known to be at high risk of being severely handicapped. Doctors may face legal action for having failed to terminate a pregnancy in such instances, but such action has been rejected in the USA and would be unlikely to succeed in England (see *Unborn Child, Rights of*).

The other and vital consideration is that even in 'high risk' cases of congenital disorders the large majority of fetuses will be normal and very few pregnancies will be terminated after the completion of antenatal tests. This means that many more couples will willingly take the risk of a pregnancy, knowing that abnormal fetuses will be aborted, and at the cost of the termination of a few abnormal pregnancies, a much larger number of normal infants will be conceived.

Congenital Malformations

TO TREAT OR NOT TO TREAT? The large majority of malformations are the first cases in a family, hence were unexpected and were not preventable. As a result of spectacular advances in medicine and surgery, many such infants can now be made to survive, even those with very gross handicaps. There is no ethical problem in offering, and indeed there is an obligation to provide, comprehensive treatment to handicapped infants and children, who, without treatment, would still live and whose lives can be made better by skilled treatment.

It is a different matter whether all the modern advances should be used for the treatment of such infants who are born with very severe handicaps or children who develop gross physical or mental defects later, for example, as a result of very severe head injury. Experience in the last 20 years has shown that all our efforts to preserve the life of babies severely affected by congenital malformations, and probably more specifically by spina bifida, causes immense suffering to the affected individuals and their families, quite apart from the huge cost to the community.

It is in these fields that most consider it ethically wrong to prolong life by a continuous succession of operations and drug therapy, when the quality of such life is below an acceptable standard. Suitable criteria for selective treatment are available and generally accepted for babies born with spina bifida[1] and these are fully supported by the parents of newborn babies. In other, less common conditions, it is not so clear where to draw the line, but there is an obligation, particularly on paediatric surgeons, to define clearly the division between what is technically possible and what is humanely desirable.

These are major emotional, intellectual and ethical difficulties in deciding whether to treat or not. Opinion is divided whether to treat an intestinal obstruction, such as duodenal atresia in a mongol baby. Without an urgent operation death is certain. With operation, survival is the rule. Is duodenal atresia an opportunity for a mongol child to die young or is it merely a surgical emergency which should be dealt with like any other surgical problem? Whatever is the decision, it should be made by the parents, with the full knowledge of all the facts. Their hands should not be forced by doctors getting a court order to override the parents' wishes, if the child is bound to remain severely handicapped in spite of successful medical or surgical intervention. Similar principles may be applied in the management of life-threatening 'medical' illnesses of severely handicapped children, such as the treatment of meningitis, or the use of haemodialysis in renal failure or the unduly prolonged use of the technique of intensive care, such as respirators, in extremely handicapped individuals.

Other ethical problems arise in patients who are not offered specific treatment for their main conditions. One is that no other 'half-treatment' should be offered so that they have a greater chance of survival, but with even more severe handicap. Another is that all 'untreated' infants and children should be given full supportive therapy against pain, discomfort or convulsions. Thirdly, that investigations are proper to enable the medical professions to come to the right conclusion whether to treat or not, but it is unethical to carry out unnecessary or painful investigations after a decision has been reached not to treat.

The ethical problems related to major congenital malformations will not be solved to anybody's full satisfaction, either by termination of pregnancy, whether the offspring is known or likely to be defective, or by the selective non-treatment of severely affected individuals, although this appears a necessity at present. There are, however, indications that true prevention of congenital malformations, that is, prior to conception, may become possible in the not too distant future. This way, ethical problems would greatly diminish to everybody's satisfaction. In this context it may be of considerable interest that preliminary results suggest that neural tube defects may be preventable by giving women, who hope to become pregnant, additional doses of Vitamin B complex with folic acid at least one month prior to conception and during the first few months of pregnancy.[2]

1. Lorber J. Ethical problems in the management of myelomeningocele and hydrocephalus. *J R Coll Physicians Lond* 1975; 10:41.
2. Smithells RW, Sheppard S, Schorah J *et al.* Possible prevention of neural tube defects by periconceptual vitamin supplementation. *Lancet* 1980; 1: 339–40.

Seller MJ. Congenital abnormalities and selective abortion. *J Med Ethics* 1976, 2:138–41.

Swinyard CA, ed. *Decision making and the defective newborn.* Springfield: C. Thomas, 1978:59–67.

John Lorber

Consent. The Oxford English Dictionary defines 'Consent' as 'Voluntary agreement to, or acquiescence in, what another proposes or desires; compliance, concurrence, permission.'

In medical and surgical practice this means that consent to examination or treatment must always be obtained, even if the fact that the patient has sought advice implies consent to what is to be done. In the case of children under 16 years of age the written consent of one of the parents must be obtained. In the case of the patient who is unconscious or of unsound mind the consent of a near relative should be obtained. When such consent cannot be obtained treatment should be confined to the minimum necessary to deal with the emergency. In the case of children it is essential that the parents should understand the reason for and the nature of the examination and treatment.

The terms 'true consent' and 'informed consent' are both used. 'Informed consent' implies that the patient has received all the information necessary to enable him to give consent. However, it may be impossible or inadvisable always to give full information, so that the term 'informed consent' is a relative one.

The medical profession has a responsibility, not only for the cure of the sick and prevention of disease, but also for the advancement of knowledge on which both the first two aspects of their work depend. This responsibility for the acquisition of new knowledge can be met only by clinical investigation and experiment on human beings (see *Clinical Trials; Human Experiment*).

Other human beings are the only mammals for which a licence to experiment is not required in this country, but on the other hand the use of one's fellow beings raises all kinds of legal, ethical and moral issues which have never been properly faced or examined. Anything which is done to a patient which is not directly to the therapeutic benefit of that patient, or which does not contribute to the diagnosis of the disease is an experiment. Thus, the random use of treatment or withholding treatment is an experiment and although the results of such random trials may ultimately produce important biological information and confer benefit on patients who are subsequently treated, they are not to the manifest benefit of the individual patient who is involved. No experiment should ever be carried out in which the investigator knows that he may not always retain complete control of the situation. The more elaborate and the more prolonged any experiment or investigation is, the more it is necessary to explain to the patient what is involved, and in particular the nature of the risks. The existence of statutory research ethical committees (q.v.) in NHS hospitals is an important safeguard but the personal attitude of the responsible doctor is even more so.

In the Memorandum on Clinical Investigations, issued by the Medical Research Council in 1953[1] and again in 1963[2] guidance is given to all those responsible for clinical research. The responsibility for determining what investigations are or are not undertaken on a particular patient rests 'with the doctor concerned, and nearly all his judgements will be accepted by the patient. Judgements are particularly difficult in relation to novel procedures and those whose value to patients are highly problematical. In very specialized situations few people may be capable of giving informed opinions about what is justifiable. Under these circumstances the Council felt that medical scientific societies and editors of journals should accept responsibility for what was acceptable and what they were prepared to publish'. In the report of 1963 the Medical Research Council[2] states that in regard to procedures contributing to the benefit of the individual, where such procedures are novel the doctor must exercise special care and that it is within the competence of the parent or guardian of a child to give permission for procedures intended to benefit that child when he is not old enough or intelligent enough to be able himself to give a valid consent. In regard to control subjects in investigations of treatment it is justifiable to give to a proportion of the patients a novel procedure on the understanding that the remainder receive the procedure previously accepted as the best. When effective treatment has not previously been devised then the situation should be fully explained to the participants and their true consent obtained. In controlled trials the patients participating in them, or their parents, should be told frankly that two different procedures are being assessed and their co-operation invited, but occasionally to do this is contra-indicated; for example, in patients with a possibly fatal illness, or when a placebo or inert substance has to be introduced into part of the trial to determine whether a particular treatment has had any effect apart from suggestion. To overcome these difficulties the Council recommend that controlled clinical trials should always be planned and supervised by a group of investigators and never by an individual alone. Any doctor taking part in such a collaborative controlled trial is under an obligation to withdraw patients from the trial and to institute any treatment he considers necessary should this, in his personal opinion, be in the better interest of his patient (see *Clinical Trials*).

When an investigation is not of direct benefit or is of doubtful benefit to the particular individual he must explicitly consent to submit to it as a volunteer in the full sense of the word; in such circumstances parents cannot give a valid consent for such a procedure to be inflicted on their child. The possibility or probability that the results of the investigation may be of benefit to humanity or to posterity offers no defence in the event of legal proceedings. The rights of the individual are protected by law and nobody may infringe them for the public good. True consent means consent freely given with proper understanding of the nature and consequences of what is proposed. Consent is valueless if it is assumed or obtained by undue influence, and particular care is necessary when the volunteer stands in special relationship with the investigator, for example, a patient and his doctor or a student and his teacher. Consent may be implied in relation to diagnostic or therapeutic procedures, but if these are complex or unusual there should be formal evidence of consent. The investigator should obtain consent himself in the presence of another person, in writing, and accompanied by other evidence that a proper explanation has been given, understood and accepted.

In the UK by virtue of Section 8 of the Family Reform Act 1969 a minor between his 16th and 18th birthdays may consent to 'any surgical medical or dental treatment' without the necessity for the parents to give consent as well. Under the age of 16 years the consent of the parents should be obtained before any operation is done, but in emergency a doctor who treats a child aged less than 16 years, especially at the request of or with the permission of the child, is unlikely to be charged with unlawful assault (see *Confidentiality*). There should, however, be evidence that the person concerned fully understood the implication to himself of the procedures to which it was given. In the case of those who are mentally subnormal ordered the reality of the consent given will be judged by similar ria to those which apply to the making of a will, contracting a riage, or otherwise taking decisions which have legal force as well as moral and social implications. When true consent in this sense cannot be obtained procedures which are of no direct benefit and which might carry a risk of harm to the subject should not be undertaken. It is the opinion of the Medical Research Council that the head of the department where investigations on human subjects take place has an inescapable responsibility for ensuring that the practice of those under his or her direction is irreproachable. (See also *Declaration of Helsinki; Nuremberg Code*).

There may occasionally be reasons for not disclosing all the possible risks or complications to a patient or to the parents of a patient in ordinary medical practice, on the grounds that this would cause worry and anxiety to the individual (see *Truth*). When, however, research is being carried out there is no justification for such concealment. All the possibilities must be disclosed to the individual or parents before consent to the procedure is sought.

It is remarkable that there has been no legal action in Great Britain by anyone who thought that research had been done on him without consent, and this may be a tribute to the high ethical standards which have been maintained in the country.

In May 1969 the United States Public Health Service issued Guidelines which stated that parents were specifically excluded from being able to consent to research on their children unless the procedure was for their benefit.

Up to the age of 16 years parents in the UK are responsible for the well-being of their child (q.v.). If anything is done to the child without the freely given consent of the parents that action constitutes an assault on the child. The parents may give or withhold their consent to anything which it is proposed to do to their child but they may not consent to anything which involves risk to the well-being of the child. On the other hand in spite of parental consent a child may refuse to submit to treatment which is frightening or which the child knows will be painful. In the conduct of clinical trials in minors each substance must be considered on its merits and properties. If there is any possible danger in its use or if its effects on a child are unknown no-one may authorize its use in a child. If the substance has not been used in a child before but it is known that in adults it produces the desired effects to a degree at least as effective as other substances which have been used for the same purpose in children, the parents may alone give permission for the trial use of the substance. If, however, the effects of the substance are unknown, after proper explanation, then it must be tried in a consenting adult before it may be used in a child. In an ill child, permission for treatment, the effects of which are known, is not required if the intention is to save life in an emergency. In common law parents have no power of disposition over their children's bodies and therefore any clinical research which is not of therapeutic value to the patient is impossible in minors because no-one can give permission for it. Consent for research on minors can be given by parents or guardians only if this can be shown to be specifically for the benefit of the individual child.

In the case of a pregnant woman, treatment which is necessary should be given and there is no reason why the mother should not consent to such treatment because she is pregnant and her consent applies to the fetus as well as to herself.

1. Medical Research Council Report 1953. London: HMSO, No. 349.
2. Medical Research Council Report 1962–63. London: HMSO, Cmnd 2382.

A. W. Wilkinson

Contraception. The attempt to prevent conception by periodic continence, or by mechanical, chemical or physiological means, is basically viewed as a postponement of conception. Abortion (q.v.) and the permanent blocking of conception by sterilization (q.v.) are dealt with under these headings.

1. CLINICAL ASPECTS. Methods of contraception include the rhythm method, *coitus interruptus* and *reservatus*, spermicides, mechanical barriers, intra-uterine devices and hormonal preparations. Only the last three require medical consultation and the majority of couples practising contraception seek no medical advice.

In some countries services are provided by para-medical personnel, but where a doctor is responsible it is his duty to give advice on a well informed basis. There is a danger that personal convictions may unduly influence the advice he gives and those who have moral objections to contraception should advise the patient to seek help elsewhere.

In the UK, persons aged 16 years and over can give consent (q.v.) to medical treatment on their own behalf and therefore have the right to professional secrecy and confidentiality in matters of contraception. It is now increasingly common for girls under the age of 16 to request advice and help with contraception and the dilemma here is twofold: whether to accede to the request and whether to inform the parents (see *Child; Confidentiality*). Some assert that this is a natural result of the lower age at which sexual maturity occurs, and would challenge the retention of 16 years as the age of consent, holding that each individual has the right to regulate her own behaviour, and that it is in the interest of society that unwanted pregnancy should be prevented and the resultant social problems avoided. Apart from the moral issues involved, they fear that by making contraceptives available to the very young the risk of promiscuity would be increased and adverse effects on the development of the child both physically and psychologically result. They stress in particular the attendant risks of acquiring sexually transmitted disease and possibly some forms of genital cancer.

There is general agreement that in such instances it is prudent to try to obtain the consent of the girl to tell her parents, especially in the case of the very young girl where the need for contraception may be only one manifestation of a larger problem. If consent is withheld, the doctor must decide what course to adopt in the light of the circumstances, the needs of the individual and of his own professional views. It remains to be established whether, in supplying contraceptives to a girl under 16 years of age, he could be held to be breaking the law by aiding and abetting unlawful intercourse.

A doctor providing contraceptive services should not seek to attract patients to himself from his colleagues by means other than the normal establishment of a good professional reputation, and when giving advice to the patient of another doctor he should refrain from saying or doing anything which might disturb her confidence in her personal physician. With the patient's permission he should notify her doctor of any relevant clinical findings detected on examination and should tell him the method of contraception advised. He should not refer the patient for opinion or treatment unless authorized to do so.

A couple's choice of contraceptive method may raise problems of an emotional and ethical nature which the doctor needs to consider sympathetically. The following methods are in use.

Abstinence from intercourse is infallible.

Natural Family Planning involves abstinence on the days when the ovum is likely to be available for fertilization. Ovulation usually occurs about 14 days before the next menstrual period but the time of ovulation may be identified more precisely by recognizing the changes which occur in the cervical mucus and in the body temperature at that time. Natural Family Planning is one of the methods acceptable to the Roman Catholic Church. It is unreliable for women who have irregular menstrual cycles, after recent childbirth or miscarriage, during lactation and at the time of the menopause.

Coitus Interruptus, withdrawal of the penis from the vagina before ejaculation, is unreliable and has a high failure rate. It depends on the self-control of the man and is therefore especially unsuitable for use by young people. Frustration in the woman and tensions and anxiety in the man are attributed to its use.

Coitus Reservatus, intercourse without ejaculation, demands a degree of self-control beyond the ability of most men. It has the same disadvantages as coitus interruptus.

Spermicides are chemical substances which destroy sperms and are usually employed as a pessary, cream, jelly, aerosol preparation or plastic film inserted into the vagina before intercourse. The failure rate is relatively high, but their simplicity and general acceptability make them a method of choice in some countries.

The Condom (sheath, protective, etc) is a sheath of latex rubber or animal tissue worn over the penis during intercourse. Some couples find that its use dulls sexual pleasure and that it disrupts spontaneity, but properly used it provides effective contraception and also gives some degree of protection against sexually transmitted diseases.

The Occlusive Pessary (diaphragm, cap) is a soft rubber or plastic barrier which covers the cervix, thus preventing the passage of sperm into the uterus. Some women find it distasteful to insert the device themselves. It has a failure rate of 2–3 per H.W.Y.*

The Intra-Uterine Device (I.U.D., coil, spiral, loop) is a small plastic or metal shape inserted into the uterus and is effective in preventing conception. The failure rate is 1–5 per H.W.Y. Its mode of action is incompletely understood but it may have a spermicidal effect. The possibility that it may prevent implantation of the fertilized ovum causes some to look on it as an abortifacient and therefore open to objection. Insertion is simple, and quick. Once inserted it requires no further action and is therefore suitable for those who find regular resort to contraceptives unacceptable or difficult. I.U.Ds may be expelled spontaneously and if this is undetected unwanted conception could ensue. They sometimes produce prolonged menstrual bleeding or intermittent spotting, which may be unacceptable particularly to those religious groups for whom menstruation is a time of uncleanness.

Synthetic Hormones are used by women in the form of the contraceptive pill, as injections, in vaginal rings, or as implants. So far no male contraceptive is in clinical use. Oral contraceptives may consist of a progestogen alone or a combination of oestrogen and progestogen. Post-coital administration of hormones may also be employed. When taken regularly, the combined pill is virtually 100% effective. The use of the contraceptive pill is associated with an increased incidence of thrombo-embolic disorders particularly among heavy smokers and older women and fatalities have been reported. However, the risk is very small, and if women recognized to be particularly susceptible are excluded it is generally regarded as acceptable. Users often derive benefit to their general health but the long-term effects of continued administration of steroid hormones are as yet unknown. (See also *Population Policy*.)

Parkes AS, Short RV, Potts M, Herbertson MA. Fertility in adolescence. *J Biosoc Sci*: Supplement No. 5.

Hawkins DF, Elder MG. *Human fertility control – theory and practice.* London: Butterworths, 1979.

Nancy B. Loudon

* Effectiveness is measured in failure rate per hundred women years (H.W.Y.) = Total accidental pregnancies × 1200/Total months of exposure.

2. RELIGIOUS AND ETHICAL CONSIDERATIONS. While the major religions, except perhaps Buddhism (q.v.), expressed in their early development a major concern for human fertility (no doubt reflecting the high incidence of infant mortality), there has also been 'since ancient times'[1] a widespread search for procedures to prevent or abort conceptions, with infanticide serving as a back-up procedure. Much of this effort expressed the special concerns of women who, despite their inferior status, were attempting to survive and to safeguard their existing children. However, it was not until the nineteenth century that contraception began to be an important social factor in Europe and America. As improved medical care allowed large numbers of children to survive the first years of life, the increase in family size became a major problem for both father and mother. Contraception became a matter of urgent concern, sometimes expressed in terms of a right or seen, especially by the mother, as part of a wider dimension of human liberty.

All the major Christian churches began to re-examine their traditional teaching on the responsibilities of parents, and on marriage in general, early in this century. There has emerged a consensus that stresses the spiritual significance of marriage, giving to husband and wife both freedom and responsibility – freedom to use the gifts of science to space their progeny and an obligation to act as responsible parents.

Eastern Orthodox Christianity is tending to modify the traditional pro-fertility stance of the Orthodox hierarchy, recognizing that an official position on contraception is lacking, and that in such circumstances couples with problems should seek medical advice.

Roman Catholic Christianity remains divided. Pope Paul VI in *Humanae Vitae* (q.v.) retreated to the position of Pius XI and XII in accepting contraceptive intent and practice (in the form of periodic continence) for serious personal or social reasons, but insisting that each marital act should be otherwise open to its procreative purpose. The majority of the papal commission urged the Pope to recognize that the procreative end of marriage need not require that each marital act be oriented to that end. The various interpretations of *Humanae Vitae* by national hierarchies, and the increasing resort to contraception by Catholic couples, show the present divided state of the Roman Catholic Church.

Christian thought in this area has focused mainly on the rights of the couple, the 'two become one', to have access to the means they judge necessary for responsible parenthood, in relation to criteria regarding effectiveness, side effects, injury to sexual companionship, cost, etc. In view of the inferior status of women in most societies, more attention is now being given to the rights of individuals, including the unmarried and the child, as well as to social considerations.

The non-Christian religions have also moved markedly towards acceptance of contraception. Muslim leaders have found sufficient basis in their traditions for a positive approach. The same is true of Hindu and Buddhist scholars. Most of the Asian countries now have government-sponsored family planning programmes; several Latin American governments sponsor or accept family planning as a lesser evil than the widespread resort to abortion; and African countries are now implementing population policies on an increasing scale. In 1975, 22 Asian countries, 21 Latin American countries and 20 African countries officially supported family planning.[2] Most of the affluent societies have extensive public and/or private programmes, but even these fail to provide adequate services in areas of poverty where the need is greatest. In fact, the main weakness of such activities in all parts of the world is that they are seldom linked to measures of social reform and the relief of poverty, without which there is unlikely to be acceptance of a small family pattern or a motive for responsible parenthood. (See also *Vegliare con Sollecitudine*.)

1. Himes NE. *Medical history of contraception*. New York: Gamut Press, 1963.
2. Norman D. *Population and family planning programs: A factbook*. New York: Population Council, 1975.
Berelson B, ed. *Family planning and population programs*. University of Chicago Press, 1966.
Fagley RM. *The population explosion and Christian responsibility*. Oxford: University Press, 1960.
Noonan JT, Jr. *Contraception*. Cambridge, Mass: Belknap Press, 1965.
Roberts TD *et al*. *Contraception and holiness*. New York: Herder & Herder, 1964.
Symonds R, Carder M. *The United Nations and the population question*. New York, McGraw-Hill, 1973.

R. M. Fagley

Controlled Trials. See *Clinical Trials*.

Cornea, Transplanting of. See *Tissue Transplant*.

Coroners. See *Death, Certification of*.

Cosmetic Surgery. Whereas the word cosmetic describes the 'art of adorning or beautifying the body', cosmetic surgery more precisely improves appearances. The improvements may range from correcting a fault such as over-prominent ears or a crooked nose, making the face look younger, reducing the width of an ugly scar, increasing or decreasing the size of the breasts, to alterations of normal ethnic features by removing the epicanthal folds of Japanese or building a nasal bridgeline and narrowing the nostrils in Africans (to make them more Western looking). There are six aspects to discuss.

(1) When people have more money to spend, some will prefer to use it on improving their looks because an affluent society usually becomes more conscious of personal appearance. However, a certain stigma is attached to both the recipient (who does not want others to know that anything has been done) and the donor (who takes money for his surgical art), and there is often public disapproval that nature is being tampered with. (2) A distinction is made between children and adults. For instance, if a child has an ugly mole on his cheek its removal is approved, but the same condition in an adult is called cosmetic surgery and receives no priority even though the mental suffering of the latter may be great. Children with overprominent ears, who may be teased at school because of their appearance, can have their ears set back without stigma; the adult who may suffer similarly is expected to seek treatment privately.

(3) Attitudes also differ according to the abnormality. For instance, the reduction to 'normal' of the overlarge female breast is accepted as a fair demand on the hospital service whereas to augment the flat-chested to 'normal' is not. The person whose nose is ugly because of injury may have a nasal reduction as of right, whereas the owner of an ugly, large, family nose obtains no sympathy. The depressed nasal bridgeline left after removal of the nasal septum can be built up by inserting a bone graft; the racial depressed nose of the African can be improved by the same procedure but that is called cosmetic surgery.

(4) In most countries cosmetic surgery is carried out mainly by those trained in plastic surgery who take account of the cosmetic result of every operation they perform, whether this be removal of excess abdominal skin or excision and reconstruction of a cancer of the face. The distinction is therefore unreal between cosmetic surgery undertaken to excise and improve a broad ugly scar made by a general surgeon and the same operation undertaken *de novo* by an expert plastic surgeon. The result will be a fine narrow scar in both cases and both are 'cosmetic surgery'.

(5) Cosmetic surgery treats disease as does any other surgery; the difficulty is to understand the disease. People who look markedly different from others are ill at ease, unhappy and hence not in good health and will demand treatment. If a skilled surgeon will not treat them, they will seek a back street practitioner. In most patients treated in plastic surgery units in hospital the results are good and everyone is satisfied. The numbers treated elsewhere are unknown as are the results (a comparison could here be made with abortion), but undoubtedly the demand is increasing.

(6) With the State and other bodies such as insurance companies now so involved in medicine, it is more than ever necessary to review the ethics of cosmetic surgery. Should all patients at least be referred to psychiatrists before treatment at public expense? This might make

the demand seem more respectable but there is a wider issue. Restoration of health should perhaps take care of those with disfigurements, deformities and disabilities which do not occur in the international index of disease. The grateful patients are commonly happier and more productive members of the community. (See *Mutilation; Resources*).

Edgerton M. The role of surgery in academic medicine. *Pla Reconstr Surg* 1974; 54:523–30.
Editorial. Cosmetic breast surgery. *JAMA* 1974; 1972; 222:1101–2.

James Calnan

Counselling. In certain medical and socio-medical fields, advice given to patients, or parents, is referred to as counselling. Genetic counselling describes the discussions held between doctors, social workers and parents where there are risks to children yet unborn because of hereditary disease in a family (see *Amniocentesis; Chromosome Disorders; Congenital Malformations; Eugenics; Genetic Conditions*). Marital counselling (see *Marital Pathology and Counselling*) is the handling of problems arising between spouses. Counselling is also given to women seeking abortion (q.v.) for whatever reason, and to both men and women where sterilization (q.v.) is proposed.

Cremation. See *Death, Certification of.*

D

Death, Attitudes to. The positive approach to death of some cultures and civilizations often proves to be healthier for the survivors than the frightened, denying and negative attitude customary in Western civilization for the last three generations. The death of the body with the apparent disintegration of the personality can be looked upon either as an act of total annihilation or as the end of one state of existence and the beginning of another. A belief in some form of existence after a man's body has ceased to function may enable him and his family to face his death as something less than the final catastrophe. Some die seeing their lives continuing in that of their children and tribe. But a total denial of a future life, or attempts to conceal the inevitable death of every man, will produce at best resignation or courageous despair, and at worst unresolvable bereavement (q.v.).

Depending on his beliefs and culture, a man's attitude to his impending death may reflect hope or despair, sadness or joy. His ability to face the end of his life on this earth may spring from the manner in which that life has been led. Faith or courage to love do not often make their first appearance at the death bed. However, if such virtues have at least been recognized during a man's lifetime it is often at the time of his dying that their reality and strength are revealed. All our lives we are preparing for death.

Although the moment of death itself may seem to be the first totally solitary experience a human being is called upon to endure, the process of dying can be greatly influenced by the attitudes of those who often feel that they are merely onlookers. Love strong enough to overcome man's natural fear of death and to keep the family by the bedside for as long as necessary is often an unused potential. The revelation of such strength, often in apparently feeble individuals, is itself one of the best reasons for seeing death as a positive event. The patient and his family, although paying a high price, are given in return a unique experience in communication and sharing.

One of the saddest results of the medical advances of the last generation is the separation of the science and art of healing from the need to comfort and succour. The separation between a dying man and his family, and between a man and the truth about his own condition, is too often initiated and perpetuated by medical and nursing personnel and their subservience to modern technology. It is never right for a member of the profession to tell a patient a deliberate lie but that is not to say that the full truth (q.v.) has always to be stated at any given moment. All hope must never be taken away and a patient should be given real opportunities for discussing his diagnosis and prognosis with his medical adviser. Often it is the patient who tells the doctor the truth. Often the truth when presented appropriately both in manner and time proves to be a powerful weapon for the patient and physician in their battle against uncertainty and the unknown. Medical teaching is orientated towards achieving a clinical cure, and the fact that death should sometimes be allowed to occur is forgotten in the effort to preserve life at all costs. The profession will change its attitude only when it re-discovers the enormous potential in the patient himself, and in his family, for accepting situations once they have been adequately explained.

With the use of modern medicine to alleviate suffering, a re-direction of old established skills and a realistic attitude to mortality, the doctor, patient and family can bring to death all that they have learnt of life, against a background of physical, mental and spiritual comfort. (See also *Declarations (Sydney)*; *Euthanasia; Hospices; Terminal Care*).

Choron J. *Death and western thought*. New York: Macmillan, 1963.
Feifel H. *The meaning of death*. New York: McGraw-Hill, 1959.
Fulton R. *Death and identity*. New York: Wiley, 1965.
Gorer G. *Death, grief and mourning*. London: Cresset Press, 1965.
Hinton J. *Dying*. Harmondsworth: Penguin Books, 1967.

Thomas S. West

Death, Certification of. Medical certification of the cause of death is the first step in the legal disposal of the dead.

A doctor who has been in regular medical attendance on the deceased during his or her last illness is bound to provide, without delay, a certificate as to the cause of death if he feels able to do so; no fee is payable for this service. The certificate of the cause of death must be written on the prescribed form, the precise wording of which differs as between Scotland and England and Wales. The correct procedure in England and Wales is for the doctor to forward the certificate to the Registrar and to hand to the informant a notice that he has done so; in practice, it is more convenient and quite competent to entrust the certificate to the informant. The Scottish certificate embodies no notice to the informant and must be passed on to him or to the Registrar within seven days of death; again, the former process is generally adopted. Although the format for describing the cause of death is international, the certificates of individual countries may contain information or affirmations by the practitioner additional to those described for Britain. The ethical principles, however, remain the same.

The English doctor certifies that he was in medical attendance during the deceased's last illness. No other practitioner can sign on his behalf and the fact that there was no regular medical attendant or, if there was, that he was not available at the time of the death contribute two of the commonest reasons for referral of cases to the Coroner. The English certificate also requires the doctor to state when he last saw the patient alive. The Registrar must inform the Coroner if this indicates an interval of more than fourteen days and if, in addition, the practitioner has not seen the body after death. Other reasons for involvement of the Coroner include indications that the death was unnatural, was associated with employment or with detention, might have been related to medical treatment or was, in general, sudden and unexpected or of uncertain cause in the opinion of the practitioner; all cases of poisoning, whether natural or unnatural, are reportable and these include deaths related in any way to alcohol.

The procedure for reporting deaths to the Coroner illustrates a conflict between legal dogmatism and practical expedience.[1] Strictly speaking, the deceased's doctor is bound to issue a certificate if he is able to state the cause of death – but, except in Ireland, there is no specific obligation on him to make such a report; statutory responsibility rests with the Registrar. If there is an element of doubt, the English Coroner almost invariably requires a post-mortem dissection and, in the event that this shows death to have been due to natural causes, he then certifies the cause of death on his own Form B. The original death certificate has, therefore, been the product of wasted effort and it has long been standard practice for the doctor to inform the Coroner of an appropriate case and to take no further action; nevertheless, it is incorrect and will remain so until the protests of the medical profession are heeded.

The propriety of direct reporting to the Scottish Fiscal is, by now, fully accepted. The procedure which has evolved is for the doctor with a concerning case to inform the Fiscal who will then either authorize the doctor to certify or will seek the assistance of his own medical adviser; the latter will then certify the cause of death either with or without recourse to post-mortem dissection. This practice is possible because there is no declaration in Scotland to the effect that the certifier was in medical attendance on the deceased during life – a certificate of cause of death may be signed by *any* medical practitioner who is able to do so; it follows that there is no '14 day rule' in Scotland.

There is no obligation on the doctor to use the International Classification of Diseases, Injuries or Causes of Death in the certificate which should reflect the considered opinion of the certifying practitioner. Pleas are made for the avoidance of indefinite terms; further enquiries will certainly be made if there is an obvious opportunity for clarification. The doctor may, however, find himself in difficulties if he tries to couch his certificate in terms which will avoid distress to the next of kin. In particular, there can be no attempt to bypass the Coroner or Procurator Fiscal; to do so by deliberately excluding a relevant antecedent cause – say, a drunken fall – would be to court criminal proceedings. There is, however, no need to include *irrelevant* conditions in Part II of the certificate which refers only to other significant conditions *contributing to the death* and it is inadmissible in Scotland to include the word 'suicide' in a certificate. It is clearly professional misconduct to sign a death certificate in anticipation of a death; a doctor in England might be requested to do so were it known that he was about to leave on holiday.

Nowhere in the United Kingdom is it obligatory for the certifying doctor to view the body after death but it is bad practice not to do so without good reason and many embarrassing results of such failure have been recorded. It is mandatory to examine the body when signing a cremation certificate and this applies to the deceased's medical attendant and to the practitioner supplying the confirmatory certificate. A false declaration by the latter would be particularly serious in view of the extra status granted to practitioners of more than five years standing. It is to be noted that completion of the cremation form is independent of death certification which must be followed in the normal way irrespective of whether the deceased is to be buried or cremated.

Some confusion has recently been introduced into death certification by the frequent use of life-supporting ventilation and by the consequent acceptance of the concept of brain stem death.[2] Although there is no law on the point, the fact of death in such circumstances should always be verified by two practitioners though the death certificate, if provided, still requires only one signature. A further complication is introduced by the increasing use of 'beating heart donors' for transplantation purposes. Many such cases will arise from natural death but others will already have been intimated to the Coroner or Procurator Fiscal who will dictate their management. It is the writer's opinion that much subsequent difficulty could be avoided in the latter circumstance if death were certified on the appropriate form before organs were removed and ventilation finally discontinued – the normal procedure by which the medicolegal authority can reject a certificate would then apply. There is, however, as yet no agreed policy on the subject. (See also: *Death, Determination of; Tissue Transplant.*)

1. Editorial. Confusion over Death Certification. *Br Med J* 1979; 1: 1662.
2. Conference of Medical Royal Colleges and their Faculties in the United Kingdom. Diagnosis of death. *Br Med J* 1979; 1:332.

J. K. Mason

Death, Determination of. The cessation of respiration, and the stoppage of the heart beat which invariably follows within a few minutes, have traditionally been accepted as criteria for the determination of death, and in the majority of cases these factors still apply. If the heart stops first, the brain rapidly becomes functionless owing to lack of oxygen, and breathing then stops also – because it depends on brain stem control. If the primary event is respiratory arrest, as usually happens with overwhelming brain damage, the heart normally stops beating within a few minutes of cessation of breathing. However, the availability of the ventilator to take over respiration has created a new possibility, in that heart action may now continue long after natural 'breathing' has stopped. If fluid intake is adequate and blood pressure maintained the heart will continue to beat, and to maintain the viability of certain organs, for only a few days at most – commonly for only 48 to 72 hours. It is in these circumstances of irrecoverable brain damage, causing irreversible cessation of respiration but with the heart still beating, that a patient is said to be 'brain dead'.

Once this state has been established by agreed criteria (see below), the patient can be regarded as truly dead, even though the function of some organs is maintained by artificial means. This was the conclusion of the Conference of the Medical Royal Colleges of the UK in 1979;[1] this is also embodied in legal statutes of several states in North America. Other states and many other countries do not consider that legislation needs to be altered to accommodate this new circumstance – a patient is dead when a doctor says so, and brain death is no more than one among several circumstances that would lead a doctor to declare that death has occurred.

Criteria for the establishment of brain death have evolved gradually over the 20 years since the phenomenon was first recognized. There are differences in detail between the criteria used in different countries and institutions; in Britain these have been published by the Royal Colleges[2], and recommended by the Department of Health. Before applying these tests it is essential to establish that the patient's state is due to irremediable structural brain damage – which is usually the result of head injury or intracranial haemorrhage. It is important also to exclude depressant or muscle relaxant drugs, metabolic disturbances and hypothermia, as possible explanations for the absence of respiration and of brain stem reflexes. Both the diagnosis of structural brain damage and the exclusion of functional (reversible) causes of cerebral depression usually depend on knowledge of the circumstances which led to the patient's present state, rather than on laboratory investigation – although this may sometimes be necessary.

Diagnosis of brain death depends on demonstrating that all brain stem reflexes are absent, and on confirming that the patient is still apnoeic (has no spontaneous respiration). Reflexes tested are the corneal (blink in response to touch); pupillary contraction in response to bright light; and oculo-vestibular. The last depends on the slow injection of 20 ml of ice water into each external auditory meatus; if the brain stem is functional, there will be movement of one or both eyes – absence of any movement, following stimulation of each side in turn, indicates that the brain stem at this level is out of action. To test for respiration, the chest is observed while the patient is off the ventilator for five minutes, during which the arterial concentration of carbon dioxide (pCO_2) will rise well above the threshold at which the respiratory centre would be stimulated if the brain were 'alive', provided that the pCO_2 was normal to begin with. If the pCO_2 is abnormally low, it must be artificially raised before disconnection. Oxygenation is maintained during this period by oxygen enrichment of the inspired gases prior to disconnection, and by administering 6L/min of oxygen through a tracheal catheter whilst the patient is not being ventilated.

In some countries clinicians seek to confirm death by a variety of laboratory tests – most of them elaborate and few of them widely available. That most commonly used is EEG (electroencephalography), the technique of recording the electrical activity of the brain. The currents generated are much smaller than those from the heart, so that interference and artefacts are commonly picked up by the sensitive equipment needed to record them. Absence of electrical activity was at one time regarded as essential for the diagnosis of brain death – but it can occur with recoverable lesions, whilst extraneous currents may be recorded in brain dead patients. These considerations, and the relative scarcity of the expensive recording machines, have led many authorities to emphasize that EEG is not necessary for the diagnosis of brain death, and this is the case in Britain (see *Declaration of Sydney*).

It is sometimes alleged that brain death has been mistakenly diagnosed[345]. Close enquiry usually reveals that the criteria have not been rigidly applied – in particular the exclusion of drugs or other causes of functional depression of brain stem function. Sometimes there has been failure to distinguish between brain death and other unresponsive states (e.g. vegetative state). That a patient who was 'given up for dead' sometimes recovers is not evidence that recovery from brain death is possible, nor that the diagnosis cannot be definitely established. The use of a figure of speech to report a grave prognosis is quite different from the confirmation of brain death by formal criteria. The fact that spinal cord function may persist after brain death, so that reflex limb movements may occur in response to painful stimuli, is not always appreciated, and sometimes leads to reports of mistaken diagnosis. It must, however, be emphasized that not all patients with brain damage who are on ventilators have brain death, and that only a limited number of patients with extensive and irrecoverable brain damage are brain dead.

If mechanical ventilation is not discontinued soon after brain death is recognized, but is continued until heart action stops spontaneously, internal organs will begin to disintegrate; in some instances the limb extremities may even begin to decompose. To allow this to happen deprives the patient of death with dignity and needlessly prolongs the distress of the family. To continue to expend effort and skill on those who cannot benefit from them is a mistaken use of resources which are almost always restricted; if this happens often it can erode staff morale in critical care and intensive therapy units. There are therefore clear humanitarian reasons for recognizing brain death and for discontinuing artificial life support once the diagnosis is made.

That some brain dead patients may prove to be suitable organ donors is a secondary matter which should not influence the conduct of the case, except in certain details of procedure and timing. Brain death was a well-recognized phenomenon before the emergence of transplant surgery, the future development of which should not be allowed to conflict with the evolution of a rational and compassionate policy for the management of brain dead patients, in most of whom the question of organ donation does not arise.

1. Conference of Medical Royal Colleges and their Faculties in the UK. Diagnosis of death. *Lancet* 1979; 1: 261–2.
2. Conference of Medical Royal Colleges and their Faculties in the United Kingdom. Diagnosis of brain death. *Lancet* 1976; 2: 1069–70.
3. Jennett B. The donor doctor's dilemma: observations on the recognition and management of brain death. *J Med Ethics* 1976; 1: 63–6.
4. Editorial. Diagnosis of brain death. *Lancet* 1976; 2: 1064–6.
5. Jennett B. The diagnosis of brain death. *J Med Ethics* 1977; 3: 4–5.

Brian Jennett

Declarations. The Declarations of the World Medical Association – those of Geneva, Hawaii, Helsinki, Oslo, Sydney and Tokyo – and the 'Nuremberg Code' are given in full in date order. (See also *Hippocratic Oath*.)

The Nuremberg Code (1947)

On August 19, 1947, a war crimes tribunal at Nuremberg rendered judgment on 23 German defendants, mostly physicians, who were accused of crimes involving experiments on human subjects. The judgment laid down ten standards to which physicians must conform when carrying out experiments on human subjects, as follows:

PERMISSIBLE MEDICAL EXPERIMENTS. The great weight of the evidence before us to effect that certain types of medical experiments on human beings, when kept within reasonably well-defined bounds, conform to the ethics of the medical profession generally. The protagonists of the practice of human experimentation justify their views on the basis that such experiments yield results for the good of society that are unprocurable by other methods or means of study. All agree, however, that certain basic principles must be observed in order to satisfy moral, ethical and legal concepts:

1. The voluntary consent of the human subject is absolutely essential. This means that the person involved should have legal capacity to give consent; should be so situated as to be able to exercise free power of choice, without the intervention of any element of force, fraud, deceit, duress, overreaching, or other ulterior form of constraint or coercion; and should have sufficient knowledge and comprehension of the elements of the subject matter involved as to enable him to make an understanding and enlightened decision. This latter element requires that before the acceptance of an affirmative decision by the experimental subject there should be made known to him the nature, duration, and purpose of the experiment; the method and means by which it is to be conducted; all inconveniences and hazards reasonably to be expected; and the effects upon his health or person which may possibly come from his participation in the experiment.

The duty and responsibility for ascertaining the quality of the consent rests upon each individual who initiates, directs, or engages in the experiment. It is a personal duty and responsibility which may not be delegated to another with impunity.

2. The experiment should be such as to yield fruitful results for the good of society, unprocurable by other methods or means of study, and not random and unnecessary in nature.

3. The experiment should be so designed and based on the results of animal experimentation and a knowledge of the natural history of the disease or other problem under study that the anticipated results justify the performance of the experiment.

4. The experiment should be so conducted as to avoid all unnecessary physical and mental suffering and injury.

5. No experiment should be conducted where there is an *a priori* reason to believe that death or disabling injury will occur; except, perhaps, in those experiments where the experimental physicians also serve as subjects.

6. The degree of risk to be taken should never exceed that determined by the humanitarian importance of the problem to be solved by the experiment.

7. Proper preparations should be made and adequate facilities provided to protect the experimental subject against even remote possibilities of injury, disability or death.

8. The experiment should be conducted only by scientifically qualified persons. The highest degree of skill and care should be required through all stages of the experiment of those who conduct or engage in the experiment.

9. During the course of the experiment the human subject should be at liberty to bring the experiment to an end if he has reached the physical or mental state where continuation of the experiment seems to him to be impossible.

10. During the course of the experiment the scientist in charge must be prepared to terminate the experiment at any stage, if he has probable cause to believe, in the exercise of the good faith, superior skill, and careful judgment required of him, that a continuation of the experiment is likely to result in injury, disability, or death to the experimental subject.

Taken from Mitscherlich A, Mielke, F. *Doctors of infamy: the story of the Nazi medical crimes*. New York: Schuman, 1949: xxiii–xxv.

Declaration of Geneva (1948; amended 1968)

At the time of being admitted as a member of the medical profession:

I will solemnly pledge myself to consecrate my life to the service of humanity;

I will give to my teachers the respect and gratitude which is their due;

I will practise my profession with conscience and dignity;

The health of my patient will be my first consideration;

I will respect the secrets which are confided in me, even after the patient has died;

I will maintain by all the means in my power the honour and the noble traditions of the medical profession;

My colleagues will be my brothers;

I will not permit considerations of religion, nationality, race, party politics or social standing to intervene between my duty and my patient;

I will maintain the utmost respect for human life from the time of conception; even under threat, I will not use my medical knowledge contrary to the laws of humanity.

I make these promises solemnly, freely and upon my honour.

Declaration of Helsinki (1964; revised 1975)
RECOMMENDATIONS GUIDING MEDICAL DOCTORS IN BIOMEDICAL RESEARCH INVOLVING HUMAN SUBJECTS

Introduction

It is the mission of the medical doctor to safeguard the health of the people. His or her knowledge and conscience are dedicated to the fulfilment of this mission.

The Declaration of Geneva of the World Medical Association binds the doctor with the words: 'The health of my patient will be my first consideration,' and the International Code of Medical Ethics declares that, 'Any act or advice which could weaken physical or mental resistance of a human being may be used only in his interest.'

The purpose of biomedical research involving human subjects must be to improve diagnostic, therapeutic and prophylactic procedures and the understanding of the aetiology and pathogenesis of disease.

In current medical practice most diagnostic, therapeutic or prophylactic procedures involve hazards. This applies *a fortiori* to biomedical research.

Medical progress is based on research which ultimately must rest in part on experimentation involving human subjects. In the field of biomedical research a fundamental distinction must be recognized between medical research in which the aim is essentially diagnostic or therapeutic for a patient, and medical research the essential object of which is purely scientific and without direct diagnostic or therapeutic value to the person subjected to the research.

Special caution must be exercised in the conduct of research which may affect the environment, and the welfare of animals used for research must be respected.

Because it is essential that the results of laboratory experiments be applied to human beings to further scientific knowledge and to help suffering humanity, the World Medical Association has prepared the following recommendations as a guide to every doctor in biomedical research involving human subjects. They should be kept under review in the future. It must be stressed that the standards as drafted are only a guide to physicians all over the world. Doctors are not relieved from criminal, civil and ethical responsibilities under the laws of their own countries.

I. Basic Principles

1. Biomedical research involving human subjects must conform to generally accepted scientific principles and should be based on adequately performed laboratory and animal experimentation and on a thorough knowledge of the scientific tradition.

2. The design and performance of each experimental procedure involving human subjects should be clearly formulated in an experiment protocol which should be transmitted to a specially appointed independent committee for consideration, comment and guidance.

3. Biomedical research involving human subjects should be conducted only by scientifically qualified persons and under the supervision of a clinically competent medical person. The responsibility for the human subject must always rest with a medically qualified person and never rest on the subject of the research, even though the subject has given his or her consent.

4. Biomedical research involving human subjects cannot legitimate-

ly be carried out unless the importance of the objective is in proportion to the inherent risk to the subject.

5. Every biomedical research project involving human subjects should be preceded by careful assessment of predictable risks in comparison with forseeable benefits to the subject or to others. Concern for the interests of the subject must always prevail over the interest of science and society.

6. The right of the research subject to safeguard his or her integrity must always be respected. Every precaution should be taken to respect the privacy of the subject and to minimize the impact of the study on the subject's physical and mental integrity and on the personality of the subject.

7. Doctors should abstain from engaging in research projects involving human subjects unless they are satisfied that the hazards involved are believed to be predictable. Doctors should cease any investigation if the hazards are found to outweigh the potential benefits.

8. In publication of the results of his or her research, the doctor is obliged to preserve the accuracy of the results. Reports of experimentation not in accordance with the principles laid down in this Declaration should not be accepted for publication.

9. In any research on human beings, each potential subject must be adequately informed of the aims, methods, anticipated benefits and potential hazards of the study and the discomfort it may entail. He or she should be informed that he or she is at liberty to abstain from participation in the study and that he or she is free to withdraw his or her consent to participation at any time. The doctor should then obtain the subject's freely-given informed consent, preferably in writing.

10. When obtaining informed consent for the research project the doctor should be particularly cautious if the subject is in a dependent relationship to him or her or may consent under duress. In that case the informed consent should be obtained by a doctor who is not engaged in the investigation and who is completely independent of this official relationship.

11. In case of legal incompetence, informed consent should be obtained from the legal guardian in accordance with national legislation. Where physical or mental incapacity makes it impossible to obtain informed consent, or when the subject is a minor, permission from the responsible relative replaces that of the subject in accordance with national legislation.

12. The research protocol should always contain a statement of the ethical considerations involved and should indicate that the principles enunciated in the present Declaration are complied with.

II. Medical Research Combined with Professional Care
(Clinical research)

1. In the treatment of the sick person, the doctor must be free to use a new diagnostic and therapeutic measure, if in his or her judgment it offers hope of saving life, reestablishing health or alleviating suffering.

2. The potential benefits, hazards and discomfort of a new method should be weighed against the advantages of the best current diagnostic and therapeutic methods.

3. In any medical study, every patient – including those of a control group, if any – should be assured of the best proven diagnostic and therapeutic method.

4. The refusal of the patient to participate in a study must never interfere with the doctor-patient relationship.

5. If the doctor considers it essential not to obtain informed consent, the specific reasons for this proposal should be stated in the experimental protocol for transmission to the independent committee.

6. The doctor can combine medical research with professional care, the objective being the acquisition of new medical knowledge, only to the extent that medical research is justified by its potential diagnostic or therapeutic value for the patient.

III. Non-therapeutic Biomedical Research Involving Human Subjects
(Non-clinical biomedical research)

1. In the purely scientific application of medical research carried out on a human being, it is the duty of the doctor to remain the protector of the life and health of that person on whom biomedical research is being carried out.

2. The subjects should be volunteers – either healthy persons or patients – for whom the experimental design is not related to the patient's illness.

3. The investigator or the investigating team should discontinue the research if in his/her or their judgment it may, if continued, be harmful to the individual.

4. In research on man, the interest of science and society should never take precedence over considerations related to the wellbeing of the subject.

Declaration of Sydney (1968)
A STATEMENT ON DEATH

The determination of the time of death is in most countries the legal responsibility of the physician and should remain so. Usually he will be able without special assistance to decide that a person is dead, employing the classical criteria known to all physicians.

Two modern practices in medicine, however, have made it necessary to study the question of the time of death further:

(1) the ability to maintain by artificial means the circulation of oxygenated blood through tissues of the body which may have been irreversibly injured and (2) the use of cadaver organs such as heart or kidneys for transplantation.

A complication is that death is a gradual process at the cellular level with tissues varying in their ability to withstand deprivation of oxygen. But clinical interest lies not in the state of preservation of isolated cells but in the fate of a person. Here the point of death of the different cells and organs is not so important as the certainty that the process has become irreversible by whatever techniques of resuscitation that may be employed. This determination will be based on clinical judgement supplemented if necessary by a number of diagnostic aids of which the electroencephalograph is currently the most helpful.* However, no single technological criterion is entirely satisfactory in the present state of medicine nor can any one technological procedure be substituted for the overall judgment of the physician. If transplantation of an organ is involved, the decision that death exists should be made by two or more physicians and the physicians determining the moment of death should in no way be immediately concerned with the performance of the transplantation.

Determination of the point of death of the person makes it ethically permissible to cease attempts at resuscitation and, in countries where the law permits, to remove organs from the cadaver provided that prevailing legal requirements of consent have been fulfilled. (See also *Death, Determination of*).

Declaration of Oslo (1970)
STATEMENT ON THERAPEUTIC ABORTION

1. The first moral principle imposed upon the doctor is respect for human life as expressed in a clause of the Declaration of Geneva: I will maintain the utmost respect for human life from the time of conception.

2. Circumstances which bring the vital interests of a mother into conflict with the vital interests of her unborn child create a dilemma and raise the question whether or not the pregnancy should be deliberately terminated.

3. Diversity of response to this situation results from the diversity

---

* Many authorities, including those in Britain, emphasize that the electroencephalograph (EEG) is not necessary for the diagnosis of brain death (see *Death, Determination of*).

of attitudes towards the life of the unborn child. This is a matter of individual conviction and conscience which must be respected.

4. It is not the role of the medical profession to determine the attitudes and rules of any particular state or community in this matter, but it is our duty to attempt both to ensure the protection of our patients and to safeguard the rights of the doctor within society.

5. Therefore, where the law allows therapeutic abortion to be performed, or legislation to that effect is contemplated, and this is not against the policy of the national medical association, and where the legislature desires or will accept the guidance of the medical profession, the following principles are approved:

(a) Abortion should be performed only as a therapeutic measure.

(b) A decision to terminate pregnancy should normally be approved in writing by at least two doctors chosen for their professional competence.

(c) The procedure should be performed by a doctor competent to do so in premises approved by the appropriate authority.

6. If the doctor considers that his convictions do not allow him to advise or perform an abortion, he may withdraw while ensuring the continuity of (medical) care by a qualified colleague.

7. This statement, while it is endorsed by the General Assembly of the World Medical Association, is not to be regarded as binding on any individual member association unless it is adopted by that member association. (See also *Abortion*.)

Declaration of Tokyo (1975)
STATEMENT ON TORTURE AND OTHER CRUEL, INHUMAN OR DEGRADING TREATMENT OR PUNISHMENT

Preamble

It is the privilege of the medical doctor to practise medicine in the service of humanity, to preserve and restore bodily and mental health without distinction as to persons, to comfort and to ease the suffering of his or her patients. The utmost respect for human life is to be maintained even under threat, and no use made of any medical knowledge contrary to the laws of humanity.

For the purpose of this Declaration, torture is defined as the deliberate, systematic or wanton infliction of physical or mental suffering by one or more persons acting alone or on the orders of any authority, to force another person to yield information, to make a confession, or for any other reason.

Declaration

1. The doctor shall not countenance, condone or participate in the practice of torture or other forms of cruel, inhuman or degrading

procedures, whatever the offence of which the victim of such procedures is suspected, accused or guilty, and whatever the victim's beliefs or motives, and in all situations, including armed conflict and civil strife.

2. The doctor shall not provide any premises, instruments, substances or knowledge to facilitate the practice of torture or other forms of cruel, inhuman or degrading treatment or to diminish the ability of the victim to resist such treatment.

3. The doctor shall not be present during any procedure during which torture or other forms of cruel, inhuman or degrading treatment is used or threatened.

4. A doctor must have complete clinical independence in deciding upon the care of a person for whom he or she is medically responsible. The doctor's fundamental role is to alleviate the distress of his or her fellow men, and no motive whether personal, collective or political shall prevail against this higher purpose.

5. Where a prisoner refuses nourishment and is considered by the doctor as capable of forming an unimpaired and rational judgement concerning the consequences of such a voluntary refusal of nourishment, he or she shall not be fed artificially. The decision as to the capacity of the prisoner to form such a judgement should be confirmed by at least one other independent doctor. The consequences of the refusal of nourishment shall be explained by the doctor to the prisoner.

6. The World Medical Association will support, and should encourage the international community, the national medical associations and fellow doctors, to support the doctor and his or her family in the face of threats or reprisals resulting from a refusal to condone the use of torture or other forms of cruel, inhuman or degrading treatment. (See also *Prisoners*.)

Declaration of Hawaii (1977)
A STATEMENT OF THE WORLD PSYCHIATRIC ASSOCIATION ISSUED AT THE SIXTH WORLD CONGRESS IN HONOLULU, 1977

Ever since the dawn of culture ethics has been an essential part of the healing art. Conflicting loyalties for physicians in contemporary society, the delicate nature of the therapist-patient relationship, and the possibility of abuses of psychiatric concepts, knowledge, and technology in actions contrary to the laws of humanity all make high ethical standards more necessary than ever for those practising the art and science of psychiatry.

As a practitioner of medicine and a member of society, the psychiatrist has to consider the ethical implications specific to psychiatry as well as the ethical demands on all physicians and the social duties of every man and woman.

A keen conscience and personal judgement is essential for ethical behaviour. Nevertheless, to clarify the profession's ethical implications and to guide individual psychiatrists and help form their consciences, written rules are needed.

Therefore, the General Assembly of the World Psychiatric Association has laid down the following ethical guidelines for psychiatrists all over the world.

(1) The aim of psychiatry is to promote health and personal autonomy and growth. To the best of his or her ability, consistent with accepted scientific and ethical principles, the psychiatrist shall serve the best interests of the patient and be also concerned for the common good and a just allocation of health resources.

To fulfil these aims requires continuous research and continual education of health care personnel, patients, and the public.

(2) Every patient must be offered the best therapy available and be treated with the solicitude and respect due to the dignity of all human beings and to their autonomy over their own lives and health.

The psychiatrist is responsible for treatment given by the staff members and owes them qualified supervision and education. Whenever there is a need, or whenever a reasonable request is forthcoming from the patient, the psychiatrist should seek the help or the opinion of a more experienced colleague.

(3) A therapeutic relationship between patient and psychiatrist is founded on mutual agreement. It requires trust, confidentiality, openness, co-operation, and mutual responsibility. Such a relationship may not be possible to establish with some severely ill patients. In that case, as in the treatment of children, contact should be established with a person close to the patient and acceptable to him or her.

If and when a relationship is established for purposes other than therapeutic, such as in forensic psychiatry, its nature must be thoroughly explained to the person concerned.

(4) The psychiatrist should inform the patient of the nature of the condition, of the proposed diagnostic and therapeutic procedures, including possible alternatives, and of the prognosis. This information must be offered in a considerate way and the patient be given the opportunity to choose between appropriate and available methods.

(5) No procedure must be performed or treatment given against or independent of a patient's own will, unless the patient lacks capacity to express his or her own wishes or, owing to psychiatric illness, cannot see what is in his or her best interest or, for the same reason, is a severe threat to others.

In these cases compulsory treatment may or should be given, provided that it is done in the patient's best interests and over a reasonable period of time, a retroactive informed consent can be presumed, and, whenever possible, consent has been obtained from someone close to the patient.

(6) As soon as the above conditions for compulsory treatment no longer apply the patient must be released, unless he or she voluntarily consents to further treatment.

Whenever there is compulsory treatment or detention there must be an independent and neutral body of appeal for regular inquiry into these cases. Every patient must be informed of its existence and be permitted to appeal to it, personally or through a representative, without interference by the hospital staff or by anyone else.

(7) The psychiatrist must never use the possibilities of the profession for maltreatment of individuals or groups, and should be concerned never to let inappropriate personal desires, feelings, or prejudices interfere with the treatment.

The psychiatrist must not participate in compulsory psychiatric treatment in the absence of psychiatric illness. If the patient or some third party demands actions contrary to scientific or ethical principles the psychiatrist must refuse to co-operate. When, for any reason, either the wishes or the best interests of the patient cannot be promoted he or she must be so informed.

(8) Whatever the psychiatrist has been told by the patient, or has noted during examination or treatment, must be kept confidential unless the patient releases the psychiatrist from professional secrecy, or else vital common values or the patient's best interest make disclosure imperative. In these cases, however, the patient must be immediately informed of the breach of secrecy.

(9) To increase and propagate psychiatric knowledge and skill requires participation of the patients. Informed consent must, however, be obtained before presenting a patient to a class and, if possible, also when case history is published, and all reasonable measures be taken to preserve the anonymity and to safeguard the personal reputation of the subject.

In clinical research, as in therapy, every subject must be offered the best available treatment. His or her participation must be voluntary, after full information has been given of the aims, procedures, risks, and inconveniences of the project, and there must always be a reasonable relationship between calculated risks or inconveniences and the benefit of the study.

For children and other patients who cannot themselves give informed consent this should be obtained from someone close to them.

(10) Every patient or research subject is free to withdraw for any reason at any time from any voluntary treatment and from any teaching or research programme in which he or she participates. This withdrawal, as well as any refusal to enter a programme, must never influence the psychiatrist's efforts to help the patient or subject.

The psychiatrist should stop all therapeutic, teaching, or research programmes that may evolve contrary to the principles of this Declaration.

Defence Societies. Practising doctors and dentists in the UK are almost without exception members of one of the three defence societies –

The Medical Protection Society, The Medical Defence Union, and the Medical and Dental Defence Union of Scotland.

These societies which are all of over seventy years standing provide medico-legal advice, legal representation at Courts and Enquiries, and most importantly indemnity in matters arising from the practice of the member's profession. The majority of claims dealt with are in negligence, but cases of assault and defamation also arise.

Membership of the societies is not limited to the UK but extends to Ireland, New Zealand, South Africa, Australia, the Far East and many parts of the world. The one exclusion is that members are not covered in respect of actions arising in the Courts of the United States.

All three societies are controlled by a Council elected by the membership and day to day matters are in the hands of a professional Secretariat.

The defence societies also have a prophylactic role in seeking to minimize the mishaps and risks which are associated with modern therapy. To this end they provide lectures at under and post graduate level. The societies also publish for their members booklets on such topics as Consent, Confidentiality, Law and the Doctor, the Mental Health Act, Complaints to F.P.C.s, the Abortion Act and Pitfalls of Practice. Films on medico and dento-legal topics are also available.

Subscription rates (1980) of the MPS and MDU are £10 for the first year after qualification and then £45 p.a. for dentists. Doctors pay £15 for the first year and this rises gradually to £95 p.a. A very small class of non-clinical members pay a subscription of £20 per annum. The MDDUS rates are somewhat lower.

Defence societies are not insurance companies, a declaration to that effect having been obtained in the case of the Medical Defence Union – v. – the Department of Trade 1979.*

Defence societies are not unique to the UK but exist also in Australia, Canada and France. In EEC countries other than the UK, Republic of Ireland and France, professional risk indemnity is arranged through insurance companies usually by national or regional medical associations. The services provided by such insurance companies are much more restricted than those of the defence societies.

J. Leahy Taylor

Defensive Medicine. The practice of medicine modified or influenced by anxiety regarding potential legal action or complaint.

Defensive medicine arises from two main causes. Firstly, there is a fear of litigation by the patient against the doctor. Claims against members of the medical profession for medical negligence have in the past been successful only if well known and accepted rules have been broken. However, partly as the result of the enormous growth in legal claims against doctors in the United States the general public

---

* The Medical Defence Union – v. – The Department of Trade 2 WLR 686, 1979.

now feel that if the profession ever makes a mistake in diagnosis or treatment someone must pay for it. The result of this according to Lord Denning[1] has been that some medical men have refused to treat patients for fear of being accused of negligence. Secondly, the demand by the patient for investigation of trivial ailments can be difficult to refuse.

These two aspects of defensive medicine have produced a very great increase in the demand for diagnostic radiology and laboratory tests. Radiologists and pathologists have long suspected that much of their work is unproductive and of no value to the patient. There is anxiety that patients are being unnecessarily irradiated. Furthermore, the gap between limited resources (q.v.) and the cost of open-ended demand is increasing. In a free National Health Service investigations do not cost the patient or clinician anything so there is no curb on the doctor's or patient's demands. Therefore, there must be an inexorable growth of defensive medicine unless the present system is changed.

There is an urgent need to assess the value to the patient of a number of diagnostic techniques. For example pre-operative chest radiographs are considered by some clinicians to be essential before giving a general anaesthetic. Recent work, however, has shown that there is little or no justification for this opinion on a routine basis[2].

It is difficult to establish clear guidelines regarding the need to investigate patients. However, costly investigations should be request-ed only if there are definite clinical indications that the result of the test will influence the management of the patient.

At a time when financial problems in the Health Service are daily becoming more acute it is opportune to consider whether limited sources are being used in the most effective manner.

1. Appeal Court Decision reversing judgement of December, 1978 in the case of Stuart Whitehouse.
2. National Study by the Royal College of Radiologists. Preoperative chest radiology, *Lancet* 1979; 2: 83.

Kenneth T. Evans

Dialysis. See *Haemodialysis*.

Disabled. See *Handicapped, Duties to; Mental Handicap*.

Disciplinary Procedures.

UNITED KINGDOM – *Medicine*. The statutory body that exercises a disciplinary function over the medical profession in the United King-dom is the General Medical Council (q.v.). It is a body largely com-posed of doctors elected or appointed by the profession and is independent of Government.

The Council receives complaints against doctors and reports of convictions in courts of law. These are first considered by the President or his nominee, who has to decide whether the matter should be referred to the Preliminary Proceedings Committee. This Committee like the Professional Conduct Committee is elected annually from the Council's membership. It sits in private and decides whether there is a case to be answered before the Professional Conduct Committee.

It has the help of the legal advisers to the Council and of a legal assessor, a Queen's Counsel who is usually a Recorder.

The Professional Conduct Committee usually sits in public but can, if it so decides, go into camera. A legal assessor sits with the Committee to advise on points of law since the whole proceedings are conducted under the rules of evidence with lawyers presenting and defending the case.

When Serious Professional Misconduct has been found to have occurred and, in the case of convictions the matters proved, the Committee may decide to conclude the case with or without admonition. It has however power to order the erasure of a doctor's name from the Register or that his registration should be suspended for up to twelve months in the first instance. Conditional registration which depends on his fulfilling certain requirements laid down by the Committee can also be imposed, or judgement may be postponed so that the doctor's conduct may be kept under review. The defendant has the right of appeal to the Judicial Committee of the Privy Council against decisions that interfere with his right to practise.

UNITED KINGDOM – *Other Professions Related to Medicine.*

Dentistry. The General Dental Council has a Preliminary Proceedings Committee and a Disciplinary Committee. The President chairs both Committees on which sit two lay members and a Legal Assessor to advise.

Eight dental members sit on the Disciplinary Committee and four on the preliminary Proceedings Committee.

Nursing. The General Nursing Council for England and Wales has an Investigating Committee and a Disciplinary Committee. The Vice Chairman of Council, a registered nurse, is the Chairman of the former and there are 8 other nursing members of Council. A nursing member of Council is Chairman of the latter and there are 9 other nursing members and 2 members (often registered medical practitioners) who are not nurses and who are appointed by the Secretary of State. There is provision for a legal assessor.

Similar arrangements apply in Scotland and in Northern Ireland.

Pharmacy. The Pharmaceutical Society of Great Britain exercises a disciplinary function through its Statutory Committee. The Chairman who is appointed by the Privy Council 'has to be a person having practical legal experience'. There are five other members appointed by the Council who need not all be pharmacists.

There is no Committee equivalent to the Preliminary Proceedings

Committee of the GMC and the GDC. The Chairman refers matters to the Statutory Committees.

Professions Supplementary to Medicine. The Council for Professions Supplementary to Medicine has boards constituted under the Council for each of the professions included in the Act – chiropodists, dietitians, and medical laboratory technicians, occupational therapists, physiotherapists, radiographers and medical gymnasts. Each board is empowered to set up its own Investigation Committee and Disciplinary Committee. There is provision for a Legal Assessor to sit with the various Disciplinary Committees.

AUSTRALIAN STATES, NEW ZEALAND, HONG KONG, SOUTH AFRICA, THE CANADIAN PROVINCES.

The statutory provisions for regulation of the medical profession in countries which have ethnic, cultural and professional ties with the United Kingdom have features in common with each other and with the General Medical Council.

1. The majority of members are doctors.

2. All are responsible for the maintenance of registers of duly qualified medical practitioners.

3. All exercise disciplinary powers and most control fitness to practise.

The disciplinary powers are similar to those of the General Medical Council in cases of conviction or where Serious Professional Misconduct, however described, has been proved; but some Canadian provinces have power to inquire into allegations of 'lack of skill or judgement in the practice of medicine' or professional incompetence. Members appointed or nominated by Ministers or Government are in a higher proportion than in the General Medical Council in most instances and in about one third the President is appointed and not elected.

EUROPE. See *European Economic Community.*

Richardson

USA. In the USA the position is extremely complex. Professional organizations may take disciplinary action but seldom do so except that the American College of Surgeons may bring a member before its Regents for inappropriate conduct. Action taken may be a reprimand, barring members from presenting papers for the college, or actual loss of membership. Proceedings are conducted according to legal measures as an individual may sue a society if 'due process was not used in evaluating the alleged episode'. Each State has a Board of Registration in medicine which has the power to revoke the licence of a practising physician or surgeon. Revocation is usually for serious unprofessional conduct. Each State also has a medical association, and these bodies can also take disciplinary action for various offences, either as the result of, or even before, a decision by the Board of

Registration. The Board of Trustees of a hospital can revoke the privilege of a physician to treat patients in that institution.

J. Englebert Dunphy

Doctor/Patient Relationship. See *Clinical Practice; Communication; Confidentiality; General Practice; Medical Science (introductory essay).*

Donation. The gift of blood, bone-marrow, organs, semen or tissue from the body of one person to that of another.
(See *Artificial Insemination; Blood Transfusion; Bone Marrow Transfusion; Tissue Transplant.* See also *Consent; Truth.*)

Double Effect. This principle, used and elaborated by moralists (mostly, but not all, Roman Catholic), in its simplest statement asserts that when an action, definable as good in terms of its object, can achieve a good effect only at the risk or expense of causing incidental but unavoidable harm, the act is licit and may be performed. Examples occur in medical practice, e.g. (1) an ectopic pregnancy threatens the life of the mother; an obstetrician may therefore remove the tube containing the fetus with the (good) object of saving the life of the mother; a secondary effect, unintended but unavoidable, is the death of the fetus. Failure of the obstetrician to operate would result in the death of both mother and fetus. (2) A patient with a terminal illness is in severe pain; a physician may therefore administer analgesics adequate to control pain, and with that object and effect, even though they may (though not inevitably) hasten the death of the patient; the proportionate administration of the drug plays no part in the legal causation of death.

The principle is not peculiar to medical practice. A ship's captain may, in an emergency, order the closing of watertight doors. The action is necessary to save the ship and as many as possible of her company. If some of the crew are trapped behind the closed doors, the captain is not culpable in law or morals for their death – though he would have delayed so long as possible to enable them to escape. Their death would be a secondary and unintended effect of a necessary act.

It is a general condition of such acts that the direct object be good in itself, and that no less drastic means be available to attain it; the evil effect is secondary, unintended, but inevitable. Moralists elaborate and refine conditions beyond the scope of the present purpose.

Dunstan GR. *The artifice of ethics.* London: SCM Press, 1978: 91ff.
Mortimer RC. *The elements of moral theology.* London: A & C Black, 1947: 51ff, 74.

G. R. Dunstan

145

Down's Syndrome. See *Mongolism* and also *Amniocentesis; Chromosome Disorders; Congenital Malformations; Genetic Conditions.*

Drug. This word has come so much to be associated with Drug Dependence (q.v.) that the term 'Medicine' is preferred for substances given to a patient for therapeutic purposes. (See *Clinical Trials; Pharmaceutical Industry; Prescribing.*)

Drug Dependence. The World Health Organization has defined drug dependence as 'A state, psychic and sometimes physical, resulting from the interaction between a living organism and a drug, characterized by behavioural and other responses that always include a compulsion to take the drug on a continuous or periodic basis in order to experience its psychic effects, and sometimes to avoid discomfort of its absence. . . . A person may be dependent on more than one drug.' Alcoholism is considered separately under that heading. For consideration of drug dependence in terminal illness see *Terminal Care.*

Treatment of a patient dependent on drugs introduces a number of conflicts: (1) between doctor and patient. The patient may request a prescription for drugs but the doctor feels it would be ill advised to grant it. (2) Within the doctor's own professional judgement. There may be some short-term advantages in giving or withholding drugs, but other less desirable long-term consequences. For example, he may accede to the request in order to avoid the potentially dangerous withdrawal of barbiturates or alcohol, or the less physically dangerous but exceedingly unpleasant symptoms of opiate or amphetamine withdrawals; or he may think it better to provide an individual with a legitimate supply of drugs when the patient's dependence is such that he would inevitably seek drugs from illicit sources, with the risk of stigmatization as a criminal and increasing alienation from legitimate society. (3) Between what the doctor feels is correct for the patient and what the consequences may be to others. The withdrawal of habitual night sedation may increase the surgery attendances and hospital referrals not only of the patient but also of other members of the family. If doctors do not provide sufficient heroin to satisfy the demands of known addicts and those immediately dependent on them for diverted supplies, there is the risk that the price of illegally commercial heroin will rise, creating a market worthy of large scale illegal commercial exploitation. To some extent this has happened in Great Britain since 1968 when prescription of heroin to addicts was restricted to special clinics with a subsequent reduction in the amounts of heroin prescribed. The result was a rise in price of the diverted heroin from 60 mg for £1 to 10 mg for £3 to £6 in 1980 and the import of heroin from southeast Asia and the Middle East. In the USA the provision of methadone for maintenance is seen more obviously as a means of controlling a social problem and is resisted less by the medical profession than by radical politicians who see it as a cynical policy of the (white) middle class to control the criminal activity and political aspirations of the (black) poor. A further conflict may arise where the provision of a prescription to one individual for valid reasons leads to a general expectation among a peer group for prescriptions to other members; it can be difficult to provide acceptable reasons for discriminating between patients who mix socially. (4) Related to the above is the diversion of legitimately prescribed drugs to others for whom they were not prescribed. The rapid increase in heroin dependence in the UK between 1960 and 1967 was based on freely available, diverted, medically prescribed heroin (but the illicit price remained stable). Information from drug users as to the source of the original supplies with which they experimented suggests that between 20% and 50% first took drugs that had been prescribed for other members of the family; these included tranquillizers, sleeping pills, stimulants and opiates. Such diversion occurs both with and without the knowledge of the person for whom they are prescribed. (5) There is sometimes a dispute between professions as to whether the problem of drug dependence is primarily medical, social, moral or penal. In this situation it is important for each professional to be aware of the limits of his own professional competence.

This variety of personal and social pressures can make it difficult for a doctor to take balanced decisions in individual cases. Some avoid taking such decisions by refusing to see drug dependent patients, but this leads to an increase in the load placed on others. The establishment of special clinics was in part a recognition of the need for, and advantage of, concentrating expertise in special centres. They are, however, barely able to cope with the number of opiate addicts and seldom have the facilities to provide a service to those dependent on other drugs. As a result, doctors whose surgeries are in certain geographical areas or whose predecessors had, rightly or wrongly, a certain reputation for lenient prescribing, come under particular pressure.

Guidelines as to the circumstances in which it was reasonable for a doctor to provide heroin or morphine to an addict were laid down by the Rolleston Committee in 1926.[1] While recent legislation has modified the application of this advice in the case of heroin, the suggestions are applicable in the majority of cases of dependence on any psycho-active drug including sedatives and stimulants. 'There are two groups of persons suffering from addiction to whom administration of morphine or heroin may be regarded as legitimate medical treatment, namely: (a) those who are undergoing treatment for the cure of the addiction by the gradual withdrawal method; (b) persons for whom, after every effort has been made for the cure of the addiction, the drug cannot be completely withdrawn either because (i) complete withdrawal produces serious symptoms which cannot be satisfactorily treated under the ordinary conditions of private practice; or (ii) the patient, while capable of leading a useful and fairly normal life so long as he takes a certain non-progressive quantity, usually small, of the drug of addiction, ceases to be able to do so when the regular allowance is withdrawn.'

It is possible at present for any doctor to prescribe methadone or other opiates (but not heroin) to addicts for the maintenance of their addiction; but in practice this is generally confined to such prescription in an emergency pending an appointment at a special clinic. In such an emergency it is suggested that a small dose of oral methadone only should be prescribed, using the preparation specifically formulated under the drug tariff formula – methadone mixture DTF. Particulars of such patients must be notified to the Home Office and a specialist opinion sought urgently. The treatment of persons dependent on stimulants and sedatives is still considered to be the responsibility of general medical services and general psychiatrists. The Rolleston Committee's recommendations can still be applied and the practitioner should consider carefully whether the short-term gains from prescribing outweigh the long-term hazards to the patient. If it is decided to offer maintenance prescribing, a long acting preparation is preferable. In general, the quicker the onset of action of a drug, the more likely it is to be abused. There is thus some advantage in prescribing only the longer acting preparations which cannot be self-injected. This is not popular with those patients whose main aim is to experience an immediate intoxicating drug effect rather than to avoid withdrawals. Thus in addition to being medically preferable, it has the additional property of enabling some estimate to be made of the motivation of the patient towards stability. Phenobarbitone is the appropriate treatment for barbiturate dependence, rather than medium and short acting barbiturates and tranquillizers. Dexamphetamine sustained release preparations are more suitable than shorter acting tablets for continual supply to patients who have been dependent for many years on amphetamines. Preparations in capsules which are readily soluble should never be prescribed; for instance, among the barbiturates Nembutal and Tuinal are particularly liable to abuse by injection.

STATUTORY OBLIGATIONS IN THE UK. The Pharmacy Act requires that many drugs may only be supplied on prescription. Certain drugs are further restricted under the Misuse of Drugs Act 1971. This Act applies throughout the UK although the regulations may differ in minor details. In general these include the stronger natural opiate derivatives and synthetic substitutes, most stimulants and the sedative methaqualone. Hallucinogens such as lysergide, and cannabis and its active principle tetra-hydrocannabinol, are also controlled and the inclusion of barbiturates in this area of control is under consideration. Regulations made under this Act lay down certain requirements for the writing of a prescription. It must be in ink or other indelible writing, and signed and dated by the person issuing it. In the same person's handwriting it must specify the name and address of the person for whose treatment it is issued, the dose that is to be taken and where appropriate the strength of the preparation, and either the total quantity in both words and figures or the number, in both words and figures of dosage units. In the case of a prescription for a total quantity intended to be dispensed by instalments, it must contain a direction specifying the amount of the drug to be dispensed in each instalment and the intervals between instalments. Except in the case of a National Health Service prescription it must specify the address of the person issuing it. The use of a stamp for these purposes is not acceptable unless the writer of the prescription has a special dispensation.

Under another regulation, which applies to England, Wales and Scotland, any doctor who attends a person whom he considers, or has reasonable grounds to suspect, is addicted to one or more of the principal opiates 'shall, within seven days of the attendance, furnish in writing to the Chief Medical Officer at the Home Office such of the following particulars with respect to that person as are known to the doctor, that is to say, the name, the address, sex, date of birth and National Health Service number of that person, the date of the attendance and the name of the drug or drugs concerned'. The regulations also prohibit doctors from supplying or prescribing cocaine or heroin for persons whom they believe to be addicted to controlled drugs except under licence of the Secretary of State or for the purpose of treating organic disease or injury. These regulations have effectively limited the maintenance prescribing of heroin and cocaine to doctors working in the special drug treatment clinics. There is a further exemption in that a doctor not specifically licensed may be authorized to administer or supply these drugs if authorized by a doctor who is acting in accordance with the terms of the licence issued to him in pursuance of these regulations. This exemption appears not to apply to the prescription of such drugs by an unlicensed doctor. Cannabis and LSD are not available for normal medical prescription except for specially approved experimental purposes.

DOCTORS PRESCRIBING FOR THEMSELVES. Since a doctor cannot register with himself for general medical care under the National Health Service, he is not able to prescribe drugs for himself on the EC 10 form. Whether a doctor may legitimately write a private prescription of a controlled drug for his own treatment is not clearly defined under statute law and has not yet been decided by the courts. In general it would be considered unwise for a professional man to treat himself for addiction. Dependence on drugs *per se* does not necessarily render a person unfit to practise as a doctor. On the other hand, as in the case of various other handicaps involving physical or mental ill health, it can impair a practitioner's professional capabilities and give rise to anxieties amongst colleagues that he or she is not fit to care for patients. Such a conflict between loyalties to a colleague and responsibilities towards patients has arisen for example in the case of an anaesthetist who acquired the habit of inhaling volatile anaesthetics during the course of an operating session. Within the hospital service there is a formal procedure whereby any member of the hospital staff should inform one of three senior doctors who are specially designated to receive and informally investigate any such suspicions; after an informal investigation they may then report the matter formally to the employing authority; there are provisions for indemnifying them against any legal action resulting from their investigation. Outside of the hospital service there is no clear structure for the informal investigation of such matters. It is suggested, however, that where there are anxieties falling short of unprofessional conduct which can constitute a complaint to the General Medical Council, or which might form a breach of contractual obligations with the Family Practitioner Committee, that concerns regarding a colleague should be informally communicated to a professional member of the Family Practitioner Committee in the first instance. (See also *Alcoholism; Anaesthesia; Competence to Practise; General Medical Council; Medical Science* (introductory essay).)

1. Rolleston Committee. Report of Ministry of Health Departmental Committee on Morphine and Heroin Addiction. London: HMSO, 1926.

Bean P. *The social control of drugs*. London: Martin Robertson, 1974.

Canadian Government. *Interim report on the non-medical use of drugs*. Harmondsworth: Penguin Books, 1971.

Connell PH. What is barbiturate dependence and who is at risk? *J Med Ethics* 1976; 2:58–62.

d'Orban PT. Barbiturate abuse. *J Med Ethics* 1976; 2:63–7.

Judson H. *Heroin addiction in Britain*. New York: Harcourt Brace Jovanovich, 1974.

Wells F. The moral choice in prescribing barbiturates. *J Med Ethics* 1976; 2:68 1–170.

Further information and reading lists from the Institute for the Study of Drug Dependence, Kingsbury House, 3 Blackburn Road, London, NW6 1XA.

Martin Mitcheson

E

Education. See *Clinical Teaching; Health Education; Medical Education; Sex Education; Teaching of Medical Ethics.*

EEC. See *European Economic Community.*

Electroconvulsive Therapy. Electroconvulsive treatment (ECT) implies the induction of a generalized elipeptiform convulsion by the application to the scalp of a measured electric current.

ECT is commonly prescribed in depressive illnesses of moderate or greater severity (particularly when suicide is considered a potential risk), in some schizophrenic illnesses (especially where affective or catatonic features are present) and for a few other less common indications.[1] Its prescription may be unethical, in the sense of negligent or rash, if due regard has not been paid to the probability of benefit,[2] or to the various well-recognized physical contra-indications.[1]

In a few severe depressives, it might be regarded as negligent to withhold a remedy widely acknowledged as quick and effective in illnesses associated with much suffering and an appreciable mortality.

Ethical considerations also arise from the damage that may sometimes accrue to the personality, or to intellectual functions. *Memory impairment* commonly follows a course of ECT but diminishes or disappears within approximately two months. Occasional 'islands' of amnesia may remain and are a handicap, particularly to those whose work is primarily intellectual. This risk is minimized by administering ECT unilaterally to the non-dominant hemisphere.[3] Dewhurst has reviewed allegations that ECT – along with other physical methods of treatment – can be used to render difficult patients more tractable or submissive, serving much the same purpose as methods of restraint during the last century. The doctor may be suspected, then, of giving vent to his own feelings, rather than being guided by his patient's welfare.[4,5] The suggestion is specially plausible where ECT has been used with excessive frequency or where many treatments appear to have resulted in an aggravated confusion. In these circumstances, both the patient and the therapeutic process itself are disparaged. Some critics have also suggested that submission to ECT invariably degrades the patient. This more extreme view ignores the benefits of a treatment which is often life-saving. Nevertheless, ECT should only be prescribed on indications that are generally acknowledged as sufficient and where the benefits that can reasonably be anticipated have been weighed against possible disadvantages.

Although the valid consent of the patient is always an ethical pre-requisite, a real difficulty arises where a patient is too ill to appreciate the arguments for treatment, or where he is unwilling. In such cases, alternative forms of treatment should be reconsidered, as well as the grounds for compulsory treatment under Section 26 of The Mental Health Act. Where ECT still seems to be indicated, it should only be administered with the written agreement of the nearest relative, with the support of a second senior colleague, and after discussion with the ward staff involved.[6,1] The administration of ECT is normally modified by the use of intravenous anaesthesia followed by an intra-venous muscle relaxant. This makes the procedure far more acceptable to the patient, virtually eliminates the risk of skeletal damage, and throws less strain on the cardiovascular system. It is therefore the desirable form of administration when ordinary anaesthetic facilities are available.

1. Hobson RF. Prognostic factors in electric convulsion therapy. *Psychiatry* 1953; 16: 275–81.
2. Costello CG, Belton GP, Abra JC, Dunn BE. The amnesic and therapeutic effects of bilateral and unilateral ECT. *Br J Psychiatry* 1970; 69–78.
3. Lodge Patch IC. Treatment or punishment? A nineteenth century scandal. *Psychol Med* 1976; 6:143–9.
4. Royal College of Psychiatrists. Memorandum on the use of electroconvulsive therapy. *Psychiatry* 1977; 131:261–72.
5. Clare AW. Therapeutic and ethical aspects of electroconvulsive therapy; a British perspective. *Int J Law Psychiat* 1978; 1: 237–53.
6. Dewhurst K. Restraining the insane. *Practitioner* 1969; 203: 658–65.

I. C. Lodge Patch

Embryo Transfer and Replantation.

LABORATORY ASPECTS

These terms are usually taken to refer to the transfer of an 'egg' from a donor female into a recipient. The stages of embryonic devel-opment used for transfer include secondary oocytes, pronucleate ova, cleaving embryos or blastocysts (when morphogenetic changes are first visible in the embryo). The technique has been widely practised during the past century in animals, including rodents, rats, farm animals and, recently, non-human primates. Embryos are obtained either from donor females after natural mating, or by maintaining fertilization and cleavage in a culture medium outside the body.

Oocytes, nucleate ova and 2- or 4-celled embryos are usually placed in the oviduct, whereas embryos at later stages are placed in the uterus. Provided the hormonal conditions of the recipient are correct, embryos develop in large numbers to full term whether obtained from a donor or after culture. There appears to be no increase of fetal or neonatal anomalies associated with these techniques.

The term 'embryo transfer' is also applied misleadingly to a method being developed clinically by which an oocyte is removed, fertilized *in vitro* with semen from the husband, and the embryo replanted in the mother's own uterus. The intention of this procedure is to bypass an occluded oviduct or obviate some other cause of infertility in the husband or wife, and a better term for it would be 'replantation of embryos' or 'replacement of embryos', since only the wife and her husband are involved.

Oocytes are withdrawn from the mother's ovary at laparoscopy, a relatively simple surgical procedure, just before ovulation is expected. Semen is collected from the husband by masturbation and a few spermatozoa are added to the oocytes. Many oocytes are fertilized, embryos develop without obvious defects and, at about day 5, they begin their transformation to blastocysts. At any time between 2½ and 5 days after fertilization, embryos can be replanted in the uterus of the mother, either through the vagina and cervical canal, without need for anaesthetic or operation, or through the uterine wall by means of laparoscopy or laparotomy.

Several pregnancies have been established by these procedures. The method has become a clinical reality with the birth of two children and the establishment of two other pregnancies when oocytes were removed from the mother during her natural cycle and replaced as embryos a few days later. All the fetuses have been morphologically normal, although one was triploid, i.e. had an extra set of chromosomes, which is a well recognized hazard of normal conception. Refinements of the method could lead to its wide-scale adoption for alleviating infertility in many couples, including men with oligospermia and other causes of infertility, and the simplicity and repeatability of the treatment may ultimately replace many current methods of operating on the oviduct.

The transfer of an embryo from one woman to another has not been undertaken. Replanting an embryo which originated from the mother's oocyte and the husband's spermatozoa has no obvious moral or legal difficulties, provided that informed consent is given, and granted the acceptance of normal monitoring of the development of the fetus. Transfer of embryos from one woman to another would raise problems similar to those arising after artificial insemination by donor (AID) (q.v.).

R. G. Edwards

Embryo Transfer and Replantation

CLINICAL ASPECTS

The use of an ovum removed from a donor fertilized by her husband's spermatozoon and replanted into a 'surrogate' mother raises serious ethical, moral and legal difficulties. First, pregnancy itself is not without danger of haemorrhages, malignancy, permanent damage to the mother's health, and toxaemia. To ask a person to undertake these risks for another's child would appear to be unethical. Secondly, problems could arise about the true paternity of the child with ensuing legal wrangles. Thirdly, no one can predict the effects of asking a woman to contribute physically and mentally to nine months pregnancy only to hand the infant over to someone else. These difficulties overwhelm any medical considerations, and 'surrogate' mothers should not be used.

Ova obtained from volunteer women undergoing sterilization procedures might be studied after fertilization for a limited period of time during organogenesis. Such research might reveal methods of control of certain familial or hereditary anomalies and diseases. Certainly such studies should be encouraged, but nevertheless the results are at present speculative. Such work ought to be carefully controlled by research committees to ensure the proper ethical management. Is it not time for a Code of Conduct of such research projects to be set up after national and international consultation?

P. C. Steptoe

ETHICAL CONSIDERATIONS

The procedure must still be classified as in an experimental stage, not yet established, not yet even developmental. It must therefore be offered as such, if at all, and assessed scientifically and ethically as such. Insofar as embryo replantation is offered as a remedy for infertility it may be classed as a clinical experiment, designed for the benefit of the patient. It has been criticized on ethical grounds by McCormick[1] and Ramsey[2,3] and defended by Edwards[4] who is especially concerned to defend the advance to clinical application despite an almost total failure with the culture of embryos in non-human primates; clinical methods have outstripped experimental studies on non-human primates; teratologists and doctors disagree about the necessity of the intermediate stage; and primates were not tested before the clinical application of kidney transplanting or of vasectomy. Other ethical considerations attend research (potentially very valuable) on the fertilized ovum and the concept of 'monitoring' the fetus. When does the developing embryo acquire human rights in the sense that it has a claim upon clinical care, with an interest of its own which may not be invaded or neglected in the interest of experimental work? This is the fundamental question which has to be faced in formulating an ethics of creating a human zygote, experimenting with it, killing it or letting it die[5]. The clinician's reply to this will be that the justification will be accorded by success – by providing a satisfying remedy for infertility by bringing a wanted child to birth. (See also *Fetuses and Fetal Material, Research on.*)

1. McCormick R. Genetic medicine. Notes on the moral literature. *Theological Studies.* Maryland: 1972; 32: 531.
2. Ramsey P. Shall we reproduce? *JAMA* 1972; 220: 1346f, 1480f.
3. Ramsey P. *The ethics of fetal research.* Newhaven: Yale University Press, 1975.
4. Edwards RG. Fertilization of human eggs *in vitro*: morals, ethics and the law. *Q Rev Biol* 1974; 49: 3.
5. Dunstan GR. *The artifice of ethics.* London: SCM Press, 1978.
Short RV. Human *in vitro* fertilization and embryo transfer. In: Department of Health, Education and Welfare Ethics Advisory Board. *Report and conclusions: HEW support of research involving in vitro fertilization and embryo transfer,* 1979.

G. R. Dunstan

Emergency. An emergency (in medical terms) is a sudden, unforeseen injury, illness or complication thereof, demanding immediate or early professional care to save life or prevent gross disability, pain or distress. It may affect one person only or, in a major disaster, cause mass casualties or many acutely and suddenly ill patients. It may involve a single member of the medical or allied (caring) professions or demand the immediate mobilization of all available medical and paramedical resources.

The immediate responsibility of the doctor faced with, or called to, an emergency is to apply his knowledge and skill to the saving of life and relief of suffering and to establish the most favourable conditions for his patients' ultimate recovery. This is the basic philosophy of medicine. (See *Hippocratic Oath* and Ref. 1.)

Recent advances in life-saving techniques and emergency care offer new expertise to doctors, ambulance personnel and nurses who may face an emergency. Increasing specialization has, however, produced experts in selected fields whose ability to deal effectively with general emergencies is limited. Such doctors might be reluctant to offer their services for fear of litigation and yet feel a moral and ethical obligation, as qualified 'practitioners of medicine and surgery', to help in a situation overloaded with emotion. The essential practical skills demanded by the occasion can only be offered by those who possess them. They can only be expected in those whose professional commitments expose them to the emergency as doctors of 'first contact', i.e. those employed in accident and emergency units, general practitioners, occupational medical officers and others in military service or with special missions.

The ethical responsibility of the doctor in an emergency is clear. He offers a service within his proper professional competence. He will supplement, within his ability, the expertise of other professionals involved. If he has no appropriate skills he will present himself as a citizen with some knowledge of emergency first aid. Nothing less would be acceptable.

No doctor need fear the consequences of such actions provided he has honestly endeavoured to keep himself up-to-date with the technical advances in his own field. No active and approved life-saving treatment given in good faith in an emergency could be regarded as an 'assault upon a person'. Nor could the doctor so acting be expected to consider the final outcome of his action. He has no more than a 'primary obligation'.[2] That the life saved should become unacceptably subnormal is irrelevant to the demands of the emergency. In the emergency, particularly the major disaster, the doctor must balance the immediate needs of his patient, within his professional conscience, against the needs of the community in the maintenance of essential services. When resources are limited, painful decisions must be taken to ensure that priority of care is given to those most likely to be rehabilitated to a full and productive life.

Emergencies vary greatly and no realistic codes of practice can be established. Each individual concerned in restoring normality will be most effective if employed in duties for which he has been specifically trained. It may be that emergency care will become a specialty to be practised only by the adequately trained, and national emergency services developed to deal with the inevitable accidents and disasters which occur in the turbulent wake of advancing technology.

1. Royal College of General Practitioners. *The future general practitioner*. London: BMA Publications, 1972.
2. Dunstan GR. *Accident casualty emergency – who cares?* Conference Report. London: Medical Commission on Accident Prevention, 1974: 155.

Stanley Miles

Ethical Committees. See *Research Ethical Committee*.

Ethics, Medical. See introductory essay.

Ethics in Science and Medicine. An international journal published quarterly by Pergamon Press, Oxford. It was established in 1973 to provide a forum for professional exchange encompassing all topics relating to the social and moral issues raised by general scientific and medical developments. These issues include the areas of morality, of the techniques governing prediction, innovation, development and change, and concerning the organization and alternative methods of planning, control, co-operation and discussion.

The Editor-in-Chief is Dr. Peter McEwan and the editorial board includes medical, philosophical and scientific representatives.

Peter J. M. McEwan

Eugenics. Eugenics applies knowledge of the genetics of man to human problems. The term was coined in 1904 by Francis Galton, one of the earliest students of human inheritance, as 'the science which deals with all influences that improve the inborn qualities of a race; also with those influences that develop them to the utmost advantage.' Galton stressed that analysis of genetic material required careful observation and measurement as well as proper mathematical tools and as a result of his writings, for example his work *Hereditary genius* (1869) in which he concluded that heredity is the major factor in human achievement, the eugenics movement developed in the latter part of the 19th century, and Galton was identified as its leader in England.

There followed a period of uninformed enthusiasm – uninformed because the fundamental genetic knowledge had not at that time been established.

Attempts were made to apply both positive and negative eugenics: positive eugenics was seen as the encouragement of reproduction by the more desirable elements of society, negative eugenics as discouragement of reproduction by the less desirable. Enthusiasts confused problems originating in social difficulties with those of heredity, but in some countries, e.g. in the United States, the results of their pressure was considerable and 'eugenic' laws requiring compulsory sterilization for feeble-mindedness, insanity, rape, habitual criminality, and other categories of the so-called 'hereditary unfit' had been passed in sixteen of the United States by 1917. Most serious geneticists, in the light of the knowledge that they were acquiring, were less enthusiastic for the eugenics movement, and it was virtually ignored for many years by the medical profession, like genetics itself despite the pioneering work on the inheritance of blood groups and Garrod's concept of inborn errors of metabolism.[1]

With the successes of the enthusiasts, the situation was ripe for political connivance; for example in the United States the Dillingham Commission of 1907 asserted that immigrants from the Mediterranean regions were biologically inferior, and, following earlier laws forbidding entry to criminals, polygamists and the mentally unsound, there came the immigration restrictions of 1924. Such misapplications reached their maximum development in Germany, where steps were taken to implement the Nazi ideals of 'preserving the purity of the race' and that 'only those who are healthy produce children', by extermination of the politically unfavoured groups and positive encouragement to breed of the politically more favoured. The 1939–45 War terminated this, and there was great popular revulsion in other countries. Meanwhile, knowledge of human inheritance had increased and many serious and informed thinkers, as for example the signatories to the Edinburgh Charter (1939)[2,3] of the genetic rights of man, felt that despite the dictatorial excesses, there was fundamentally hope for the application of genetics for the betterment of mankind and that eugenics was not to be forever brushed aside by prejudice due to its earlier mismanagement.

In its modern phase eugenics has accomplished much, for today it is firmly based on a strong body of knowledge from a number of scientific disciplines. Genetic theory has established that the frequencies of deleterious genes in populations are balanced in a variety of ways; that for the crude mechanism of mortality can be substituted equally efficacious control through restricted reproduction; and moreover that deleterious genes are much more widespread throughout the population than is apparent, so that every individual carries a concealed burden of deleterious genes, recessive or polygenic in effect. Medical genetics in particular has made great advances in the recognition of the genetic element in a large number of disease states, monogenic, multifactorial and chromosomal, while the techniques of carrier state detection of recessive traits, presymptomatic diagnosis, dietary and chemotherapeutic control to prevent the manifestation of inherited conditions and antenatal screening and diagnosis, have between them made massive advances, unthought of even 15 years ago. Research on fertility control has been particularly effective, and family planning services are in Britain so widespread that practically nobody need be beyond the reach of fertility control. With the implementation of the abortion laws, so that a high risk of a child with a serious defect provides legitimate grounds for termination of pregnancy, has come the possibility of control of population quality by selective termination. Social studies have demonstrated the relationship between impaired development and poor environmental circumstances, while demography has elaborated better methods of measuring population trends. Drawing heavily on all these fields, the major successes of modern eugenics have come through preventive medicine and community medicine. It recognizes that the fundamental right to decide whether to produce offspring, and how many, is personal to the parents, that most parents decide responsibly, and in taking that decision often seek advice. The development of genetic advisory services in many parts of Britain means that such advice can be made available, either directly or through their family doctor, to those who know of or fear hereditary defects in their families. There is seldom conflict between what is desirable in the short term for the health of the family and in the long term for the health of the population at large. Certainly by improved education about matters affecting human reproduction and inheritance, through either the press and television or the formal education system, by the genetic advisory services of the National Health Service and a variety of supporting social services, progress has been achieved responsibly and ethically far beyond the ideas of the early eugenics movement. These developments in Britain have been actively encouraged by the Eugenics Society, which was founded by Galton in 1907 as the Eugenics Education Society, and which adopted its present name in 1926.

These developments have posed a number of ethical problems, of quite a different order of delicacy from the grossly unethical misapplications of several decades ago. Modern ethical issues fall into three categories:—

First, genetic knowledge allows the prediction of the characters of a developing baby before it is born; in some conditions, for example in the chromosomal abnormalities and some metabolic disorders, modern techniques allow this to be done with 100% accuracy. A major issue, in Britain today, less heated than several years ago, is whether abortion is justified when the fetus is found to be defective, or when there is a high risk that the fetus is defective.

A second very different set of issues concerns the use for genetic purposes of methods of procreation other than the normal process of intercourse, such as artificial insemination by a donor, or extracorporeal fertilization with subsequent reimplantation of the fertilized ovum into the mother's uterus, both of which have been carried out successfully though in differing numbers of individuals. In this category also, practicable though not yet practised, is extracorporeal fertilization with implantation in the uterus of a different woman; and, at a stage further removed, nuclear replacement (the removal of the nucleus from an ovum and its replacement by a nucleus from some other body cell of the same or some other individual), and the procedure of cloning (q.v.) which can be used to produce as many genetically identical individuals as desired.

Some of these issues, though discussed today, lie for their practical applications far in the future. Most modern ethical problems concern a third category, the grey areas where the situation is not clear-cut. Few would dissent from the termination of a pregnancy if the fetus is shown to have a severe spina bifida, a trisomy of chromosome 13, or one of the mucopolysaccharidoses. The decision is less easy where the defects are less severe, say XXY karyotype or a terminal deletion of an X chromosome; it is more difficult still when the patient may or may not be apparently quite normal, say with an XYY or an XXX karyotype. Particular problems are posed where the parent is herself of low intelligence and unable to take a decision on termination. Another ethical problem still unresolved is that of identifying in its early stage a disease for which there is no treatment. If one identifies such a defect presymptomatically, should the patient be told the result, and should such information be made available if requested by an insurance company?

There is extensive literature about the ethical issues, and the views expressed are as diverse, irrespective of whether they come from

159

professional ethicists, clinicians, or the public at large. A short selection is given below. (See *Abortion; Amniocentesis; Artificial Insemination; Chromosome Disorders; Cloning; Congenital Malformation; Embryo Transfer; Genetic Conditions; Genetic Engineering; Population Policy.*)

1. Garrod AE. *Inborn errors of metabolism.* Oxford: University Press, 1909.
2. Bajema C, *Eugenics then and now.* Dowden, Hutchinson and Ross. New York: Wiley, 1976.
3. *Eugen News* 1939; 24: 63–4.
Harris H. *Genetic screening and selective abortion.* London: Nuffield Provisional Hospitals Trust, 1975.
Hilton B, Callahan D, Harris M, Condliffe P, Berkley B. *Ethical issues in human genetics.* New York: Plenum Press, 1973.
Jones A, Bodmer WF. *Our future inheritance: choice or chance?* Oxford: University Press, 1974.

D. F. Roberts

European Economic Community (EEC). The European Economic Community provides a unique opportunity for the comparative study of medical ethics. Despite the universality of medical science the practice of medicine is influenced by the history, laws and customs of the different countries. Each of the nine member states has its own long established professional attitudes and standards of behaviour. Some countries define their medical ethics in detailed written codes while others express only general principles supported by tradition. The latter derive from the Common Law system, the former from Roman Law. This fundamental philosophical difference presents difficulties when those following one system try to understand those following the other.

A 'European Guide to Medical Ethics and Professional Conduct' is being prepared by the *Conférence Internationale des Ordres et des Organismes d'Attributions Similaires.* The members of this unofficial professional body are representatives of all the registering authorities in the EEC. The Dutch, who have no such authority, and the Portuguese and Spaniards, who are not yet members of the Community, attend regularly as observers.

This Guide will provide practical information for doctors, particularly those migrating, reminding them of their obligations to their patients, to other individuals, to society and to their colleagues. It will be a reference book recording the ethical principles of each member state. Apart from some differences of attitude, for example in regard to abortion, there are fundamental ethics which all states can accept: That medicine is based on the knowledge and personal conscience of every doctor; that in protecting health and relieving suffering doctors must always respect the human person in regard, for example, to professional secrecy, experiments and drug trials, and the rights of persons deprived of their freedom; that doctors must not act without the consent of the patient or against his interest or without accepted medical indication, and must be strictly truthful in their statements and certificates. Without these basic principles, which have remained intangible across the centuries, doctors could not maintain their professional independence and freedom of decision.

In most countries the Hippocratic Oath (q.v) or one of its modern revised versions, is sworn on graduation or before registration. Only in Denmark, Germany, Holland and Italy does this appear to be a legal requirement. Attitudes to the unauthorized practice of medicine vary from prohibition, 'the absolute protection of the public agent charlatans' as in Belgium, France, Holland, Italy and Luxembourg, to the limited and controlled recognition of 'healers' (*Heilpraktiker*) in Germany. Denmark also has prohibition with the interesting exception that in times of emergency the Minister may allow otherwise unauthorized persons to practise medicine. In Ireland and in the United Kingdom any person may 'heal' but it is an offence falsely to represent oneself as a registered medical practitioner.

Disciplinary control of the profession in some states lies with Government, with litigation in the civil courts, or prosecution in the criminal courts. In others the profession may be said to be self-governing with statutory authority to exercise its own disciplinary powers. These may be administered centrally (as in Denmark, Ireland the United Kingdom) or regionally (as in most of the other countries). Appeals may be taken to higher professional councils, to tribunals of doctors and lawyers sitting together, to the ordinary Courts of Appeal, or to such supreme tribunals as the *Conseil d'Etat* in France or the Judicial Committee of the Privy Council in the United Kingdom. The ultimate sanction in all states, whether by erasure from a Register or otherwise, is withdrawal of the right to practise. Lesser punishments include warning, reprimand or censure, and suspension of varying duration and extent. In Denmark, Germany and Holland fines may be imposed. Doctors are usually defended before tribunals by lawyers, and the rules of evidence are observed. In some countries hearings are in public and the findings are published, in others both are secret. (See *Disciplinary Procedures*.)

Belgium

The Provincial Councils of the *Ordre des Médecins* control registration (*Inscription au Tableau*) and discipline. Sanctions are warning, censure, reprimand, suspension for a maximum of two years, and permanent erasure. Appeal may be made, first to a mixed Council of Appeal (5 doctors appointed by the *Ordre* with 5 Counsel of the Court of Appeal appointed by the King), and then to the *Cour de*

Cassation. All proceedings are held *in camera* and the findings are not published.

Denmark

The National Health Service, under the Minister of the Interior, controls registration (authorization) and discipline. Authorization is not granted to, and may be withdrawn from, 'persons assumed to be dangerous to their fellow-beings when practising medicine', either on account of physical or mental abnormality due to accident or illness or the abuse of alcohol or other drugs or on account of gross incompetence. Withdrawal of the right to practise is made by the Minister on the advice of the National Health Service after consideration by the Medico-Legal Council. Unless the doctor accepts the Minister's decision the case is decided by a judge in the civil court. The Public Prosecutor may start criminal proceedings against a doctor for gross or repeated negligence.

France

The Departmental Councils of the *Ordre des Médecins* control registration (*Inscription au Tableau*), and if a doctor moves to a different Department he must re-register there. The Regional Councils of the *Ordre* control discipline, with appeal, first to the National Council of the *Ordre*, and then to the Council of State (*Conseil d'Etat*). The sanctions are: warning, reprimand, temporary prohibition from practice in the Social Security, suspension from practice for a maximum of three years, and erasure.

Germany

The Minister of Public Health of each Province (*Land*) controls the right to practise (*Approbation*). The Chamber of Doctors (Ärztekammer), membership of which is obligatory for all doctors practising in the Federal Republic, may initiate proceedings against a doctor, leading to possible loss of the right to practise.

Holland

The right to practise is controlled by the Minister of Social Affairs. 80% of doctors belong to the Royal Netherlands Medical Association (*Koninklijke Nederlandsche Maatschappij Tot Bevordering Der Geneeskunst*), which has its own disciplinary procedure operating mainly in regard to professional relationships. In other matters discipline is administered by the five Disciplinary Colleges. The members, four doctors and two lawyers acting as Chairman and Secretary, are all appointed by the State. They control doctors in their relations with patients in the interest of the public. As well as warnings, reprimands and fines, sanctions imposed include loss of the right to practise. Appeal lies to a central Disciplinary College, and thereafter to the competent Court of Appeal. Proceedings and findings are secret.

Ireland

The Medical Council advises the medical profession generally on all matters relating to ethical conduct and behaviour. The Council may decide, after inquiry by its Fitness to Practise Committee, that a doctor is guilty of professional misconduct, or is unfit to practise by reason of physical or mental disability. Sanctions range from advice, admonition, or censure, to the attachment of conditions to registration, or to suspension of registration or erasure. There is a period of 21 days for appeal to the High Court. When it is in the public interest the Council may apply to the High Court for an order for immediate suspension of registration. The Council may also erase from the register the name of a practitioner convicted of a criminal offence. There is separate machinery for offences against the Social Security.

Italy

The Provincial *Ordini dei Medici* control registration and discipline. Sanctions are warning, censure, suspension for one to six months, and erasure. Decisions of the *Ordine* may be published. There is separate machinery for offences against the regulations of the Social Security.

Luxembourg

The Minister of Public Health controls the right to practise, but acts only on the advice of the Medical College. The College also acts as the Disciplinary Council. Sanctions are warning, reprimand, suspension for a maximum of two years, and temporary or permanent loss of the right to practise in the Social Security. Appeal is to the superior Disciplinary Council of three magistrates and two doctors.

United Kingdom

The General Medical Council (q.v.) has power to provide advice for members of the medical profession on standards of professional conduct or on medical ethics. Its Professional Conduct Committee judges cases of alleged serious professional misconduct, or of criminal conviction, and may order erasure or suspension, or impose conditions on registration. If its Health Committee judges that a practitioner's fitness to practise is seriously impaired by physical or mental conditions, it may order suspension, or impose conditions on registration. Either Committee has power to order immediate suspension if necessary for the protection of the public or in the best interests of the practitioner (who may appeal to the High Court). In all cases appeal within 28 days may be made to the Judicial Committee of the Privy Council. There is separate machinery for offences against the regulations of the Social Security.

Anrys H. *Les professions médicales et paramédicales dans le Marché Commun.* Bruxelles, 1971.
Berufsordnung für die deutschen Ärzte. *Deutscher Ärztetag.* Dusseldorf, 1976.
Code de Déontologie Médicale. Paris, 1979.
Code de Déontologie Médicale. Bruxelles, 1975.
General Medical Council. *Professional conduct and discipline.* London: GMC, 1977.
Koninklijke Nederlandsche Maatschappij Tot Bevordering Der Geneeskunst. Gedragsregels Voor Artsen. Utrecht, 1978.
Medical Act 1978. London: HMSO, 1978.
Medical Practitioners Act 1978. Dublin: Stationery Office, 1978.
Minister of the Interior. *Order concerning the Practice of Medicine Act.* Copenhagen, 1970.
Vergragt JH, de Vries J. *Uitoefening der Geneeskunst.* Zwolle, 1967.

David Mitchell

Euthanasia. Euthanasia literally means death without suffering. The word is now generally restricted to mean 'mercy killing', the administration of a drug deliberately and specifically to accelerate death in order to terminate suffering. This can be either voluntary or involuntary. Voluntary euthanasia, requested by the sufferer, has been described as assisted suicide or homicide by request. Involuntary euthanasia implies a decision by society or by an individual to end the life of the sufferer who cannot signify volition, for example, the severely handicapped infant and the demented. In no country is either form of euthanasia legal.

In recent years, discussion relating to voluntary euthanasia has been complicated by the introduction of the term 'passive euthanasia'. This is defined as withholding certain medical treatment intended to lengthen the lives of the incurably sick, in other words, 'letting nature take its course'. It does not involve the administration of a drug to accelerate death and, therefore, should not be described as euthanasia. Moreover, the use of the term derives from a failure to distinguish between acute and terminal illness. The two are distinct pathophysiological entities and what is appropriate to one may not be appropriate to the other. Gastric tubes, intravenous infusions, antibiotics, respirators and cardiac resuscitation are all supportive measures for use in acute or subacute illnesses to assist a patient through a critical period towards recovery of health. Generally, to use such measures in the terminally ill, with no expectancy of their return to health, is inappropriate treatment and therefore bad medicine. A doctor has a duty to sustain life where life is sustainable; he has no duty – legal, moral or ethical – to prolong the distress of a dying patient.[1,2]

Contrary to popular belief, it is possible to relieve pain in terminal cancer.[3] Further, it is seldom necessary to dull consciousness in order to relieve such pain. The term 'indirect euthanasia' has been used to describe the administration of pain-relieving drugs to patients with terminal cancer. This is incorrect; giving a drug to lessen pain cannot be equated with giving a lethal dose deliberately to end life. It is generally agreed that should life be shortened by the use of such drugs, this is an acceptable risk in the circumstances. *All* treatment has an inherent risk; a greater risk is acceptable in more extreme situations. However, it is axiomatic that, even in extreme situations, the least drastic remedy necessary should be employed. Moreover, correctly used, narcotic analgesics are much safer than commonly supposed and there is some evidence that those whose pain is relieved may outlive others whose nutrition and rest are disturbed by persistent pain.

The case for voluntary euthanasia depends ultimately upon whether a man has, or should have, the right to decide how much suffering he is prepared to accept and, when that limit is reached he has 'the right to die' in order to terminate the suffering. The phrase 'right to die' is, however, used in a variety of ways including a patient's right not to be subjected to 'meddlesome' or inappropriate treatment and his right to receive drugs to control pain even at the risk of shortening life. Such ambiguity limits the value of the expression in serious discussion.

The case against voluntary euthanasia rests on the denial of the right to have life terminated. Such a denial has been based on philosophical, moral and religious considerations. The 'right to live' was defined legally by the European Convention of Human Rights in 1953. Section I, Article 2 reads: 'Everyone's right to live shall be protected by law. No one shall be deprived of life intentionally save in the execution of a sentence of a court following his conviction of a crime for which this penalty is provided by law.' In 1950, the World Medical Association declared that voluntary euthanasia is contrary to the spirit of the Declaration of Geneva and, therefore, unethical. This was endorsed by national Medical Associations throughout the world.

The two viewpoints are, by definition, irreconcilable and, in consequence, discussion is generally conducted on a practical level. Given a high standard of medical and geriatric care, how many patients would choose voluntary euthanasia? Would legislation result in a change of attitude by society towards the life of the individual, towards the elderly and the infirm, towards the mortally sick? Would a patient feel obliged to apply for euthanasia rather than remain a burden on his relatives or society? Doctors and nurses, instead of acting only to conserve and to relieve, would acquire a second role.

Would this jeopardize the relationship with their patients? Would voluntary lead to involuntary euthanasia? Some supporters, both in Britain and in the United States, undoubtedly regard legislation for voluntary euthanasia as but the first step. It is generally agreed that safeguards to prevent abuse would be necessary. Are the practical problems insurmountable?

Two Voluntary Euthanasia Bills have been presented to Parliament in the United Kingdom. In 1936, the situation envisaged was one in which the doctor could no longer control pain and was therefore faced with the choice of ending the patient's life or failing to relieve the pain. The 1969 Bill provided that the patient or prospective patient should be able to sign in advance a declaration requesting the administration of euthanasia if he was believed to be suffering from 'a serious physical illness or impairment reasonably thought in the patient's case to be incurable and expected to cause him severe distress and render him incapable of rational existence.' In a later Bill, the requirement that the condition be fatal was omitted and the words 'incapable of rational existence' added. These modifications would have allowed a considerable extension of the range of cases eligible for euthanasia and, theoretically, could have included senile dementia and certain forms of chronic mental illness. Lord Raglan, who introduced the 1969 Bill, has since concluded that the problem of drawing up a suitable declaration may be insuperable: 'All attempts that I've seen at drawing up a declaration had too many weaknesses for my liking and had too many holes picked in them.'[4]

A third bill 'to enlarge and declare the rights of patients to be delivered from incurable suffering' was introduced in the House of Lords in February 1976.[5] It sought to establish the incurable patient's right to full relief from pain and physical distress; to remove the stigma of suicide should such a patient decide to end his life; and to give legal status to a person's written wish not to have life-sustaining treatment should he subsequently suffer from irreversible brain damage or degeneration. The bill, which was defeated by 85 votes to 23, appeared to be based on two misconceptions, firstly that terminal pain cannot be relieved, and secondly that doctors must preserve life 'at all costs'. That such misconceptions are sufficiently widespread to form the basis of suggested legislation is disturbing, and underlines the need for continuing education in the area, not only of the general public but also of the medical and nursing professions.

1. Devlin, Lord Justice, quoted by Addison. Voluntary euthanasia Paper read at Third World Congress on Medical Law. Ghent, Belgium, 1960.
2. Healy EF. *Medical ethics.* Chicago: Loyola University Press, 1956.
3. Twycross RG. Relief of terminal pain. *Br Med J* 1975; 4: 212.
4. Raglan, Lord. The case for voluntary euthanasia in The problem of euthanasia. *Contact* 1972; 39:9.

5. Incurable Patients Bill. *Hansard*. London, HMSO: 368:196.

Church Information Office. *On dying well*. An Anglican Contribution to the debate on Euthanasia. London: CIO, 1975.

Downing AB. *Euthanasia and the right to death – the case for voluntary euthanasia*. London: Peter Owen, 1969.

Trowell H. *The unfinished debate on euthanasia*. London: SCM Press, 1973.

Twycross RG. Relief of pain. In: Saunders CM, ed. *The management of terminal disease*. London: Arnold; 1978.

Vere DW. *Voluntary euthanasia – is there an alternative?* London: CMF Publications, 1971.

Voluntary Euthanasia Society. *A plea for legislation to permit voluntary euthanasia*. Voluntary Euthanasia Society, 1970.

Winget C, Kapp FT, Yeaworth RC. Attitudes towards euthanasia. *J Med Ethics* 1977; 3:18, 25.

Robert G. Twycross

Exorcism. Disordered thoughts, feelings or behaviour or bodily discomforts may be attributed either by the patient or by others to possession by a spirit. Exorcism is a method of healing which depends on the use of spiritual power, e.g., through appeal or adjuration, to expel the spirit. It is a special case of spiritual healing (q.v.).

Possession is not necessarily regarded as evil. It may be licensed in some cultures where it has a therapeutic function.[1] But it may be used to explain a wide spectrum of disorders. At one extreme are the hallucinations of schizophrenia, which a person may describe as voices in his head intruding against his will from outside as a result of malignant influences. These he may identify as evil spirits if this has been suggested to him or is part of his culture. With feelings of possession tend to go feelings of passivity, being under the control of others, and of not being oneself. By no means all the disorders attributed to possession amount to mental illness. At the other extreme a person may offer as an excuse for an infelicitous practical joke that there is a puck in him, or for an offence against law or propriety that something has got into him. The psychological mechanisms in all these cases are denial, or dissociation, and projection.[2]

That it has been practised in many different societies throughout history is evidence that exorcism has been found effective in some cases at least.[1] To what processes its effects are due is uncertain. It may be that it relieves guilt by transferring the responsibility to the evil spirit, or reflects a quest for forgiveness, the expulsion of the evil spirit representing confession and atonement. The patient may say that he has been cleansed. Interaction between healer and patient is complex. Healer and witnesses suffer stress through their involvement in the patient's conflicts. There are dangers that the patient may become more seriously disturbed, and then inflict harm on himself or others. The dangers are less if the healer has taken care in the selection of cases, and has sufficient experience and sense of responsibility to be alert to warning signs.[2]

Exorcism is not a medical method, and depends on ideas, e.g. possession by spirits, which are not acceptable to doctors and are metaphysically objectionable to others.[2] Yet it is not far removed from the psychoanalytic methods of catharsis and abreaction or from psychodrama. The distress from which the patient seeks relief tends to be of a kind for which medicine provides no sure remedy. The orthodox position is that the doctor plays no part in the practice of exorcism. The responsibility must lie wholly with the religious healer. The decision to seek exorcism is for the patient to take for himself. The doctor, if his advice is asked for, should warn patient and exorcist, should he regard the patient as liable to serious breakdown. In practice this is a difficult judgement to make.

This account assumes that the phenomena surrounding exorcism can be described adequately in the psychological terms acceptable to contemporary Western medicine. Those who practice exorcism, on the other hand, accept the factual existence of spirits and the spiritual as distinct from the psychological effectiveness of the rite. There is indeed evidence that behavioural symptoms which in Western cultures yield to pharmacological or psychological treatment, in other cultures yield only to spiritual techniques.[3] If sufficient evidence were to accumulate that in the West also certain conditions yielded to exorcism but not to psychotherapy, there would be a case for revising the orthodox position.

1. Lewis IM. *Ecstatic religion.* Harmondsworth: Penguin Books, 1971.
2. Crown S, Davis DR, Moore EG. Exorcism: a symposium. *J R Soc Med* 1979; 72: 215–21.
3. Maclean U. *Magical medicine.* London: Allen Lane, 1971.

Grayston K. Exorcism in the New Testament. *Epworth Review* 1975 2: 90–4.

Petitpierre R. ed. *Exorcism.* London: SPCK, 1972.

Trethowan WH. Exorcism: a psychiatric viewpoint. *J Med Ethics* 1976; 2: 127–37.

Welbourn FB. Exorcism. *Theology* 1972; 75: 593–6.

D. Russell Davis
F. B. Welbourn

Experiment. See *Animal Experiment; Fetuses and Fetal Material, Use of for Research; Human Experiment.*

F

Faith Healing. See *Spiritual Healing.*

Family Planning. See *Abortion; Contraception; Population Policy; Sterilization.*

Fee Splitting. See *Malpractice; Pregnancy Advisory Services; Sterilization.*

Fertilization in vitro. See *Embryo Transfer.*

Fetishism. A sexual deviation in which erotic feelings are aroused by inanimate objects, such as articles of clothing or parts of the body, e.g. hair. Fetishism is largely confined to males. See *Sexual Deviations or Variations.*

Fetuses and Fetal Material, Use of for Research. A fetus is a human embryo from the time of conception to delivery. Fetal material refers to the other contents of the uterus which result from pregnancy, i.e. placenta, fluids and membranes. Research using human subjects is broadly divided into two categories – therapeutic and non-therapeutic. The former is the use of new techniques, drugs etc. designed to improve the condition of the subject, with no known or only minimal harmful effects. The latter is research designed to find out the effects of certain procedures or drugs which may not benefit the experimental subject, but may advance medical knowledge and yield information which can be applied in treating others.

It is generally accepted that research on human subjects is only justifiable ethically if all other channels, including human experiment, have been explored, and the information required can only be obtained in this way (see *Human Experiment*).

The use of fetal material and of fetuses born dead has been accepted for many years as ethical in research related to such a wide variety of subjects as the study of viruses, cancer, immunology, vaccine preparation and congenital abnormalities. Invaluable results have been obtained thereby, and no legal or ethical problems arise.

Legalized abortion has made available much more material for fetal research. Its potential is considerable in order to study the growth and development of the fetus, both normal and abnormal, during pregnancy, to test out new methods to improve the survival rate of prematurely born infants, and to gather new knowledge in a wide range of conditions affecting the well-being of the fetus both before and after birth.

An aborted fetus is usually dead, but may be living although pre-viable i.e. although the heart may be beating, parts of the brain on which consciousness depends are not fully developed and show no signs of electrical activity. Therefore such fetuses are incapable of surviving, even with all modern technical and scientific aids. It is universally accepted that any non-therapeutic research on a viable fetus would be both illegal and unethical, but views are sharply divided in regard to the ethics of carrying out research on the pre-viable fetus after abortion or while still *in utero* prior to an agreed abortion. There has been much concern and wide debate on these aspects of the problem. In the United Kingdom the Department of Health and Social Security set up a Working Party in 1971 to report on the ethical, medical, social and legal implications of using fetuses and fetal material for research[1], and in 1974 in the USA the Department of Health, Education and Welfare established a similar Commission[2]. Both Reports are in substantial agreement, although there are some differences in detail. All the medical evidence shows that the whole pre-viable fetus offers an important opportunity that cannot be obtained in any other way for making observations of great value on the transfer of substances across the human placenta, on the reaction of the immature fetus to drugs and on the endocrinological development of the fetus. Observations on the pre-viable fetus, of necessity of very short duration, have already contributed significantly to our understanding of vital physiological and biochemical processes before birth, on which the development of a fetus into a normal child essentially depends.

The consensus at present appears to be that, subject to a very strict code of practice and control by research ethical committees (q.v.), non-therapeutic research may be permitted on the pre-viable fetus[3]. However, it remains a grey area and there are many who argue that in permitting such research we are denying the fetus protection against non-therapeutic research that is normally granted to human subjects. When is a fetus a human being? (See *Embryo Transfer; Unborn Child, Rights of*).

Another area of disagreement concerns the question of consent (q.v.), the normal prerequisite of any form of research on a human subject. As the fetus cannot consent, has the mother the right to give or withhold consent once she has agreed to the destruction of the fetus by abortion? Again, the consensus is that she still has that right, and that therefore her consent should be sought, but differing views have been expressed.

Dialogue and debate will continue, and in the light of advancing medical science on the one hand, and changing social conscience on the other, new aspects will almost certainly emerge.

1. *The use of fetuses and fetal material for research*. London: HMSO, 1972.
2. *Protection of human subjects*. Part 3. Bethesda, Md.: Department of Health, Education and Welfare, 1975.
3. Ramsey P. *The ethics of fetal research*. Newhaven: Yale University Press, 1975.

John Peel

Fluoridation. Epidemiological studies have shown that, where drinking water contains one part per million or more fluoride ion*, the prevalence of dental caries is reduced by approximately half in those individuals consuming it during tooth development[1]. This benefit is lifelong[2].

Fluoridation is thus the raising of the fluoride content of a water supply to the optimum concentration of one part per million.

There is still a strong, and vocal, body of opinion that argues that fluoridation is unethical because (a) it infringes the rights of the individual to choose his own 'medication' and enjoy a supply of 'pure' water and (b) it constitutes a hazard to health[3]. (See *Health Education; Social Pressures*).

However, fluoride ion is normally present in many water supplies and all diets although usually in amounts insufficient for dental health. In fluoridation, therefore, no substance foreign to the body is introduced. Moreover, it is possible to remove fluoride from the water.

In these circumstances, any intrusion on individual freedom can only be slight and must be balanced against the other ethical consideration, namely, that it is equally unethical to deprive the population of an urgently needed preventive measure, when that measure has such an overwhelming body of scientific evidence to show its safety and effectiveness[1,4].

This well documented evidence, the results of nearly forty years investigation and research, has been upheld by the World Health Assembly[5] and almost every reputable body in the field of Public Health.

The Royal Commission on the National Health Service in their Report[6], concluded that the prevalence of dental disease remains at an unacceptably high level and recommended as an immediate requirement, the full implementation of water fluoridation in Britain.

Fluoridation has also been upheld in regard to ethical and legal considerations by the Dublin High Court[7] and the Judicial Committee of the Privy Council[8].

---

* *Ion*: One of the electrically charged particles into which the atoms or molecules of certain chemicals (especially salts, acids and bases) are dissociated by solution in water.

No comparable dental benefit can be achieved by any alternative preventive measures.

1. WHO. *Fluorides and human health.* Geneva: World Health Organization, 1970.
2. Murray JJ. Adult dental health in fluoride and non-fluoride areas. *Br Dent J* 1971; 131: 191.
3. New Zealand Government. *Report of the Commission of Inquiry on the fluoridation of public water supplies.* Part IX, Wellington: Government Printer, 1957; 135–43.
4. *Fluoride teeth and health.* Report of the Royal College of Physicians of London. London: Pitman Medical, 1976.
5. World Health Assembly (1969) Twelfth plenary meeting, 23rd July.
6. Royal Commission on the National Health Service. *Report* London: HMSO, 1979, Cmnd 7615, p. 123, para 9: 72 and 73.
7. Ireland, Republic of, (1963) *Fluoridation Judgement delivered . . . in the High Court, Dublin, 1963* (1962 No. 915P, Gladys Ryan and the Attorney-General) Dublin, High Court.
8. *The Times* (1964) 23rd July.

J. N. Mansbridge

Forcible Feeding. See *Declaration of Tokyo; Prisoners.*

Forensic Psychiatry. Forensic psychiatry is a central part of general psychiatry and deals with the many legal aspects of psychiatric practice. A few practitioners may specialize in psychiatric legal work but the majority of assessments for courts, appearances in court, treatment of mentally abnormal offenders, and so forth, is carried out by psychiatrists with ordinary health service practices. Forensic psychiatry is also conducted within prisons, in Special Hospitals, and in private practice. Special Hospitals are separate from the National Health Service and are run directly by the Department of Health and Social Security in England and by the Scottish Home and Health Department in Scotland. The four English ones are Broadmoor, Rampton, Moss Side, and Park Lane, whilst Scotland has Carstairs State Hospital. Regional Health Authorities are now being urged in England and Wales to develop specialized forensic units within the National Health Service.

A central ethical issue for any psychiatrist is the question of responsibility. In the ordinary way a general practitioner, physician or surgeon is the servant of his patient and can be dismissed by his patient. He gives advice to his patient which can be accepted or rejected. Any treatment that is prescribed is within the control of the patient. These arrangements apply in most cases because the patients are adults who are considered to be responsible and capable of making decisions for themselves. This is the basis on which one person ordinarily deals with another. Each one of us attributes blame or praise to our fellow man and works on the assumption that he is capable of accepting such responsibility. However we all recognize that some individuals are less responsible than others and therefore require a different approach, an approach embodying a lesser or greater degree of paternalism. Examples of such individuals are children, the mentally handicapped, those suffering from senile dementia, and the mentally ill. It is part of a psychiatrist's task to evaluate degrees of mental handicap, senile dementia, and mental illness and determine the degree of surveillance which should be applied to the sufferers to ensure that they are protected from the consequences of their disability. This may mean overriding the patient's expressed wishes and indeed detaining such an individual in an institution against his will.

The psychiatrist dealing with forensic matters is especially aware of these problems as he will be asked to comment upon matters of responsibility during a hearing of the case against an accused person. At such a hearing the psychiatrist will need to determine whether the patient is so mentally deranged that he is 'unfit to plead' (ie to stand trial). To be fit to plead the defendant has to understand the proceedings of the trial, to understand the evidence, and to be able to challenge a juror. Unfitness to plead is a serious issue that has to be put to a jury in a Crown Court because if proven the court has to commit the defendant, on an indefinite basis, to a mental hospital. The defendant is denied his trial and cannot be released without the sanction of the Home Secretary. During the trial the question of legal responsibility may be raised.

Under English law (unless specifically excluded by statute) *mens rea* or guilty intent has to be present before a defendant is proved guilty. If he suffers from a psychiatric disturbance he has open to him the defence (which he has to prove) that he could not form the necessary intent at the time of the offensive act, because he was mentally unbalanced. If he is found not guilty by reason of insanity then he is committed to a mental hospital on an indefinite basis and can only be released with the sanction of the Home Secretary.

In the United Kingdom it is also possible, if charged with murder, to raise a defence (which again has to be proved by the defendant) that, whilst there was some responsibility for the homicidal act, there was sufficient mental abnormality present at the time substantially to impair or diminish responsibility so that manslaughter is the more appropriate conviction. The advantage of this decision is that the mandatory sentence of life imprisonment for murder is avoided and the judge can give any sentence appropriate to the case and the offender's needs.

Finally, and more usually, psychiatric issues can be raised at the sentencing stage in mitigation. If the court is convinced of the relevance and significance of these factors then punishment can be lessened, or even replaced entirely by a psychiatric disposal, such as a compulsory commitment to a mental hospital under the Mental Health Act, or to a course of psychiatric treatment voluntarily accepted whilst on probation.

It is sometimes believed that special ethical problems are raised in forensic psychiatry because of the possibility of applying compulsory treatment to offenders specifically to change their pattern of behaviour. Whilst it is true that medical abuses of this kind have been reported in other countries, notably the Soviet Union,[1,2] in the United Kingdom these are unlikely as an individual only receives *treatment* against his wishes if this is for clear cut mental disorder and there is a very high likelihood that the treatment will improve the mental disorder and restore the patient to full responsibility. The only area of concern is the length of duration in an institution which can be applied to people designated as subnormal or psychopathic who have committed an offence. Under British laws such individuals cannot be committed to a hospital unless they have committed an offence, but a court, with the recommendation of two doctors, can send them, on an indefinite basis, to hospital for medical care. The problem arises because these conditions are notoriously difficult to treat and improvement is slow or non-existent. It is therefore possible for such people to be detained for long periods, longer than they would have been detained by penal criteria alone.

However, national attitudes determine, to some extent, the ways in which doctors behave and it happens that the biggest ethical issue facing psychiatry in Britain is of an opposite nature but very relevant to forensic psychiatry. With the increasing liberalization of ordinary mental health services there has been increasing rejection of mentally abnormal offenders as unsuitable for care in open hospital environments[3] with no secure facilities. This has meant greater numbers of severely ill patients being sent to security institutions, such as Special Hospitals, and particularly to prisons.[4] Some such patients will be denied medical care altogether. It is in response to this problem that a series of recommendations, the Butler Committee proposals being the best known,[5] have suggested that each NHS region builds special medium secure forensic inpatient facilities, or in some other way mental hospitals must re-introduce psychiatric care with a degree of security. (See also *Declaration of Hawaii; Mental Illness; Mental Illness, Certification of.*)

1. Lader M. *Psychiatry on trial.* Harmondsworth: Penguin Books, 1977.
2. Block S, Reddaway P. *Russia's political hospitals.* London: Gollancz, 1977.
3. Gunn J. Management of the mentally abnormal offender: integrated or parallel. *Proc R Soc Med* 1977; 70: 877-70.

4. Orr JH. The imprisonment of mentally disordered offenders. *Br J Psychiatry* 1978; 194–9.
5. DHSS. *Report of the Committee on Mentally Abnormal Offenders.* London: HMSO 1975, Cmnd. 6244.

John Gunn

Fringe Medicine. A term covering various paramedical practices, often, but not always, used with a derogatory connotation to imply non-recognition by the medical profession of the procedures in question. Acupuncture, chiropractic, homeopathy and osteopathy are all sometimes included under this title; each is dealt with under its own heading. Some would also include faith healing or spiritual healing (q.v.). (See *Medical Science*, introductory essay.)

G

General Medical Council. The General Medical Council (GMC) was created in Great Britain as a statutory body by the Medical Act of 1858, to register those qualified to practise medicine. Until that time there was great confusion about the nature and significance of medical qualifications, and quackery was rife. The establishment of a register quickly brought order out of chaos and a decline in quackery, but the maintenance of the register created special duties for the Council.

The Council has a duty to register qualifications in a responsible manner, and the educational standards of those admitted to the register must therefore be satisfactory and conform to minimum standards. A registering body must also be able to remove from the register those who for various reasons are unfit to remain upon it. The Council has thus inevitably been involved in giving advice and determining standards in undergraduate education and in matters concerning professional discipline.

The GMC has never been concerned with medical ethics as such, but with conduct that used to be described as 'infamous' in a professional respect, and is now characterized as 'serious professional misconduct'. Although the two terms sound somewhat different they have the same meaning in terms of the Council's disciplinary judgments.

Direct abuse of professional relationships with patients will always raise the question of serious professional misconduct, as will actions that threaten the reputation of the profession, and thus the regard and confidence of the public.

Not all misdemeanours affect a practitioner's professional integrity to the same degree. Drunkenness, for instance, although always discreditable to the man and therefore to his profession, is, if repeated, and especially if perpetrated in connection with his professional work, more than discreditable and can amount to serious professional misconduct. Theft or dishonesty is highly discreditable, but there are circumstances where it could be argued that neither involved serious professional misconduct as the act was totally unconnected with professional activities. If, however, the dishonesty was practised upon a patient, or came about as a result of the practice of medicine, such an argument is unlikely to be upheld.

A proper relationship between members of the profession is essential to the maintenance of its professional status, and infringement of this principle can be damaging to public regard and so to the patient, and thus can amount to serious professional misconduct.

The GMC publishes a booklet entitled *Professional Conduct and Discipline*, which gives information about disciplinary procedures and indicates areas of conduct which can lead to offences being committed. It is not a code of conduct as such, as each circumstance has to be judged on its merits. A code could also be unacceptably restricting to the Council's area of enquiry, which can and should change with changing circumstances and attitudes. Any abuse by a doctor of any of the privileges and opportunities afforded to him, or any grave dereliction of professional duty or serious breach of medical ethics, may give rise to a charge of serious professional misconduct.

The GMC is the only body with the statutory power to remove a doctor's name from the Medical Register and thus prevent him from following his profession. Other bodies can and do advise on standards of behaviour, and can exclude from their membership those judged to have transgressed or not to have met these standards. This serious and humiliating procedure does not, however, have the same practical and financial results as does erasure from the Register.

The Medical Act of 1978 has for the first time given the General Medical Council a statutory place in the field of postgraduate education 'with the general function of promoting high standards of Medical education and co-ordinating all stages of Medical education' (section 15(i)). The duty of promoting high standards in the undergraduate period is also new as previously the Council was required to ensure minimum educational standards.

These new functions together with a new power 'of providing in such a manner as the Council thinks fit, advice for members of the Medical profession on standards of professional conduct or on Medical Ethics' (section 5) will be put into effect by the newly established and greatly enlarged Council with its built in majority of elected members.

The Council will also as a result of the Act of 1978 be required to establish a Health Committee which will examine a doctor's physical and mental fitness to practise outside the disciplining machinery and in private. The main objective is, as with all those of the Council, the protection of the public by making it less disturbing for a colleague to question a doctor's fitness to practise by ensuring that the behaviour of a sick person is subjected to scrutiny by an appropriate tribunal sitting in private.

The Council is anxious to inform itself of the views of the public and the members of the profession on matters that concern medical conduct. Some of these may change rapidly in a changing society; others are less mutable. What is immutable is the principle of preserving the integrity of the profession and enhancing the quality of its service to the public. (See also *Clinical Practice*; *Competence to Prac-*

tise; Disciplinary Procedures; European Economic Community; General Practice; Quality Assurance.)

Richardson

General Practice. General practice (primary care) is a distinct medical specialty with its own special features and methods that influence ethical concepts and behaviour.

The special features that distinguish it from other specialties are:– (1) direct access and availability of the doctor to the patient; (2) first-contact primary care, with the patient bringing an undefined and unclassified package of problems for the general practitioner to assess, diagnose and manage; (3) the work-involved care for a relatively small, 2000–2500 patients per general practitioner, and static population; (4) long-term care is the rule rather than the exception, with the practitioner caring for, and coming to know, 2 or 3 generations of families; (5) the morbidity and mortality patterns are those that can be expected to occur in a population of 2000–2500 persons, no more and no less. Common disorders and problems occur commonly and rare diseases are seen rarely. (6) With 9 out of 10 episodes and consultations in general practice being managed by the practitioner, the process of referral to, and collaboration with, other medical and paramedical specialties is an important role in coordinating and manipulating the available services for the good of the patient. (7) In many health care systems, including the British National Health Service, the general practitioner is an independent contractor able to organize and to manage his work as he thinks best and without too many directives. (8) The ways in which the general practitioner is paid will influence the ways in which he works. Fees-for-services will encourage more consultations and more investigations than a capitation or salaried system.

Certain ethical issues relate to all these features.

ACCESSABILITY – AVAILABILITY. *Whose patient?* In the British National Health Service persons register with a general practitioner. This provides a legal basis for defining a doctor-patient relationship. In other systems patients tend to 'shop around' and ethical rules are necessary to avoid the confusion and dangers that can occur when more than one doctor is involved in treating a patient at the same time without close professional collaboration.

Out of hours cover. In theory the general practitioner is responsible for providing a continuing 24-hour service. This is not possible. There have to be arrangements for sharing the care with other colleagues.

The best way in organizing such out of hours cover is by a *regular rota* shared among practitioners in the same practice or with neighbouring practices in the area. All the practitioners are known to one another and they are familiar with the local community and the local services that are available.

In many countries including UK *commercial deputizing services* have been created particularly in urban areas to provide out of hours cover in primary care. The doctors usually are young hospital doctors who visit patients in their homes when called in an emergency. They tend to be untrained for and inexperienced in general practice and are unfamiliar with the local community and the local health services. They are unknown to the patient and to the doctor who employs them.

Appointment systems and other barriers have arisen which make easy contact between patient and doctor difficult.

An essence of good general practice is speedy access to the doctor. Appointment systems, which now are the rule in British general practice, have been introduced to provide a more manageable organization. However, they must ensure that any patient has to be able to consult the doctor within 24 hours, if his or her condition so requires.

In addition to appointment systems the patient now has to negotiate the barrier of a secretary-receptionist before he is able to meet his doctor. It is important therefore that the secretary-receptionist is sensitive to the patient's needs, anxieties and personality in acting in the front-line of medical practice, and the general practitioner has a responsibility to see that this is so.

FIRST-CONTACT CARE. In his role in providing such care the general practitioner now tends to work as a member of the *primary health care team* that includes among others his partners, nurses, health visitors (public health nurses), social workers, secretary-receptionists and doctors' wives.

In addition, if the practice is involved in teaching, there are *trainee-practitioners* and *undergraduate medical students* who may participate in seeing and treating the patient.

The ethical issues involve the degrees of *sharing and delegation of care* among the team. The underlying principle must be that no one in the team must be expected to undertake care and treatment for which he or she has not been trained, but in which he is experienced and in which he is covered by the law.

SMALL AND STATIC COMMUNITY. Working and living as a member of a small practice population the doctor must take special care to observe the *ethics of professional doctor-patient relations*. He must look upon his patients as friends but not encourage and develop too close and too familiar personal relations. This exposes him to many unnecessary risks.

In such a small and static population strict *confidentiality* is all important. Not only must confidentiality be maintained within the practice team, but professional confidences must not be divulged to members of the patient's near and extended family without permission.

The doctor's own family also has to be considered. It is natural for him to discuss his work with his wife and family, but patients' confidences must be maintained at all times in all places.

LONG-TERM CARE. There is a nice line which the general practitioner has to tread. He has to be aware of and assume appropriate *social and community responsibilities* and interpret wisely and widely his role as a family doctor. He must beware of becoming too involved in the lives of his community and in the lives of families for whom he cares.

Home visiting is a part of general practice that has declined with social and medical advances. There still is need for home visiting of the house-bound, the terminally sick and of those with acute medical illness.

Home visiting is a privilege for the doctor and must be treated with respect. Requests for home visits are one of the most frequent causes of friction between patients and general practitioners. Sometimes the practitioner does not consider a home visit necessary and sometimes the patient demands a visit for what proves to be a relatively trivial complaint. This can lead to a breakdown of good doctor-patient relations.

Prescribing of drugs by doctors increases in volume and in price each year. Each person in Britain on average receives 6.5 prescription scripts per year at an average annual cost of £15 per person.

It is difficult to decide ethically how many of these prescriptions are really necessary and how many are useful to the patient's welfare. It is often difficult for the doctor to resist the patient's demands and expectations for drugs.

The British National Health Service *Records* for general practice are not conducive to good record keeping. They are too small to include much detail and their folders are too small to contain life-long reports of investigations and specialists' reports. Nevertheless, good practice demands good records and it is the doctor's duty to ensure that these are kept within the constraints of the methods available (see *Medical Records*).

MORBIDITY. The general practitioner is a specialist in the morbidity of common physical, emotional and social problems. He also must be an expert in the early diagnosis of major diseases and in continuing care. He has to accept these responsibilities and to realise the limits of his expertise.

RELATIONS BETWEEN GENERAL PRACTITIONERS AND OTHER SPECIALISTS. The general practitioner is the chief link between the patient and the other medical and surgical specialists. Except in a system where there is free access to all specialists it is through the practitioner's referral that the patient is seen by a specialist.

The general practitioner has to decide when a referral is necessary and to whom the patient should be referred.

The specialist must respect his role as a consultant; the patient should be referred back to the general practitioner, with a report, once his special tasks have been completed. The specialist must not take over the long-term care of the patient except with the agreement of the general practitioner.

The patient may be referred to a specialist who is employed in a health care system where no fees are paid or the patient may be referred to a specialist privately who will receive fees which may or may not be covered by prepaid insurance. Whatever the system the same ethical principles apply. (See also *Advertising; Clinical Practice; Communication; Confidentiality; Drug Dependence; Health Education; Interprofessional Relationships; Medical Science* (introductory essay); *National Health Service; Prescribing; Teamwork; Unqualified Practitioners.*)

John Fry

Genetic Conditions. New knowledge brings with it a responsibility to use the new knowledge wisely. The community as a whole, and parents individually, accept that they have a duty to see that, as far as possible, children experience an environment which will favour healthy growth and development. Increasingly, both community and parents also now feel that children have a right, as far as is possible, to be born without serious genetically determined handicap, in so far as this may be achieved by ethically acceptable procedures.

At present about four children in a thousand are born with disorders due to chromosomal anomalies (q.v.), about 10 in a thousand are born with disorders due to mutant genes (see below) of large effect (about 7 per thousand dominant, 2.5 per thousand recessive, and 0.5 per thousand X-linked), and about 20 in a thousand are born with serious congenital malformations (q.v.). In addition many other children will be born genetically predisposed to develop some of the common serious diseases of adult life; for example about 10 in a thousand will develop schizophrenia as young adults.

While both the community and parents share the responsibility for providing a good environment for children, responsibility for freedom from genetic handicap in children is primarily a responsibility of individual parents. The final decision on whether or not to plan children should rest with the parents. The duties of the medical profession in this respect include: to inform parents of any special risks of genetic disease; to put these risks into perspective both as regards random risks and the prognosis for an affected child, including the prospects for effective treatment; to discuss with them the alternative courses of action open to them; finally, to help the parents, once they have made their decision, to carry these out, with the proviso that parents should not expect a doctor to carry out any procedure which he regards as unethical. Specialist genetic clinics to advise on the more difficult problems have been set up in association with most University medical schools in Europe and the United States.

The majority of children with *chromosome abnormalities* are born to chromosomally normal parents, and are unpredictable except that they occur with increasing frequency at increasing maternal age. No way is yet known of primary prevention by controlling the non-disjunction of chromosomes in germ-cell formation that is the cause of most of these cases. Any reduction in their birth frequency must depend on secondary prevention by prenatal screening by amniocentesis (q.v.) and abortion (q.v.) where the fetus is found affected. There is already an increasing demand for such screening from mothers pregnant over the age of 40 years, who know of the risk of about 1 in 50 (including a 1 in 100 risk of Down's syndrome) of the birth of a chromosomally abnormal child at that maternal age. It is likely that the age limit will be extended downwards as more facilities become available and the procedure is made safer. Most couples consider ethical and wish for the abortion of a fetus having trisomy 21 (Down's syndrome) with the inevitable and usually severe degree of mental retardation associated with the syndrome. Parental decisions will be more difficult and variable when the fetus is found to have, for example, trisomy of the sex chromosome of type XXY where the expectation is of a son with only mildly reduced intelligence, and sterility. In the minority of instances where the chromosome abnormality has not arisen *de novo*, but is inherited from one or other parent who has a similar abnormality in balanced form, the risk of recurrence in a later child is relatively high, and parents usually feel able to plan further pregnancies only if offered the cover of prenatal screening.

Conditions due to mutant genes* of large effect, so-called *monogenic or unilocal disorders*, are conveniently divided into (autosomal) dominant, (autosomal) recessive and X-linked. Individually most such conditions tend to be rare, but they include many hundred different disorders. Dominant conditions are defined in medical genetics as those in which the mutant gene concerned causes clinical abnormality in the heterozygote (with a single dose of mutant gene). Recessive conditions are those in which the heterozygote is clinically normal and only homozygotes (that is those with a double dose of the mutant gene) are clinically affected. X-linked conditions are those which are due to a mutant gene on the X-chromosome.

The cases of dominant conditions which are due to fresh mutation are unpredictable and therefore at present unpreventable. No way is known of primary prevention by controlling gene mutation, and secondary prevention by prenatal screening and abortion is not practicable where there is only the low random risk of a particular condition. However, the transmission of the condition to second, third and later

---

* Genes are the individual units of inheritance. They are strung along the chromosomes. They are present in duplicate at the corresponding sites on the two members of a chromosome pair. They are normally stable and transmitted from parent to child unchanged. Occasionally, however, the copying of the gene in reproduction is imperfect and the altered, or mutant, gene may show loss or partial loss of its function. Some mutant genes have little effect on health, some have a large effect.

generations may be substantially reduced if patients are told of the 1 in 2 risk to their children and most of them decide not to take the risk. Men or women who themselves have dominant conditions, for example classical achondroplasia, or the adult form of polycystic disease of the kidneys, are well placed to decide whether they wish to take the high risk of having similarly affected children. The doctor giving genetic advice may, however, need to warn about the variability in severity of many dominant conditions even within a family. There is a special difficulty in parental decisions where serious dominant conditions have a late onset, as for example is the case with Huntington's chorea which usually has an onset in the fourth or fifth decade. The offspring of patients will often be young adults, and perhaps already married, when a parent develops the disease. They have a 1 in 2 chance of having inherited the gene (and of later developing the disease) and, if they do develop it, there is a 1 in 2 risk to any child they have. In this situation most men and women decide to have no children, while others take a chance on a small family of one or two children. Prenatal diagnosis is, as yet, possible for only a few dominant conditions even in high risk situations, but in time will offer patients the opportunity, if they so wish, of planning children with the intention of allowing the pregnancy to go to term only if the fetus is unaffected. Some couples, where it is the husband who is affected, may choose to make use of artificial insemination by donor (q.v.). From the viewpoint of eugenics (q.v.), genetic counselling is particularly important where a serious dominant condition may be effectively treated, as for example multiple polyposis of the colon by total colectomy. The resultant increase in potential reproductive fitness of patients with such dominant conditions will lead to a rapid increase in the birth frequency of the condition, unless treated patients plan a family size below replacement rate.

In the case of recessive disorders parents, though nearly always healthy themselves, are almost always both heterozygous carriers of the mutant gene concerned. They are usually unaware of their risk and not known to be at risk until they have had one affected child. Thereafter there is a 1 in 4 risk for any further child of the couple. Recessive disorders usually show less variety in clinical severity than do dominants and so the handicap of the first affected child is usually a good indication of the prognosis for an affected younger sib. With serious recessive conditions experience shows that, after counselling, some three quarters of parents feel they should plan no further children. They prefer the alternatives of adoption or, now that few children are available for adoption, may consider artificial insemination by donor (q.v.). However where prenatal diagnosis is available, as it is already for about 60 serious recessive conditions, many couples at risk feel it ethical to plan further children with the intention of having the pregnancy terminated if the fetus is shown to be affected. However the prevention of the birth of the first affected child can come only from the detection of parents at risk at or before marriage. Such carrier detection is already possible for many recessive disorders and is appropriate for the unaffected brothers and sisters of a child with the recessive disorder; such sibs have a 2 in 3 chance of being carriers. It is, however, worthwhile developing voluntary screening programmes of the whole population at or before marriage only where a particular recessive disorder has a relatively high frequency in that particular population. Such programmes are already in operation for a few conditions, for example: in many American and Canadian cities for Tay-Sachs disease* in the Ashkenazi Jewish populations, in whom the carrier frequency is about 3 per cent; in certain areas of Italy for beta-thalassaemia, where the carrier frequency is about 10 per cent; in the black population of certain American cities for sickle-cell anaemia, where the carrier frequency is about 10 per cent. It is important that such screening programmes are accompanied by full explanation to the public, and full counselling of those identified as carriers. Such programmes are best carried out by doctors and nurses who are themselves members of the ethnic group at special risk. It will be desirable to institute such programmes for carrier detection of the gene for cystic fibrosis all over Europe, once a method becomes available, since the carrier frequency appears to be about 5% in most European populations. The carriers who are detected before marriage will have the option of avoiding marriage to another carrier, and if they do marry another carrier will know from the start of the risks to children. Effective treatments are becoming available for many recessive conditions, either dietary, as is the case with classical phenylketonuria, or by replacement therapy as with congenital adrenal hyperplasia. This does not, however, present the same eugenic problems as with dominants, since any resultant increase in the gene frequency is exceedingly slow, giving ample time for countermeasures where these are appropriate.

With X-linked conditions the serious genetic risk is the 1 in 2 chance to any son of a woman who carried the mutant gene on one of her two X-chromosomes. Such women are usually clinically unaffected. In families in which males with X-linked disorders have already been born some women will be seen from the pedigree to be certain carriers, others will be possible carriers. The latter may often be further distinguished, with the help of biochemical tests, into those who have a high probability, and those with a low probability, of being carriers. Such biochemical tests are available, for example, in the case of the severe X-linked form of muscular dystrophy and of classical haemophilia. In practice almost every woman who knows that she has a high probability of being a carrier of the gene for

---

* Tay-Sachs disease, a serious genetic disorder, has its onset shortly after birth and is characterized by progressive mental deterioration, blindness and paralysis and is usually fatal by the age of 2 or 3. There is no effective treatment.

muscular dystrophy feels that she should not take the risk of having an affected son. She and her husband then have the difficult decision to make whether to plan to have no children, or to plan a pregnancy with the aim of having the pregnancy terminated if the fetus is male. Their decision will be less difficult once it becomes possible to distinguish the affected from the unaffected male fetus. The successful treatment of patients with X-linked disorders, for example haemophilia, raises eugenic problems since, while their sons will be unaffected and will not transmit, their daughters are certain carriers. Few would regard as ethical the termination of pregnancy where the fetus is female, but preconceptional sex determination, not yet available, would enable haemophiliac men to plan to have only sons.

Part genetic disorders may have relatively high birth frequencies, for example about 5 per thousand in the case of neural tube defect (anencephaly and spina bifida) and congenital heart malformation, and about 10 per thousand in the case of schizophrenia. The genetic element in the aetiology of such conditions is probably complex and includes a substantial contribution from environmental factors. Risks to sibs and offspring of patients are much raised above the random risk, but usually appreciably less than for monogenic conditions. For example the risks are about 10% for the first degree relatives in the case of schizophrenia, about 5% in the case of neural tube malformations, about 3% in the case of the more common heart malformations. Nevertheless these are risks which responsible parents often feel able to take. For example, most parents who have had one child with spina bifida feel it right to plan further children, but wish for prenatal screening now that this has become possible by α-fetoprotein estimation in amniotic fluid followed by abortion of an affected fetus. However only a minority of cases may be prevented in this way and to achieve a substantial reduction in the birth frequency of affected children with neural tube malformations, by prenatal diagnosis and abortion, it will be necessary to develop screening methods applicable to all pregnancies. This is already possible for neural tube malformations by measuring α-fetoprotein in mother's blood at 17 weeks of pregnancy. Prenatal diagnosis of congenital heart malformations is not yet practicable, but should be possible within, say, a generation. True primary prevention of congential malformations should in the not too distant future be possible by finding means of recognizing parents genetically at risk and protecting their offspring from the additional environmental triggers, once these have been elucidated.

Ash P, Vennart J, Carter CO. The incidence of hereditary disease in man. *J Med Genet* 1977; 14: 305–6.

Carter CO, Evans KA, Fraser Roberts JA, Buck AR. Genetic clinic: a follow-up. *Lancet* 1971; 1: 281–5.

Carter CO. *Human heredity.* 2nd edn. Harmondsworth: Pelican Books, 1977.

Hilton B, Callahan D, Harris M, Condliffe P, Berkley B. *Ethical issues in human genetics*. New York: Plenum Press, 1973.

Stevenson AC, Davison BCC. *Genetic Counselling*, 2nd edn. London: Heinemann Medical, 1976.

C. O. Carter

Genetic Engineering. Genetic engineering, also referred to as genetic manipulation, gene cloning and recombinant DNA technology, is defined in the UK as, 'the formation of new combinations of heritable material by the insertion of nucleic acid molecules, produced by whatever means outside the cell, into any virus, bacterial plasmid, or other vector system so as to allow their incorporation into a host organism in which they do not naturally occur but in which they are capable of continued propagation'. Recombinant DNA technology can produce hybrid (recombinant) nucleic acid molecules containing DNA derived from organisms that would not normally be expected to hybridise. Therefore it will by-pass the restrictions imposed by sexual incompatibility, the lack of DNA sequence homology and the other chemical, mechanical, physical and biological barriers which confine hybrid formation to closely related species or, occasionally, genera. Genetic manipulation owes its origins to a series of recent developments in molecular biology and microbial genetics[1]. Of major importance has been the discovery of a large class of enzymes known collectively as restriction enzymes. Present in many micro-organisms, these enzymes have the property of cutting double-stranded DNA molecules at a specific sequence of 4 to 6 base pairs. Each enzyme recognises a different base sequence and for a particular restriction enzyme the cleavage sites occur with a frequency of about one site every few thousand base pairs[2]. Any two DNA fragments produced by cleavage with a particular restriction enzyme can be joined under appropriate conditions and the joint resealed. Thus molecules composed of DNA segments from totally unrelated organisms may be artificially recombined together to produce combinations of genes which rarely, if ever, occur in nature.

Another essential feature of current practice is the use of a cloning vehicle or vector into which the foreign DNA can be inserted. The purpose of the vector is to maintain and replicate the cloned fragment and the two most commonly used vectors are plasmids and viruses. Plasmids are self-replicating, extra-chromosomal DNA elements found usually, though not exclusively, in bacteria. Their small size and circular form, plus the fact that they can be extracted as free DNA and subsequently re-introduced into viable bacteria where they will be replicated and even genetically expressed, makes them ideal as vectors. Viruses have equally useful properties. Vectors with single cleavage sites for particular restriction enzymes have been constructed specifically for cloning purposes. Having opened the vector molecule at this site by restriction enzyme cleavage, a linear segment of foreign DNA produced by cutting with the same enzyme can be inserted (spliced) between the free ends and the recombinant molecule closed to reform the circular structure. Genetic selection techniques are available which permit identification of those recipient bacteria into which the vector has been introduced. The inserted DNA can be excised from the vector DNA and isolated by a reversal of this process. A number of variations to this basic technique are now available, e.g. for cloning RNA molecules. Genetic engineering offers several real and potential advantages. 1) Specific DNA sequences from any organism can be produced in large amounts with a very high degree of purity using microbiological methods. This circumvents the very expensive, time-consuming and complicated methods normally used to obtain purified fractions of eukaryotic gene sequences. 2) The structure and function of specific DNA regions can be analysed. This approach has been used with DNA sequences for human foetal γ globin[3,4] and the insulin genes from rat[5] and man[6,7]. 3) The potential for industrial production of compounds such as human insulin, antibodies, blood clotting factor, interferon and vaccines[8]. 4) The potential for the production of plants with new synthetic capabilities, of which nitrogen fixation is a good example[9]. 5) The possibility for the construction of hereditary disease replacement systems. Undoubtedly, the advent of genetic engineering has opened up new and far reaching areas of study in science, medicine and agriculture. The possibility of constructing recombinant DNA molecules from grossly dissimilar organisms (bacteria and man, for example) has led some scientists to express concern about the potential health hazards of genetic engineering[10]. Among the lay public there is considerable confusion and ignorance. Ethical issues have been raised questioning the right of scientists to tamper with the natural biological order in the light of our past experiences, for example, with radiation and thalidomide. The development of potentially hazardous technologies for building scientific careers and the ability of scientists to regulate wisely the use of their findings have also been criticised. However, it is the potential risk to health rather than the moral aspects of genetic manipulation that has stimulated such widespread discussion since publication in 1974 of the Berg letter calling for a cessation of genetic engineering work to permit assessment of the possible dangers[10]. One outcome of this debate is that in most countries there is government control over work using recombinant DNA techniques (see entry for GMAG). The discussion of conjectural hazards centres on the possibility that the presence of foreign genetic elements may adversely affect the normal functions of cells or groups of coordinately-expressed cells. Foreign genes introduced into human cells could alter their differentiated state, immunological response, metabolic functions, could interfere with hormone activity or cell division or cause the expression of a cryptic virus. Bacteria or viruses carrying foreign genetic material might have increased pathogenicity or host range. Genes coding for antibiotic resistance cloned in non-pathogenic organisms might be transferred to dangerous pathogens. All living organisms would be at risk. Two types of safety measure are used to minimize the risk of infection by a host organism carrying foreign genetic elements. The first is physical containment and involves the use of refined micro-biological techniques and equipment designed to prevent the escape of the host organism. The second, referred to as biological contain-ment, minimizes the chance of survival of a host organism outside of the laboratory. This is achieved by using host cells carrying a series of deleterious mutations which permit their growth only under highly artificial laboratory conditions. Furthermore, data accumulated from experiments specifically designed to analyse risks suggest that hybrid organisms constructed by genetic manipulation constitute no greater risk than that of the constituent organisms. A cogent and rational view of these issues was presented recently by Szybalski[11].

(See *Cloning: Eugenics; Genetic Conditions; Genetic Manipulation Advisory Group.*)

1. Old RW, Primrose SB. *Principles of gene manipulation.* Oxford: Blackwell Scientific, 1980.
2. Roberts RJ *Gene* 1978; 4: 183–93.
3. Humphries P, Coggins LW, Old RW, Mitchell JM, Coleclough C, Paul J. *Mol Gen Genet* 1978; 165: 65–71.
4. Smithies O, Blechl AE, Denniston-Thompson K, Newell N, Richards JE, Slightom JL, Tucker PW, Blattner FR. *Science* 1978; 202: 1284–9.
5. Ullrich A, Shine J, Chirgwin J, Pictet R, Tischer E, Rutter WJ, Goodman HM. *Nature* 1977; 196: 1313–9.
6. Goeddel DV, Kleid DG, Bolivar F, Heyneker HL, Yansura DG, Crea R, Hirose T, Kraszewski A, Itakura K, Riggs AD. *Proc Nat Acad Sci USA.* 1979; 76: 106–10.
7. Gait MJ. *Nature* 1979; 277: 429–31.
8. Johnson IS, Burnett JP Jr. In; Boyer HW, Nicosia S, eds. *Genetic engineering.* Amsterdam: Elsevier-North Holland Biomedical Press, 1978: 217.
9. Postgate JR. *Philos Trans Royal Soc Lond* 1977; 281: 249–60.
10. Berg P, Baltimore D, Boyer HW, Cohen SN, Davis RW, Hognes DA, et al. *Nature* 1974; 250: 175.
11. Szybalski W. In: Boyer HW, Nicosia S, eds. *Genetic engineering.* Amsterdam: Elsevier-North Holland Biomedical Press, 1978: 253–75.

D. A. Ritchie

Genetic Manipulation Advisory Group (GMAG). GMAG was set up in December 1976 by the Secretary of State for Education and Science following a recommendation of the Working Party on the Practice of Genetic Manipulation under the Chairmanship of Sir Robert Williams[1]. GMAG now constitutes the central advisory committee for all matters relating to the use of genetic manipulation techniques in the UK. Its terms of reference include: 1) giving advice to those undertaking activities in genetic manipulation, including activities related to animals and plants, 2) undertaking the continuing assessment of risks and precautions and of any newly developed techniques for genetic manipulation and to advise on appropriate action, 3) to maintain contacts with the Health and Safety Executive and the Dangerous Pathogens Advisory Group, 4) to maintain records of containment facilities and of the qualifications of Biological Safety Officers, 5) to provide advice on general matters connected with the safety of genetic manipulation, including health monitoring and the training of staff[2]. The group has nineteen members and contains not only scientific and medical experts but also members appointed to represent the interests of the public, employees and management. In addition, there are nine assessors representing various relevant Government departments. Five sub-committees have been set up under GMAG to consider the following specific aspects of the group's work: 1) Validation of Safe Vectors, 2) Medical Monitoring, 3) Confidentiality of Proposals, 4) Genetic Manipulation in Plants, 5) Risks of Scale-up[2,3,4].

GMAG is an advisory body, the legal framework within which the control of genetic manipulation is operated being provided by the Health and Safety at Work etc. Act 1974[5]. In practice, a scientist wishing to use recombinant DNA technology must notify GMAG of this intention and provide detailed information about the proposed experiments. GMAG, having considered the proposal, will advise on the level of the safety precautions under which the work must be conducted. This advice is given in the form of a containment categorization based on the guidelines set down in the Williams Report. There are four containment levels, CI – CIV, corresponding to increasingly stringent levels of physical containment. GMAG does not give advice on the scientific merit of a proposal. Recently certain types of genetic manipulation work have been made exempt from this categorization procedure. (See *Genetic Engineering*.) Further details may be obtained from: Genetic Manipulation Advisory Group at Medical Research Council, 20 Park Crescent, London, W1N 4AL.

1. Williams Working Party. *Report of the Working Party on the Practice of Genetic Manipulation*. London: HMSO, 1976, Cmnd 6600.
2. *First Report of the Genetic Manipulation Advisory Group 1978*. London: HMSO, 1978, Cmnd 7215.
3. *Second Report of the Genetic Manipulation Advisory Group 1979*. London: HMSO, 1979, Cmnd 7785.
4. Richmond M. Some notes about the work of the British Genetic

189

Manipulation Advisory Group during its first year of life. In: Boyer HW, Nicosia S, eds. *Genetic engineering.* Amsterdam: Elsevier North Holland Biomedical Press, 1978:289.
5. *The Health and Safety (Genetic Manipulation) Regulations 1978.* Statutory Instruments. London: HMSO, 1978, No 752.

D. A. Ritchie

Genetic Registers. If genetic counselling is to realize its full potential in reducing the incidence of genetically determined disease it is necessary that there should be registers of individuals and families at risk. Then, when an individual at risk of transmitting genetic disorder reaches reproductive age, he or she may be informed of the risk and have this put into proper perspective before they plan a family. Such registers would be most valuable at present for dominant conditions, such as Huntington's chorea or multiple polyposis of the colon, and X-linked conditions such as early onset muscular dystrophy or haemophilia (see *Genetic Conditions*).

Such registers however raise serious problems of acceptability and confidentiality. Unauthorized access to such a register might gravely prejudice an individual's employment. The following criteria have been suggested:

1. Registers should be set up for the express purpose of tracing and counselling individuals at high risk of transmitting genetic disease.

2. They are best maintained on a regional rather than a national basis and linked to treatment centres for specific disorders.

3. Entry to a register should occur only with the full knowledge and approval of the individual concerned.

4. Strict safeguards for confidentiality must be incorporated, with personal medical information available only to the consultant in charge of the register. (See also *Confidentiality*; *Medical Records.*)

Emery AEH, Brough C, Crawfurd M, Harper P, Harris R, Oakshott G. A report on genetic registers. *J Med Genet* 1978; 15:435–42.

C. O. Carter

Geneva Declaration. See *Declarations.*

Geriatrics. The term geriatrics covers the medical care of elderly people and especially the rehabilitation of old people suffering from long-term illnesses. The management of the elderly sick is often complicated by their family and social circumstances and raises problems different from those posed by younger patients. Varying degrees of incapacity are caused by the process of ageing and by disease, in particular vascular disorders (strokes and heart diseases), respiratory, rheumatic and mental disorders. There are limits to the efficacy of treatment in many cases, although occupational therapy and physiotherapy will often restore some degree of independence. Otherwise the requirement is for nursing skills: all patients need to be kept clean and comfortable, to be fed, to have proper attention paid to bladder and bowel functions, and especially they must not be allowed to become dehydrated. With such care their dignity and humanity can be maintained.

Medical or surgical intervention in the elderly requires careful judgement. It may be justifiable to withhold certain forms of medical treatment, for example by not giving antibiotics to treat bronchopneumonia in a patient with total mental incapacity following a stroke. It may well not be right to attempt to resuscitate a moribund elderly person. Before undertaking major operations, surgeons must consider whether the procedure is justified and whether the likely benefit outweighs the disadvantages and the risk. Will the extension of life be matched by the quality of life in the extra months and years? On the other hand, modern treatment of painful illness and the care of the dying have been so much improved that there is no justification in the call for unnecessary extinction of life in an old person. In all cases the question of consent (q.v.) arises, and if the patient is incapable of rational decision, the wishes of the relatives must be considered.

Many elderly folk with some degree of illness or incapacity live alone well beyond the time when this is either prudent or safe. Removal should always be by consent and with full awareness of the situation. Doctors and social workers should take into account all the factors involved – personal, social, economic and legal. Families can sometimes take on responsibilities of care, but they may need advice on whether they should attempt this in what may be unsuitable accommodation, where the interests of children may be adversely affected, and where the demands of the patient may exceed the ability of the family to meet them. It may be right to encourage fuller use of local authority services. Each case has to be treated on its merits and there are no hard and fast rules, but careful handling will often help to produce a satisfactory solution. Care of the elderly has become a bigger problem in some societies where the principle of the extended family has tended to be undermined. In less developed countries the problem may be mitigated by a lower expectation of life. In the West, with falling birth rates, the elderly will form an increasing percentage of the population, demanding a growing share of the resources available. In the home this will put an increasing strain on families, physicians and the social services. In hospitals increasing numbers of elderly patients will stay until they die, since they need nursing care which cannot be given outside, or they have no capable person to look after them at home. This will call for a larger allocation of hospital beds and nursing staff at a time when, especially in the UK, a general reduction of services is taking place, and will pose difficult problems in national planning. Private institutions, because of their cost to the patient, can make little contribution, and private fund-

raising organizations are increasingly in competition with other simila
bodies for such monies as are available.

While many elderly people require medical treatment, all requir
care. Meeting this need may call for sacrifice at family, profession,
and national levels. (See also *Euthanasia*; *Handicapped, Duties to
Psychogeriatrics*; *Resources*; *Terminal Care*.)

Agate JN. *Geriatrics*. 2nd edn. London: Heinemann, 1963.

Anderson WF. *Practical management of the elderly*. 2nd edn. Oxfor
Blackwell, 1971.

British Medical Association. *Medicine in old age*. London: BM.
Publications, 1974.

Brocklehurst JC. *Textbook of geriatric medicine and gerontolog*
Edinburgh and London: Churchill Livingstone, 1973.

Church Information Office. *On dying well*. London: CIO, 1975.

Editorial. Is geriatrics the answer to the problems of old age? *J Me
Ethics* 1976; 2: 193–206.

Amulre

Geropsychiatry. See *Psychogeriatrics*.

H

Haemodialysis. Patients whose kidneys have ceased to function can be kept alive by intermittently circulating their blood on one side of a semipermeable membrane while an electrolyte solution similar to that of plasma filtrate circulates on the other. The substances which the kidneys have failed to excrete dialyse across the membrane and are thereby removed. If this procedure is used repeatedly it is called maintenance haemodialysis (chronic, intermittent or regular). The process takes place in what is called an artificial kidney or dialyser.

Contra-indications to this treatment vary within countries and within units in the same country. In the USA, where it is the law that any patient with terminal renal failure should be dialysed, the senile, the demented, the paralysed and those who are cardiac cripples, or who are totally unfit psychologically for haemodialysis, may have to be treated. In Britain selection is decided by those in charge of the dialysis unit. The dilemma of whom to choose is always present. The majority of patients with terminal renal failure are over 50 years of age; their prognosis is not so good as that in younger patients, and they are less likely to be bringing up a young family. There is, therefore, a natural inclination to choose the younger patients. In some units the policy is not to dialyse any person over 35 years of age whereas others will take on much older patients, excluding only those who have other infirmities which might prevent a good measure of rehabilitation. Some units will not initiate treatment of a patient who is a carrier of the hepatitis B antigen because of the risk of hepatitis to the other patients and staff. It is still debatable whether children should be dialysed unless it is in preparation for transplant with a kidney from a living related donor.

The optimum duration for maintenance haemodialysis per week is still uncertain. It depends mainly on the size of the patient, his diet, and the size and properties of the semipermeable membrane. It is customary to dialyse two to three times a week for a total of 10 to 20 hours during the week. It is reasonable to suppose that up to a point the better the patient eats, the more frequent his dialyses, and the longer he dialyses the better he will feel. On the other hand an inexperienced patient will wish to have infrequent, short dialyses. Unfortunately facilities for treatment are always less than the number of patients needing treatment, and in certain countries the financial rewards of the medical attendant increase with the number of patient on dialysis. Thus the patient's natural inclinations, though they may not benefit his health, may, if they are acceded to, enable more patients to be treated and increase the doctor's remuneration. Morbidity and survival are mainly related to age and the patient's capacity to adapt to dialysis. In the best dialysis units 5 year survival for patients up to the age of 30 years is about 90%, while for patients over 50 years it is nearer 45%. Some units will only dialyse a patient after he has agreed to have a transplant when a cadaver kidney becomes available. If the patient changes his mind after having been placed on maintenance haemodialysis, the flow of patients through the unit is curtailed, so that other patients who need treatment will not be able to be treated and will inevitably die. Such units usually try and transfer the patient to another unit that has a home dialysis programme.

In the United Kingdom the necessity to cut the costs of dialysis and the limitations on hospital dialysis has led to an expansion of home dialysis facilities, which now provide treatment for 60% of chronic renal failure patients in Britain. The revenue costs are a quarter to a third of those for hospital dialysis, and patients seem to benefit considerably from their independence of hospitals. Recent experience has shown that small local dialysis centres can also provide a cheaper and convenient way of dispensing haemodialysis:the patient dialyses himself with the help of a relative or spouse, and the saving in staff together with the re-use of dialysis circuits cuts the cost of centre dialysis to approximately that of home dialysis. Because of the limitations of such developments, centre dialysis can only be offered to those patients who agree to transplantation. Such a dynamic arrangement maximises the number of patients treated by one machine, and thus increases the number of patients to whom dialysis treatment can be offered.

Advances in peritoneal dialysis (a hitherto very expensive option but now of the same order of cost as home dialysis) have resulted in 'chronic ambulatory peritoneal dialysis' (CAPD), a process which is carried out by the patient at home and at work. This is another valuable alternative which allows treatment of patients who are unsuitable for haemodialysis, or for whom no haemodialysis equipment can be provided. Early experience in transplanting these patients has proved encouraging. (See also *Resources; Tissue Tranplant*).

Curtis JR, Williams GB. *Clinical management of chronic renal failure* Oxford: Blackwell Scientific, 1975.

H. E. de Wardener

Handicap, Mental. See *Mental Handicap.*

Handicapped, Duties to. The handicapped may suffer from one or more of a wide range of conditions of varying degrees of severity. The greatest functional disturbances result from disorders of (1) the nervous system, including the sense organs of sight and hearing; (2) the locomotor system, including bones, joints and muscles; (3) the heart and lungs and (4) the mind. Most disorders causing functional disability are likely to persist with little hope of improvement or specific cure and the chief duties of those concerned with the care of the handicapped are the comfort, relief and support of the afflicted person and the family.

The object of care must be to achieve maximum function compatible with the disabilities; the principles of hope, endeavour and enthusiasm must never be forgotten and apply to both adults and children. Medical, social and community services should be mobilized to greatest effect. The immediate and subsequent effects on the family of the affected person should be recognized and understood. First there is shock and anxiety, fear and uncertainty for the future; then reaction with anger, guilt and self-pity. A period of rejection of the handicapped person may follow, usually succeeded by a process of adaptation, adjustment and acceptance, provided that help and support are available.

Dilemmas arise in meeting the requirements of both patient and family and in balancing the duty of care and the emotional response to disability with clear medical judgement and assessment of social considerations. The presence of the handicapped within the community leads to pressures being exerted by powerful groups with public support. The choice whether the patient is best cared for at home or in an institution will be affected by the medical condition of the patient, the availability of care and welfare services, the economic and social state of the family and how they cope with emotional reactions.

In wider terms, decisions are called for at national level on the allocation of resources to the care of the handicapped. In underdeveloped countries much preventable handicap exists as a result of lack of total health care, and the welfare of those afflicted may have low priority in medical planning. Severe foreseeable handicap, arising from genetic or other prenatal causes, may, if thought fit, be dealt with by termination of early pregnancy, which raises different ethical considerations. The desire to allow the physically handicapped to lead as normal a life as possible has led to the view that sexual relations between handicapped couples in institutions should be assisted by the caring staff if coition cannot be achieved without such help. The practice is more widespread in some European countries and in North America than in the UK. In Sweden, staff sometimes wear clothing matching the bedding and room furnishings so as to camouflage their presence. In Britain views are divided and some staff find the practice repugnant. There are particular difficulties if the obligation to assist is made a condition of employment. (See also *Abortion*; *Congenital*

Malformations; *Genetic Conditions*; *Haemodialysis*; *Mental Subnormality*; *Resources*; *Social Pressures*.)

John Fry

Hastings Center. The Hastings Center is a research and educational organization devoted to exploring ethical problems of medicine, biology, the behavioral sciences, and the professions. The work of the Center encompasses research on a variety of substantive issues – death and dying, genetics, human experimentation, behavior control, and health policy – and it tries to amplify its research work by a variety of educational programs. The Hastings Center has three main areas of concentration: 1) ethical issues of biomedicine; 2) ethical issues of the behavioral and social sciences; 3) ethical issues of the professions. In addition to its research work, the Center publishes a journal, the *Hastings Center Report*, and organizes regular summer workshops, consultations, and other activities designed to make the work of the Center and the issues in the field of bioethics better known to the general public.

Address: Institute of Society, Ethics and the Life Sciences, 360 Broadway, Hastings-on-Hudson, New York, N.Y. 10706.

Daniel Callahan

Hawaii Declaration. See *Declarations*.

Health (Hospital) Advisory Services. The Health Advisory Service in England and Wales formerly known as the Hospital Advisory Service was established in 1969 and is an independent body reporting direct to the Secretary of State on certain aspects of the organization of the National Health Service.

The Scottish Hospital Advisory Service was established in 1970. It is part of the Scottish Home and Health Department and reports simultaneously to the Secretary of State for Scotland and to the relevant Health Board.

The objectives of both Services are to maintain and improve the standards of management and the organization of patient care in hospitals for mental illness, mental handicap (Scotland and Wales only), for the elderly and the young chronic sick. In England and Wales the remit extends to the relevant community services, while in Scotland advice is limited to the Hospital Service but includes the relationship between hospital and community services.

The Services are concerned to encourage and disseminate good practices, new ideas and constructive attitudes. They act as information centres on the long-stay hospitals and endeavour to promote effective co-ordination between health and local authority services. They are not inspectorates and they seek rather by persuasion and influence to assist in the local solution of local problems. They assist in future planning of facilities for patients in such hospitals. Matters of clinical judgement are excluded from the remits.

The methods of working are slightly different in the two Services. In England and Wales, since 1976, visits are undertaken jointly with the Social Work Service of the Department of Health and Social Security and include the community health services and the complementary services provided by the Social Service Departments of Local Authorities. Members of visiting teams are drawn from National Health Service or Local Authority staff in current or recent practice by secondment and serve only short periods before returning to normal duties. Teams consist typically of a consultant in the relevant specialty, a senior administrative nurse, a Health Service administrator, an occupational therapist or a physiotherapist and a social worker. Reports are confidential and, after agreement as to factual content, are submitted formally to the Secretary of State. Reports are followed up by enquiry and sometimes by further visits.

In Scotland there is one team which makes all the visits over a period of years in order to give continuity. The team consists of a Director and one other doctor from the Scottish Home and Health Department, an administrator and two nursing advisers seconded for two to four years from the National Health Service and two social work advisers from the Scottish Office. Reports are not confidential and are submitted to the Secretary of State for Scotland and the appropriate Health Board.

In England and Wales and in Scotland health authorities are encouraged to make the reports available to the health councils.

Annual reports of the Services are available to the public.

Visits raise many questions about the treatment and the quality of life of vulnerable people. For example, whether a consultant gives enough time to chronically ill patients, whether the health authority has balanced its priorities between high technology medicine and the continuing care of frail old people, what happens in a particular town to one of its citizens who becomes mentally ill. Some hospitals have a nursing style that is so kindly that people remain dependent who might be able to cope on their own if challenged. Institutions may be so staff-centred that they have lost the understanding of their real purpose. The Advisory Services often have to act as advocates for services which are otherwise unheard in the clamour for resources. Although recommendations may not be met immediately there is little doubt that reasoned argument has altered priorities in health care and led to shifts in national priorities. (See *Geriatrics*; *Handicapped, Duties to*; *Health Councils*; *Health Service Commissioners*; *Hospitals*; *Mental Handicap*; *Mental Illness*; *Psychogeriatrics*; *Quality Assurance*; *Resources*; *Teamwork*.)

Annual Report of the Health Advisory Service. London: HMSO, 1976.

Baker AA. The future of the Health Advisory Service. *Br Med J* 1979; 1: 967–8.

DHSS Circular HC(76)21.

Klein R. An alternative approach to audit, *Br Med J* 1976; 2: 597–8.

Scottish Hospital Advisory Service. Quinquennial Report. SHHD, 1977.

SHHD Circular 1975(Gen)97.

Welsh Office Circular WHC(76)19.

D. H. Dick
W. T. Thom

Health Care Systems. Health care can be provided either by private enterprise or by the State or by elements of both. Private systems may be paid for by the individual, usually through insurance schemes, and the benefits obtainable are proportional to the ability to pay; those who can pay neither directly nor by insurance are covered by charity. In general, therefore, completely private systems are unsatisfactory since they make inadequate provision for the needy and the tendency has been towards the development of State systems of one kind or another.

The involvement of the State may take one of three forms. (1) It can be minimal, leaving most people to provide for their own care out of their own resources but providing services for the needy using funds obtained by taxing those more able to pay. (2) It can allow a mixed system, one type of which exists in the UK. Here the State provides services for all, and the costs are met by taxation and compulsory contributions, but those who wish to do so may pay for private care. It is not possible in Britain to avoid paying for State-run services, but this is a variation of the mixed system which could be adopted. (3) It may be total, and all private medicine be abolished by law.

It can be argued that the provision of care by the State inhibits the exercise of charitable giving, but in a mixed system at least there are many causes which need support and which provide practical care and promote research which the State service cannot or does not offer. A further objection lies in the threat which could exist to a doctor's clinical autonomy (q.v.) from the fact that the State is virtually a monopoly employer and could (and has, for example, in the case of some transplant operations) lay down limits to freedom of practice and the prescription of drugs.

It is said that the provision of care is so important that it demands the most efficient system to sustain it and should not depend on people's goodwill. This begs the question whether a State system *is* the most efficient. Apart from the problems of an overlarge administrative and 'back-up' staff, it is debatable whether a State system provides the best basis on which a doctor can exercise his skills and initiative to the greatest advantage, and also whether it encourages the most efficient use of resources by the public (see *Health Education*; *Patients*).

However, in view of the costs involved, it is certainly doubtful whether anybody other than the State could offer a comprehensive service without imposing unacceptable financial burdens on those who use it. Equally, the principle of a State medical service requires that its costs should not in general be directly linked to the provision of care, so as to avoid the possibility of patients being saddled with heavy expenses at a time of physical or mental distress, which might deter them from using the service at all. However, such directly linked systems of payment are successfully applied to some of the less costly features of health care such as dentistry and to optional items such as prophylactic inoculations for foreign travel, although the deterrent effect in the case of dental care may be greater than is desirable.

These arguments can be employed not only against a totally free system, but also against the first of the mixed systems referred to above. The North American pattern, which comes into that category, provides examples of how serious and prolonged illness can bring severe financial hardship to the sufferers.

The main arguments now centre on whether State intervention should be partial or total. Considerations here have, in the past, been mainly political, with socialists stressing equality and the abolition of privilege while non-socialists assert that all-embracing State systems are wasteful, an infringement of human liberty and discourage human responsibility. Increasingly today, however, it is being found necessary to reappraise the methods of funding medical care, as rapidly increasing costs threaten to outstrip the resources (q.v.) available, thus calling into question the practicability of total provision of care by the State. (See also *Private Practice*; *State Health Services*.)

Steiner H. The just provision of health care: A reply to Elizabeth Telfer. *J Med Ethics* 1976; 2: 185–9.
Telfer E. Justice, welfare and health care. *J Med Ethics* 1976; 2: 107–11.

John Rivers

Health Councils. Community Health Councils (CHCs), and in Scotland Local Health Councils (LHCs), were set up by statute[1,2] to represent the local community's interests in the health service to those responsible for managing it, and to give the public a statutory right to advise in the planning and provision of health services.

A Health Council has no executive power but is a consultative body with a statutory duty to 'keep under review the operation of the health service in its district and make recommendations for the improvement of such service or otherwise advise the area health authority'. In turn the health authority has a duty to provide information to the HC about the planning and operation of the health service in its district and is required to consult the HC about any proposals for the development and alteration of services.

CHCs have between eighteen and thirty-six members, of whom at least one half are appointed by relevant local authorities, at least one third by voluntary organizations with an interest in the NHS, and the remainder for their special knowledge or experience by Regional Health Authorities.[3] LHCs have between twelve and thirty members of whom at least one third are appointed by local authorities, and the remainder by Health Boards, the majority following consultation with voluntary organizations and Trade Unions, and two or three for their special knowledge or experience[4]. Members do not act merely as spokesmen for the particular groups from which they are drawn, but are expected to share a common concern for the quality of health care provision in their district and to represent the interests of the community as a whole.

It has been suggested that, since HCs are the creation of those responsible for providing health care, they cannot unequivocally represent the interests of consumers, and since members are not democratically elected to office, they cannot claim to represent the public in their district. In view of the substance of both these objections, HCs have sought to establish their autonomy and to demonstrate their freedom and independence over against the authorities which set them up. They have also encouraged members of the public, both individually and in groups, to communicate with them and have sponsored public meetings and surveys of opinion to determine the views of the public in their district on specific issues.

HCs are expected to consider: the quality, effectiveness and adequacy of services; forward planning and alterations; cooperation between the health services and local authorities; facilities for patients and relatives; waiting lists; catering and other supporting services in the NHS institutions; specialist groups and services; the relationship between the health authority and the public it serves, in health education, for example. HCs have not been given the function of investigating and reporting on individual complaints which remain the direct responsibility of health service management and, where appropriate, the Health Service Commissioner (q.v.). They do not consider the clinical treatment of individual patients, but are ready to give advice to complainants on how and where to lodge complaints, and to act as 'patient's friend' when requested. They are also entitled to information about the volume and type of complaints received about a service or institution.

HCs, on their own initiative or at the request of the health authorities, have frequently discussed ethical issues including clinical autonomy, abortion and abortion counselling, sterilization of children under 16, the availability of oral contraceptives, fluoridation of public water supplies, male midwives, the right of patients to know the diagnosis of their illness, consent procedures, parents' refusal to consent to blood transfusions, psychosurgery, complaints procedures, repeat prescriptions, organ transplants, homoeopathy, confidentiality, general practitioner deputizing arrangements, drug safety, seat belt legislation, tobacco and alcohol advertising, and priorities in health care. It is not clear what factors influence the opinions of HC members on these issues. Some canvass local opinion through surveys of the general public or consultation with local organizations. Some feel they are themselves competent to comment without consultation.

Health authorities have been asked (DHSS Circular HSC (1S)153) to consider appointing a lay member of a HC to serve on its ethical committees, which deal with submissions for clinical research. Many such appointments have now been made.

The Association of CHCs in England and Wales (ACHCEW) and the Association of Scottish LHCs (ASLHCs) have been set up to provide a forum for the exchange of information and opinion and to create a strong consumer voice at national level.

The fundamental issue underlying the purpose and function of HCs is how far the public (through HCs) can or should determine the style and quality of health care provision. There is now world wide recognition of the need for public participation in health care policy making. The World Health Organization has set out its approach in seven basic principles, the fourth of which states: 'The local population should be actively involved in the formulation and implementation of health care activities so that health care can be brought into line with local needs and priorities. Decisions upon what are the community needs requiring solution should be based upon a continuing dialogue between the people and the services.'[5] Wilson[6] maintains that 'in any discussion or conference on health, truth is best served by a wide representation of civil interests' and Hallas and Fallon[7] state that a health service should be developed 'from the bottom up' and that it is vital that 'professionals take account of the non-professionals.'

The apathy of the healthy towards health services and the understandable reluctance of patients to complain about deficiencies in the service are major problems for HCs. It is to be hoped that HCs will not only reflect public opinion on health matters but help to shape it; that they will not only monitor the operation of the NHS in their district but seek new and better ways of promoting health through increased public awareness and participation, and through a heightened sense of responsibility on the part of members of the community. The right of access of every person in Britain to NHS care is assumed, but can a citizen claim this right unless he also claims the responsibility for promoting health in his personal and corporate life?

(See also *Health Education*; *Hospitals*; *Patients' Association*; *State Health Services*; etc.)

1. National Health Service Reorganisation Act 1973, Sections 7 and 9. London: HMSO, 1973.
2. National Health Service (Scotland) Act 1972, Section 14. London: HMSO, 1972.
3. The National Health Service (Community Health Councils) Regulations 1973: Statutory Instruments 1973, No 2217.
4. National Health Service (Local Health Councils) (Scotland) Regulations 1974: Statutory Instruments 1974, No 2177 (S.200).
5. World Health Organization Assembly, May 1975.
6. Wilson M. *Health is for people*. London: Darton, Longman & Todd, 1975: 90.
7. Hallas J, Fallon B. *Mounting the health guard – A handbook for CHC members*. London: Nuffield Provincial Hospitals Trust, 1974: 13.
8. Bochel D, Maclaren M. Local health councils: 'Institutionalising the consumer voice.' In: Clarke M, Drucker H, eds. *The year book of Scottish Government*, 1979.
9. Hallas J. *CHCs in action*. London: Nuffield Provincial Hospitals Trust, 1976.
10. Klein R, Lewis J. *The politics of consumer representation – a study of community health councils*. London: Centre for Studies in Social Policy, 1976.

T. Stewart McGregor

Health Economics. See *Resources*.

Health Education. Health education in some form has been used for more than a century in all countries with developed services. The message was first about environmental conditions and was backed up by powers of enforcement related especially to nuisances, unfit food and the control of communicable disease. The development of personal health services by local government agencies needed a more persuasive approach, but still involved some powers of enforcement, for instance in the School Health Service. Britain had compulsory vaccination against smallpox until 1908 and some enforcement up to 1948, but from then on immunization programmes in this country have been developed by persuasion, not by compulsion such as some other countries still use. The large recent improvements in protection against infectious disease have therefore required much greater attention to education of the public about health. Campaigns for specific prophylaxis against particular infections are relatively simple affairs which can be supported by firm scientific evidence about the anticipated benefits. They involve the use of simple technical procedures with only very small risks. Nevertheless they still illustrate the ethical problems that occur with other educational programmes which are intended to produce modifications of life style or environment for the improvement of health. There are risks, small though they may be, in any immunizing procedure and parents and others must be told about them. It is easy for the professional to appreciate that the one in a million risk of cerebral involvement after administration of measles vaccine is trivial compared with the risks of clinical measles, but failure to explain this could well discredit immunization as a whole and is unfair to parents.

The explanation of straightforward technical procedures is not sufficient unless it is backed by constant vigilance in controlling the safety and efficacy of the agents used, and in assessing the continued need for their use. For example, routine vaccination during infancy against smallpox ceased to be recommended in Canada, Britain and the USA as soon as the risk of smallpox from abroad had fallen far enough, and well before other European countries relaxed their requirements. The ethical obligation on the health educator is to ensure that the message is justified and the action commended to the individual is in his own interest. The principle was illustrated by the way in which vitamin concentrates for infants were advocated for years despite the fact that progressive change in the content of infant foods and in patterns of feeding increased the supply from ordinary dietary sources until some infants were even endangered by excessive intakes of vitamin D. The message must be right initially; it must be discontinued or changed if circumstances change, even though the educator must then eat his words.

Health education is now changing because the simpler procedures in preventive medicine have become part of the accepted pattern of living in countries such as Britain. What is now needed is reaffirmation and adjustment from time to time rather than crusades. The new targets are factors in the accepted pattern of living which can be varied with advantage to health and may be components in ordinary social exchanges to which many people attach value. There are still new factors with specific ill effects of which the public needs to be informed such as new harmful chemicals, and there are problems of abuse of other chemicals such as LSD, but modification of life style offers the greatest opportunity of health promotion. However, this raises an ethical problem, since in trying to modify life styles the health professional may fail to pay due regard to the impact of that change on the life of the individual. The addicted smoker is damaging his health but the extent to which he should be made to accept guilt, perhaps in regard to his family, is not a simple decision to be made by his professional adviser who happens to be a bitter opponent of tobacco smoking.

The arguments against the use of tobacco and alcohol can be deployed with vehemence adjusted to the occasion, and official pronouncements in these areas are reinforced by those of voluntary agencies such as Action on Smoking and Health (ASH) and of temperance societies. The arguments for other changes, such as the reduction of fats in the diet or the substitution of polyunsaturated for saturated fats, are on less secure bases. There is a great temptation to be seen to be active against the leading cause of death, cardiovascular disease, but the health educator must ask himself how far he is justified in pressing the case beyond a balanced statement of the evidence. One can choose a measure oneself on incomplete evidence, but it is not right to promote national changes at quite so low a level of assurance. There is never unanimous support, but there is an obligation on the health educator to make the best synthesis of informed views he can, and to subject it to expert scrutiny. The level of probability of both the safety and effectiveness of the course commended in the public context in which it is to be used must be high. Even the safe and effective measure of fluoridation of drinking water is open to the objection that the objector cannot avoid using something he may think unsafe. The campaigner may be frustrated but he must accept that there is this opposing viewpoint.

In the UK the central responsibility rests with the Health Departments of the four countries, advised by their expert advisory machinery and in consultation with relevant professional bodies. The peripheral responsibilities rest with Area Health Authorities which are expected to have Health Education staff. The autonomous Health Education Council and the Scottish Health Education Unit mount programmes at the national level, provide material and advice for Health Authorities and conduct research into methods and efficacy. For much effective health education the individual doctor or other health professional uses his own direct influence with patients and for this he needs a great deal more help and information than he is given.

Health education against smoking, the abuse of alcohol and the wrong choice of foods is made far more difficult by the freedom accorded to industry to present the use of these products as desirable and socially advantageous. Some other governments (thirteen in all, including the Republic of Ireland) have enacted laws to prohibit or restrict severely the promotion of tobacco products. The British Government has so far refused to do so, relying on 'Health Hazard' warnings and on the voluntary collaboration of an industry which is naturally resistant to its own contraction. It is at least arguable that the advocacy of anti-health behaviour at a cost more than a hundred-fold the funds available to promote health should be restricted in the interest of personal freedom of choice. (See *Communication; Fluoridation; Immunization; Pharmaceutical Industry; Sex Education; Tobacco Smoking.*)

Campbell AV. *Moral dilemmas in medicine*. 2nd edn. Edinburgh and London: Churchill Livingstone, 1975.
Cohen, Chairman, *Health education*. Report of a joint committee of the Central and Scottish Health Services Councils. London: HMSO, 1964.

Dalzell-Ward AJ. 1964. *A textbook of health education.* London: Tavistock, 1975.

DHSS. *Reorganisation of National Health Services and of Local Government: operation and development of services.* Circ. HRC(74)27, 1974.

Tones BK. Professionalism, ethics and behaviour change. *Health Education Journal* 1974; 33:2.

World Health Organization. Report of an Expert Committee on Health Education. *Technical Report Series 89.* Geneva: WHO, 1954.

World Health Organization. *Research in health education. report of a working group.* Technical Report Series 432. Geneva: WHO, 1954.

George Godber

IN GENERAL PRACTICE. Health promotion through education is increasingly recognized as a central component of good general practice involving not only modifications in behaviour and life-style but also in promoting in the individual greater personal responsibility for health and an informed use of the health services. The general practitioner, who on average has a one-to-one consultation with three quarters of the population each year, is particularly well placed to modify public behaviour and this form of health education becomes an integral part of routine consultation. The health visitor has a primary role as a health educator with particular responsibility to mothers in pregnancy, children up to the age of five, the handicapped and the elderly.

A. G. Donald

Health Service Commissioners. Health Service Commissioners for England, Wales and Scotland were established under the NHS (Scotland) Act 1972 and the NHS Reorganization Act 1973. The offices have hitherto been held jointly by a single person (who has also in fact been the Parliamentary Commissioner for Administration (Parliamentary Ombudsman)).

The Health Service Commissioner (Health Service Ombudsman) opened his office for the receipt of complaints in October 1973. He is empowered by Statute to investigate complaints from people who claim that they have sustained injustice or hardship as a result of an alleged failure of a regional or area health authority to provide a service which it was a function of that body to provide, or as a result of an alleged failure in a service provided by such a body, or as a result of maladministration in the provision of a service by such a body. Actions of all employees of health authorities, professional or not, are investigable by the Commissioner. The actions of family practitioners (who are not employed by health authorities but have a contractual relationship with them) are not investigable. The actions of Family Practitioner Committees, but not of their Medical Service Committees, are investigable.

Moreover, there is a further important and relevant limitation on the Commissioner's powers. He is not empowered to investigate complaints into matters which, in his opinion, involve the exercise of clinical judgment. The limitations on the Commissioner's powers, which exclude the investigation of complaints against family practitioners and of all questions involving clinical judgment, mean that broadly speaking questions involving medical ethics fall outside his jurisdiction and continue to be dealt with by the Medical Service Committees of Family Practitioner Committees, the professional associations and, in extreme cases, the law. The Commissioner's investigations generally concern complaints of administrative and managerial failure or inefficiency, bad communications and poor standards (other than of medical treatment) in hospitals – food, cleanliness, nursing care, etc. Even in such complaints, however, the actions of doctors and nurses frequently fall to be examined, for instance where questions of lack of communication or of courtesy are alleged. Moreover, the Commissioner may frequently seek information about actions taken in the exercise of clinical judgment where such information seems to him to be essential background to the case which he is investigating. The Commissioner may then report the information he has been given in his case report to the complainant without, however, commenting on it in any way. Within these limitations, experience has shown that doctors and nurses are ready to discuss frankly with the Commissioner's investigating officers all aspects of a case which is under investigation.

Serious questions of medical ethics almost invariably involve questions of clinical judgment. The Act excludes from the Commissioner's jurisdiction questions which 'in his opinion' involve the exercise of clinical judgment. There are obviously border line cases which arise from time to time and, to assist the Commissioner in settling the question of jurisdiction in such cases, he has a group of advisers nominated by the Presidents of the Royal Colleges. In one case, involving a complaint about the sterilization of a young girl, the Commissioner consulted a member of the group of advisers as to whether the operation was decided upon on clinical, rather than social, grounds: and, in that case, the Commissioner investigated the complaint in its entirety. Cases which come so close to this sensitive ground are rare but there are many cases where the Commissioner's case report will comment on actions taken by a doctor in connection with that case, though remaining silent on the purely clinical aspects.

Many complaints addressed to the Commissioner are concerned in substance with clinical treatment. The Commissioner always explains to the complainant that he cannot investigate this but offers explicitly or implicitly to investigate other issues which arise out of the complaint. At the end of what may often be a lengthy investigation, the Commissioner's Report gives little satisfaction to the complainant, since the main issue that concerned the complainant remains uninvestigated. What changes, if any, should be made in this present system has been the subject of reports by the Davies Committee and the Select Committee of the House of Commons on the Parliamentary Commissioner for Administration. Any change would require legislation which, so far at least, seems likely to be opposed by the medical profession. Any substantial change in the powers of the Commissioner would completely change the nature of his office and the calls upon it. (See also *Clinical Autonomy; Health (Hospital) Advisory Services.*)

1. DHSS and the Welsh Office. *Report of the Committee on Hospital Complaints Procedures* (the Davies Committee). London: HMSO, 1973.
2. Select Committee on the Parliamentary Commissioner for Administration. *Independent review of hospital complaints on the NHS* (First Report). London: HMSO, 1977.

I. V. Pugh

Heart Transplant. See *Tissue Transplant.*

Helsinki Declaration. See *Declarations.*

Hereditary Disease. A condition transmitted from parents to children and already manifest or latent at birth. Some infections, such as syphilis, are transmissible in this way, but these are less commonly found where treatment of the adult is available. Most hereditary disease now occurring in developed countries is genetically determined. The ethical implications are discussed under: *Amniocentesis; Chromosome Disorders; Eugenics; Genetic Conditions.*

Hindu Medicine. The medical lore (*Ayurveda*) of India from ancient until modern times. The traditional texts, attributed to Charaka, Susruta, and Vagbhata, were settled before about AD 700. They handle certain ethical questions incidentally. Ethics is the proper concern of the *dharmasastra* (the 'science of righteousness'). Physicians were required to be dextrous, learned in the precepts of the science of healing from a teacher, tried in practice, and pure. 'Pure' means uncorrupt. They were required to cure, or at any rate to treat, even the poor and the stranger: but the payment of the fee was recognized as a factor in effecting the cure. Although the physician was to treat the patient honestly, he was under no obligation to treat the terminally sick: on the contrary he should not treat one who is (apparently) incurable, one who is hostile to physicians, or who is the subject or object of enmity on the part of the 'king' (i.e. the executive).

In return for the physician's acceptance of the duty to treat him, the patient must comport himself obediently, and *in general* regard the physician as a privileged person like his parent or preceptor, e.g. abstrain from dispute with him in any context. The physician must respect totally the confidence of the patient, and it is for this reason that in ancient times spies masqueraded as physicians. There was an exception. Wounds and self-inflicted complaints should be reported to the 'king', lest the physician be accused of complicity in crimes. This rule (the regularity of which is not beyond doubt) stems from the fact that physicians were licensed by the 'king', or are at least supposed to have been. In the case of a difficult operation, or treatments hazardous to life, even where the patient gives his consent, a previous notification to the 'king' was recommended, and perhaps even regular, in order to protect the physician. It will be observed that a physician was held, by the *dharmasastra*, to be immune to suit for damages on the part of a dissatisfied patient, but was liable to a fine for 'falsely' treating him. This is perhaps more practical than it seems at first sight. Incompetence, negligence, and malice are all embraced by the term 'falsely', and no doubt the fine would be proportionate to the nature of the offence.

A physician, according to the medical texts, must not attend persons belonging to the following classes: hunters, fowlers, outcastes, and evil-doers. The reasons are complex. He might be infected with their anti-social or violent ways, and become, at second hand, guilty of violence against life. As we have seen, the patient's fee had its psychological significance in the cure; the physician could sue for a reasonable fee where one was not previously agreed. But the fee once obtained was not suitable for gifts in charity, etc., since the earnings by his profession were tainted by the ritual impurity involved in the function of medicine, and the spiritual condition of the patients. Granted that Hinduism accepts the belief that, though many sicknesses are due to the current faults of the patient, many are due to unexpiated sins incurred in previous lives, the Hindu physician was still expected to treat a patient, provided he was not incurable, and provided he did not belong to one of the disqualified classes (above). Yet his earnings were tainted.

The topic of abortion figures in medical texts in the context of saving a mother's life, which, it is agreed, takes precedence over the life of a fetus in a case where a choice has to be made. Non-medical abortions naturally did occur, and there is no question that to procure an abortion was a sin (Manu VI, 90, VIII.87, 317, XI.88). The physician does not figure in such contexts or such discussions. Suicide, deprecated by the *dharmasastra*, was allowed, until the early 19th century, on various religious grounds. The terminally sick were allowed to end their lives in prescribed ways. The physician neither partook of, nor prevented, such measures. The medical art had as one of its prerequisites the patient's will to live.

Medical experiments were unknown. Surgeons could practise upon decomposed corpses (if available), and, more frequently, upon suitable inanimate objects in order to acquire dexterity with the instruments. Experiments with animals were (it seems) unknown, since the similarity between animal and human doctoring was not regarded as better than superficial.

Ayurvedic medicine is widely practised today and the indigenous systems of medicine (Ayurvedic and Unani) are, along with homoeopathy, widely popular. The practitioners are, in general, within the purview of professional associations set up by or under certain statutes, but these do not affect professional ethics. The public are not conscious of any discrepancy between the ethics of Western-trained physicians and those trained in the indigenous systems, e.g. regarding relationships with female patients.

Though an Ayurvedic and Unani College (1912) is affiliated to Delhi University, training in India is haphazard. Indian 'allopathic' (scientific) medicine still fights for international recognition, and it is not surprising that there is no common professional standard of medical practice as between foreign and indigenous systems.[1] There are no women practitioners of Ayurvedic medicine, and this is among the reasons limiting the scope of medical services. Provincial governmental agencies tend to back Ayurvedic training, but the results lack uniformity and conviction.[2] The Medical Termination of Pregnancy Act, 1971, which extends the right to terminate to cases where contraception has failed, is criticized as only partially countering back-street abortions, but it is remarkable that only practitioners qualified under the aegis of the Indian Medical Council (i.e. in 'western' medicine) may terminate under the Act.[3]

1. Jeffery R. Recognizing India's doctors: the institutionalization of medical dependency, 1918–39. *Modern Asian studies* 1979; 301–26.
2. Brass P. The politics of Ayurvedic education. In: SH Rudolph, L. Rudolph, eds. *Education and politics in India.* New Delhi, 1972.
3. Bose AK, Chattopadhyay S, Jacob A. Articles on the Medical Termination of Pregnancy Act, 1971. *Journal of the Indian Law Institute* 1971:16.
Basham, AL, Dunn FL. In: C Leslie, ed. *Asian medical systems: a comparative study.* Berkeley, 1976.
Dash B. *Fundamentals of Ayurvedic medicine.* Delhi, 1978.
Jolly J. *Indian medicine* (Trans C. G. Kashikar). Poona, 1951.
Kane PV. *History of Dharmasastra*, III, 939; IV, 302, 308, 525, 604–6. Poona, 1946.
Mukhopadhyaya G. *History of Indian medicine*, vol. II. Calcutta, 1926:1–89.

Sternbach L. *Juridical studies in ancient Indian law*, I, Chap. 6. Delhi, 1965.

Zimmer HR. *Hindu medicine.* Baltimore, 1948.

Zimmermann F. From classic texts to learned practice: methodological remarks on the study of Indian medicine. *Soc Sci Med* 1978; 12:97–103.

J. Duncan M. Derrett

Hippocratic Oath. Various versions of the *Oath* exist, but the following text can be taken as representative:

'I swear by Apollo the physician, by Aesculapius, Hygeia and Panacea, and I take to witness all the gods, all the goddesses, to keep according to my ability and my judgement the following Oath:

'To consider dear to me as my parents him who taught me this art; to live in common with him and if necessary to share my goods with him; to look upon his children as my own brothers, to teach them this art if they so desire without fee or written promise; to impart to my sons and the sons of the master who taught me and the disciples who have enrolled themselves and have agreed to the rules of the profession, but to these alone, the precepts and the instruction. I will prescribe regimen for the good of my patients according to my ability and my judgement and never do harm to anyone. To please no one will I prescribe a deadly drug, nor give advice which may cause his death. Nor will I give a woman a pessary to procure abortion. But I will preserve the purity of my life and my art. I will not cut for stone, even for patients in whom the disease is manifest; I will leave this operation to be performed by practitioners (specialists in this art). In every house where I come I will enter only for the good of my patients, keeping myself far from all intentional ill-doing and all seduction, and especially from the pleasures of love with women or with men, be they free or slaves. All that may come to my knowledge in the exercise of my profession or outside of my profession or in daily commerce with men, which ought not to be spread abroad, I will keep secret and will never reveal. If I keep this oath faithfully, may I enjoy my life and practise my art, respected by all men and in all times; but if I swerve from it or violate it, may the reverse be my lot.'[1] (See also *Declarations; Hippocratic Tradition.*)

1. *Dorland's American illustrated medical dictionary.* 25th edn. Philadelphia: Saunders, 1974.

Hippocratic Tradition. None of the deontological writings that bear the name of Hippocrates (fl. 420 BC) can be ascribed to him with confidence, although the earliest of them, the *Oath*, was probably written during his lifetime. Its religious tone and language (see *Hippocratic Oath*) and its emphasis on secret knowledge suggests that it was written for a restricted group of adepts and had no universal application. Although its injunctions about the doctor's personal morality and conduct can be parallelled in later texts in the Hippocratic Corpus, the *Law*, the *Doctor*, *Decorum*, *Precepts* and *Epidemics VI*, their advice is almost always from the point of view of the utility of appropriate and decorous conduct to the doctor in securing the patient's recovery and continued approbation. The *Oath* is introspective, the other texts more socially orientated.

The earliest extant references to the *Oath*, by Scribonius Largus (fl. 40 AD) and Erotian (fl. 60 AD), show that to them it represented an ideal, not an essential prerequisite, especially in a society where both abortion and suicide were commonplace. Nor is there anything in the fragments of Galen's commentary on the Oath (c. 180 AD) to suggest that he regarded it as obligatory. Not until a rhetorical discourse of Libanius (c. 370 AD) is it implied that all doctors must assent to its clauses before practising. Yet its form was not fixed, and the ease with which details could be changed enabled it to be smoothly adopted by Christians, Jews and Muslims alike (see *Islam*). It is under the Arabs that it is first administered by the civil power as an entry requirement and guarantee of competence for the medical profession; and where we first hear of conflicts between the state and doctors basing themselves on the words of the *Oath*. A similar development occurred in Western Europe, where Christian versions were administered on entry to the medical profession, and continued to be sworn by intending physicians in Scottish and continental medical schools down to this century. Although its opening invocation and its limitations on the spread of medical knowledge are no longer relevant to modern practice, its spirit influences much of the ethics of health care (see e.g. *Medical Ethics*; *Abortion*; *Confidentiality*; *Doctor/Patient Relationship*; *Euthanasia*; *Professional Practice*) and it is frequently invoked as normative by the layman.

The emphasis in the Hippocratic tradition on the individuality of the patient's illness and on the need to co-operate with nature is still influential, but the other ethical tracts, together with an Arabic *Testament of Hippocrates*, although studied as examples of good conduct and effective practice, were never regarded as providing a general code of medical morality.

Deichgräber K. *Medicus gratiosus*. Wiesbaden: Steiner Verlag, 1970.

Edelstein L. *The Hippocratic Oath*. Baltimore: Johns Hopkins University Press, 1943.

Edelstein L. The professional ethics of the Greek physician. *Bull Hist Med* 1956; 30: 391–419.

Harig G, Kollesch J. Der Hippokratische Eid. *Philologus* 1978; 122: 157: 76.

Jones WHS. *The doctor's oath*. Cambridge University Press, 1924.

MacKinney LC. Medical ethics and etiquette in the Early Middle Ages. *Bull Hist Med* 1952; 26: 1–31.

Vivian Nutton

Homoeopathy. A system of medicine based on treatment with very small amounts of drugs which in high dosage cause symptoms similar to those of the disease. The founder of homoeopathy, Samuel Hahnemann (1755–1843), was a German physician who found contemporary forms of medical treatment such as bleeding and drugging barbaric and ineffective. A chance observation that cinchona – the Peruvian bark from which quinine is extracted – caused symptoms similar to those of malaria led him to experiment with other drugs and to develop the principle that effective remedies should stimulate an artificial disease as similar as possible to the illness to be treated. This principle he summed up in the Latin phrase *similia similibus curentur* – 'let like be treated with like'.

Next, in a long process of practical experiments, he developed the theory of potentiation by dilution. This requires the dose of the drug to be lessened by repeatedly blending it with a neutral substance such as pure sugar or water, discarding 90% on each occasion. In this process either the drug is each time ground with pestle and mortar or, in the case of liquid tinctures, is violently shaken. It is then further diluted and the process repeated. Clearly in time the amount of drug remaining becomes infinitesimal, but homoeopathic physicians have great faith in these so-called high potencies. For example, Hahnemann himself treated a child with scarlet fever with a dose of 1/432,999 of a grain (about .000013 mg) of belladonna but in retrospect he thought the dose too large. Since Hahnemann's day the range of homoeopathic remedies has been much increased, but the principle of treatment remains the same: essentially the belief is that the body will heal itself if encouraged and assisted by remedies proved effective by practical experience and tailored to the physical and psychological characteristics of the individual patient.

However, homoeopathy differs from other non-orthodox systems of medicine in the extent of the areas of overlap. In Britain most homoeopathic physicians have had a conventional medical training and are on the *Medical Register*. Homoeopathy is taught as a postgraduate course, and shares with orthodox medicine the use of modern diagnostic methods. The Royal National Homoeopathic Hospital is part of the National Health Service, and the surgical treatment given to its patients is exactly the same as that given in any other hospital. Indeed some doctors combine the practice of homoeopathic and conventional medicine: they may use antibiotics for bacterial infections such as pneumonia but prefer a homoeopathic remedy for a condition such as rheumatoid arthritis for which there is no specific, curative treatment.

In consequence there need be no ethical conflict between homoeopathy and orthodox medicine. A doctor's ethical obligation to his patient is to recommend the treatment he thinks best on the basis of his training and experience. That treatment may be homoeopathic; but so long as the doctor explains to his patient that he is prescribing non-conventional treatment and the patient accepts it, his ethical obligation is discharged. It would not be right, however, for a patient to be treated with homoeopathic remedies without some evidence that he or she understood the differences between conventional and homoeopathic theories. In some cases a patient may ask his or her general practitioner for referral to a homoeopathic physician; and again the GP's first obligation is to explain to the patient that homoeopathy is out of line with conventional medicine. However, if he believes that homoeopathic treatment will not benefit the patient, he should say so; and he may reasonably refuse to make the referral requested.

Referral to or treatment by a homoeopathic doctor who has no registrable medical qualification is affected by the same ethical restrictions as referral to fringe practitioners: a doctor who sends patients to such a non-qualified practitioner may expose himself to a charge of formal 'covering.' (See also *General Practice*.)

DHSS Circular. *Role of Homoeopathy in the NHS*. London: DHSS, 28 March 1979, No 79/89.

Tony Smith

Homosexuality. The terms homosexual and lesbianism refer to the tendency, in men and women respectively, to be sexually aroused by persons of their own, rather than the opposite, sex.

A widely accepted statistic[1] is that 4% of males are exclusively homosexual and a further 37% have had significant homosexual experience between adolescence and old age. There is no accepted figure for lesbianism. Kenyon[2] estimates that 1 in 45 of the adult female population are persistently and exclusively homosexual.

HOMOSEXUALITY

People can be more or less homosexually orientated. Kinsey *et al*[1] used a 7-point rating scale with the extremes occupied by 'wholly' heterosexual or homosexual persons; the mid-point by persons equally orientated towards both sexes (bisexual) and intermediary positions by those who are more homo- than heterosexual, or more hetero- than homosexual. Ratings for this scale are made on the person's behaviour and thoughts regarding homosexuality.

Homosexuality also involves different levels of a person's functioning which do not always co-relate. Thus a behaviourally heterosexual man might have a predominantly homosexual phantasy life. He may, for example, use homosexual thoughts in order to be sexually potent with his wife. If the reaction of that part of the nervous system subserving sexual functioning (autonomic nervous system) is also considered, penile erections may be stimulated by explicitly homosexual display material although the person concerned practises heterosexual behaviour and professes a heterosexual phantasy life. This might occur, for example, after apparently 'successful' treatment for homosexuality based on planned (and agreed) modifications of the orientation of sexual behaviour and sexual thoughts.

Origins of homosexuality

Human patterns of expression of the major drives, sexuality and aggression, are varied indeed. There are inborn components and both have a long psychological, familial and social learning history so that their expression is diverse. A highly aggressive man may commit murder or suicide; become a criminal or a policeman. A highly sexed man may succeed as a husband and father; as a gigolo or as a celibate priest.

The origins of male homosexuality are probably multidimensional: inborn, psychological and social factors are involved but the precise 'mix' is uncertain. The possibility of inborn factors is a current interest. These relate to the mode of action and timing ('sensitive periods') of the male sex hormone testosterone on the intrauterine sex-typing of the central nervous system and the effect of this on adult sexual orientation.[3] As yet, however, this potentially exciting area of research is of little clinical relevance.

The contribution of the environment, particularly early family experiences which may have both conscious and unconscious ramifications, seem to many psychotherapists overwhelming in their importance particularly the frequently described family constellation of dominant mother and ineffective, negated or absent father.[4] The role of chance environmental events, such as homosexual seduction leading to the development of homosexuality or unfortunate heterosexual experience leading to heterophobia, are favoured by behaviouristically inclined observers[5] but seem unconvincing because over simple; too much is left to chance. In fact a criticism of all psychological explanations to date is that over-simple explanatory hypotheses are used to account for extremely complex behaviour. This inadequacy in relation to homosexuality is perhaps emphasized by asking the reader a simple but opposite question: why are the majority of persons sexually orientated towards the opposite sex? Is this inborn (e.g. to preserve the species) or is it in some way psychologically or socially acquired, for example by sex role stereotyping?

Can homosexuals be characterized?

Can any useful generalizations be made about male homosexuals? Psychiatrists see only a small, highly selected group of homosexuals often because of problems which may be only indirectly related to their homosexuality e.g. depression, suicide attempt, occupational problems etc. Information is however available from surveys made of homosexuals and lesbians in the community, contacted through homophile organizations. A carefully planned and executed research is that of Saghir et al[6,7,8]. Apart from sexual orientation there is remarkably little in terms of social-demographic or psychiatric criteria reliably differentiating homosexual from single heterosexual men used as a control group. These social and psychiatric findings are complemented and confirmed by the direct study of homosexual behaviour in the laboratory.[9]

LESBIANISM

Psychiatrists relatively seldom see lesbians. In an article orientated towards ethical issues it is not profitable to discuss possible reasons, although these may well lie in the social, rather than the psychiatric area. Thus male homosexuals, particularly under the stimulus of assertive homophile organizations, tend to be more publicly admitting of homosexuality even to the extent of behaving in what sociologists call a 'secondarily deviant' manner, i.e. not only being homosexual but playing the part of being homosexual. These pressures are sometimes helpful to male homosexuals who are clear about their wish to 'come out' in the gay world. For some young men however who are unsure of their sexual orientation such pressures may add to their sexual identity crisis. They may be dissuaded, for example, in their desire to discuss their attitudes and confusions with a counsellor or psychotherapist. So far as a comparison between the sexual behaviour of the male and female homosexual is concerned Saghir et al[7] confirmed in particular that homosexual relationships were strikingly different between male and female. Homosexual men were significantly more involved in casual and frequent homosexual relationships than homosexual women, and the female homosexual is more faithful and more concerned about fidelity while having an affair than the male homosexual.

ETHICAL CONSIDERATIONS

Perversion, deviance or variant?

Both from a psychiatric and from an ethical point of view there are problems in finding an appropriate concept from which to structure our attitude to homosexual orientation. Is homosexuality a perversion of normal sexuality?[10] Is it a deviant response?[11] Is it a normal variant of sexuality?[12]

The psychoanalytic view has always been that homosexuality must be regarded as a sexual perversion. One component of normal sexuality, attraction to the same sex, takes over the whole of sexuality and 'perverts' the sexual instinct from its 'normal' heterosexual channelling and, by implication, also from the perpetuation of the species. The sociological term 'deviance' in a sense sits on the fence merely saying that homosexuality is a form of behaviour which is different but committing itself to no value-judgement. In many ways deviance is the best term because the least causatively committing and the least socially offensive. The homophile organizations challenge with a suggestion that homosexuality is merely a 'variant' of normality. Certainly it is impossible to defend heterosexuality on the spurious ground that it is more mature: the relationships of many heterosexuals are emotionally infantile; of many homosexuals extremely mature. In terms too of contribution to men's permanent good, especially men's creativity, the contribution of male homosexuals has been almost overwhelming. Almost at random one can think of homosexuals throughout the creative worlds of art, music, poetry, opera, literature, ballet – all areas of creativity. If in some respects men's creativity, their originality, their ability to surprise, is what establishes the difference between us and the higher primates on the one hand and electronic gadgetry on the other, then this creative contribution is perhaps a major platform upon which to claim homosexuality is a sexual variant rather than a perversion or deviance.

A crucial way, in the opinion of the present writer, in which male homosexuality differs from other expressions of sexuality perhaps more readily accepted as perverse or deviant is that a loving relationship is made with a whole and appropriate person, not with parts of a person (as in fetishism or transvestism), with an inappropriate person (as in paedophilia), in solitary self-damage (as in transsexualism or self-mutilation) or in degradation (as in sexual intercourse with dead bodies). (See *Sex Education; Sex Therapy; Sexual Deviations or Variations*.)

Societal attitudes: Stigma and exclusion

Practical ethical issues arise because in society, despite significant social advances, homosexuals are still pressurized by two processes of social stigma and exclusion. Should homosexuals be discouraged or prevented from being teachers, doctors, lawyers, judges, psychiatrists, psychotherapists, scout-masters, ministers of religion? All these bring them into contact with other male persons but, just as the blind are also assumed to be deaf so that people speak loudly to them, so the sexual proclivities and inbuilt controls of homosexuals are assumed to be less effective than those of heterosexuals so that clients, patients or the lay public are held to be somehow at greater risk from them. There is surely no psychological or ethical justification for this assumption?

Taking this argument further is there any reason to suppose that homosexuals of either sex should not be acceptable adoptive or foster parents? No heterosexual parent could surely be so immodest to suggest that bringing up children in a conventional marital pairing is easy or that success is achieved without hard work? In this sense homosexual pairings may be as effective (or as ineffective) parents as the rest of us. A client of the writer's, in a stable lesbian relationship, decided with her partner who should have a baby (by AID) and they brought this child up stably and successfully.

Ethics of treatment

Relatively few male or female homosexuals come to psychiatrists for treatment to change their sexual orientation. If they do the results of both psychoanalysis and behaviour therapy are similar. With psycho-analysis approximately one-quarter become exclusively heterosexual but of those men who were exclusively homosexual only 19% become heterosexual whereas with initially bisexual clients about 50% become exclusively heterosexual.[4] Factors particularly affecting the outcome of treatment are initial bisexuality, staying in treatment longer, being certain of the desire to change sexual orientation at the outset of treatment, relative youth and less severe father-son psychopathology. There have been a number of trials of direct behavioural modification for homosexuality. McConaghy[13] showed that, with all forms of aversive treatment, about one-quarter of the clients reported an increase in heterosexual feelings and heterosexual intercourse.

If however the results of treatment of symptoms such as anxiety, depression and social difficulties arising in relationship to homosexuality are considered, rather than change in homosexual orientation, and these problems are the usual reasons for homosexuals coming to therapy, then there is no reason to expect any difference between the results of psychotherapy in homosexuality compared with the same symptoms occurring on a background of heterosexuality. In this case the best available estimate of therapy improvement rate is that of Bergin and Lambert[14] which is 65%.

Bancroft[15] has emphasized the ethical dilemma towards which 'treating' homosexuality leads. If a condition is potentially 'treatable' then it may be conceived as an illness. Thus if a psychotherapist attempts to help a homosexual client he tacitly accepts and encourages society's stigmatizing attitudes towards homosexuality. If, however, he encourages genuine involvement and self-determination on the part of the client in designing the treatment contract the therapist probably comes as near as humanly possible to resolving the ethical and therapeutic dilemma.

1. Kinsey AC, Pomeroy WB, Martin CE. *Sexual behaviour in the human male.* W. B. Saunders, 1948.
2. Kenyon FE. Female homosexuality – a review. In: Loraine JA, ed. *Understanding homosexuality: its biological & psychological bases.* London: Medical & Technical Publishing, 1974.
3. Ehrhardt AA, Meyer-Bahlburg HFL. Psychosexual development: an examination of the role of prenatal hormones. In: CIBA Foundation Symposium 62. *Sex, hormones and behaviour.* Oxford: Excerpta Medica, 1978.
4. Bieber I. *Homosexuality. A psychoanalytic study.* Basic Books: New York, 1962.
5. Mackay D. Modification of sexual behaviour. In: Crown S, ed. *Psychosexual problems: psychotherapy, counselling and behavioural modification.* London: Academic Press, 1976.
6. Saghir MT, Robins E. Homosexuality I: sexual behaviour of the female homosexual. *Arch Gen Psychiatry.* 1969; 20: 192–201.
7. Saghir MT, Robins E, Walbran B. Homosexuality II: Sexual behaviour of the male homosexual. *Arch Gen Psychiatry* 1969; 21: 219–29.
8. Saghir MT, Robins E, Walbran B, Gentry KA. Homosexuality III: psychiatric disorders and disability in the male homosexual. *Am J Psychiatry* 1970; 126: 1079–86.
9. Masters WH, Johnson VE. *Homosexuality in perspective.* Boston: Little Brown, 1979.
10. Socarides CW. The psychoanalytic theory of homosexuality: with special reference to therapy. In: Rosen I, ed. *Sexual deviation* 2nd edn. 1979: 243–77.
11. Crown S. Male homosexuality: perversion, deviation or variant?. In: CIBA Foundation Symposium 62. *Sex, hormones and behaviour.* Oxford: Excerpta Medica, 1979.
12. Tripp CA. *The homosexual matrix.* London: Quartet Books, 1977.
13. McConaghy N. Is a homosexual orientation irreversible? *Br J Psychiatry* 1976; 129: 556–63.
14. Bergin AE, Lambert MJ. The evaluation of the therapeutic outcomes. In: Garfield SL, Bergin AE, eds, *Handbook of psychotherapy and behaviour change: an empirical analysis.* 2nd edn. 1978: 139–90.
15. Bancroft J. Ethical considerations involved in the modification of homosexual preferences. (Abstract). *Br J Sexual Medicine* 1979; 6: 23–7.

Sidney Crown

Hospices. The mediaeval hospice was a place of refreshment for pilgrims and travellers which welcomed all who reached its doors, sheltered them until ready to continue their journey, and cared for the sick and wounded. When the Irish Sisters of Charity opened Our Lady's Hospice in Dublin in 1846 and St Joseph's Hospice in London in 1905 they included many long-stay patients but made the dying so much their special concern that the term 'hospice' came to be equated with this work. The modern hospice has become a skilled community which aims at improving the quality of life remaining for patients with long-term as well as mortal illnesses and sometimes for the frail and elderly. It accepts the patient with his family as the focus of its concern, involving them when possible as part of the caring team and supporting them in their bereavement.

The present ideal has grown from the work of Homes or hospices founded at the turn of this century on both sides of the Atlantic for patients with terminal cancer and tuberculosis. As hospitals became more involved with acute care such patients tended to be discharged and could only turn to Poor Law or equivalent institutions if they were unable to remain in their own homes. Hospice therapeutics may be traced back to the classic *The Care of the Aged, the Dying and the Dead*, written by a family doctor for students of Harvard Medical School,[1] to a Harveian Oration[2] and to a few articles from the Homes.

That little of this knowledge was being passed on was made plain by surveys by the Marie Curie Memorial Foundation,[3] Hinton and others[4] which revealed how much suffering was still endured by dying patients in hospital and in their homes.

Advances in the treatment of malignant disease had offered longer term control, better palliation and sometimes cure to many patients; but for others it had greatly lengthened the time of ill health and dependence and had led to much physical and mental suffering. The trend for death to occur in hospital rather than in the patient's home isolated him from all that was familiar, often without offering him understanding or treatment appropriate to his special needs.[4]

Work on the control of terminal pain in advanced cancer observed in St Luke's Hospital from 1948 onwards was developed in St Joseph's Hospice between 1958 and 1965.[5] It was then possible to exploit the therapeutic advances of the 1950s: new psychotropic drugs, cancer chemotherapy, palliative radiotherapy, the techniques of the new Pain Clinics and a greater knowledge of family responses to stress and bereavement.

The focus of the modern hospice movement thus began with attention to the nature of terminal pain, to its better understanding and therefore more effective treatment. Alongside this came a revival of the old concept of a 'good death' and attention to the achievements that a patient could still make in the face of physical deterioration. A hospice aims by skilled and experienced awareness of a patient's symptoms and feelings to help him live to the limit of his potential in physical strength, mental and emotional capacity and in social relationships. It offers an alternative form of treatment to the acute care of the general hospital, not in opposition but as a further resource for those for whom that is no longer appropriate. It is the alternative to the negative and socially dangerous suggestion that a patient with an incurable disease likely to cause suffering should have the legal option of hastened death, or 'euthanasia.'

The research and teaching hospices, opened from 1967 onwards, set out to establish recognized standards of care which could be interpreted in the home, as well as in other settings and cultures, and become a part of general medical and nursing teaching. They aimed to identify some of the common problems, to find solutions and to spread this knowledge as widely as possible. As the work spread, a wide variety of interpretations and innovations grew into the 'Hospice Movement'. Different titles, such as Palliative or Continuing Care Units, Homes named after local founders, converted houses keeping their former names, Home Care teams, Symptom Control or Support teams in hospitals, all emphasize different approaches and appear under the umbrella term 'hospice'. Most of these are outside the National Health Service in the UK, although some are closely related in policy and practice and have considerable financial support. A few are totally within the NHS. In none have patients to pay for their care. The present position of terminal care in the NHS. in general was reviewed by Ford and Pincherle.[6] Information concerning the movement in the U.S.A. is obtainable from the National Hospice Organisation, 765 Prospect Street, New Haven, Connecticut 06511, U.S.A.

A major aim of any hospice is that its experience and teaching should be so accepted that the professions as a whole will carry out the care needed by dying patients, the majority of whom will always die in their own homes or in general hospitals and not in special centres. In practice, however, it has been found that such centres continue to be needed for patients with those intractable problems, physical, emotional or social, that are almost impossible to deal with except by a specially trained staff and, sometimes, in a specially planned milieu. It has been important to define the standard of relief that should be achieved so that those in the general field may assess their own practice and recognize the expertise of the special unit or team and when it should be involved. Only such a standard and such integration will ensure that wherever patients are dying they will receive the best treatment available.[7] A survey comparing places and policies for terminal care records that patients were least depressed and anxious in a hospice, preferring the more frank communication available there.[8]

Whether it is a geographically separate unit, part of a hospital campus, a separate ward or a home care or hospital team, a hospice should establish the following principles, some of them common to any branch of medicine or nursing, others specific to hospice care.

1. An integrated clinical team is needed for expert control of symptoms, both common and uncommon.

The expertise of oncologists, radiotherapists, anaesthetists and psychiatrists may all be called upon by the hospice doctors, who in turn have special knowledge to offer.[9]

2. The hospice team itself will involve the para-medical disciplines. Such a team is not unlike those that arise in any unit which is grappling with complex physical and emotional problems.

3. Skilled and experienced team nursing will call for confident leadership by the ward sister and easy communication among its members. The days are passed when doctors could step back and consider that the nurses should take over, (or even the unsupported family) but nursing is the cornerstone of hospice care.

4. Methodical recording and analysis should monitor clinical practice and, with relevant research where possible, lead to soundly based practice and teaching for the management of terminal distress. Successful practice has been spread widely, for example in the work of the Palliative Care Unit in Montreal.[10]

5. According to local facilities and customs home care should be developed and integrated with the community services already established. Although the amount of care the hospice itself should undertake will vary, help must be available 24 hours a day and 7 days a week from someone who knows the family. This will normally be in consultation with the patient's own doctor, who remains in charge, using the hospice team as a resource. At least half of the patients of a hospice are likely to be in their own homes and, as a patient's condition changes, movement between his general hospital, his home and hospice beds if available gives continuity of care. The passage back from terminal to acute care is made more frequently as effective symptom control develops.

6. There must be a bereavement follow-up service. The family has to recover and the hospice team must identify those in special need. Good neighbours, social workers, chaplains and family doctors have been able to fill this role but the need for unhurried listening, especially from a member of a group which helped the family deal with the patient's illness and death, may help to reduce the considerable morbidity recorded in several studies of bereaved people. Many hospices use trained volunteers for this service.

7. Teaching must be given in all aspects of terminal care: the competent control of symptoms first, and the use of analgesics and the many forms of adjuvant therapy. These are passed on in writing,[11,12] in lectures and seminars. Hospices are used as a resource in both formal and informal consultation.

8. Imaginative use should be made of architecture. Some hospices work effectively as teams with no beds of their own, others have a few allocated to them in a general hospital; only the minority are likely to be able to build. Buildings old and new must be adapted to combine much-needed privacy for patients, families and staff with the equally important sense of openness and community and to maintain a sense of home alongside efficient and easy operation.

9. A competent and approachable administration, essential to any field of human need, is here required to give security to patients, families and staff. Efficiency is comforting. Hospices have shown that their operation is cost-effective as well as appropriate and humane.

10. Although the current interest in hospice care in the United States is especially concerned with the dying cancer patient and his family, a good community is usually a mixed one and hospices may include in their concern those with other long-term progressive illnesses, chronic pain and, in some cases, frailty and old age. There are many disadvantaged groups who need the same focus and attention.

11. There must be a readiness for the cost of commitment and a continual search for meaning. Devotion has been an outstanding characteristic of past and present hospices. Willingness to face this demand has a fundamental bearing on the way the work is done and upon the stability and support of the staff. Affirmations of faith may be made but never imposed; each individual has to grow into a fuller (though never complete) realization of the truths he accepts. In such a climate, patients and families are encouraged to reach out towards what they see as true.

To see that such care is available has become an essential part of our commitment to every patient with a progressive illness whose care we undertake. Competence in helping the patient and his family to handle the situation that faces them, together with the philosophy suggested above, give to the modern hospice a positive and dynamic atmosphere. (See *Death, Attitudes to; Declaration of Sydney; Euthanasia; Terminal Care.*)

1. Worcester A. *The care of the aged, the dying and the dead.* Springfield: Thomas, 1935, and New York: Arno Press, 1977.
2. Gavey CJ. *The management of the 'hopeless' case.* London: H. K. Lewis, 1952.
3. Marie Curie Memorial foundation. *Report on a national survey concerning patients nursed at home.* London; Marie Curie Memorial Foundaton, 1952.
4. Hinton J. The physical and mental distress of the dying. *Q Med J* 1963; 32: 1–10.
5. Saunders CM. *Care of the dying. Nurs Times* Reprint. 2nd edn. London: Macmillan, 1960.
6. Ford GR, Pincherle G. Arrangements for terminal care in the National Health Service (especially those for cancer patients). *Health Trends* 1978; 10: 73–6.
7. Saunders CM. *The management of terminal disease* London: Arnold, 1978.
8. Hinton J. Comparison of places and policies for terminal care. *Lancet* 1979; 1: 29–32.
9. Saunders CM. The challenge of terminal care. In: Symington T,

Carter RL eds. *Scientific foundations of oncology*. London: Heinemann, 1976: 673.

10. Melzack R, Ofiesh JG, Mount BM. The Brompton mixture: effects on pain in cancer patients. *C.M.A. Journal* 1976; 115: 125–8.

11. Baines MJ. Control of other symptoms. In: Saunders C. ed. *The management of terminal disease*. Arnold, 1978:99.

12. Twycross RG. Relief of pain. In: Saunders CM. ed. *The management of terminal disease*. London: Arnold, 1978.

13. Dunphy JE. Annual discourse – on caring for the patient with cancer. *N Engl J Med* 1976; 295: 313–9.

Cicely Saunders

Hospital Chaplains. Chaplains are employed in hospitals on either a full-time or a part-time basis according to the number of patients of their denomination. Their primary function is generally assumed to be ministry to those whose stay in hospital deprives them of contact with their home churches. The chaplain's duties have thus traditionally included the pastoral visiting of patients, the administration of the sacraments, and the conduct of worship in the hospital. The chaplain is also frequently seen in the hospital as having special responsibility for patients and their relatives at times of crises and when issues of life and death arise. More recently there has been a revived recognition of the chaplain's role in the pastoral care of hospital staff and of the fact that in a society which may be very confused about its values, the minister of religion may usefully represent to people of little or no formal religious faith the fixed points for which they may feel need.

The chaplain's role in the hospital was originally well-defined and included many functions now taken over by other professions such as social work. The fact that the chaplain's role is not a technical one may give him considerable freedom to make contact with individuals in the hospital without being unduly affected either by their diagnostic category, or by their place in a professional hierarchy. He may be able to examine and raise wider issues concerned with health care in the hospital and the community which it serves, and to be involved in the process of health education from a general, rather than a clinical, point of view, and informed both by his pastoral relationships and theological background.

The chaplain is usually employed and paid by the hospital in which he (or she) works but licensed or authorized by the appropriate religious authority. The chaplain has responsibilities both to the hospital and, for example, in the case of a Christian chaplain, to the Church of which he is a minister or priest, and this can very occasionally raise conflicts of loyalty for him. Much more frequently, however, the dual accountability of the chaplain can mean that he is in a key position to reflect on, and sometimes interpret, the language, terms of reference, needs and methods of the hospital in the light of his own theological understanding and pastoral experience. For example, a hospital chaplain who has experience of working with patients facing abortion (q.v.) and the staff who care for them may be aware of the complex ethical and pastoral issues involved and be able to contribute in an informed way to ethical discussion in church, hospital and community.

The Judaeo-Christian tradition has been much concerned with the tension between the needs of the individual and of the society of which he is part. As a representative of this tradition the chaplain's professional skill and theological expertise may provide him with a different dimension to offer his colleagues when clinical or planning decisions are made. His work may variously involve the care of a patient on a life support system who is being considered as an organ donor (and of his relatives) and contact with those who have to manage other people or distribute scarce resources. In these settings the chaplain may appropriately use skills practised by others, for example counselling or group work, but as a pastor his concern is to explore how decisions, whether made by the formally religious or not, frequently presuppose a whole set of theological assumptions about the nature and value of human beings.

A chaplain's basic training in theology and pastoral care is frequently supplemented by supervised clinical pastoral training in hospital prior to appointment, which would include some introduction to clinical and ethical issues. In his work he may be asked to share his own practical experience and the insights of his theological tradition into ethical questions. This would include working with medical and nursing students, theological students, clergymen and others in both formal and informal teaching settings. Many hospitals and health districts have an ethical committee with medical and non-medical members to which new and experimental procedures have to be submitted, and a chaplain is often a member of such a committee.

A chaplain is frequently in close contact with patients, relatives and staff, and is also understood to be independent of formal hierarchies in the hospital. He may receive, in confidence, from patients, members of staff or others (see Confidentiality) personal or clinical information which may become relevant to the care of the patient. Because there are no formal rules governing the chaplain's course of action in his intermediate position between patients and staff, he needs to use considerable sensitivity and discretion in handling and sharing such information.

Ethical issues are frequently implicit in routine pastoral care and counselling. For example, a person during a pastoral encounter may become aware of the previously unexamined ethical implications of a particular course of action. It should be part of the professional skill of the chaplain to help himself and others to recognize these issues whilst being able to work closely with others, both staff and patient.

whose views and actions may differ widely from his own, without loss of integrity.

The chaplain's position of trust in the hospital will depend both on his ability to make relationships with others and also on his faithful representation of his tradition. Equally, however, he may find that if he becomes identified with external bodies, particularly *vis à vis* issues of practice where there is no ethical consensus, the whole basis of integrity on which his pastoral care of patients and staff depends is undermined. (For this reason many chaplains have resisted vigorously attempts by some anti-abortion groups to involve chaplains in their information-gathering.)

Ethical problems may also arise in the relationships between chaplains of different denominations, especially when they differ in the emphasis they give to the social or corporate dimensions of their faith or in their understanding of the theological and philosophical grounds on which ethical decisions are made. Respect for denominational boundaries may deprive the hospital of co-operation and interaction between chaplains in situations where hospital and community might benefit considerably from both.

Faber H. *Pastoral care in the modern hospital.* London: SCM Press, 1971.

Wilson M. *The hospital – a place of truth.* University of Birmingham: Institute for the Study of Worship and Religious Architecture, 1971.

Ian Ainsworth-Smith
John Perryman

Hospitals. (1) Important considerations apply both to the provision of hospitals and to their activities.

A modern hospital is extremely expensive to construct and equip, and few countries have the financial resources available to meet these costs on other than a limited scale. Large hospitals need large staffs and may attract to themselves an unduly high proportion of health personnel available. It can be argued that, especially in the developing countries, the money would be better spent on providing preventive and primary health care for large numbers of the population, by setting up numerous health centres and by encouraging the wider spread of health personnel among the population; in many countries these principles are being applied.

On the other hand, increase of primary health care will lead to a demand for more sophisticated hospital treatment as more and more seriously ill people are discovered. Decisions have to be taken whether or not the care they need is to be provided, and to what extent – and if provided, how it is to be paid for. If limits are to be set on what can be done for the sick, there must be general acceptance of this constraint by the population as a whole. If the level to be set is higher than that which has applied hitherto, few difficulties will arise, but there may be problems in countries such as the UK where economic recession is making impossible the constant growth in spending on health and social care which most people have taken for granted.

We need to reassess the purposes for which hospitals exist because hospitals to some extent both reflect and re-inforce social values. Priority seems to be given to treatment of the acutely ill patient: intensive care units, by their very nature, require funding which seems disproportionate to provision for the care of the elderly, and the chronic and mentally sick. It can rightly be said that special care is not possible without special equipment, and equipment for geriatric wards can be much simpler and less costly, but the public may need re-education in its attitudes. The principle of community care of the mentally ill is already established, and economic pressures may lead to the necessity of families taking greater care of their elderly and infirm, so relieving hospitals of this obligation. Such care in the home may be desirable anyway. These considerations need to be taken into account in planning for the future.

The dedication of hospital staffs to the care of their patients has never been in dispute, but doubts arise whether the best interests of the patient are always paramount. While the majority of patients are grateful for hospitals and their work, the fact that complaints and criticisms are so often expressed suggests that insufficient attention is paid even now to the needs of the patients and relatives. Hospitals are bureaucratic institutions to a greater or lesser degree, depending on their size; the larger the unit the greater the risks of impersonal treatment. In short-stay units the staff, and in long-stay units both patients and staff are liable to institutionalization. Criticisms include (1) problems of communication between staff and patient and in particular between staff and relatives; (2) complaints that the interests of the organization take precedence over the interests of the patient – reflected in the past (and sometimes still) by e.g. over-zealous discipline in the ward, unwillingness to allow freedom of visiting or visits by children, or for a mother to accompany a child into hospital; (3) an authoritarian attitude on the part of doctors and nurses. A patient's entry into hospital is too easily assumed to carry with it consent for unforeseen treatment. (See also *Consent; Childbirth, Intervention in; Patients.*)

In hospitals devoted to treatment, staff may find the care of those 'for whom nothing more can be done' difficult, particularly care for the dying, and this is reflected in the establishment of hospices for this purpose. (See *Hospices; Terminal Care.*)

It can be fairly argued that the examples quoted above are illustrations of a system of values that rates the 'cure of disease' as more important than the 'care of patients'. The charge is a severe one, and if put to the test may very often be found, by and large, to be true.

Of course there is overlap; the care of the patient must include cure of his disease. But hospitals have something to learn in their general daily practice from the services which care for people for whom there is little expectation of clinical cure. Hospices for the dying, Christian-inspired, are distinguished for their caring competence. Where there is no expectation of cure, bedside care is something of value in itself. Relationship of the hospital to the neighbourhood is another testing factor. The urban hospital tends to be alien. Visitors are seldom regarded as part of the patient's health or illness, or capable of sharing in nursing procedures. They and the patients are commonly treated somewhat as children. Again, despite knowledge of mother-deprivation, only some UK hospitals make provision for the admission of mothers with small children or *vice versa*.

The assumed values on which a hospital is built powerfully operate on people's minds with social consequences for the future care of the sick and dying. But the hospital has been described as a 'living learning arena' where patients, staff and families experience joy and sorrow together. Living and learning together implies a way of reviewing the values which underlie the health service and keeping social and medical ethics alive (see also *Hospital Chaplains*).

Friedson B, ed. *The hospital and modern society*. New York: Collier-Macmillan, 1963.

Goffman E. *Asylums*. Harmondsworth: Pelican Books, 1970.

Lambourne RA. The hospital as a source of standards and values. *Contact* 1966; 16:3.

Martin DV. *Adventure in psychiatry, social change in a hospital*. Oxford: Bruno Cassirer, 1962.

Menzies IEP. *The functioning of social systems as a defence against anxiety*. London: Tavistock Institute of Human Relations, 1970.

Shoenberg E. *A hospital looks at itself*: Oxford: Bruno Cassirer, 1972.

Willard H, Kasl SV. *Continuing care in a community hospital*. Harvard University Press, 1973.

Wilson M. *Health is for people*. London: Darton, Longman and Todd, 1975.

Michael Wilson

Hospitals. (2) Most civilizations seem to have accepted from their early beginnings that there existed a need to accommodate the sick; in most cases such accommodation was provided under the auspices of religious authority and evolved through somewhat different routes to the present-day concept of a hospital. In England, with which this article is primarily concerned, despite the foundation of the Hospital of St. Peter by the Canons of York Minster in A.D. 947 (probably more as a hostel for the traveller or pilgrim than for the care of the sick) and St. Batholomew's Hospital in London in 1123, it was not until the

19th century that hospitals fulfilling in general terms their present function began to be built in any quantity. This, despite the clear lead given by St Thomas More in *Utopia* (1516) 'Special care is taken of the sick who are looked after in public hospitals. . . .' a statement which retains its significance to the present day.

Our Victorian forebears believed in size and this belief has continued until very recently.

The word 'Hospital' is itself a generality and the providers of residential care have to consider the very different needs of the acutely sick, the mentally ill, the physically or mentally handicapped and those who need care during a terminal illness.

In all developing countries the point is soon reached when there is a realization on the part of the providers (though not always on the part of the population in general) that while the demand for health care is infinite the resources available for its provision are finite.

The pattern of hospital care for acute illness has been seen to change perceptibly. The acute phase of an illness requires in-patient treatment nowadays in a sophisticated and highly expensive General Hospital. Once the acute phase has passed less intensive specialised and expensive care becomes appropriate, ideally being made available at smaller community hospitals nearer to the patient's home.

Our forebears, when they accepted belatedly that 'care' and not 'custody' was appropriate for the mentally sick and the handicapped, believed that they should receive such care in institutions, later to become hospitals, remote from towns and frequently of enormous size. Happily these misguided ideas have largely disappeared and in their place has arisen a general acceptance that mental and physical illness are not different in kind and in their acute phases should not be separated, the District General Hospitals providing for the short-term treatment of the mentally ill.

The long-term problem of the intractably mentally ill and the mentally and physically handicapped requires a different solution. Humanity, and indeed common sense, both dictate that the chronically sick and handicapped should receive their care in small hospitals or if possible hostels near their homes where relatives can be encouraged to visit and to maintain contact with patients over long periods of time. There is a need to provide skilled and humane care for the dying. While of course such skills and such humanity must be made available at any hospital, the hospices (q.v.) are providing a degree of skill and dedication in the care of the dying that many hospitals are not yet able to match.

In general the future is unlikely to see the building of more large hospitals which, with the very necessary extension of primary care and hostel accommodation, will no longer be required to act as a repository for the chronically sick and handicapped and those people who should and could be treated in the community without leaving their own homes.

In which direction the development of hospital provision will proceed in the immediate future is difficult to forecast as the ethical and moral problem of the allocation of resources – limited as they are – between acute medicine, long-stay needs and community care remains to be resolved in a way which will command general acceptance.

Ives AGL. *British hospitals.* London: Collins, 1948.
Woodward J. *To do the sick no harm.* London: Routledge & Kegan Paul, 1974.

John Donne

Human Experiment.

1. CLINICAL ASPECTS

All clinical investigations are experiments in man. Those with direct diagnostic or therapeutic relevance to the individual patient seldom pose serious ethical problems and indeed a doctor may be said to have failed in his duty to his patient if he does not undertake such investigations. Clinical investigation carried out primarily to advance knowledge and from which the subject, whether patient or volunteer, may not derive any personal benefit includes:

(a) Studies of physiological function in health or disease. These studies may be (i) by observation – recording movements of an adult in sleep or the responses of a child to sound; (ii) by 'non-invasive' procedures – measurement of pulse rate, respiratory rate or the volume of urinary output in a variety of conditions; or (iii) by 'invasive' procedures – causing a nasogastric tube to be swallowed so that gastric secretion may be measured, inserting an electrode through the skin into muscle fibres to record their electrical activity or passing a cardiac catheter from an arm vein into the heart to record the flow of blood and the pressures in the chambers of the heart and the differential pressures across the heart valves. Many 'invasive' investigations are simple; others such as cardiac catheterization should be carried out only by skilled staff.

Much of the great body of knowledge of human physiology obtained over the last two hundred years has been derived from such investigations and has been of great importance in improving our knowledge of normal function and our understanding of what goes wrong in disease.

(b) Investigation of new drugs. The first use of a new drug in man is usually carried out in a very small number of subjects under close supervision. Preliminary animal work will have predicted the likely effect of the drug and the purpose of early studies will be to confirm that the drug has this effect in man, and to determine how it is absorbed, whether it is bound to protein in the blood, how it is metabolized and how it is excreted. Such knowledge will determine

what further work needs to be done in animals before the drug is more extensively administered to man.

Procedures appropriate for testing a new drug vary greatly, depending on its nature. There should be close co-operation between those who have studied its actions and toxic effects in animals (see *Animal Experiment*) and those who carry out the first studies in man. Many investigations are best carried out in normal volunteers; for instance measurements of the rate of absorption, plasma levels and speed of excretion of a new penicillin may require continuous sampling of blood and urine for 24 to 48 hours and it may be desirable to repeat the investigation several times in the same subject at different dose levels. Other studies must be done in patients: it would be unjustifiable to give a new cytotoxic drug of potential value in the treatment of leukaemia or cancer to a normal subject.

After studies of a new drug have characterized its pharmacological properties in man, further studies usually have to be undertaken to compare the new treatment with that which already exists – drug therapy, surgery, radiotherapy or perhaps no therapy at all. This last may be especially important when testing psychotropic drugs. It is now widely accepted that properly planned clinical trials (q.v.) are usually the most effective and rapid method of determining whether a drug is or is not more effective than existing therapy.

There are some situations in which the pharmacological effectiveness of a new drug is easy to determine, but the value of its use in man may be difficult to assess. The oral anticoagulant drugs, for instance, reduce the liability of blood to clot, but there has been considerable controversy as to whether their administration to patients who have had a myocardial infarction gives protection against further infarcts. Most physicians now believe that because properly controlled trials were not carried out when these drugs were first introduced in the 1950s many thousands of patients have received drugs which have not helped them greatly but which have sometimes caused serious adverse reactions. Moreover, because it was complacently accepted that this treatment was valuable, other forms of therapy were not explored as vigorously as they should have been.

(c) The use of new and untried procedures. Many procedures such as needle biopsy of the liver, cardiac catheterization, vaccination and renal transplantation when first introduced were considered to be unjustifiable. This is likely to be the case whenever a new procedure or operation is introduced until sufficient evidence has become available to allow assessment of the benefits and to show that these outweigh the disadvantages or dangers.

Usually such procedures are introduced cautiously and are first used where it is hoped that an individual patient stands to derive some definite benefit. Only after extensive experience of the procedure does evidence accumulate to suggest that it is safe enough to allow its more general use.

Consent

It is widely accepted that patients or volunteers should be fully informed about any experiment in which they participate. When this is either impossible, or might destroy the validity of an investigation, it is especially important that an investigator safeguards the interests of his patients by obtaining the approval of a Research Ethical Committee (q.v.).

Dependent subjects

Special care is required if students, soldiers, employees or prisoners (q.v.) are asked to volunteer for experimental work. They may acquiesce because they fear they may suffer in some way if they do not. However, what is considered unacceptable in one community may be looked on as normal in another or in different circumstances. In the USA prisoners have for some years co-operated in medical research and there has been little anxiety that exploitation of these volunteers has occurred, although in Britain such a practice would not be acceptable.

Mortally ill patients

It is considered repugnant to carry out experiments of any sort in patients near to death. It is certainly unwise to conduct clinical trials of a new drug in such patients, for the effects of the drug are likely to be masked by the disease and when death occurs the blame may be laid on the treatment rather than the disease.

Children

If experimental work is to be done in children the consent of the parents is essential. The extent to which parents are entitled to make decisions on behalf of their children has never been tested in law in Britain but there is no reason to suppose that the Courts would penalize those who undertake sensible and reasonable investigations to throw light on or to improve the treatment of diseases which occur in children. New therapy for certain forms of leukaemia, for infectious diseases of children or to alleviate certain genetic errors in metabolism can only be tested in children, as can vaccines to protect against illnesses such as measles or whooping cough. It is a field of research where the integrity of the investigator must be of the highest calibre to justify the trust of parents and to protect the rights of the child (see *Child; Immunization*).

Considerable controversy on this issue was aroused by the publication of studies of the natural history of infectious hepatitis at Willowbrook, a residential school for mentally defective children in New

York State.[1] Because most children admitted to the hospital became infected, the medical staff felt justified in giving the children hepatitis virus and isolating them in a special unit so that they were at less risk. It is claimed that this policy, possibly justified when it was started in 1956, was continued because the medical staff wished to carry on their research on hepatitis, and new measures which might give protection to children from infective hepatitis were not used.

Rewards

Any system of reward to a patient or a volunteer who participates in experimental work must be such that there can be no question of subjects being bribed to submit to unreasonable hazards. On the other hand it is unreasonable to ask subjects to give up a whole day and a night to take part in a pharmacokinetic study of a drug without offering some compensation.

Similarly it is highly desirable that those who plan and conduct clinical research should not have their judgement in any way perverted by monetary reward or expectation of professional advancement. Professional staff, doctors, nurses and technicians should be paid at standard rates of remuneration for the work they do, and payment should not in any way depend on a 'successful outcome' of their study as for instance when carrying out studies on new drugs.

Public Liability policies

If experimental work is done on normal volunteers an institution should carry a public liability insurance policy, in case something untoward happens to a volunteer as a result of negligence. Insurance companies will give such cover, but will not extend it to cover studies of new drugs which have not been given clearance by the Committee on Safety of Medicines and are not marketed and in ordinary use. If work is being done with a new drug, research workers should obtain a statement of indemnification from the firm with which or for which the investigation is being carried out.

With investigations carried out by or under the supervision of qualified medical staff in Britain, the subject has the additional safeguard that doctors carry personal professional insurance and claims may be met by their medical defence society. This does not apply when investigations are carried out in institutions where there is no supervision by medically qualified personnel as for instance in a School of Pharmacy or a Department of Physiology without medically qualified teachers. These institutions or departments should ensure that they have public liability insurance policies and that their insurance company is informed that experimental work in humans is being carried out and is to be included under the policy. The possibility has recently been discussed of universities or other institutes obtaining 'no fault' liability insurance so that volunteers may still receive compensation in the unlikely event of their coming to any harm when there is no fault on anyone's part.

The principle here is that the investigator is greatly privileged by the volunteer who trusts his competence and sincerity. In return the investigator must take every possible precaution to ensure that nothing untoward occurs to the volunteer, and must also arrange for financial compensation to be available if anything untoward does occur. Accidents in the hands of competent and experienced research workers are rare, but they do occur and they may leave a subject severely crippled.

Conclusion

The planning and execution of experimental work in man demands the highest professional scientific and ethical qualities of individual research workers. Because the skills of a number of different disciplines are required, research often requires the coordinated efforts of a skilled team of workers. It is unethical to conduct badly planned or poorly executed research from which no conclusions or, worse, wrong conclusions may be drawn.

Although codes, regulations and laws are of value in promoting the highest standards of ethical behaviour, experience has shown that the greatest safeguard for volunteers and patients is a high level of concern, compassion and skill among those carrying out research and those who are members of research ethical committees. If this is maintained, there should be no cause for concern that unreasonable or unjustifiable procedures or experiments are being undertaken. The welfare of the subject must come first, and experiments should not be performed on a man if they are likely to harm him even if the result might be highly advantageous to science and to the health of others. The difficulty is to decide what constitutes 'harm', and how one assesses whether an experiment is 'likely' to harm. Although the subject needs protection, the community needs knowledge.

Kurgman S, Giles JP. Viral hepatitis. New light on an old disease. *JAMA*, 1970; 212: 1019–29.

Bliss BP, Johnson AG *Aims and motives in clinical medicine*. London: Pitman Medical, 1975.

Proceedings of a Conference on the Ethical Aspects of Experimentation on Human Subjects. Boston: American Academy of Arts and Science, 1967.

Ramsey P. *The patient as person*. Newhaven: Yale University Press, 1970.

Wade OL, Beeley L. *Adverse reactions to drugs*. 2nd edn. London: Heinemann, 1976.

Weber HR. *Experiments in man. Report of an ecumenical consultation*. Geneva: World Council of Churches, 1969.

O. L. Wade

2. PHILOSOPHICAL PROBLEMS.

There are two distinct kinds of experimental intervention, each of which produces its own moral problems: (1) an experiment on a human subject which is expected to benefit that patient; (ii) an experiment on a human subject which is not expected to benefit that patient.

The *general* issue of experiment on human subjects raises a possible clash between two moral values, the precise nature of the clash being dependent on whether the experiment is of type (i) or (ii).

On the one hand, health seems to be a basic good, whatever one's moral views may be, just because it is usually a precondition of attaining any other good. Consequently, if medical experiment is an efficient means of promoting health, a rational man will approve of it because it is irrational to will the end – good health – and not will the means to it.

At the same time, experiment also seems to act as a threat to human dignity and the inviolability which this dignity seems to require. Human dignity on this view consists in a man being seen as an end in himself and not being used as a means to the ends of others. Medical experiments have been held to threaten this value, particularly when performed without consent and where the individual cannot benefit from the research. The clearest and most extreme example of this would be experiments conducted on non-Aryans by the Nazis, but even in far less extreme cases people often talk of being 'used', or being 'guinea pigs'.

The values involved in medical research and the principle of inviolability need not conflict. In a case where the experiment is expected to benefit the patient, and where the patient, in full knowledge of the situation and the risks involved, has consented to it, the values are compatible. Granted that the patient's consent is genuine and he has not been coerced into giving it, then this kind of case is not morally problematic. Similarly, in a case where a patient consents to an experiment when he fully realizes that it cannot be reasonably expected to benefit him, but will help others, there seems to be no moral difficulty. In both cases the principle of inviolability is secured by informed consent (q.v.). It is important to notice that there can be no *obligation* in this latter case, nor has society the right to demand co-operation in this kind of situation, unless it is argued that a person's body is a social asset over which society has rights which can override the individual's entitlement to decide what shall happen to him. Some forms of utilitarianism might allow for compulsory conscription of experimental subjects because on a utilitarian view the welfare of society can outweigh the claims of the individual. However, it is not clear that this way of treating people ultimately makes sense and it is, on the face of it, incompatible with respect for persons.

In the clear-cut cases, it seems to be consent which removes the elements of manipulation from the picture. However, there may be individuals who are in such a physical or psychological position that true consent is impossible: children, the mentally ill, prisoners (q.v.), those in great pain. The most usual form of argument to justify experiment without consent in these cases would be that, since health is a basic good, a rational man will desire health and those experiments which are a means to health; therefore, if the patients concerned were capable of making a rational choice (which they are not) they could decide to be subjects of experiment. This argument contains difficulties – the connection between rational choice and health might be contested, e.g. by Jehovah's Witnesses, and also, if the argument does work, it does so only when the experiment is expected to help the patient concerned. There is no ground for thinking that a rational person would *necessarily* choose to be the subject of an experiment which would be of benefit to others, and in the UK it is considered unethical to conduct such experiments on those who cannot give their consent, although under the Helsinki Declaration (see *Declarations*), the consent of the parents or guardians is considered to be sufficient.

The other problematic case of experiment is where there is either some incentive or threat attached to the consent. Certainly threats are usually thought to be infringements of an agent's freedom, and if used to secure consent would infringe the principle of inviolability. The situation with incentives is not so clear cut. Payment for participation in experiments or remission of sentence for prisoners (q.v.) who agree to participate, although they may appear to be incentives and offers, can usually be thought to be manipulative and in certain contexts may constitute offers which the agent concerned can hardly refuse. Certainly both threats and offers considerably cloud the notion of consent which is pivotal in reconciling the values involved in experiment and the principle of inviolability.

Benn SI. Freedom and persuasion. *Australasian Journal of Philosophy*, Vol. 45.

Downie RS, Telfer E. *Respect for persons*. London: Allen and Unwin, 1969.

Freund PA. Ethical problems in human experimentation. *New England Journal of Medicine* 1965; 273, 687–92.

Hart HLA. Are there any natural rights? *Philosophical Review*, 1955: 64.

Jonas H. Philosophical reflections on experimenting with human subjects. *Daedalus*, 1969.

Milne AJM. *Freedom and rights*. London, Allen and Unwin, 1968.

Nozick R. *Anarchy, state and utopia*. Oxford: Blackwell, 1975.

Rawls J. *A Theory of justice*. Oxford: University Press, 1973.

Human Life, Sanctity or Sacredness of

Smart JJC, Williams B. *Utilitarianism, For and against.* Cambridge: University Press, 1975.
Wolstenholme GEW, O'Connor M, eds. *Ciba Foundation symposium on ethics in medical progress.* London, Churchill, 1966. (Paperback edn, 1968, under the title *Law and Ethics of Transplantation.*)

Raymond Plant

Human Life, Sanctity or Sacredness of. See under *Sanctity.*

Human Rights. Human rights is a modern name for what was known in the Age of Reason as natural rights or the rights of man. They are rights which are claimed on behalf of all men in all situations, and are thus to be distinguished from positive rights, which are either bestowed only on the men who have earned them, or are conferred only on those who fall under the jurisdiction or a particular system of positive law. Human rights are essentially moral rights: they are not the rights that men necessarily *do* enjoy, but the rights they ought to enjoy. They are based on what is traditionally known as natural law, which has the distinction, and perhaps the disadvantage, of being unwritten and often unenforced. Many philosophers have considered both natural law and natural rights to be mere metaphysical abstractions, but belief in the validity of some such supreme principles of justice, higher than the laws of princes, has played an important role in the evolution of Western culture.

The main human rights that have been claimed one way or another since Stoic times are the rights to life and liberty; more recent Declarations of Human Rights have added such rights as happiness and property, and even rights to social security, medical care and holidays with pay. While these more 'economic' rights are generally admitted to belong to the realm of Utopian aspiration, the traditional political and civil rights have always been thought of as being morally compelling in the present world, and to offer, at the very best, an objective and universal standard of justice by which to appraise the merits of positive systems of law. The current use of the word 'rights' to name both 'ideals' and 'real moral entitlements' lends a certain equivocation to much contemporary discusion of the subject.

Conflicts between one right and another are not uncommon; even between those so well entrenched in the Western consciousness as the rights to life and liberty. Some philosophers, such as Thomas Hobbes, have given priority to the right to life over liberty; others such as John Locke, to the right to liberty over life. There has also been an enduring uncertainty over the interpretation of such abstract rights at the level of practical action. Most natural law theorists have favoured the doctrine of the just war, according to which the protection of the liberty of the community justifies depriving certain individuals of their right to life. Others have held that if the right to life is paramount, killing is never permissible. Correspondingly a principle of the right to life can be invoked both to justify capital punishment (on the ground that a murderer forfeits his own right to life in depriving another of that right) and to justify the abolition of capital punishment (on the ground that all life, including a murderer's, is sacred).

In medical ethics, the importance to the physician's profession of the diminution of pain and the postponement of death prompts particular emphasis being given to the right to life. But this right can be understood in different ways. Thus, whereas the right to life in Stoic times was held to entail the right to terminate one's own life, both Christian and modern utilitarian opinion have interpreted the right to life as imposing a duty both to stay alive oneself and to keep alive others, including those who may wish to die. But in itself, the assertion of a right to life entails no precise judgement in such matters as suicide (q.v.) and euthanasia (q.v.), but does impose on the physician a *prima facie* duty to minister to the wounds and maladies of criminals, enemy soldiers, and prisoners, whose needs 'as mere human beings' constitute a claim for his services (See *Military Medicine; Prisoners*).

A belief in human rights may produce opposing opinions on the question of abortion (q.v.). The right to life is often invoked by opponents of abortion, on the ground that the right to life of the fetus is being violated (see *Unborn child, Rights of*); while champions of abortion argue that the fetus, being only a potential and not an actual human being, is not a subject of rights; and further that the pregnant woman, being a fully developed being, can assert her right to liberty against the right to life of the undeveloped being. No theory of human rights can alone resolve the contradictions and disagreements which the concept of human rights necessarily generates. All systems of law need authorities to interpret them at the level of daily practice, and human rights rest largely on the authority of reason and conscience.

Cranston M. *What are human rights?* London: Bodley Head, 1974.
Melden A. *Human rights*. Belmont: Wadsworth, 1969.
Raphael DD. *Political theory and the rights of man*. London: Macmillan, 1967.

Maurice Cranston

Humanae Vitae. An encyclical letter of Pope Paul VI, officially dated 25 July 1968. It reasserted the prohibition of artificial methods of contraception in these terms: 'The Church, calling men back to the observance of the natural law, as interpreted by her constant doctrine, teaches that each and every marriage act (*quilibet matrimonii usus*) must remain open to the transmission of life'. The grounds for this teaching were the inseparable connection, willed by God and unable to be broken by man on his own initiative, between the two meanings of the conjugal act, the unitive meaning and the procreative meaning. The 'safe period' did not offend against these principles. It was held to be an instance of using 'nature' rather than interfering with it. Consequently the safe period remained the only officially permitted method of contraception for Roman Catholics (see *Rhythm Method; Vegliare con Sollecitudine*).

While some welcomed the encyclical as clearing up confusion, others were surprised because they had been led to expect a change in Catholic teaching. This mistaken expectation was based on the existence and work of the Pontifical Commission on Population Questions. Originally set up by Pope John XXIII in 1962, its membership was gradually enlarged and the range of its medical and psychological competence was strengthened. But the Commission could not reach agreement on the central issue. A minority of four moral theologians thought that the Church could not modify its judgement on the morality of artificial contraception without damagingly contradicting its previous clear teaching. The majority produced a report – leaked to the press in April 1967[1] – which argued that new knowledge and new conditions justified a fresh approach. They held that biology alone could not determine morality, and that one should see morality in the unselfish pattern of a marriage taken as a whole rather than in individual acts of intercourse.

But *Humanae Vitae* dashed the hopes of change. The Commission, said Pope Paul, had proposed 'criteria' and 'solutions' which departed from traditional teaching, and no group of advisers could dispense him from a personal study of the matter (*Humanae Vitae*, 6). The Church had asked the Pope a question: the Pope had given his answer.

Much subsequent discussion has concentrated on the nature of papal authority rather than on the morality of contraception. And yet the encyclical was never presented as 'infallible'. Within a day of its publication, a Vatican spokesman had explained that although it was 'authoritative teaching', binding upon Catholics, it was not 'irreversible teaching'.

But whatever the status of the encyclical, there were immediate practical problems about how priests or Roman Catholic doctors should deal with couples who disagreed with its teaching and wished conscientiously to use contraceptives. Liberal-minded priests found themselves at odds with their bishops. There was confusion. Most of these quarrels quietly subsided with the passage of time. Disagreement is now tolerated or ignored.

Even those who accepted the encyclical provided two contrasting readings of it. The 'maximalists' tried to make literal fidelity to *Humanae Vitae* the norm of Roman Catholic orthodoxy. The 'minimalists', on the other hand, stressed that *Humanae Vitae* had not abolished the rights of the individual conscience, and they sought various 'pastoral solutions' for those who had difficulty with it.

The difference of emphasis was reflected in episcopal presentations of the encyclical. The Indian Bishops called upon everyone to give unquestioning obedience to *Humanae Vitae*, and hoped that the government would not impose penalties on those who disagreed with its family planning campaigns. Elsewhere the minimalist approach was used; the encyclical was treated with respect as one factor to be considered in reaching a moral decision, but not the only one. The Canadian Bishops declared their solidarity with the troubled laity, and said that 'the dignity of man consists precisely in his ability to achieve fulfilment through the exercise of a knowing and free choice'. The Scandinavian Bishops insisted that 'no one should be considered a bad Catholic because of his dissenting opinions'.

Some moral theologians have adopted a casuistical approach to the encyclical. Bernard Häring is an example. He exploits the opening provided by the following passage: 'The Church . . . does not at all consider illicit the use of those therapeutic means truly necessary to treat diseases of the organism, even if an impediment to procreation which may be foreseen should result therefrom, provided such impediment is not, for whatever reason, directly willed.' Häring gives 'therapy' a wide interpretation: it embraces the overall well-being, physical and psychological, of the woman, and there will be many cases in which the avoidance of another pregnancy can be recommended.[2]

Other theologians have not been content with casuistry. A non-infallible document, they claim, stands or falls on the validity of the arguments that it uses. Reuss[3], for example, follows Noonan[4] in conceding that the constant tradition of the Church has been against contraception, but insists that this is not enough to justify continued opposition, since many of the reasons previously advanced are now discredited or abandoned. Thus contraception was once opposed because intercourse could be justified only if directed to procreation: but the adoption of the safe period undermined this argument.

There has been, then, enough diversity of response to justify any position except irresponsible and selfish use of contraceptives. The actual views of Roman Catholics, maximalist or minimalist, casuistic or dissenting, cannot be known in advance. (See *Contraception*.)

1. Harris P, Hastings A, Morgan J et al. *On Human Life*. London: Burnes and Oates, 1968.
2. Häring B. *Medical ethics*. Slough: St Paul Publications, 1972: 87.
3. Reuss JM. *Familienplanung und empfängnisverhütung*. Mainz: Matthias-Grünewald-Verlag, 1976.
4. Noonan J. *Contraception*. Cambridge, Mass, 1965.
Delhaye P, Grootaers J, Thils G. *Pour relire Humanae Vitae*. Duculot: Belgium.

St John-Stevas N. *The agonising choice*. London: Eyre and Spottis-woode, 1971.

Peter Hebblethwaite

Hypnosis. The hypnotic state is a temporary state of altered attention in which the subject is in a condition of increased suggestibility.[1]

Hupnos is the Greek word for sleep but the hypnotic state is not identical with normal sleep as shown by, among other things, the differing electro-encephalogram recordings.

METHODS OF INDUCING HYPNOSIS

The hypnotic state can be produced in various ways, e.g. eye fixation, cataleptic hold, hand levitation and progressive relaxation. Often combinations of these methods are used, varying with operator, subject and circumstances. The co-operation of the subject is probably essential for successful hypnosis. It is said that only 10% of the population cannot be hypnotized. The more intelligent the subject and the more his ability to concentrate, the greater the likelihood of his being susceptible.

USES OF HYPNOSIS

Disorders treated by hypnosis fall roughly into three groups.[2]

(1) Psychosomatic disorders

Those conditions in which emotional and psychological factors result in disturbance of bodily function. Almost any system of the body can be affected and dramatic relief may result from suggestion under hypnosis.

(2) Psychiatric disorders

Hypnosis has been used by psychiatrists in the treatment of various conversion neuroses, anxiety states, phobias, obsessions and hysteria, but not usually in the treatment of psychotics

(3) A miscellaneous group of conditions.

In particular the relief of pain in childbirth and dental extraction and the alleviation of chronic pain such as that due to terminal cancer.

In psychosomatic and psychiatric disorders, the removal of symptoms by hypnosis without identifying or treating the cause is likely to result merely in replacing one set of symptoms by another. Treatment with hypnosis does not replace thorough psychiatric assessment and treatment.

In the third group the mechanism of production of symptoms is not in doubt and removal of such symptoms by hypnosis is fully justified.

DANGERS OF HYPNOSIS

Conn[3] discussed 3000 of his cases and compared his results with the current opinions of experts; he concluded that there were no significant or specific dangers associated with hypnosis *per se*. Bramwell[4] was certain that hypnosis increased the moral sense and came to the conclusion that his subjects would refuse to carry out suggestions under hypnosis which they would have rejected in their waking state. Martin Orne[5] after very many experiments stated that, 'the view that hypnosis is able to exert a unique form of control over the individual must be rejected.' However, other authorities assert[6] that hypnosis can be used to compel a subject to comply with actions against his wishes, and that any subject who fails to respond is *not* sufficiently hypnotized.

Others[7] maintain that any subject who would comply has the wish to do so and this gives him the opportunity to fulfil his wish. Watkins[2] states that the hypnotist who induces a subject to commit a crime would inevitably be an accomplice before and after the fact and, in law, equally culpable. Reiter[8] gives an example which is the one documented criminal case where a bank robbery was committed following a post-hypnotic syggestion. The hypnotist was convicted as an accomplice while the subject was considered mentally deranged.

Another danger of hypnosis is its effect on the hypnotist, particularly if he is unqualified in its use. The more skilled he becomes, the more he tends to confuse himself with the Almighty and eventually he may come to believe he can cure most conditions with his 'Magic Power'.

Last year (1979) two identical Bills, mainly aimed at restricting stage hypnotism, were introduced in the Lords and Commons. The sponsors, however, gave undertakings that the bills would not limit established lay hypnotists from conducting their business. This, in effect, means 'that lay hypnotists will continue to be allowed to advertise their skills as a cure for everything from smoking to sexual impotence'.[9]

CONCLUSION.

Orne[5] states that, 'Hippocrates realized that there is a unique quality in the doctor-patient relationship which makes the patient vulnerable and permits the sick and unscrupulous physician to use such a relationship in the service of his own gratification'.

There is general agreement with the conclusion of the American Psychiatric Association that 'the utilization of hypnotic techniques should be restricted to those individuals who are qualified by background and training to fulfil all the necessary criteria that are required for a complete diagnosis of the illness which is to be treated.'

1. Mason AA. *Hypnotism for medical and dental practitioners*, London: Secker & Warburg, 1960:17.
2. Watkins JG. *Int J of Clin Exp Hypn* 1972; 20: 95–100.
3. Conn JH. *Int J Clin Exp Hypn* 1972; 20: 61–79.
4. Bramwell JM. *Hypnotism: its history, practice and theory*. London: Grant Richards, 1903.
5. Orne MT. *Int J Clin Exp Hypnosis* 1972; 20: 101–17.
6. Wells WR. *J Psychol* 1941; 11: 63–102.
7. Erickson MH. *Psychiatry* 1939; 2: 391–414.
8. Reiter PJ. *Antisocial or criminal acts and hypnosis: a case study.* Springfield, Ill., Charles C. Thomas.
9. Ezard J. Lay hypnotists will continue to be allowed to advertise their skills as a cure for everything, *Guardian* 1979 Aug 27: 4.

M. D. Arwyn Evans

I

Iatrogenic Disease. Disease caused by a doctor or by the process of diagnosis or treatment.

In the last fifty years our therapeutic armamentarium has been enormously enlarged in all fields, e.g. internal medicine, psychiatry and surgery. Powerful new drugs are in the hands of the physician and the psychiatrist; the surgeon is able, with the aid of modern anaesthesia, antibiotics and bioengineering, to perform constructive and destructive operations not previously possible.

Powerful weapons such as these can cause harm as well as good and must, like a motor car, be kept under control. It is now more than ever essential before embarking on a course of treatment, medical or surgical, to consider not only whether it may do the patient good but whether it may do harm. In certain treatments it is accepted that some detrimental effect may be inevitable to achieve some other relief, and the treatment is given nevertheless (see *Double Effect: Psychopharmacology; Psychosurgery*). More often the disease is the untoward result of, or reaction to, treatment designed to relieve the patient's existing disorder.

Naturally any patient who realizes that his condition has become worse as the result of investigation or treatment will be bitterly resentful. Errors of omission are more easily forgiven than errors of commission, though the ethical issues for the doctor may be the same. The question of legal liability may arise as a related issue. (See also *Clinical Practice; Malpractice, Medical; Medical Science* (introductory essay); *Negligence*).

J. Halliday Croom

Immunization: (syn. vaccination) – the introduction of live or dead antigenic substances into the body in an attempt to stimulate immune responses and provide protection against disease.

It would always seem beneficial to increase resistance to disease and the resulting wide use of immunization bears witness to this thinking. The ethics of immunization concern not so much whom one should immunize, but rather whom one should refrain from immunizing. In general it is easier to make a vaccine than to know to whom it should be given. The fact that a manufacturer has a vaccine available (which

243

he is pressing to sell) may not be a good reason to use it for a disease which is unimportant and carries no serious morbidity or mortality.

Since harm ought not to be inflicted on a healthy person, all vaccines must be shown to be safe and effective. In fact, no vaccine can be absolutely safe, but it must be shown that the risks of damage as a result of immunization are much less than those associated with the disease itself. This becomes particularly important when the use of a vaccine has markedly reduced the incidence of a disease; for example, some countries stopped routine smallpox vaccination when it was realized that more people were dying as a result of vaccination than would have died from the disease itself. Nowadays there is no need to vaccinate anyone against smallpox except laboratory workers who are working in laboratories where the virus is under investigation. Because of the risk of vaccine complications and death from vaccines it would seem quite unethical for any physician to carry out routine elective vaccination of anyone in a world where there has been total global eradication of the disease. (The last case of naturally transmitted smallpox occurred in Somalia on 26th October 1977: in spite of intensive surveillance it has not been found elsewhere and the WHO Global Commission for the Declaration of Smallpox Eradicaton concluded in December 1979 that smallpox has been eradicated from the world).

If an individual accepts vaccination not so much in his own interest as with a view to the induction or maintenance of herd immunity, any untoward effect, if proved to be due to the vaccination, should be compensated by society. Compulsory immunization is considered by many to be ethically unacceptable.

While preliminary tests of the safety and efficacy of an immunization procedure can be made in animals, the final tests must be made in human beings. The animal tests show that the vaccines contain no contaminating agent, that inactivated vaccines contain no living agents and that the agents in live vaccines show no evidence of reversion to virulence or likelihood of spread. Only when these animal tests have been completed is it ethical to carry out tests of safety and effectiveness in man.

It seems right and proper that the first humans tested with a new vaccine should be susceptible (non-immune) members of the team of investigators who have developed the vaccine and that they should be kept under observation by an independent physician. In the case of vaccines containing live micro-organisms, the family contacts of those vaccinated must also be observed and tested for any evidence of spread of the agents. If there are no problems, an increasing number of colleagues of the investigators may be immunized and they and their contacts observed. If the material is to be used mainly in children the final tests of safety must be in children for there may be differences in susceptibility to some virus vaccines in children and in adults (e.g., the danger of encephalitis in infants who are given 17D yellow fever vaccine – one of the safest vaccines ever known – is well recognized).

When oral poliovirus vaccines were first tested in the United Kingdom the investigators first studied them in themselves (following a series of tests in non-human primates) and then in a gradually increasing number of their colleagues. Following what appeared to be a satisfactory outcome of these tests in adults, how could they be sure of the safety and efficacy of the vaccines in babies and children? It seemed unethical to offer these relatively untested vaccines to children unless they were sufficiently confident about their safety to give them to their own children and this was done. These tests in their own children indicated that certain attenuated viruses were quite unsatisfactory for further vaccine production and they were discarded.

When it came to testing quadruple (dip/tet/pert/polio) vaccine, the preliminary studies were made in babies – how else could they have been tested? Care was taken to ensure that, after all these trials, any baby in the trial was provided with as good a state of immunity as possible, and much better than the majority of the population in the community of similar age.

An important ethical consideration supporting the choice of doctors or their offspring in the early stages of a trial is that the doctors, whether as subjects or as parents, are in a favourable position to weigh up the risks and to give or to withhold consent which is genuinely 'informed' (see *Consent*). After a gradually increasing number of normal children have been tested in the community and all tests have shown that the vaccine is safe and effective, it would seem ethical to carry out studies of safety and effectiveness in closed communities of infants and children where opportunities of spread are greater and where the babies and children can be more carefully observed.

Some have supported the idea that a vaccine which spreads is of great advantage in that it can produce an 'epidemic of immunity', but others consider it unethical to introduce any agent into a community the spread of which could not be controlled, and wrong to subject any individual to immunization by a naturally spreading vaccine virus, particularly as there can be no certainty that in some circumstances such live agents might not regain virulence.

If the vaccine being tested is a new development of an existing vaccine, all babies and children taking part should, after the trials, be immunized with the existing routine vaccine and if necessary re-immunized to ensure that they are at least as well, if not better, protected than other individuals in the community at large.

Following preliminary trials a controlled blind trial should be carried out in the community in order to measure the degree of protection to natural challenge. This has not always been done when the vaccine seemed to have an obvious protective effect. Contra-indications to the administration of a vaccine must be clearly stated and known to those who use it; failure to observe such contra-indications could be considered as negligence.

It is wrong to introduce a vaccine into a community without considering the logistics of continuing immunization programmes. Thorough and long-term surveillance of the antigenicity of the product and the effectiveness of the immunization programme must be carried out. Failure to do this, as happened with the administration of whooping cough vaccine, has led to uncertainties about its value in some countries. The cost effectiveness of a vaccination programme requires consideration. A decision not to use a vaccine, e.g. in a developing community, has to be measured against its influence on overpopulation and a limited health budget. (See also *Clinical Trials; Health Education; Resources.*)

George Dick

Industrial Medicine. The practice of medicine within an industrial or commercial organization, and/or medical research associated with environmental problems arising from industry or commerce. (See *Occupational Medicine*).

Infanticide. The first thing to note about the term 'infanticide' is its equivocal character. On the one hand, it refers to killing an infant: one initiates an action or series of actions which cause the infant's death. On the other hand, infanticide sometimes refers to letting an infant die: one never initiates or one discontinues actions which might have saved the infant's life with the result that it dies, usually from some life-threatening defect. This entry will consider the ethical dimensions of both 'active' and 'passive' infanticide.

The ethical dimensions of infanticide are complicated by the unsettled moral status of infants in Western culture. It has not always been clear to us, now as well as in much of our history, whether infants generally should be accorded the same moral (and hence legal) standing as adult, intact human beings. Defective infants are an even greater conundrum as the older term used to denominate them, 'monster', clearly indicates. It should, therefore, come as no surprise that much of the contemporary discussion of the ethics of infanticide focuses on the moral status of the defective infant. To be sure, we are no longer moved by the superstitious and, by our lights, far-fetched accounts of that moral status offered in the past. Nevertheless, our scientific explanations of birth defects only compound the moral problems. There is only cold comfort to be had from the knowledge than an infant is defective because of a random and misfortunate roll of the genetic dice. What are the various ways in which the moral status of defective infants has been understood?

One view, which seems clearly to be in the minority, is that the defective infant, as for infants generally, is a full person with full moral status. On such a view the infant is possessed of a full right to life and hence an absolute right to treatment. Since the usual exceptions to respecting another's right to life, namely self-defence, fighting in a just war, etc, never apply to the defective infant, we always act improperly if we do not treat intensively such infants. *A fortiori*, the active killing of such infants will be entirely out of the question. This position is buttressed by pragmatic considerations. Exquisite as the skills of diagnosis of defective infants might be, prognosis is another matter. Any claim to know the future of a defective infant, especially with regard to its mental capacities and certainly with regard to its quality of life, is but a guess and thus subject to error. Since we cannot predict at birth what the outcome of treatment will be, except that the infant will have a chance to life, then prudence demands that we err, if at all, on the side of life.

Another view, on which there are variations, is that the moral obligations owed to infants are not absolute. Instead, the defective infant's right to treatment is limited, principally by quality of life considerations. The main elements of this view are the following. The defective infant, like normal infants, has a presumptive right to treatment: we should always begin by assuming (1) that we are obliged to treat such infants and (2) that the burden of proof falls on those who think that the infant should not be treated. That is, compelling reasons must be given to justify withholding or discontinuing treatment. The debate on this matter has centered on questions concerning (1) the efficacy of treatment for the defects, particularly life-threatening ones, and (2) the quality of future life, assuming intensive treatment, of the defective infant.

(1) Efficacy of treatment. One corrective to the view that all defective infants should be treated is that for some conditions treatment is not efficacious. Either there is no known treatment or what treatments we possess will only prolong the infant's dying. In such cases, therefore, we must accept that some infants will die no matter what we do. It is a commonplace of moral reasoning that 'ought' implies 'can'. That is, if one cannot fulfill an obligation one is under no such obligation. When there is no efficacious treatment for the infant's defect we do no wrong by allowing defective infants to die.

(2) Future quality of life. For many birth defects there are treatments that are more or less effective. The qualification is important because it should give us pause. We may be able to repair a defect, usually physical, but still not be able to make the infant whole by doing so. Sometimes the best we can do is to restore the defective infant only to some diminished degree of well-being. It is sometimes thought that when that diminishment is very severe, the obligation to treat the defective infant diminishes correspondingly. That is, the quality of the defective infant's future life may be so severely compromised that it will do little more than struggle to survive. Or, it may be both

severely mentally and physically handicapped, so that whatever developmental capacities it possesses will be constantly frustrated. In short, it will suffer terribly. Other defective infants in less severe straits, however, should be intensively treated. In the most severe circumstances as described above, though, it seems unreasonable to treat intensively the severely defective infant. Thus, we do no wrong by withholding or discontinuing treatment.

Some have argued that in these most severe cases we indeed do wrong by choosing the infant for 'passive' infanticide, because the dying process itself will be more severe than the future quality of life that non-treatment was intended to avoid. In such cases, because the death of the infant is the intended outcome, the distinction between 'passive' and 'active' infanticide collapses. Since the former, moreover, may violate the duty to avoid severe pain and suffering while the latter fulfills that duty 'active' infanticide for some very few defective infants may be morally justified.

There are at least two objections to this conclusion, even if its logic is intact. The first is that there are serious and well-founded legal barriers to such a practice. Secondly, one might object that a practice of active killing, even in the very limited circumstances of the above argument, will fundamentally compromise the life-preserving orientation of medicine. Hence, when argued in the broader moral context of medicine as a powerful social enterprise, the conclusion favouring a limited practice of active infanticide for some defective infants may not be acceptable.

Finally, even if we could settle the substantive ethical issues, serious procedural issues remain. These focus on the question of who should have the final authority to decide the medical fate of defective newborns. Traditionally, these matters have been left to doctors and parents to decide. But there is clearly a trend to question this practice. Hospital ethics committees, court review, or even regulatory remedies may also be appropriate. What seems clear is that there is dissatisfaction with the view that the final moral authority in these matters should devolve upon doctors alone, and physicians in particular. (See also *Abortion; Antenatal Diagnosis; Congenital Malformations.*)

Hauerwas S. Truthfulness and tragedy. University of Notre Dame Press, 1977.
Reich WT, ed. *Encyclopaedia of bioethics.* New York; Macmillan, The Free Press. See entries on infants, death and dying, mentally handicapped and acting and refraining.
Swinyard CA. Decision making and the defective newborn. Springfield: Charles C. Thomas, 1978.

Laurence B. McCullough

Infertility. The inability to produce living offspring[1]. Female sterility implies the inability to conceive due to some physical or psychological condition in the woman. In the male it is the inability to procreate. Sterility implies an absolute bar to conception whereas infertility signifies an impairment of normal reproductive capacity. The partners of a marriage may be considered infertile when pregnancy has not occurred with a year of regular coitus without contraception[2]. In Britain approximately 12% of couples are involuntarily infertile; the female being responsible in about one third, the male partner in a third and both in the remainder.

Some couples accept infertility without complaint but others are greatly distressed. While the stigma of infertility is declining in the West, women especially still face social, cultural and, in some countries, economic pressures to have children. As society is increasingly conscious of the obligation to provide education, work, good housing and health care, so that all may attain their full potential, it seems valid that assistance should be given, when desired, for individuals to achieve their reproductive capacity; for the urge to reproduce is a very basic one. Lack of resources (q.v.) may limit the amount of help available but there is no ethical reason to deny it, provided it does not entail methods[3] (see below) beyond normal corrective medical means. The aim should be achievement of conception through normal sexual union, or exceptionally through artificial insemination (q.v.) with the husband's semen (AIH), although this practice may be unacceptable to members of some religious faiths. Furthermore, nothing should be done which might hazard the rights or health of the child not yet conceived. It is sometimes argued that it is improper to use scarce resources to increase the birth rate because of the world population crisis (see *Population Policy*). In fact, successful treatment of infertility contributes insignificantly to total world population[4]. The conflict, however, between individuals' desire to reproduce and other health and welfare interests may pose dilemmas in selecting priorities.

Investigation of the infertile couple is recognized to be difficult, time consuming, sometimes rewarding but often disappointing. A reasoned assessment of their chance of success should be given. If there is uncertainty it is often advisable for the prognosis to err on the optimistic side. Apportionment of responsibility should, in general, be avoided. The risks of treatment, when feasible, must be weighed against the handicap of the infertility itself; for example, ovulation induction* in the female[5], and operations in both sexes carry recognized risks. Strict clinical criteria must be the yard-stick against which therapeutic regimes are measured. The extent to which, on occasions, medical help is requested may raise legal and ethical considerations. For example, the *desire* for childbearing by the partner of a sterile male, or by a woman with irreparably blocked oviducts, can

---

* *Ovulation induction*: Drug or hormone treatment designed to stimulate release of an ovum from the ovary.

be satisfied only by recourse to artificial insemination by donor (AID) (q.v.) in the former, and possibly by *in vitro* fertilization[6] (see *Embryo Transfer*) in the latter. Adoption is more acceptable, but fewer couples can now solve their problem in this way because of decreasing numbers of children available for adoption.

1. Browne FJ, Browne JC McC. *Postgraduate obstetrics and gynaecology*. 3rd edn. London: Butterworth, 1964: 391.
2. Kleegman SJ, Kaufman SA. *Infertility in women*. Philadelphia: FA Davis, 1966: 5.
3. Montgomery DAD, Welbourn RB. *Medical and surgical endocrinology*. London: Arnold, 1975: 223.
4. McNaughton MC. Treatment of female infertility. *Clin Endocrinol Metab* 1973; 2: 545.
5. Ramsey P. Shall we 'reproduce'? *JAMA* 1972; 220: 1346–50; 1480–5.
6. Steptoe PC, Edwards RG. Birth after the reimplantation of a human embryo. *Lancet* 1978; 2: 366 (Letter).

D. A. D. Montgomery

Informed Consent (see *Consent*). Consent is necessary before any therapeutic or experimental procedure is undertaken on a patient. Informed consent implies that the patient has been made fully aware of what he is agreeing to. Inasmuch as it is often impossible, or inadvisable, to give complete information, it is thought by some that the term 'informed consent' should not be used and that 'true consent' is a better term, for it recognises the trust in which the patient holds the doctor and the fact that consent is granted in the light of such explanation as he has been given and has been able to understand. For full discussion see entries on *Child*; *Clinical Trials*; *Human Experiment*; *Truth*.

Case Conference. The limits of informed consent. *J Med Ethics* 1975; 1: 146–9.

John Rivers

Insemination, Artificial. See *Artificial Insemination*.

Institute of Society, Ethics and the Life Sciences. See *Hastings Center*.

Insurance. See *Defence Societies; Human Experiment; Malpractice; Negligence; Private Practice*.

Intensive Care Units. Intensive care has been defined as the use of mechanical or electronic aid to support or maintain a vital function until the disease process, which caused the vital function to fail, is arrested or ameliorated. Frequently, more than one vital function fails, but the commonest one to do so is the respiratory system. Thus the first Intensive Care Units (ICUs) were respiratory units set up to deal with outbreaks of poliomyelitis. They were medically unique because patients were grouped according to their medical and nursing dependency rather than the interest and specialty of the responsible physician.

ICUs are also used often for intensive *observation* of vital functions in patients who may recover without intensive *therapy*, but who may need it at short notice.

The concentration of equipment and skilled staff in one area is therefore rational. Up to 3% of acute admissions to a general hospital may require intensive therapy and the provision of such facilities may deplete finance available for more traditional forms of medicine (see *Hospitals; Resources*). Recent advances in the Servo-control of equipment used in intensive therapy has decreased the numbers of highly trained and salaried staff required. Units now run efficiently with up to 60% of relatively untrained auxiliaries.

The admission of patients to an ICU should be controlled by one committed specialist, who can refuse admission if the patient is unlikely to benefit, or if his acceptance would so overload the resources of the unit that patients already there would be put at risk.

The ease with which certain vital functions can be supported has led to their deliberate therapeutic withdrawal, so that the systems providing them can be rested. For example, complete ventilatory support can be given to patients with severe asthma or chest injury or to those with tetanus who are receiving paralysing doses of curare for the prevention of fatal muscular spasms.

Intensive care has serious psychological effects on patients and their relatives and on the staff, and everyone concerned should be made aware of them.

The patients suffer in three ways:

1. Sensory deprivation. Critically ill patients sleep little because of the activity and noise of the units. The noise level is not constant; sudden excessive noise (above 70dB (A)) is common and causes arousal and may increase disorientation. Patients become lost in time and space because there are no familiar objects, no indications of the passage of time, no changes in the intensity of lighting by day or by night, and often no windows.

2. Lack of communication. During lucid moments some patients cannot speak, owing to the ventilatory machines to which they are attached, and visiting is very restricted.

3. De-personalization. As the techniques become more complex, the medical staff can or can appear to become more interested in pathophysiology than in the patients as persons.

The staff should make every effort to prevent distress from these causes.

The nursing staff may suffer in two ways:

1. Failure to understand the equipment or techniques used leads to a feeling of inadequacy and insecurity. This can and should be overcome by careful teaching and training.

2. The high mortality rate in ICUs (often over 50 per cent) throws a great strain on the nurses, especially if they become emotionally involved with patients and their relatives. Although there is great need for such close human relationships, for the reasons mentioned, it seems wise to have an equal number of apparently uncaring technocrats to even out the periods of elation and depression so characteristic of ICUs. Attempts have been made to prevent such problems by moving nursing staff temporarily to other parts of the hospital, but this has not been successful because they resent being moved and are not welcomed in other departments.

There have been several reports of severe depression and even suicide among nursing staff working in ICUs. The specialist in administrative charge of the unit should maintain close personal relationships with the staff and transfer to other work those who show real evidence of being unable to cope with the unusual demands.

1. Bentley S, Murphy F, Dudley H. Perceived noise in surgical wards and an intensive care area: an objective analysis. *Br Med J* 1977; 2: 1503.
2. *British Medical Association Planning Unit Report No. 1. Intensive Care*. London: B.M.A. Publications, 1967.
3. Robinson JS. The design and function of an intensive care unit. *Br J Anaesth* 1966; 38: 132.
4. Robinson JS. Psychologische auswirkungen der intensivpflege. (Psychological effects of intensive care – a personal account). *Der Anaesthetist*, 1975; 24: 416.

J. S. Robinson

Interprofessional Relationships. The era of medicine which saw the doctor enjoying what has been called a charismatic role has been changed over the last two decades by the advances in medical technology. This has opened up new areas for investigation, research and a reassessment of the role of the doctor and his position *vis à vis* other professionals working in his field. These advances have stimulated the development of departments and services which in their turn have demanded the setting up of professional bodies who are responsible for their professional and ethical standards. The result has been that while the doctor may well be the head of a team, he is nevertheless dependent upon the skills and integrity of the professionals working with him within the team for much of what is done in both curative and preventive medicine.

Areas of conflict can arise where poor communications exist between individuals and groups or when strongly held views are impossible to modify. This conflict may well occur in the field e.g. of abortion (q.v.) between doctor and nurse or between surgeon and anaesthetist. It has to be recognized that the maintenance of the profession's ethical standards may become strained as the result of competing priorities for resources (q.v.). The classic example is the competing claims upon resources for the acute and dramatic specialties and the resources required for the elderly, the long-stay and the handicapped (see *Geriatrics; Handicapped; Hospitals; Resources*).

In all countries the doctor assumes clinical responsibility and it is for this reason that whatever team mechanism is set up the doctor must take the final responsibility. Even within the medical profession specialization has now become so extensive that no single disease group is without its specialists and therefore interprofessional relationships have become extremely important to ensure that the combined skills of all are brought to bear on the patient requiring care. For many years the medical and nursing professions in many countries have enjoyed a very special relationship not only in the hospital but also in the community. This special relationship has been enhanced as nursing assumed a more technical and extended role but with both the advances in medicine and the subsequent increase in the professional groups, the need for some more formal relationship has become apparent. This more formal relationship has taken different shapes in different countries having different methods of working. The sheer size of the problem is exemplified by the wide spectrum of expertise in the fields of occupational therapy, dietetics, orthoptics, physiotherapy, radiography, medical laboratory technology, chiropody and those working in the remedial gymnastic field. In addition to those there are other professional groups such as speech therapists, operating room technicians, clinical psychologists, social workers, physiologists and ministers of religion. Even though the doctor may be ultimately in charge, technical and basic nursing, administration of drugs, occupation, diet, X-rays, the testing of intelligence, the working up to a point at which he can be discharged home and the involvement of the social worker, are all important parts of the care of the individual.

Although in teamwork the doctor must in most cases take the final responsibility, there are activities which are rightly the responsibility of other professionals. Teamwork leads to the need for delegation and ethical problems may arise as to how much is acceptable. In addition, for team members to be able to play a full role they need to share information about a patient which was formerly regarded as confidential between patient and doctor (see *Confidentiality*).

There are two areas of particular importance for the development of teamwork and team care. The more advanced forms of cardiac surgery and neurosurgery require a whole host of supporting staff in order to enable the surgeon to carry out his technical skills. It is however in the long-stay field that the development of teams of other professionals has taken on a new significance. Not only are there many more patients for one doctor to care for but their length of stay is measured in months and years rather than in days. The progress of patients is therefore more closely observed by the other professionals and their ability to comment and to suggest has become important. The care of the dying must not be overlooked for it is in this field that the supportive role of the clergy and others is so important (see *Death, Attitudes to; Hospices; Hospital Chaplains; Terminal Care*).

The method of achieving good interprofessional relationships is basically one of mutual trust with the recognition of each other's abilities, expertise, techniques and responsibilities. Many use case conferences and seminars to achieve this but in the final analysis the development of this team approach demands not only a clear definition of the objectives of the respective teams but the will to make it work.

One of the problems is that many doctors are unaware of some of the skills which can be contributed by members of the other health professions. For instance in one large teaching hospital occupational therapists used to be dismissed as 'raffia ladies'. This frequent ignorance is common among both hospital doctors and general practitioners. Those doctors who have built up a knowledge about the potential of other health professions have done so by having regular meetings to discuss patients' problems. The benefits of group meetings of this kind are not limited to the exercise of specialised skills. Not uncommonly the nurse or physiotherapist or occupational therapist has picked up a vital social problem which the patient has not revealed to the doctor or sometimes even to the social worker. Often in a rehabilitation problem, increasingly important with an aging population, physiotherapist, occupational therapist and social worker may have far more to contribute than the doctor and their opinions should be listened to. Such meetings, when they become part of the ward routine, do not take up much time and it is soon obvious how valuable they are to patients.

Relationships between specialties within medicine could be regarded as in some sense interprofessional. Theoretically the reorganization of the National Health Service was intended to lay the foundation for an integrated service serving both the patient and the community by close co-operation between hospital doctors, general practitioners and community physicians. In fact this has been given little attention, except, to some extent, by the Royal Colleges and Faculty of Community Medicine in Scotland. In particular the development of continuity of care in chronic diseases, designing a comprehensive service which fully utilizes the co-ordinated skills of hospital and general practice, is a challenge which has not yet been met.

Even within hospitals interspecialist relations may leave much to be desired. Communication between clinician and radiologist or laboratory worker purely by written forms gives rise to many misunderstandings and misinterpretations. Many units now find it of immense value to have regular interspecialty meetings where patients' problems are discussed. Those who take part in such meetings agree that all specialties have much to learn from them and that they can prevent a great deal of unhelpful, redundant and expensive investigation. They also lead to greatly improved personal relations. (See *Communication; Quality Assurance.*)

1. Annual Community Medicine Conference. *Integration of patient care.* Glasgow: Greater Glasgow Health Board, 1975.
2. *Challenge for change,* No. 7. London: Nuffield Provincial Hospitals Trust, 1971: 216.
3. Circular H.M. 67. London: Department of Health and Social Security, 1968.
4. DHSS. *Organisation of medical work in hospitals*: 1st Report 1967; 2nd Report 1972; 3rd Report 1974. London: HMSO.
5. Royal College of Physicians of Edinburgh. *Co-operation between medical and other health professions.* A Series of Six Reports: Chiropody, Dietetics, Medical Use of Laboratories, Occupational Therapy, Physiotherapy, Speech Therapy. Edinburgh: Royal College of Physicians, 1976.
6. Royal College of Physicians of Edinburgh. *Co-operation between medical and other health professions.* Second Series of Reports: Nursing, Pharmacy, Radiography, Social Work. Edinburgh: Royal College of Physicians, 1979.

The late Keith Porter
revised by John Crofton

IN GENERAL PRACTICE. Within the medical profession the relationship between the general practitioner and the hospital-based specialist has traditionally been based on the referral system whereby the general practitioner consults the opinion of a specialist regarding the management of his patient. In Britain, except in cases of emergency, the consultant does not normally see a patient without such a referral for the general practitioner, as doctor of first contact, acts as the patient's representative in all his dealings with specialist services in the medical or para-medical professions. It is for this reason that the general practitioner acts as the co-ordinator of patient care, and good inter- and intra-professional relationships can only be maintained if this fundamental role of the general practitioner is recognised. (See *General Practice.*)

A. G. Donald

Intersex. An intersex individual is one who does not clearly belong to either sex by reason of ambiguous sexual development. Such patients are: (a) Genetic females whose external genitalia have been masculinized by congenital adrenal hyperplasia *in utero* or from some other rare androgenic source. (b) Genetic males imperfectly masculinized by poor testicular function in the early embryo. (c) True hermaphrodites with ovarian and testicular tissue present; such patients may be genetic males or females or may have a gross sex chromosome anomaly.

Investigation as soon after birth as possible is required to determine the more appropriate sex of rearing, after which plastic surgical measures are needed to convert the genitalia to those of the chosen gender role. If recognized early in life, masculinized genetic females should always be brought up in the female role regardless of the degree of external masculinization present; undermasculinized genetic males and true hermaphrodites should be assigned to the gender role more appropriate to the functional possibilities of their external genitalia. If seen only later in life, the orientation of the individual to the sex of upbringing so far must be seriously taken into account before any decision on the subsequent sex of rearing is made.

There are other individuals without anatomical ambiguity of genitalia whose true sex may be in question by reason of their sexual behaviour. Included in this category are patients who get sexual satisfaction by dressing in clothing of the other sex – transvestites – and others whose psychological disturbances are deeper – transsexuals – who seek to live in the opposite gender role and seek sex re-assignment surgery to convert their genitalia to those of the opposite sex (see *Sexual Deviations or Variations; Sex Change, Reassignment or Reversal*).

Intersexual individuals with an anatomical ambiguity adapt admirably to the chosen sex if this decision is made wisely and early in life and if doubt is not cast thereafter on their sexual identity. Transsexual individuals remain a formidable problem for which a satisfactory solution is not yet available.

With increasing knowledge of intersexual conditions among the general public, a particular ethical – and medico-legal – difficulty is emerging. It is medically advantageous for certain male individuals to live in the female gender role (patients with testicular feminisation for example). It is also desirable that such patients do not know that they have fundamental male features such as male chromosomes and testes since their acceptance of the female role is better if they do not. When an explanation is given to these patients about their problem and its management, information may require to be withheld or presented in very general terms to hide its true nature. In some countries – the USA for example – withholding such information may leave the doctor vulnerable to litigation so that his interests and those of his patient may conflict. With even greater understanding and acceptance by the public of intersexual states, the need to withhold such information may diminish or disappear.

An interesting relationship exists between intersexuality and sport. Some intersexual individuals, who are phenotypically, wholly or predominantly female, may have a considerable physical advantage over a normal female. Thus, it is common to find that phenotypic females with androgen insensitivity (testicular feminization) who possess testes and a male chromosome complement, often possess a degree of athletic prowess. The additional androgen secretion by the adrenal of a female patient with congenital adrenal hyperplasia, would not only cause some masculinization of the external genitalia, but would, in some circumstances, give that individual additional physical strength.

Considerations of this kind have evidently led sporting authorities to attempt to grasp the nettle of intersexuality by insisting upon the examination of buccal smears in an attempt to identify the genetic male taking part in women's events; it is to be presumed that physical examination, to attempt to detect the competitors with clinical evidence of doubtful sex, is undertaken as well. Such authorities are, of course, at liberty to make their own rules for competitors, and ethical considerations come into it only in so far as examining doctors may be invited to pass on to a third party information concerning a patient. It may be presumed that an individual agreeing to a buccal smear and to a physical examination demanded by an athletic board was also agreeing to the information obtained being passed to the board requesting it, but in view of the very serious consequences, if an abnormality is detected, it would seem wiser for the doctor to obtain written consent (q.v.) from those tested before doing so.

Dewhurst CJ, Gordon RR. *The intersexual disorders.* London: Baillière, Tindall & Cassell, 1969.

Green R, Money J. *Transsexualism and sex reassignment.* Baltimore: Johns Hopkins Press, 1969.

Jones HW Jr, Scott WW. *Hermaphroditism, genital anomalies and related endocrine disorders.* Baltimore: Williams & Wilkins, 1971.

Overzier C, ed. *Intersexuality.* London and New York: Academic Press, 1963.

Jack Dewhurst

FURTHER ETHICAL ASPECTS. Personal satisfaction and considerations of social function and confidence would both favour a clear sexual identity where it may be had. But nature denies it to these individuals in varying ways and degrees. Professional intervention is called for (a) in advance of particular demand, e.g. when the intersex condition is observed very early in life and the doctor's general awareness of future problems would lead him to advise appropriate corrective measures; or (b) upon request, when a patient is dissatisfied with his condition, whether intersex or transsexual, either because of the limitations it imposes upon his personal fulfilment, or because of social misunderstanding, intolerance or lack of acceptance. The ethical possibilities for the practitioner seem to be: (1) to intervene surgically, pharmacologically or psychiatrically, when clinically appropriate, subject to the normal considerations of probable benefit, proportionate risk, side effects, etc; (2) to counsel the patient with a view to enabling him to accept what cannot be altered or could not be altered without disproportionate harm; (3) to seek to increase public understanding of the problem, and so to modify social attitudes which add to the difficulties of the individuals concerned; (4) to record his cases with careful detail in order to further clinical understanding and research for the benefit of others.

G. R. Dunstan

Ionizing Radiation. The term refers to radiation from a group of high energy particles or electromagnetic waves which have the property of ionizing the atoms through which they pass. It includes X-rays, produced in X-ray sets; α and β-particles, and γ-rays, emitted from radioactive substances; and neutrons, electrons, protons, and other nuclear particles, produced in nuclear reactors or accelerators.

In medicine, X-rays are the most commonly used, but there is an increasing use of radio pharmaceuticals for diagnostic tests. All these types of radiation are used in radiotherapy.

Because of their high energy, ionizing radiations can destroy the tissue through which they pass. This property – which is purposely employed in radiotherapy to destroy cancer cells – introduces an element of risk (q.v.) whenever radiations are used in medicine. With high doses delivered to the whole body the hazard is acute and death may ensue within a few weeks; however, such exposures are unlikely to occur except in an accident. The main concern is about small doses which are given to patients in X-ray diagnostic investigations, particularly in barium swallows, pelvimetry, cardiac catheterization, or repeated fluoroscopy. The chief hazard is the induction of cancer (q.v.), which may appear years after the exposure. When the gonads are exposed there is also the risk of genetic damage to future generations (see *Genetic Conditions*).

Because of these hazards, any exposure of patients to ionizing radiation has to be carefully considered and the risks weighed against the benefits.

The difficulty in making such a balance is that it is impossible to give an accurate quantitative assessment of the risk of small doses of radiation. It can only be estimated by extrapolating from effects observed at high doses, and by making certain assumptions, e.g. that the increase in risk is proportional to the increase in dose, and that there is no threshold or safe dose. For the carcinogenic effect the best data available lead to a figure for the increase in the probability of occurrence of cancer of one in fifty thousand (2×10^{-5}) for each milligray (mGy) of absorbed dose. (The Gray (Gy) is the unit of dose and corresponds to the absorption of 1 Joule per kilogram of tissue.) For genetic effects there is a very wide range of damage, but the overall risk is of the same order of magnitude as for the somatic effects. For comparison purposes it is useful to note that the natural background of radiation, to which we are all exposed all the time, amounts to 0·8 mGy per year. (1Gy = 100 rad.)

The average dose, as far as carcinogenic action is concerned, from all X-ray procedures in medicine is about 0·4 mGy per capita per year. The average increased risk of cancer is, therefore, about one in 120,000. However, it should be remembered that some diagnostic procedures result in doses 100 or even 1000 times greater than the average, with a corresponding increase in the risk of cancer to the individual. Moreover, the sensitivity to radiation is greater in childhood, and particularly so in the fetal stage. For this reason no X-rays are given to pregnant women unless other considerations make it necessary. To avoid the risk of unrecognized early pregnancy, the 10-day rule has been introduced, i.e. that women in the reproductive age may be given X-rays only during the 10 days following the first day of the last menstrual period.

It should also be noted that the harmful effects of radiation are cumulative, i.e. each further dose adds proportionately to the risk (except at old age). For this reason all exposures of patients should be recorded, and no exposure is supposed to be made without the patient's record card being available.

Care is also necessary to protect the personnel operating X-ray equipment or other appliances involving ionizing radiation. The present regulations for persons occupationally exposed to radiation stipulate a dose limit of one milligray per week. In hospital practice, however, one aims not to exceed one tenth of this figure. All personnel are obliged to wear radiation monitors which are read regularly.

While in the case of patients the possible risks from radiation – if all care is taken to reduce the exposure to the necessary minimum – is usually justified by the objective of immediate benefit to his health, such considerations do not apply to radiation research conducted on volunteers. Since it is often impossible to extrapolate from animals to man, some experiments involving human beings are probably necessary; the knowledge acquired from such experiments may help to alleviate suffering. There are no definite rules which could serve as guidelines for ethical committees (see *Research Ethical Committees*) which have to approve such experiments, but the British Institute of Radiology has made some suggestions based on an unpublished document of the World Health Organization. Several categories of research projects are considered, each with specified limits of the radiation dose and the corresponding committee from which approval should be sought. The free consent of the volunteer, which includes an explanation of the amount of the radiation to be given and the possible risk, is of course essential (see *Consent; Human Experiment*).

British Institute of Radiology, Irradiation of human subjects for medical research. *British Institute of Radiology Bulletin* 1975; Vol 1, No 2.
Coggle JE. *Biological effects of radiation*. London: Wykeham Publications, 1971.
National Academy of Sciences. *The effects on populations of exposure to low levels of ionizing radiations*. Washington, 1972.
United Nations Scientific Committee on the Effects of Atomic Radiation. *Ionizing radiations, Vol II, Effects*. New York: United Nations Organization, 1972.
World Health Organization. *Health hazards of the human environment*. Geneva: WHO, 1972.

Joseph Rotblat

Islam. In Islam there is no intrinsic medical system comparable, e.g., to the Ayurveda in Hinduism. Together with philosophy and the other secular sciences, medical science as a whole was taken over from the Greeks by translating the available texts of Hippocrates, Rufus, Galen, Dioscorides and others in Arabic. These translations, together with later adaptations, commentaries and additions, led to a hey-day of Greek medicine in the Arab world. Later, however, Islamic orthodoxy attempted to build up an Islamic or 'prophetic' medicine on the basis of the Koran and the corpus of sayings ascribed to the prophet Muhammed. Its object was defined as the knowledge of the beginnings of the human body, its condition in health and sickness, the causes and symptoms of the latter, and the means of warding off disease and preserving good health.

If 'prophetic' medicine blurred the rationalistic attitude of the Greek heritage by introducing and sanctifying the use of talismans, potions from the washed off ink of Koran verses and other magical lore, it also helped to defend medicine against opponents from within the ranks of the so-called 'people of the trust in God' and the extreme predestinarians. Prophetic medicine was in fact only one aspect of the Islamic attitude towards medicine. The other and more brilliant aspect is represented by a multitude of broad-minded Muslim promoters of the healing art among caliphs, scholars and other high-ranking personalities. It must be said, however, that during the first four or five centuries of Islam, the majority of physicians were Christians and Jews.

The basic ethical text for the Arabic physician, regardless of his religion, was, therefore, the Hippocratic Oath (q.v.). Other important

Greek sources, the influence of which can be traced in the pertinent Arabic literature through the centuries, were Galen's probably spurious commentary on the Oath, his 'On that a really good physician be (at the same time) a philosopher', where the physician is warned against being inveigled by worldly goods and pleasures, and the same author's 'On examining the physician', which is in fact a guide book for laymen instructing them how to assess a good doctor and laying the main stress again on the behavioural side: 'A good physician should not be a courtier nor a lickspittle of rich people. He should not indulge the cravings of his patients as long as any possible damage to their health was involved. And he should watch over the preparation of drugs he prescribed and let nobody interfere with his prescriptions and treatments except responsible and reliable persons. His main concern should not be how to become rich and famous, but how to cure men's illnesses, and he should be ready to treat the poor without fees.'

These ideals were handed on by Arabic physicians, but relevant writings are few, one of the most important being the book *Adab at-tabib*, or practical ethics of the physician, by a Jewish author of the 10th century AD. As always where the history of social ideas is concerned, it is difficult to know how far these ideals were put into practice. That some, if not the majority, did so is shown by the example of the great philosopher-physician Rāzî (died 925) who is expressly reported to have cured poor people gratuitously.

One issue where differences between theory and practice are clearly indicated is abortion. Though prohibited in the Hippocratic Oath, many abortifacient drugs are described in the pharmaceutical text-books. This may be because abortion was not so strictly prohibited in Islamic law as in medical tradition.

Medicine also lent its art willingly to the sterilization (see *Castration*) of eunuchs, and apparently raised no objections to the amputations and the bastinado which were ordered by Islamic law as a punishment for some offences. Chopping off of the right hand, under medical supervision, is still the official Koranic punishment for a thief in Saudi Arabia (see *Mutilation*).

It should be kept in mind that medical ethics in Islam – as well as in ancient Greece – were on the whole more concerned with the profession than with the patient. Many of its instructions are in fact directed against charlatanism (a much more potent rival in those times than it is today) and concerned more with the honour of the art than with the welfare of the ill. Thus physicians were warned not to take up or continue treatment of a patient whose disease appeared to be incurable.

Although there was little actual control of medical practice and ethics, there were two systems by which, at least in theory, they could be supervised. On the one hand the doctor in a town was under some sort of supervision by the *muhtasib*, or controller of market and public morals, to whom, according to some sources, he would swear the Hippocratic Oath. But as in general this man would have no knowledge of medicine, it is unlikely that his control was very effective. On the other hand, the hierarchical structure which existed in the towns may have served, at least casually, as a kind of control system. Writers on standards of medical ethics put forward lack of state control as one of the principal reasons for the decline of the medical art. There is no evidence of an official ethical code for the medical profession prior to the Othmanic era when, with the introduction of Kanunnames, official legislation on a broader scale began and included some rules for the conduct of medical men.

Orthodox Islam has not moved its position, but individual Muslims have at various times adopted the results of the scientific investigations of their day rather than those of scholastic theology. As a result, modern medicine in Islamic countries which have come under Western influence tends to follow the Western pattern.

J. Christoph Bürgel

J

Japanese Medicine. See *Shinto*.

Jehovah's Witnesses. A religious sect whose members do not accept blood transfusion for themselves or for their children. Ethical issues are discussed under *Blood Transfusion*.

Journal of Medical Ethics. The *Journal of Medical Ethics* is published quarterly by the Society for the Study of Medical Ethics (q.v.). It was established in 1974 to promote the study of contemporary medico-moral problems and to influence the quality of both professional and public discussion.

The Editorial Board includes leading members of the medical specialties, together with representatives of the Law, the Church, and disciplines such as moral philosophy and sociology.

Edward Shotter

Journal of Medicine and Philosophy. See *Society for Health and Human Values*.

Journalism. See *Medical Journalism*.

Judaism. In spite of the Biblical reproach of King Asa who 'sought not to the Lord, but to physicians' (II Chronicles 16:12) and notwithstanding that the second century teacher Rabbi Judah declared that 'the best of doctors will go to Hell' (Mishnah end of tractate Kiddushin), Judaism looks upon the craft of healing with very few exceptions as a great good and an instance of man's partnership with God. Some of the most distinguished Rabbis were themselves physicians. The governing principle in Jewish medical ethics is the supreme importance of the preservation of life so that things otherwise prohibited by Jewish law must be set aside in order to save life. Thus even though it is forbidden to mutilate a corpse, heart and kidney transplants as well as corneal grafting are permitted, provided of course that the utmost care is taken to be sure that the person whose body is being used for the purpose is really dead (see *Tissue Transplant*). On euthanasia (q.v.), the weight of authority is against any direct intervention for whatever reason, but conscious failure to keep a dying person alive by the use of artificial methods is viewed less severely. Reform Judaism permits all methods of contraception (q.v.) whereas Orthodoxy only permits those that involve 'wasting of seed' where there is danger to the life of the wife if she becomes pregnant. However, this is usually interpreted in a liberal manner and the tendency is emerging to permit the use of oral contraceptives even for social and family reasons. Feticide is not considered to be homicide in Jewish law; nevertheless, abortion (q.v.) is severely frowned upon except where there is a strong possibility that the child will be born grossly deformed. Some authorities permit the abortion of a fetus conceived through the rape of a married woman. Artificial insemination (q.v.) where the donor is not the husband (AID) is held to be forbidden by the vast majority of the authorities but only a very few see any objection where the donor is the husband (AIH). Sterilization (q.v.), whether of men or women, is strictly forbidden according to Orthodoxy. No objections have been raised to plastic surgery (see *Cosmetic Surgery*). The use of animals for medical experiments, the aim of which is the increase of knowledge resulting in an increase of human health, is permitted, provided care is taken to reduce animal suffering to the minimum (see *Animal Experiment*).

Freehof B. *Current reform responsa.* New York, 1969. *Modern reform responsa.* New York, 1971. *Reform responsa and recent reform responsa.* New York, 1973. *Contemporary reform responsa.* New York, 1974.

Jacobs L. *What does Judaism say about . . .?.* Jerusalem and New York, 1973.

Jakobovits I. *Jewish medical ethics*, 2nd edn. New York: Bloch, 1975.

Jakobovits I. Some recent responsa of medical subjects . In: Zimmels HS, Rabbinowitz J, Finestein I, eds. *Essays presented to Israel Brodie, Chief Rabbi.* London: Sancino Press, 1967: English section 183–203.

Louis Jacobs

K

Kidney. See *Haemodialysis*; *Tissue Transplant.*

King Edward's Hospital Fund for London. The Fund, generally known as 'The King's Fund', was founded on the personal initiative of King Edward VII, while he was still Prince of Wales, in 1897. It became an independent charity incorporated in 1907 by Act of Parliament, which stated its purpose as:

> the support benefit or extension of the hospitals of London or some or any of them (whether for the general or any specific purposes of such hospitals) and to do all such things as may be incidental or conducive to the attainment of the foregoing objects.

This remit is generously interpreted and the Fund has traditionally concerned itself with measures for the improvement of standards of hospital practice. Whilst this does not extend to provision for clinical research it has always been accepted that projects aimed at the preparation of doctors, nurses and administrators for the better undertaking of their responsibilities in the work of hospitals (and indeed of the health service generally) is a necessary and important element in the fulfilment of the Fund's trust.

For this purpose the Fund maintains a residential college in Bayswater (the King's Fund College); and the King's Fund Centre in Camden where numerous conferences and study groups are arranged and where there is an extensive library and information service.

The Fund supports projects and investigations in health affairs. Other activities include publications on numerous health topics and the provision of bursaries to enable professional men and women to gain wider experience through study abroad.

It is perhaps in the context of education in the organization and practice of health systems and the support of related projects that the interests of the King's Fund most closely coincide with the aims of those whose particular concern it is to encourage recognition of the importance of ethics in the care of the sick.

Address: 14 Palace Court, London W2 4HT.

G. A. Phalp

L

Lesbianism. Female homosexuality. Lesbian activities were never made a statutory crime in the UK as the practice of male homosexuality was. (See *Homosexuality; Sexual Deviations or Variations.*)

Leucotomy. Cutting certain white matter fibres of the brain. *Lobotomy* is cutting into one of the lobes of the brain. These operations are performed with the aim of producing personality change as a treatment for certain illnesses. (See *Psychosurgery.*)

Leverhulme Trust. The Leverhulme Trust was founded by the first Viscount Leverhulme at his death in 1925. The Trust's income, from its holding of shares in Unilever Limited, is currently some £2½ million a year.

The purposes of the Trust are research and education without restriction of field but the Trustees as a matter of policy avoid projects within the ambits of, e.g. the Medical Research Council and specialist foundations. They have recognized the importance of the study of medical ethics by financing, 1975–78, a research fellow and associate for experiments in study and teaching by the Edinburgh Medical Group and by providing, 1978–81, a senior educational fellowship for the Director of Studies of the London Medical Group.

Address: 15–19 New Fetter Lane, London EC4A 1NR.

Ronald C. Tress

Life, Prolongation of: Ordinary and Extraordinary Means. The language of 'ordinary' and 'extraordinary' means is used by moralists to distinguish between obligatory and discretionary procedures for the preservation of life. When the terms occur in medical usage, their connotation differs from that in moralists' usage. The intention in both, however, is the same: to insist that it is the patient's ultimate interest which should determine the treatment he receives, that interest being seen in relation to his unique being and his unique human and social environment. Both usages enhance the discretion (and therefore the responsibility) of the physician in deciding appropriate management for each patient, having in mind not only his medical condition but also his spiritual and emotional capacity, his religious conviction, the degree of affective interaction between him and those nearest to him, his personal and social commitments, and what can be afforded (by his family or by the State) on his behalf.

For a moralist, 'ordinary' procedures would include all those which, in a particular setting (e.g. in the vicinity, it may be, of a London teaching hospital or of a Tanzanian village health centre), offer a patient a reasonable hope of benefit, without excessive expense, pain or other serious inconvenience. These procedures the patient is under obligation to seek (and the physician is under obligation to provide) because of his general duty to live as healthily as he can, in his own interest and that of the society of which he is a member. 'Extraordinary' procedures are those which do not satisfy these criteria of 'ordinariness', which would impose on the patient undue suffering or expense, or, it may be, an undue distortion of his personality or a barrier in his relationships with his kin, a lessening of his human capacity, and all without a reasonable hope of benefit. These he is not bound to seek nor his physician bound to administer – except in particular circumstances, e.g. of a patient requiring a little more time for his spiritual or religious preparation for death, or of a monarch, statesman or soldier on whose continued living great public issues are seen to depend.

In medical usage, 'ordinary' would indicate what is normal, established, well-tried; of known effectiveness, within the resources and skills available; of calculable and acceptable risk; of generally low mortality; involving pain, disturbance, inconvenience, all within predictable limits of acceptability and control; and all proportionate to an expected and lasting benefit to the patient. These procedures the patient has a right to require and the physician a duty to undertake. 'Extraordinary' means would include investigatory and experimental procedures of uncertain efficacy, or even carrying a high mortality rate; those involving a heavy disproportion between the pain, mutilation, disfigurement or psychological disruption of the patient and any immediate or long-term benefit reasonably predictable; or of disproportionate cost. These, though eligible on a basis of consent, the patient is not bound to ask for nor the physician bound to provide. The criteria for decision relate primarily to the patient, not to the remedy: thus to prescribe an antibiotic for the control of pneumonia in a young patient with the prospect of a full life before him would now be 'ordinary'; for another person in extreme old age, burdened with other severe and irremediable disorders, it would be 'inappropriate management'.

'Extraordinary' means may become 'ordinary' as experimental procedures become established, as risks, costs, inconveniences etc. are reduced, or as acceptability grows. General anaesthesia, analgesia in childbirth and many surgical interventions have passed through this transition; others like transplant surgery (see *Tissue Transplant*) are in transit now.

267

Linacre Centre for the Study of the Ethics of Health Care

The distinctions have come into prominence in recent years in the context of intensive and terminal care, especially in the management of patients who, because of a brain lesion, would suffer respiratory collapse and cessation of circulation but for the support of a ventilator or respirator (see *Death, Determination of; Intensive Care Units; Terminal Care*). Pope Pius XII, in an allocution to anaesthetists on 24 November 1957, used them in answer to questions posed. In general (though with qualifications) he designated the ventilator, after an adequate period of trial to test the possibility of spontaneous function, an 'extraordinary' means of sustaining life (or, rather, circulation) without which life would cease; no patient was bound, therefore, in normal circumstances, to require its continuance, nor the physician to continue it. It was licit for him to withdraw the ventilator before circulation had ceased, even though circulation would then cease and the patient would die. While excluding from ecclesiastical competence the question of how or when the moment of death is determined (since it cannot be deduced from any moral or religious principle), he maintained that while the vital functions – as distinct from simple organic or biological life – continued either spontaneously or with support, the patient should enjoy the presumption of having a human life, with all the personal consideration and ethical protection which is thus its due.

Blomquist C. Moral and medical distinctions between 'ordinary' and 'extraordinary' means. In: *Decisions about life and death: A problem in modern medicine*. London: Church Assembly Board for Social Responsibility, 1965, Appendix 4.

Kennedy I. The Karen Quinlan Case. *J Med Ethics* 1976; 2: 3–7.

Piux XII, Pope. Allocution to anaesthetists, 24 November 1957. French tr, Wolstenholme GW, O'Conner M. *Ethics in medical progress*. London: Churchill, 1966.

G. R. Dunstan

Linacre Centre for the Study of the Ethics of Health Care. A charitable trust (Reg. No. 274327) formed by the Roman Catholic Archbishops of England and Wales.

The Centre was founded in 1977 to help Catholic health-care practitioners to deal with moral problems arising in their work and to present their moral views to colleagues. Its governing body includes doctors, nurses and theologians. Discussion papers are published on topics causing difficulty. These represent joint work by clinicians and moralists. Topics studied include 'prolongation of life', resulting in three LINACRE CENTRE PAPERS published in 1979; 'trends towards euthanasia', conducted by a multi-disciplinary working party; and 'the ethics of co-operation', in relation to clinical practices that conflict with Catholic moral principles. The Centre collaborates with Christian and other organizations in seeking to apply ethical principles to health care. A Newsletter is issued. Speakers are obtained for local discussion groups. The Centre has offices in the Convent attached to the Hospital of St John and St Elizabeth. Its library is housed at Heythrop College, University of London.

Enquiries should be addressed to The Linacre Centre, 60 Grove End Road, London NW8 9NH (Tel 01–286 5126).

F. D. K. Williams

Liver Transplant. See *Tissue Transplant.*

Local Health Councils. See *Health Councils.*

London Medical Group. See *Society for the Study of Medical Ethics.*

M

Malpractice, Medical* Unskilful, faulty, injurious, or unauthorized medical acts.

Any medical act may have a result which is less than the ideal or different from what the patient expected, and the question may be raised whether a mistake was made or an unauthorized act performed. In the United States, when an injury has occurred for which no compensation is available, redress is often sought by trying to establish tort liability through trial by jury. Such large awards have been made that liability insurance is becoming extremely expensive and difficult to obtain. Premiums for professional liability insurance range from $6,000 to $40,000 a year, depending on the specialty involved. 'Expectation', as the basis for claims for negligence is one of the points of difference between the USA and the UK in relation to malpractice. NEGLIGENCE (q.v.). Negligence is an unintentional tort resulting in personal injury for which compensation (q.v.) may be claimed. The *prima facie* case for negligence has four components: duty, breach, causation, and damages. Although the tort of negligence is essentially the same, there are certain developments in the United States which merit mention.

1. 'Good Samaritan acts' which protect the physician from the charge of negligence while rendering emergency (q.v.) treatment outside the scope of his own practice have been enacted in virtually all of the States. To date there have been no judgements for malpractice against 'good Samaritans'.

2. The concept of the standard of care which a physician can reasonably be expected to provide has been broadened from the 'locality rule' to 'a national standard.' Unless a physician provides care comparable to the best in the nation he may be liable to a charge of negligence.

3. The physician's duty of disclosure of risks, so as to obtain 'informed consent' (q.v.), has been subjected to such scrutiny in the courts that even very 'remote risks', commonly understood to be

* This entry relates to practice in the USA since the term malpractice is used infrequently in the UK. For UK practice see *Negligence; Assault* and the other Cross References.

remote, are being explained to patients by some physicians (see also *Truth*).

4. The doctrine of *respondeat superior* makes the physician or surgeon responsible for the acts of all members of the medical-surgical team over whom he has direct control, although each member may have direct legal and moral responsibility for certain aspects.

5. The doctrine of *res ipsa loquitur* (the thing speaks for itself) may make a negligent act so obvious that defence in court is not feasible. Such cases may be settled out of court. For example, if a swab is left in the wound, and appropriate precautions were not taken, negligence is evident.

ASSAULT AND BATTERY are intentional torts which may have purely civil cause for action or, in exceptional circumstances, may be classed as criminal. Intentional torts, even though regarded as civil causes of action, may not be covered by professional liability insurance. Although civil assault and battery are always intentional, some cases may be claimed as negligence, such as when the wrong leg is amputated.

Failure to obtain appropriate consent (q.v.) may make a medically justifiable act an intentional assault and battery. If the surgeon, with the best of intentions, proceeds with an elective operation which is clearly indicated, but for which the patient has not given consent, he may be charged with assault and battery. In an emergency or an unanticipated condition where immediate action is necessary to preserve the life or health of the patient, consent is not necessary, and it is the duty of the surgeon to do what the occasion demands.

THE LEGAL PROCESS. The legal process in the United States is an adversary system which attempts to reconstruct what happened before the court, but the result depends upon the skill of the lawyers and the experience and performance of plaintiff, defendant and witnesses. The jury or judge decide what they think is proved rather than what actually happened. Thus, even when negligence is not clearly established but the injury is severe, a skilful lawyer may persuade a sympathetic jury to decide for the plaintiff. Compensation may amount to millions of dollars. Likewise a skilful lawyer may be able to protect an incompetent doctor. In all cases the judge has the authority to reduce or increase the amount of compensation awarded by a jury for a negligent act.

With the increase in malpractice suits it is not unknown for an attorney to represent a client on the understanding that if the case fails there will be no fee (contingency fee arrangement). Such a practice clearly encourages patients to bring even frivolous actions since they have nothing to lose. This in turn undermines confidence between patients and doctors and alters the attitudes of doctors in their practice.

Many physicians and surgeons in the United States are arranging with patients for arbitration of any incident which might be considered negligence or malpractice. Some groups of physicians have established their own insurance companies for the specific purpose of arbitration and settlement of such claims.

The best defence of the physician against suit is a close personal and sympathetic relationship with the patient (see *Clinical Practice*) and carefully documented records (see *Medical Records*).

FEE SPLITTING, ITINERANT SURGERY AND ADVERTISING TO THE PUBLIC are regarded as professionally unethical practices (ie. they offend against professional etiquette) but are not necessarily illegal. Doctors who engage in such practices are subject to disciplinary action by professional societies.

Fee splitting implies that the specialist, usually a surgeon, shares his fee with another doctor to encourage referral of patients. Fee splitting also occurs if a physician refers his patients to a particular pharmacy or optical firm for which he receives a secret payment or otherwise profits financially from the transaction.

If a referring doctor actually participates and contributes to the care of the patient, he may receive an appropriate fee, but this must be with the knowledge of the patient and separate billings should be made. The American College of Surgeons requires its members, on admission, to pledge not to split fees; proved fee splitting is a ground for withdrawal of membership.

Itinerant surgery is the practice of operating on patients in a hospital so far away from the surgeon's usual place of practice that he cannot provide proper postoperative care. Itinerant surgery may lead to a malpractice suit for negligence if harm comes to the patient because of the unavailability of the surgeon.

Public appearances by physicians are often requested by news and television media. In such circumstances it is essential for the individual to limit his presentation to the facts and carefully avoid statements which might be favourable to him and his hospital but prejudicial to others. Advertising and deliberate seeking of public appearances are unethical, particularly if the practitioner pretends to have a new or unusual skill or form of treatment. (See *Advertising; Communication*.)

Releasing the name of a patient and the nature of his illness or operation to the press or other media makes a practitioner liable to a charge of invasion of privacy unless he has obtained the specific written permission of the patient. (See *Confidentiality*.)

Recently the Federal Government has been investigating professional societies and questioning their right to prevent physicians from advertising on the grounds that this represents 'restraint of trade'. The Government is arguing that if physicians advertised, competition might result in a reduction of fees and a lowering of the costs of medical care. (See also *Clinical Practice; Defensive Medicine; Disciplinary Procedures; European Economic Community; General Medical Council*).

Bergen RP. The confusing law of informed consent. *JAMA* 1974; 229: 325.

Curran WJ, Shapiro ED. *Law, medicine and forensic sciences*. 2nd edn. Boston: Little, Brown & Co., 1970.

Holder AJ. *Medical malpractice law*. London and New York: John Wiley, 1975: 56.

Moritz AR, Morris RC. *Handbook of legal medicine*. 3rd edn. St Louis: C. V. Mosby, 1970.

Waltz JR, Inbau FE. *Medical jurisprudence*. New York: Macmillan, 1971.

J. Englebert Dunphy

Marital Pathology and Counselling. The essential characteristics of marital pathology are those of sustained and persistent tension in the relationship of a couple which, if not reversed, will lead to the break-down of their marriage and the dissolution of an attachment or human bond. The idea that a science can emerge which is capable of examining and explaining the reasons for marital breakdown is still foreign to society as a whole and to medical circles in particular. Nevertheless, research has been proceeding for nearly fifty years along these lines and, despite the tentative nature of the findings, a picture is emerging which is likely to be increasingly influential in clarifying the social and psychological basis of marital pathology and providing the foundations for greater understanding. This, it is hoped, will lead ultimately to the *prevention* of marital breakdown rather than to measures to deal with the situation once it has happened. The relationship between this research and the ethics of marital breakdown and divorce is very close. Marriage and the family are uniquely important in every society and have a special significance for Christianity with its emphasis on the permanency of marriage as the Christian ideal.

Tension may be expressed in physical or psychological terms. Physical manifestations are tiredness, headaches, insomnia; symptoms referable to the chest such as chest pain, breathlessness, intensification of asthma in those predisposed to it; to the heart with pain near the cardiac territory and palpitations; to the gastro-intestinal tract with the presence of pain or change of bowel habit; to the skin with exacerbations of existing disorders or new symptoms; to the back with backache and disorders of menstruation in women. Psychologically there will be evidence of anxiety and depression with all the familiar symptoms of those disorders. If the stress is unrelieved, suicidal attempts and sometimes suicide (q.v.) itself may follow.

Children in the family may also suffer with either somatic or psychological complaints, difficulties at school or social problems such as juvenile deliquency, and beyond this there lies the shadow of the long-term effects on the personality of the child if the situation is not resolved or the marriage is ended in divorce or separation.

The size of the problem is not always appreciated. It is impossible to gauge exactly the dimensions of marital pathology which remains a private matter until it reaches the point when a couple seek a divorce, but figures for divorce petitions in England and Wales show a huge rise since 1959, when they were at their lowest postwar level. From 26,327 in that year, the figure more than doubled to 55,007 in 1968 and again to 110,017 in 1971 when the new Divorce Act came into effect. In 1974 the number was 130,900 and shows no sign of falling. A current estimate of likely marital breakdown in the years to come is that between one sixth and one quarter of existing marriages will break down. This involves millions of men and women and there can be little doubt of the seriousness of marital pathology in Western society because the pattern observed in the UK is widespread throughout most Western countries.

Why is such a change occurring? Firstly, the status of women is changing and the man-woman relationship is altering, moving in the direction of equality of worth and complementarity, which is changing traditional husband-wife roles. Secondly, the role of the wife primarily as a child bearer has altered with the advent of contraception, and we have now acquired such control over the timing of fertilization that, with or without contraception, the overwhelming majority of sexual activity is no longer directed towards procreation, resulting in a reduction in family size. Thirdly, and perhaps most important of all, with the material progress made in industrial countries, the emphasis has shifted to the need for an equivalent fulfilment in the quality of personal relationship focusing on such matters as the expression of emotion, affection, sexual satisfaction and the equality of opportunity for social and psychological satisfaction of both sexes. This rise in personal expectation impinges heavily on the institution of marriage which is bound to bear the brunt of these social and psychological changes as it moves from being a contract to a relationship with the emphasis on personal fulfilment. Furthermore, in Western society where expectation of life has increased, this relationship is likely to last between 40 and 50 years, imposing a great strain on, for example, the traditional Christian values of permanency and exclusiveness.

The disturbance of this personal relationship, marital pathology, can be clarified if first we describe accurately the five components of the relationship – social, physical, psychological, intellectual and spiritual – and secondly we recognize that marriage is not a static entity; its quality alters over the years and marital pathology must be related to the various phases of the marriage which, for the sake of simplicity, I have described as: (1) the first five years, (2) from about the age of thirty to when the last child leaves home, and (3) the final phase when the couple return to their original one-to-one relationship.

First Phase. There is much evidence that the first five years are the most crucial for the viability of the marriage and it is estimated that 40% of all divorce originates from problems in this period. Social factors of significance include (1) the age of marriage – marriages under the age of 20 are particularly vulnerable; (2) pre-marital pregnancy – this is always a handicap and associated with a youthful marriage makes a very fragile combination; (3) persistent family opposition to the relationship; (4) lack of independent accommodation; and (5) financial difficulties. However, not all couples with such social problems succumb and the other vital factor is the presence of a persistently unsatisfactory sexual life and lack of affection which creates a crisis.

Second Phase. In the period when the children are growing up, the initial sexual dissatisfaction may continue or the earlier satisfactory sexual life deteriorate. There may be specific sexual reasons, e.g. in the male, lack of sexual drive, premature ejaculation or sexual deviations such as homosexuality or, in the female, persistent tension during sexual intercourse which gradually becomes a phobia for intercourse itself, or postpuerperal syndromes with persistent tiredness, irritability or loss of sexual desire or a deteriorating personal relationship affecting the sexual life. The latter may arise from lack of affection or its demonstration, or persistent unacceptable behaviour such as physical violence, alcoholism, gambling, or promiscuity with unfaithfulness. During this phase there may also be unilateral social or emotional development in which one partner alters markedly in his attitude to life in a way that the spouse cannot match, e.g. the wife's need for independence or the husband's social success which brings him into a different circle of associates with whom his wife cannot relate.

Third Phase. When the children have left home the couple have to face each other afresh and examine the quality of their relationship. It is a time of assessment and reckoning. For example, they may find that one or both has lived primarily through the children and not through each other, or now that these responsibilities are over they seek fulfilment sexually and emotionally in an otherwise prolonged deprived relationship. In addition there may be specific sexual problems for the husband as sexual drive diminishes in the male and permanent impotence may set in from the fifties upwards. This is infrequent but, unlike impotence in the first half of life – which is almost invariably psychological and reversible – in later years it is a much more serious problem. Marital breakdown at this period is a greater problem for women than for men. It is easier for a man to enter a second relationship with a younger woman than for a woman to accept a much younger man.

During each phase, the couple need to make sense of each other intellectually and spiritually. They need to be able to communicate their social and intellectual objectives and share a common spiritual outlook in which their values, although not necessarily identical, do not clash violently with the meaning and objective of life.

MARRIAGE COUNSELLING. When a couple have persistent difficulties, it is likely that one or both will seek help from someone they trust, maybe a relative, friend, doctor, priest or family solicitor. Their advice may be useful and constructive or it may be totally irrelevant.

Marriage counselling, whose principles of assistance are different from traditional advice, has now been in existence for over 30 years. The counsellor is trained to listen with great care, avoid advice or the passing of judgement on either spouse's actions, and thus remain free and impartial. The aim of counselling is to help clients clarify the nature of their difficulties and assist them to make their own decision regarding the next step. Since most people still expect to be guided and directed, a number leave the counsellor's office disappointed and may never return, but those who persist find that there is an orderly unfolding of the value of counselling as follows:

1. Initially the spouses may be seen alone or, more usually, as a couple. They begin to express their criticism, hostility or confusion, are keen to justify their own actions and seek to change the behaviour of their partner to conform with their own sense of what is right. The counsellor's task is to avoid taking sides and simply to help the couple clarify accurately the nature of the difficulty in their relationship. The problem may be clear but often the presenting difficulty hides something else. For example, the sexual or financial complaint may hide an urgent need for affection which can only be understood in terms of sexual intercourse or material goods. The counsellor's first task is to identify accurately the nature of the conflict.

2. When the couple have grasped the real nature of their problem, the task of reconstructing the relationship begins. The means here are various. One couple may need to go on talking for a long time before they really understand each other's feelings and needs. Another may need to concentrate on particular items of behaviour. The husband may need to spend more time with his wife, express greater affection, stop drinking, as the only way of reassuring his wife that he loves her. The wife may need to demonstrate affection afresh, be prepared to be more flexible over sexual intercourse, or take greater interest in her husband's job. Both may have to concentrate far more on being reassuring, appreciative and affirmative instead of critical, cynical and devaluing each other. Some problems resolve quickly, others need a long time, sometimes years.

3. Successful counselling means that a new relationship has emerged in which the couple have come to terms with each other's present and evolving needs. Sometimes this is not possible and all that can be accomplished is a partial accommodation to one another.

Common difficulties in counselling include: lack of involvement of one partner, absence of any real desire to change, desire but inability to change, or the presence of so much distress that hope of change has disappeared. Unfortunately too many couples avoid seeking help for so long that they reach this point of despair and see divorce as the only outcome. Despite these obstacles, every attempt should be made to reach the unwilling partner and encourage either or both to over-come their difficulties.

MARITAL BREAKDOWN. When the couple have decided to proceed to a permanent separation or divorce they still need help. Separation or divorce may be an acrimonious affair or may be handled with respect and care for each other and the children. At parting there is added to the initial tension a considerable degree of social isolation, and depres-sion may intervene. If an alternative relationship is available, the loneliness may be overcome more easily but otherwise the depression may need supportive counselling or even drug therapy until the sep-arated person recovers from the loss and readjusts his life. Suicidal attempts and suicide are particularly liable to occur during this period between the actual separation and the reconstruction of a new rela-tionship. The pain may be revived at the time of the divorce proceed-ings, particularly if the couple have to attend the court. The departure of a partner is a personal loss and, until there is compensation in another relationship or adjustment is made, some form of counselling to cope with the distress, remaining hurt, anger and/or confusion may be necessary.

ETHICAL PROBLEMS IN COUNSELLING. Marital counselling partici-pates in the general principles of counselling, namely unconditional, non-judgemental acceptance of the client. The specific process, how-ever, is that in marriage counselling the counsellor has to gain the trust of both spouses. One of the special problems is the suspicion of one partner that the counsellor is colluding with the other spouse, seeing things in his way. It is for this reason that marital counselling is increasingly carried out with couples so that the counsellor can encourage the dialogue between the partners, facilitating, encouraging, clearing misunderstanding and avoiding being placed in a position of holding the secrets of one partner. Counselling is a process of frank-ness and, if the counsellor is used to avoid communicating painful material, the avoidance of tackling awkward subjects by the couple perpetuates the problem. Counsellors avoid becoming the recipients of secrets of one of the couple kept from the other, and, if they are given these secrets, every effort is made to encourage an open discus-sion. Sometimes the secret is an affair and then care is taken to ensure that revelation does not cause more harm. There are therefore some secrets which should remain so, but each one should be evaluated and every effort should be made to confront and clarify the matter.

Another major ethical question faced often in counselling is whether the couple should stay together for the sake of the children. This is not a decision that the counsellor should make for a couple. He can assist with the clarification of the decision. Knowledge regarding the break-up of families, the likely impact on the children, depending on their age and attitude to their parents, can all be shared, always remembering that generalizations have to be applied with care to individual couples. Another factor is the presence of acute hostility in the home. Evidence suggests that overt hostility is damaging to the child. Finally there is the quality of the relationship of the spouses. If they have nothing but indifference, hatred and enmity for each other, the model they will present to their child is not a good one. Often parents have made up their minds that they will not keep the marriage going for the sake of the child only, and want confirmation of this decision from the counsellor. The counsellor must make sure that ultimately the decision emanates from the couple, because in all marriage counselling the greatest risk is for the counsellor to accept responsibility for decisions which properly belong to the couple.

If the marriage is to be maintained for the sake of the children, it is necessary for the couple to accept genuine sacrifices in their own relationship so that the children experience a minimum social and emotional harmony in the home. Children need a living model of harmony and love, not simply two people sharing the same abode. If the parents are going to stay together, they have to act as parents and resist expressing their hostility and indifference in front of the children. Above all they have to resist using the children to manipulate the marital relationship.

In the debate between staying together for the sake of the children or not, there needs to be a minimum physical, emotional, social, intellectual and spiritual relationship between the couple in order for the children to have something positive to receive. Mere cohabitation does not reflect marriage or family life.

A practitioner may sometimes feel advised to refer a couple or patient with marital difficulties to an agency specializing in help for such. He will be sensitive to the risk of being misinterpreted as rejecting his patient. Ways of doing this, and the subsequent relationship between him and the agency accepting the referral, are under constant study in the Institute of Marital Studies in London, a unit of the Tavistock Institute of Medical Psychology. Issues of ethical and practical importance arise.

Occasionally a *sub poena* obliges a practitioner or non-medical counsellor to appear in court in proceedings following matrimonial breakdown. Insofar as the law recognizes privilege at all in these circumstances (and the recognition is at most discretionary, not established by rule), the privilege is that of the spouse who has been counselled: if permission to disclose is refused, the counsellor's presumptive ethical obligation is not to disclose.

Dominian J. *Marital breakdown*. Harmondsworth: Penguin Books, 1968.

Dominian J. Marital Pathology. A review. *Postgraduate Medical Journal* 1972; 48: 517–28.

Dominian J. *Marital pathology: an introduction for doctors, counsellors and clergy.* London: Darton, Longman & Todd, BMA, 1980. (From articles in *Br Med J* 1979; 2.).

J. Dominian

Mass-medication. The administration of a substance to all or part of a populaton for preventive or therapeutic purposes. Normally this can only be done through the public water supply (see *Fluoridation*) or by means of a foodstuff which is widely used and the manufacture of which can be controlled. Examples of the latter are the addition of calcium to the flour used for bread making and of vitamins A and D to margarine. While there are strong arguments – although these are not universally accepted – in favour of mass-medicaion for beneficial reasons, its use as a manipulative procedure would not be ethical, nor could it be condoned even for therapeutic purposes if there were other than a negligible risk. Those who object on principle do so on the basis that freedom of choice is removed and that the risk is greater than is admitted.

John Rivers

Medical Education, Ethics of. The ethics of medical education, as distinct from the teaching of medical ethics (q.v.) involves selection of students, manpower planning and careers advice, objectives and relevance of the course, teaching methods and assessment.

In selection, most medical schools rely heavily on academic performance. They accept that motivation, kindness and sound judgement are important attributes for a doctor, but these are difficult to measure and the final judgement of whether the product of a school is a 'good doctor' cannot be made till many years later. Studies are in progress as are attempts to draw medical students from a broader range of social class and background and from minority groups. The question is posed whether doctors brought up in artisan homes are better able to deal with the medical problems of the underprivileged or whether the less well educated prefer to have a god figure rather than a social peer as their doctor. Applicants for medical study contain a large proportion of the highest intellects among school leavers. Can nations afford to have so many of their best intellects creamed off into medical practice when for so many branches of medicine a lesser degree of intellect is entirely adequate? Would it be ethical either in selection or in career guidance to direct applicants away from their own choice on the basis of manpower needs?

In countries without legislation against sex discrimination, the admission of women to medical schools may raise ethical problems. If there is great competition for limited places and if the cost of education is borne largely by the State the question arises of the return to the community for the investment made by it. With cultural changes and greater opportunities for part-time post graduate training and part-time appointments women are enabled to combine a career in medicine with family responsibilities. When women are accepted for medical schools, there is a moral responsibility on the authorities to ensure adequate opportunities for further training and satisfactory careers, and on the entrant to make proper continued use of the expensive and highly competitive opportunity given to her.

Many medical schools now publish the objectives of their courses and most refer to high ethical standards and to humanitarian as well as scientific approach. Until recently nearly all teaching was in the hospital setting and the apostolic urge of teachers, together with escalation of scientific advances, tended to glorify specialization to the detriment of primary care and preventive medicine which are economically and morally of greater importance to the majority. A better balance is now being achieved and many medical schools throughout the world, especially new ones, are gearing their teaching programmes very specifically and quantitatively to the needs of the community they are to serve. Even in such everyday matters as sexual difficulties, the medical graduate of less than a generation ago was in no way equipped to help his patients and it could be said that, until recently, medical courses were unethically neglectful of the vocational needs of the student. The teacher of today should sense his wider responsibilities and must not abuse his privilege by forcing his own dogma on his apprentice.

In assessment, the examiner in medicine must not only test academic attainment but must safeguard the public. The need for continuing education is now fully accepted and in some countries periodic recertification after testing is under consideration. From the ethical standpoint, there would seem to be no objection to insistence on such tests provided they were limited to the area of practice professed by the individual doctor (see *Competence to Practise; Quality Assurance*).

Medical students are often invited to volunteer as subjects in human experiments (q.v.) or clinical trials (q.v.). They form a readily available captive group; they may be scientifically interested in the experiment; they may not feel it expedient to decline a request from their teachers. Experimenters thus have special ethical problems and responsibilities in relation to students (see also *Consent*).

Antonovsky A. Student selection in the School of Medicine, Ben Gurion University of the Negev. *Med Educ* 1976; 10: 219–34.

Editorial. Women in medicine: the avoidance of wastage. Br J Med Educ 1973; 7: 143–5.

Johnson ML. Non-academic factors in medical school selection. *Br Med Educ* 1971; 5: 264 1–18.

Sheldrake P. How should we select? – a sociologist's view. *Br J Med Educ* 1975; 9: 91 1–17.

WHO Working Group. *The selection of students for medical education.* Copenhagen: WHO Regional Office for Europe, 1973.

A. S. Duncan

Medical Ethics. See p. xxviii.

Medical Journalism. Twenty years ago, when surgeons at the Hammersmith Hospital London were attempting to separate a pair of
Siamese twins, news-hungry reporters attempted to disguise themselves as orderlies to get into the operating theatre. More recently,
reporters covering the birth of the first test-tube baby besieged the
hospital and attempted to trick staff into disclosing the names of other
patients being treated for infertility. These exceptions to the generally
high standard of press behaviour in Britain reflect the pressures sometimes placed on journalists when a human-interest story has all the
national papers in competition. Doctors brought into contact with the
press on such occasions should remember that their patients have a
right to privacy and that no reporter has any right to information
about an individual patient, whether or not he or she is in the public
eye. Again, when a case report is published in a medical journal the
consent given by the patient to publication of photographs or personal
details does not imply consent to the doctor concerned discussing the
case with the non-medical press.

Most medical journalism is, however, not concerned with individual
case histories but with reports of advances in treatment or diagnosis.
Here science journalists writing for national newspapers or broadcasting on TV or radio pride themselves on the accuracy of their
reports and the clarity of their presentation. Nevertheless, doctors
(and sometimes their patients) are often highly critical of the way that
journalists cover medical stories, accusing them of raising false hopes
or causing unnecessary alarm and distress. Have medical journalists
ethical obligations to the public that do not apply to other science
writers?

Conflicts arise most often with reports about cancer and diseases,
such as multiple sclerosis, for which there is no known cure. Patients
with these disorders – and their families – are often ready to grasp at
straws if any hope is offered that a new treatment may be a substantial
advance. In such circumstances a journalist might be expected to be
very cautious about giving publicity to unconfirmed claims of break-
throughs in treatment: yet all too often newspapers carry headlines
such as 'New hope for leukaemia victims,' and almost every year a
clinic in some distant country is reported as 'curing' patients with
diseases such as retinitis pigmentosa, leading to fund-raising appeals
to send sufferers on futile journeys.

Part of the problem comes from the competitive nature of modern
journalism and the convention of news reporting. Most news editors

take the view that if a hospital consultant or a scientist in a reputable research unit claims to have made an advance in treatment then that fact is news; and if one paper carries the report the others will follow suit. Journalists are not, they say, qualified to assess the validity of the claim, nor should they attempt to do so: they should simply report the fact that the claim has been made. Furthermore, many news editors are willing to report unconfirmed claims by patients to have been cured or had their symptoms relieved by an unorthodox treatment.

One example of the ill-effects of this policy was the results of the widespread press coverage given in the early 1970s to claims that a specific diet (one containing none of the wheat protein, gluten) could relieve the symptoms of multiple sclerosis. Patients who claimed to have benefited from the gluten-free diet were given prominent publicity. Despite the lack of any scientific basis for the claims, doctors and hospital authorities were heavily criticized for not treating their patients with the diet. So loud did the clamour become that the Multiple Sclerosis Society set up pilot studies in Edinburgh and Newcastle to evaluate the treatment: no benefit was shown. A gluten-free diet is not very pleasant, and several of the patients taking it became ill or lost weight – but even so some victims of the disease believed the diet did them good despite the clear evidence to the contrary.

Is there any way that disasters of this kind can be avoided? In general, experienced medical reporters are less likely to write enthusiastic accounts of untried new treatments, no matter how respectable the source of the claims, than are colleagues new to the business. Unfortunately few British newspapers have specialist medical reporters – and even those that have, rarely keep the same journalist covering medicine for more than a year or two. Ideally, newspapers and broadcasting services (especially local radio stations) should have well-informed medical experts to whom they can turn for advice – even if it is mainly negative. (See also *Cancer; Communication.*)

Tony Smith

Medical Records. A medical record consists of the written notes established by a doctor on the past medical history of a patient, on the subjective and objective signs of his present illness, on the treatment prescribed and the patient's response to that treatment. In general practice (q.v.) it may include a note of the patient's fitness for work and record the issue of certificates. The record may also contain entries by other health professionals to whom the doctor may have delegated certain investigations or treatment. Until comparatively recently such records were brief both inside and outside hospital, serving only as *aide-mémoires*. The size of many records today reflects the increased number and sophistication of investigative and therapeutic procedures available, which in turn indicate the many skills involved and carry the implication that access to the details of a patient's illness are no longer limited to members of the medical profession. (See *Teamwork*.)

A medical record is sometimes put to uses other than the immediate clinical care of the individual patient and provision for his future care. It can be used for clinical, epidemiological or archival research. It can fulfil obligations for legal purposes and it can provide information for management. In some countries it may be used to assess standards of professional care. Whenever there is a departure from its use for the benefit of the individual patient ethical problems may arise. These are mainly those of confidentiality and the conflict between individual interest and community interest. These issues are discussed under *Computers, Confidentiality* and *Quality Assurance*.

Until the advent of the National Health Service medical records in the UK were the property of the doctor responsible for the care of the patient within the voluntary hospital or outside of it. Today in private practice records remain the property of the doctor, but within the NHS the law (NHS Act 1946; NHS Scotland Act 1947) provides that the medical records are the property of the Minister of Health (now Secretary of State for Health and Social Security) and the Secretary of State for Scotland. Their agents are the Area Health Authorities (England and Wales) and Area Health Boards (Scotland) who respectively delegate custody to the District Records Officer and the District Medical Officer – to whom the Records Officer is responsible for custody. Similar provision is made in Northern Ireland. Within the Health Service X-ray films and reports form part of the medical record. Outside the NHS ownership of X-ray films is undetermined but it seems likely that they remain the property of the private radiologist who has in the past always maintained custody.

There is no statutory obligation upon a private or hospital doctor to maintain records but medical undergraduate and postgraduate students alike are taught by precept and example that the maintenance of adequate records is conducive to good patient care. There is however a contractual obligation upon the general practitioner in the Health Service to keep records for which a card is provided and is initiated by the area authority.

In any case it can be cogently argued that a doctor fails to fulfil an ethical obligation to protect his patients from avoidable harm unless he maintains adequate records of illnesses, consultations with colleagues, treatment and responses to drugs. There is a parallel and acceptable proposition that doctors have an obligation to make such records available to any deputy engaged to look after their patients. There is, of course, an element of self-preservation in the maintenance of good records. Adequate evidence of good care will refute allegations of negligence and will go far to avoid unfavourable criticism of doctors by courts of law.

From the days of Hippocrates to the present there has been authority prescribing almost unqualified confidentiality in regard to matters learned in the course of professional relationships. (See *Hippocratic Oath*.) There is a statutory obligation on management to maintain confidentiality in regard to venereal disease records. The General Medical Council warn that *improperly* disclosing information may give rise to disciplinary proceedings on the grounds of 'serious professional misconduct.' Outside hospital the obligation on doctors might well extend to their ensuring that a place of safe custody is available and that any delegate to whom custody or sight of records is entrusted signifies their awareness of the need for secrecy. Inside hospital the obligation is on management to appoint and supervise trained records staff, to provide safe custody and to ensure that there is a known and agreed policy covering the issue of records for any purpose other than the medical care of the individual patient.

Public anxiety has perhaps been raised by the very efficiency in records linkage envisaged by computer systems which will proceed from the present hospital level to area and eventually national level. Anxiety stems from the possibility of linkage being established with other national computer systems with the records being raided in the name of law and order or possibly by ill-wishers for other reasons. Such anxieties must be judged against the benefits to the community of immediate availability of an ill patient's records, no matter where else in the country he may have received treatment and secondly of the ease of production of special registers e.g. of immune status or special risk. Patient response to a computerized health centre at Livingston seems to suggest that it is the number of local people who handle records rather than the system which arouses anxiety. In any case the ethical situation remains the same and the onus is on management to ensure that the system suitably safeguards individual identity with medical details in the same way as the census authorities have done on a similar scale in compliance with their statutory obligation.

Stemming in part from similar anxieties and perhaps with particular regard to childrens' records there has been a demand that patients or parents should have a right to see records on a quasi open government argument and to ensure that it contains nothing inaccurate or arguable and possibly to discourage recording value judgements. Another reason for such a demand is certainly to further a possible claim against a doctor or health authority alleging negligence in care. Tradition in the United Kingdom is against this and 'Not to be seen by patient' is commonly printed on the case folders. Elsewhere in Europe it has been acceptable for patients to have custody of their medical dossier and to make the rounds of different doctors seeking views on their condition. There is therefore no universal ethical argument against patients' sight of records although in terms of good management there are arguments against it. Uninitiated perusal is more likely to arouse anxiety than to dispel it. Early confirmation of utter hopelessness is rarely for the majority of patients good medicine. Although it may well be that records should contain no judgements other than purely medical, writers might well omit possibilities of future value to the patient if he knew that he was then going to hand the record to the patient. Some support for this view can be gathered from a recent statute in that where a claimant gives consent to his medical records being made available to a Medical Appeal Tribunal (Social Security Act 1975) such records must also be made available to the claimant but there is provision for non-disclosure where knowledge of any particulars in the record is felt to be undesirable in the person's interest.

There remains the situation where a court of law orders the production of a patient's medical record. Such an order is usually for the production of such records as are relevant to the incident which is the subject of litigation and the order is served on the custodian of the records. Such records are today usually in folders which contain details of other incidents, knowledge about which might disadvantage the individual concerned. There therefore remains an ethical obligation to deliver to the court no more than what is ordered.

Acheson ED. *Record linkage in medicine*. Edinburgh: Livingstone, 1970.

Committee on Privacy. Report. London: HMSO, 1972, Cmnd 5012.

Hadfield SJ. *Law and ethics for doctors*. London: Eyre and Spottiswoode, 1958.

General Medical Council. *Professional conduct and discipline*. London: GMC, 1979.

Scottish Health Service Studies No. 29 (The Livingston Project), Edinburgh: SHHD, 1973.

Walker Committee. *Hospital records in Scotland*. SHHD, HMSO, 1967.

Donald McIntosh

Medical Research Council (MRC). The MRC is the main government agency in the United Kingdom for the promotion and support of medical research (see *Research, Funding of*). Most members of the Council and of its Boards and Committees are distinguished independent medical scientists, who give much time to Council business for little or no remuneration. For these reasons the Council is widely respected and carries great authority.

The MRC is not a government department, but receives an annual grant in aid from Parliament. Council initiates research in fields which it regards as important, supports work proposed by scientists, which it considers worthwhile, and undertakes research, on a customer-contractor basis, commissioned by the Health Departments, the Health and Safety Executive and the Department of Employment. One fifth of its income was received from these sources in 1979–80.

The MRC supports research mainly in the universities, in its own research establishments and in hospitals in the UK. It also support some research abroad, particularly in tropical medicine in developing countries.

The constitution of the Council, its relationship to Government and the principles which govern the framing of its policies all affec human welfare and raise ethical issues. Most scientists regard th independence of Council as of paramount importance, while many politicians consider that it should be controlled much more closely by Government departments. In framing its policies, the MRC has to strike balances between extreme views about research. One concern the relative merits, on the one hand, of committees planning and directing research centrally and, on the other, of the identification and support of good (and if possible exceptionally talented) scientists with original ideas. Another issue concerns the relative priorities to b given to long term research in the basic sciences, without any obviou applications, and to the investigation of immediate practical problems A third involves the relative amounts of money to be spent in the UK and in poorer and less well developed countries.

In the 'dual support' system for higher education the teaching component and a small amount of research in the universities ar supported by the University Grants Committee, while the bulk o research is dependent on the medical and other research councils charitable grant-giving bodies and industry. This arrangement help to maintain the mutual independence of the MRC and of th universities.

The MRC has issued two statements to guide scientists in the ethica conduct of their work. One concerns 'Responsibility in investigation on human subjects' (1962–63) (see *Clinical Trials; Consent; Huma Experiment; Research Ethical Committees*) and the other, 'Responsi bility in the use of medical information for research' (1972) (se *Confidentiality*). In addition the Council stated its policy in relatio to research on '*In vitro* fertilization' in its annual report, 1978–79 (See *Embryo Transfer and Replantation*'.) Council requires researc workers to obtain approval from their local Research Ethical Com mittees for work involving human subjects, but reserves its indepen dent right to decline or withdraw support on ethical grounds.

Address: Medical Research Council, 20 Park Crescent, Londo W1N 4AL.

R. B. Welbour.

Medical Science. See p. xviii.

Medicines. As the word Drug has come to be used mainly in the contex of drugs of dependence, it is recommended that 'medicines' should b used to describe substances administered for therapeutic purposes

(see *Medicines Commission; Pharmaceutical Industry; Prescribing.* See also *Pain; Terminal Care.*)

Medicines Commission. This United Kingdom body was established in 1969 under the Medicines Act of 1968:

(a) to make recommendations to the Ministers of Health and Agriculture with regard to the number, functions and composition of Committees dealing with medical substances (such as the Committee on Safety of Medicines and the Committee on the Review of Medicines).

(b) to advise the licensing authority (i.e. the Ministers individually or jointly) when a company appeals against the decision of either of these Committees that a product should not be marketed or that a licence should be withdrawn.

(c) to consider representations against any order that prohibits the sale, supply or importing of medicinal products or medicated animal feeding stuffs.

(d) to direct the body responsible for preparing the British Pharmacopoeia with respect to the revision of that publication and the booklet entitled *Approved Names.*

(e) to direct, if considered expedient, the preparation of other compendia of standards regarding substances or articles used in human or veterinary medicine.

(f) to undertake functions on matters of safety, quality or efficacy and the monitoring of adverse reactions in so far as they are not already carried out by the Committees referred to above.

Members of the Commission are usually doctors or pharmacists and the normal term of appointment is four years. They are advisers, not Government employees. (See also *Medicines, Safety of, Committee on; Pharmaceutical Industry; Prescribing.*)

Ronald H. Girdwood

Medicines, Safety of, Committee on. This United Kingdom body was first established in 1972 by the Health Ministers under the Medicines Act of 1968 (a) to give advice with respect to safety, quality and efficacy in relation to human use of any substance or article (not being an instrument, apparatus or appliance) to which any provision of the Act is applicable and (b) to promote the collection and investigation of information relating to adverse reactions for the purpose of enabling such advice to be given. The members of the Committee and its Sub-Committees are mainly University Professors, Readers or Senior Lecturers; they give advice which is transmitted to the Health Ministers, but are not employees of the Government or of drug companies. New drugs or compounds have to undergo rigorous testing by the companies before the Committee will issue a Clinical Trial Certificate. There may have been years of laboratory studies followed by assessment on animals, and such studies may include mutagenic tests and investigations on pregnant animals for evidence of fetal deformities. Only about one out of 8000 potential therapeutic agents are considered further, but the few that remain are, in most instances, then tested on humans. Unless there are contraindications (e.g. with cancer chemotherapeutic agents), these tests are carried out on normal volunteers, *not* patients, this stage of the testing not being under the control of the Committee, although unethical studies would not be tolerated. The clinical trials come next if the Committee agrees to them and, if successful, the company may apply for a Product Licence, provided, of course, its manufacturing premises and processes satisfy the inspectors. Without this Licence the substance cannot be marketed in the United Kingdom. Clinical trials must meet strict ethical criteria.

Adverse reactions should be reported to the Committee by doctors, and information about any such reactions notified direct to drug companies must thereafter be passed to the Committee. This information is kept strictly confidential. If there are reports of serious adverse reactions, the Committee may ask that the drug be withdrawn. If they are less severe, a warning notice is sent to all doctors. In addition, occasional bulletins are sent when there is only suspicion that a clinical event is drug related.

In 1975 a Committee on the Review of Medicines was established to undertake a general review of the safety, quality and efficacy of the 36,000 products that were on the market before the Committee on Safety of Medicines was formed. (See also *Medicines Commission*; *Pharmaceutical Industry*; *Prescribing*.)

Ronald H. Girdwood

Mental Handicap. Mental handicap is a condition of arrested or abnormal development of mind leading to a varying amount of social disability. The terms Mental Deficiency, Mental Retardation, Mental Subnormality are to all intents and purposes synonymous; the term Mental Deficiency is the legal designation in Scotland and Mental Subnormality in England and Wales. The term Mental Handicap is being accepted in the United Kingdom as the term that covers these differences.

The ethical problems connected with such handicap fall broadly into two categories: (1) issues concerned with prevention, and (2) issues concerned with the management of existing residual handicaps.

We should distinguish between those ethical issues which are broadly based in the culture within which care is provided and those which have a more immediate and close professional impact.

In certain cases, it is society at large that takes the basic decisions on the quality of care and indeed the survival of the handicapped (q.v.), and the amount of effort and money that should be lavished on their care is not a professional but a socio-political decision. The role of members of the professions concerned with the care of the mentally handicapped is to supply society at large and its policy makers with factual data to allow them to reach an informed opinion. For example, the compulsory sterilization (q.v.) of the mentally handicapped based on the supposition that the majority of handicap occurs through the reproduction of affected individuals was abandoned when it was shown to be scientifically erroneous.

1. *Prevention.* The following considerations are relevant to pre-natal prevention.

Genetic counselling is generally acceptable if measures are taken before conception. After that different cultures lay different constraints on the prevention of the birth of a handicapped child. Contraception and early termination of pregnancy when the diagnosis of an affected fetus is possible are normally accepted in most Western countries, although there is some opposition from religious and cultural groups within them. In the Western democracies the decision to avail oneself of contraception or to have a pregnancy terminated for valid medical reasons is left to the potential parents; the professional involvement is limited to the provision of factual information and advice, although it must be realized that the professional worker exercises considerable influence upon the parents who, in some cases, are glad to have the support of professional advice.

The problem becomes more controversial if the diagnosis becomes delayed until the fetus is viable and there have been attempts to control the temporal limits of termination of pregnancy by legislation. Although infanticide is not countenanced by any existing legal system, the role of the physician becomes more central when he has to decide whether or not to treat a potentially fatal condition – a decision which presents considerable moral problems and on which there are still considerable differences of professional opinion, for example, whether or not to operate on a severe case of spina bifida and whether to treat with determination an anencephalic baby.

Absolute guidance cannot be given in such cases and the final decision will be determined by the parents' attitudes and reactions and the doctor's ethical judgement. Although in principle the parents should be involved in many cases, it is unkind and unfair to expect them to carry the heavy burden of such a decision in times of emotional stress, and it falls on the doctor to decide on the course of action – guided always by the understanding of the emotional situation and by a primary concern for the parents' emotional wellbeing. (See *Abortion; Genetic Conditions; Spina Bifida.*)

2. *Care and Management.* In the last 20 years many have come to hold the view that the handicapped have a moral and legal right (as stated in the UN Declaration of Human Rights), to optimal care, including special facilities for living, working, and above all for training and education. There can be no doubt that they are entitled to such benefits; but their claims have to be related to those of other

sections of society. The decision is a political one and should be argued out by the interested parties (such as parents' organizations and government bodies). The function of the professionals is to provide data, distinguishing between assumptions and established fact, to attempt to assess needs and priorities and to assess the cost effectiveness of any measure by determining the maximum benefit to be derived from such measures (see *Resources*).

Doctors and other professionals are responsible for ensuring that the life of the patient is as satisfying as possible and that he is given the opportunity to be independent and to take his own decisions so far as is consistent with his limitations. This includes, both for children and adults, the provision of adequate preparation for independence in a supporting environment. It is now recognized that the handicapped have sexual needs and they are entitled to have as much liberty as possible, while being protected from exploitation and emotional hurt. Nowadays when it has become customary to give the handicapped much greater liberty of action and decision they sometimes have to be protected from assuming responsibilities they cannot shoulder. In particular the children of mentally handicapped women present a special problem, and have sometimes to be taken into care both for their own and for their mothers' sakes. Sterilization (q.v.) of women who have shown themselves uninterested in and incapable of child care has at times to be considered – though it must never be enforced on an unwilling subject (see *Consent*).

Treatment or training may be unpleasant or painful, and here a careful balance must be struck between the unpleasant effect of therapy and the benefits derived from it. For example it has been shown that modification of behaviour (see *Behaviour Therapy*) can be achieved through negative conditioning by giving the patient painful electric shocks. The use of such therapy is justifiable if it can control self-mutilation in disturbed patients (e.g. when patients bite off their finger tips or lips, or inflict on themselves large disabling wounds). On the other hand this would not be justifiable merely for the elimination of objectionable habits.

It is particularly important that some forms of medication with unpleasant side effects (such as heavy sedation), putting to bed and isolation from disturbing stimuli should not be used as punitive measures. Particular care should be exercised with punishments – social sanctions exist and are universal in all human groups. They have a place in the management of the mentally handicapped if only by the withdrawal of privileges, but these sanctions should be kept under constant supervision and used with great moderation (see *Psychotherapy*).

The question of experimenting on the mentally handicapped is fraught with emotional attitudes (see *Human Experiment*). Clear distinction should be made between the trial of new methods of treatment and medication which may be of benefit to the patient and using the handicapped for academic experiments on human beings. The former is acceptable because it may benefit the patient, though if there is any danger of adverse reactions the handicapped and his family should be participants in the decision to submit the patient to the trial. In the latter case experiment is unobjectionable if there are no dangers or unpleasant reactions – there is no reason why experiments on e.g. colour vision or sound discrimination should not be carried out, particularly if the individual can be interested in the test. No other experiments should be countenanced, but should be confined to volunteers who are capable of forming an opinion and expressing consent.

When discussing the rights of the individual suffering from mental handicap their families must also be considered and the community at large also has its claims for consideration in cases of social or delinquent behaviour. It may then be necessary to move the handicapped into residential care with varying amounts of control, to relieve the stress of caring for very disturbed or dependent individuals or in order to contain their unacceptable behaviour (see *Mental Illness, Certification of*).

A very special function and duty of the professional worker is to protect the families of the handicapped from charlatanism. Devoted families are prepared to spend beyond their means and to subject the handicapped to operations and stressful regimens in a fruitless search for non-existing cures. It is the duty of the professional worker to assess these claims and to present the facts fairly and firmly so as to protect their patients and their families.

The custom has grown of pressing the claims of one or other type of care as an expression of moral imperatives. For example, 'it is the moral duty of a community to care for its handicapped in its midst'. Such 'ethical' considerations are not valid. The only guiding principle should be the emotional satisfaction, happiness and the quality of life of the handicapped. (See also *Handicapped, Duties to; Human Rights*.)

A. Shapiro

Mental Illness. Disorder in such mental processes as perceiving, thinking and remembering takes several forms, corresponding in some respects to its causes, which are various: external, the application to the body of factors such as violence, drugs including anaesthesia, alcohol and perhaps hypnotic influences; brain disease, the loss of nervous tissue as a result of disease of the blood vessels or other causes; and disease in other organs such as the heart, kidneys, or liver affecting brain function. There is another form of disorder characterized by delusions and hallucinations, the essence of which lies in a failure to distinguish fantasy from fact and to test experience against reality. This may be described as psychosis or, when departing sufficiently from a generally accepted standard of health, as mental illness. By analogy with physical illness, mental illness may be held to be susceptible to explanation in terms of underlying biological abnormalities, which lie not in any structural change in the brain but in a subtle imbalance or malfunctioning of nervous tissue. This view is derived from a 'disease model'[1] – sometimes called 'the medical model' – support for which comes from the apparent success of drug and electroconvulsive (q.v.) treatments. Schizophrenia, mania and some types of depression are commonly discussed in the terms of a disease model and are then properly described as mental illness.

Mental illness has replaced unsoundness of mind as a term in legislation[2] and is one of the categories of mental disorder which justify the use of the powers given by the Mental Health Act, 1959, to compel, amongst other things, admission to hospital in the interests of the patient's own health or safety or with a view to the protection of other persons (see *Mental Illness, Certification of*). Mental illness is given as the grounds in 96% of compulsory admissions to hospital; the remainder are covered by the other categories; severe subnormality, subnormality, and psychopathic disorder. Mental disorder is defined in the Act in terms of its categories. Mental illness is not defined, the questions at issue in each case being left to professional judgement. Patients suffering from brain disease are put into the category of mental illness for the purposes of the Mental Health Act and also patients who, although free from delusions, are yet regarded as 'insane on account of conduct alone'.[2]

Explanations of psychosis without resort to a disease model have been put forward. An achievement of psychoanalysis has been to show that symptoms of mental illness may become comprehensible when the full context of past experience and present circumstances has been revealed. Another explanation regards the symptoms of illness as attempts to resolve the problems arising out of a crisis in a relationship with another person. Although potentially adaptive, they may be poorly organized, even chaotic, self-defeating or destructive. Forms of help, such as psychotherapy or behaviour therapy, may then be more appropriate than treatments based on a disease model. At any rate, a patient regarded as mentally ill may be reluctant or unwilling to accept a disease model. He is of course entitled to refuse the medical treatments which go with it. In these circumstances the doctor has a duty to continue to offer support and to seek ways of helping which are acceptable to the patient. If the dangers warrant it, and if he judges the patient's capacity to act responsibly to be impaired by mental illness, he should use the powers given by the Mental Health Act to do what he in good faith judges to be in the best interests of the patient's health or safety or to be necessary to protect other persons. Under the procedure of the Act, his recommendation that the patient be compulsorily admitted to hospital ordinarily requires the concurrence of a medical colleague and either the nearest relative or an approved social worker.

1. Wing JK. *Reasoning about madness.* Oxford: University Press, 1978.
2. Royal Commission on the Law relating to Mental Illness and Mental Deficiency 1954–1957. Report (Percy Report). London: HMSO, 1957, Cmnd 169.

D. Russell Davis

Mental Illness, Certification of. Process of legal documentation which enables people with mental disorder to be detained in designated hospitals against their will. In the United Kingdom the latest legislation is contained in the Mental Health Act (1959)[1], Mental Health Act Scotland (1960)[2] and the Mental Health Act Northern Ireland (1961)[3].

Part 4 of the 1959 Act, Sections 29 and 25, 135 and 136, and Section 30 (2) provide the administrative framework for detaining people with mental disorder for observation. Section 30 (2) can be used to detain informal patients in hospital by order of the responsible medical officer. The purpose of these sections is to deal with emergency situations where a person is thought to be suffering from mental disorder and needs to be detained in the interests of his own health and safety and/or with a view to the protection of other persons.

In Sections 29, 135 and 136, and 30 (2) the period of detention is 72 hours with a view to subsequent discharge, informal admission, a further period of detention for observation not exceeding 28 days from the date of admission (Section 25) or detention for treatment under Section 26. Detention under Section 26 may last for a period of up to one year and then be extended for longer periods if warranted under the Act. Two doctors are involved in completing the documents for Section 25 and Section 26, one previously acquainted with the patient (preferably a family doctor) and the other recognized as a specialist under Section 28 of the Act.

Part 5 of the Mental Health Act deals with admission and certification procedures where the individual is suffering from mental disorder and has been involved in criminal proceedings. Sections 60 (65) and 72 deal with compulsory admission to hospital for treatment and are equivalent to Section 26 in Part 4 except that Section 65 places special restrictions in relation to discharge which involve the Home Office. Patients have the right to appeal to Mental Health Tribunals[4].

Ethical issues that arise:

1. Is certification for mental disorder ever justified? This reflects the conflicting issues of civil liberty, social hazard and the physician's role as a therapist. Defending the freedom of choice for the individual Szasz'[5] questions whether the doctor should be involved in controlling the lives of people with psychiatric syndromes of unknown aetiology and pathology. This would imply that people with depression or schizophrenia should not be certified despite suicidal and homicidal potential. Such a concept would be unacceptable to most psychiatrists

293

who would maintain that these mental disorders require treatment and in most instances respond to treatment. They would justify certification for patients who otherwise would be denied treatment because their capacity for judgement and insight had been impaired by the presence of mental disorder. Szasz's[5] theoretical arguments are authoritatively refuted by Roth[6]. The Mental Health Act (1959) however does not state that certification is warranted only when behaviour is likely to be affected by treatment. It also produces a difficulty for the doctor in relation to the clause 'for the protection of others' as doctors are ethically bound to the patient's needs and may find that judgements about community protection conflict with the interests of the patient. For some the ethical choice will be resolved by placing emphasis on the patient's health and safety.

Gostin[7] in his treatise 'A Human Condition' says that if a state has the right to exercise compulsory powers it also has the duty to ascertain that less restrictive means are not available by which to achieve the same purpose. He raises issues about safeguards for the mentally disordered child and greater use of Mental Health Tribunals and proposes a system of advocacy for patients. In the 1960 Mental Health Act Scotland, reviewed by Elliott et al,[8] a Mental Welfare Commission was substituted for the old Board of Control (abolished by the Mental Health Act 1959) to safeguard patient interests.

2. Non-consent to treatment. Many certified patients are not willing to consent to treatment procedures that seem appropriate to the doctor. The Royal Commission[9] took the view that society had the right to impose treatment on a mentally disordered person against his will and it follows from this that it ought to be possible to override the patient's refusal. At present doctors and nurses can control or treat certified patients without their consent so long as they do not act in bad faith or show negligence (Section 141, Mental Health Act 1959). The Department of Health and Social Security legal department, however, advises doctors to obtain the consent of the patient and also of the nearest relative before beginning a form of treatment that involves risks (undefined). This is also the legal advice of the medical defence unions. The Butler Commission[10] recommended that treatment should be given if the patient is unable to give valid consent so long as treatment is not irreversible or hazardous (terms still undefined), when a second consultant opinion should be obtained. Treatment, other than nursing care, should not be imposed without consent if the patient is able to appreciate what is involved, except where it represents minimum interference to prevent violence, saves life or prevents deterioration of illness. These matters and other aspects of the Mental Health Act (1959) are being considered in a review of the Mental Health Act (1959)[11]. Certification and treatment without consent raise concern about the possible abuse of psychiatry[12] (cf. treatment of dissidents in the Soviet Union), hence the need for clear guidance and adequate safeguards for both doctor and patient. (See *Psychiatry*,

Misuse of. See also *Declaration of Hawaii; Forensic Psychiatry; Human Rights.*)

1. Mental Health Act, 7 and 8 Eliz 2, Ch 72. London: HMSO, 1973.
2. Mental Health Act Scotland. London: HMSO, 1960.
3. Mental Health Act Northern Ireland. Belfast: HMSO, 1961.
4. Mental Health Review Tribunal. Review of the Mental Health Act, 1959. London: HMSO: 39–40.
5. Szasz TS. Schizophrenia and sacred symbols of psychiatry. *Br J Psychiat* 1976; 129: 308–16.
6. Roth M. Schizophrenia and the theories of Szasz, T. *Br J Psychiat* 1976; 129: 317–26.
7. Gostin LO. A human condition: the Mental Health Act from 1959–1975. In: *Mind*: 1. London: NAMH.
8. Elliott WA, Timbury GC, Walker MM. Compulsory Admission to Hospital: An Operational Review of the Mental Health (Scotland) Act 1960. *Br J Psychiat* 1979; 135: 104–14.
9. Report of the Royal Commission on the Law relating to Mental Illness – Mental Deficiency. Cmnd. 169, Para 316. London: HMSO, 1957.
10. Committee on Mentally Abnormal Offenders. Report (Butler Report). London: HMSO, 1975, Cmnd 6244, Para 3.54–3.56.
11. *A review of the Mental Health Act, 1959.* DHSS: London: HMSO, Sept. 1978.
12. Royal College of Psychiatrists. Plyushch L. *Br J Psychiat* Sept. 1976; News and Notes 1–2.

B. Mandelbrote

Military Medicine. The tasks of a military medical service are the prevention of disease and the care of sick and wounded and the ethics of its medically qualified personnel, that is their moral standards, professional conduct and etiquette conform to those observed by their civilian colleagues. At all levels the service commander is responsible for the health of the officers and soldiers serving under him. The medical officer's role is advisory to the commander.

In the British forces medical officers have to be registered with the General Medical Council: they are non-combatant and are subject to military discipline and law. There is a well-defined doctor/patient relationship (see *Clinical Practice*) in which confidentiality[1] (q.v.) including that of medical records (q.v.) is respected although such records are government property. Strict confidentiality is, however, modified in that there are occasions when a medical officer is required to discuss cases with his commanding officer in the interests of the unit. Although it is understood that a medical officer would not be required to undertake treatment which he believes is not in his patient's best interests, it is possible that he could receive a command which would conflict with his ethical responsibilities. Where a medical officer's duty to his patient conflicts with his duty to the service he should bear in mind any risk of danger to his patient's comrades and the service. In these circumstances he would be wise to consult with a medical colleague, preferably senior, or, if one is not available, the commander.

Unit medical officers will, especially overseas, often have the care of service dependants towards whom they have a responsibility similar to that of a civilian general practitioner. Training in general practice in the services conforms to the standards set by the Joint Committee on Postgraduate Training in General Practice. The special relationship between the serviceman, his medical officer and the commanding officer does not, however, extend to the family but it should be borne in mind that the health of the family could affect both the serviceman and his unit.

In peace the ethical problems which can arise are, in general, those which occur in civil life: these concern confidentiality, dangerous drugs (see *Alcoholism; Drug Dependence*), life and its prolongation (q.v.), death (q.v.), sex and reproduction (see *Abortion; Contraception; Sexual Deviations; Sexually Transmitted Diseases*) and matters relating to research[2] (see *Human Experiments*).

In war service medical officers and their medical personnel are protected by the Red Cross Geneva Conventions.[3] Article 12 of the first (1864) Geneva Convention dealt with the protection of wounded and sick of the armed forces of all parties in conflict, and stated that only urgent medical reasons would authorize priority in the order of treatment to be administered. Discrimination, or more appropriately, selection, of patients for priority in treatment, also referred to as triage, may be necessary, in terms of urgency and remediability when the simultaneous occurrence of a large number of casualties strains or overwhelms the immediately available staff and resources (e.g. medical supplies including blood plasma). In these circumstances the interests of the many must come before those of the individual to ensure the best chance of survival for as many as possible.

The Geneva Conventions of 1949 introduced further ethical responsibilities to deal with new moral dilemmas created by wars and scientific progress. In 1977 the Geneva Conventions[4] were brought up to date by two Protocols which applied to international and non-international armed conflicts (the term 'War' being avoided). Protection was extended beyond service medical personnel to cover those concerned with any medical duties indicating that no person would be punished for carrying out medical practice compatible with medical ethics.

Protocol I formulated more comprehensive rules for the protection of civilians covering civilian wounded, sick and shipwrecked persons, medical personnel and medical units, bringing them into line with military medical units. It also dealt with medical transportation including transportation by aircraft. Outrages of personal dignity and discrimination in treatment on the basis of race, religion, nationality or on political grounds were forbidden (see *Declarations; Prisoners*). Also prohibited were physical mutilations, medical or scientific experiments and the removal of tissue or organs for transplantations except where medically justified as in blood transfusion and skin grafting. The compulsory assignment of personnel to work on or develop weapons of war was also prohibited.

Although the presence of a doctor during the interrogation of a prisoner is unethical, doctors in the armed forces may undertake the medical monitoring of personnel who have agreed, as an informed voluntary act, to be trained in techniques of resistance to intensive interrogation.

Protocol II related to the protection of victims of non-international armed conflicts and the application of principles of humane conduct to conflicts occurring within a state.

1. British Medical Association. *Handbook of medical ethics*. London: BMA, 1980.
2. Royal College of Physicians of London. Report of Committee on the Supervision of the Ethics of Clinical Research Investigations in Institutions. London: Royal College of Physicians, 1967.
3. Geneva Conventions Act 1957. First schedule (Geneva, 12 August 1949). Public General Acts and Measures of 1957. London: HMSO, 1958.
4. Final Act of the Diplomatic Conference on the Reaffirmation and Development of International Humanitarian Law Applicable in Armed Conflicts, with Protocol I, Protocol II and Resolutions adopted at the Fourth Session. Red Cross Miscellaneous No 19. London: HMSO, 1977, Cmnd 6927.

J. M. Matheson

Miscarriage. See *Abortion*.

Mongolism. This term was introduced by Dr. Langdon Down in 1866 to cover a class of severely retarded children who showed certain facial features which resemble mongolians, and has been in widespread use since. However, several Chinese cytogeneticists have made exceptional contributions to the study of such disorders and have objected to this term, and the term Down's Syndrome – called Down Syndrome or D.S. in the USA – has become established in English-speaking countries. This term has the disadvantage of claiming national precedence for the discovery, as well as confusing a difficult subject, and the term Mongolism rarely causes disturbances to parents, excepting a small minority who resent the implication of Asian admixture or who confuse Mongolism with Mongrelism. The terms mongolian idiot and mongolian idiocy are needlessly offensive, and the term 'mongoloid' devoid of scientific meaning. A steady replacement of the word by Down's Syndrome seems likely, although the established and harmless use of the word 'mongol' is likely to continue, as, indeed are such terms as German measles, Asian 'flu and Bornholm disease, since no descriptive and acceptable word, free from any nationalist claims, is available. If Down's syndrome is established, a move for its removal is likely to follow in view of some anti-negro implications in Down's original paper and this would cause great confusion if the relatively innocuous term 'mongol' was allowed to die out. The ethical issues do not differ markedly from those involved in congenital mal-formations (q.v.).

J. H. Edwards

Moral Autonomy. Autonomy (Gr. *autos* – self, *nomos* – law) refers to the capacity for, or the right to, self-determination. The classical description of *moral* autonomy is given by the philosopher Immanuel Kant: willing what is right, out of respect for universal law. All rational beings, Kant believes, have the capacity to act in a consistently moral manner and to avoid *heteronomy* (acting under external influ-ence or duress). Autonomy must be distinguished from libertarianism (acting in any way one chooses) and from individualism (assertion of one's rights against those of others). The phrase 'respect for persons' is often used to express the notion of safeguarding *every* individual's integrity (including one's own) which is the central feature of this ethical approach.

Criticisms of the concept come from both Determinism (the view that every human action is causally conditioned) and from Social Benefit Theory (the view that good consists in maximizing the benefit of the majority). According to the former, freedom is an illusion and therefore the concept of autonomy vacuous. According to the latter, personal liberty may impede the good of society as a whole and therefore cannot be regarded as a moral absolute. A combination of these views would put forward the ideal of efficient social conditioning to maximize happiness as an alternative to individual autonomy.

The debate about autonomy is central to medical ethics. The doctor/patient relationship (see *Clinical Practice*) entails both mutual benefits and mutual obligations. Autonomy in the relationship is safeguarded by professional independence (see *Clinical Autonomy*) on the one hand and consent (q.v.) to treatment on the other. Under the general framework of law, the doctor is free to advise in the light of his clinical judgments and the patient is free to determine the definition of his own well-being. Examples of denial of autonomy are the use of doctors as agents of state control (see *Psychiatry, Misuse of*), com-pulsory eugenic programmes (see *Eugenics*), release of medical information detrimental to the patient (see *Confidentiality*) and use of patients for clinical research (see *Clinical Trials; Human Experiment*) without obtaining adequate consent. In all these cases the voluntary mutual commitment or covenant between patient and doctor is replaced by an externally imposed demand from 'the state' or 'society at large'.

Codes of medical ethics (see *Declarations; Hippocratic Oath*) emphasize the benefit of the individual patient as a first principle and (implicitly or explicitly) oppose the use of medicine as a form of social control (see *Immunization; Mass Medication*). Such an emphasis may be challenged, since the assertion of personal freedom and individual rights cannot be conclusively demonstrated. (No more can the assertion of total determinism and state rights.) But if social benefit is taken as the final arbiter, the consequence must be accepted that there is *no* individual whose rights are sacrosanct. It seems preferable to adopt autonomy as the central value in medical ethics, at whatever cost to 'efficient' social engineering.

Downie RS, Telfer E. *Respect for persons.* London: Allen and Unwin, 1969.

Hampshire S. *Freedom of the individual.* London: Chatto and Windus, 1965.

Kant I trans. Abbot TK. *Fundamental principles of the metaphysics of morals.* (Library of Liberal Arts Edition). New York: Bobbs-Merrill, 1949.

Skinner BF. *Beyond freedom and dignity.* Harmondsworth: Penguin Books, 1973.

A. V. Campbell

Muslim. See *Islam.*

Mutilation. Removal of part or parts of the body, especially those on or near the surface, as a result of accidental injury or of surgical operation. Examples include amputation of digits or limbs, excision of a breast, jaw, eye, larynx or penis, and removal of the contents of the pelvis (bladder, uterus and rectum) with the creation of artificial openings for urine and faeces. The most extreme form of surgical mutilation compatible with life is removal of the lower part of the body, including both legs and the pelvis.

Castration, Circumcision and Sterilization are dealt with under those headings.

When mutilation is the result of an accident, the surgeon does everything appropriate to repair the damage, including plastic procedures and the provision of prostheses. Mutilating surgical operations are not undertaken lightly, nor are they eschewed when they are considered to be necessary. Opinions differ about indications, and clearly the advantages, which include relief of symptoms, eradication of disease and prolongation of life, must be weighed against the disadvantages, which include physical disability and psychological trauma.

Patients' reactions to mutilating procedures vary greatly, but should never be underrated. At one extreme they are accepted in a stoical or even cavalier manner, while at the other they cause feelings of shame and depression and may lead to suicide. Mutilation should never, except in unavoidable circumstances, be undertaken without accurate diagnosis and as full a discussion as is appropriate with the patient and relatives. The patient's consent (q.v.) to the specific procedure should always be obtained. The old view, sometimes voiced, that this degree of consultation with the patient was undesirable, since he might refuse an operation which the surgeon considered necessary, is no longer tenable (see *Communication* and *Consent*).

The Muslim religious law, the *Shariat*, requires punishment of certain offences by amputation of hands or feet, which is supposed to be performed under anaesthesia by surgeons. Although the law has been revived recently in some Islamic countries[1], all sentences of amputation appear to have been commuted. However, doctors may be required to undertake these procedures and should be aware of the ethical implications. The Declaration of Tokyo (q.v.) states specifically that they should not 'countenance, condone or participate' in them. It can be argued that, if an amputation is to be performed, it should be done with the least possible discomfort and mutilation and that only a doctor can ensure this. However, most would agree with *The Lancet* that no doctor should use his skill to participate in mutilation as an act of punishment. (See also *Cancer; Circumcision; Cosmetic Surgery; Islam*)

1. *Lancet* corresp: Doctors and the Islamic penal code. Lykkeberg J. 1979; 1: 440. Hashmi KZ. 1979; 1: 614. Naqvi NH. 1979; 1: 614.

R. B. Welbourn

N

National Health Service. In this country there has been a long tradition to help the sick, and much was done before the NHS was introduced by the former voluntary hospitals and local authority hospitals. For those ill at home there was the panel practice introduced by Lloyd George, but this covered only the men at work and not their families. Friendly Societies provided rudimentary mutual insurance for medical treatment at very small charges to contributors and for nominal fees to practitioners. During World War II there was growing concern about the patchy and often inadequate provision for illness, and this led to the passing of the National Health Service Act in 1947 as part of a great wave of social legislation introduced after the end of the Second World War. It enabled the whole population to have free access to medical services when required. This was achieved by better organization of the health care services and by State financing.

When the NHS began in 1948 it was organized into three parts: first, the family practitioner services; secondly, a group of health services provided by the area health authorities and partly paid for by central government; and thirdly, the hospital specialist services.

The family practitioner services included not only the general practitioner (family doctor) service, but also the dental service, the supplementary ophthalmic service and the pharmaceutical service. These were all administered by executive councils.

The local area health services provided a wide range of facilities. These included the ambulance service, the maternity and child welfare service, vaccination and immunization, local mental health services, and health visiting and domiciliary midwifery. In addition they had general responsibilities for the public health and for the prevention of illness.

The hospital service. With the exception of a small number of 'disclaimed' hospitals, all former voluntary and municipal hospitals were incorporated into the National Health Service.

It was a grand concept aimed to provide medical care free at the point of delivery for all who wished to take advantage of it. At the same time there was freedom for independent medical practice. It was financed mainly by taxation and also to some extent by compulsory insurance. There was a further important but subtle benefit. Hitherto much of the medical care had been given on a charitable basis. Indeed, very fine work had been achieved by the voluntary services, but too often the recipients were made only too aware that they were the objects of charity. Under the NHS medical care became their right as taxpayers and at last they could have some representation in the organization of the medical services (see *Voluntary Work*).

Hospitals made a slow start, for in the early post-war years homes, factories and schools rightly had priority, and the two per cent extra 'new money' each year was far less than was needed when one considered the dilapidations of hospitals as a result of war-time neglect. Nevertheless, quickly there was a much better distribution of consultant skills around the country, and this was particularly noticeable for anaesthetics, gynaecology and orthopaedics, and there was also considerable improvement in the casualty and accident services.

An ambitious plan for rebuilding hospitals was begun in the early 1960s, and during this decade some six per cent 'new money' was coming into the Health Service each year. Unhappily this programme slowed down for economic reasons and furthermore the new hospitals proved extremely expensive to run. Most of the older busy general hospitals were not refitted because they were under 'planning blight' while awaiting their turn, which never came, for rebuilding. Hence, many of the problems which persist to this day.

In 1974 an apparently sensible reorganization was approved by Parliament. It aimed to organize health services on a District and Area basis with close links between general practitioners, social services and hospitals. Unfortunately the introduction of a new administrative layer, the Area Health Authority, resulted in great slowing down of decision-making, and the building up of much frustration. This contributed to the industrial unrest which became such an unhappy feature in the NHS in the winter of 1978.

The National Health Service was reviewed by a Royal Commission reporting in 1979. They redefined the objectives for the NHS as follows:

> It should encourage and assist individuals to remain healthy;
> provide equality of entitlement to health services;
> provide a broad range of services of a high standard;
> provide equality of access to these services;
> provide a free service at the time of use;
> satisfy the reasonable expectations of its users;
> remain a national service responsive to local needs.

The Commission showed that much social and geographical in equality in health and health care still persists, but they appreciated that good health depends on much more than a good Health Service. Health systems cannot be looked at in isolation from the society they serve or from the way the society chooses to behave. In the course of their survey they found much which they did not like at all, but in general they felt that the country need not feel ashamed of its Health

Service and that there were many aspects of it of which they could be justly proud. The Royal Commission made a well-balanced assessment of the NHS, making valuable comments.

It seems likely, as a result of this report, that the area health authorities will be disbanded and that the health services will be organized as single district areas serving between 150,000 and 500,000 people. Many will hope that these districts will be related to the natural flow of patients and not determined by arbitrary lines on the map, as had previously been the case.

During the first two decades the NHS made steady progress at varying rates and there were few political overtones. In the third decade strong political overtones developed, leading to divisive reactions and industrial unrest. There is much to be said for keeping the National Health Service out of the political arena and letting the professionals get on with the much-needed build-up of the service. Fortunately in this country there are a great many first-class administrators. Fortunately, again, most people working in the NHS are self-selected by their desire to help other people. Furthermore, the National Health Service is in tune with the historical approach to illness in this country, and there is every expectation that it will persist in the general form as we now know it, and within measurable time it will truly become a fine hallmark for a civilized society. (See also *Health Care Systems; State Health Services.*)

Godber G. Problems in the delivery of health care. *Community Health*. 1976; 8: 2–10.

Jones FA. Getting the NHS back on course. *Br Med J* 1978; 2: 5–9.

Royal Commission on the National Health Service. *Report*. London: HMSO, 1979, Cmnd 7615.

Watkin B. *The National Health Service, the first phase 1948–1974 and after*. London: Allen and Unwin. 1978.

F. Avery Jones

Natural Law. See *Christianity; Human Rights.*

Necessity. Necessity is the term applied by English lawyers to the proposition that an act which is *prima facie* unlawful may in fact be lawful if performed as the only way of achieving another, more desirable and lawful result. Thus, the firemen who destroy someone else's house in order to prevent the spread of fire to a whole city are thought to be justified by the doctrine of necessity. The doctrine, like much else in the Common Law, is based on ethical and practical considerations. Its ethical aspect bears a close relationship to the moral theologians' concept of the law of double effect (q.v.), and may indeed in its practical results be identical with it. But, while moral theologians are likely to assent to the doctrine in the realm of ethics, its validity in English law is uncertain. In the leading case of *R. v. Dudley and Stephens*[1] the defence of necessity was held by five judges of the Queen's Bench Division not to be available to two shipwrecked sailors who, in order to preserve their own lives, had killed and eaten the cabin-boy. The *ratio decidendi* of the case is by no means clear, and in each of two further cases[2,3] (at first instance only) the judge was of the opinion that what, under the law as it then was, would otherwise have been an illegal abortion could be justified by the necessity to preserve the life or health of the mother. It is generally agreed, however, that, if necessity does provide a defence, two conditions are required, namely, (1) that no more wrong is done than is in fact necessary, and (2) that the evil sought to be averted is greater than the evil committed. One of the strongest arguments in support of the view that necessity does provide a defence is the negative one which rests on the fact that it does not occur to anyone to prosecute a surgeon for performing an appendicectomy or other surgical operation. Yet, *prima facie*, even if the patient consents, the surgeon is performing an unlawful act by cutting the patient's body with a knife. If a surgeon were to be charged with an offence, there would seem to be no defence open to him other than necessity – the need to avert the greater evil of the threat to the patient's health by means of the lesser evil inherent in even a properly executed operation. It is also arguable that the defence of necessity is recognized by law under some other name. The law imposes the obligation, even, if necessary, by killing, to keep or restore the Queen's peace and to restrain and arrest persons guilty of some grave crimes. Since this is an obligation, to fail to perform it is itself an offence, so that a failure to shoot in order to repel the Queen's enemies may be an offence, regardless of whether the failure is due to qualms of conscience, cowardice or any other cause. The law also recognizes the right, and perhaps the obligation, of self-defence. Other examples could be given. They may all be examples of the operation of necessity as a defence to what would otherwise be an unlawful act.

1. (1884) 14 QBD 273.
2. *R. v. Bourne* (1939) 1 KB 687, and (1938) 3 All ER 615.
3. *R. v. Newton and Stungo* (1958) Crim. LR 469.
Smith and Hogan. *Criminal law.* 1st edn: 120–6; 245–6; and the authorities there cited.
Bacon. *Maxims V.*
Mortimer RC. *The elements of moral theology.* London: A & C Black, 1947.

E. Garth Moore

Negligence. A failure to use reasonable skill and care resulting in damage. Negligence is a tort, i.e. a civil wrong as opposed to a crime. The term 'criminal negligence', refers to negligence so gross and so damaging in its effects as to amount to a crime. For practical purposes it does not exist in the medical context.

There are four essentials to give grounds for an action in negligence: a duty of care, a breach of that duty, damage to the plaintiff, direct causation between the breach of duty and the damage.

In the context of medical negligence the word 'damage' refers to the harm suffered by the patient, the word 'damages' to the amount awarded by the court.

A doctor owes a duty of care to any patient he attends or advises and there is no distinction in the duty owed to a fee-paying patient, a National Health Service patient or a patient treated gratuitously. A doctor does not however guarantee to cure or alleviate nor to be correct in his diagnosis or treatment. He undertakes to use reasonable skill and care.

Not every doctor has or can have the highest degree of knowledge or skill in every specialty. The standard of care depends therefore on the experience and position held by the doctor. The patient is entitled to expect a higher standard of care from a specialist working in the field of his own specialty than from a general practitioner. On the other hand, lack of staff and facilities at night time, over weekends and in emergencies, may lower the standard of care that can reasonably be demanded.

The court in assessing whether or not there has been negligence will take all relevant facts into consideration.

The purpose of the court in a negligence action is not to punish the defendant but to put the patient, so far as money can achieve this aim, in the position he would have occupied, had it not been for the negligence. It follows that the same act or omission may be met by widely differing awards.

Two small children might be affected by the same act of negligence, one dies and the other survives with severe physical and mental disabilities. About £750 would be awarded for the death, but for the surviving child an assessment would be made of the cost of caring for him throughout his anticipated life span.

Damages are divided into general and special. Special damages compensate for items which can be quantified such as loss of income, medical and nursing expenses, transport costs, etc. General damages deal with matters such as pain and suffering, loss of expectation of life, and loss of enjoyment of life.

Loss of future earnings is a major factor in many cases. This has tended to replace dependency as a head of claim and is one of the factors which has led to the recent increase in court awards. The claim takes into account the plaintiff's original state of health, prospects of promotion, age, and other relevant factors.

Actions must in general be brought within three years of the act complained of, or if the plaintiff was not aware of his having suffered harm within the three years, then he may bring his action within three years of his becoming so aware.

Most negligence actions in England are heard in the High Court, though where the damages claimed do not exceed £2000 the county court has jurisdiction. The cases are heard by the judge sitting alone, who, having heard the evidence and the opinions expressed by the expert witnesses called by either side, determines liability and damages.

In Northern Ireland, the Republic of Ireland, New Zealand and other countries, negligence actions come before a jury and the damages awarded tend to be higher. The USA also has a jury system and the damages are extremely high by UK standards.

In New Zealand the Accident Compensation Act took away the right to sue in negligence in respect of any injury compensatable under the Act. In general, injury arising from acts of commission is compensatable whereas that resulting from acts of omission such as a failure to make a diagnosis or a failure to give proper advice is not. Should the accident compensation commission turn down a claim, then the patient may sue.

In Sweden no-fault compensation is provided by a patient insurance system and harm resulting from pharmaceuticals by a drug insurance scheme. The difficulty in compensating for injury due to inadequate diagnosis is dealt with by a provision that if examination results have been incorrect or if observed clinical signs have been inadequately interpreted and the patient has suffered harm as a result then compensation is payable. Where the County Council makes payment for the injury the patient's right to damages is surrogated to the County Council.

In the USA 1975 saw a crisis due to the withdrawal of certain insurance carriers from the professional risk field. Such an event appears unlikely to occur in the UK where negligence actions are dealt with by professional societies, not insurance companies, lawyers do not work on a contingency fee basis, amounts awarded are assessed by a judge and therefore both parties are more able to forecast the value of a claim.

The Royal Commission on Civil Liability and Compensation for Personal Injury which reported in 1978 whilst recommending a no-fault scheme for road accidents, felt that compensation for personal injury arising from other causes including medical, should continue to be based on proof of negligence. (See also *Compensation; Defence Societies; Malpractice.*)

Bingham R. *All modern cases on negligence.* London: Sweet and Maxwell, 1978.

Martin CRA. *Law relating to medical practice.* London: Pitman Medical, 1979.

Nathan. *Medical negligence.* London: Butterworth, 1957.

Speller SR. *Law relating to hospitals and kindred institutions.* London: HK Lewis, 1978.

Taylor JL. *Doctor and negligence.* London: Pitman Medical, 1971.

J. Leahy Taylor

Nell'Ordine della Natura. See *Vegliare con Sollecitudine.*

Neonatal Care. See *Child; Childbirth, Intervention in.*

Non-accidental Injuries. See *Battered Wives; Child Abuse.*

Notification. See *Compulsory Examination and Treatment; Confidentiality; Death, Certification of; Mental Illness, Certification of.*

Nuffield Provincial Hospitals Trust. The purposes of the Trust, which was founded by Lord Nuffield in 1940, are defined in the Trust Deed as 'the co-ordination on a regional basis of hospital, medical and associated health services throughout the provinces; the making of financial provision for the creation, carrying on or extension of such hospital, medical and associated health services as are necessary for such co-ordination, and the promotion of improved organization and efficient development of hospital, medical and associated health services throughout the provinces'.

The general line of approach adopted by the Trust from its inception has been to act as an independent observer of health services and to commission studies, demonstrations and experiments designed to help their improvement. More recently the policy has been to act more and more as an independent agent in the brokerage and development of ideas and for the encouragement of ever-sharper critiques of underlying concepts concerning the maintenance of the health of individuals relating to cure, care and prevention.

Central to this policy is the belief that the best atmosphere for advances in well-being and health is an understanding of the vital forces affecting health in our society. The main thrust of the Trust's enquiries, an important part of the mechanism of which is a private seminar programme, has been devoted to a succession of probes into issues which are fundamental to a better understanding of what determines ill-health in the individual and what can be done about it by way of public policies, not just in reviewing the effect of existing institutions and underlying beliefs but by seeking a better conceptualization of the issues embracing health in all its aspects. To do this involves the mobilization and analysis of the best available 'intelligence' and the sharpening of techniques to explore concepts, review activities, synthesize conclusions and to point to further directions for future action.

All the activities of the Trust since its inception have indicated that progress towards better health may be in part dependent on progress in resolving certain major problems involving personal ethics, such as changes in the behaviour of health professionals, the external circumstances behind such changes, and the increasing complexity of the management arrangements which tend to superimpose constructions on the one-to-one idea of doctor/patient relationships. These issues have been specially pointed up in many of the more recent interests of the Trust, for example quality assurance in care, manpower, collaboration between the NHS and other authorities concerned with care, the framework for prevention covering as it does many areas external to DHSS interests, the social causation of ill-health, the application of technology to medicine, and the implications of these for medical education, particularly in its postgraduate and continuing aspects.

As a necessary complement to this, a major policy has been to develop a publications programme in an effort to help the creation of a literature for the wide dissemination of ideas covering the range of issues raised by the expansion and ever-burgeoning complexities of health services. This programme leads to the highlighting of gaps in knowledge and to the stimulation of speculation and projections about future developments.

The address of the Trust's offices is 3 Prince Albert Road, London NW1 7SP.

G. McLachlan

Nuremberg Code. See *Declarations*.

Nursing (1). Historically nursing has had a nurturant, mother-surrogate role, giving general care and comfort to the ill; it owed its origins to the dominant religious system of each country.

Later nursing became allied with and subordinate to medicine, from which its changing perspective largely derived and a 'preventive' aspect evolved, notably in the field of public health, as science became increasingly applied to medicine.

Claims to professional status developed alongside national qualifications and controlled training courses. There is now a growing tendency for the 'first-level', 'professional' nurse to specialize, either in clinical work or, increasingly, in education or management where higher status and greater material rewards are found, while general, non-specific, care is undertaken more and more by 'second-level' or untrained personnel.

The claim to professional status is difficult to satisfy, especially on three important criteria: (1) the existence of a central, non-derived, body of knowledge, (2) the development of research and (3) the (status) position of the practitioner. Attempts to define the role of nurses have proved unsatisfactory since their activities are largely tied to culture, context, demand levels and the social position of related groups, especially medicine. Definitions which are generally accepted tend to be generalized and qualitative, e.g. 'the unique function of the nurse is to assist the individual, sick or well, in the performance of those activities contributing to health or recovery (or to peaceful death) that he would perform unaided if he had the necessary strength, will or knowledge'[1].

The professional claim is further complicated by the difficulty of maintaining a distinct border line between nursing and medicine. Training syllabuses tend to be strongly orientated towards the physical sciences while many nursing activities are related to the social sciences, so that it is difficult to establish and measure standards of nursing care except where the requirement of care can be scientifically identified, as in transplant surgery or renal dialysis. The ethical position is therefore largely anchored to general concept of life and death, or to existing social/religious attitudes to such procedures as therapeutic abortion and resuscitation of the elderly and to the nurse's involvement in these matters. Since these concepts vary, so do nurses' attitudes.

The International Council of Nurses (ICN) was first organized in 1899 and its membership is one national association from each country. In 1953 its Grand Council adopted an international code[2] of ethics for nurses which describes the fundamental reponsibilities of the nurse as fourfold: to promote health, to prevent illness, to restore health and to alleviate suffering. The code is written under five headings: nurses and people; nurses and practice; nurses and society; nurses and co-workers; and nurses and the profession. The statements are, again, largely qualitative and non-specific except in two instances: 'the nurse holds in confidence personal information' and 'the nurse takes appropriate action to safeguard the individual when his care is endangered by a co-worker or any other person'.

Twenty three years later (1976) the Royal College of Nursing (Rcn) (the UK member association of the ICN) published a 'code of professional conduct'. Although the headings are similar to the ICN code of ethics – responsibility to patients/clients, responsibility for professional standards, responsibility to colleagues, and professional and personal responsibility – other areas of specific difficulty are emphasized. For example, handling potentially violent patients; attitudes to strike action ('which can never be justified'); the patient's right to information concerning his own case ('the active participation of patients in their own treatment should be facilitated by means of open and sensitive communication'); and certain moral values which 'as private individuals, nurses should defend and pursue, . . . namely individual autonomy, parity of treatment and the pursuit of health'.

Specific problems of nursing involvement with medical practice are not mentioned in this document but are discussed in a second publication *What the Rcn stands for*. Here the question of 'switching off' life maintaining machines is stated as being the sole responsibility of the doctor; decisions on abortion are said to be essentially medical, but abortion should not be regarded as a form of contraception and should not be available on demand; and the Rcn takes its stand firmly against the introduction of any legislation permitting euthanasia (q.v.).

The American Nurses Association (ANA) (the USA member association of the ICN) adopted a code of ethics in 1950 which was last revised in 1968.[4] This 10 point document makes general statements similar to those already discussed but two new points emerge: 'The nurse participates in research activities when assured that the rights of the individual subjects are protected' and 'The nurse refuses to give or imply endorsement to advertising, promotion or sales for commercial products, services or enterprises.'

The latter is covered in England and Wales by a regulation of the General Nursing Council (the registering body) which defines clearly the limits regarding advertising; registered or enrolled nurses can be disciplined for professional misconduct if these regulations are broken. This statutory body has the legal right to remove a nurse's qualification for grave professional misconduct; it has not, however, published guidelines on the subject and treats each case on an individual basis. The largest group of 'removals' nowadays is for misuse of drugs, but others result from action against patients such as theft or physical ill treatment.

It is likely that, in the next decade, nurses will be faced with ethical questions which are more sharply defined than in the past.

'In caring for people of all ages the support and maintenance of human dignity and personality is important. In Western society it is not esteemed because we value the care of disease and the deferment of death more highly. It is possible that nursing will succumb to our present value system and become more and more technical: geriatric nursing will not then be fulfilling. Care for people without hope of recovery will have to be done by a different kind of nurse altogether: one who takes seriously the fact that non-nursing duties . . . are often the way in which a nurse cares and gets to know her patients. But menial work in this country is increasingly being done by immigrants: is it they who will care for us in our old age, the underprivileged cared for by the underprivileged in mutual understanding? Or nursing will recognize that its very *raison d'être* is threatened by a value system that is alien to its nature: namely the preference for the cure of disease to the care of people'.[5]

1. Henderson V. The nature of nursing. *Am J Nurs* 1964; 64:63.
2. International Council of Nurses. *Code for nurses*. Geneva: ICN, 1953.
3. Royal College of Nursing. *The Rcn code of professional conduct*. London: Rcn, 1976.

4. Spalding EK, Notter LE. *Professional nursing*. Philadelphia: Lippincott, 1970: 446.
5. Wilson M. *Health is for people*. London: Darton, Longman & Todd, 1975: 12.

E. Bendall

(2). In the first edition of this Dictionary, Miss Bendall suggested that ethical issues to be faced by nurses might be more sharply defined in the next decade. Now, 3 years later, the issues are far from defined but they are fast becoming more clearly illuminated if one is to judge by the number of recent articles, books, codes and guidelines on the subject of ethics for nurses.

Since 1977 there have been 44 additions to the *index medicus* category 'Ethics – Nursing'. Increasing emphasis on the need for research in nursing and for practice to be based upon nursing research has led to an awareness of the inherent ethical considerations. In 1977 the Royal College of Nursing (Rcn) issued a Code of Ethics for Nursing Research and since then there have been several articles and books on the subject. By the end of 1979 the *Nursing Times* published a Bibliography of Nursing Research Methodology which included a separate sub-section on ethics.

The International Council of Nurses (ICN) published a book in 1977 which discussed some of the issues which nurses face in their daily work with patients and co-professionals. It describes real-life situations of ethical conflict and the issues include resuscitation, the mechanical maintenance of life, and genetic counselling. At about the same time the Rcn produced a Code of Professional Conduct. The most recent addition to the list is a set of guidelines on ethics for nurses by the ICN which was issued in 1979 to nursing associations of member countries. As is usual with International Agreements the guidelines are stated in very general terms and members are warned that they will have to interpret them in the light of the local cultural, social, religious and legal framework within which nurses operate in various countries.

It is not merely the volume of published material which has changed: the method of discussion and presentation has altered to some extent. Where previously codes and agreements were stated at a broad level of generality many recent publications rely heavily upon discussion of case material which highlights dilemmas and grey areas of inter and intra-professional conflict. The issues contained in previous publications continue to be matters of concern for nurses but in addition new areas are being examined as dilemmas of life and death increase. As nurses participate in multidisciplinary teams, they are becoming increasingly aware of their involvement in joint decision making. They are, in addition, beginning to identify areas in which the nursing contribution is unique. The quality of life, and the giving of care where no cure is possible are issues of importance to nurses.

In 1979 the National Health Service passed through its first experience of major industrial action with strikes which involved and affected nurses of all grades. This period of unrest highlighted the ethical and professional issues contained in the right of the individual worker to withhold his labour versus the responsibilities and duties of members of a profession. In April 1979 Rcn members voted once more against strike action by nurses for industrial or any other reason. Subsequent to this the General Nursing Council for England and Wales issued a statement to the effect that 'if a nurse put the health, welfare and safety of his or her patients at risk by taking strike action he or she would have a case to answer on the score of professional misconduct just as he or she would if the health, welfare or safety of a patient were put at risk by any other action on his or her part'. The debate on these issues continues. As we enter the 1980s we are no nearer to a sharp definition of ethical issues to be faced by nurses but there is ample evidence of an increasing awareness among nurses of their involvement in and contribution to the debate on this subject. (See *Interprofessional Relationships; Research Ethical Committee; Right to Strike; Teamwork.*)

A nursing research methodology bibliography. *Nurs Times* (Occ Paper) 1979; 27: 109–11.

Dunn A ed. The Rocky Path of Professionalism. *Nurs Times* 1979; 31: 1289.

General Nursing Council for England and Wales. *Statement on professional misconduct*. London: GNC, July, 1979.

International Council of Nurses. *Guidelines on nursing research for national nurses associations*. Geneva: ICN, 1976.

International Council of Nurses. *The nurses' dilemma: ethical considerations in nursing practice*. Geneva: ICN, 1977.

International Council of Nurses. Guidelines on ethics. *Nurs Times* 1979; 75, vol. 47.

Royal College of Nursing. *Ethics related to research in nursing: guidance for nurses involved in research*. London: Rcn, 1979.

Royal College of Nursing. *Code of professional conduct: A discussion document*. London: Rcn, 1979.

Royal College of Nursing. Resolution against change of Rule 12 (Power to call industrial action). 26 February 1979.

W. W. Thomson

O

Occupational Medicine. Certain diseases are specifically of occupational origin. The prevention of these diseases and of accidents at work has become a major objective of all industrial nations and has led to a great increase in the importance of occupational medicine. However, the position of the physician specializing in this field presents special ethical difficulties.

In essence these derive from conflicts of loyalty. In normal medical practice a patient seeks the advice of a doctor and the relationship between the two is private and unambiguous. Most doctors in industry are employed by management, however, and conflicts of interest can readily occur. Some examples help to illustrate the problem. Suppose a physician suspects that an employee is developing an incapacitating illness. If revealed to the company it might jeopardize that employee's prospects of promotion or even of retaining his job. Supposing a physician forms an opinion that there is a certain health hazard in an industry which management decide is unimportant and which is concealed, should he publicize his views and, possibly, lose his job? Another widespread problem concerns certification of incapacity to work by practitioners who have no direct occupational responsibilities. In this familiar example the patient may be in a position to bring very considerable pressure to bear on the doctor by his ability to withdraw his patronage, that of his family and of a wide circle of acquaintances.

Dilemmas of this nature occur whenever the interests of an individual worker conflict with those of the employing agency whether this be a private company, a government organization or a corporate state. Accusations that physicians have failed to maintain an ethical position have been freely made. It has been suggested on the one hand that they have been more than willing tools of management and have co-operated in the deliberate concealment of health hazards, and on the other that individual doctors distort the truth in order to please trades unions. It is the experience of the writer that most physicians specializing in occupational medicine attempt to preserve an ethical position. Ideally they should be independent and without contractual obligations to any one side, but this is seldom possible. Certain guiding principles receive general support in the literature. Health records must remain absolutely confidential. Under no circumstances should they be disclosed without the written consent of the patient.

Some medical reports are of a statutory legal nature and disclosure is not an ethical matter. Trade secrets learned during the course of the doctor's work must remain confidential. The physician should resist the temptation to sign inaccurate documents, even if they appear to assist a 'hard luck' case. He must never interfere with the relationship between a patient and his family physician.

If the employer offers a private consultant opinion at the expense of the company, the company doctor should, before making such a referral, inform the family physician and preferably obtain his consent. Where emergency treatment is given, the family physician must be kept fully informed.

The publication of research results is a particularly sensitive question. In the long term, a healthy work force and an efficient industry are interdependent. Research in which freedom to publish is restricted is thus highly undesirable. Where a company or government appears to be suppressing results deliberately, the physician must make every effort to persuade them to alter their policy. The facts usually emerge in the end and are less likely to cause problems if discussed openly from the very beginning. Where policy is unresponsive to these considerations, the doctor is undoubtedly in difficulties and faces unpleasant decisions.

In essence, it is accepted that the doctor should try to preserve the normal codes of medical ethics which govern the conduct of any physician. In entering occupational medicine he sells his professional expertise to industry but not his ethical independence.

There is one topic where the ethical position is uncertain – whether or not the profession should co-operate in pre-employment medical examinations, other than for safety reasons. While all organizations prefer to recruit healthy employees, doctors may fear that knowledge of diseases or disabilities discovered at medical examination may be used as an excuse to exclude from employment some who ought not to be turned down. In the UK the position is to some extent mitigated by a regulation requiring employers of more than 25 persons to include among their staff, if practicable, a percentage of disabled workers. (See *Clinical Practice; Communication; Compensation; Confidentiality; General Practice; Medical Records.*)

Eckhardt RE. Annals of industry – non-casualties of the work place. *J Occ Med* 1974; 16: 472–7.

Murray R. Ethics in occupational health In: Schilling RSF, ed. *Occupational health practice*, London: Butterworth, 1973: 421–30.

Roberts NJ. The question of ethical standards in occupational medical practice. *J Occ Med* 1972; 14: 632–5.

Tabershaw LR. Whose 'agent' is the occupational physician? *Arch Environ Health*, 1975; 30: 412–6.

D. C. F. Muir

Ombudsman. See *Health Service Commissioners*.

Ordinary and Extraordinary Means. See *Life, Prolongation of*.

Organ Transplant. See *Tissue Transplant*.

Oslo Declaration. See *Declarations*.

Osteopathy. Osteopathy originated as a system of healing based on the idea that spinal displacements are the cause of disease. Strictly speaking, osteopathy has nothing to do with manipulation; it is a theory on how diseases arise. It is true that the corollary is reduction of the displacement, and this is indeed what osteopaths attempt, but doctors and bonesetters have been manipulating successfully for more than two thousand years, as a local treatment for a local phenomenon.[1] In 1874 in the USA, Still, who was not a doctor, decided that a displaced vertebra could impinge against a blood vessel, causing damage by reducing blood flow to the relevant organ. This he named the 'Rule of the Artery', reviving a concept put forward by Harrison of Edinburgh in 1824[2]. This was later changed to pressure on a nerve[3,4], whereby an organ was deprived of life-force. Here he came close to the truth, for an intervertebral disc protrusion can indeed compress a nerve root. This sets up pain radiating to the area served by that nerve, but not of course to disease elsewhere. Later still, the mechanism whereby spinal manipulation afforded relief was expanded to include lasting alteration of autonomic tone – the excitability of nerves controlling internal organs. This tenet is scarcely viable today since drugs now exist (e.g. those for reducing blood pressure) that abate such tone, but without producing the effects that osteopaths postulate.

The latest available edition (undated) of the *Osteopathic Blue Book* issued in London declares that in practice osteopathy is 'a system of therapeutics which lays the major emphasis on the structural and mechanical derangements within the framework of the body.' The 'osteopathic lesion' is fixation of a vertebra within its range of movement without irreversible change. This is description by result, and does not indicate how the fixation arose. The book contains a remarkable list of diseases that osteopaths consider suited to manual treatment. All this matter came up for review in 1935 at the enquiry into osteopathy at the House of Lords[5]. The opinion of osteopaths could not withstand medical interrogation and the hearing brought them such embarrassment that they pleaded, and were granted, permission to withdraw their petition. State recognition putting them on a par with the medical profession is no mere outworn pretension, for a further attempt to secure official registration was made in the House of Commons in 1976. The osteopaths' intention was to achieve recognition as an autonomous group, not as auxiliaries to medicine like nurses. Again, the Bill was withdrawn by its sponsor.

Manipulation and osteopathy are not synonymous. The former represents a manual treatment that has been widely employed for centuries for local disorders in the case of fractures, dislocations, adhesions about a joint, hernia, or abnormal intrauterine presentation of the fetus, no less than in spinal disorders. The practice of these manoeuvres involves acceptance of no particular theory of the causation of disease. If osteopaths had accepted the physiotherapists' ethics and had maintained merely that they were capable manipulators – as some of them undoubtedly are – ready to treat such patients as doctors sent to them for this purpose, all reproach against them would by now have ceased. Curiously enough, the lack of medical recognition of lay manipulators has redounded to osteopaths' benefit. Their near monopoly has been maintained by doctors' illogical passing on from dislike of treatment by laymen to dislike for what they do: i.e. manipulation. Hence, large numbers of patients attend hospitals all over the country requiring a simple spinal manipulation. But, in vain; for neither the doctor nor the physiotherapist working there knows enough about this measure. Later on, the patient visits a layman, receives a few simple twists and recovers at once.

Naturally, if all medical and physiotherapy students were grounded in this work, the need for laymen would soon come to an end. It would be carried out by doctors and physiotherapists, who have been taught the indications and contra-indications of manual methods, and realize that many of the diseases today treated by laymen are not in fact suited to these manoeuvres. The work of the orthopaedic physician is to set out the pros and cons of manipulation, so that a perfectly simple subject becomes clear to students in both professions. Then diagnosis leading to suitable treatment in lesions of the soft moving parts will become tomorrow's orthodoxy.

With the advance of medical knowledge, the time must surely come when osteopaths will forget their 'lesion' and their outworn theories and concentrate on becoming skilled manipulators of the joints of the spine and limbs,[6] thus achieving the respectability that the efficacious part of their work warrants. Doctors would then be prepared to study and advocate those methods which they both found successful. Patients would no longer have to go outside the medical profession for a few simple twists, and treatment widely recognized as successful would become fully available through the hospitals of Britain. Since the disorders treatable by spinal manipulation constitute one of the commonest causes of absence from work, the finances of the Health Service, the nation and the insurance companies would benefit greatly. But as long as osteopaths make diagnoses to suit themselves and treat non-spinal as well as spinal lesions, they are spreading their net so wide that medical men tend not to countenance their work, effective though in part it is.

OSTEOPATHY IN OTHER COUNTRIES. Osteopathy has taken an entirely opposite turn in the USA. In 1955 a medical committee found that the six main osteopathic colleges had revised their dogma, had accepted normal medical knowledge, and were offering such satisfactory general tuition that they were accorded official recognition on a par with medical schools. Nowadays they put less and less emphasis on manipulation and turn out fully qualified doctors. In the USA, Medicare defrays the cost of adjustments by chiropractors up to a certain sum. This is surprising; for they claim that, since all tissues have nerves (in fact the intervertebral disc has none), manipulating the joints of the spine must influence almost all disease. This reasoning is indeed hard to follow. In France and Belgium spinal manipulation except by medical men is illegal. By contrast, in Australia, Denmark and Switzerland chiropractors have secured a measure of State recognition. In South Africa they are barred from manipulation for gain. In Britain, just as it is lawful for anyone who chooses, doctor or not, to induce anaesthesia and perform surgical operations, so is it open to everyone to call himself osteopath, chiropractor or bonesetter, and manipulate all comers without further ado. Insofar as three thousand people are estimated to earn their living by manipulation, and the osteopathic register contains some three hundred names, it is clear that the wholly self-styled predominate.

1. Schiötz EH, Cryiax J. *Manipulation: past and present*. London: Heinemann Medical, 1975.
2. Harrison E. Effects of spinal distortion on the sanguineous circulation. *London Medical and Physical Journal* 1820; 44: 373.
3. Brown T. Irritation of the spinal nerves. *Glasgow Medical Journal* 1828; 158.
4. Riadore JE. *Treatise on irritation of the spinal nerves*. London: Churchill, 1843.
5. Report from the Select Committee of the House of Lords appointed to consider the Registration and Regulation of Osteopaths Bill. London: HMSO, 1935.
6. Cyriax J. *Textbook of orthopaedic medicine*. 17th edn. London: Baillière, Tindall, 1975: Vol 1.

James Cyriax

P

Paediatrics. See *Child.*

Paedophilia. See *Sexual Deviations or Variations.*

Pain. Pain is what hurts – it is an experience which is essentially incapable of definition. It is grouped with pleasure as being a primary motivator of action, but like pleasure little is known about the fundamental nature of the processes involved in the production of pain. A popular publication on this subject is aptly called *The Puzzle of Pain*[1]. The *Concise Oxford Dictionary* describes pain as 'suffering, distress of body or mind'. The origin of our word is from Old French *peine* and Latin *poena* meaning penalty. Thus pain is not simply a physical affliction; it can affect the mind and all our behaviour and until comparatively recently it was associated with the thought of punishment.

There is reason to believe that it is inherent to any life linked with consciousness and that the *via dolorosa* is as old as man, as is man's search for an escape from it.

Pain is a sensation which is built up by experience. Scientifically speaking pain, like vision and hearing, is a complex perceptual experience, but because of the diversity of causes (trauma, burning, pressure, ischaemia, etc) it is obviously not a single quality of experience which can be specified in terms of a defined standard stimulus. Perhaps the most helpful definition is that of Melzack[1] who considers that the word pain 'represents a category of experiences, signifying a multitude of different qualities varying along a number of sensory and affective dimensions'.

The obvious biological value of pain is as a signal of tissue damage; it may in fact be the first sign of impending trouble. It does not always occur after injury, and to complicate matters when it does occur, the severity will not necessarily be in proportion to the extent of the damage. In some circumstances elimination of pain may mask a warning signal which would guide treatment.

The terms used to describe pain are varied depending upon its nature, its intensity, its duration as well as to related effects referring to the significance of the pain to the patient. Such adjectives as dull, sharp, gnawing, pinching, tugging, pulling, burning, hot, scalding and rasping tend to describe pain sensation in relation to other experiences, while terms such as mild, distressing and excruciating are used in an attempt to evaluate its severity. Allied effects on the body may also be used for descriptive purposes, e.g. tiring, suffocating, exhausting, blinding and sickening. The significance of pain is conveyed in terms such as frightening, terrifying, punishing and cruel.

ATTITUDES TO PAIN. In addition to the original pain sensation there is the all important factor of its meaning to the sufferer. The patient's psychological reaction is often related to the significance of the pain and may be the dominant factor in whether it is described as mild or severe. It is well known that battle injuries are often considered as a 'passport home' and only a minority of casualties request pain relieving drugs[2], while pain from malignancy may conjure up more sinister thoughts in the mind of the sufferer and lead to a constant demand for drugs. The relevance of the cause of pain to the family and dependants indirectly may influence what the patient 'feels' and determines his general attitude to pain. Thus a niggling pain in a patient whose mother has recently died from cancer under distressing conditions may cause more 'suffering' than the severe battle wounds referred to above. In one the pain conjures up thoughts of leaving a family of small children while the other held out hopes of returning home to the family.

The pain threshold varies not only from patient to patient but also from culture to culture and in differing circumstances. The difference between Oriental and Western attitudes to childbirth is a good example of this. Differences in pain tolerance reflect different ethnic attitudes to it and this also includes attitudes resulting from different religious backgrounds, possibly involving the concept of guilt. In practice individual variations may affect dosage of analgesics, but differences due to apprehension and related factors can often be minimized by appropriate sedation.

Despite all our attempts to explain variability in appreciation of pain (and liability to 'complain' of pain) there still remains a great unexplained individual variation which is part of the 'puzzle of pain'.

CONTROL OF PAIN. Pain from surgery or childbirth can be controlled by general(ized) or local(ized) anaesthesia. The former acts principally on the brain and is associated with loss of consciousness, while the latter affects the nerve pathways from the site of injury to the brain where the sensation is consciously appreciated. Local anaesthesia, nerve section or pain tract section (cordotomy or tractotomy) can be used in the relief of intractable pain, particularly from that of malignancy. Its results are however sometimes disappointing and this may be partly due to the 'reaction' component of the pain affecting the patient's general outlook.

Pain relieving drugs are referred to as analgesics and their effects are somewhat akin to low-grade general anaesthesia. They affect the whole of the body and may leave the patient with a 'drugged' feeling.

Despite this they are a great help to the suffering patient as they often allay apprehension and relieve mental suffering. They should not be withheld in severe pain which is not amenable to other forms of relief and their legitimate use is one of the greatest boons of modern medicine. Patients often develop tolerance to analgesics, requiring ever increased doses for adequate pain relief. This may be a problem in terminal malignancy, where doses which could normally be lethal may have to be given. The prime object of the treatment is to alleviate pain and this end should be achieved even if the possible indirect, unintentional but inevitable result is acceleration of death. Drug therapy is discussed elsewhere (see *Terminal Care*). Ideally, when controlled, the pain must not be allowed to return and the memory and fear of it must be broken[3] (see *Hospices*). The use of special units for this purpose has much to commend it[4].

The potent pain relieving drugs may be derived from opium (morphine, diamorphine-heroin, papaveretum) or synthetic (pethidine, methadone, pentazocine) and they can be taken by mouth or given by injection. When there is a predominance of the anxiety or apprehension factor in pain, the administration of sedatives or tranquillizers (such as chlorpromazine or diazepam) is of great value.

With individual attention to dosage, frequency, route of administration of analgesics and rational use of other drugs, adequate pain relief can almost always be achieved. This requires time and patience and is not always given the priority it deserves. (See also *Acupuncture, Anaesthesia; Palliative Surgical Operations*.)

1. Melzack R. *The puzzle of pain*. Harmondsworth: Penguin Books, 1973.
2. Beecher HK. Pain in men wounded in battle. *Ann Surg*. 1946; 123: 96–105.
3. Saunders CM. The challenge of terminal care. In: Symington T, Carter Rd, eds. *Scientific foundations of oncology*. London: Heinemann, 1976: 673.
4. Leading Article. Pain and the dissatisfied dead. *Br Med J* 1978; 1: 459–60.
Bonica JJ. *The management of pain*. London: Kimpton, 1953.
Keele KD. *Anatomies of pain*. Oxford: Blackwell, 1957.
Soulairac A, Cahn J, Charpentier J. *Pain*. London: Academic Press, 1968.
Twycross RG. Relief of pain. In: Saunders CM, ed. *The management of terminal disease*. London: Arnold, 1978: 65–98.

John W. Dundee

Palliative Surgical Operations. Surgical operations performed for the relief of symptoms, without hope of cure of the underlying disease. Common examples are relief of pain and/or other symptoms by removal of the primary growth from a patient whose cancer is known to have spread already, the relief of intestinal obstruction in a patient with abdominal cancer, which cannot be removed, and the preservation of a limb by mechanical clearance or bypassing of an obstructed segment of artery in a patient with widespread arterial disease.

Use of the term may be extended to include operations which do not restore health and expectation of life completely. These include operations for spina bifida (q.v.), the transplantation of organs (see *Tissue Transplant*), and operations for those forms of cancer which, while apparently removed completely, have probably extended already in an occult form and are likely to recur overtly later.

Most surgeons undertake palliative operations only when they expect them to provide greater relief of symptoms than other palliative measures, such as drugs, and when they are likely to prolong life *in an acceptable form*. Some forms of palliation, such as colostomy (artificial abdominal opening for the bowel), may be quite unacceptable to some patients.

Sometimes a curative operation involves a mutilating procedure (see *Mutilation*), which is unacceptable to the patient. In these circumstances it may be preferable to perform a palliative operation, even when a curative one is possible.

If the issues involved are discussed, as far as appropriate, with the patient and his relatives, and if their wishes are respected, the best decisions can usually be made without difficulty. (See also *Cancer; Life, Prolongation of; Pain; Terminal Care; Truth*.)

R. B. Welbourn

Parasuicide. See *Attempted Suicide*.

Patent. A conditional and limited monopoly granted by the State as a reward for the introduction into the realm of new technology.

With few exceptions every country of the world has its own patent law. The United Kingdom Statute[1] grants patents for a maximum duration of 20 years. A prerequisite of such a grant is the disclosure of a detailed description of the invention which becomes public property when the monopoly ceases. Legal arguments involving the infringement and validity of patent monopolies proceed by way of High Court litigation.

Inventions in the medical field patentable under British law include new drugs *per se*, processes for making drugs, synergistic combinations of drugs, and surgical appliances. Methods of medical treatment of human beings are not patentable in the United Kingdom as they are in the USA and some other countries. Recent UK jurisprudence has, however, allowed patents for methods of contraception and of medical diagnosis, although refusing a patent on a method of inducing abortion in human females. Additionally, under the new Patents Act patents are permitted for substances or compositions for use in a method of treatment of the human body by surgery or therapy or of diagnosis practised on the human body, even if such material is known, provided there has been no previous disclosure of the use of that material in any such method.

A recent study[2] of the economic effects of the patent system in industry as a whole reached the conclusion that pharmaceuticals stood out as the industry which is most heavily dependent on patents. The pharmaceutical industry (q.v.) asserts that the existence of a patent law provides a positive incentive to the discovery of new drugs and without it the present high level of Research and Development expenditure in the industry could not be maintained, whereas its opponents allege that some companies make excessive and unjustified profits by virtue of their patent monopolies. These arguments have been studied by various UK Government appointed committees. The Sainsbury Committee,[3] although considering the question of patent monopoly in the pharmaceutical industry, made no positive recommendations and referred the issue to the Banks Committee. This Committee in its report[4] reached the conclusion that there was no good reason why drugs should be treated differently from other patentable things and that patent protection for pharmaceutical products was necessary to the existence of a research-based pharmaceutical industry evolving new and valuable remedies.

When new patent legislation was enacted in the United Kingdom during 1977 the special rules relating to the compulsory licensing of pharmaceutical patents under the then existing Patents Act, 1949 were abolished, but the provisions giving the Crown power to use and authorize the use of patented inventions in the pharmaceutical field were extended. These provisions enable a Government Department to make, use and exercise any patented invention for the services of the Crown, and are such as to enable the Department of Health and Social Security to obtain supplies of a patented drug or medicine for the National Health Service should a patentee be abusing a strong market position, e.g. by overcharging the Service.

In recent years patents on pharmaceuticals have been the subject of worldwide controversy dependent largely on whether or not the country concerned has an indigenous innovating pharmaceutical industry. Thus, whilst Brazil, Peru and Turkey have abolished drug patent protection altogether and Canada, India and Mexico have substantially weakened such protection, the new European patent legislation and the new Japanese patent law considerably strengthen it. An exception to this is in the United States where the activities of the Department of Justice against pharmaceutical manufacturers exercising their patent monopolies often seriously undermine the value of US drug patents.

The proposals for the abolition of patents in the pharmaceutical field may be said to be based on the humanitarian view that new and improved medicines should be readily available to all peoples of the world. However, history has shown that one of the most important factors in the worldwide conquest of disease is the continuing flow of new drugs, and this would cease without patent protection to support the research effort.

Although in the short term the erosion or abolition of pharmaceutical patent protection may enable the developing nations to obtain access to drugs and medicines at low cost, in the long run the answer to the economic and social needs of these nations must be the transfer to them from the developed countries of the necessary technology and know-how to enable them to set up local pharmaceutical manufacturing facilities which ultimately will become inventive and innovative in their own right. Effective patent protection acts as a great incentive to such transfer.

1. Patents Act 1977. London: HMSO, 1977.
2. Taylor CT, Silberton S. *The economic impact of the patent system.* Cambridge: University Press, 1973.
3. Report of the Committee of Enquiry into the Relationships of the Pharmaceutical Industry with the National Health Service, 1965–1967. London HMSO, 1967, Cmnd 3410.
4. *The British patent system.* London: HMSO, 1970, Cmnd 4407.

Ronald Smither

Patients. Patients are, or believe themselves to be, in need of care and attention. By putting themselves in the hands of doctors or of hospitals, they voluntarily subject themselves to others in the belief that, by so doing, they will benefit. Patients are often fearful, the anxiety being an additional factor to the physical illness, or they may have a mental disorder which alters their normal emotional make-up. The physical examination which they have to undergo may be distasteful, embarrassing or tiring. Patients are, therefore, especially vulnerable people, yet they retain their own rights as individuals – rights which are matched by responsibilities.

The doctor/patient relationship (see *Clinical Practice*) is one of special trust and confidence. The standard of expertise and professional conduct among the medical profession should ideally be such that patients believe that the treatment they will get is the one best suited to their own interests (not necessarily to the interests of society at large, since no patient would like to think that his doctor might sacrifice him to the general good). The doctor in those circumstances has the right, in turn, to expect the patient to understand what is being done for him, and to cooperate intelligently. That the system so often works well is a tribute to the effectiveness of such a relationship; it is inevitable that it sometimes fails. That failures are now more common – or more often publicized – warrants examination of the causes.

There is no doubt that, in recent years, the expectations of patients have increased. When people are ill, they are inclined to regard their doctors as god-like and able to work miracles, and to be disappointed by failure. As treatments have become available for more and more diseases, patients have been less willing to accept that all diseases cannot be cured. That medical care is now a right through the National Health Service means that doctors are called upon for help for even the most minor complaint, which might well have been ignored if payment had to be made. Increased publicity for medical matters, through radio and television, newspapers, books and magazines, produces a demand for treatment which may or may not be reasonable. The patient must accept that his rights are not unlimited and that he has a duty to exercise responsibility, especially in the demands he makes on the doctor's time. He has a responsibility also to try and ensure, by his manner of life, that he does not unnecessarily become a patient (see *Health Education*).

On the doctor's side, the very personal relationship with the patient which once existed has been whittled away. Group practice, which makes the life of the general practitioner more normal and manageable, means that it is harder for a patient to get to know any one doctor. Home visiting has been reduced and doctors are sometimes over-ready to refer a patient to hospital rather than deal with difficulties themselves. It is open to question whether a return to older styles of practice might not in itself reduce some of the doctor's workload by re-establishing some of the mutual confidence which seems to have been lost, provided that this could be matched by an increase in patient responsibility. At the same time medical knowledge has greatly increased. The amount of scientific facts which have to be absorbed and understood during medical training, and the emphasis in hospital on the acute and rarer cases, have meant that students often fail to appreciate the day to day problems with which they will be confronted in general practice.

The main right of patients is the right to information about their own or their children's condition. Failure on the part of doctors to talk intelligibly and sensibly to patients is an ethical as well as a practical failure (see *Communication*). Learning how to do this must therefore be a main part of a doctor's education, if anything like the ideal relationship is to be achieved. The need for information is especially apparent in hospitals (q.v.) for operations and procedures have also arisen, with patients apparently unaware in some cases of exactly what they have agreed to (see also *Childbirth, Intervention in*).

Doctors for their part may reasonably complain of the attitudes of some patients. Either through ignorance or fear, many people remain unaware of the true nature of their illnesses, however much explanation is given, and complaints that the treatment is of longer duration, or is more painful, or carries more risk than expected may not be justified. Likewise, a substantial proportion of patients – reported to be as high as 40% in some psychiatric cases – fail to take the full course of medicines which have been prescribed[1].

There are thus duties and responsibilities on both sides, and if mutual trust does not exist, either party may be to blame. If patients become hostile and resentful, they may take legal action against doctors in cases of failure, sometimes alleging negligence when they had not understood the risks involved. This leads to great expense and also to ineffective medicine, since doctors will be inhibited from doing all that they might for their patients if legal action in the event of failure is likely (see *Malpractice*). Also, clinical success is less probable in an atmosphere of mutual suspicion. If doctors wish to retain the respect of their patients, they must in turn treat their patients with respect and recognize not only their needs but also their sensitivities and their rights. Doctors have long had societies to represent and protect their interests. There now exist patients' associations to represent the rights and voice the complaints of patients. (See also *Health Councils*.)

1. Willcox, DRC, Gillan R, Hare EH. Do psychiatric out-patients take their drugs? *Br Med J*, 1965; 2: 790–2.

Mary Warnock

Patients' Association. The Patients' Association is an advice service and collective voice for patients, independent of Government, the health professions and the drug industry, and financed by members' subscriptions, by donations and recently by a small government grant.

The Association aims to represent and further the interest of patients; give help and advice to individuals; acquire and spread information about patients' interests and promote understanding and goodwill between patients and everyone in medical practice and related activities.

The Association produces information leaflets on subjects such as patients' rights, changing doctors, and complaints procedure.

The Association was founded in 1963, as a result of concern about reports of unethical experiments on patients without their knowledge or consent, and about the tragedies following the use of thalidomide. Since then its campaigns have led or contributed to action in such areas as the appointment of an NHS Ombudsman (see *Health Service Commissioners*); a code of practice for the medical profession in using patients for teaching; improved hospital visiting hours; improvements in drug safety and more information for patients. Campaigns continue on waiting, privacy, teaching and many other issues. (See also *Clinical Teaching; Health Councils*.)

The address of the Association is 11 Dartmouth Street, London SW1H 9BN. Tel. 01-222 4992.

Elizabeth Ackroyd

Paul VI, Pope. See *Humanae Vitae.*

Peer Review. See *Quality Assurance.*

Perinatal Care. See *Childbirth, Intervention in.*

Personality Change. This may be (1) iatrogenic, i.e. produced intentionally or as a side effect by brain operations, drugs or psychotherapy (see *Psychopharmacology; Psychosurgery; Psychotherapy*), or (2) the result of illness, trauma, or any other condition affecting the brain.

Pharmaceutical Industry. The industry has often been subjected to adverse criticism and now that governmental health schemes have become almost universal, with the State their chief customer, the industry encounters increased political antagonism and bureaucratic control.

Ethical objections to the industry are based on the following beliefs that (1) money should not be made from the cure of disease; (2) the profits of the industry are excessive; (3) the promotion of its products is extravagant, inaccurate and exaggerated; (4) it battens on human fear, gullibility and suffering, motives of salesmanship predominate over what is best for medicine, and research workers in the industry are subject to commercial pressures; (5) to promote their products bribes are offered in the shape of lavish hospitality to the medical profession, and the provision of scholarships and lectureships; (6) to circumvent patents (q.v.) the industry floods the market with drugs, hardly differing from each other and called by a bewildering variety of brand names which is confusing to the medical profession; (7) great economies would result without detriment to the patient if prescribing was confined to generic drugs.

The industry strongly refutes these charges and it is apparent that the problem of the economics, profits and ethics of the pharmaceutical industry and the promotion of its products is not a simple but a very complex one. A comment on the seven charges is adumbrated in the following seven paragraphs.

1. Many others beside the pharmaceutical industry – doctors, nurses, builders, food manufacturers, hospital porters and so forth – make a profit from the sickness of their fellows, though not perhaps on such a lordly scale. The industry has conferred the greatest benefits on society, for the great advances in chemotherapy which have occurred in the last 50 years have, with a very few notable exceptions, been due to its scientists. There is nothing essentially wicked in making a profit. In some future Utopia non-profit-making motivations may produce the same results without side effects. Till then we must take the world as we find it and remember that since the October revolution the State-owned industries in the USSR and its satellites have hardly produced a single new medicine of therapeutic importance.

2. It is difficult to know what is an 'excessive profit'. Economists seem unable to agree on basic rules of assessment. The vast sums expended by the industry on research and innovation and the great financial risks involved in a major development programme may justify the substantial profits on successful products. Though new medicines may be expensive the overall price index of pharmaceuticals has remained remarkably steady at a time of high inflation. Further, the industry is subjected in the UK to firm control by the Voluntary Price Regulation Scheme through which prices are negotiated with the Department of Health and Social Security.

3. Advertising is essential for all industries, including nationalized ones, and while half of all advertising expenditure may be wasted nobody knows which half! Were pharmaceutical advertising to be forbidden it would reduce the price of medicines in the UK, by less than two per cent, and this would ultimately be self-defeating, for lacking industry's marketing techniques few medicines could be afforded at all. The strict codes adopted in recent years by the Association of the British Pharmaceutical Industry and the Proprietary Association of Great Britain and the data sheets approved by the Safety of Medicines Committee which must accompany all product licences and to which all subsequent advertising must conform, now control standards of promotion and eliminate excessive claims (see *Medicines, Safety of, Committee on*). These measures have undoubtedly greatly improved the quality of pharmaceutical advertising, and few would deny the need for improvement, but doctors still resent, justifiably, the volume of advertising they receive by mail, especially as such promotion is seldom very educational but rather a means of impressing by frequent inculcation or admonition. Nevertheless, information on medicines must be disseminated and manufacturers cannot be expected to rely on doctors hearing about them by reading journals or attending scientific meetings which they may not do.

4. The pharmaceutical industry in the UK has, in comparison with other industries, the highest proportion of scientifically qualified men and of employees engaged in research. No profession or trade lacks its quota of black sheep and doubtless the pharmaceutical industry is not exceptional in this respect. It can, however, be claimed that it includes as high a proportion of intelligent, educated, altruistic and idealistic men as most other industries.

5. The meetings at which hospitality is extended to doctors may be divided into three types. (a) An important new chemical entity may have been marketed relatively recently and the firm responsible may organize a national symposium addressed by authorities in this and possibly other countries who have had experience of the new medicine, to discuss its indications, contra-indications, methods of administration and adverse effects. During the day of the discussion the firm not only defrays the expenses of the active participants but also provides refreshments, luncheon and dinner to the invited audience of

experts. (b) In the same way a firm may support meetings in hospitals or postgraduate centres on some broad topic such as urinary tract infections, hypertension or diabetes, in the treatment of which the firm's own products as well as those of others may be used. (c) A firm may organize short lunch-time or supper meetings of local practitioners or junior hospital staff to view a film strip or listen to one of their own staff extolling one of their products. The ethics of the first two types of meeting at which hospitality is extended seem unexceptionable. Indeed without this type of support by the industry the advance of therapeutics and postgraduate instruction would suffer significantly; but the third type is more questionable. It is often said with perhaps some justification that the audience comes not so much for instruction as for the refreshments provided. The likelihood that an academic centre would be biased in favour of a firm's products because the firm responsible has established a scholarship or lectureship in one of its departments is surely remote, though it is imperative that such academic participants should be warned of the danger should they be undertaking a clinical trial of the firm's products. The Association of the British Pharmaceutical Industry would welcome such warnings. In comparison with this slight risk the advantages of a close association between academic medicine and research by the pharmaceutical industry is apparent. The benefits of such an association were obvious in Germany and Switzerland at the turn of this century. Their industries were more alert in recognizing the significance of synthetic chemicals and received the close co-operation in research of academic medicine. On the other hand in the UK a rather highbrow distaste for anything connected with 'trade' was exhibited by academic workers which has not entirely dissipated even to this day. Consequently we had to rely heavily on Germany for pharmaceutical products till the first World War enforced the rapid expansion of our own industries.

6. We must not unduly denigrate the minimal molecular manipulation of well established products which often results in significant improvements on their originals. For example, no one would today use Sulphanilamide or Sulphapyridine in preference to modern Sulphonamides or the original Cortisone rather than modern Corticosteroids. Further, though branded medicines are usually more expensive than generic ones, it is not invariably the case that the active agent, to which the generic name only refers, constitutes the sole basis for the medicine's efficacy. The extent to which the active agent becomes available for absorption is influenced by a variety of compounding factors, crystal size, disintegration time, diluents, excipients and other pharmaceutical aids. The nature of those other substances mixed with the active agent, the manner in which this is done and the number and type of quality controls applied at each step of manufacture, can affect the therapeutic efficacy of the product.

7. As producers of generic medicines are not burdened by the cost

of research and development their products are usually cheaper than branded ones but may differ in therapeutic effect. Such differences are seldom very important but it would be a mistake to assume that generically equivalent products are invariably of equal therapeutic potency to branded products.

Code of Practice for the pharmaceutical industry. 5th edn. London: ABPI, 1979.

Cooper MH. *Prices and profits in the pharmaceutical industry.* London: Pergamon Press, 1966.

Davies W. *The pharmaceutical industry.* London: Pergamon Press, 1967.

Dunlop DM. *Medicines in our time.* London: Nuffield Provincial Hospitals Trust, 1973.

Happold FH. *Medicines at risk.* London: Queen Anne Press, 1967.

Inglis B. *Drugs, doctors and disease.* London: André Deutsch, 1965.

Macleod N. *Pharmaceutical medicine.* London: Longmans, 1979.

Reekie WD, Weber MH. *Profits, politics and drugs.* London: Macmillan, 1979.

The late Derrick Dunlop

Physician/Patient Relationship. See *Clinical Practice; Confidentiality; General Practice; Medical Ethics* and *Medical Science* (introductory essays).

Pius XII, Pope. See *Life, Prolongation of; Vegliare con Sollecitudine.*

Placebo.

DEFINITION 1. A treatment, given to please the patient, which has a psychological rather than physical effect.

2. A dummy substance, e.g. tablet or capsule, used in comparison with a potentially active treatment in a clinical trial.

BACKGROUND. In addition to organic features, many illnesses and symptoms have psychological aspects; for example, angina pectoris, bronchial asthma, cough, and pain due to disease or injury. When interest is shown by a doctor, particularly if combined with a physical treatment or medicine (which has no therapeutic effect of its own), improvement will occur in slightly over one-third of patients. This phenomenon, termed a placebo response, has led to the mistaken belief that such treatment is effective and hence to the introduction of remedies which are of little or no value. In order to distinguish the effects of treatment from a placebo reaction, it is necessary to compare results of the test treatment with those obtained using a dummy substance. Recent research suggests that the placebo response may be produced by the release of naturally occurring opiate-like substances (endorphins and enkephalins) within the brain.

The placebo has been used in practice either to reinforce or as a substitute for physical methods, especially when the latter are either ineffective or unnecessary. The results of placebo therapy depend upon the attitude of the clinician, the type of informaton given and the conviction with which he prescribes the dummy substance. Age, ethnic origin and the colour and shape of medicines used can also affect the response.

ETHICS. Opinions differ on the ethics of giving placebos to please patients. Cabot has stated that 'placebo-giving is quackery', while Handfield-Jones and Benson and Epstein regard placebos as having a small but definite place in practice. Many physicians believe that placebos may be used as a means of reinforcing a patient's confidence in his recovery provided that the diagnosis is undoubted and no more effective treatment is possible: placebos may also benefit the dying or incurable. There is general agreement that placebos should be withheld if the diagnosis is in doubt and that they are no substitute for proper psychotherapy.

Some physicians dislike prescribing remedies which are pharmacologically useless and resort to using semi-placebos such as vitamins in the hope that they may do good. This practice seems undesirable as the prescriber deceives not only the patient but himself as well, and these treatments are frequently expensive. Toxic substances should never be used as placebos.

The use of dummy treatments in clinical trials (q.v.) is important in determining the true effects of drugs apart from placebo responses and bias on the part of the patient or observer. Nonetheless, the hazards of leaving a patient untreated for hours, days or weeks must be carefully considered before clinical trials of this type are undertaken. A dummy treatment would be unacceptable in patients with most malignant disease, severe hypertension or bacterial meningitis, but an initial comparison with a dummy might be acceptable in the early evaluation of a new treatment for mild hypertension or rheumatoid arthritis. In comparing the efficacy of surgical operations a simple incision without surgery would not be ethically acceptable as a placebo. As with placebos given to benefit or please a patient, their use in clinical trials should be discontinued as soon as possible; that is, once efficacy has been demonstrated.

Beecher HK. The powerful placebo. *JAMA* 1955; 159: 1602.

Benson H, Epstein MD. The placebo effect. A neglected asset in the care of patients. *JAMA* 1975; 232: 1225.

Bok S. The ethics of giving placebos. *Sci Am* 1974; 231: No 5, 17.

Cabot RC. The physician responsibility for the Nostrum evil. *JAMA* 1906; 47: 982.

Handfield-Jones RPC. A bottle of medicine from the doctor. *Lancet* 1953; 2: 823.

Wolf S. The pharmacology of placebos. *Pharmacol Rev.* 1959; 11: 689.

Charles F. George

Population Policy. Rulers and governments throughout the ages have sought as a matter of policy to manipulate the size and structure of the populations which they controlled. The reasons were variously racial, nationalistic or religious, and examples range from the many expulsions of Jewish peoples over the centuries to that of the Asians from Uganda in the 1970s, and from the religious persecutions in Europe in the sixteenth century to the attempts at tribal dominance in Burundi today. Peoples have been held captive for economic reasons, as were the Israelites in ancient Egypt – a situation matched in modern times by the extensive use of slave and convict labour in Nazi Germany and the USSR. The segregation of black and coloured populations in South Africa and Zimbabwe is partly racial and partly economic. The execution of such policies is now almost universally condemned as inhumane and contrary to human rights.

Population policies are now mainly concerned with the control of population growth. At present there are more than 4000 million people in the world and the latest United Nations projection is for a figure of 6200 million by the year 2000 A.D. Population experts view the problem with alarm from both social and economic standpoints; but there is little agreement among the nations as to how it should be tackled. Some even assert that reduction in population growth is not the most important factor in the future material well-being of the world's inhabitants.

Where living standards are very high, as in the developed and well populated countries of e.g. Western Europe, populations have become almost static. The desire to maintain high living standards, scarcity and cost of housing and the risk of unemployment have all been limiting factors on family size and have made population policies as such largely unnecessary. In some developed countries such as Australia and Canada, where population densities are very low, immigration, once freely allowed, has been increasingly restricted for economic reasons and some degree of racial selection has also been imposed. This has aroused far less criticism than have the coercive policies outlined above, but it may yet be called in question whether it is justifiable to use such restrictive policies to maintain high standards for a few when a more even distribution of population and a wider sharing of resources throughout the world would seem more equitable. It goes without saying that this argument applies with equal force to the economic activities of wealthy nations in respect of poorer ones.

It is in relation to the countries of the Third World that control of population is most often discussed. Some countries (e.g. Ethiopia, Libya) consider themselves underpopulated and discourage limitation of births other than as a means of improving the health of mother and child. The manufacture or import of contraceptives may be limited or forbidden, abortion illegal or severely restricted. In some countries of Eastern Europe where populations are relatively small and growth negligible, social and financial incentives have been offered to those prepared to have large families. However, the picture is more commonly that of rapid growth of population, especially in urban areas, leading to problems of overcrowding, insufficient food and unemployment. Attempts are being made, with varying success, to limit population growth, usually by encouraging the use of some form of contraception. In 1976 the Indian Government of Mrs Indira Gandhi attempted to tackle the country's population problem by introducing compulsory sterilization by vasectomy in some states. This was bitterly resented by the populace and was a major factor in the defeat of the Congress Party in the General Election of 1977. Since then the number of sterilizations has decreased markedly and the image of family planning in India has been somewhat tarnished.

The UN World Population Conference held in Bucharest in 1974, at which two-thirds of the countries of the world were represented, emphasized the seriousness of unlimited population growth, especially its effect on employment in urban areas in underdeveloped countries. Argument turned mainly on the relationship of population size to the socio-economic outlook, with the richer countries and most Asian states stressing the need to reduce population growth and with African and Latin American states laying more importance on fighting poverty and underdevelopment. In the plan put forward at that meeting two principles were enunciated which are likely to be in direct conflict: (1) that couples must have the basic right to decide 'freely and responsibly' the number and spacing of their children, and (2) that each country must have the right to formulate its own population policy tailored to its own needs. These statements appear to ignore the problem that a population policy, either to encourage or to restrict growth, is almost certain to deprive a couple of freedom of choice, or at least to influence it unduly, while the word 'responsibly' could have unfortunate overtones of compulsion in some political contexts. On the other hand, the view that the state has no right to bring influence to bear on what should be a personal and private matter can be countered by the fact that nowadays in all countries the state impinges on personal freedoms to an increasing extent, and that such a contraction of human rights is justified if it is for the general good. Acceptance of compulsion will also depend on the nature of the political system. For example, the discouragement of marriage in China until the late twenties for men is apparently accepted as a means of population limitation.

However, unless a world policy on population can be adopted by all nations – and the Bucharest conference showed how far from realization that was – there are dangers that one country will attempt to manipulate the policies of another for its own ends, perhaps by means of economic sanctions. That the developed countries are seeking to hold down the populations of Third World countries in order to maintain their own economic and racial dominance is a frequently expressed fear, the reality of which is evident in some areas of the world.

Family limitation may present problems in that the methods offered to achieve it may run counter to traditional cultural and religious beliefs. Where governments have achieved success in 're-educating' their people to accept contraception in one form or another, it is usually because care has been taken in the choice of family planning methods to ensure that they disturb as little as possible the customs and traditions of the people.

Where drastic measures are proposed, such as compulsory sterilization, involving complete withdrawal from the individual of freedom of choice and the carrying out of procedures which, from a purely medical point of view, are unnecessary, doctors and other personnel will be faced with decisions for which it is difficult to provide unqualified recommendations. This is an area where discussion and further experience are needed. (See also *Abortion; Contraception; Sterilization.*)

Davis K. Population policy: will current programmes succeed? *Science* 1967; 158: 730.

Loraine J A. Bucharest and its aftermath. *Towards survival* 1975; 28: 11.

Loraine J A. Doctors and the global population crisis. *Br Med J* 1977; 2: 691.

Loraine J A. Twenty-five years of the World Population Crisis. *Contemp Review.* 1977; 231: 208.

Loraine J A. *Syndromes of the seventies.* London: Peter Owen, 1977.

Loraine J A. World overpopulation. In: Scott A, Loraine J A, eds. *Here today . . .* Edinburgh: EUSPB, 1979: 15.

Loraine J A. *Global signposts to the 21st century.* London: Peter Owen, 1979.

Policies on population around the world. *Population Bulletin* 1975: 29, No 6.

Population Reference Bureau. *World population growth and response 1965–1975: a decade of global action.* Population Reference Bureau, 1976.

Population Reference Bureau. *World Population Data Sheet,* 1978.

John A. Loraine

Pregnancy Advisory Services (PAS). A generic term designating private fee-charging agencies primarily concerned to advise women about abortion (q.v.) and, when appropriate, to refer them to doctors willing to terminate pregnancy in private institutions licensed for abortion by Britain's Health Ministers.

PASs are a heterogeneous group ranging from altruistically managed charitable services to frankly commercial agencies. They originated from the workings of the abortion law and the state of public medical care after 1968. In principle the National Health Service (NHS) provides any necessary medical care without charge for British residents. In practice only a half of residents obtaining abortion do so through the NHS[1]. The other half, usually unwillingly, buy private treatment; and the proportions of public and private patients vary widely from place to place.

These variations chiefly reflect features of the Abortion Act 1967. While not permitting first-trimester abortion without medical indications on request (as in the USA and several West European nations), the Act does allow any two doctors to authorize abortion on specified grounds which can be narrowly or widely interpreted and which often involve non-clinical indications; and it leaves every doctor free to refuse to assist women wanting abortion, however clear their legal grounds (save for his overriding duty to help if life or health are gravely endangered). In some areas and hospitals NHS abortion may be obtainable only for strong clinical indications, while in others most women who, after seriously considering the alternatives, still request abortion may be granted treatment at public expense.

These and other limitations on NHS capacity to meet the demand revealed by the Act soon resulted in a large lucrative 'domestic' market in abortion facilities doubled in size and still more in profit by a 'foreign' market of women (chiefly French and German) coming to Britain for treatment forbidden in their own countries. Expecting the emergence, initially at least, of an abortion market in which British women would be exposed to commercial exploitation, concerned reformers in 1968 founded the two original PASs, in London and Birmingham, to provide a non-profit medically and socially responsible alternative service for women treated outside the NHS. Starting as simple advice services with no treatment facilities, these two charities (now the London and the British PASs) grew eventually to dominate the 'domestic' market and, by their low charges, to deprive commercial operators of much of their earlier profits; while after 1973 liberalized abortion laws on the Continent resulted in a rapid and continuing decline in the 'foreign' market.

In Britain in 1975 (a transitional year) the NHS provided abortion for 58,700 UK residents and 200 foreigners; the two charities for 31,700 and 3800 respectively; commercial agencies for 25,600 and 27,700. The BPAS had become a self-contained nationwide professional service, managed by a charitable trust, dealing with pregnancy testing, contraception (q.v.), vasectomy and female sterilization (q.v.) as well as abortion through a network of local advice centres and its own treatment facilities. At the centres trained non-medical counsellors see each woman enquiring about abortion and assist her to reach her own decision about the outcome of her unwanted pregnancy. If after counselling she decides for abortion, she is then examined by 'referring' doctors who decide whether abortion may be permitted. If it is, treatment is then given in one of the BPAS nursing homes by 'operating' doctors who have not participated in selecting the patients. The pay of BPAS medical and counselling staff in no way depends on whether they advise women for or against abortion. Patients' payments go exclusively to the organization, which grants loans or waives charges in necessitous cases. The procedures of the smaller London PAS are similar.

The nomenclature and outward forms of the two charities – but not their purposes or spirit – were rapidly copied in the first few years following the Abortion Act by a variety of commercially motivated entrepreneurs working on the fringes of private medicine. Numerous agencies with similar sounding titles, and others ostensibly offering only pregnancy testing for high fees, were created in most urban centres, some being linked directly or indirectly with particular commercial nursing homes, others with certain doctors in private practice. Some even attempted, unsuccessfully, to gain respectability by seeking registration as charities. Neither the official inquiry into the working of the Abortion Act (Lane Committee, 1974)[2] nor the Parliamentary Select Committee on Abortion (1975–76)[3] reported an adequate survey of commercial PASs. But it was agreed that it was among these agencies and their medical associates, with their tendency to pursue maximum profit for minimum service and their special interest in foreign patients, that most of the much publicized early abuses of the Act were prevalent – abortion on demand regardless of the law, neglect of counselling, social needs and after-care, touting for customers at airports and advertising abroad, fee-splitting and tax evasion.

Pending legislation proposed by both the Lane Committee and the Select Committee, the Health Ministers had no direct power to check such abuses by introducing a licensing system to control or close down unethically conducted PASs. But in 1975 and 1976 Ministers found that indirect control was feasible through the conditions they could impose in the licences of nursing homes approved for abortion. This culminated in 1976 in official inspection of all PASs, the preparation of an approved list of those conforming to certain standards, and the forbidding of nursing homes to accept patients referred by agencies not on the list.

1. Laffite F. The abortion hurdle race. *Fam Plann* 1976; 24: 4.
2. Committee on the Working of the Abortion Act (Lane Committee). *Report*. London: HMSO, 1974, Vol 1, Cmnd 5576.

3. Select Committee on the Abortion (Amendment) Bill, Session 1974–75. *Third Report and Minutes of Evidence*, 20 Oct 1975. HC 692 – I and II. London: HMSO, 1975.

Birth Control Trust. *Abortion: the NHS and the charities.* London: Birth Control Trust, 1977.

British Pregnancy Advisory Service. *A charitable rejoinder to the Select Committee.* Birmingham: BPAS, 1976.

François Lafitte

Pregnancy, Termination of. See *Abortion.*

Prenatal Diagnosis. See *Antenatal Diagnosis.*

Prescribing. A prescription is a physician's written order to a pharmacist to supply medicinal substances to a patient. In Britain there are four categories of medicines.

1. *Controlled drugs.* Subject to the requirements of the Misuse of Drugs Regulations (1973) these can only be obtained by doctor's prescription which must be written in ink, or be otherwise indelible, must give the name and address of the patient and the quantity of the drug to be supplied in both words and figures and must be signed with the doctor's full signature. The group includes the narcotic analgesics, cocaine, certain appetite suppressants and amphetamines.

2. *Prescription-only medicines.* This includes the majority of potent drugs used in medical practice such as digoxin, antibiotics, hypnotics, hormones and vaccines.

3. *Over-the-counter remedies* that can be purchased without a prescription at a pharmacy.

4. *Over-the-counter medicines* which are on the 'general sales list' (Medicines Act 1968) and may be sold in shops other than pharmacies and may be obtained without a doctor's prescription.

The cost of the British National Health service in 1978 was approximately £8000 million. The cost of the pharmaceutical services was about 9% of this total, being mainly due to the prescribing by general practitioners which accounts for a much greater proportion (90%) of the cost of the pharmaceutical services than does the use of drugs in hospital (10%).

Studies in Northern Ireland, Norway and Sweden, [1,2,3] have shown that there are great variations in the use of drugs from area to area, within a country. In Britain the cost of prescribed drugs per head of population per annum is highest in rural areas and areas of great unemployment such as West Wales and Northern Ireland.[4] The pattern of drug prescribing by doctors varies within countries and there are greater differences between countries. It is not easy to define what is the appropriate use of drugs. The differences observed in the prescribing of oral hypoglycaemic drugs*, for instance, may depend on:

a) The concept held by physicians on what constitutes diabetes.

b) The incidence of diabetes in the community (related to the age structure).

c) The concepts held by doctors about appropriate therapy: some may be content to eliminate symptoms, others attempt to lower the blood sugar to a predetermined level.

d) The demands made by patients. Their expectations may differ greatly. In some communities dietary therapy is unacceptable and drug prescribing may be expected.

A survey in the USA in 1967[5] showed that 98.3% of prescriptions were for precompounded drugs. It was disturbing that, of the 200 most frequently prescribed drugs, 80 were combinations and there was criticism about 'the use of drugs without demonstrable efficacy; the use of drugs with an inherent toxicity not justified by the seriousness of the illness; the use of drugs in excessive amounts or for excessive periods of time or inadequate amounts for inadequate time; the simultaneous use of two or more drugs without appropriate considerations of their possible interaction; the multiple prescribing by one or several physicians for the same patient of drugs which may be unnecessary, cumulative, interacting or needlessly expensive'.

There are many difficulties for the prescriber. More than 90% of the prescriptions written by doctors today are for medicines which did not exist 30 years ago[6]. It is often difficult to assess the therapeutic value of drugs of undoubted pharmacological efficacy. For instance, the lipid lowering properties of clofibrate and related drugs are indisputable but whether they protect patients from the complications of atherosclerotic disease is far from proved[7,8,9] and whether it is justifiable to give these drugs as a prophylactic measure to healthy men is a matter of further controversy. There are tremendous promotional pressures on doctors by the pharmaceutical industry (q.v.) and pressures of competition within the industry which have resulted in the marketing in many countries of unnecessary and meretricious preparations. It is a reflection on the industry and on the medical profession that doctors can be persuaded to prescribe by uninformative advertisements and by the patronizing and aggressive methods of some sales representatives. A special problem arises in countries with state health services: it is difficult to arrange a cheap and economical supply of effective drugs without restricting the doctor's choice of preparations (see *Clinical Autonomy*). Such restriction is resented by doctors and is disliked by the drug industry, although it can be argued that it is justified if it allows resources to become available for other important services. There is concern however that such restriction

---

* Oral hypoglycaemic drugs: Drugs taken by mouth to lower the blood sugar: usually prescribed to elderly patients with mild diabetes.

may impair innovation and the development of new drugs. (See *General Practice*.)

There is controversy over the names of drugs: whereas industry would prefer trade names to be used, it would be easier, especially for nurses and students, if only official names were used. The system of alternative names is bad; sooner or later, for safety, agreement will have to be reached by which drugs are known by one name only.

In Britain the doctor is helped in his prescribing by the *British National Formulary* (published by the British Medical Association and the Pharmaceutical Society of Great Britain), by *Prescribers Journal* and by the *Compendium of Data Sheets* which firms now have to issue under the Medicines Act.

1. Bergman U, Elmes P, Halse M, Lunde PKM, Sjoquist F, Wade OL, Westerholm B. The measurement of drug consumption. *Eur J Clin Pharmacol* 1975; 8: 83–9.
2. Wade OL, Beeley L. *Adverse reactions to drugs*. 2nd edn. London: Heinemann Medical, 1976.
3. Wade OL, Hadden DR, Hood H. The prescribing of drugs used in the treatment of diabetes. *Br J Prev Soc Med* 1973; 27: 44.
4. *Prescribing sickness benefit costs in Northern Ireland*. Report of a Health Advisory Committee. (1969). Cmnd 528 Belfast, HMSO. 1969: 528, Cmnd 528.
5. *National prescription audit and general information report*. 6th edn. Dedham, Mass., Gosselin, 1967.
6. Spalton LM. Medicine legislation and the health of the community. *Lancet* 1971; 1: 180.
7. Dewar HA, Oliver MF. Secondary prevention trials using clofibrate: a joint commentary on the Newcastle and Scottish trials. *Br Med J* 1971; 4: 784.
8. Physicians of Newcastle upon Tyne Region. Five-year study of clofibrate in the treatment of ischaemic heart disease. *Br Med J* 1971; 4: 767.
9. Research Committee of Scottish Society of Physicians. Ischaemic heart disease: a secondary prevention trial using clofibrate. *Br Med J* 1971; 4: 775.

O. L. Wade

Pressure Groups. See *Social Pressures*.

Prevention. See *Amniocentesis; Fluoridation; Health Education; Immunization; Resources*.

Primum non nocere. An elementary maxim that the doctor's first care must be to do no harm. (See also *Hippocratic Oath*.)

Priorities. See *Resources*.

Prisoners. A prisoner is one who is in custody by legal process. The definition includes those of any age subject to custodial remands or sentences, on civil or criminal charges. Some of the documents referred to in this contribution use the wider concept of 'arrested person' which includes any person under arrest or detention by any authority for any cause, and the place of detention includes any police station, interrogation centre or other place where an arrested person is held.[1]

A prisoner is invariably at the centre of conflict; his needs and desires are pitted against those of another party or more usually of society in general. By the process of imprisonment society temporarily delegates its role in the contest to others, and appoints a judicial referee to see fair play and to reach what is usually a compromise solution. The prisoner is the subject of a number of often conflicting objectives: to make sure that the order of the Court for his detention is carried out; to collect information about him; to extract information from him; to use him as an object lesson to others; to change his behaviour in some way; to get him through his detention with as little damage to himself and with as little stress for the guardians as possible. These objectives are in a constant state of flux not only in individual prisons, but in national policy. Our generation has seen many variations in the priority of these objectives, including attempts to apply the current therapeutic method, and revolt against these endeavours requiring 'that prisoners be protected against potentially deleterious methods used to bring about changes in prisoner attitudes'[2], and recently a world-wide somewhat defeatist tendency towards 'humane containment' coupled with an attempt to find alternatives to imprisonment. The general public may look upon prisons as places for punishment which some will regard as too lenient and others as a cruel anachronism; some prisoners will dread imprisonment, others will treat it as a haven; only a few will know that prison has only recently evolved as an alternative to infinitely harsher measures: death, banishment, mutilation, transportation, flogging, branding. All of us, whatever our status, have double feelings about prisoners and prisons. Doctors, nurses, pharmacists, social workers and other specialists have to work in prisons; they are not immune to the inevitable conflicts, and are indeed peculiarly susceptible, being members of society yet dedicated to the relief of suffering. If a prison medical service is managed separately from community health services its members will be influenced by the same processes of institutionalism which affect other staff and prisoners. An alternative would be for intra and extrapenal medical staff to have a single employer and for those who are most involved in such work also to have a commitment outside the penal setting.

PROFESSIONAL CONFIDENCE. The conflict is well exemplified in the matter of professional confidence. The Hippocratic Oath (q.v.)[3] states

'Whatever in the course of practice I see or hear (or even outside my practice in social intercourse) that should never be published abroad I will not divulge, but consider such things to be wholly secret'. And the International Code of Medical Ethics (see *Declaration of Geneva*) included the strict endorsement of this principle. But the doctor can be compelled by law, not only to reveal what his patient said but to produce the medical records (by a *subpoena duces tecum*). If the doctor communicates confidences to a nurse (or prison officer) and the nurse hands them on, both would be liable to breach of secrecy[4]. Some have held that it is impossible for a doctor to work for a health authority or prison medical service and at the same time maintain strict secrecy. There are many pronouncements which may or may not salve the doctor's conscience. Lord Mansfield's dictum in 1776 reassures the doctor '. . . but to give that information in a court of justice which, by the law of the land he is bound to do, will never be imputed to him as any indiscretion whatever'. The British Medical Association[5] stresses that the over-riding consideration must always be the benefit of the patient and the protection of his interests, but adds 'The complications of modern life sometimes create difficulties for the doctor in the application of the principle (of secrecy) and on certain occasions it may be necessary to acquiesce in some modification.' It is thus left to the conscience of the individual doctor, and so it usually is with the numerous other ethical problems surrounding the prisoner. It is ethical for the examining doctor to introduce himself and declare his purpose clearly, warning the prisoner if there is to be any verbal or written report, so that he may decide for himself upon the extent of his cooperation. Most adult prisoners are able to appreciate such an approach, but the greatest care should be taken with juveniles in remand homes or centres. In difficult cases, it is wise to consult senior colleagues and to record the fact.

Despite the high morbidity among prisoners and the disabilities induced by the process of imprisonment, the medical officers should strive to produce a system of care that is at least equal to that available in the community. These difficulties are compounded by extra-penal health resources which are reneging on their responsibility to provide a spectrum of care, particularly for the mentally ill.[6]

AIDS TO THE DOCTOR. There are numerous codes of ethics to which he may refer, starting with Hippocrates' teaching of some two thousand and four hundred years ago, through Magna Carta (1215) and the French Declaration of the Rights of Man (1789) to the codes of the 20th century. The Standard Minimum Rules for Prisons are now 50 years old, and the Universal Declaration of Human Rights (1948) following the Nuremberg Trials of National Socialist atrocities upon prisoners, is highly relevant (See *Nuremberg Code* under *Declarations*). The Declaration of Helsinki (q.v.) dealt with experiments on human subjects, and the recent Declaration of Tokyo (q.v.) on Arrest and Detention is highly important in this context. (See also *Declaration of Hawaii.*)

Item 3 of the Tokyo Declaration which states that 'the doctor shall not be present during any procedure during which torture or other forms of cruel, inhuman or degrading treatment is used or threatened' will certainly raise difficult problems for certain doctors, for instance in countries where there is still capital or degrading punishment, or where interrogations are being conducted in time of war perhaps, with the use of wall-standing, hooding, noise, reduced diet or deprivation of sleep. Although such methods were condoned[7] they were later shown to result in physical and mental injury and were declared to be illegal. A British Official Report[8] on such interrogation relies heavily on the doctor: 'We think that a doctor with some psychiatric training should be present at all times at the interrogation centre, and should be in a position to observe the course of the oral interrogation.' The United Nations[1] recommendation 20, in this connection is rather less stringent: 'An arrested person shall be examined by a physician before and after interrogation.' Rules 32 and 33 of the Standard Minimum Rules for the Treatment of Prisoners deal with the required involvement of doctors before and during the more severe forms of punishment[9]. The passive participation of physicians in procedures which are detrimental to health (perhaps even imprisonment itself) is questionable since the very processes deprive the prisoner of his right to conditions favourable to health. This is not to recognize that discomfort and hardship are clearly matters which a person involved in crime will suffer.

British policy towards hunger strikes among prisoners anticipated item 5 of the Tokyo Declaration, requiring that the prisoner's capacity for rational judgement must not be impaired by illness, mental or physical, but leaves the ultimate decision as to whether to force-feed to the individual doctor who is best able to weigh the many factors involved.

DEGRADING TREATMENTS. It has been questioned whether there is any difference between torture and execution, in particular in its effect on those who have to carry it out. The legal distinction is perfectly clear. Execution is by order of a court and the ultimate remedy against it must be by democratic legislation. Torture is illegal and the remedy therefore relies upon discipline, morale, and watchfulness within the service concerned. The effect on persons who have to carry out executions is not easily measured because it will depend on variables, especially the perceived necessity and justice of the process. The Gowers Commission on Capital Punishment[10] went, somewhat superficially, into the effect on prison staff and prison inmates of executions, concluding that, except in the case of some prison chaplains, the effect is 'short-lived and has no adverse effect on health.' (p. 271). The Commission did not comment on the effect upon prison medical officers, nor upon their recruitment to the service, and did not comment on the effect upon the institution as a whole. History shows that agents of the state cannot indefinitely be made to execute orders which are generally abhorrent, so that even if only on grounds of expediency, authority should be prepared to vary the consequences of misbehaviour in accordance with the dangers occasioned thereby. Heavy penalties or cruel methods can often be shown to have arisen in times of crisis, and quickly to have become useless, or even harmful, anachronisms.

Institutions, especially closed institutions, can be observed to show conflicting tendencies towards on the one hand the custodial function (which if not opposed becomes oppressive and even destructive), and on the other reformation and treatment (which if unopposed leads to selection of nicer and nicer inmates to the point at which they need not be there at all). It is always a struggle to maintain a balance between these tendencies, and thus to achieve a useful institution. If degrading activities are permitted within the institution it makes the task of maintaining this balance more difficult, widening the gap between inmate and staff, and running the risk of encouraging the more oppressive elements. The fashionable objective of prison systems is 'humane containment'; it is very important to recognize that this worthy and apparently simple objective will not be reached without positive caring endeavours by the staff; as with the trajectory of a bullet, the rifle must be aimed in a direction far higher than the target. Degrading activities may have widely deleterious effects beyond their immediate context.

EXPERIMENTS ON PRISONERS. Some of the points made in the Declaration of Helsinki are that, in the case of legal incapacity or incompetence, consent should be procured from the legal guardian. 'The subject of clinical research should be in such a mental, physical and legal state as to be able to exercise fully his power of choice.' The personal integrity of the individual must be respected 'especially if the subject is in a dependent relationship to the investigator' (which of course will always obtain in prisoners). (See also *Consent*.)

Reference to the age at which consent can reasonably be given is made in an MRC Report.[11] 'Courts will not regard a child of 12 years or under (14 years or under for boys in Scotland) as having capacity to consent to any procedure which may involve him in an injury.' Katz, Capron and Glass[12] have provided a standard text in this area of experimentation on humans. According to Hersch[13] the final criterion should be 'would I do this to Einstein or Picasso?', to which one might add '. . . or a Member of Parliament fully aware of his legal rights.'

1. United Nations Economic and Social Council. *Torture and other Cruel, Inhuman or Degrading Treatment or Punishment in Relation to Detention and Imprisonment.* (EC/CN. 4/NGO/191) New York: United Nations, 1976.

2. United Nations Fifth Congress on the Prevention of Crime and the Treatment of Offenders, Toronto, Canada. A/Conf. 56/6. New York: United Nations. 1975: 1.

3. Jones WHS. *The doctor's oath.* Cambridge: University Press. 1924.

4. The patient's right of confidence. *Br Med J* 1962; 2: 615.

5. British Medical Association. *Members handbook* London: BMA, 1965: 59.

6. Fifteenth Report from the Expenditure Committee. *The reduction of pressure on the prison system.* London: HMSO, 1978, Vol 1.

7. Enquiry into Allegations Against the Security Forces of Physical Brutality in Northern Ireland Arising out of Events on 9th August, 1971. London: HMSO, 1971, Cmnd 4823.

8. Committee of Privy Counsellors appointed to Consider Authorised Procedures for the Interrogation of Persons Suspected of Terrorism. London: HMSO, 1972, Cmnd 4901, para 41.

9. United Nations Department of Economics and Social Affairs. *Standard minimum rules for the treatment of prisoners.* New York: United Nations, 1958.

10. Royal Commission on Capital Punishment. *Report* (Gowers Report). London: HMSO, 1953, Cmnd 8932.

11. Medical Research Council. *Annual Report 1962–3.* London: HMSO, 1963, Cmnd 2382.

12. Katz H, Capron AM, Glass ES. *Experimentation with human beings.* New York: Russel Sage Foundation, 1972.

13. Hersch J. Quoted in Editorial, When is consent? *Lancet* 1967; 2: 813.

The late P. D. Scott
revised by Paul Bowden

Prisoners of War. See *Military Medicine.*

Private Practice. The National Health Service (NHS) (q.v.) was planned to provide medical care for the whole UK population and, after retirement pensions, was perhaps the most important social advance of this century. Hitherto the voluntary hospitals and the local authority hospitals had provided hospital services. The consultant staff in voluntary hospitals were all honorary and this meant that the distribution of consultant skills around the country largely related to their ability to earn an income from private practice in their specialty. As a result there was an uneven distribution, particularly in relation to paediatrics. The NHS has gone a very long way towards providing a fair distribution of consultant skills across the country. It has been less successful in the upgrading of the hospitals and this has been particularly true of the mental health services. Although a number of new hospitals have now been built, the majority of hospital work in

Great Britain is still done in Victorian buildings and there is still a great deal of basic re-fitting to be done. The relatively poor fabric and facilities have been a significant factor in encouraging a portion of the public to seek their medical care outside the NHS.

The concept of the NHS was to provide free care for all those who needed medical help – taking the economic sting out of serious illness – and, in spite of the many physical defects and financial stringencies, it has made great progress, largely owing to the appreciation by the profession of the importance of providing this service. Nevertheless, those who wished to have private insurance cover could do so.

For a minority of the public there is a need for extra privacy in hospital and the ability to have single rooms. This could be achieved by having a modestly priced 'amenity bed'. In addition some wish to retain control over the arrangements for their treatment, with the right to choose their consultant. For this it was necessary to have a private bed paying full hospital cost plus the consultant's fees. In the former voluntary hospital service, the tradition for private treatment had been well established and such treatment was available either in a private nursing home or in a private wing built in association with a voluntary hospital. With the introduction of the NHS the decision had to be taken whether or not private practice could be kept within its framework. The consultants strongly pressed for this because it helped to concentrate their professional activities by reducing travelling. The important fact that it would retain the goodwill of the consultants was appreciated by Mr. Aneurin Bevan (then Minister of Health) who allowed a total of about 2% full pay private beds within the NHS and also introduced the amenity beds which, for a small charge, provided more congenial accommodation together with the general medical service provided by the NHS.

Medical care to be successful needs the full confidence of patients (q.v.). For the great majority of the population the reputation of the hospital is sufficient to provide this sense of confidence, but there is a small proportion who, realizing that health is their most important capital asset, feel the need to ensure that their specialized investigation or operation is undertaken by a consultant who has acquired a special reputation in this field and who will provide continuity of care. The NHS can undertake to organize only an adequate medical service and it is impossible to guarantee the services of nominated individuals. Where the demand represents only a small proportion of the total, there is no difficulty in meeting it by getting the patient to pay the full cost of the hospital care and in addition the consultant's professional fees. In this way the freedom of the individual can be maintained without any threat to the efficiency of the service as a whole.

The ethical objection to private beds is based on the dislike of a system which allows patients to obtain treatment more quickly by payment than if they waited their turn under the NHS. Accelerated admission, or queue-jumping, seems to be open to very proper objection in relation to a comprehensive National Health Service. Little attempt has been made to quantify its incidence, however, and it has been the general experience of doctors in all parts of the country that it invariably takes longer to get a moderately ill patient into a private bed than into an NHS bed, and indeed acute emergencies can hardly ever be admitted privately. It seems surprising, then, that the occupation rates of private beds are often quoted at 60 to 70%. Except in special private wings, private beds are used for NHS patients when not occupied by private ones. The reason is the small demand for certain specialist units such as psychiatry and maternity where the private beds are not interchangeable. However, in relation to non-urgent but nevertheless often troublesome disabilities, such as hernia, haemorrhoids and some orthopaedic disorders, the long NHS waiting lists mean that quicker treatment can be achieved privately at full cost. The majority of consultants have been scrupulously fair, but there is a small minority, as in all walks of life, who have selfishly taken advantage of the situation and deliberately encouraged the choice of private care, or who have admitted out of turn to ordinary NHS beds patients seen in private practice. In 1979 plans were introduced for having common waiting lists for NHS and private patients.

Under the Health Services Act of 1976 a Health Service Board was set up, which led to the progressive closure of private beds in NHS hospitals. By the end of 1979 over a third of them had been phased out. However legislation also required that they could not be closed until adequate alternative private facilities were available and this has led to an increase in the number of smaller private hospitals. After 1979 the arrangements for private beds were to be left for final decision locally. Now (Dec. 1979) a new Health Service Bill has been introduced which proposes the abolition of the Health Services Board, the restoration of private beds to NHS hospitals and transfer of the control of private hospital developments to the Secretary of State.

Should pay beds be divorced entirely from the NHS? On the one hand they are a potential cause of industrial unrest and of attack by some political activists: on the other the pay beds are a vital protection against the full development of a two-tier standard of medical care. If the private practice develops entirely outside the NHS, it will always move more quickly and more effectively than the NHS, with its inevitable bureaucracy. New developments will be introduced more quickly and standards of comfort and service will be better. It would only be a matter of time before going into an NHS hospital was equated with the second best, and indeed would be second best. As long as there are private beds within the NHS there is far less risk of two-tier standards ever developing to any important extent.

The small amount of private practice – only 1% – has been a positive advantage to the NHS because consultants spend much more of their time within the main hospital and are more easily available. They spend less time on unproductive and often difficult travelling.

Privilege

In academic centres, where there is special expertise, the full-time university staff, who (like whole-time NHS staff) do not accept fees, have always attracted private patients whose payments support departmental research funds. These provide extra technical staff, research assistants, equipment and so on. If the present trends are continued, it would seem likely that private practice within the NHS will disappear from the smaller units, but will remain in the larger ones where the advantages to the hospital can be apparent to all.

In general practice (q.v.) there are still a few doctors who do not take NHS patients and who operate privately, with the patient paying for services provided. Others can undertake private practice in addition to NHS practice, subject to financial limits. They are not, however, allowed to charge fees to those on their own NHS lists, except for some special services for which the British Medical Association publishes a list of recommended fees. General practitioners may refer their NHS patients to consultants for private treatment. One of the advantages to the patient of private care is that the doctor is usually prepared to make domiciliary visits to a much greater degree than is now usual in NHS practice. In the case of doctors who work solely on a private basis, the arrangement is a personal contract between doctor and patient; where the practice is mixed, problems could arise in that fee-paying patients might be given preference over NHS patients purely on financial grounds. However, this objection is more theoretical than practical, as the great majority of doctors give the patient the medical attention needed, irrespective of whether he is an NHS or a private patient. There is a very deep-rooted tradition in the medical profession to help the patient without any consideration of his circumstances.

Jones FA. Getting the N.H.S. back on course. *Br Med J* 1978; 2: 5–9.

Merrison A, Chairman. Royal Commission on the National Health Service. London: HMSO, 1979.

Watkin B. *The National Health Service: The First Phase 1948–1974 and after.* London: Allen and Unwin, 1978.

F. Avery Jones

Privilege. See *Private Practice.*

Professional Practice. See *Clinical Practice; General Practice.*

Prolongation of Life. See *Life, Prolongation of.*

Prophylaxis. Protection from disease; preventive treatment. (See *Health Education; Immunization; Mass-medication; Screening.*)

Proportion. Proportion is a term sometimes used to indicate that there

346

must be some reasonable relationship between the unpleasant means taken to effect some good end and the good end itself. Thus, to amputate a leg in order to eliminate a corn on the toe would offend against the principle of proportion, whereas the temporary discomfort caused by an inoculation against typhoid would be well within the bounds of proportion. In English law the principle of proportion finds some place in the doctrine of Necessity (q.v.). Thus, while it may be legitimate to shoot a man who is about to throw a bomb into a crowded building, the principle of proportion would forbid the shooting of a child who was about to discharge a pea-shooter at someone. Similarly, while gross provocation can reduce a homicide from murder to manslaughter, 'the instrument with which the homicide was effected must also be taken into consideration; for, if it were effected with a deadly weapon, the provocation must be great indeed to reduce the offence to one of manslaughter; if with a weapon or other means not likely or intended to produce death, a less degree of provocation will be sufficient; in fact the mode of resentment must bear a reasonable proportion to the provocation . . .' (*Archbold. Criminal Pleading, Evidence and Practice.* 37th edn. p. 783).

E. Garth Moore

In professional practice the test of proportion should be applied to many complicated interventions or procedures, e.g. to sophisticated techniques in induction and monitoring in childbirth (q.v.); to multi-system intensive care (see *Intensive Care Units*). The question is: are these means, with their attendant risk, discomfort, disturbance to patient and staff, cost, etc., proportionate to a good end reasonably attainable in each individual case?

G. R. Dunstan

Psychiatry, Misuse of. Misuse of psychiatry involves domination of individuals by the improper application of information or power derived from the professional relationship or from psychiatric skills. The term has come particularly to refer to political abuses of psychiatry although it is justifiable to use it in a wider context.

Taking improper advantage of the professional relationship for social, sexual or other use to which the psychiatrist would not properly be entitled represents domination of the patient for the personal purposes of the psychiatrist. The use of psychological knowledge derived from medical practice to further the purposes of, say, subliminal advertising can also be construed as unethical, if individuals are thereby persuaded to purchase articles or take other steps which they would not normally do. It may be argued that medical knowledge derived from professional relationships should not be utilized to plan campaigns of advertising or for psychological warfare. It is hard to draw a precise line and much rests with individual opinion.

The major application of the term misuse of psychiatry today is to the use of psychiatric procedures for the suppression of political dissent.

Psychiatric procedures can be specified as (1) Interviews; (2) Attribution of diagnoses; (3) Recommendations for compulsory detention in psychiatric hospitals; and (4) Administration of drugs and other treatments.

STANDARDS OF NORMAL PRACTICE. In most democratic countries compulsory admission to psychiatric hospitals is only undertaken (1) in the interests of the patient's own health or safety; (2) for the protection of others. These criteria are specified in Britain in the Mental Health Act (1959) and the Mental Health Act (Scotland) (1960), and it is unusual to enforce compulsory admission unless there is either some likelihood of effective treatment being provided or of significant harm occurring to the patient or others. The consent of the next of kin must normally be sought unless admission is the result of court proceedings (See *Mental Illness, Certification of*). In the United States a minority, e.g. Szasz[1], Ennis[2], and the New York Council for Civil Liberties take the view that compulsory admission to psychiatric hospitals ought never to be undertaken. The American Council for Civil Liberties and the majority opinion throughout the Western world hold otherwise: that it is humane and desirable to oblige some patients to accept treatment which usually takes the form of residence and care in hospital with the administration of medication. In Britain other treatments, such as behavioural management (see *Behaviour Therapy*), electro-convulsive therapy (q.v.), and brain surgery (see *Psychosurgery*) are not usually undertaken against the wishes of the patient. Good practice also requires the consent (q.v.) of the patient's next of kin to any major procedure, even though it is not strictly necessary in law. Political opinions as such never constitute grounds for psychiatric detention. A patient with delusions which may have a political bearing, e.g. that he is the sovereign, might be diagnosed as having mental illness, and could, or would, be detained in the event of the above criteria being satisfied. An individual who planned forcibly to remove the sovereign and parliament in order to establish a dictatorship of the proletariat would not be held to show *prima facie* evidence of mental illness justifying detention, although many would regard such ideas as indicating a need for psychiatric investigation. A plot to plant bombs for such purposes, if discovered, would lead to police intervention, possible psychiatric examination and trial. In the absence of delusions of the type described above, psychiatric intervention would normally be undertaken to provide an opportunity for the defence to offer evidence in mitigation. Psychiatrists would be called independently by both prosecution and defence (see *Forensic Psychiatry*).

Abuses of psychiatry occur sporadically in all cultures. They may arise because those concerned with the care of the mentally or physically ill are hasty, inconsiderate, ill-informed or negligent in their work. Some may even act with malice. Most often it is a case of poorly-trained staff, working in poor conditions, responding to irritating behaviour on the part of patients. Such abuses are not part of the concept of misuse of psychiatry. That term has been adopted to cover systematic abuse of psychiatric procedures to detain opponents of government, who are only held to be insane because of their political opinions, or because of deliberately false diagnoses attached to them.

Interviews are improper in which attempts are made to persuade a sane individual to change his political views – although it would not be improper to point out that the latter can lead to practical difficulties. Diagnoses are improper which use the special characteristics of political dissenters as the sole or main ground for diagnosis, e.g. the diagnosis of schizophrenia on the grounds of 'reformist delusions'[3], or because of 'a heightened propensity for conflict, the desire for self-assertion, the rejection of traditions, opinions, standards, etc',[4] or 'anti-social actions . . . prohibited by law, such as disturbance of public order, dissemination of slander, manifestation of aggressive intentions, . . . with a cunningly calculated plan of action'[5]. Recommendations are improper which follow from fraudulent diagnoses or which recommend detention, even of sick individuals, where alternative facilities may be available. The impropriety of using irrelevant drugs and other treatments, which carry hazards even in normal practice, speaks for itself.

The country in which the misuse of psychiatry is said most often to occur is the USSR, where it is claimed that such misuse has been applied to members of the democratic (dissident) movement, Buddhists, Ukrainian nationalists and Jewish would-be emigrants, among others. Sane people, accused of political offences, are, say the critics, kept from open trial by means of fraudulent certification by official psychiatrists; diagnoses of schizophrenia are falsely given, and recommendations are made for compulsory treatment in prison mental hospitals so that political dissidents are kept indefinitely in hospitals for mentally abnormal offenders.[6,3,7,8] In such places they find themselves together with insane murderers, rapists, and other violent patients. Some of the dissidents, e.g. Leonid Plyushch[9], have been subjected to heavy doses of drugs (against their wishes and the wishes of their families).

Replies from the USSR have been made in the lay[5] and medical press[10]. Part of the argument turns upon criteria for the diagnosis of schizophrenia which vary from country to country, even outside the USSR[11]. If Western critics, including the writer, are correct, several of the leaders of Soviet psychiatry have deliberately sought to make the diagnosis of schizophrenia where it was not applicable; and in any case, even if the diagnosis was correct, the compulsory detention and treatment of the political offenders was unjustified. In extenuation of the Soviet practice it might be argued that the doctors save the 'patients' from a worse fate in prison camps. This is not the general view either of the dissidents or their families who consider that detention in mental hospitals under Soviet conditions does injustice to their ideas and their sanity, amounts to a worse experience than a labour camp and constitutes an indefinite sentence.

In November 1973 the Royal College of Pscyhiatrists in Britain passed a resolution deploring the current use of psychiatry in the Soviet Union for the purpose of political repression and condemning the activities of the doctors who lend themselves to such work.

In 1977 the Sixth World Congress of the World Psychiatric Association meeting in Honolulu passed the following resolution by the narrow margin of 92–89. 'That the WPA take note of the Abuse of Psychiatry for political purposes and that it condemn those practice in all countries where they occur and call upon the professional organisations of psychiatrists in those countries to renounce and expunge those practices from their country and that the WPA implement this resolution in the first instance in reference to the extensive evidence of the systematic abuse of Psychiatry for political purposes in the USSR'. The result was determined by the fact that different member societies of the WPA had votes in proportion to their paid up membership so although an actual majority of societies voted not to condemn the USSR specifically the motion was carried on the votes of the larger groups of psychiatrists from the English speaking countries and Western Europe supported by a much smaller number of votes from some 'Third World' areas[12].

The WPA also voted by a much larger majority to set up a committee to enquire into reported abuses and at the time of writing (September 1979) this committee has been constituted and has received some complaints. Meanwhile other countries have also been incriminated in the question of the abuse of psychiatry, particularly Romania and Czechoslovakia, but no response has been heard from them. The present writer has argued[12] that the controversy over the part played by the WPA involves a particular principle concerning international relationships in medicine and science. Whereas professional diplomats are expected to hold converse with people from other countries whose behaviour may be ethically objectionable this should not be acceptable in relationships between doctors or scientists. The purpose of diplomacy is to seek adjustments between national interests for the sake of peace, etc. The purpose of international relationships between professional and learned societies and their members is to further the disciplines which depend upon the observance of medical and other professional ethics. Co-operation with societies whose leaders violate medical ethics is not a help but is a hindrance to medical progress. Promoting international harmony is a secondary function of co-operation between professionals from different countries. It cannot and should not be achieved at the price of violating the first principle which is that ethically correct work must be the basis for international medical and scientific exchanges (see *Declarations, Declaration of Hawaii*).

1. Szasz TS. In foreword to Ennis, op. cit.
2. Ennis BJ. *Prisoners of psychiatry*. New York: Harcourt Brace Jovanovich, 1972.
3. U.S. Senate Sub-Committee on the Judiciary. *Abuse of Psychiatry for Political Repression in the Soviet Union*. Washington DC: Govt. Printing Office. (Stock No 5270–01653.)
4. Timofeyev NW, Timofeyev LN. Problems of medical deontology in clinical forensic psychiatry. *Korsakow Journal of Neuropathology and Psychiatry* 1973; 5: 13.
5. Schmidt Y *et al. Guardian* 1973, Sept 29.
6. Reddaway P. *Uncensored Russia*. London: Jonathan Cape, 1972.
7. U.S. Senate Sub-Committee on the Judiciary. *Abuse of Psychiatry for Political Repression in the Soviet Union*. Vol 2. Washington DC: Govt. Printing Office.
8. Bukovsky V, Gluzman S. *A manual on psychiatry for dissidents*. Survey, London: Eastern Press Ltd, 1975: 179–99.
9. Chronicle of Current Events. London: Amnesty International 1973, No 29.
10. Morozov GV. Psychiatry in the Soviet Union. *Br Med J* 1974; 3: 40.
11. World Health Organization. *The international pilot study of schizophrenia*. Geneva: WHO, 1973.
12. Merskey H. Political neutrality and international co-operation in medicine. *J Med Ethics* 1978; 4: 74–7.
13. Amnesty International Document Eur 39/11/78. London: Amnesty International, 1978.
14. Bloch S, Reddaway P. *Russia's political hospitals: the abuse of psychiatry in the Soviet Union*. London: Gollancz, 1977.
A Chronicle of Human Rights. No 1 et seq. New York: Khronika Press, 1973.
A Chronicle of Current Events. London: Amnesty International, 1973.
Prisoners of conscience in the USSR – their treatment and conditions. London: Amnesty International Publications, 1975.
Amnesty International supplies additional current information on the topic.

Harold Merskey

Psychiatry of Old Age (or of Late Life). See *Psychogeriatrics*.

Psychogeriatrics. As in the case of 'geriatric' (q.v.) this term has been subject to very loose usage. For many the 'psychogeriatric' patient is the 'geriatric' (frail elderly person) who presents additionally with confusion or difficult behaviour, often with the implication that he is demented. Adaptation by psychiatrists of the principles of Geriatric Medicine to the needs of such patients is leading to the development of a parallel sub-specialty of Psychogeriatrics. Some prefer the term Geriatric Psychiatry or Geropsychiatry or Psychiatry of Late Life or of Old Age to emphasize the trend to involvement with the whole range of psychiatric disturbance (functional and organic) in the elderly, though the original term and its derivative 'Psychogeriatrician' tend to persist through habit and convenience.

Careful history-taking and examination (embracing the environmental, social, psychological and physical status of the patient) form the basis of the psychogeriatric assessment. The prospects for treatment may range from the dramatic recovery, through variable response to painstaking rehabilitation, to the preservation of dignity and comfort during a period of rapid or gradual terminal illness. The expected future quality of life is a major factor in the choice of goal, which itself may need to be modified in turn by changes in the patient's circumstances and conditions and those of his family. In the case of the demented patient the aim will be to balance independence and support as the disorder advances, to help the patient and his supporters in crises and to allow comfort and palliation of symptoms to the fore as the disease advances or life threatening complications arise. At the other extreme the particular efficacy of Electro-convulsive Treatment (ECT) (q.v.) in certain types of depression in old age may face the psychogeriatrician with the dilemma of how firmly to recommend such treatment for his often frail patients against a climate of growing public unease about such therapy.

The impairment of judgement associated with advanced dementia frequently leaves the psychiatrist with the decision as to when the point has been reached at which the patient is no longer able to manage his own affairs, or at which others should intervene to protect him from himself or his environment. Such decisions must incorporate a large measure of common sense, preserving the right to eccentricity on the one hand but also taking note of the extent to which the patient risks others apart from himself.

In countries such as Britain where resources (q.v.) and especially hospital beds are limited, the psychogeriatrician has to balance his traditional role of personal physician to his patient against the needs of rival candidates for these resources. This may involve leaving patients in, or discharging them to, situations of real risk, or rehabilitating reluctant patients simply to create the space (e.g. beds) to admit others. With this pressure on resources increasing it becomes more crucial that such considerations play no part in moulding the individual doctor's attitudes to the management of the life threatening conditions mentioned earlier. It should be added that in this field (with the impaired judgement of the demented patient on the one hand and the pathological and usually reversible despair of the depressive on the other) the arguments against euthanasia (q.v.) are perhaps, if paradoxically, at their strongest.

Pitt B. *Psychogeriatrics. An introduction to the psychiatry of old age.* Edinburgh and London: Churchill Livingstone, 1974.

Colin Godber

Psychopathy. A severe disorder of personality, of emotional adjustment or maturation whereby a person behaves in an extreme manner, either violently or in a bizarre, heterodox way, and has gross inability to relate, namely to initiate, develop and sustain a non-destructive and productive social and emotional relationship. The condition is persistent and intractable to classic forms of medical and psychiatric treatment, e.g. analytical or supportive psychotherapy, behaviour therapy and physical methods.

While psychopathy may exist in a setting of subnormality and mental illness, it also exists as a clinical entity apart from these conditions and without organic brain lesion.[1]

It is seen in people who have not learned to relate and in whom persistent attempts to relate have led to a worsening and a destruction of any ability to relate in accepted emotional and social terms. Reactions of others – anger, disgust, oversympathy, over-mothering – perpetuate and worsen the condition; as the person develops from childhood into adolescence and adulthood the condition becomes fixed and eventually obdurate to treatment.

The term psychopath or psychopathy is unsatisfactory. It is imprecise as a medical diagnosis; it has variable legal significance, and it expresses more the emotional state of the user, namely exasperated hopelessness, tinctured with anger and even contempt. The American substitute sociopath, a near synonym, is free from these latter emotional connotations, but is no more precise. Those who work with this group of people use a diagnostic term 'personality disorder', followed by a description of the predominant features in the individual.[2]

Certain factors are present in all cases to a greater or lesser degree:
1. Periods of emotional and social deprivation in infancy and childhood.[3]
2. Long periods spent in institutions, perhaps because of the need to control a difficult or unmanageable child or adolescent, leading to ambiguity in the forming and development of relationships.
3. A highly exaggerated need for reassurance of identity, sexuality, sanity and existence. 'I don't feel I am me'.
4. A misdirection of aggressive drives seen in offences of arson, burglary and assault.

5. A misdirection of sexual drives, seen in offences of rape, sexual assaults, deviancy and exposure.

6. A marked feeling of unworthiness, uselessness, lacking in value as a person underlies the extreme behaviour.

7. An appearance of coldness and lack of feeling. A dissociation at the time of committing extreme violence, murder or rape.

8. A dehumanization and, at times, feelings of internal elation during the process of hostage holding, wounding, feelings of all-powerfulness, but lack of ability to relate to the victim or to the police.

9. Almost total lack of judgement in behaviour even though the person is of normal intelligence and is not suffering from any psychotic or organic illness. This lack of judgement is the result of inability to perceive his own needs and the needs and responses of others and is interpreted as a lack of conscience.

10. A low level of anxiety which is uncovered in treatment. It is apparent that the person prevents the anxiety coming into consciousness by more and more repetitive acting out. A typical sequence of events is taking and driving away a car, a police chase, accident, arrest, court case and subsequent imprisonment, fight, wrist slashing, drugs, drink and unawareness of the social pressure of his peers, the police, his parents, his wife.

11. Impulsivity. He reacts to inappropriate social stimuli by impulsive behaviour which he rationalizes from his own primitive needs. It is in this phase that, when examined either by the judiciary, the police or psychiatrists, he is observed to have no remorse.

12. Lack of response to ordinary learning methods, to early childhood punishments, and to the birching, isolation, confinement and deprivation of over-exaggerated bodily needs, that may be necessary for his management and containment, but which reinforce his feelings of unworthiness and isolation. This person is unable to learn from his mistakes.

13. Lack of trust in extreme cases is almost complete, but particularly during periods of crisis during the commission of a crime.

14. Lack of social skills. Inability to use the telephone; to apply for a job; deficiencies in social relationships; inability to organize and enter into an outing or a social evening. These people cover up this deficiency by taking drugs, becoming drunk and prevent themselves facing their social deficiencies by causing a diversion, such as picking a fight.

AETIOLOGY. There are constitutional and environmental components in the definitive conditions, but exploration of hereditary pre-disposition, chromosomes, organic underlying causes, lesions in the temporal or frontal lobe have yielded little help in diagnosis, prevention or treatment. In most cases no definite hereditary predisposition or organic lesion is seen. An 'immature' electroencephalogram shows a variable and ill defined pattern and there is no correlation between presence or degree of violent behaviour and EEG patterns.

TREATMENT. Medical treatment depends on an implicit commitment between the physician and the patient based on trust and good faith, but this person cannot enter into such a commitment because of lack of ability to trust. Impulsiveness and lack of judgement prevent his attending clinics, taking medicines (the effects of which are dubious) or entering into a classic psychotherapy (q.v.) relationship. Management is also a problem since his impulsive acting out behaviour will be accentuated during any process of change in treatment. This person is intractable to treatment by psychoanalysis, supportive psychotherapy and physical methods; in conventional hospital treatment regimes he disrupts the treatment of other patients and staff management and has to be expelled. At the same time in these settings he has ample opportunity to act out his distorted, destructive methods of relating and therefore his pattern of behaviour is perpetuated. The only satisfactory regime which allows him to grow, experiment with emotional and social relationships and so develop an awareness of himself and his behaviour in relation to others is the therapeutic community directly designed for the treatment of personality behaviour disorders. The therapeutic community system for the treatment of behaviour disorders was set up by Maxwell Jones at the Henderson Hospital about 30 years ago.

Emphasis is placed on the individual's responsibility for his behaviour and on providing a milieu to allow him to examine his emotional needs, the emotional needs of others, his effect on the feelings and behaviour of others, their effect upon him to allow him to form and reform and readjust to others and explore and correct his faulty mechanisms of relating. He tests out the boundaries of the structure and others in relationship to his own emotional needs and behaviour. Permissiveness and boundary drawing enable him to grow and establish a less faulty and destructive method of operating.

The principles of treatment were instituted at HM Prison Grendon 16 years ago under the Home Office and the direction of William Gray.[4] Both systems have evolved and progressed in their understanding of the behaviour, emotional structure and relationship faults in the psychopath. The treatment regime at Grendon is now being evaluated in terms of change, growth and reduction of destructive behaviour. Goals are:- the prevention of repetitive, escalating, extremely violent behaviour patterns; improvement in social and emotional methods of operating; ability to form satisfactory, deeper relationships in a domestic setting; understanding and directing of sexual and aggressive drives in a non-destructive manner; growth and development in the patient's feeling of his own worth; finding and developing aspects of his personality that are of value to himself and others. In coming to an appreciation of the needs of others he is able to reinforce a poorly developed conscience, a sense of his own responsibility, to develop social and emotional skills, an appreciation of his own worth, an ability to learn from his past errors, and feelings of real regret andre-morse in a caring environment. At the same time, he is protected from his own destructive impulses but contained predominantly by the pressure from his peers.

GRENDON TREATMENT REGIME. Grendon is made up of 6 therapeutic communities and an Assessment Unit. Each of these communities consist of inmates, prison officers, psychiatrists, a psychologist and a probation officer or social worker.

Philosophy. A person is considered to be responsible for his behaviour. He must have some degree of self motivation for change. His aim is to become aware of his behaviour and how this is regulated by his emotions/feelings. How these two affect his relationships:

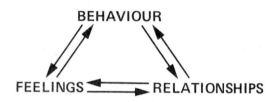

To develop and correct social skills by involvement in the community.

To completely examine and bring about an alteration in life style.

A person is in treatment in the community. He is not sick, being treated by a doctor and nurses. He is a person allowing himself to share in the support, examination, confrontation of his peers in his whole life situation.

To develop and enhance those positive qualities he may possess and so produce some feeling of worth.

Treatment methods. No psychopharmacology is used; no psychotrophic drugs nor night sedation. (Drugs for medical conditions are of course prescribed as required, e.g. penicillin).

Reasons.

1. A person is considered responsible for his behaviour and he and the community have resources to control this behaviour without the protection of medication.

2. In the intensive treatment he must be aware of his feelings relating to his behaviour and how this affects his interpersonal relationships. This perception is dulled or altered by medication. There are (a) group meetings involving staff and men with community meetings, small group meetings, encounter groups, role-playing groups, psychodrama – with audio visual aids, work groups, discharge groups, operatic groups, family groups, committee meetings, transactional analysis, areas of decision making, management and control groups using therapeutic community principles such as democratization, boundaries

and limit drawing, role mobility, communication. The community or wing meeting is the central point of the treatment.

Evaluation. In 1972/73 Professor John Gunn *et al* conducted a survey of the Grendon treatment regimes. They found that evaluation of treatment regimes in terms of reconviction rate was not valid. 'Reconviction depended upon a myriad of personal, environmental and situational factors, many of which the prison psychiatrist cannot be expected to influence.'[5] In all the main areas that were measured – psychiatric state, symptomatology, personality, attitudes to authority figures and self – large changes were recorded between the first and subsequent assessments. They also showed significant reduction in neurotic symptoms, anxiety, tension and depression. Using methods involving semantic differential several areas of therapeutic significance emerged.

There was a rise in the esteem of 'myself element' and fall in the unrealistic high estimation of psychiatrists. Changes show the men gain increase in self-confidence and worth. They found that the results reflected the orientation of the Grendon therapeutic regime with a primary emphasis laid on the people's own ability to help themselves.

ETHICAL ISSUES

1. All anti-social behaviour, even of an extreme nature, does not presuppose psychopathy or a psychopathic personality. The majority of offenders are assumed to be responsible for their behaviour and are treated as such by the law. Others are not responsible because they suffer from a clearly diagnosed mental illness within the terms of the Mental Health Act 1959. The small, though persistently recurring group in the courts who are neither 'bad' nor 'mad' are recognised by the law in charges of murder and manslaughter by the finding of diminished responsibility because of personality disorders or psychopathy.

2. The Mental Health Act 1959 included psychopathic disorders as a mental disorder, describing this as a persistent disorder or disability of the mind (whether or not including subnormality of intelligence) which results in abnormally aggressive or serious irresponsible conduct on the part of the patient and requires or is susceptible to medical treatment. This has been, with a few exceptions, totally unsatisfactory in providing treatment for this group of people. The exceptions were those whose behaviour was not normally aggressive or their conduct seriously irresponsible.[6] If their behaviour was of this nature, they were discharged from the hospitals and, as described earlier, have not been able to use outpatient facilities. The Henderson Hospital has been able to treat many who were untreatable in the formal mental hospital. In 1975 the Butler Committee issued a report on mentally abnormal offenders. After careful exploration and evaluation, the conclusion of this committee was that treatment of the personality dis-

order with aggressive behaviour and gross irresponsibility would be better treated within the penal system and proposed a number of training regimes.[7] Running parallel it suggested removal of the term 'psychopathic disorder' from the Mental Health Act. The committee recommended that these units for the training and treatment of dangerous anti-social psychopaths be on a voluntary basis in special units within the penal system. The ethics of such regimes depends on the voluntary clause for persons entering or leaving treatment.

3. There is a conflict between the needs of treatment, the rights of the individual and the safety of the public. A psychopath is not invariably dangerous. He may be potentially dangerous but other factors play a very important part such as social situation, marriage, housing and drinking habits. Careful evaluation is required in each case and at regular short intervals. Doctors refute the criticism by some sociologists that they are not curing or caring but simply acting as agents, sometimes repressively, of social control.

4. It has been found that destruction of brain tissues can reduce aggressive drives and violent behaviour, although these techniques are still imprecise and are irreversible. They have been used in the past for treating impulsive aggression, but are not in use today in most countries. Because of their irreversible nature such techniques pose serious ethical problems and patients must be aware of the direct and side effects of the treatment and enter voluntarily into it. (See *Psychosurgery*.)

5. All patients entering into the Grendon treatment have a choice of continuing treatment or of removing themselves from treatment and they are continually offered this choice. The principle of voluntary co-operation is strictly adhered to in the Therapeutic Communities of Grendon and Henderson.

6. A fear is often expressed, both by sociologists and in literature,[8] that if the authorities or the medical profession take away a person's aggressive drives they leave him unprotected from the aggression of society or his peers in the open situation and result in his being unable to protect himself. The aim of psychotherapy is not to defuse aggression but to enable a patient to use his drives in a non-violent non-impulsive manner. Steps should be taken in each case to enable the patient to understand his new situation and be aware of areas of vulnerability which he should avoid.

7. The medical practitioner who uses the word psychopath as a diagnostic term and places this on a patient's record should be aware of perhaps unintended far reaching consequences to the patient.

   a. The term has implications with the general non-medical public: the repetitive portrayal in cinema and television of the 'psychopathic killer'.

   b. It is clinically inexact to place this diagnostic label on a child or adolescent who behaves extremely, even persistently. For example the cases of children who kill children. The imprecise non-predictable diagnostic term on the records can result in misinterpretation at some later date by other practitioners, legal, medical and administrative authorities, and result in perhaps unnecessary custodial or other measures to the detriment of the health of the patient.

c. The diagnostic label implies an intractability or untreatability and so the management can reinforce an already damaged personality. On the other hand, without using this label the practitioner must be aware of the danger of the patient to others at certain times and under certain circumstances.

1. Scott PD. Psychopathic personalities. *Current Medical Digest* 1962; 2: 19.
2. Committee on Mentally Abnormal Offenders. *Report* (Butler Report). London: HMSO, 1975, CH 5–5.19–2–24.
3. Bowlby J *et al*. The effects of mother-child separation. A follow-up study. *Br J Med Psychol* 1956; 29: 211.
4. Gray WJ. *Medical care of prisoners and detainees*. Amsterdam: ASP, 1973.
5. Gunn J. *Psychiatric aspects of imprisonment*. London: Academic Press, 1978.
6. Mental Health Act, 1959. 7 and 8 Eliz 2, Ch. 72. London: HMSO, 1959. Part I Section 4 Sub-sect (4).
7. Committee on Mentally Abnormal Offenders (Butler Committee). *Report*. London: HMSO, 1975, Ch. 5–5.19–5–24.
8. Burgess A. *The clockwork orange*. London: Heinemann, 1962.

B. J. Barrett

Psychopharmacology – Uses and Abuses. Psychopharmacology: the scientific study of the interrelations between drugs and the mind. (Neuropharmacology is concerned with interactions between drugs and the nervous system.) Mind and brain have many inseparable aspects that must be studied together. When drugs are used for this purpose, the resulting discipline is that of neuropsychopharmacology.

Some psychopharmacologists are interested chiefly in the use of psychological methods to investigate the mode and site of actions of drugs. Others study the use of drugs to unravel mental events and processes and their interrelationships with those in the brain. A major application of both approaches is the development of drugs that can be used in clinical medicine by general practitioners, psychiatrists and other specialists.

The term psychopharmacology was first used before World War II, although the specialty did not exist as a science at that time. Since then, an enormous amount of laboratory and clinical research has produced a large number of chemicals with demonstrable effects upon the central nervous system and upon human and animal behaviour.

Many of these have subsequently found medical as well as non-medical use.

The clinical study of the brain and mind poses special problems in definition: of diagnosis, of symptomatology and also of treatment. Thus, for example, the boundaries between ease, unease and disease, and between legitimate use, misuse and abuse of drugs, are often unclear. Legitimate use of a psychopharmacological agent may be said to be the treatment of correctly diagnosed mental disorder, including common neuroses, psychoses and other disturbances, the existence of which is generally recognized although there may be disagreement about their manifestation in an individual. But use of a drug is not necessarily legitimate because it has been medically prescribed, nor is abuse an inevitable consequence of self-prescribing of medical or non-medical substances improperly obtained. Some abuse is also due to the medical profession in over-prescribing psychopharmaceutical preparations; not all can be attributed to over-consumption by patients and society at large. In so far as some maladaptive behaviour can be diagnosed without recourse to medical advice, some self-prescription can be legitimate (see *Self-medication*). On the other hand, some employment of many social drugs – alcohol and cannabis, if not heroin or tobacco – may be useful, if not *necessarily* illegitimate, and is certainly not abusive by definition. All these substances are dangerous, however; and different degrees of familiarity with their effects are neither a guarantee of their relative safety nor an excuse for the inconsistency of social attitudes to their use (see *Alcoholism; Drug Dependence; Tobacco Smoking*).

At present, the relationship between medicine and society is changing in such a way as to redefine the frontier between use and abuse. Proponents of the 'medical model' are retreating from over-inclusion of many kinds of behaviour in psychiatric disorder; on the other hand, the desire of many people to use modern technology to maximum effect for prophylaxis against tension and stress is increasing, as is that to 'normalize' behaviour under their own and not medical control. But because the concepts of normal, average, typical, desirable and ideal are seldom clearly differentiated, the consumer may fall into error as easily as the physician; either may mistake statistical deviation for sickness or social deviance. Perhaps for such reasons it is sometimes difficult to decide whether medical treatment in a given case was designed to restore health or to facilitate behaviour more acceptable to the society in which the patient lives. However, the use of therapeutic agents as an act of social policy for the purpose of changing group (as distinct from individual) behaviour may certainly be regarded as improper. Thus it is essential for any investigator to ensure, by consultation with colleagues or if necessary specialists in other disciplines, as well as with the subject that his own actions are controlled by full intention to achieve the patient's welfare, rather than by the intention to control behaviour. Particular care is needed when, as will frequently be the case with psychiatric patients or with those already influenced by drugs, the motives, changed sense of responsibility or even power of comprehension modify the subject's ability as a partner in the discussion. Parallel dangers, and therefore safeguards, are especially important in experimental (non-therapeutic) situations, in which the incentives to participate – financial reward, remission of sentence, acceptance by peers – may be even stronger and therefore more easily manipulated than the desire to recover health.

Drugs by themselves are not abusive, and neither are people, but when drugs are administered or self-administered by the wrong people for invalid reasons, abuse unquestionably results. (See also *Drug Dependence; Human Experiment; Psychiatry, Misuse of.*)

Blaney PH. Implications of the medical model and its alternatives. *Am J Psychiatry* 1975; 132: 911–4.

Joyce CRB. Can drugs affect personality? in Ramsey IT, Porter R, eds. *Personality and change.* London: Churchill Livingstone, 1971: 65–72.

Kendall RE. The concept of disease and its implications for psychiatry. *Br J Psychiatry* 1975; 127: 305–15.

Trethowan WH. Pills for personal problems. *Br Med J* 1975; 292: 749–51.

C. R. B. Joyce

Psychosurgery. The surgical treatment of some psychiatric illnesses by means of localized lesions made in specific sites in the brain.

It has been pointed out[1] that the definition of pyschosurgery given in a World Health Organization booklet[2], is unacceptable. In most instances no detectable abnormality of brain function has so far been discovered but pharmacological work suggests that there could well be biochemical abnormalities present in some major mental illnesses. These illnesses are inherited and this lends support to the possibility that inheritance involves the transmission of a biochemical defect. With such a defect, physical treatments, including medication, (see *Psychopharmacology – Uses and Abuses*) electroconvulsive therapy (q.v.) and psychosurgery would be expected to be of value although we do not yet know the precise means by which these therapies produce amelioration. It seems clear that surgical lesions made in the brain could interrupt abnormal nerve pathways and so ameliorate some mental disorders.

When considering the controversial subject of psychosurgery, it is essential to specify which operation is being performed and for which conditions. All too often the first operation devised is still the subject of condemnation when in fact it has been obsolete for many years. This original operation was called Standard Prefrontal Leucotomy. It was conceived by Freeman and Watts[3] in the USA and was first carried out in 1936, becoming very widely used over the next fifteen years or so. This procedure was used mainly as a treatment for schizophrenia, a potentially severely disabling and often very chronic psychiatric illness for which there was virtually no other treatment at that time. The operation was extensive and involved separation of the frontal lobes from the remainder of the brain. Reviews showed that a proportion of schizophrenics benefited significantly but there were risks of serious side-effects, including major and disabling personality changes. In retrospect the operation can be seen as being too widely used and being insufficiently refined. Ethical doubts arose and persist but in the context of its time, before the advent of effective medication for schizophrenia, prefrontal leucotomy was probably more valuable than it appears now and the risks could then have been regarded as worth taking, considering the grave nature of the illness. The operation became obsolete in the 1950s with the discovery of effective medication.

Since then psychosurgery has been more selectively used and the operations have become much more limited and precise. The contemporary techniques involve a localized lesion, the size of which is carefully controlled and which is placed in the selected part of the brain by stereotactic means[4], allowing of considerable accuracy. There is now a very low chance of producing troublesome side-effects with these restricted lesions. Psychosurgery is now mainly used for the alleviation of severe depression, tension, anxiety and obsessional symptoms when all other treatments have failed. Schizophrenia is an uncommon indication for contemporary stereotactic psychosurgery.

A recent survey has shown that a total of 431 operations took place in the British Isles during 1974–76[5]. Two-thirds of the operations were carried out in four centres and the most common indications were the four general illnesses given above. A similar study carried out in the United States[6] showed that during 1971–3, 195 neurosurgeons had performed a total of 1039 operations for psychiatric conditions. Four neurosurgeons each performed more than twenty psychosurgical operations in any one of the three years.

Now that refined techniques are employed, many ethical problems have been resolved. In addition, psychosurgery is best carried out in relatively few units where experience can be accumulated, and this seems to be current practice in most cases. From the published studies there appear to be eight such units performing the majority of operations, four in the USA and four in the UK. With these modern operations personality change of any kind is very rare and when it occurs it is minimal. In relation to helping patients with, for example, severe depression, known to be associated with a high risk of death by suicide, there may be much to gain and consequently the inevitable surgical risks, which are very rare, are worth taking. Informed consent (see *Consent*) is required but there can be practical problems with this aspect. Most patients with depression or anxiety are able to understand the treatment suggested and should be able to give free agreement or otherwise. But sometimes the patient is so ill as to be unable to communicate or unable to comprehend fully the nature of the illness or the treatment suggested. When the patient is too ill to be able to give consent, it may be regarded as ethically acceptable to operate with the full consent of relatives and with the agreement of several experienced doctors. One of the ethical problems concerns the reliability of the therapeutic value of this treatment, which is irreversible. Reviews of postoperative results suggest that these operations can produce good results with carefully selected patients[7,8], but the evidence so far available does not convince everyone.

For severe psychiatric illnesses associated with intense distress and carrying a high risk of suicide, psychosurgery may be acceptable but the ethics are more questionable in a recent development towards psychosurgical modification of socially aberrant behaviour. The operation for reducing abnormal aggressiveness involves a lesion placed in part of the brain called the amygdala[8] which is in the temporal lobe. This operation has been used for severely disturbed subnormal patients where informed consent is likely to be unreliable. Furthermore, there have been attempts to use this operation in the USA on aggressive criminals, and this obviously is open to grave ethical objections. In these circumstances it may be doubtful in some cases whether true un-pressured consent can be obtained at all. There have also been reports of psychosurgery being used for cases of sexual deviation (q.v.). Most doctors would regard such conditions more as the patients' personal problems in relation to general social attitudes rather than as conditions serious enough to justify the risks of a neurosurgical operation. So this use of psychosurgery raises major ethical doubts.

Some ethical objections depend more on personal attitudes. There are those who are antagonistic to all forms of physical treatment in psychiatry, including medication and electroconvulsive therapy as well as psychosurgery. This is associated with a minority view that all psychiatric patients need to adjust more effectively to life and need to be helped to do so only by discussion of their problems. This does not take into account chronic and severe psychiatric illnesses which are not amenable to such treatment which is in any case expensive to provide and not widely available.

Further, those who feel that there need not be great concern if a patient kills himself, since he has a personal free choice to do so, have to answer whether that attitude is not ethically questionable.

There will be more than one doctor involved in the decision whether to recommend psychosurgery for a patient and this involves balancing the advantages it may offer against its disadvantages, both of which are now known with some accuracy. Looked at in this way, the best ethical control may be provided by the medical profession itself, as suggested by the *Stanford Law Review* in 1949, which concluded that, 'the greater good will be achieved by avoiding legislative fetters and relying for protection on the high standards of the medical profession and the individuals who compose it'. Legal redress is nonetheless available in these circumstances. Another means of control is that devised by the state of Oregon, USA, which passed a law in 1971 setting up a Psychosurgery Review Board, consisting of individuals from various specialties. Ethical problems then arise as to whether a Board is the best means of dealing with the needs of an individual patient. The third, and undesirably inflexible method, is to prohibit all psychosurgery. This has obtained in the Soviet Union for many years and the Dutch Parliament is at present considering the possibility of controlling by law some physical treatments for psychiatric illnesses, including psychosurgery.

1. Bridges PK, Bartlett JR. Psychosurgery: yesterday and today. *Br J Psychiatry* 1977; 131: 249–60.
2. World Health Organization. *Health aspects of human rights.* Geneva: WHO, 1976.
3. Freeman W, Watts J. *Psychosurgery.* Springfield: Charles C. Thomas, 1941.
4. Knight G. Stereotactic tractotomy in the surgical treatment of mental illness. *J Neurol Neurosurg Psychiatry* 1965; 28: 304–10.
5. Barraclough BM, Mitchell-Heggs NA. Use of neurosurgery for psychological disorder in the British Isles during 1974–76. *Br Med J* 1978; 2: 1591–3.
6. Donnelly J. The incidence of psychosurgery in the United States, 1971–1973. *Am J Psychiatry* 1978; 135: 12, 1476–80.
7. Göktepe EO, Young LB, Bridges PK. A further review of the results of stereotactic subcaudate tractotomy. *Br J Psychiatry* 1975; 126: 270–80.
8. Mitchell-Heggs N, Kelly D, Richardson A. Stereotactic limbic leucotomy. *Br J Psychiatry* 1976; 128: 226–40.
Hitchcock E, Cairns V. Amygdalotomy. *Postgrad Med J* 1973; 49: 894–904.

P. K. Bridges

Psychotherapy. Psychotherapeutic methods of treatment are those in which one person (the therapist) helps another person (the client or patient) to resolve problems or to achieve personal fulfilment. A major factor in psychotherapy is the relationship between patient and therapist. The psychotherapeutic process is not assisted artificially, for example, by prescribing drugs. It may take place in a one-to-one situation or in a group.

Psychoanalysis is an intensive form of psychotherapy in which definite rules are laid down for the length (50 minutes) and the number of sessions per week (four or five) and also for the actual conduct of the interaction between patient and therapist (for example, when and how to 'interpret' the material brought by the patient). From an ethical point of view, however, there is no difference in principle between the psychotherapies so that this article is applicable also to psychoanalysis.

Ethics relates to morals and moral questions, to the regulation of behaviour which is self-imposed rather than by an outside authority such as the law. In medicine and surgery tools of great power have been placed in men's hands so that ethical issues have had to be faced[1,2]. While no less important in psychotherapy, the ethical problems are not so obvious and relatively little has been written about them. 'Talking treatment' is considered less powerful than physical treatment in psychiatry, not least by the patients. It is therefore particularly important that psychotherapists, aware that the influence of persons upon one another can be extremely powerful, should be clear about ethical issues affecting their subjects.

CONTRAINDICATIONS AND DANGERS OF PSYCHOTHERAPY. Not all persons who come for psychotherapy should receive it. Psychotherapy is capable of disrupting those whose personalities are fragile or those whose hold upon reality is tenuous. Exact criteria of unsuitability cannot be specified in a short article, but it is not ethical to apply any form of psychotherapy if the client is likely to be made worse. For psychotherapy to be helpful a person must have the basic personality strength to be able to recognize and face up to personal problems and inadequacies. This does not mean that psychic pain should be avoided; personal fulfilment is not possible without the painful process of looking at weaknesses and false or partly false solutions to the problems of life. But the person with a threatened psychosis (insanity); the person with an impulsive component to his personality expressing itself perhaps in repeated suicide attempts or in drug dependency (q.v.); the person in whose personality, perhaps through poor interpersonal relationships in earlier life, there are few strengths to work with and many weaknesses; these are examples of people who are usually not suitable for an 'uncovering' type of psychotherapy. It is, however, ethical to advise the type of help, including other psychiatric treatment, that may be correct and to help them to obtain this.

NEGOTIATING A PSYCHOTHERAPEUTIC CONTRACT. By a psychotherapeutic 'contract' is meant the arrangements the psychotherapist and the patient or client make both with regard to practicalities such as spacing of sessions, type of psychotherapy, payment if in the private sector; and the aims and goals of psychotherapy, whether this is to be symptom resolution, or something more ill-defined but nevertheless meaningful such as self-realization, self-actualization or self-fulfilment. Ethical considerations enter into the initial decisions as well as ongoing changes in the contract as patient and therapist get to know one another. In psychotherapy patient and client should be as honest as possible with one another so that in negotiating the psychotherapeutic contract the patient should be aware of the factors taken into account by the therapist. This is particularly so where other significant persons are concerned as in marital or family therapy. These other persons may be adults but they may also be children; the psychotherapeutic contract for a couple with young children may pay attention to factors different from those in a contract with a couple whose children have grown up. To pretend, as do certain of the 'encounter' therapies, that personal fulfilment, 'doing your thing', is permissible in any circumstances regardless of the consequences for others seems ethically unacceptable.

PSYCHOTHERAPEUTIC INTERVENTIONS. Between negotiating a psychotherapeutic contract and termination of treatment, the therapist makes a series of technical interventions aimed at producing changes in the patient's behaviour and experience. These may include questioning and information-gathering; reflecting back to the client his problems in an effort to make them clearer to him; or 'interpreting' the client's problems and difficulties by suggesting to him other, unconscious or unrecognized, motives behind some of his behaviour so that he comes to know himself better.

There are a number of ethical problems here. First there is the influence of the therapist's attitudes, his personal values and adjustment to life. Häring[1] and Szasz[3] have both emphasized the possible dangers of manipulation in psychotherapy. The technical problem is that communication between therapist and the patient, including the therapist's interventions, takes place at both verbal and non-verbal levels. While the therapist can be aware of his verbal interventions and can modify or control these to some extent, non-verbal communication, through gesture, facial expression, nods or noises of approval or disapproval, can be almost unconscious and yet there is ample evidence that a patient or client can be conditioned (caused to learn) by the application of these rewarding and punishing contingencies.

Secondly, there is the danger of reductionism[6]. To the psychoanalyst or behaviourist, behaviour and experience may be treated as 'nothing but' something else, the expression, for example, of sexuality or conditioning. Yalom[4] has emphasized in this situation the need in psychotherapy for a 'third force'. This is the existential contribution which emphasizes the irreducibility of much human experience, responsibility for one's own activities and self-determining behaviour.

It is a matter of controversy whether, as psychoanalysts believe, the personal psychoanalysis of therapists will prevent non-ethical manipulation of patients. Some form of systematic opportunity for the therapist to achieve increased self-understanding, as, for example, a period of individual or group psychotherapy or the opportunity to enter a sensitivity training group, is helpful. It may also be ethically desirable in order that the therapist should impose his values as little as possible on the patient but allow the patient to realize himself and develop his own aspirations, goals, gratifications and fulfilments in work, in social relationships and in sexuality.

EXTRA-THERAPEUTIC CONTACT. Should therapist and patient meet outside therapy? There are two aspects to this: the social and the sexual. So far as sexual contact is concerned apologists, particularly in the USA[5] defend reports that a small percentage of therapists either have sexual relationships with patients or at least verbally approve of this possibility. Rationalizations (excuses) are made that, for example, this might help a female patient with a sexual problem (frigidity) to overcome this problem. Most responsible therapists, however, both in the USA and in the UK consider that this form of contact is never ethically justifiable. The relationship between the therapist and the client is, in many ways, so unequal that advantage must not be taken of one by the other.

The issues regarding social interaction are not so clear-cut. Although little definite information is available, it seems undoubted that some expatients continue to meet the therapist and the therapist's family on a social basis. It also seems probable that, having tried this once, many therapists discontinue the practice! It is extremely difficult, probably impossible, to normalize a relationship in which, for months or perhaps even years, issues such as the amount known by one person about another, and dependency issues, have been so one-sided.

A more difficult area arises from the spontaneity of the 'new' therapies[6] often called 'encounter' therapies, in that a number of these use structured exercises involving touching between patients or between patient and therapist although not specifically sexual touching. This is a somewhat ambiguous area. There seems little doubt that, for example, a shy female client may, by simply stroking a young man's face, achieve a feeling of closeness to a human being greater than she has ever achieved before and this may not only be helpful but of fundamental importance to achieving her goal in psychotherapy. It seems likely that, provided a clear idea is retained of the possible dangers of these techniques, their therapeutic advantages outweighs their potential ethical disadvantages.

TERMINATION OF THERAPY. All therapies must finish and ethical considerations enter into the decision when to terminate therapy. The basic argument is between the psychoanalytic aim for fundamental personality change and resolution of symptoms compared with the aim of other psychotherapies which tend to limit therapy to perhaps ten or fifteen once-weekly sessions and therefore to have more modest goals. 'Perfection' should not be imposed on a client whose manifest imperfections of personality are such that a lesser goal would be more appropriate. The other ethical consideration is that, no matter how long or short the therapy, the therapist should give the client advance warning, related to the client's personality, when treatment is to cease.

THE PROFESSION OF PSYCHOTHERAPY. The need for a more effective profession of psychotherapy and counselling[7] is underlined by the Foster Report on Scientology[8]. '. . .those who feel they need psychotherapy tend to be the very people who are most easily exploited

. . .' '. . .I have become convinced that it is high time that the practice of psychotherapy for reward should be restricted to members of a profession properly qualified in its techniques and trained – as all organized professions are trained – to use the patient's dependence which flows from the inherent inequality of the relationship only for the good of the patient himself . . .'

Practical problems are particularly acute in judging non-orthodox psychotherapies, and deciding which do and which do not fulfil ethical standards. Many unorthodox and new therapies may appear experimental or even outrageous but may catalyse later progress and development in orthodox psychotherapies. This is well illustrated by the influence of the encounter movement on orthodox group psychotherapy.

1. Häring B. *Manipulation: Ethical boundaries of medical, behavioural and genetic manipulation.* Slough: St Paul Publications, 1975.
2. Ramsey IT, Porter R, eds. *Personality and Science. An interdisciplinary Discussion.* London: Churchill Livingstone, 1971.
3. Szasz TS. *The Ethics of Psychoanalysis.* London: Routledge and Kegan Paul, 1974.
4. Yalom ID *The Theory and Practice of Group Psychotherapy.* New York: Basic Books, 1975.
5. Kardener, SH Sex and the physician-patient relationship. *Am J Psychiatry* 1974; 131: 1134–6.
6. Marteau L. Encounter and the new therapies. *Br J Hosp Med* 1976; 15: 257–65.
7. Blackham HJ, ed. *Ethical Standards in Counselling,* London: Bedford Square Press, 1974.
8. Foster JG. *Report on Scientology.* London: HMSO, 1971.

Sidney Crown

Publication. See *Communication; Medical Journalism.*

Q

Quality Assurance. The terms quality of care and quality assurance are being increasingly used both by health professionals and by the public. Whatever the system of delivery of care the objective is to give a service of high quality both technical and interpersonal.[1] The question arises as to whether well established practices already form adequate safeguards of quality of medical care or whether more formal mechanisms are necessary.[2] One of the attributes of the profession is that it is self-monitoring but the increasing knowledge and awareness of the general public about medical matters, increasing demand for public accountability and increasing litigation point towards the need for the health professions to be seen to be keeping their standards under continuous review. Some regard this as threatening their clinical autonomy but many welcome it as a means of ensuring good patient care.

The term 'Quality Control' is used in the laboratory services as in industry but it relates more to accuracy than to the more sensitive areas of interpretation and judgement. 'Medical Audit' is increasingly used and although it has a connotation of accountancy it does indicate what is required. Similarly the term 'Peer Review' stresses that the audit or control should be exercised within the professions rather than imposed from without. In some countries, notably the United States, formalised procedures have been introduced by legislation but in the United Kingdom any arrangements for quality assurance are left to local initiative. There are exceptions such as the Confidential Enquiry into Maternal Deaths which is conducted on a national basis. Cost containment is an important feature of the Professional Standards Review Organization (PSRO) in the USA. This, together with utilization review and patient satisfaction are closely related to quality assurance but have less ethical component. On the other hand if resources are poor the doctor may have to declare that without better facilities his performance will reach unacceptably low standards. If in spite of exemplary treatment a patient is not satisfied, the doctor must look at his communication skills and at other interpersonal factors.

All those with responsibilities for the health of the people have ethical responsibilities to ensure that the standards of care are as good as are economically possible and that professional standards are high and are maintained throughout a lifetime of practice. In the United

States, voluntary, and in some states compulsory, periodic recertification or relicensure has been introduced. Continuing medical education[3], self assessment[4] and ongoing evaluation of care conducted with colleagues would seem to be more appropriate ways of achieving these objectives. Discussion within the team of unusual or problem cases has been common practice in hospitals, but regular reviews of routine work are equally important. The isolation of general practice has inhibited this type of activity but the Royal College of General Practitioners is active in fostering innovations and action.[5] Anxiety about whether criticism in closed meetings of a colleague's handling of a patient remains legally privileged has inhibited frank review. Similarly publications in a medical journal of reports of local assessment of care may be picked up by the lay press and presented in a critical way, whereas the unit should be commended for taking stock of its procedures.

Ultimately the individual has the ethical responsibility of ensuring his continued professional standards and of the quality of care which he gives but he can be greatly helped by medical audit and peer review.

(See *Clinical Autonomy*; *Clinical Practice*; *Communication*; *Competence to Practise*; *Health (Hospital) Advisory Services*; *National Health Service*; *Resources*; *State Health Services*; *Teamwork*.)

1. Donabedian A. The quality of medical care: a concept in search of a definition. *J Family Practice* 1979; 9: 277–84.
2. Duncan A. Quality assurance: what now and where next? *Br Med J* 1980; 1: 300–2.
3. Richards RK. *Continuing medical education*. London: Yale University Press, 1978.
4. Matthews MB. Self-assessment programmes and aspects of audit. *J R Coll Physicians Lond* 1979; 13: 139–42.
5. Editorial (and Special Number). Medical audit in general practice. *J R Coll Gen Prac* 1979; 29: 699–700.
McLachlan G, ed. *A question of quality? Roads to assurance in medical care*. Oxford University Press for Nuffield Provincial Hospitals Trust, 1976.

A. S. Duncan

R

Radiation. See *Ionizing Radiation*.

Radical Surgery. See *Mutilation*.

Random Blood Testing. See *Blood Testing, Random*.

Randomized Trials. See *Clinical Trials*.

Registers, Genetic. See *Genetic Registers*.

Registers Risk. See *Risk Registers*.

Religions and Medical Ethics. See under names of various religions: *African Medicine; Buddhism; Chinese Medicine; Christianity; Hinduism; Islam; Judaism; Shinto*. See also *Medical Ethics* (introductory essay).

Reproduction. See *Abortion; Artificial Insemination; Contraception; Embryo Transfer; Eugenics; Infertility*.

Research. See *Animal Experiment; Clinical Trials; Consent; Fetal Material, Research on; Human Experiment; Medical Research Council; Pharmaceutical Industry; Research Ethical Committee; Research, Funding of*.

Research Ethical Committee. The purpose of a Research Ethical Committee (REC) in Britain is to safeguard patients and healthy volunteers who take part in clinical research. It must also protect the research worker and the good reputation of the hospital or institution in which research is carried out. It is the responsibility of a REC to ensure that no unreasonable or unethical project is undertaken and to encourage all concerned with research in human beings to have a strong sense of responsibility to their subjects.

HISTORY OF RESEARCH ETHICAL COMMITTEES IN BRITAIN. The need for such committees derives from the substantial increase in clinical research since World War II. In 1963 the Medical Research Council (q.v.) issued a statement entitled *Responsibility in Investigations on*

Human Subjects[2]. This expressed the view, shared by all responsible research workers, that whenever a procedure or investigation was undertaken in either a patient or a healthy subject solely or mainly to contribute to medical knowledge and not to benefit the individual in which it was performed, (1) the investigator had the responsibility to ensure that the subject's agreement with the procedure was obtained (see *Consent*), (2) that no harm should come to the subject and (3) that, if there was any doubt about the propriety of the procedure, the opinion of experienced colleagues would be sought before starting.

However, in 1967 Pappworth[3] reported a large number of research procedures to which patients had been submitted which he thought unpleasant, hazardous or unjustified. Although his book was written in emotive style and most experienced clinicians felt that much of Pappworth's criticism was unreasonable, he did reveal some research investigations, mostly outside Britain, which should never have been carried out. A similar conclusion had been reached in a more temperate paper by Beecher[1] in the USA.

In 1971 the Royal College of Physicians of London[4] recommended that in every institution in which clinical investigation in human beings was carried out, arrangements should be made for all projects to be approved by an independent group of persons, some of whom should be experienced in carrying out investigations in humans. As a result, Research Ethical Committees were established, immediately in some hospitals and by 1973 in almost all hospitals where clinical investigation is carried out.

THE PRESENT SITUATION. Further recommendations were made in a report by the Royal College of Physicians in 1973[5]:

1. A REC should be a small committee set up solely to supervise the ethics of clinical research.

2. The medical members should be experienced clinicians with knowledge and experience of clinical research.

3. The REC should have a lay member (see *Health Councils*).

4. To remove any uncertainty about which procedures should be submitted to a REC, all proposed research investigations in human beings should be submitted.

5. Whenever a research investigation was not expected or intended to benefit the individual patient a full explanation should be given and the patient should be free to decline to participate or to withdraw at any stage.

6. That whenever possible the consent of a patient should be obtained in the presence of a witness.

7. That when there are circumstances in which it is genuinely inappropriate to inform a patient fully, it is the duty of the REC to examine the situation with special care.

8. That particular care is needed if clinical investigation is proposed in children or mentally handicapped adults who cannot give informed consent. The parents or guardians should be consulted.

9. That particular care is needed if clinical investigation is proposed on a subject or patient who has any sort of dependent relationship to the investigator, e.g. student, laboratory technician or employee (see also *Prisoners*).

The REC of the writer's own hospital is typical of many such committees now functioning. It has six members: four are medical, two of whom are full-time clinical professors in the medical school, one is a layman and one a nurse. It is responsible for the supervision of all clinical research in the hospital, in the community (by general practitioners) and in the medical school (where it is informed of all procedures undertaken by students for education purposes in practical classes). It also acts on behalf of non-medical Departments in the University where occasional studies in human beings may be carried out (Departments of Psychology, Sociology, Physics, etc.).

This REC examined 392 submissions between its formation in 1971 and April 1979. Only one submission was rejected but modifications of the protocols usually of a minor nature were quite frequently made. It has been suggested that this clean record shows that the Committee is a 'whitewashing committee'. A more generous and I think a more accurate comment is that this reflects the high standards of care and the responsible attitudes with which physicians and surgeons in our hospitals undertake research work in patients or human volunteers, and this is the experience of most other research ethical committees throughout the UK.

Some RECs have a Junior Hospital Doctor as a member. To have a nurse is still unusual but is valuable because it reassures the nursing staff of the hospital about the propriety of research projects in which they often play an important part.

Two important developments have strengthened the position and influence of a REC: (1) it is now virtually impossible for a research worker to obtain financial support from the Medical Research Council or any other grant aiding body unless his proposed research has been approved by his local REC and (2) no reputable medical or scientific journal in Britain will publish research for which the approval of a REC has not been obtained.

The Royal College of Physicians (London) continues to play an important part in the field. An informal meeting of Chairmen of RECs was held at the College in October 1974 at which issues that had arisen in different Committees were discussed and explored and the President of the College has proposed that similar meetings should be held in future years.

In the USA review committees with similar functions operate in centres of medical research.

1. Beecher HK. Ethics and clinical research. *New Engl J Med* 1966; 274: 1354–60.
2. Medical Research Council. Responsibility in investigations on hu-

man subjects. In: *Report of the Medical Research Council for 1962–63*. London: HMSO, 1963: 21–5, Cmnd 2382. Reprints available from the Council. (See also *Br Med J 4*: 177–8.)
3. Pappworth MH. *Human guinea pigs: experimentation in man.* London: Routledge and Kegan Paul, 1967.
4. *Report of Committee on the supervision of the ethics of clinical investigation in institutions.* Royal College of Physicians of London, 1971.
5. *Report of Committee on the supervision of the ethics of clinical investigation in institutions.* Royal College of Physicians of London, 1973.

O. L. Wade

Research, Funding of. The approximate distribution of funds available for medical research in the United Kingdom is as follows:

	Government agents		Others	
	Medical Research Council	Health Depts.	Private charities, foundations, trusts	Pharmaceut. Industry
Proportion of total expenditure on medical research	21%*	4%**	11%	64%

* Includes funds transferred from Health Departments.
** Mostly on health services research, but also comprising a locally organized small research grant scheme operating at regional level.

These proportions are estimates, and vary somewhat from year to year. In addition, substantial Government funds are provided through the University Grants Committee, chiefly in the form of 'core support' to university medical departments.

In the financial year 1979–80 the approximate income of the MRC (q.v.) was £68.5 million, including £13.0 million received from the Health Departments ('transferred funds' following a government decision in 1972 to transfer a proportion of research council budgets to 'customer' departments); the remainder is derived from the Science Vote, distributed mainly between the five research councils (Agricultural, Medical, Natural Environment, Science, Social Science) by the Secretary of State for Education and Science on the advice of the Advisory Board for Research Councils. The Advisory Board recommends financial allocations on the basis of broad research proposals put forward by the Councils but is not involved in their detailed implementation and is therefore not normally concerned with ethical issues in biomedical research. MRC expenditure is divided in the ratio of about 2:1 between research conducted in MRC establishments and research grants to people working in universities, hospitals etc.

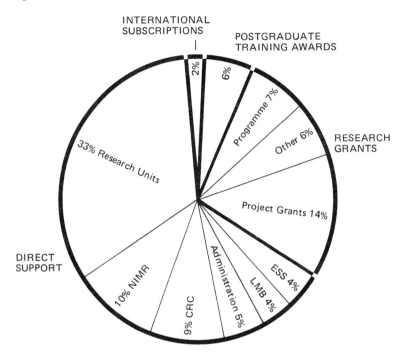

INTERNATIONAL SUBSCRIPTIONS

POSTGRADUATE TRAINING AWARDS

2%

6%

Programme 7%

Other 6%

RESEARCH GRANTS

33% Research Units

Project Grants 14%

DIRECT SUPPORT

10% NIMR

9% CRC

Administration 5%

LMB 4%

ESS 4%

Medical Research Council Expenditure

NIMR: National Institute for Medical Research
CRC: Clinical Research Centre
LMB: Laboratory of Molecular Biology
ESS: External Scientific Staff

Policy on ethical aspects of MRC-supported research is defined in the Council's statement on Responsibility in Investigations on Human Subjects first published in its Report for 1962–3 (Cmnd 2382) and recently reaffirmed. Clearance by local research ethical committees (q.v.) is required; and even when such clearance has been obtained the Council reserves the right to decline or to withdraw support on ethical grounds. The Council also carries out research in various countries in the developing world, chiefly in West Africa, East Africa and West Indies; and in these countries seeks also to conform with whatever ethical requirements may be in operation as well as to meet UK ethical standards.

Agencies which provide funds for medical research are confronted with the often conflicting considerations of scientific excellence and scientific opportunity on the one hand, and social need and economic relevance on the other. The extent to which the latter shall determine the distribution of money is one of the central ethical issues in research funding. The Government White Paper of 1972, *Framework for Government Research and Development* (Cmnd 5046) which adopted the main recommendations of the Rothschild Report on which it was based, and which gave the Health Departments control over part of the MRC's budget, was designed to move the balance of research expenditure in the direction of social need as reflected in utilization of National Health Service resources. The following table shows how 67% of MRC expenditure on medical research in 1978–9 was divided between the main diagnostic groups of the International Classification of Disease (ICD). The remaining 33% is related to a number of disease categories and therefore not classifiable in this way.

ICD Chapter	Title	MRC Research Expenditure (67%) £'000	% of Total
I	Infective and parasitic diseases	5,720	16.08
II	Neoplasms	4,924	13.84
III	Endocrine, nutritional and metabolic diseases	3,036	8.54
IV	Diseases of blood and blood-forming organs	569	1.60
V	Mental disorders	3,918	11.02
VI	Diseases of the nervous system and sense organs	5,601	15.75
VII	Diseases of the circulatory system	1,622	4.56
VIII	Diseases of the respiratory system	1,282	3.60
IX	Diseases of the digestive system	740	2.08
X	Diseases of the genito-urinary system	365	1.03
XI	Complications of pregnancy, childbirth and the puerperium	1,032	2.90
XII	Diseases of the skin and subcutaneous tissue	363	1.02
XIII	Diseases of the musculo-skeletal system and connective tissue	2,161	6.08
XIV	Congenital abnormalities	401	1.13
XV	Accidents, poisonings and violence	3,833	10.77
		35,567	100.00

The above arrangements for the funding of medical research do not of course necessarily apply to countries outside the UK, though arrangements in a number of other Western European countries are broadly similar. Elsewhere, the main government financial support for medical research may come through the government department responsible for health care; this is the case, for example, in the USA, where the National

Institutes of Health receives its support through the Department of Health, Education and Welfare.

It is not possible to generalize usefully about the ethical aspects of research funding in other countries, since requirements and codes of practice, where they exist, vary; the Helsinki Declaration (q.v.) provides guidelines which are probably widely observed. It may be noted in this respect that observers outside the UK have sometimes held that the MRC statement (see above) is unduly restrictive in that it prohibits research, except when undertaken incidentally to a diagnostic or therapeutic procedure, in those legally incapable of giving informed consent, i.e. in children and the mentally disordered. (See *Child; Consent.*)

S. G. Owen

Resources. Resources include economic goods such as money, buildings and manpower (which can be valued in financial terms) and professional standards of competence and ethics (which cannot be similarly quantified, but are at least as important). (See *Competence to practise; Quality assurance.*) The former only are considered here, but their deployment raises many ethical issues. The provision of health care is now a major preoccupation of society, involving not only the medical profession but also a whole range of other professions and occupations, and the necessary interaction between health services and personal social services makes it difficult to define what should be considered as a 'health service resource'. However, the availability of resources is one limiting factor in the provision of health care, a consideration which raises major problems in all societies.

Provision of resources. The cost of health care is already very high and it continues to grow with increases in public demand and in the sophistication of medical care; for example, in the financial year ended 31 March 1974, expenditure on the health and personal social services in England and Wales amounted to £3032 million, an increase of £420 million over the previous year, and this amount omits not only what was privately spent on health care but also the cost of undergraduate medical training and biomedical research. The increase quoted is deliberately chosen to represent 'natural growth', as it antedates the present major inflationary trend. Even so, there are still unmet demands and unfulfilled needs. The range of what is medically possible is extending all the time with substantial increases in cost; the gap between what is possible and what we can afford is constantly widening. Further inevitable burdens are being added to the health services, in some countries by an increase in the population who have passed the age of retirement, in others by a rapid growth in the birth rate. Decisions on how to make the best compromise between limited resources and a virtually open-ended demand must ultimately lie with society as a whole, but the medical profession has particular responsibilities over and above their general social responsibility, by virtue of their knowledge of and participation in health care.

In countries with a national health service, it is the responsibility of Government to decide what proportion of public expenditure can be provided for health needs. In other countries, resources are obtained on a 'free market' basis or from charitable resources. Historically, there has been an evolution from predominantly charitable provision of health care through the stage of a market economy to predominantly corporate provision; but vestiges of the earlier system remain, even when the great mass of health care is provided nationally (see *Health Care Systems*). Within national systems there are also variations of funding, the main patterns being a salaried service, a 'fee for item of service' system and one in which doctors are in contract to provide specified services. The ethical implications of these various patterns of resource provision are mainly social rather than medical. The ultimate arbiter of the pattern of medical care must be society as a whole, influenced by the advice of those who are professionally involved, but not bound by it, provided that this pattern is consistent with professional standards and motivation in the medical and other health professions.

After considering possible alternatives, the Royal Commission on the National Health Service[1] considered that the responsibility of assessing the 'right' level of NHS expenditure and of allocating it to Health Authorities must remain with central government. They recommended that experiments with budgeting should be made by authorities, to encourage more efficient use of resources, and to place responsibility for resources more firmly on those who use them.

Allocation of resources. In a market economy, sometimes misleadingly described as a free society, the best – or at least the most expensive – health care goes to the wealthy, with some mitigation of the lot of the indigent from charitable resources. The inherent inequity of this situation in relation to health has prompted attempts to allocate resources more evenly, but the problems in doing so are formidable and incompletely solved. The nature of these problems can be expressed in a series of questions, to none of which is there a simple answer, and all of which have ethical implications.

1. Should resources be allocated on the basis of the 'client group', e.g. children, the aged, the mentally and physically handicapped? By what criteria are we to judge their relative priority?

2. Alternatively, should we attempt to allocate resources to medical categories of illness? If so, should we take account of mortality, of the misery which chronic disease causes, disfigurement (see *Cosmetic Surgery*), or of the burden of services which care of these conditions imposes? An attempt at a composite index on these lines, in the context of biomedical research priorities, has been reported[2], but it leaves unanswered the fundamental question of how the different indices are themselves to be weighted.

3. How do we judge the conflicting claims of acute hospital medicine (which expensively attracts inquiring minds but which may also be the most effective preventive measure against chronic illness), of preventive approaches[3], including health education (q.v.) and of care within the community?

4. What steps can be taken to lessen the inequalities in resources which have developed historically between different regions of the country? A first approach has been made in the form of RAWP[4] (England) and SHARE[5] (Scotland), but there has been some criticism of the use of standardized mortality rates (SMR) as an indicator of relative need; and of an inadequate allowance for the increased cost of a teaching hospital. (See *State Health Services*.)

The answers to such questions (and these are only examples) are for society to determine in the light of what is currently possible both medically and economically. Paradoxically, more work has been done on how to assess the resource implications of the answers to such questions than on how to arrive at the answers themselves, but certainly one component of the debate must be the resource implications of the various choices. What is quantifiable can be subjected to cost-benefit analysis,[6] or can be studied by the techniques of operational research,[7] but a rigidly economic approach is only one component of decision-making, which must also take account of professional attitudes and uncostable benefits, such as the difference between living and mere survival. The disadvantages of a planned system, while far from negligible, seem to be less than those of random response to professional predilections and to the advocacy of pressure groups, and the best road ahead probably lies in building on our existing system of allocation of resources, accepting and testing, as they become available, refinements in decision theory and economic analysis.

Consideration of resources cannot omit those which lie within the power of each individual. We can all contribute towards health care, and a vital use of financial resources is in educating people to take care of themselves and to make proper use of the services that are available, so that money and manpower can be freed for other important needs. Avoidance of excesses in diet and in the use of alcohol, abstention from smoking and from extramarital sexual relations could all save much unnecessary illness. Proper dental hygiene and diet would generally reduce the expenditure on dental care, while some infectious disease still occurs because immunizations and vaccinations are neglected. Prevention of accidents on the roads and in the home is frequently within the power of the individual.

It is not reasonable to expect society to use scarce resources to make good all the ills and deficiencies which we bring upon ourselves and others through lack of responsibility, nor should we seek to burden the health services with trivial complaints which could often be dealt with without recourse to professional medical advice (see *Patients*).

1. Royal Commission on the National Health Service. *Report.* London: HMSO, 1979, Cmnd 7615.
2. Black DAK, Pole JD. Priorities in biomedical research; indices of burden. *British Journal of Preventive and Social Medicine* 1975; 29: 222–7.
3. *Prevention and Health: Everybody's Business.* London: HMSO, 1976.
4. DHHS. *Sharing Resources for Health in England.* Report of the Resource Allocation Working Party (RAWP Report). London: HMSO, 1976.
5. Scottish Home and Health Department. *Scottish Health Authorities Revenue Equalisation* (SHARE). Edinburgh: HMSO, 1977.
6. Williams A. The cost-benefit approach. *Br Med Bull* 1974; 30: 252.
7. McDonald AG, Cuddeford GC, Beale EML. Balance of care: some mathematical models of the National Health Service. *Br Med Bull* 1974; 30: 262.

Douglas Black

Respiration, Artificial. Artificial ventilation of the lungs, either by conventional or mechanical means, by which it is possible to maintain life in a person who would die without such support. Where brain death has occurred, the propriety of continuing life support is questioned. The problem is discussed under *Death, Determination of; Intensive Care Units; Life, Prolongation of; Tissue Transplant.*

Responsibility. See *Clinical Practice; Interprofessional Relationships; Teamwork.*

Resuscitation. See *Intensive Care Units; Life, Prolongation of; Ordinary and Extraordinary Means.*

Rhythm Method. A method of contraception which involves abstention from sexual intercourse for some days before and after the time of ovulation. It relies on the fact that conception usually occurs only in the few days immediately after ovulation, the timing of which can be established by daily accurate recording of body temperature, or by observation of changes in cervical mucus, or by other signs or symptoms; but as the 'rhythm' of the menstrual cycle is liable to upset, the method is not always reliable. Further details are given under *Contraception* and ethical issues are discussed under *Humanae Vitae* and *Vegliare con Sollecitudine.*

Risk. The essence of a civilized society is that certain risks can be reduced by public planning, as through smoke control, public supplies of clean water, or inoculation, through legislation, as in speed limits and control of firearms, and through private choice, as in defining and communicating the hazards associated with such activities as smoking or motor-cycling.

Ethical problems enter when risks to one group can be minimized only at a cost of increasing risks to another group or limiting its freedom. One classical argument relates to destructive obstetric procedures designed to ensure maternal survival by crushing or dismembering a fetus which resists all attempts to achieve a successful birth.

A more topical problem is that involved in the immunization (q.v.) of populations, when the strategy ensuring minimal total death or disability is usually that in which more death or disability is due to the immunization than to the disease. Similar problems are involved in screening (q.v.), e.g. for cervical cancer, where without screening we have, say, a deaths from cancer, and with screening, b deaths and c removals of uteruses which are not cancerous. Improved techniques can make b and c smaller, but cannot make c zero. Any rational policy must involve an explicit 'exchange rate' between avoidable cancer and unnecessary mutilation.

In amniocentesis (q.v.), in which similar decisions are taken on behalf of a fetus, which is thereby exposed to a small risk of eviction and an even smaller risk of injury as a result of the test, the situation is even more difficult than when there is no third party.

In theory high risks imposed by absence of medical action are usually accepted as equally culpable as those following excessive or inappropriate medical action. In practice non-intervention in the presence of disease is a part of traditional medical practice, especially in Northern Europe, and does not impose on those responsible the same practical difficulties as would be involved in actively advancing or encouraging death.

Risks are normally expressed in percentages, or in simple fractions (the risk of the next child being a boy is 50% or 1 in 2; the risk of another child having spina bifida is 3% or 1/30). Sometimes the odds ratio is used; in the above case this would be one to one or thirty to one against it happening (twenty-nine to one would imply a misleading precision, although more consistent).

Third party risks can cover future generations, but this important matter is seldom considered, and even excluded by some authorities on radiation protection.

J. H. Edwards

Risk Registers were first introduced as a means of detecting physical and mental handicaps early enough in childhood for treatment to be most effective. Babies born underweight and those who have difficulty or delay in breathing immediately after birth, those who need intensive care in the first week of life, and those who have jaundice or other perinatal disorders are all known to be more than usually likely to have developmental defects or spasticity. If the names of these babies are put into a risk register at the time of their discharge from hospital, the local health authority can arrange for regular visits from a health visitor and regular assessment from a paediatrician.

Ethical problems arose when the concept was enlarged to include babies at risk of injury from their parents. Some local health authorities have asked GPs, casualty officers, social workers, and anyone else who may come into professional contact with small children to cooperate in forming risk registers of children who may have suffered non-accidental injury. If this is done, a doctor seeing for the first time a child with a suspicious injury could check with the registry to find out if similar suspicions had been noted before. While such a procedure may cause some misgiving, if duty to safeguard the child's interests is seen to override the risks inherent in such registration, there should be no ethical conflicts so long as steps are taken to ensure that access to the register is restricted to the health professionals concerned. (See also *Child Abuse; Genetic Registers.*)

Tony Smith

Royal Colleges. The Royal Colleges (of Physicians, Surgeons, Obstetricians and Gynaecologists, Radiologists, Pathologists, Psychiatrists and General Practitioners) in the British Isles are established by Royal Charter and are concerned primarily with promoting the standards of medical practice and training. They do so by teaching, research, approval of training programmes and examination. They grant diplomas and certificates of competence to practise medicine in general and in its many special branches, in some ways duplicating and in other ways complementing the functions of the Universities. The appropriate Royal Colleges, like the Universities, are represented on committees which appoint consultants in the National Health Service. Unlike the British (and Irish) Medical Associations and some other professional bodies, they are not concerned with terms and conditions of service and do not engage in political activities. However, at a time (in November, 1975)[1] when some professional bodies were advocating or engaged in 'industrial' action (see *Strike, Right to*), the Royal Colleges issued a statement, which included the following: 'Above all the Presidents share their colleagues' concern, which they know to be sincere, at the effect of the proposed actions on the care of patients. This concern must, for the Colleges, override all other considerations (as indeed their Charters require) and it is for this reason that they cannot associate themselves with the profession's proposals to limit their services to the treatment of emergencies. They must and will give priority, even at this crisis in the affairs of their profession, to the preservation of standards of patient care and of training'.

A joint working party of the Conference of Medical Royal Colleges and their Faculties in the UK and the British Medical Association published in 1977 a 'Discussion document on ethical responsibilities of doctors practising in National Health Services'[2]. They maintained that, in a national health service, doctors retained ethical responsibility to their own patients, but that Government shared with the medical profession as a whole joint ethical responsibility to the community. This could only be discharged if it was acknowledged and if effective machinery for consultation and conciliation was established to resolve conflicts when they arose. Such acknowledgement and action are still awaited. (See *National Health Service; Private Practice; Strike, Right to.*)

The Conference of Medical Royal Colleges and their Faculties in the UK published two authoritative reports on the 'Diagnosis of Brain Death'[3] and the 'Diagnosis of Death'[4]. (See *Death, Determination of*).

The Royal College of Physicians of London published in 1973 a report on the ethics of clinical research[5].

All the Royal Colleges publish from time to time reports and statements about the practice of individual specialties in relation to the national interest.

Professional colleges in many other countries have similar functions to those in the British Isles.

1. Presidents and Deans of Royal Colleges and Faculties. Hospital dispute – Royal Colleges statement. *Br Med J* 1975; 4: 601–2.
2. Joint Working Party of the Conference of Medical Royal Colleges and their Faculties in the UK and the British Medical Association. Discussion document on ethical responsibilities of doctors practising in National Health Service. *Br Med J* 1977; 1: 157–9.
3. Conference of Medical Royal Colleges and their Faculties in the United Kingdom. Diagnosis of brain death. *Lancet* 1976; 2: 1069–70.
4. Conference of Medical Royal Colleges and their Faculties in the United Kingdom. Diagnosis of death. *Lancet* 1979; 1: 261–2.
5. Committee on the Supervision of the Ethics of Clinical Research Investigations in Institutions. *Supervision of the ethics of clinical research investigations in institutions.* Royal College of Physicians of London, 1973.

R. B. Welbourn

S

Safe Period. See *Contraception; Rhythm Method.*

Sanctity or Sacredness of Human Life. Phrases, having overtones taken from religious terminology, used to express the presumptive inviolability of the human person, his right to life, with its attendant right to protection in the enjoyment of his total integrity. The principle is implicit in the Hippocratic tradition (q.v) and was heavily reinforced by Jewish and Christian theology (see *Christianity; Judaism*). It finds modern expression in the Geneva Declaration of the World Medical Association, 'I will maintain the utmost respect for human life from the time of conception, even under threat. I will not use my medical knowledge contrary to the laws of humanity' (see *Declaration of Geneva*). In Judaism, every moment of life is infinitely precious, and has therefore an inviolable claim to protection. The words 'sanctity' and 'sacredness' imply – indeed, taken literally, they assert – a divine sanction for this inviolability as in itself divinely willed for man, proper to the created nature of man and the divine purpose of his existence. *Sanctity* (from the Latin *sanctus*) denotes 'holiness', a word which, in its historic evolution, denoted the numinous separateness of God, then his ethical purity, then the ethical purity, or saintliness, of those 'separated' or dedicated to God; thence a claim to religious reverence and protection, inviolability. *Sacredness* (from the Latin *sacer*) has a similar meaning: set apart, dedicated to religious use; holy by association; and therefore to be respected, protected.

The words are sometimes used in controversy, e.g. about abortion (q.v.), as though they self-evidently gave *absolute* protection, or imposed *absolute* prohibitions on the taking of life. The supposition cannot be supported from the moral tradition in which the concepts themselves have been preserved. The Jewish Law, for instance, which forbade murder in the Sixth (Fifth) Commandment (Exodus 20:13), also enjoined capital punishment for a number of crimes. The principle, properly used, asserts a human right to enjoy protection in life and bodily integrity; that right may be violated only for just cause approved by the general moral sense and by public authority. It is for society itself to work out and maintain the second-order conventions and rules by means of which the principle can operate in professional practice as in the other activities of ordered human life.

G. R. Dunstan

Science, Medical. See introductory essay.

Screening. The presumptive identification of unrecognized disease or defect by the application of tests, examinations or other procedures which can be applied rapidly.[1]

Wilson and Jungner[2] drew attention to the interest in population screening as a public health measure. Screening for disease aims to identify those among the apparently healthy who are affected or likely to be affected by disease. More specifically screening seeks the early detection of those diseases for which treatment is either easier, more economical or more effective when undertaken at the earliest possible point in time. Ethically there is a promise implicit in the invitation to be screened that those who volunteer are likely to benefit, i.e. that they will be followed up with exact diagnosis and long-term care if necessary and will receive treatments of proved efficacy.

The pressure for screening comes mainly from two sources: firstly, the public who think that by going for a test early enough possible disease will be identified and its severity lessened; and secondly, clinicians who, frustrated by the ineffectiveness of treatment, seek prevention.

In developed countries screening is now more important in the prevention of non-communicable disease (particularly in middle-aged adults) e.g. cancer, coronary heart disease and chronic bronchitis. Screening procedures which may identify, for example, those who are at risk through infection to other members of society or of the community, may still be valid in the developing world.

Screening for genetic defects has possibilities which have only been exploited adequately in the case of rhesus incompatibility. Other aspects of genetics are discussed under *Amniocentesis; Chromosome Disorders; Genetic Conditions* and *Spina Bifida.* Many of the conditions for which screening should be undertaken are not life-threatening (e.g. hearing and visual defects) yet identification of individuals with such defects may improve the quality of life of the individual. Multiphasic screening, i.e. the application of a number of different tests at one time, has often been advocated, particularly in the United States and Europe. It must be introduced as part of a larger health programme which also provides follow-up diagnosis and therapy: yet recent investigations, e.g. the South East London Screening Study,[3] have demonstrated that there is little, if any, benefit to be gained from multiphasic screening in terms of reduction of mortality, morbidity or levels of function. For example, individuals who do not feel ill may be invited to be examined and abnormalities found, e.g. raised blood pressure. Effective treatment may be available, but the individual may not wish to undergo this treatment or may be unwilling to participate in long-term health maintenance regimens[4].

1. Before screening is undertaken, each screening procedure must satisfy certain ethical, scientific and financial criteria[5].

2. Screening requires personnel and equipment to carry out tests and it is right to question whether this is an appropriate use of these resources. Many of the tests used in screening, although cheap in themselves, become expensive because very large numbers of individuals have to be tested before a single case is identified.

The introduction of any screening procedure should be accompanied by availability of effective methods of treatment and adequate resources to deal with those cases that are found through screening. For example, it would be inappropriate to introduce screening for rhesus incompatibility unless adequate supplies of rhesus antigens are available.

3. The treatment must be acceptable to the individual who may have no personal evidence in the form of symptoms that he has a condition.

4. The screening programme should reach those groups who are most at risk. For example, women in the lower socio-economic groups who have a high incidence of cervical cancer may find a cervical smear test unacceptable.

5. The natural history of the condition including development from latent to declared disease, should be adequately understood.

Otherwise screening will merely achieve longer known illness and the production of anxiety states in those who fear, perhaps groundlessly, that they are suffering from a serious medical condition.

1. Commission on Chronic Illness. *Chronic illness in the United States, Vol I, Prevention of chronic illness.* Cambridge, Mass: Harvard University Press, 1957: 45.

2. Wilson JMG, Jungner G. *Principles and practice of screening for disease.* Geneva: World Health Organization, 1968.

3. The South-east London Screening Study (1977). A Controlled Trial of Multiphasic Screening in Middle-age; Results of the South-east London Screening Study. *J Epidemiol* 1977; 357–63.

4. Sackett DL, Haynes RB, Gibson ES, Hackett BC, Taylor DW, Roberts RS, Johnson AL. Randomised clinical trial of strategies for improving medication compliance in primary hypertension. *Lancet* 1975; 1: 1205–7.

5. Cochrane AL, Holland WW. Validation of screening procedures. *Br Med Bull* 1971; 27: 3.

Haynes RB, Sackett DL, Taylor DW, Gibson ES, Johnson AL. Absenteeism from work after the detection and labelling of hypertensives. *New Engl J Med* 1978; 299: 741–4.

Walter W. Holland

Self-Medication. See *Warning on Self-Medication.*

Semen Donation. Semen, obtained by masturbation, given either by the husband (AIH) or by a donor (AID) for the purpose of artificial insemination (q.v.). If given for research purposes, the ethical principles governing human experiment (q.v.) apply.

Sex Change, Reassignment or Reversal. These terms, which are strictly inaccurate because no 'reversal' takes place, refer to the administration of hormones to, and the performance of operations on, persons of equivocal sex to make their external characteristics conform as nearly as possible to the most appropriate gender role. They include similar procedures in transsexuals – undoubted males (usually) or females, who wish to acquire the physical characteristics of the opposite sex. (See *Intersex; Sexual Deviations or Variations.*)

Sex, Determination of. By means of amniocentesis (q.v.) it is possible to establish the sex of an unborn child. The risk of the procedure makes its use inadvisable in circumstances other than in which sex-linked disorders of chromosomes (q.v.) and other genetic conditions (q.v.) are suspected and where the sex of the child is a material factor in its future health or survival.

Sex Education. Sex education has now been firmly established as an important part of child, adolescent and adult education. It is generally agreed that, in order to develop happy and stable relationships in adult life, human beings need a loving family background, information concerning the biology of sex, reproduction and contraception, and an opportunity to relate this to their own personality.

Parents can offer their children the experience of love, caring and consideration for others along with an acceptance of the value and goodness of sex and sexual feelings. This includes the acceptance by the parents of the normality of erotic feelings and behaviour in childhood. They should be able and willing to answer their children's questions as they are asked, upon any matter to do with sex and reproduction. Frequently these questions begin as early as 3 years old.

When the child enters school, teachers now accept that they have a part to play in the child's understanding of sex, and, on the whole, from primary school into secondary school, plan courses which are becoming more and more integrated into the school curriculum, offering children, first information, and then an opportunity, as adolescence develops, to use this information in understanding their own feelings and in taking responsibility for their own feelings and actions in relation to others. In this way, confusion of young people, offered a bewildering choice of behaviour norms by the media, their families and the rest of society, can gradually become less profound.

It is important that educators recognize that information is not enough; neither should they attempt to force their own moral system upon the children: the young person should be encouraged to find ways to use the information in his own way. Contraception, problems of abortion, of sexually transmitted diseases, and anxieties concerning, for example, homosexuality or masturbation, can then be dealt with.

Most parents now are fully in accord with the programme of the schools and indeed welcome them. It is particularly helpful if there is a close collaboration between parents and staff.

The biological information can, presumably, be given in ordinary classroom teaching; the discussions have to take place in small groups, either single-sex or preferably mixed. Some schools employ outside personnel, marriage guidance counsellors, family planning doctors or health visitors, for example; but it is probably best for staff to be selected and trained to do this work themselves, which adds to its integration into other school activities. If this is not possible, then the staff should work closely with visiting staff.

Some young people, either because of unhappy home experiences or for other reasons, have particular anxieties and problems and have now an opportunity to discuss these in various settings – either in the school with a nurse, counsellor or tutor, or at a youth club or youth counselling centre. The young person should be free to make his own choice.

Various studies have shown that young people, particularly boys, still feel that they would like more opportunity to learn about sex and family life in schools.

Adults also have a need for education at times, not only in order to help their children, but to help in their own relationships. Some general practitioners, family planning doctors and marriage guidance counsellors undergo special training so that help is becoming more available for these enquirers.

It is not suggested that adequate sex-education at school will prevent all problems in later life, nor will it prevent the damaged individual from using his sexuality inappropriately; but there is evidence that, with greater freedom of discussion about sex, less, rather than more, sexual offences take place – and where at a positive level people are able, free of guilt, to work towards achieving a better quality in their relationships.

Fit for the future. Report of the committee on Child Health Services. London: HMSO, 1976.

Tables from National Child Development Study, 1958 and 1974.

Unplanned pregnancy. Report of a working party of RCOG. February 1972.

World Health Organization. *Pregnancy and abortion in adolescents*.

Report of World Health Organisation meeting. Geneva: WHO, 1975.

Faith Spicer

Sex Therapy. Sex therapy is predominantly concerned with problems of dissatisfaction, lack of interest or enjoyment, or dysfunction (e.g. erectile or orgasmic failure) within sexual relationships. The past ten years have seen a substantial growth in this type of help. This reflects not only changing attitudes to sex and the accompanying increased expectations over recent years, but also a much greater therapeutic optimism. Whereas in the past there was a tendency to see most sexual problems as symptomatic of serious or relatively intractable personality difficulties, with consequently little attempt at treatment, it is now recognized that many such problems are relatively simple to understand and easy to treat. To some extent, the initial wave of optimism is being tempered by the re-acceptance that a fair proportion of these problems are indeed difficult, either from the psychological or the physical point of view.

Masters and Johnson[1] have played a central part in these developments, bringing together a comprehensive approach to treatment, apparently more effective than its predecessors. They have concentrated exclusively on the treatment of the couple rather than the individual. Their contribution has initiated a wide variety of further elaborations and modifications, particularly in the United States where the rich variation of sexual values is well represented in these treatments. Treatments aimed at the couple, the individual or groups of either couples or individuals are all being used.

Nevertheless, most variants of modern sex therapy share in common the assignment of specific sexual tasks (usually to be carried out in the patient's home) combined with counselling or psychotherapy to overcome the psychological factors that obstruct those assignments[2,3]. Modern sex therapy is therefore 'directive'.

The popularity of these new approaches, their relatively profitable status within private practice and the sexual nature of the problems dealt with raise a number of important ethical issues.

1. *The sexuality of the therapist-patient relationship*

The nature of the clinical material and the usual need for genital examination at some stage introduces a degree of vicarious sexuality into the therapeutic relationship. Most therapists regard this as an important opportunity for 'permission giving', encouraging positive attitudes and desensitizing sexual anxieties, providing that this 'within-treatment' sexuality is kept within safe limits and is not exploited for the therapist's benefit. Thus the taboo on explicit sexual contact between the therapist and patient is almost universally accepted. There are a few therapists who see such contact as therapeutically justified.

Most professional organizations of sex therapists explicitly prohibit such activity.

The use of surrogate partners, provided by the therapist, has been seen by some as a way of obtaining the benefits of sex with the therapist whilst avoiding its disadvantages. The use of surrogates remains a complex ethical issue. Does it divorce sex from personal relationships? If it does not, can the relationship with the surrogate partner present its own problems? What are the legal implications for patient or surrogate if either is married? Anxieties have been expressed about confidentiality in these circumstances and the trend for surrogates to see themselves as therapists (with their own 'professional' organizations) is serving to blur the distinction that possibly justified them in the first place.

2. *Influencing the patient and 'informed consent'*

Methods of sex therapy vary and some are more or less acceptable to particular patients. Some therapists may be inflexible in imposing their own values through their treatment methods, e.g. the use of masturbation techniques. Fully informed consent to the treatment at the outset is therefore desirable and, when sought, often leads to rejection of treatment by patient or couple.

3. *Influencing social attitudes to sex*

Sex therapists also vary in the emphasis that they place on sexual function as opposed to the sexual relationship. The burgeoning of sex therapy, both in its contact with patients and in its interpretation through the mass media, may have altered sexual expectations, provoked sexual dissatisfaction and fostered anxiety about 'performance' by replacing one set of sexual 'norms' with another. It often has clear cultural or social class origins which may make its implantation into different cultures or classes problematic.

4. *Confidentiality*

Intimate details of patients' sex lives pose special problems of confidentiality, both between patient and therapist and in the recording of such information in case files.

When working with couples, particular problems may arise when one partner gives the therapist information that is to be concealed from the other. There is a general tendency, especially by the less experienced, to elicit as much information as possible in the belief that this will enhance the effectiveness of treatment. In the absence of evidence to support this assumption the therapist should limit his history taking to what would appear to be relevant.

5. *Professional qualifications of sex therapists*

The current vogue for sex therapy has produced large numbers of therapists, many with minimal professional qualifications or training. The fears of exploitation of the public by self-styled, incompetent or unethical therapists is leading to attempts to establish and maintain 'professional' standards in this multi-disciplinary field. At the same time, there is some disagreement about these standards, particularly between professional groups. The main controversy centres around the need for medical training and qualifications. Whereas there are some aspects of sexual problems which undoubtedly require medical skills, the bulk of sex therapy does not. The sex therapist requires a degree of personal comfort with the topic, reasonable understanding of normal sexual responses and skills in counselling. These requirements are as likely (if not more so) to be found in non-medical professionals such as clinical psychologists or in other appropriately trained counsellors. On the other hand the point is often made that there is protection of the public in the case of professional bodies which establish and enforce ethical guidelines. It is to be hoped that these issues will be resolved by the proper appraisal of appropriate experience rather than by professional demarcation disputes. (See *Confidentiality; Consent; Homosexuality; Medical Records; Psychotherapy; Sexual Deviations and Variations; Teamwork.*)

1. Masters W, Johnson VE. *Human sexual inadequacy.* Boston: Little, Brown, 1970.
2. Kaplan HS. *The new sex therapy.* New York: Brunner/Mazel, 1973.
3. Bancroft J. Sex therapy. In: Bloch S, ed. *Introduction to psychotherapies.* Oxford: University Press, 1979.
Bancroft J. The treatment of sexual problems. In: Bloch S, Chodoff P, eds. *Psychiatric ethics.* Oxford: University Press, 1980.
Masters W, Johnson VE, Kolodny RC, eds. *Ethical issues in sex therapy and research.* Boston: Little, Brown, 1977.

John Bancroft

Sexual Deviations or Variations. The progression in terminology from sexual abominations, perversions or deviations to the currently fashionable 'sexual variations' depends less upon precise knowledge of the roots of these behaviours than upon the current tolerance exercised by society at large. Current views reorganize several different aspects of what has in the past been encompassed by the term 'sex'. The sex of an individual in terms of his existence as man or woman involves congruence among a number of factors, namely: (1) Chromosomal sex (2) Gonadal sex (3) Internal morphology (4) External morphology with secondary sex characteristics (5) Gender identity (psychological identity).

Sexual behaviour refers to venereal or procreative activity or a clear substitute for this and usually involves reversible physical changes. Such behaviour may be heterosexual, homosexual or narcissistic, any or all of which may be exhibited by the same individual.

Gender identity is the individual's inner sense or conviction of maleness or femaleness, is largely influenced by environmental factors and is said to be fixed early in life. A transsexualist has a disorder of gender identity and despite the full biological attributes of masculinity is convinced that he is or should be female or *vice versa.*

Gender role is manifest in behaviour as masculinity or femininity. An individual of stable gender identity may be more or less masculine or feminine (effeminate when attributed to a male).

Sexual behaviour, gender identity and gender role are usually assumed to be largely independent. There is however an alternative view that the three are interrelated and that the need within an individual to maintain harmony or to avoid dissonance results in changes in one area having repercussions likely to result in adaptive change in other areas. Thus a change to homosexual behaviour in circumstances which encouraged or facilitated effeminacy in gender role might result in gender uncertainty with pressure for change from male towards female gender identity.

In many religious traditions, including the Christian, any sexual union without procreation as its primary object was held to be immoral. Contemporary Christianity now recognizes sexual union as having a dual role in procreation and in cementing the marital relationship though Churches differ in the degree of independence which they permit between these two factors. Even the Roman Catholic Church allows the avoidance of conception by what it terms 'natural' means (see *Humanae Vitae*).

Most societies have a wider but changing view of what is normal or acceptable. Changes in society, such as the availability of effective contraception and female emancipation, have resulted in an increasing separation between sexual pleasure and procreation and may result in an increasing acceptance of a wide range of sexual behaviour. Practice is to some extent defined by law with penal sanctions, but social convention is a much more powerful determinant of acceptable behaviour. Masturbation, although widespread as personal and private behaviour, has in the past been roundly condemned by church and society at large. Now despite a residuum of guilt the practice is regarded as universal and harmless.

Oral-genital sex has been regarded with near universal revulsion and categorized by many as deviant practice. Recent gourmet guides to sexual behaviour, handbooks, films and lectures with entirely praiseworthy aims in terms of public education, recommend oral sex as a pleasurable, healthy and normal practice. The widespread current emphasis upon the pleasures of sexuality may increase the pressure for acceptance of a range of practices which are currently regarded as deviant.

Normal sexual behaviour may be defined as any form of sexual activity between two adults which is acceptable to both and does not involve degradation or exploitation, or – if performed otherwise than in private – public affront.

Deviant sexuality would then be defined as any form of sexual expression in which the exclusive practice of the particular behaviour was preferred to or regarded as an essential concomitant to normal sexual activity.

The following is an arbitrary classification of sexual perversions or deviations and related sexual abnormalities based entirely upon overt behaviour and carrying no implications for aetiology.

1. *Not requiring a human partner*
   Substituting objects (fetishism) may involve a part of another individual, e.g. breasts, ankles, buttocks, or more commonly inanimate objects such as clothing, hair, excreta. Fetishism appears to be virtually confined to the male and most commonly involves items of the clothing of the opposite sex.
   Substituting an animal (bestiality)
   Making do with the self (narcissism) with or without transvestism, mirrors etc.
2. *Not requiring a willing partner* (stealing or forcing a sexual experience)
   Vicarious enjoyment of others' sexual behaviour ('peeping tom', troilism*)
   Voyeurism*
   Exhibitionism*
   Frotteurism*
   Rape
   Use of insensible or dead partner (necrophilia).
3. *Requiring a willing partner* (homo or heterosexual)
   i) orgasm without genital copulation; oral-genital contact (fellatio* or cunnilingus*) anal intercourse, mutual masturbation, etc.
   ii) requiring unusual conditions before satisfaction is attainable.
     a). special sort of partner, for example of the same sex, prostitute, child, cripple etc.
     b). forbidden category of partner, for example, incest.
     c). special mental state of subject, for example, intoxicated, imagining another partner.
     d). special relationships with partner, for example, sadomasochistic.
     e). special consequences, for example, punishment, symptoms.

Hypersexuality is certainly deviant in a statistical sense and may cause distress to the affected individual and those about him, perhaps leading to perverted sexual practices as a means of securing relief. Transves-

---

* Troilism – the involvement of three individuals in simultaneous sexual congress.
* Voyeurism – the desire to observe other people or animals engaged in sexual activity.
* Exhibitionism – public genital exposure usually with intent to shock or alarm.
* Frotteurism – the practice of rubbing the genitalia against another person – often undertaken in crowded situations.
* Fellatio – insertion of the penis into the mouth of a partner.
* Cunnilingus – oral stimulation of the female genitalia.

tism* is frequently fetishistic in origin but some cases appear to be entirely devoid of an overt sexual element.

Transsexualism* is regarded as a disorder of gender identity rather than of sexual behaviour but the situation may be more complex than suggested by this formulation and associated deviant sexual activity is common.

The task and responsibilities of the physician in connection with sexual deviance are poorly defined and affected by individual attitudes and susceptibilities as well as by wider social pressures. Perhaps the most controversial issues are raised by the problems of treatment or intervention.

Many who request medical advice about deviant practices do so under pressure from a partner, relatives or friends, through fear of discovery or because of impending prosecution. In some cases the request for intervention may come from the courts or within the penal system and some offenders are presented with a 'treatment or else' proposition.

There can be no doubt of the appropriateness of a physician's involvement when a person presents himself with distressing symptoms directly related to the deviant sexual practice and requests alleviation. Some argue that the main task of the physician in this circumstance is to help the individual to adjust to his deviance without any attempt to treat or modify the deviant practice while others maintain that even such symptomatic treatment should be regarded as a poor substitute for changing the structure or attitudes of society to secure a reduction of the stigma or guilt associated with the practice.

Such views often imply that the deviant practice emerges or is exposed as a pre-formed, even pre-ordained, behaviour pattern rather than one which evolves and is modified by learning experiences. Nor is there at present any certainty of the consequences to society of modification of current social attitudes. A different view is that each pattern of behaviour must be assessed in terms of its likely effects upon the individual, upon those directly affected by his behaviour and upon society as a whole. Where the balance of evidence suggests that the practice is or may become harmful the physician has a responsibility for communicating the facts to the individual and suggesting possible interventions. The treatment or behaviour modification is often distorted by the ambivalent commitment of the majority of those who enter therapy and the sensitivity of the male sexual response and its shaping by phantasy. When treatment is initiated as an alternative to loss of freedom the issue of full and informed consent (q.v.) may be obscured.

* Transvestism – the desire to wear the clothing of the opposite sex.
* Transsexualism – the conviction that the individual's own sex or gender identity is at variance with his or her biological characteristics.

In some cases, for instance paedophilia* or genital exhibitionism, the individual may sincerely desire to change or avoid his practice yet be unable to resist the impulse in reality or in phantasy. Control may be secured by the use of an antiandrogen, a drug counteracting the effect of androgens (male sex hormones) which virtually suppresses sexual activity but may have a variety of undesirable side effects such as breast enlargement. If the offender is in prison and his release is conditional upon medical recommendation can he give full, informed and free consent to such treatment? (See *Forensic Psychiatry.*)

Where the others involved are victims, legal sanctions are often applied and the transgressor may accept the implied limitation of his freedom and accept treatment to ensure his conformity with the law. Where the others are sexual partners or relatives they must jointly consider the situation and reach informed decisions on possible treatment.

The effects of individual deviance upon the community are more problematic particularly where no breach of the existing law is involved. Does overt homosexual behaviour with the possibility of modelling, identification or other influence on indirect contacts constitute a risk to vulnerable or developing individuals who might be diverted from eventual maturation of heterosexual attitudes? Does publicly condoned transvestism or transsexuality increase the distress of those with gender uncertainty who with clear societal guidelines might avoid such difficulties?

Even if the problems associated with compulsion or coercion can be resolved there remain the physician's role as culture carrier or opinion modifier and the inevitability of the use of authority, based on professional knowledge and skill, to influence the individual's decision to seek or to accept intervention.

Transsexualism poses particularly difficult problems for the diagnosis is often made and the treatment prescribed by the patient himself. Since this treatment may involve, in the male, removal of the external genitalia, the prescription of potentially hazardous hormones and the construction of an artificial vagina the ethical problems are complicated by at least three practical issues: (1) is the required treatment the most appropriate means of dealing with the problem? (2) is the risk of death or injury acceptable? and (3) is it justifiable to utilize scarce medical and surgical resources in providing these procedures? These and many other questions in this field remain unanswered and some may be unanswerable. Although often couched in medical terms the debate and the ultimate solutions must extend outside the medical profession. Society must determine what is acceptable; yet it cannot compel practitioners to undertake procedures which they personally reject upon moral or medical grounds. (See also *Homosexuality; Sex Education; Sex Therapy.*)

---

* Paedophilia – a preference for children as sexual partners.

Bancroft J. *Deviant sexual behaviour: modification and assessment.* Oxford: Clarendon Press, 1974.

Catholic Truth Society. *Casti connubii.* London: CTS, 1930.

Scott PD. Definition, classification, prognosis and treatment. In: Rosen I, ed. *Pathology and treatment of sexual deviation.* Oxford: University Press, 1964.

Storr A. *Sexual deviation.* Harmondsworth: Penguin Books, 1964.

West DJ. *Homosexuality.* Harmondsworth: Penguin Books, 1960.

Sydney Brandon

Sexually Transmitted Disease. Discussion of the sexually transmitted diseases and the patients who suffer from them frequently provokes an emotional response which is often of a disapproving and condemnatory nature. Patients sometimes feel that there is a moral stigma related to their attendance at a specialist clinic and the attitudes of some doctors and nurses may reinforce this impression. Despite more liberal outlooks in recent years, this group of diseases is one in which it is difficult to achieve a dispassionate, informed and scientific approach.

Extra special confidentiality is assured for patients by the National Health Service (Venereal Disease) Regulations of 1948. No information about a patient should be given to a third party without the written consent of the patient and the hospital notes should be kept in a specially secure area. Some patients, especially girls, may be under the legal age of consent, namely 16. It is the usual practice to examine them, take tests and treat without asking for parental consent. Whether the mother should be informed if the girl is found to be infected is debatable. Some argue that it is wrong to do this without the agreement of the girl herself, while others believe that enlisting the aid of the parents is vitally important in the proper care of the patient.

In the past a double standard of morality has prevailed in sexual matters. It implied that men had premarital sex with girls who were often their social inferiors or with prostitutes, whereas women were not usually expected to have had premarital sexual experience. This double standard was carried over into medicine and is illustrated by the fact that a man with gonorrhoea will always be told the exact diagnosis but a married woman not infrequently has the diagnosis concealed from her, especially if she is known to have been infected by her husband. The changes in sexual attitudes and behaviour in recent years are wearing down the double standard of sexual morality.

Contact tracing is one of the most important methods of controlling the spread of sexually transmitted diseases. Persons found to be infected have a moral responsibility to see that their sexual contacts are examined medically. The moral stigma attached to a sexual infection is often related to the fact that it is caught as a result of an act of sexual infidelity. There is a transfer of guilt and shame from the sexual act to the disease itself and sometimes to the hospital clinic, causing difficulties in obtaining the attendance of the consort. The husband is usually told that all the facts of his case are confidential and will not be revealed to his wife. But he cannot be assured that his wife will not be informed of her own diagnosis as she is entitled to know the full diagnosis of her own case. Frequently it is obvious that she does not wish to know the details and in this case the information is not forced upon her.

State controlled prostitution is sometimes proposed as a method of controlling sexually transmitted diseases. Ethically the method is totally unacceptable as it would create a group of second-class citizens recruited by the State, who would be recorded in a special register, would practise their trade in special places, would require repeated examination and treatment and would be exposed to exploitation. The evidence from many areas of the world indicates that it is completely ineffective.

Recent research work has been orientated towards the possibility of immunization against the sexually transmitted diseases. Although there are immense technical problems a vaccine may eventually become available and its use would produce many difficult new ethical and moral problems (see *Confidentiality; Consent*).

Dunlop EMC. Some moral problems posed by the sexually transmitted diseases. *Br J Vener Dis* 1973; 49: 203.

Morton RS. *Sexual freedom and venereal disease*. London: Peter Owen, 1971.

Nicol CS. Venereal diseases. Moral standards and public opinion. *Br J Vener Dis* 1963; 39: 168.

R. D. Catterall

Shinto. Shinto is a religion unique to Japan. Its origin dates from prehistorical times, and it has continued till today. There are still a great many Shinto shrines throughout the country, where Japanese people go to worship the gods of Shintoism, as a custom and not necessarily by rational thinking, and to pray for fortune, e.g. to avoid disease or to seek its cure, or for success in passing school entrance examinations, etc.

We find relatively few references to medical ethics in Shinto literature. The oldest chronicles of Japan are *Kojiki* and *Nihonshoki*. In both of them we read that the predecessors of medical practitioners in Japan were 'Oonamuchi-no-mikoto' (more commonly called 'Okuninushi-no-mikoto') and 'Sukunahikona-no-mikoto'. They worked together to relieve people and domestic animals from diseases and injuries. In the *Kojiki* there is a well-known story of 'Inaba-no-Shirousagi' (that is, a white hare of Inaba Province). At first a god of the name 'Yasogami' treated the wounded hare very poorly, so that it became worse, but then 'Oonamuchi', who was Yasogami's younger brother, helped to cure the hare by applying powder of the cat tail (gama-no-ho). This story, though it belongs to myth, means mercy of the god to all creatures, even to animals. It coincides with 'Zihi' (benevolence) of Buddhism.

In Shintoism the cleanliness of body and soul is highly respected, and this must have great hygienic value. As 'Kegare', meaning defilement or dirtiness, is most hated by the gods, people have to clean or purify themselves before they pray. Bathing in clear water is the most effective. 'Harai', meaning cleaning of body and soul, is performed ceremonially by Shinto priests for people, often with various forms of incantations or charms.

During the Tokugawa era, when Japan was strictly closed to foreigners, except for a limited number of Dutchmen and Chinese (who were restricted to small areas in Nagasaki), there occurred a remarkable development in Shinto medicine. It was called 'Waho-igaku', meaning pure Japanese medicine, and was a counteraction against the then prevailing medical knowledge which was mostly of Chinese and partly of European origin. One prominent figure in this field was Atsutane Hirata (1776–1843). His contemporaries, Nobutomo Ban and Hotei Sato, were more or less connected with Hirata in their doctrines. Norinaga Motoori (1730–1801), a physician in Matsuzaka of Ise Province, and the most famous nationalist scholar, was the forerunner of them all.

Hirata's book *Shizu-no-iwaya* (1811) tells of the mythical origin and historical manners of Waho-igaku with passionate expressions, and it is especially notable that Hirata strongly insisted on medical ethics. At the beginning of this book Hirata says, as one of the five cardinal items, that 'physicians do not know Ido', that is, the 'way of medicine'. He continues, 'The medical occupation is very difficult to perform, and besides it is a very distasteful occupation, because it is concerned directly with the problem of life and death. Needless to say, all human beings want to continue their life. All physicians should think deeply of the solemnity of their task, study to their utmost ability the medical matters, and treat the patients. But in our country at the present time true physicians are very few in number, while most of them are thief-physicians, etc.' This was Hirata's criticism when he wrote the book. He practised medicine in Edo, but abandoned it a few years later; soon afterwards this book appeared in the style of his lectures, compiled by his students.

From the *Shizu-no-iwaya* we can see that Hirata had studied many medical books of Chinese origin, some from Buddhism and also some of European origin, especially anatomical books, translated by scholars from the Dutch. He laid importance on anatomical and physiological knowledge imported through Holland, but opposed dissection of the human body, which is not good in the holy country created by his 'true gods'. He considered some of the medical knowledge which entered Japan during its long history from foreign countries as useful, but regarded it as subsidiary to the Waho-igaku.

The word 'Ido' appears in mediaeval Japanese literature and for a long time it had the meaning of medical practice, including ethics to a small degree. Later, in the latter half of the Tokugawa era, largely we believe by the influence of Hirata's writings on Shinto medicine, the Ido has come to have a greater weight in medical ethics. The word 'Ijutsu' is now commonly used for medical practice; this shows an example of historic differentiation of a language.

Seitaro Higuchi
Teizo Ogawa

Shock Therapy. A popular term for the treatment used in psychiatry known as Electro-convulsive Therapy (ECT) (q.v.).

Situational Ethics. See *Christianity.*

Smoking. See *Tobacco Smoking.* The wider issue of dependence on drugs is dealt with under *Alcoholism* and *Drug Dependence.*

Social Pressures. Social pressures can be grouped under two heads – the demand by particular groups of the public for selective support for the provision of more or less of a particular kind of service, and demand for the use of a particular medical technique or course of action by physicians some of whom doubt the validity or the ethical propriety of the action desired. The health professions, including medicine, may have divided opinions and they, like the public, may be violently swayed towards one or the other side of the argument. Since physicians cannot and should not attempt to be autocratic in such situations they are often drawn into political discussions.

For nearly 30 years it has been an assumption of British society that service which is justifiable and practicable within our means will be publicly provided (see *Health Care Systems; National Health Service; State Health Services*). Since resources (q.v.) are finite and insufficient to meet all needs, much less all demands, social pressures can be generated on slight provocation. The NHS then has to meet or resist them as best it can, since the market situation of a self-rationing system does not exist. This may mean that a Health Authority's or even Parliament's assessment of public feeling may determine which developments of medical science are to be selectively supported from available resources. Since medicine is there to serve and not to control the public this is not unreasonable, so long as the clinician's freedom to decide whether he himself will use a particular method of treating a willing patient is not subject to outside non-professional control (see *Clinical Autonomy*). Even this assurance of individual clinical freedom has to be qualified now that medical science has become so complex that decisions must often depend on a consensus of professional and scientific views not always of medically qualified persons. Clinical freedom is a right of patients which should ensure that medical decisions are reached without intervention by some other authority; it must not be a capriciously used autocratic right of a physician, although it must protect him from being required to do what he believes to be wrong.

Social pressures have been used recently to block the fluoridation (q.v.) of water, a preventive measure which is endorsed by a large majority of medical and dental opinion. This is an example of a straightforward arousal of public emotional reaction preventing what those who can make a scientific appraisal believe to be in the public interest. There is an ethical argument about imposing a practice on everyone, but its weight should be impartially and unemotionally assessed.

On a different level social reaction has helped to clarify and simplify the medical policy on such procedures as the surgical treatment of spina bifida (q.v.) (and see *Congenital Malformations*). Social pressure has caused substantial NHS resources to be used for the provision of free contraceptive services including sterilization (q.v.) on social grounds at a time when this use of funds must mean that other, medically perceived, needs cannot be met. Substantial use of NHS funds for a cytological service for the detection of uterine cancer (see *Screening*) and for provision of intermittent haemodialysis (q.v.) in the management of end-stage renal failure were the result of public response to medical presentation of a new technique. They have been kept within bounds by a sensible balance between technical and social judgements without autocratic decision on either hand, whereas some other countries have pushed both services beyond the limits the best allocation of resources would suggest. This kind of decision requires give and take between 'medical' and 'lay' opinion, including the other health professions comprised in the term 'medical'. In general such mutual tolerance does obtain, as for instance in the acceptance of a neutral attitude towards the use of influenza vaccines the value of which is not yet proved.

Social pressures for redistribution of services are less reliable because judgements on such questions as the effectiveness of small local hospitals become clouded by emotional and historical associations which are not helped by conflicting medical opinions. But medical preference for 'acute' services as opposed to long-stay care cannot override public wishes (see *Hospitals*). A public authority may face pressure for expansion of a particular service, for example family planning in Britain or treatment of end-stage renal failure in the USA, and yield to something which depletes funds for other needs. Public pressure may also force Parliamentary action through private members' bills as in the Abortion Act, in requiring access for the handicapped to buildings or the wearing of crash helmets by motor cyclists. Equally pressure may lead to the withdrawal of health promoting legislation, as in some States in the USA where seat belt legislation has been withdrawn despite proven benefit.

As indicated above, social pressure should never influence a physician to use a technique or method he thinks wrong or unethical. We are still faced by controversy about termination of pregnancy despite a reported medical majority view in favour of the more liberal approach allowed by the present Act. Yet no gynaecologist who has ethical objections should be under compulsion to terminate pregnancies – nor any other health professional to assist (see *Abortion*). But social pressure which succeeded in reversing a recent decision to sterilize a child is understandable and acceptable (see *Sterilization*). The argument about induction of labour on social grounds (see *Childbirth, Intervention in*) presents the picture in reverse and reflects unwillingness on the part of some mothers to allow the medical profession to adopt measures it may wish to use for the sake of convenience. The problem is likely to be solved by compromise, but not at the expense of a mother's personal choice.

The management of spina bifida brings social pressures directly on the individual doctor – sometimes for, sometimes against intervention – and can lead to overriding decisions by the Courts for or against the medical view. The recent protracted legal wrangle in the USA over continuation of life-support systems for a young woman in coma for many months[1] is a dilemma not yet encountered here because similar problems have been solved by agreement. Yet such concerns have arisen and are important factors in our failure to secure the use of sufficient cadaver organs for transplant (see *Tissue Transplant*). The individual physician caught in such a dilemma can consult his professional colleagues and must have open dealings with relatives.

Social pressures on decisions about health provision are inevitable in the NHS as in any other pattern of health service, from the Tanzanian health programme with minimal resources to the predominantly market system of the USA. The NHS needs to promote better understanding by the public of the aims and attainable goals of the health professions, and by those professions of public aspirations in the health field. Non-political dialogue is essential and the Community Health Council is the place for it (see *Health Councils*). The pressures are different in a market economy such as that of the USA or where, as in West Germany, an insurance system controls payments to physicians. Formal assessment systems such as the American PSRO may be required or a professional association, as in Germany, may scrutinise claims. A fee per service system of payment always imports more detailed scrutiny of claims and therefore more documentation, as notably in Canada. (See *Quality Assurance*.)

Social Workers

1. Kennedy I. The Karen Quinlan case. *J Med Ethics* 1976; 2: 3–7.

George Godber

Social Workers. Activities in which social workers are involved and the skills demanded of them cover a wide range. Their training is undertaken as part of higher education and varies in content in different countries. Social workers may be employed in the social welfare services of central and local government (including hospitals); as probation officers; in residential and day centres, e.g. for children, elderly or disabled people or offenders; in school welfare and child guidance work; in non-statutory bodies, local or national, formal or informal, for assisting families under stress or for helping mutual aid groups in deprived areas. In some European and Asian countries social workers are based on industry.

In large multi-service organizations for welfare, such as local government authorities, and especially in countries which combine the social security system with personal social services, social work tasks need to be distinguished from other activities, e.g. the provision of home helps or police court liaison. Just as doctors do not perform all tasks in a health service, so social workers have specific roles and functions which require definition. These may, for example, include responsibility in cases of major changes in the life styles of clients, often with diminution of liberty. The allocation of such tasks within a complex service for human problems will be difficult and sometimes irrational; it will be influenced sometimes by basic principles and at other times by expediency; it will be subject to national variation and constant evolution.

Public services for health, housing, education and welfare have many common and inseparable interests, and require organizational change from time to time. Whatever the national and regional structure, it is important that the welfare service, including the social workers, should be able to relate freely to the other services both in individual cases and in broader matters of social policy.

Social work ethics, like medical ethics, originate outside the public services in which they are practised and which they often influence. The aims of social work are to enhance individual functioning and to promote community welfare. Roots spring partly from social reform movements, partly from associations with medicine. Social work education is strongly influenced by psychology, sociology, and social policy and administration; and only less so by philosophy, law, medicine, economics and history. To its mainly Western, liberal, Christian and capitalist traditions, social work adds influence from Marxism, existentialism and somewhat from Zen Buddhism.

Contemporary turmoils in the social sciences over their own values, and the values which other bodies put upon them, assail social work.

The modern development of social services into politically significant institutions, together with world-wide economic dislocation and the continuing ethical and political debates in Western societies about their own nature and prospects, expose social workers, like other professionals, to fundamental ethical conflicts and uncertainties.

Social work ethics have hitherto been expressed in terms of social casework, but many think that this method is now over-narrowly based and possibly over-influenced by assumptions such as the supremacy of the family and of the individual, and by unquestioning attitudes to education and work. There is, however, no agreement on alternative statements of values and modern views expressed have been controversial, self-conscious and diverse. Social workers' authority and power are considered to derive partly from the law, partly from professional knowledge and skill, and above all from the readiness of clients to invest social workers with authority to help them. The persistence of poverty and the difficulties of ensuring that those who need assistance obtain it bring the boundaries between social workers and politicians very close together. Many social workers are conscious of the opposing arguments (1) that social work is an instrument of social control designed to protect the *status quo* against change, and (2) that it undermines traditional social values by its softness, permissiveness and radical influence on public morality and the redistribution of resources; they would consider it consistent with their goals to contribute in part to social change and in part to social control.

The dominant belief of social work is in the value of a human being *per se* – not just in the value of life itself but of a person capable both of some degree of self-determination and of functioning as a member of groups in society. The emphasis on individual rather than communal values is typically Western, and may require correction. The principle contains a challenge: which individuals or which groups do social workers in fact devalue, and why?

There follows a belief in the value of self-determination for the client or client group (client or consumer – for relationships, roles and functions are open to debate); people's considered choices are seen as likely to be the right ones for them. To try to increase choices in solving problems, to make clients more aware about choices, and to try to reduce inner and outer pressures which may inhibit such choices, are long-standing aims of social workers, requiring recognition of social, economic, physical and intra-personal opportunities and limitations. The tendency is towards greater openness with clients about processes, power, possible conflicts and consequences. The results of greater power for clients (e.g. for a residents' committee in a hostel) can be surprising to a bureaucratic organization or to a social worker, as people may make unexpected choices. Their own skill in limiting choices makes traps and conflicts for social workers.

Interprofessional collaboration brings together different traditions of caring. Social workers often reinforce the doctor's leaning towards greater openness with patients, believing that it may reduce stress but often requires emotional and practical support to both patients and medical workers, who can be trusted to signal their readiness or reservations to a perceptive collaborator.

The confidentiality of clients' affairs, long regarded as essential, can be threatened by the growing complexity and size of organizations and the needs of interprofessional co-operation. Social workers believe that they should keep clients informed of events and of those who are involved in handling them at times when to seek clients' permission to share information would be to imply a measure of choice which in reality is not available.

Finally there is ethical concern about the nature of caring organizations, and anxiety that large hierarchical and bureaucratic welfare institutions may not meet the needs of clients directly, flexibly and economically and with openness to public opinion. Alternative methods are being sought and preferences expressed for neighbourhood semi-autonomy and consumer participation. Likewise, social workers are in conflict about 'professionalism' and the choices between maintaining standards of practice and furthering knowledge on the one hand, and undue self-protection on the other. (See also *Interprofessional Relationships; Teamwork.*)

Bartlett H. *The common base of social work practice*. Washington DC: National Association of Social Workers, 1970.

BASW. *A code of ethics for social workers*. Birmingham: British Association of Social Workers, 1975.

CCETSW. *Values in social work*. Social work curriculum study. CCETSW Paper 13. London: Central Council for Education and Training in Social Work.

Younghusband E. *Social work and social values*. London: Allen and Unwin, 1967.

Jean M. Snelling

Socialized Medicine. See *Health Care Systems; National Health Service; Private Patients; State Health Services.*

Society for Health and Human Values. The Society for Health and Human Values is a professional association whose primary objective is to encourage and promote informed concern for human values as an essential, explicit dimension of education for the health professions. To accomplish this objective, the Society seeks, through a variety of endeavours, to facilitate communication and cooperation among the professionals from diverse principles who share such an objective and to support critical and scholarly efforts to develop knowledge, concepts and programmes dealing with the relation of human values to education for the health professions.

The Society was formally organized in 1969. Members are primarily educators who are involved in teaching or administration of health professional schools and teachers in various of the humanities disciplines who are also involved in contemporary problems in medicine.

The Society holds its Annual Meeting and Program in conjunction with the Annual Meeting of the Association of American Medical Colleges. Through its Institute on Human Values in Medicine it provides resource services to medical and health science schools to assist in curriculum development in human values studies and also promotes the dialogue between medicine and the humanities disciplines. It also produces various publications, including the Reports of the Institute, and sponsors the *Journal of Medicine and Philosophy*.

The address of the Society for Health and Human Values is 925 Chestnut Street, 6th floor, Philadelphia, PA 19107 USA.

Ronald W. McNeur

Society for the Study of Medical Ethics. An independent non-partisan body which promotes the multidisciplinary study of issues raised by the practice of medicine. It publishes quarterly the *Journal of Medical Ethics* (q.v.).

The Society was founded in 1972 as a development of the London Medical Group, which, as a student organization, has, since 1963, sponsored in the twelve London teaching hospitals the study of issues raised by the practice of medicine which concern other disciplines, such as the law, moral philosophy, moral theology, and the social sciences. Since 1967 similar independent groups have been formed in Edinburgh, Newcastle, Sheffield, Glasgow, Bristol, Birmingham, Manchester, Liverpool, Cardiff, Aberdeen, Dundee, Southampton, Oxford, Cambridge and Leicester. Through these groups, which the Society has inaugurated, lectures and symposia are arranged in a majority of the British medical schools and university teaching hospitals. Addressed primarily to medical students and nurses they are open to others professionally interested. The Edinburgh Medical Group has, with external funding, appointed in conjunction with the University of Edinburgh, research fellows in medical ethics and reports have been published on the *Dilemma of Dying* and the *Ethics of Resource Allocation in Health Care*. The Society has initiated a study of the Ethics of Clinical Research Investigations on Children. Regional conferences are sponsored by the Society, in conjunction with the Medical Groups, and details are given in the *Journal of Medical Ethics*.

Address: Tavistock House North, Tavistock Square, London WC1H 9LG.

Edward Shotter

Spina Bifida. Spina bifida is a condition in which there is failure of fusion of the arch of bone which normally encloses and protects the spinal cord. The severity of the condition varies from a simple bony defect with no nerve involvement (spina bifida occulta) frequently detected only by accident, through the relatively rare meningocele, in which there is protrusion of fluid-filled membranes forming a lump on the back, to myelomeningocele with involvement of the spinal cord, which is often split open and exposed on the surface. The extent of the neurological problem even in myelomeningocele varies from isolated urinary incontinence to total lower limb paralysis and weakness of the lower abdominal muscles. The most severely affected children face a permanent wheel chair life with bladder incontinence and problems with bowel control. Three quarters of the children with myelomengingoceles also develop progressive hydrocephalus (abnormal accumulation of fluid in the brain, causing enlargement of the head).

This range of disability has complicated discussions on management. Those with only a bony defect require no treatment, and meningoceles should be repaired; but the management of the baby with a myelomeningocele requires more consideration.

Before 1956 repair of the more severe back defects was pointless since the majority of the babies developed and died of hydrocephalus. The invention of a constant opening pressure non-return valve by Holter and Heyer[1] led to the introduction of programmes for early repair. By the late sixties it was evident that, with immediate (within 24 hours of birth) repair of the back and control of the hydrocephalus by a valve,[2] the survival rate of these babies at age one year had been increased from 10% to 90%.

It was also clear that many of these survivors were severely crippled, despite having been through many operations, and faced a life punctuated by further operations. In the most severe cases it could be fairly said that intensive treatment rather than saving life had only prolonged the process of dying. Careful review of the extent of the disability at birth[3] suggested that those babies destined to be severely handicapped could be identified at birth. A policy of selection for operative treatment has now become fairly general. Criteria for deciding against early operation are:

1. Severe paralysis, 2. severe hydrocephalus, 3. the presence of other major birth defects or brain damage, and 4. severe spinal deformity. Since the introduction of these criteria there has been a wide variation in the reported progress of babies from uniform early deaths, through deaths of all within 9 months, to a significant percentage of survivors.[4,5]

Considerable controversy has also arisen over the treatment given in some centres of heavy sedation and feeding only on demand.

If those babies considered unsuitable for early operation are fed in the normal way[6] they do not appear to suffer and in 20 to 30 per cent skin grows over the back defect. Most of these survivors develop hydrocephalus. As death from hydrocephalus is slow and the constantly enlarging head is a burden to the baby and very upsetting to those caring for him, it seems reasonable to control this by insertion of a valve drainage system. The back defect can be repaired later as a cosmetic procedure.

These children can then be brought into the full treatment regime without harm from the early decision not to operate. The leg paralysis was complete at birth and the brain has been protected by the valve.

It is therefore possible to approach the child's parents with a relatively unemotional decision. Preservation of function, not life or death, is the aim of early operation. Some babies die after early operation, and some live without. All babies and their parents can be taken into a total care régime in which early operation is advised for only 30 to 40 per cent, and not undertaken for the remainder. At all stages in the subsequent treatment the benefits of any operation must be assessed and, as at birth, there will be occasions where an operation will not offer any reasonable improvement and should not be performed. The parents are consulted and given psychological and social support throughout.

Survival into adolescence brings problems of depression and obesity as these children contemplate their future with their physical and mental handicaps affecting their prospects for employment and sexual fulfilment. The risk of death from valve complications, as a result of blockage or infection of the system, persists throughout life. Renal failure becomes an increasing problem and multiple bone and joint operations are often required to straighten deformities of the legs and spine. The most severe spinal deformities can lead to death from difficulties with breathing. Problems arising from the long-term care of these patients in society are discussed elsewhere (see *Handicapped, Duties to*).

The search for the causes of these severe anomalies has so far failed to uncover more than genetic and general poor environmental factors.[7] Screening programmes with abortion of affected babies at 16–18 weeks have begun to reduce the number of these tragic births. A specimen of amniotic fluid is taken by amniocentesis (q.v.) from those mothers found to have raised serum fetoprotein levels or to have given birth previously to children with spina bifida or anencephaly (congenital absence of the brain and skull, a condition incompatible with life). The fetal abnormality can be confirmed before abortion by an ultrasound examination. (See also *Amniocentesis; Congenital Malformations*.)

1. Pudenz RH, Russell FE, Hurd AH, Shelden CH. Ventriculoauriculostomy. A technique for shunting cerebrospinal fluid into the right auricle. *J. Neurosurg.* 1957; 14: 171.
2. Sharrard WJW, Zachary RB, Lorber J, Bruce AM. A controlled trial of immediate and delayed closure of Spina Bifida Cystica. *Arch Dis Child* 1963; 38: 18–22.

3. Lorber J. Results of treatment of myelomeningocele: an analysis of 524 unselected cases, with special reference to possible selection for treatment. *Dev Med Child Neurol* 1971: 13: 279.

4. Lorber J. Early results of selective treatment of Spina Bifida Cystica. *Br Med J* 1973; 4: 201–4.

5. Robards MF, Thomas GG and Rosenbloom L. Survival of infants with unoperated myeloceles. *Br Med J* 1975; 4:12.

6. Habgood JS, Arthur HR, Burrow JM *et al.* Ethics of selective treatment of Spinda Bifida. *Lancet* 1975; 1: 85–8.

7. Campbell S, Pryse-Davies J, Coltart TM, Seller MJ, Singer JD. Ultrasound in the diagnosis of Spina Bifida. *Lancet* 1975 1: 1065–8.

Carter CO. Clues to the aetiology of neural tube malformations. *Dev Med Child Neurol* 1974; 16: 3.

Zachary RB. Life with Spina Bifida. *Br Med J*; 1977, 2: 1460–1462.

J. A. S. Dickson

Spiritual Healing. The term is commonly used to assert the importance, in healing, of transcendent factors not accessible to the normal disciplines of physical and psychological medicine. Less commonly it refers to healing of the soul with relief of physical symptoms as a possible bonus. Rarely is it intended to suggest that scientific medicine ignores spiritual considerations. In many traditional African societies disease is attributed to the complementary action of 'natural causes' and of a spiritual agency directing these causes against a particular individual. Cure requires that both the natural causes be treated with traditional remedies and the spiritual agency be reconciled, often by different practitioners.[1,2] In contemporary Western cultures the interest in spiritual healing has recently increased despite the expansion of science-based health services. Proponents of spiritual healing may be broadly grouped on a continuum as (1) those who, in common with African cultures (see *African Medicine*), see spiritual treatment as complementary to medical treatment and wish for co-operation between doctors and spiritual healers at every point; (2) those for whom scientific medicine is useless or forbidden for religious reasons; and (3) those who regard medical and spiritual diagnoses as additive and seek medical help to exclude physical and psychological factors before resorting to spiritual methods. For Christian Scientists (see *Christian Science*), for example, sickness is a state of mind to be cured by right belief, while Jehovah's Witnesses oppose blood transfusion (q.v.) on alleged biblical grounds.

The power to heal spiritually may be regarded as a normal function of a religious body. Healing services, which may, but do not necessarily, include exorcism (q.v.) or laying on of hands, are then held as a special extension of prayers for the sick which occur at all services. Very large numbers of people attend particular places of pilgrimage in many parts of the world where such services are held, the most famous being Lourdes. Other examples are to be found in the older forms of Pentecostalism, the contemporary Christian Movement[4] and many of the new healing churches in Africa. On the other hand, healing power may be attributed primarily to individuals. It may be a gift from God or derived from spirits, as for instance with Spiritualism[5]. Or it may be claimed by individuals without any overt religious belief.

The doctor should respect, although he may not share, the religious beliefs of his patients. Spiritual healing, whatever its basis, may exert a beneficial influence on the patient's emotional state, e.g. by relieving anxiety or guilt, and in its way contribute to recovery or the relief of symptoms. It does not usually interfere with or preclude medical treatment. However, the patient has the right to refuse medical treatment on religious, as on other, grounds. The doctor's duty is to point out as clearly as he can what the consequences of refusal might be, and he would be prudent to record such advice in his case notes. He may find himself in the dilemma of not providing essential treatment or having to administer treatment without consent (q.v.). The doctor might be justified in the latter course if the patient's withholding of consent is shown to be invalid by reason of unsoundness of mind. In these circumstances he would be wise to consult a near relative or a member of the patient's church as well as professional colleagues.

The theoretical problems arising out of the practice of spiritual healing are basically the same as those discussed under exorcism (q.v.). It may frequently be difficult, in both theory and practice, to distinguish between the spiritual and the psychological. (The word *psyche*, from which 'psychological' is derived, is used to describe putative forces both within and without bodily persons.) What appears to a believer to be spiritual healing may by a non-believer be either termed 'spontaneous recovery' or 'recession'[2] or attributed to psychological processes.

1. Asuni T. Death of a child in Nigeria. In: Anthony EJ, ed. *The child in his family.* New York: Wiley, 1973.
2. Evans-Pritchard EE. *Witchcraft, oracles and magic among the Azande.* Oxford: Clarendon Press, 1937.
3. *Divine healing and co-operation between doctors and clergy.* London: British Medical Association, 1956.
4. MacNutt F. *Healing.* Notre Dame: Ave Maria Press, 1974.
5. Skultans V. *Intimacy and ritual: a study of spiritualism, mediums and groups.* London: Routledge and Kegan Paul, 1974.

D. Russell Davis
F. B. Welbourn

Sport, Intersex in. See *Intersex.*

Sport, The Problem of Drugs in. Drugs have been misused in sport for many centuries. In the past few decades, the pressure on competitors to be successful has increased as more potent drugs have been developed and thus the misuse of drugs in sport had assumed serious proportions before international action was taken. From 1960, informed opinion was mobilized, and in 1965 France and Belgium introduced anti-doping laws, while the new International Olympic Committee Medical Commission was established in 1967 with dope control as one of its terms of reference. The pressure for action increased as deaths in sport occurred as a result of drug misuse.

The Council of Europe in 1963 defined doping in sport as 'the administering or use of substances in any form alien to the body, of physiological substances in abnormal amounts and with abnormal methods by healthy persons with the exclusive aims of obtaining an artificial and unfair increase of performance in competition. Furthermore, various psychological measures to increase performance in sport must be regarded as doping'. However, this definition involves intent and ignores the practical methods of control and the identification of the person with the intent, namely competitor, physician or coach. Many competitors will take products given to them by the physician or coach without knowledge of the contents or the true purpose of the administration.

Why should certain drugs be classed as doping agents? Some answer, 'because their use contravenes the basic characteristics of sport – the matching of the natural capabilities of the participants'. However, many have a more pragmatic approach: (a) competition should involve competitors not pharmacologists and physicians, (b) competitors should not be used as guinea-pigs, (c) the use of some drugs can cause aggression and loss of judgement – hazards to other competitors, spectators and officials, (d) the danger of bad example to young people, (e) the danger of drug dependence. These seem adequate arguments to use against those who stress that the attempt to control the misuse of drugs in sport is an undue restriction of the rights of the individual to use anything to improve performance so long as he understands the risks. How can he understand the risk if he is unaware of the contents of the agents used? Sometimes the competitors deliberately use a 'doping agent' but often others are involved in the administration.

However, medication may be required for competitors at sporting events. Where shall the line be drawn between such medication and doping? The policy of the IOC Medical Commission in this difficult field is (a) to prevent the use of those drugs in sport which constitute dangers when used as doping agents, (b) to prevent drug abuse with the minimum of interference with the therapeutic use of drugs, (c) to ban only those drugs for which suitable analytical methods could be devised to detect the compounds unequivocally in urine (or blood) samples, (d) to ban classes of drugs based upon the pharmacological actions of members of the classes but not to attempt to produce a complete list of banned drugs.

In pursuance of the policy the following list of banned *classes* of doping agents was approved for the 1972 Olympic Games: (a) psychomotor stimulant drugs, e.g. amphetamine etc. (b) sympathomimetic amines e.g. ephedrine etc. (c) miscellaneous central nervous system stimulants e.g. nikethamide, strychnine etc. (d) narcotic analgesics e.g. morphine etc. In 1975, anabolic steroids were added to the classes. In all classes, the words 'and related compounds' were included after a variety of examples of each class. This is essential because otherwise compounds not intended as drugs but with the desired pharmacological effect would be used to circumvent the control based upon a comprehensive list of drugs.

The sympathomimetic amine class represents a special problem because of the use of some of the compounds of this class to treat colds and allergies. If, however, ephedrine were allowed as medication, in some sports a large dose would be used immediately to produce a stimulant effect. The policy is now to allow certain *specified* compounds to treat these problems so long as notification is made by a physician of their proposed use in a specified competitor.

Local anaesthetics are sometimes misused in sport to allow competition after injury; serious irreparable damage sometimes results. However, in most sports, their use is allowed by injection provided declaration of the use is made at the time of injection.

The control of doping in sport is based upon the unequivocal identification of the presence of a drug of one of the banned classes in a competitor but not the amount. The increasing sensitivity of tests presents a problem for medication by physicians using slowly eliminated drugs belonging to the banned classes, and it is advisable that such drugs should not be used within a week of competition.

Can the elaborate and costly dope control in sport be justified? Without this there would be an increasing number of deaths at international events. Unfortunately many young competitors at low levels of sport have become involved in drugs in sport. Today our control procedures are essential if young people are to be protected against themselves and against those who would risk damaging them by drug misuse. The emphasis in doping control at sporting events is on preventing problems rather than taking punitive measures.

In 1976, at the Winter Olympics in Innsbruck, action was taken against the physician who administered the drug as well as the competitor who took the drug belonging to one of the banned classes.

The problem of control of misuse of drugs in sport will be a continuing war rather than a final battle as new misuses are controlled with countermeasures.

Beckett AH. The work of the Medical Commission. In: *The Olympic*

Games. Killanin, Lord, Rodda J, eds. London: Barrie and Jenkins, 1976: 166–70.

International Olympic Committee Medical Commission. *Doping*. Lausanne: IOC, 1972.

Williams MH. *Drugs and athletic performance*. Springfield: Charles C. Thomas, 1974.

Arnold H. Beckett

State Health Services. The interest of the state in health services is part of its concern for the social well-being of the population. The individual can function best neither as a member of his family nor of his social or employment group if he is handicapped by disease or the result of injury. If his social or economic effectiveness is reduced he or his family may become dependent upon the rest of his social group and thus limit their enjoyment of the resources available to them.

Health services can only be developed to the level now practicable if they are supported (as in most countries only the state can support them) in such a way as to provide the costly central services while ensuring the general availability of simple primary care for prevention and treatment. Where this generalization of services has been accepted as a national obligation as in Eastern Europe, Scandinavia, Britain and New Zealand, coherent systems for health care are provided by government. Some countries recognize the need, but have ideological resistance to a state-ordered system in which it is feared that personal initiative of patients or health professionals will be hampered by an integrated health care system (q.v.); they use various devices to prevent financial barriers to care. In general the integrated systems rely mainly on payment by salary, capitation and often small part payments by patients for medical services. The rest pay established doctors on some fee per service system. Developing countries tend to have a simple level of local services by various kinds of medical, midwifery or nursing aides backed by such sophisticated secondary and tertiary level services as they can afford.

Many countries have such limited systems as to give little more than remote emergency support or infrequent visitation. Often a large part of the professional and financial resources is concentrated in the main urban centres and is hardly available at all to rural areas. The People's Republic of China (PRC) and the Republic of Tanzania are examples of countries in which government control has overridden professionals' desire to concentrate at expensively equipped centres and forced the diffusion of health care to rural areas. People have a right to health and these countries are trying to use their resources to meet it (see *Chinese Medicine*). Some state intervention in the provision of health services is now universal and is even more necessary in countries with the least resources than in those with the highest sophistication of health care. In all systems there may be large gaps in service, particularly for rural populations and some occupational groups may receive special preference.

Accounts of different services are too numerous to be listed. Each country necessarily provides for its people in its own idiom and within a framework largely determined by its own central and local government structure and historical development. Development is evolutionary, and revolutionary change occurs only as a part of social and political revolution as in the USSR in 1917, Eastern Europe in 1945 and the PRC in 1947. The ideal framework for health may be seriously distorted to fit a local government pattern derived from different considerations, as in England in 1974. Or it may be that the system devised for other local government as in the rayon – oblast – republic – union sequence of the USSR or the commune – region – province – republic sequence of the PRC is well fitted to health organization. Whatever the governmental organization, there are certain levels at which functions must be fulfilled for purely health reasons and the way in which that is arranged varies according to the idiom of the country concerned.

Over a hundred years ago nearly all personal health care was private, but state intervention had begun in the wealthier countries to control the worst pollutions of the physical environment. Denmark had, and Germany was about to have, the earliest prepayment schemes for medical care. Facilities for segregation of patients supposedly dangerous because of infection or mental disturbance were appearing, but to protect the public rather than the sick. Insurance systems developed most rapidly in continental Europe and were so powerful and effective that in such countries as France and West Germany they are still the main financial instruments. They came later to Britain, Australia and North America and have now become a main instrument under national supervision in Canada and Australia; Britain and New Zealand have relied more upon tax funding, governmental control and part-salaried rather than fee per service payment of physicians. The USA has used voluntary insurance systems without, as yet, effective control of health care delivery, and supported by such categorical centrally financed programmes as for the old, the poor or those with renal failure (see *Haemodialysis*). Some South American countries have had industry-based insurance systems largely without extension to their big rural populations. China has developed an integrated system available free or at minimum charge to workers, relying heavily on the commune and modestly trained workers from it.

Many developing countries are still struggling to extend their services beyond their main population centres and are burdened with a top-heavy organization of acute hospitals which drain their limited resources (see *Hospitals*). Yet they must have a cadre of fully trained physicians and are only likely to retain enough if most are at least trained within the region. It is not possible to manage health services to best advantage without a minimum of supporting specialized medical resources. But it is disastrous misuse of limited resources (q.v.) to concentrate them upon the provision of highly specialized medicine without general provision of the best quality of care available for the population within the resource constraints.

Visitors to various countries and individuals who have worked in them have written accounts of different systems or of parts of those systems. Various publications of WHO[1,2] and of the Fogarty International Centre in Bethesda, USA[3], provide details of other countries' service. The *Lancet/NPHT* publication *Health Service Prospects*[4] collected a number of short accounts. The National Health Service in the UK has been described by many people in terms ranging from the ecstatic to the profoundly depressed. Many countries have produced more or less objective development plans or forecasts. Perhaps the most interesting commentaries concern outcome rather than structure, as typified by those of Lalonde[5] (Canada) and Hetzel[6] (Australia). The position is never static and most compendia at one time will be found to be sadly out of date. An account of many countries is provided by Stephen.[7]

Britain accepted the right of all to health care and the duty of the state to provide it in the 1946 National Health Services Acts. This was no more than the culmination of a trend through nearly a century, moving on from responsibility for the indigent and for public safety from those sick of infectious or mental illness to acceptance of a duty to all. There is no serious challenge to this principle in Britain today; the argument is about method. The sophistication of medicine has long since made it impossible for all conceivable forms of medical and allied care to be fully available to everyone. Such an open-ended commitment could divert professional attention to procedures offering ever-diminishing returns for the few, instead of applying the same effort to securing greater returns from simpler service to more people. Moreover, health care is not simply medical care, but requires the participation of many others including nurses, midwives, members of the professions associated with medicine, scientists, technicians, social workers and domestic helpers. Within medicine, increasing specialization results in sharing of responsibility (see *Interprofessional Relationships; Teamwork*).

The National Health Service (NHS) (q.v.) depends mainly upon the development of services at a district level shared between community care, based on group medical practice in which nurses and others take part, and institutional supporting care provided by an even more complex professional and technical group. In the treatment of individuals physicians must therefore face choices which are affected by the needs of other patients for a share of the same facilities. Most care can be compounded in different proportions from the same range of professional contributions without disadvantage to the outcome. The traditional concern for the individual must be effected by an equal concern for others, a fact which complicates the ethical judgement of the practitioner. There is also a dual responsibility: to the patient, to provide the service best for him, and to the state as the source of funds which must not be squandered on the individual at the expense of other participating professionals and their individual patients. This ends with a collective medical judgement on clinical policies guiding the choice of the individual clinician. This could be considered as an invasion of clinical freedom were it not of the same kind as the choice to be made where complex alternatives present themselves and individual judgement without guidance may too often be at fault (see *Resources*).

In modern medicine specialization is inevitable and shared responsibility is its sequel. The patient has a right to enjoy his chosen adviser's freedom of choice on his behalf, but society has the right to expect that freedom to be exercised without trespass on the interests of its other members in the share of its resources which they need. The decisions must be made on a balanced appraisal of needs and not demands. The doctor's contract with the state must leave him free to exercise clinical choice without imposed constraints upon his judgement. His side of the contract is the same as that with the patient – that he exercise due care. In hospital practice appointment of doctors is by selection, which involves the judgement that the individual appointed has the requisite skills, and it becomes terminable if at some later time this judgement is proved wrong. So far as the patient is concerned the doctor has the same independent responsibility to exercise all necessary care and skill and is answerable at law independently of his employer if the patient suffers by his failure to do so. (See *Competence to Practise; Malpractice; Negligence*.)

The nature of a service's contract with the participating doctor can affect the service provided. This is well seen where out-patient consultations with specialists take place away from hospitals in which supporting services make for greater efficiency. In particular, commercial pathology services in New Zealand or Australia may become so lucrative as to endanger the service in and to hospitals. The commercial gains from a 'nursing home' type of provision for the elderly sick may make the development of modern geriatric services difficult or impossible in the USA or Australia. A fee per service arrangement may be deliberately slanted by the employing authority so as to concentrate professional effort in a particular clinical field on that to which the authority attaches higher priority. This could be seen in the NHS in the differential fees favouring conservative dentistry or the limitation of fees for cervical cytology or particular immunizations to procedures adjuged to be 'public policy'. When funds are insufficient, as now in the NHS, the decision to use a part of them to pay for contraception (q.v.) or sterilization (q.v.) on social grounds is an intervention in choice for reasons appealing to Parliament rather than to the health professions.

In short, a comprehensive NHS is now inevitably prevented by lack of resources, financial, human and physical, from meeting every need or meeting it in the way which might be the first professional choice. Without subordinating the ethical standard of the individual to central policy, there should be some concession from complete independence to consensus judgement by the group. That consensus should be susceptible to societal views on objectives, but not exposed to pressure for purely electoral interests of national or local political bodies (see *Social Pressures*).

Within the overall inadequacy of resources for the NHS there is still serious inequality in allocation to regions in England, though much less than in the early years. Within the UK there is serious inequality in the allocations to the four countries, with England and to a less extent Wales as the sufferers. The Royal Commission on the NHS calls attention to this and commissioned a study by Buxton and Klein[8] which has been published. A report of a working party on re-distribution (RAWP) has been accepted for England despite the uncertainty in some of the factors given mathematical expression in the formula developed. The resulting process has been most painful in some areas. No such levelling process between the countries of the UK has been attempted.[9]

A considerable literature on services in other countries is available and interesting recent trends are now to be seen, notably in Denmark, Italy and Portugal. Regional planning and control is an increasing feature in most countries.

1. Newell K, ed. *Health by the people*. Geneva: WHO, 1975.
2. WHO Regional Office for Europe. *Health services in Europe*. 2nd edn. Geneva: WHO, 1975.
3. Fogarty International Center. *Health care in Scandinavia*. Bethesda, Md., National Institutes of Health, 1976.
4. Douglas-Wilson I, McLachlan G. *Health Service prospects*. London. *The Lancet* and the Nuffield Provisional Hospitals Trust, 1973.
5. Lalonde M. *A new perspective on the health of Canadians*. Ottawa: Ministry of National Health and Welfare, 1974.
6. Hetzel BS. *Health and Australian society*. Harmondsworth: Pelican Books, 1974.
7. Stephen WJ. *Primary medical care*. Cambridge: University Press, 1979.
8. Buxton MJ, Klein RE. *Allocating health resources: a commentary on the report of the Resources Allocation Working Party*. Research Paper No 3, Royal Commission in the National Health Service. London: HMSO, 1978.
9. Maynard A, Ludbrook A. *Lancet* 1980; 1: 85–6.
   DHSS. *Priorities for Health and Social Services in England*. London, HMSO, 1976.
   DHSS. *Sharing resources for health in England*. Report of the Re-

sources Allocation Working Party (RAWP Report). London: HMSO, 1976.

Ginzberg E. *The limits of health reform.* New York: Basic Books, 1977.

Glaser WA. *Health insurance bargaining: foreign lessons for Americans.* New York: Halsted Press, 1978.

Godber GE. *Health Services, past, present and future.* London: Athlone Press, 1974.

Mechanic D. *Future issues in health care: social policy and the rationing of medical services.* London: The Free Press, 1979.

Ministry of Health. *A health service for the nation.* London: HMSO, 1944.

Royal Commission on the National Health Service. *Report.* London: HMSO, 1979, Cmnd 7615.

Titmuss, RM. *Social policy.* London: Allen and Unwin, 1974.

George Godber

Sterility. Absolute inability to reproduce. See *Castration; Infertility; Sterilization.*

Sterilization. Any procedure which renders a person incapable of reproduction. The term is usually applied to the surgical operations of vasectomy in the male, or tubal occlusion in the female. Hysterectomy (removal of the uterus), for whatever reason it is performed, inevitably results in sterility. Other operations such as castration (q.v.) and some forms of radiotherapy sterilize both men and women but have other serious consequences. They are undertaken for specific medical reasons only and not with the object of causing sterility.

Throughout human history the ability to procreate was, and in some cultures is, greatly valued. For societies whose economy is based on peasant agriculture children, especially male children, are the principal source of economic, social and physical security. But the scale of infant and child mortality and, until recently, the brief span of adult life meant that only the highly fertile could hope to maintain their family's numerical strength and influence from one generation to another. Inability to procreate, therefore, is looked on with pity or even contempt, and until recent years sterilization was regarded in law as an intrinsically serious assault which could only be justified when performed for the most compelling reasons, especially in males, who are not themselves exposed to the dangers of childbirth.

Industrialization, urbanization, education and above all demographic pressures have changed these attitudes, at least in the affluent countries of the world. People are more ready to seek sterilization voluntarily, and doctors to perform the operations with little hesitation, or even with enthusiasm. However, despite these changing intellectual attitudes, many individuals associate sterilization with a fear of loss of sexual function and, for this and other reasons, some may not make a satisfactory adjustment after the operation.

Under the Nazi regime in Germany compulsory sterilization on ethnic grounds was sometimes performed. In India, beset by over-whelming problems of population growth, the legislature of the state of Maharashtra enacted (1976) a law to enforce sterilization whenever a couple had three children (or four if they were all of the same sex). Public reaction extended to sporadic riots, and is considered to have influenced the outcome of the subsequent Indian General Election. This coercive approach has now been abandoned (see *Population Policy*).

VASECTOMY. Vasectomy is a minor surgical operation involving di-vision and ligation of the two vasa deferentia which conduct sper-matozoa from the testicles. This prevents sperm from being included in the fluid ejaculated during sexual intercourse and thus causes ster-ility. Vasectomy is the principal method used for sterilization of the male and is usually done under local anaesthesia as an out-patient procedure. It has few, minor complications. Short lengths of the vasa are removed so that their identity can be confirmed microscopically. Some sperm may persist in the ejaculate for weeks or months after the operation, so it is usual to examine the semen after two months and then at intervals until two consecutive specimens are found to be free.

Vasectomy does not alter secondary sexual characteristics. When undergone willingly it does not interfere with libido, potency or sexual intercourse; its psychological effects are usually beneficial and seldom harmful. No serious effects upon health have been recognized, though some individuals develop antibodies to spermatozoa. Their signifi-cance is unknown. Although the pathway to the urethra is blocked, the formation of sperm (spermatogenesis) continues in many subjects, but not in all.

Sterility is virtually absolute once sperm have disappeared from the ejaculate. Very seldom the operation may fail owing to spontaneous restoration of continuity between the divided ends of a vas. Couples should accept that sterility is likely to be permanent. However, frozen semen, collected before operation, can be stored (in a cryobank) in the hope that it might possibly be used for impregnation in later years, but there is no certain prospect of success. Surgical restoration of the vasa is a difficult operation and results in restoration of fertility in less than half of cases.

FEMALE STERILIZATION. In the female, sterilization is effected by blocking the oviducts (Fallopian tubes). Formerly the operation was performed through an abdominal incision (laparotomy), the tubes being divided and ligated. If the operation is done shortly after deliv-ery, which is not the best time for the patient to make a settled decision (see below), only a very small incision is necessary. A similar technique (mini-laparotomy) has been adapted for use at other times.

Most female sterilizations in the UK are now performed using a laparoscope (endoscope), which reduces the discomforts and dangers of the operation, and necessitates a very brief stay in hospital, though this technique calls for special skill and is not devoid of risk. The tubes are occluded either by diathermy coagulation or by application of clips or rings.

To avoid abdominal surgery, attempts have been made to block the tubes from below via the uterine cavity, using electrocoagulation or a chemical sclerosant. These methods have not proved adequately reliable.

Operative reversal of female sterilization can be attempted, and may be successful in about half the cases, though special skill and meticulous technique are called for to achieve such results.

COUNSELLING AND CONSENT (q.v.). Ideally husband and wife are interviewed together and their motives and attitudes explored. The decision as to which partner should be sterilized is based largely on the wishes of the individuals concerned. If the health of one partner is already impaired or threatened, it will seem rational to sterilize that partner. However, emotional adjustment to sterilization in these circumstances is often worse than when the primary determinant is the individual's own choice.

In a family where relationships are already strained, either the birth of an unwanted child or the sterilization of one partner may precipitate more serious stress, so that the choice is not clear-cut.

Joint written consent is usually obtained. A husband undergoing vasectomy without his wife's consent might be open to divorce proceedings. On the other hand, if further pregnancies would be a clear threat to a wife's health, it is doubtful if the husband's refusal of consent would be regarded as valid in Britain, or if he would have legal grounds for action against the surgeon who sterilized his wife.

Several ethical issues arise in contemporary practice. In the many countries where infant and child mortality remain high (20 – 50% may fail to survive beyond puberty), the decision to sterilize is not easily made unless the size of the couple's family is already large enough to provide them with a 'reserve' of children. The mother who now has three or four children may next year have none, such is the toll of infectious disease among the malnourished. However, if sterilization is postponed until the survival of children is assured, the opportunity to control population is missed altogether. Thus there is a conflict between the best interests of the individual couple and of society at large.

A woman's attitude towards sterilization is likely to vary from one time to another. Immediately after she has experienced the pain of labour, and conscious of her new responsibility with the addition to her family, she may welcome an offer of sterilization, whereas later, when life has regained a more even keel, she may have no wish to renounce her fertility. In terms of population control the puerperium may be looked upon as a 'motivational opportunity'; in terms of the mother's and family's long-term happiness, it is generally a time when irreversible decisions are better avoided, since follow-up studies have shown that regret or remorse is more common after postpartum sterilization.

It is even more difficult to make settled decisions regarding steriliz-ation when financial or other inducements are offered to the patient or the doctor. Such schemes have been adopted in several developing countries to help contain population growth, and may include pay-ment to the 'motivator' who induces an individual to undergo steril-ization. In the United Kingdom, fees are paid to surgeons, anaesthetists and pathologists (who examine specimens) for steriliza-tion operations, as well as for other family planning procedures. (Fees are also paid for attempted reversal of sterilization.)

In the past, when sterilization was performed only because of the most serious threats to health, or when family size was already very large, surgical technique was directed to achieving maximum reliabil-ity, i.e. eliminating all risk of future pregnancy. But where sterilization is carried out on relatively young and healthy individuals with only small families, there will inevitably be requests (following divorce, bereavement or a change of heart) for subsequent operations to at-tempt reconstruction of the tubes or vasa.

The surgeon performing sterilization, therefore, has to choose bet-ween a technique that ensures maximum reliability, but reduces re-versibility, or *vice versa*. To protect himself from possible litigation he may prefer to achieve reliability at the expense of reversibility.

In Britain until the present decade, in a considerable proportion of cases of termination of pregnancy, sterilization was carried out at the same time. Often the gynaecologist's willingness to perform the abor-tion was conditional upon the woman agreeing to be sterilized. This attitude is perhaps a legacy of the time when therapeutic abortion was only permitted in the face of a serious and usually continuing threat to the woman's life or health. The gynaecologist knows that another pregnancy is not unknown after termination, despite contraceptive advice. To prevent this, he may therefore feel justified in putting pressure on the woman. But there is also good evidence that combin-ing sterilization with abortion adds considerably to the danger of the abortion. To reduce the physical risks, as well as to promote the long-term happiness of the woman, the temptation to offer only a 'package deal' has to be resisted.

The sterilization of mentally defective people and minors presents special problems. A feeble-minded young woman may already have demonstrated her inability to protect herself from pregnancy and, sometimes, her inability also to provide adequate maternal care for children she has borne. However, there is good evidence that the development of the mentally backward may be dependent upon op-portunities for education and training, and that many such individuals never achieve their full potential. In most cases of mental deficiency the validity of consent must be questioned.

The sterilization of female minors whose genes carry grave hereditary disorders such as Huntington's Chorea may be requested by their parents or guardians, if they are at risk of pregnancy. There is little ethical justification for an operation of this sort before the child is old enough to give willing and informed consent herself. This view was upheld by Mrs Justice Heilbron in a recent judgement involving an 11-year-old girl suffering from a rare hereditary condition. (See also *Abortion; Child; Contraception.*)

Anon. Legality of sterilisation: a new outlook. *Br Med J* 1960; 2: 1516.

Kleinman RL, ed. *Male and female sterilisation.* London: International Planned Parenthood Federation, 1973.

Liston WA, *et al.* Female sterilisation by tubal electro-coagulation under laparoscopic control. *Lancet* 1970; 1, 382.

Livingstone ES. Review of 3200 vasectomies. *Can Med Assoc J* 1971; 105, 1065.

Margaret Pyke Centre. 1000 vasectomies. *Br Med J* 1973; 4: 216.

Morris N, Arthure H. *Sterilization as a means of birth control in men and women.* London: Peter Owen, 1976.

Presser HB. *Voluntary sterilization: a world view.* Reports on Population/Family Planning. No 5. New York: Columbia University, 1970.

P. R. Myerscough

Strike, the Right to. There was no right to strike under the feudal system. Nor is there a right to strike in autocracies and dictatorships. In them the consequences of the organized withdrawal of labour are physical and economic punishment. Oppression, real or imagined, in the conditions of employment in such societies has to be very severe before the risks of strike action seem less than those privations suffered at work. Striking is therefore only a right in certain types of democracy. Other forms of society believe that strikes are too disruptive of their functions to be condoned so that riots and *coups d'état* may be the alternative. Strikes may therefore have the merit of drawing attention to serious grievances before they have become so deep as to issue in violence.

Strikes result from serious disagreements between the workforce and management, mainly about pay or conditions of employment, but they may also arise from inter-union disputes or from sympathetic action supporting other strikes, and rarely for political purposes.[1] With the national organization of Trade Unions the right to strike is generally accepted, though until recently it was not legally extended to the armed forces, the police, merchant seamen and public utility workers.[2] However the constraints of the criminal law in the United Kingdom were removed for merchant seamen in 1970 and for gas, electricity and water employees in 1971. There have been some moves urging the freedom to strike for the police, and some have pressed for the need to establish a Trade Union for the armed forces, though it may not be the intention to ask for a right to strike for them.

For doctors and nurses, the traditional health care workers, the question of the right to strike did not arise until after the beginning of the National Health Service in 1948. This introduced a near-monopoly employer[3] as a third party into the formerly private transaction between the doctor and patient. Of course there were third parties prior to this in various charity and local government hospitals, and in various insurance systems. But there were several of these and an aggrieved doctor always had the option to resign his employment and take up work in some more personally congenial way. The National Health Service, with nation-wide terms and conditions of service, severely restricted this form of escape from a particular employer. Now doctors with contracts of service in hospitals or doctors in general practice may find themselves in serious disagreement, especially over pay and conditions of work, with the near-monopoly employer, which is essentially the government. Even in smaller local disputes the chain of accountability and responsibility of the employer extends up through a variety of government agencies, which are District, Area and Regional Health Authorities. The predictable response in the face of such potential power has been the formation of employee groups, similar in nature to Trade Unions, if not actually so. Indeed the largest such body, the British Medical Association, is a Trade Union having negotiating rights with the near-monopoly employer.

There is little doubt that doctors have the freedom and the right to strike, though there are some constraints under both the criminal and civil law.[2] These are unlikely to be invoked for they are so hedged round with legalism and difficulties of proof of doctors' negligence, or conspiracy resulting in injury or damage to any aggrieved patients. The question then is not the legality of doctors striking so much as its morality. In what circumstances may a strike by doctors be ethically justifiable? If a strike is called, what are the limits allowable beyond which action must not be taken since it may result in injury, damage or neglect of patients?

Strikes which withdraw all medical services from all patients are still deemed indefensible. At the very least the acutely ill and the injured must be cared for. In industry there may be substituted for the all-out strike various kinds of go-slow or work-to-rule. For medicine there have been advocated the work to contract, the refusal to work overtime, the refusal to sign certificates and other kinds of action. Any or all of these, however, cause inconvenience, anxiety, apprehension and possibly direct damage to patients and other people. It is then argued that this is precisely the reason for the strike, what ever its diluted form. The distress caused to others is the intention so that the government may be forced to act to redress the grievances of the strikers. It is a battle of threats, counter-threats and posturing with each side trying to force the other to yield. The weapon used by strikers is the distress they cause to others or the threat of causing that distress. It is probably true that most protagonists hope that threats will be enough and that the threatened action will not eventuate. Herein lies the skill of negotiation and brinkmanship, each side jostling the other in the hope that they will not actually become locked in real combat. Failure in negotiation may precipitate the use of the strike weapon. Each side is then responsible for the breakdown for both have misjudged the situation, and how much all the parties will stand. Each, of course, claims to represent the ultimate benefit of patients, the mainly silent sufferers.

The traditional view is that there is never any moral justification for a strike by doctors, for however limited the action, any distress caused to patients, and that is always inevitable to some degree, is not acceptable to the ethos of the profession. The recent more radical view is that doctors should sometimes strike to preserve and improve their standards of work because it is on these that the welfare of patients finally depends. In striking for themselves doctors may believe that they are also fighting for the greater ultimate good of their patients. The traditional and radical views are not reconcilable when starkly presented. There is therefore now a commencing search for better methods of conciliation when doctors feel they must confront their near-monopoly employer with grievances.[3] One solution may be the use of machinery for arbitration between government and the medical profession which is binding on both sides.[4] This might give a lead to others in strike torn industries and it has been suggested[2] that doctors should, for moral reasons, give such a lead.

Nurses now have stated that they will not strike in furtherance of industrial disputes. Other health care workers, rather more distant from the immediate problems of sick people, have begun to use the strike weapon more freely than before. They too might have less easy recourse to striking or industrial action if the medical profession could show that there was a better way, bringing just as good results for the workforce as disruption of the service, and without harming the patients for whom it exists. (See also *Nursing; Voluntary Work.*)

1. *Encyclopaedia Britannica*. Micropaedia IX, 1975; 614.
2. Dworkin G. *J Med Ethics* 1977; 3: 76–82.
3. Joint Working Party of the conference of medical Royal Colleges and their Faculties in the United Kingdom and the British Medical Association. *Br Med J* 1977; 1: 157–9.
4. Taylor, Lord. *World Medicine*, June 2nd 1979: 17–22.

Working Party on Human Rights established by the Bishops' Conference of England and Wales. *The right to strike*. London: Catholic Truth Society, 1979.

Philip Rhodes

Subnormality, Mental. See *Mental Handicap*.

Suicide. An act of deliberate self-destruction. 'There is but one truly philosophical problem and that is suicide.'[1] The Judaeo-Christian and Islamic traditions saw scant problem: life given by God could only be taken by God. For Jews, suicide was permissible only, as in the dramatic case of the 970 suicides at Masada, if the alternative was to be forced by an enemy into humiliation and conduct contrary to the Law. Christian dogma followed and St. Augustine laid down that suicide, as self-murder, was sinful – spurred on, perhaps, by the mass suicide of certain Christian sects in search of an early release to Heaven and of the armies of Josephus after defeat by the Romans. Islam holds suicide to be a major sin, pardonable, possibly, but only by Allah, in respect of good deeds. Secular authorities endorsed the prohibitions for purely the material reason of seizing the property of suicides for the State. Nevertheless, the act of suicide, as a rejection of the world, a slap in the face of humanity, evoked and still evokes aggression in survivors and has led to desecration of the body. The last burial of a suicide in England at a crossroads with a stake through the heart was as late as 1823.

Suicide, however, appears to be ubiquitous, as old as man, and often socially approved. The Mayans had a god of suicide, shown as a person dying by hanging. Greece and Rome varied between condemnation and admiration (note the death of Socrates) and ritual suicide was expected in many cultures – the widow, for example, in Hindu society (suttee). Japan had clear-cut rules; ceremonial suicide, hara-kiri, was obligatory and heroic for failure in one's duty to the Feudal Lord. There are echoes of this across India with suicide epidemics as examination results emerge and in Western military tradition where Prussian generals shot themselves after losing battles.

The mass suicide of 911 people at Jonestown (1979) was by far the most remarkable suicidal event of modern times. Jonestown was over 100 miles into the jungle and there is evidence that the cult leader, the Rev. Jim Jones, was psychotic from about 1974. Suspicion of the outside world was preached, and the escape by mass suicide was regularly rehearsed as it was anticipated that outside forces, such as the CIA, would overwhelm and force them to change their way of life. The arrival of a Congressman and the press, followed by a bungled attempt to shoot the entire party, precipitated the final act with parents poisoning their children and then themselves, while Jones preached (a tape recording survives). It is held that other eccentric groups could follow a similar course.

Suicide epidemics on a small scale can follow press publicity either of a particularly sensational suicide or the reported suicide of a prominent person. Single-vehicle car fatalities rise throughout California when the latter event occurs. A striking photograph of an Australian girl dying by fire, for obscure political reasons, in Geneva was followed by reports of other deaths by fire. Such deaths are normally reported about once every three months: on this occasion there were 11 in six weeks, according to the *Evening News* Library Service. It is surmised that such people were death-orientated, and that this piece of press reporting was the final precipitating factor.

These are far from Durkheim's 'altruistic suicide',[2] which stands apart, since the desire is *not* for death, but is rather an act calculated to benefit others. Captain Oates and the kamikaze pilots were mentally 'normal' examples: psychotic depressives, with delusions of sinfulness and loss of hope, who believe their deaths will leave the world a cleaner place are 'abnormal' ones. Life-threatening behaviours, such as motor-racing, rock-climbing and heavy use of drink or drugs are sometimes regarded as 'suicide-equivalents' and so they may be at the unconscious level; but those who behave thus seldom if ever wish *consciously* to die and, as such, are properly excluded from these clinical considerations.

The civil law has followed the ecclesiastical law, that against suicide being abolished first in France in 1790[3]. It has been abolished, state by state, across the USA although several southern states still retain it. The Act against suicide in England was repealed in 1961, but it is still an offence to aid or abet suicide and survivors of suicide pacts may be prosecuted. Nowhere has the existence or abolition of the law been shown to affect suicide rates though attempted suicide is another matter. Suicide and 'attempted suicide' (q.v.) are different, albeit overlapping, phenomena in that 85% of attempted suicides are glad still to be alive and probably only a minority are determined to achieve death. Innumerable motives enter in – the cry for help, manipulation, revenge or just the desire 'to opt out' for a while. Self-injury became a national epidemic from around 1961, is the commonest cause of admission to medical wards and seems still to be on the increase. Actual suicide, on the other hand, declined by over one-third in England and Wales from 1963 to 1975 (though it has risen very slightly since). This decline is unique throughout the world and came at a time when economic predictors would have foretold a rise. Unconvincing attempts have been made to explain why suicide in Britain went down and in most other countries, up. The one unique 'intervening variable' is the massive coverage of Britain by Samaritan suicide preventive effort, but their role is hotly contested by some medical authorities. In 1977, despite a 3.2% reduction in all deaths from accidents and violence compared with 1976, only suicides increased, by 3.4%.

Stepping from the theological and moral context to the scientific, there are the determinist 'medical' and 'social' models of suicide, each of which divorces the act from freewill, and elevates the deceased to a victim of circumstance. The medical model equates suicide with depressive illness, constitution, brain biochemistry, inheritance. The social model looks at the environment – social isolation, significant recent loss, imitation (e.g. of Marilyn Monroe), political protest (e.g. Jan Palach, the Vietnam Buddhists). The truth lies in an impenetrably complex interplay of these two, from which freewill cannot be excluded. There are as many 'causes' of suicide as there are suicidal deaths, though research has conjured from them certain patterns. To devise a universal, humanistic, ethics based on known fact is thus not possible, and it is similarly not possible to discern clear ethical grounds for the use of Compulsory Treatment Orders for possibly suicidal people. Though at times these may be justified in the *short* term, to allow a person to come to terms with his or her situation and see if help can be brought, there are grounds to believe that the harder one tries by coercion to prevent suicide, the more one raises the resistances of the suicidal person and makes it more likely to occur (see *Mental Illness, Certification of*).

Samaritans are never associated with Compulsory Treatment Orders, maintaining as the 18th of their 20 Principles that 'the caller remains at all times in charge of his own destiny and is free to reject the help that is offered and to break contact without fear of being sought out against his will, even if it is felt certain that he intends to take his own life or to commit some other act which The Samaritans would deprecate'. Every effort is made, however, to dissuade a person from a suicidal act. It is usual experience that when people leave a Samaritan Centre intent on suicide, they later change their minds and return. This is in contrast to the practice at USA suicide prevention centres. There, many would call the police to such a person and have him taken to a closed, psychiatric establishment.

It is not possible to take a morally neutral stance on suicide, since it is the most significant of all deaths in its impact on survivors, causing long-lasting grief and guilt and a high suicide-expectancy: in spouses, around one thousand times the average according to one study[4]. J. S. Mill's view of the moral innocence of suicide on the ground that it does not damage the lives of others cannot, therefore, be sustained. No man, with suicide especially, is an island unto himself; or, more pithily, suicide is 'the skeleton left by the deceased in the survivors' closet'[4],[5]. Nonetheless there must be few now who maintain an absolutist view and who would condemn the old person who, say, amid the pain and stench of inoperable pelvic cancer, 'accidentally' took a fatal dose of pain-relieving tablets. Even in strongly Roman Catholic areas, refusal now of ecclesiastical burial to suicides seems to be rare and diminishing.

1. Camus A. *The myth of Sisyphus*. London: Hamish Hamilton; Harmondsworth: Penguin Books, 1955.

2. Durkheim E. *Suicide: a study in sociology*. London: Routledge and Kegan Paul, 1952.
3. Shneidman ES. *Suicidology: contemporary developments*. New York: Grune and Stratton, 1976.
4. Cain AC. *Survivors of suicide*. Springfield: Charles C. Thomas, 1972.
5. Perlin S. *A handbook for the study of suicide*. Oxford: University Press, 1975.

Farberow NL. *Suicide in different cultures*. Baltimore: University Park Press, 1975.

Mortality Statistics: Cause, 1977. London: HMSO, 1979, Series DH2 No 4.

Shneidman ES. *The psychology of suicide*. New York: Science House, 1970.

Stengel E. *Suicide and attempted suicide*. Harmondsworth: Pelican Books, 1970.

Varah C. *Samaritans in the 70s*. London: Constable, 1973.

Richard Fox

Sydney Declaration. See *Declarations*.

T

Tao. See *Chinese Medicine.*

Teaching, Clinical. See *Clinical Teaching.*

Teaching of Medical Ethics. In the last decade there has been a striking change both in the extent and in the nature of the teaching of medical ethics in medical schools. Formerly such teaching as there was related more to legal medicine, to professional etiquette and to an unwritten code of honour based on the Hippocratic Oath (q.v.). Only recently has it become recognized that the real ethical problems relate to moral dilemmas generated by scientific and technical advances. In the United Kingdom the General Medical Council (q.v.) in their 1967 Recommendations as to Basic Medical Education[1] made special mention of the need for teaching in this subject. In their 1974 survey the GMC[2] indicate that 25 out of 34 schools have formal arrangements in their curriculum for the teaching of ethics. In the United States the number of schools with special programmes tripled between 1972 and 1974.[3]

In spite of these declared increases doubt remains on fundamental issues: can the subject be taught and if so, in what ways and by whom? Some say it is not a discipline like physiology or dermatology and that it can only be acquired 'by osmosis while sitting at the feet of other physicians'. Certainly there is much to be said for the ethical problems being discussed in the context of the individual case rather than in the abstract. Unless, however, students have been introduced first to the nature and origins of the ethical arguments they will be ill-equipped to appreciate the problems as they affect an individual patient or set of circumstances. Too often the only teaching given is by individual clinicians in the course of teaching their own discipline. In the USA survey already quoted the number of staff devoting at least half their time to the teaching of medical ethics in 1974 was 31 in 53 schools. In the new medical school in Maastricht, Netherlands, there is a Chair of Medical Ethics.[4] In the United Kingdom in 1974, 11 out of 25 schools had a member of staff specifically charged with the responsibility for teaching the subject. In many countries (including the UK) much of the study of the subject has been extra-curricular and often at the instigation of the students themselves. Medical groups have been formed and are affiliated to the Society for the Study of

Medical Ethics (q.v.) which has since 1975 published the *Journal of Medical Ethics* (q.v.). These extra-curricular activities have the advantages of enthusiasm and of inter-disciplinarity: ethical problems are best discussed in groups which include other health professionals, theologians, lawyers, social workers and others.

As to who should teach, the attributes of the individuals are more important than the nature of their professional background. It is important that all teachers in a medical school should emphasize the ethical aspects of their subjects, but there is also required an individual who has made a special study of the subject and who has a clearly defined responsibility for introducing and co-ordinating the teaching. 'The time has long passed when medical ethics could be taught only by the good example of elderly colleagues. Nor can it remain just a hobby for busy clinicians or an amateur job for retired doctors. A strong scientific foundation is mandatory.'[5] (See also *Medical Ethics; Medical Science* (introductory essays).)

1. General Medical Council. *Recommendation as to basic medical education.* London: GMC, 1967: 18.
2. General Medical Council. *Survey of basic medical education in the British Isles.* London: NPHT, 1977.
3. Veatch RM, Sollitto S. Medical ethics teaching. *JAMA* 1976; 235, 1030 (and editorial p. 1043).
4. Sporken P. The teaching of medical ethics in Maastricht; the Netherlands. *J Med Ethics*, 1975; 1: 181–3.
5. Blomquist C. The teaching of medical ethics in Sweden. *J Med Ethics* 1975; 1: 96–8.
   Boyd K, Currie C, Thompson I, Tiernay AJ. Teaching medical ethics: University of Edinburgh. *J Med Ethics* 1978; 4: 141–5.
   De Wachter MAM. Teaching medical ethics: University of Nijmegen, the Netherlands. *J Med Ethics* 1978; 4: 84–8.
   Goldman SA, Arbuthnot J. Teaching medical ethics: the cognitive-development approach. *J Med Ethics* 1979; 5: 170–81.
   Moore AR. *The missing medical text.* Melbourne: University Press, 1978.

A. S. Duncan

Teamwork. In the past much, perhaps most, medical care was provided by doctors working on their own. They had strictly confidential relationships with their patients and provided personally all the therapeutic measures which were needed, including the dispensing of medicines.

Today, however, medicine is so complex that it cannot be undertaken single-handed either in general practice or in hospital. The so-called 'multi-disciplinary clinical team' (MDCT) has now become an integral feature of most medical practice, at least in developed countries. This has brought with it new ethical issues, especially those affecting final responsibility, clinical autonomy (q.v.), and confidentiality (q.v.). (See also *Clinical Practice; General Practice; Hospitals; Interprofessional Relationships; Medical Records; Nursing; Social Workers.*)

IN GENERAL PRACTICE. Many general practitioners work as members of a team, the nuclear members of which consist of the doctor, the community nurse and the health visitor but which can extend to involve allied professions including social work. Nevertheless the general practitioner is the person with whom the patient must be registered and it is he, therefore, who must accept final responsibility for matters delegated or referred to members of the team. The team in general practice is both an administrative arrangement and a functional unit with collective responsibility. For this reason, from the administrative point of view, it is essential that information obtained by the doctor in the course of a consultation is not disclosed to other members of the team without the patient's permission. On the other hand when there is collective responsibility it would not be in the patient's best interests for information not to be shared and discretion must be used as to tacit consent by the patient for communication within the team.

IN ACUTE HOSPITALS. In hospitals in the UK medical teams are essentially functional units, designed to provide optimal medical care, training of staff and efficiency. A patient attends a clinic or is admitted to a ward under the care of a consultant, who takes ultimate responsibility for his medical welfare. The consultant's name is recorded in the case sheet, often displayed in the clinic and usually shown over the bed so that the patient and staff know who is responsible. During temporary absences the consultant arranges with a colleague to act for him.

The consultant is assisted by junior doctors of varying seniority and he delegates appropriate degrees of responsibility to them. He should ensure that each member of the team understands what decisions and actions he may take independently and when, and from whom, he should seek advice. All members have the right, and should be given the opportunity, to express their views about patients, but the consultant must make the decisions about the information and advice which is given to them (see *Communication*). A consultant often asks a colleague for advice about a patient, but he takes the decision himself. If he wishes the colleague to assume responsibility, this must be agreed clearly between them and the patient must be advised accordingly. For example, a physician may refer a patient to a surgeon who advises, and agrees to undertake, an operation. The surgeon then assumes responsibility for as long as is appropriate.

Doctors in hospitals work closely with other professionals, for example nurses, physiotherapists, dieticians, pharmacists, laboratory workers and social workers. All the members of the team can contribute their own knowledge, skills and standards to the work of caring for patients. Normally all co-operate in a relationship of mutual confidence. Although each member is a specialist in his or her particular field, the leadership and ultimate responsibility of the consultant is not questioned, for clinical decisions, especially in emergencies, cannot be taken by consensus management.

IN LONG STAY AND PSYCHIATRIC HOSPITALS. Special problems may arise in geriatric hospitals and units, in psychiatric hospitals and in institutions for the mentally handicapped (see *Health Advisory Services* and references cited there).

The following sentences quoted from a report adopted by the Royal College of Psychiatrists naturally refer primarily to teamwork in psychiatry but are equally applicable to other long-stay units:

The responsibilities of a Consultant Psychiatrist are similar to those of other consultants within the National Health Service. The few differences arise from the special circumstances within the specialty, particularly relationships with other disciplines.

Consultant status within the National Health Service is created by the National Health Service Act, 1946, and the Advisory Appointments Committee procedure arises from this Act. Other disciplines within the National Health Service are not so clearly legally defined. This arises from the nature of medical responsibility and is to ensure for the public adequate specialist consultant standards.

The Consultant has, by virtue of professional qualification, Acts of Parliament and contract, the authority and responsibility to diagnose and prescribe medical treatment, and this responsibility cannot be wholly devolved elsewhere.

In the Hospital Service the Consultant associates with a variety of other disciplines of widely differing professional status. These relationships have been subject to considerable publicity and discussion in recent years under the general title of 'multi-disciplinary teams', particularly when dealing with in-patients at ward level. The multi-disciplinary policy is being stressed throughout the Service particularly in relation to the long-stay specialties; the emphasis being less in the general specialties. The policy generally lacks clarity and is liable to different interpretation, depending on the point of view of the particular discipline. By some it is thought of as a 'democratic way' of arriving at the best method of treating patients, whilst in others it is regarded as giving the status of equality in all matters to each member of the team. There is confusion between team-functioning of disciplines at management and administrative levels, and team functioning at clinical levels. Administrative or management issues can be decided on a corporate basis because the standing between the disciplines is on a basis of equality in arriving at a management decision. This method generally cannot be applied to professional opinions relating to individual patients. The confusion rests on the validity of corporate decisions as opposed to individual professional decisions.

The legal, professional, ethical, diagnostic and prescriptive responsibilities of the medical profession cannot be delegated to a multi-disciplinary group when treating an individual patient. Each doctor (Consultant) must formulate his own opinion, whether assisted in this process by others or not. Multi-disciplinary in this context, from the medical point of view, is a process of consultation, the final decision resting with the Consultant on matters where the Consultant has the final responsibility. Similar conditions may apply to other professions when the central responsibilities germane to these disciplines are involved.

The relationship of hierarchical management to multi-disciplinary teams at ward level is not clear. Can a senior officer of one discipline put aside the decision of the team? Can the authority of any one person override the team decision? Has a team decision any real authority when opposed to hierarchical management authority? If it has, then there will have to be changes in hierarchical management authority, both in structure, contract and philosophy. True multi-disciplinary teamwork at clinical levels can be recommended as probably the most efficient way of staff cooperation in the treatment of patients only provided that each member of the team is given full powers to make decisions.

Whilst employing authorities may express views on good practice to obtain improved care of patients, they can only express an opinion. There is no way to legislate on how a variety of differing disciplines can or should relate to each other. The issue is too complex and successful relationships only occur where the local personalities allow their development. The present policy of multi-disciplinary functioning is creating uncertainty and interferes with inter-professional relationships which may have evolved over many years and which have always been flexible. The multi-disciplinary concept can be introduced in an ill-considered way; it can be too idealistic; in many situations it is impracticable; and it may ignore professional responsibilities. In these circumstances the policy can only be expected to function in most hospitals partially, and in some areas it may even be disruptive and counterproductive. Multi-disciplinary team functioning should be seen as an option, not as a rigid pattern, and there should be discretion at ward level.

Appleyard J, Maden JG. Multidisplinary teams. *Br Med J* 1979; 2: 1305–7.

De Wachter M. Interdisciplinary teamwork. *J Med Ethics* 1976; 2: 52–7.

Leading Article. Who carries the can? *Br Med J* 1979; 2:1245.

Merrison A. Royal Commission on the National Health Service. *Report*. London: HMSO, 1979, Cmnd 7615.

Royal College of Psychiatrists. Statement. *Br J Psychiat* 1977: Bulletin Sept: 4. (Used by permission.)

A. G. Donald
A. S. Duncan
R. B. Welbourn

Terminal Care. The need for terminal care arises when the ageing or disease process in a human being no longer responds to curative or palliative medical or surgical procedures. For most people the end of life should be a time in which specialized care or skills are not called for and in which, with simple professional advice and support, the loving presence of the family and friends of the dying person will be all that is wanted. However, for those who find dying neither natural nor easy, special knowledge in the control of physical, mental, social or spiritual pain should be available.

Terminal care can be said to begin when medical intervention can no longer be curative. The decision when to abandon aggressive therapy and to begin symptomatic control may be difficult, but increasing expertise in the control of such treatable symptoms as pain, nausea, vomiting and breathlessness, all part of proper terminal care, has made it clear that these skills are also called for earlier in the disease process. They could be introduced with benefit to the patient while active treatment which may be distressing is still being administered, and will make easier its withdrawal when it is no longer appropriate. It must be stressed that terminal care concerns primarily the person dying, whereas often the treatments proposed are in fact therapy or legal insurance for the medical team, or aimed at the family rather than the patient. What should be clearly understood is that in the patient with terminal illness care is turned on and not switched off.

The natural place for a person to die is still in his own home and with his own people – of all generations. When admission to an institution is unavoidable the importance of the relatives during this major event in the life of the family must still be upheld. An increasing number of people die in hospitals, and the majority of *hospital* deaths are in acute hospitals, where less time and attention can be given to dying patients than in hospices (q.v.). In this context it is important to know of the new concept of a hospital team consisting of doctors, nurses, social workers and chaplain or other spiritual adviser, available on request to advise in the care of any patient with terminal disease whose pain is not being adequately controlled. Such teams have now been set up in several centres and have been shown to raise the standards of pain control throughout. Furthermore, hospital doctors (and nursing staff) are learning to refer to hospices when they are faced with difficult problems in their own wards.

Professional help will be needed (though it is often not available) to control distressing physical and mental symptons and to mobilize sources of social and spiritual support for both patient and family, such as family doctor, district nurse, social services and minister of religion. Friends, neighbours and the local community can also provide support.

Terminal care uncomplicated by the need to control distressing symptoms may still call for support by those mentioned above. It includes simple instructions to the family and an acceptance of the fact of death which will allow them, by their unfrightened presence, to sustain the patient as he reaches the end of his life.

However, in uncontrolled disease processes and with modern society's wish to banish the face of death, skill and understanding are needed if the patient is to be allowed a seemly death.

The proper use of drugs in terminal care may be different from the use of the same drugs in other circumstances. The art of controlling a patient's symptoms without clouding his mind, experience in diagnosing the often varied causes of a patient's pain and treating them appropriately, skills in nursing care and some confidence that death is not the final disaster, can transform what is too often the worst period of a family's life into something that is splendid and can be remembered with pride. At this stage in a patient's life addiction cannot be considered a serious problem. In fact the proper use of drugs, titrating the amount of drugs given against the pain experienced, never allows the mechanism of addiction to take control.

Advance in medical techniques and skills has outdistanced proper discussion on the appropriateness or otherwise of applying these skills to a particular patient. The availability of a whole range of scientific expertise does not of itself make its use mandatory. Too often it is forgotten that both life and disease have their own natural course and the artificial prolongation of one may result in the distressing prolongation of the other.

The human race has a special regard for life, believing that it should only be taken in exceptional circumstances such as war. It is ironical that, at a time when medical skills have advanced so far in the control of distress, the demand for euthanasia (q.v.) is being so loudly expressed. Modern terminal care, if available, invalidates almost every call for euthanasia. Appropriate care of the person with terminal disease, anticipated and discussed by the professional team, and including the family, will take account of signals of distress and obviate artificial medical prolongation of life.

Dying children need special consideration. Not only must a child have his symptoms well controlled, but the family and staff must also be well cared for. Here again knowledge of what can be achieved will go a long way in counteracting the feeling of impotence that too often results in turning care off rather than switching it on.

The treatment of a patient, as a person and as a member of a family or group, allows truth (q.v.) to be revealed in a situation in which manipulation and deceit become more and more irrelevant.

Browning HN, Lewis SP, eds. The dying patient: a nursing perspective. *Am J Nurs* 1972.

Calman KC, Paul J. Terminal care and pain control. In: *An introduction to cancer medicine*. London: The Macmillan Press Ltd., 1978.

Cartwright A, Hocket L, Anderson JL. *Life before death*. London: Routledge and Kegan Paul, 1973.

Chapman JA, Goodall J. Dying children need help too. *Br Med J* 1979; 1: 593–4.

Dunphy JE. Annual discourse – On caring for the patient with cancer. *N Engl J Med* 1976; 295: 313–9.

General Synod Board for Social Responsibility, *On dying well*. London: Church Information Office, 1975.

Kubler-Ross E. *On death and dying*. London: Tavistock Publications, 1970.

Saunders C, ed. *The management of terminal disease*. London: Edward Arnold, 1978.

Saunders C, ed. *The management of terminal illness*. London: Hospital Medical Publications, 1967.

Thomas S. West

Test Tube Babies. See *Embryo Transfer*.

Tissue Transplant. Tissue transplant is a surgical procedure whereby tissues or organs are moved from one person to another with the expectation that they will survive and replace the function of a diseased, damaged or lost organ or tissue in the recipient. Most organ grafts are designed to replace functions vital for survival, which cannot be artificially provided by any other means. Transplant of tissues or organs from one part to another part of the same person will not be considered, although this is important to plastic surgery (see *Cosmetic Surgery*), nor will the insertion of non-living tissues or prosthetic substances.

Ethical considerations stem largely from these factors:

(1) the results and the risks of the procedure;

(2) the origin of the material – whether from a living or dead donor; and

(3) the expressed wishes of the potential donor or of his relatives after death.

Improved results of certain types of transplant operation have removed ethical objections in some cases; the converse is also true. For example, in transplant of the *cornea* from a dead person to restore the sight of one who is blind, the majority of grafts take properly and are not rejected since the graft is normally avascular. The technique is well established and the recipient requires no treatment with potentially dangerous drugs. Removal of the cornea from the dead is not disfiguring, and as it can be removed in a healthy condition some hours after death, there is usually little difficulty in obtaining permission. On the other hand, all grafted *lungs* have done badly, probably because of susceptibility to infection. The publicity attending *heart* transplants has confused the issue. It has been argued that the results so far achieved do not justify the high demands on resources (q.v.) and manpower which the operation and aftercare require. Nevertheless patients are alive more than nine years after heart grafting. *Skin grafts* are usually quickly rejected unless the donor is an identical twin. Skin from close relatives may survive two to three weeks and from unrelated donors for ten days; even such short survival times have been of critical value to severely burned patients in preventing infection. *Liver* transplant is a dangerous operation, but rejection is mild. One patient is alive nine years after the procedure. *Kidney* transplant between identical twins has excellent results because there can be no rejection, but ethical difficulties based on predictable success become more common when the persons are not identical twins. The results depend largely on consanguinity and matching of tissue types between donor and recipient. Tissue matching occurs in 25 per cent of brothers and sisters, and grafts from parent and child do better than grafts between unrelated individuals. Most transplant surgeons would consider it unethical to transplant a kidney from an unrelated, living, volunteer donor, since the results are no better than from an unrelated dead donor.

A living donor will suffer the pain and risk of a major operation and he must fully understand the nature of the sacrifice he is making. Family responsibilities or the wishes of his family must be considered. Pressure may be put upon him by other members of the family and he may agree with reluctance or feel a sense of guilt if he does not offer. Doctors must satisfy themselves that the donor knows exactly what is involved and is consenting freely.

For the recipient, the offer of an organ graft assumes that all other treatments of a less drastic nature have been undertaken, and in the case of kidney disease that regular haemodialysis (q.v.) is not preferable. It assumes also that, without an organ graft, the patient will soon die or his quality of life be so poor as to make continued existence intolerable. There is no guarantee that a graft will succeed and all grafting operations involve hazards of varying magnitude. Unless the donor is an identical twin, the recipient will require treatment with potentially dangerous drugs to prevent immune reactions leading to rejection. Drugs employed include the steroids, which cause stunting of growth and a moon-face appearance and make the patient susceptible to infections. There is also the pain and discomfort of the removal of numerous blood samples and other tests. All these factors must be taken into account, and while an adult may be able to appreciate and accept them, a child cannot easily do so, and the quality of life for a child with an organ graft can be very unsatisfactory. The writer is therefore reluctant to perform organ grafting in young children although parents frequently request it as a last resort. Many surgeons would disagree with this view. If a non-steroidal effective immunosuppressive agent were available, the writer's reservations on organ grafting in children would be removed, but it would still be very difficult to obtain organs of the correct size to transplant into small children.

For the transplant of unpaired vital organs, the only possible donor is a dead person. Many deaths from accidents and some other conditions, such as brain tumours and brain haemorrhages, leave kidneys, heart and liver unaffected. Many more transplant operations – particularly kidney grafts – could be undertaken if more donor material were available. The shortage is due to medical, social and legal problems.

The principal difficulty is the short time after death in which it is possible to salvage organs for transplant. Kidneys must be removed within 90 minutes of the circulation ceasing if they are not to be irreversibly damaged; liver and heart within 15 minutes. To transplant a damaged heart or liver would cause the death of the recipient; to insert a damaged kidney is also disastrous. A dead person brought into hospital as the result of an accident is unlikely to be a suitable donor as there will be insufficient time to contact relatives or the coroner before the organs are also dead. More suitable as donors are patients in whom the brain has been completely and irreversibly destroyed and whose lungs are being inflated by machine to keep his body 'alive'. Once the diagnosis of brain death (see *Death, Determination of*) has been made, it is usual to switch off the mechanical ventilator so that the heart stops beating and the circulation ceases. It must be stressed that the decision to stop the ventilator should never be taken on account of the possibilities of transplantation.

The concept of brain death (*coma dépassé*) has now been accepted in the USA and in most European countries, including the United Kingdom, as a determinant of death sufficient for the removal of organs for transplant; to wait until the heart stopped would cause unnecessary risk to the graft and thus danger to the recipient. Certain cases are specifically excluded – patients who have suffered from cold exposure or who have received particular drugs, since in such cases the diagnosis of brain death may be difficult. If, after full examination and tests, doctors independent of the transplant team are satisfied that the brain is completely destroyed, permission may be given to remove organs while artificial ventilation is continued and the circulation is intact. All heart and liver grafts and most kidney transplants are now taken from this kind of donor, sometimes called 'heart-beating cadavers'.

Permission to remove organs presents another problem. If the donor's wishes during his lifetime are known, the law states that they should be respected. If his wishes are not known, enquiries must be made from relatives. If the potential donor is a 'heart-beating cadaver', there is usually ample time to consult the relatives. If, 'having made such reasonable enquiry as may be practicable', the relatives have not been contacted, the person 'lawfully in possession of the body' – assumed in the UK to be the hospital – can give permission for organ removal. The relatives of a fatal accident victim brought into hospital dead can seldom be contacted quickly, and even if they are available it may be cruel to add to their unhappiness by raising the question of organ donation. This is not always the case, and the possibility of good coming from their personal tragedy may sometimes make their sadness easier to bear (see *Bereavement*). Coroners in England and Wales have a statutory duty to investigate any sudden and unexplained death. This almost always calls for full postmortem examination, against which the objections, either of the deceased in his lifetime or of relatives, are powerless. The coroner's appointed pathologist, with agreement of the coroner, may permit removal of organs in such cases, provided that the relatives approve, but the whole of transplant law in the UK is untested and liable to varied interpretations, although it was framed to help to produce tissues for transplant. In April 1977 a circular was sent by the Home Office to coroners in England and Wales asking them to facilitate the removal of organs for transplant surgery and to use their discretion as regards consent[1]. Recommendations for clarification and amendment of the law were made by the (MacLennan) Advisory Group on Transplantation Problems and presented to Parliament in July 1969[2]. They await implementation. *Inter alia* it was recommended, by a bare majority, that there should be a presumption of agreement to donate organs, in the absence of any evidence to the contrary, a practice which already exists in some countries of Europe.

The Department of Health and Social Security issued in December 1979 a new Code of Practice for action to increase the supply of kidneys for transplantation, based on the report of a working party chaired by Lord Smith of Marlow.[3] The recommendation is that the best way of increasing the supply of kidneys is to make doctors and nurses more aware of the need and the procedures to be followed. It was considered that an 'opting-out' change in legislation was not necessary in view of the legal advice concerning interpretation of the 1961 Human Tissue Act[4], which is partly an opting-in and partly an opting-out arrangement. The Code of Practice concerns the safeguards to establish for certain that total and irreversible brain destruction has occurred and the procedure to be adopted in requesting permission from available next-of-kin. This document should be helpful in making progress to achieve an improved awareness of the medical profession of the need for organs for transplantation.

1. Home Office Circular No 65, 29 April 1977.
2. MacLennan H. *Advice from the advisory group on transplantation problems on the question of amending the Human Tissue Act 1961.* London: HMSO, 1969, Cmnd 4106.
3. Smith R. *The removal of cadaveric organs for transplantation: a code of practice.* Working party on behalf of the Health Departments of Great Britain and Northern Ireland. London: HMSO, Oct. 1979.
4. Human Tissue Act, 1961. 9 and 10 Eliz 2, Ch 54. London: HMSO, 1961.

DHSS Chief Medical Officer. Guidance circular to NHS Authorities – Human Tissue Act 1961. Health Service Circular Interim series 156. London: DHSS, June 1975.

British Transplantation Society. Shortage of organs for transplantation. *Br Med J* 1975; 1: 251–6.

Transplantation (various papers). *J Med Ethics* 1975; 1: 59–72.

Kennedy I. The donation and transplantation of kidneys: should the law be changed? *J Med Ethics* 1979; 5: 13–21.

Sells RA. Live organs from dead people. *J Roy Soc Med* 1979; 72: 109–17.

R. Y. Calne

Tobacco Smoking. In the last 25 years it has been shown that tobacco smoking is a potentially lethal addiction responsible, in economically developed countries, for much disability and mortality in middle age, as well as for harm to children whose mothers smoked during pregnancy. Clearly this ill-health and mortality would be prevented if people did not smoke, but the necessary change in attitude is difficult to achieve in the face of a habit previously, and quite reasonably, regarded as harmless, manly and socially acceptable, and which is often an addiction hard to break.

The need for alteration in social attitudes is a challenge to the sense of responsibility of doctors and other health workers, as well as to that of all thinking members of the public, especially as they themselves may have acquired the habit before its dangers were appreciated. Objectively their responsibility for unremitting dissemination of information and for persuasion, both of the public and of individuals, might seem clear, but a number of factors make this ideal hard to achieve. The climate of opinion among clinicians, and perhaps among some other health workers, is only slowly evolving towards the recognition both of their responsibility and of the degree of their authority in the field of prevention and health education. A doctor or health worker who has not himself given up the habit is liable to be hampered by a sense of guilt or an unconscious bias against accepting the facts. He will also, of course, carry very much less authority with his patients and the public. Moreover there is an understandable reluctance to seem to moralize about a habit so recently regarded as harmless. It is tedious to have to go on day after day repeating the same advice to patient after patient and to the patients' relatives. It is tedious to have to talk repeatedly on the subject to the public. It is easier to think it is someone else's business, perhaps the Health Educationists' (q.v.). But all evidence shows that official health education needs reinforcement for the individual by someone whose judgement he respects, so all health workers face a challenge to their sense of responsibility.

Smokers may insist on their right to indulge in a potentially lethal habit. Their legal right is undoubted but they have to consider that they may injure their young children directly by increasing their chances of pneumonia, that mothers may injure their unborn babies, that children may copy a lethal habit from their parents, that the family may be deprived of its bread-winner by early death or by invalidism from chronic bronchitis and that many doctors and nurses may have to spend much of their time caring for patients who have earlier deliberately decided to court disaster. Of course doctors and nurses will probably consider it their duty to care for any patients, however foolishly they have behaved.

Most lifelong smokers start the habit in their schooldays; schoolteachers and all those concerned with children therefore also face this challenge. National governments also face this problem. In economically developed countries smoking is often a major source of revenue yet governments have a public health responsibility for discouraging it. Democratic governments may hesitate to antagonize smoking voters, though this risk seems smaller than was once thought. Official policy varies greatly from country to country. Governments of developing countries face, among their many other public health concerns, the increasing popularity of smoking; the foreign exchange cost of importing cigarettes might be an added incentive to action. At present Britain and the USA provide most of the imported cigarettes to these countries. These cigarettes, in general, have a higher tar content, and are therefore more dangerous, than those sold in the home countries. Except where local laws insist, the packets lack the health warning and indication of tar content which are mandatory in Britain and USA.

Although there is no evidence that 'second-hand' smoke in the atmosphere causes serious illness to others, apart from infants who are more liable to severe lung infections if their parents smoke, it may cause headache or irritation of the eyes and throat, besides being aesthetically unpleasant for non-smokers. Asthmatics usually find a smoky atmosphere intolerable and it may precipitate a severe attack.

Anginal attacks may also be induced in susceptibles owing to the high carbon monoxide content of the atmosphere in smoke-filled rooms. There is therefore increasing public pressure to have more non-smoking compartments or sections in public transport, and non-smoking areas in public places such as theatres, cinemas and restaurants. They are being increasingly provided, but in this respect Britain lags behind many other countries. Although it is government policy that hospitals should in general be non-smoking, except for special areas set aside for smokers, and that cigarettes should not be sold in hospitals, this policy is very far from being generally implemented, owing to local opposition or, more often, lethargy. It is apparent that many health professionals and health administrators fail to live up to their ethical responsibilities in this field.

Most of those who are aware of the facts would regard the advertising of tobacco products as immoral. Banning of advertising and other forms of promotion, as has now been done in a number of countries, would be an important signal to the public that the government takes the smoking menace seriously.

Anonymous. Norway: The Tobacco Act. *Lancet* 1975; 2: 122.
Bewley BR, Day I, Ide L. *Smoking by children in Great Britain*. Social Science Research Council/Medical Research Council. London: 1973.
Bynnet JM. *The young smoker*. London: HMSO, 1969.
McKennell AC, Thomas RK. *Adults' and adolescents' smoking habits and attitudes*. London: HMSO, 1967.
Royal College of Physicians of London. *Smoking or health*. London: Pitman Medical, 1977.
World Health Organization. *Controlling the smoking epidemic*. Report of the WHO Expert Committee on Smoking Control. Technical Report Series 636. Geneva: World Health Organization, 1979.

John Crofton

Tokyo Declaration. See *Declarations*.

Torture. See *Prisoners; Tokyo Declaration* (under *Declarations*).

Tranquillizing Agents. Tranquillizers are a heterogeneous group of pharmacological agents, conventionally separated into major tranquillizers (syn. antipsychotic or neuroleptic drugs), commonly used for the treatment of schizophrenia and affective psychoses, and minor tranquillizers, used for sedation, anxiety relief and as hypnotics. However, major tranquillizers are also anxiety relieving in low dosage.

Whilst antipsychotic drugs are unquestionably the most effective drugs for treating schizophrenia and associated disorders the treatment is not curative and maintenance therapy is usually needed. Ethical problems arise because long-term therapy predisposes to a syndrome of abnormal movements called tardive dyskinesia, for which at present there is no adequate treatment. Tardive dyskinesia is an iatrogenic disease (q.v.).

Benzodiazepines are the main group of minor tranquillizers, and one of them, diazepam (Valium), is the most commonly prescribed drug in the world. Prescriptions of benzodiazepines and similar drugs are increasing year by year and concern has been expressed that doctors may be contributing to this by irresponsible prescribing, although many other factors are also involved. Although they are safe and effective antianxiety drugs, they can affect judgement and co-ordination (e.g. in driving). Because there is such a demand for minor tranquillizers the pharmaceutical industry (q.v.) is under commercial pressure to introduce new compounds that are no advance on existing ones. This unnecessary increase in new drugs, representing molecular manipulation in its worst form, combined with clever advertising, tends to lead to wasteful prescribing (q.v. See also *Drug Dependence*).

Crane GF. Persistent dyskinesia. *Br J Psychiatry*, 1973; 1: 116–21.
Leading Article. Profits from Drugs. *Br Med J* 1973; 2: 132.
Skegg DCG, Richards SM, Doll R. Minor tranquillizers and road accidents. *Br Med J* 1979; 1: 917–9.
Tyrer P. The benzodiazepine bonanza. *Lancet* 1974; 2: 709–10.

Peter Tyrer

Transcendental Meditation (TM). The TM programme of Maharishi Mahesh Yogi is a world-wide movement, which is said to bring about 'enlightenment', defined as the 'supreme awakening to the true nature of life'. The progamme 'involves a simple mental technique, practised for 15 to 20 minutes twice daily, that quickly establishes a state of deep relaxation together with increased alertness'. Courses of instruction by qualified teachers cost varying amounts for different classes of students.

Claims have been made that TM induces a deeper level of rest than sleep, reduces high blood pressure significantly, increases intelligence rapidly in schoolchildren and reduces the crime rate in cities when practised by 1 per cent or more of the population. Unlike the claims of many forms of fringe medicine, these are based on scientific research. Results, however, are not uniformly in favour of TM and claims for such benefits must be treated with caution. It is not known, moreover, whether the practice of meditation in the Western traditions would, if tested, yield similar results. (See *Fringe Medicine; Medical Science*.)

Andre ST. Some evidence that the practice of Transcendental Meditation increases intelligence as measured by a psychological test. In: *Scientific research on Transcendental Meditation; Collected Papers Vol. 1.* Los Angeles: MIU Press, 1976.

Benson H, Wallace RK. Decreased blood pressure in hypertensive subjects who practised meditation. *Circulation 1972*; Suppl. II to 45 and 46, 516.

Pollack AA, Weber MA, Case DB, Laragh JH. Limitations of transcendental meditation in the treatment of essential hyptertension. *Lancet* 1977; 1: 71–3.

Wallace RK, Benson H. The physiology of meditation. *Sci Am* 1972; 226: 516.

R. B. Welbourn.

Transfusion. See *Blood Transfusion; Bone Marrow Transfusion.*

Transplant. See *Tissue Transplant.* See also *Artifical Insemination; Blood Transfusion; Bone Marrow Transfusion; Embyro Transfer.*

Transsexuality. See *Sexual Deviations or Variations; Sex Change, Reassignment or Reversal.*

Transvestism. Sexual pleasure obtained from wearing clothes of the other sex. See *Sexual Deviations* or *Variations.*

Triage. See *Military Medicine.*

Trials. See *Clinical Trials.*

Truth, Telling the. Truth as it relates to medicine may be considered in two ways. Firstly, a patient has a legal right to expect his medical adviser to take all proper steps to elucidate the truth about his condition. A doctor who fails in this is morally wrong and legally liable; it is part of the requirement of his professional practice (see *Clinical Practice*).

Secondly, the physician or surgeon has to decide how much of this truth to impart to the patient and it is here that problems arise and different views are expressed.

With one exception, a doctor is under no *legal* duty to tell his patient the truth about his condition. The exception arises when a patient consults a doctor about his condition because he contemplates making dispositions of his property or giving other directions to a lawyer dependent on the doctor's diagnosis. The doctor may be in a dilemma, but if the patient makes his point clear, it is up to the doctor to decide whether or not to act as his adviser. If he does, he is legally obliged to tell the whole truth as he sees it; if he does not tell the truth and damage ensues, he is actionable and it would be no defence to say that he thought he was acting in the best interests of the patient. Likewise, in a compensation (q.v.) case, the patient is entitled to know the full truth of his condition so that he can decide, with legal advice, what steps to take.

Differences of opinion on the extent to which the truth should be told rest on the clinical judgement of the medical adviser and sometimes on his own moral and religious views. The law has even been known to defend a lie.[1] A surgeon told a patient about to be operated on for goitre that the operation carried no risk to her voice. He knew in fact that there was some risk but said there was none in order not to cause his patient distress. At operation damage was caused and the patient sued for negligence. At trial the judge, in summing up, declared that what the surgeon had said had been for the patient's good and was in the circumstances justifiable. The surgeon was acquitted.

Taking the other view, Rodney Smith[2] has stated: 'While we may edit the truth in the sense that favourable aspects are discussed at more length than unfavourable, we should answer the patient's questions with truth and never with a lie. The fact that his surgeon has lied almost invariably at some stage becomes clear to the patient, and from then on the chances of helping him have gone.'

The issue is what truth, and how much truth, should be told. This will vary from person to person and from time to time in the progress of an illness. Through suffering, some patients develop an inner tranquillity which enables them to accept truths which earlier could not have been borne. If the patient is dying, a hint that he should set his affairs in order may lead him to seek further advice which he might otherwise have neglected to take.[3] (See *Death, Attitudes to; Terminal Care*.)

Where questions of consent (q.v.) arise, the patient must be *adequately* informed of what is involved. What a doctor tells will depend on the circumstances, but if the truth is withheld, the layman is in no proper position to give his consent. He needs to be told three things in words he can understand. He needs to be told what is wrong with him, what it may possibly mean in the future and what medical science has to offer him. If these things are advanced carefully, the patient can make some reasonable arrangements and may also bring his usual defences to the situation at whatever level he finds necessary.[4] A patient must be capable of comprehending the truth when it is told to him. If mentally debilitated, his consent is worthless. In transplant cases the truth about the risks involved must be forced upon the healthy donor whether he wishes to hear it or not.

A conventional view is expressed as follows[5]: 'Far older than the precept, "the truth, the whole truth and nothing but the truth", is another that originates within our profession – so far as is possible, do no harm. You can do harm by the process that is quaintly called telling the truth. You can do harm by lying. It will arise also from what you say and from what you fail to say. But try to do as little harm as possible.' (See also *Communication*).

1. Br Med J 1952; 2: 106.
2. Smith R. *J Coll Surg Edinb* 1968; 15: 63.
3. Hinton J. *Dying*. Harmondsworth: Penguin Books, 1967.
4. Elland J. *Med J Aust* 1968, 1: 979.
5. Henderson HJ. *New Engl J Med* 1935; 112: 819.
Bok S. *Lying: moral choice in public and private life*. Sussex: Harvester Press, 1978.
Edmund-Davies Lord. The patient's right to know the truth, *Proceedings of the Royal Society of Medicine* 1973; 66: 533–6. (From which this article is condensed by kind permission of author and publishers.)

Edmund-Davies

Tubal Ligation. See *Sterilization*.

U

Unborn Child, Rights of.

LAW. It has always been a feature of English law that an unborn child is not a legal person. This being so, the unborn child has no legal rights. Such rights may only be asserted by someone (or some entity like a commercial company) which has legal personality and birth is the necessary precondition for asserting them in the case of a child. 'The fetus cannot in English law, in my view, have any right of its own at least until it is born and has a separate existence from the mother . . . [T]he fetus has no right of action, no right at all, until birth.' This was how the then President of the Family Division of the High Court put it in *Paton v. Trustees of BPAS*.[1]

The two most significant legal consequences of this lack of legal personality arise in the context of the law relating to (a) abortion and (b) compensation for personal injury, tort law.

(a) The abortion of a fetus cannot be legally challenged on the ground that it violates any legal rights of the fetus. This is so whether or not, in all other respects, the abortion satisfies the legal criteria laid down first by the Courts and then by Parliament in the Abortion Act 1967. Obviously, the closer in time the fetus is to full term the more reluctant the Courts and Parliament have been to countenance abortion, out of concern not only for the threat to the health of the mother, but also because it is deemed wrong to bring to an end a fetal life when so close to birth. Indeed, the Infant Life Preservation Act 1929 makes it a crime to bring about the death of a viable fetus (*prima facie*, one over twenty-eight weeks old, although the period may well soon be reduced to twenty-four weeks), except where this is necessary to preserve the life of the mother, and this Act's provisions are not affected by the later Abortion Act. Nonetheless, whatever the law on abortion, whether an abortion be lawful or not, it remains the case that there are no rights vested in the unborn child. This can easily be tested by asking whether a Court would entertain the suit of someone acting on behalf of a fetus seeking to enjoin the proposed abortion of the fetus. The clear answer is that the Court would not entertain such a suit, on the ground, *inter alia*, that the fetus has no standing before the Court, or put another way, has no right recognized by the Court. Admittedly, there exists a criminal sanction if the abortion is carried out unlawfully. If it were known that an abortion was contemplated

446

which was patently unlawful, it may be (although it is unlikely) that the Court would grant an injunction beforehand rather than leave the criminal law to impose a sanction after the event. But even in this case, the basis of the suit would be some general ground of public policy in favour of enforcing the criminal law rather than the special interest of the fetus.

(b) If a person is injured by the wilful or negligent conduct of another or in circumstances where the civil law imposes strict liability, the law of torts ordinarily provides a remedy in the form of a suit for damages. It was always assumed that this principle of law did not apply to the circumstances in which a child was born disabled because of harm suffered while *in utero*, despite the fact that the Law Commission[2] and the Pearson Report[3] both argued that an action does lie at common law. Various legal rationales were advanced; for example, that no duty was owed to the fetus which was a non-person, or that the damage was too remote. These are patently rationalizations of the Court's desire to draw some limit by choosing birth as the point at which rights and liabilities could begin to accrue. The significance of this limitation grew in recent years as the teratogenic effects of drugs became known and the possibility of a child seeking damages for disabilities induced by drugs taken by the mother while the child was *in utero* became a reality with the thalidomide tragedy. One effect of this tragedy was legislation, enacted in 1976, the Congenital Disabilities (Civil Liability) Act, whereby English law now follows most other systems of law in allowing a remedy, provided that the child is born alive. Even so, this does not confer a right on the unborn child since live birth is essential. All it creates is a 'contingent prospective right'. Thus, there is no conflict between this development and the contemporaneous existence of a law permitting abortion, for the simple reason that, 'no birth, no right'. Conflict, at least superficially, does exist, however, in the USA where the tort remedy has been taken further. In about two dozen jurisdictions the relevant Wrongful Death Statute allows the action the child would have had if born alive to pass to its next of kin if the harm caused to the fetus is so severe as to cause the child to be still-born. This looks very like the idea of a right vesting in an unborn child because it can only pass to the next-of-kin if it had already accrued. The US Supreme Court in its famous abortion decision of *Roe v. Wade*[4] dismissed the problem, perhaps a little too easily, by describing the Wrongful Death action as apparently 'one to vindicate the parents' interest and . . . thus consistent with the view that the foetus, at most, represents only the potentiality of life'.

A further tort remedy has attracted much attention recently in the USA. It is of particular medico-legal significance because it parallels developments in genetics and the practices of genetic screening and genetic counselling. A number of Courts have considered whether a child born disabled because of some genetic abnormality may sue his mother's doctor or counsellor on the ground that, had the mother been properly advised that the child was at risk, she would have been able to opt for abortion rather than giving birth. The child's claim, sometimes called a 'wrongful life' action, that he should have been aborted rather than born disabled, that there exists a right to be aborted in the fetus, if, at birth, it would be less than whole, has not yet been accepted by the US Courts. Nor has the even less attractive notion of a similar suit against the mother on the ground that her careless or reckless behaviour during pregnancy caused the subsequent birth defect. It is likely, however, that such actions will succeed relatively soon, at least against doctors or counsellors, not on the ground that the child should have been aborted but that, given he was not, he needs money and what it will buy to cope. With no developed social security system to provide it, the Courts may use the tort system as the only device whereby money may be made available and the cost spread through the community by operation of market forces. For these same reasons, such actions are unlikely to succeed in England, for, quite apart from the unattractiveness of the notion, a social security system exists as a net to catch the needy. Indeed, although this is not the place to pursue the point, a powerful argument exists for eliminating the tort system completely as a means of compensating the needy. It is expensive, very wasteful, time-consuming and unpredictable. A system of automatic rights to compensation is, perhaps, preferable based on the fact of disability rather than on a right contingent on there being someone to blame who has funds or insurance enough to meet the claim. The Chronically Sick and Disabled Persons Act 1970 makes some gesture in this direction but is grossly underfunded. It could have been hoped that the Pearson Report would have opted for this approach following the precedent set in New Zealand by the Accident Compensation Act, 1972, 3, but, apart from the numerically insignificant but politically sensitive issue of vaccine damage, the Report chose to recommend in large part the *status quo*.

Further demonstration of the lack of legal status of the fetus can be found in the practices of *in vitro* fertilization and the use of a fetus or fetal material for research. Several states in the USA, for example, California, have been persuaded to outlaw research on fetal tissue regardless of whether the fetus is viable *in utero* or is pre-viable, and whether the research is conducted either *in utero* or after abortion (whether as a fetus or as fetal material). Where there is no statute, regulations laid down by the Department of Health, Education and Welfare closely restrict the area of permitted research. Critics attack this legislation as being too extensive, prohibiting even the collection and use of fetal blood, while calls are concurrently made for research to discover the causes of, and thereby reduce, peri-natal deaths. In England no legislation exists, but it is expected of the researchers that they will comply with the detailed recommendations of the Peel Report. Although this is not a case of vesting rights in a fetus, it can be seen as seeking to protect the fetus, by law or Code of Practice, reflecting the view that, while the fetus may not be a legal person, it must be treated as something more than a thing. Some regard the issue of consent as important in this context, posing the question, whose consent as a matter of law is required before research on the fetus, if permissible, may be undertaken. Leaving aside the obvious point that the fetus cannot consent, the better answer is that if the fetus is *in utero* the consent of the mother is required since her body is involved, whatever the ultimate fate of the fetus may be. If the fetus is to be aborted, this is clear, because, if the mother can consent to abortion, she can surely consent to other invasions of the fetus. (If the circumstances did not meet the criteria for a lawful abortion, then the criminal law could be invoked, but only after the fact.) If the fetus is not to be aborted, the relevant consent is still the mother's but there are clearly limits to what she may consent to, in order not to endanger the fetus. If the fetus is not *in utero* and is pre-viable, then no consent is called for.

In the case of *in vitro* fertilization, the nature of the exercise is such that embryos are routinely discarded rather than implanted in the uterus of the participating woman. It follows from what has been said that nothing unlawful is involved. The embryo, though a potential child, has no legal personality until born.

ETHICS. Quite apart from discussions of the law, questions may be asked whether the fetus has or should have any rights such that ethical constraints should be placed on how the fetus is treated. Answers arrived at may serve both as the basis for conduct, regardless of what the law prescribes, and as grounds for urging change where necessary in the law. The difficulty in asserting rights is that they tend to represent an attempt to translate into something more worthy of respect what are in essence intuitions. Some may argue with total conviction that at the moment of conception, or, at least, the moment of implantation of the fertilized egg in the uterus, a human life has come into being. This is already a troublesome argument, turning as it does on what is intended to be conveyed by the use of the words "human life" and "come into being", (or whatever alternative words are used). And the same difficulties exist whatever criterion, e.g. viability, is used. The argument becomes more difficult when it is deduced from such assertions that the embryo or fetus has rights. Various factual statements concerning the presence of a discernible entity in the uterus are seen as compelling normative propositions that, therefore, this entity has rights, or ought to be viewed as a human being, with the necessary implication that it is endowed *ipso facto* with the various rights enjoyed by human beings who have been born.

Others, who do not accept these premises, whether secular or religious, have no difficulty in arguing that the attribution of personality to the unborn is a normative decision resting on a choice among differing and, perhaps, conflicting interests. All that can be demanded, according to this argument, is a choice which is rationally defensible and not repugnant to the enjoyment of other interests. This approach may well produce the result that personality with its attendant claims and interests should only be endowed on the child who has been born. This is a rationally defensible criterion although others may vehemently condemn and reject it. One of the advantages of choosing the point of live birth is that it allows weight to be given to the interests of the pregnant mother who may claim to do with her body (pregnant or not) what she wishes. That this claim may not be and is not wholly gratified is only to say that there are points of proper limitation. It merely thrusts the argument back to the consideration whether the fact of pregnancy should mean the total favouring of the interests (assumed) of the unborn and the total rejection of the claims of the mother. Of course, those who argue that rights are not endowed but exist *sua sponte* or by supernatural grant will reject this approach, and if they hold to the view that the unborn has rights from some particular point after conception, no further argument is necessary or possible. It is, indeed, doubtful whether this question, one of the more politically controversial topics of the age, is susceptible of resolution by resort to reason alone. (See also *Abortion; Antenatal Diagnosis; Congenital Malformations.*)

1. *Paton v. Trustees of BPAS.* 1978. 2 All. ER. 987. 89, 90.
2. Law Commission. Report on Injuries to Unborn Children. London: HMSO, 1974, Cmnd 5709.
3. Report of the Royal Commission on Civil Liberty and Compensation for Personal Injury. London: HMSO, 1978, Cmnd 7054.
4. *Roe v. Wade.* 1973. 93S. Ct. 705, 410, US 113.
California Health and Safety Code, 25956. St Paul, Minnesota: West Publishing.
Capron. *The continuing wrong of wrongful life.* Unpublished; delivered as paper, Boston, Mass., at Second National Conference on Genetics and the Law.
Edwards RG. Fertilization of human eggs in vitro: morals, ethics and the law. *Q Rev Biol* 1974; 49: 3.
Kennedy L, Edwards RG. A critique of the Law Commission report on injuries to unborn children. *J Med Ethics* 1975; 1: 116.
Park v. Chessin. NY 1978. 386 NE. 2nd 807.
Woodhouse-Meares. Report on compensation and rehabilitation in Australia. Canberra, 1974.
Vaccine Damage Payments Act, 1979.

Ian Kennedy

Unqualified Practitioners. A term used in the UK to describe those who practise various arts which are grouped together under the heading Fringe Medicine (q.v.). The term unqualified refers to their non-possession of a medical qualification or of membership of a paramedical body recognized by the medical profession in the UK. In some countries, certain of these categories (e.g. osteopaths (q.v.)) have their own association and qualification and, although they are 'unqualified' medically, enjoy a higher status *vis à vis* the medical profession in their own country than do their British counterparts. These relationships involve matters of etiquette and professional status rather than medical ethics, but when a practitioner refers a patient for further opinion it must be on the basis of a guarantee of recognized competence. That guarantee cannot be extended to unqualified practitioners and this point must be made clear when patients request such referrals. It is proper however to discuss with the patient the possibilities of benefit provided the limitations and possible dangers are also mentioned.

A. G. Donald

V

Vaccination. See *Immunization.*

Vasectomy. See *Sterilization.*

Vegliare con Sollecitudine. An Address of Pope Pius XII to the Italian Association of Catholic Midwives, 29 October, 1951, in which, while repeating the authoritative condemnations of 'birth prevention' as well as of direct sterilization, abortion and all artificial insemination, the Pope first declared the use of the 'infertile period' lawful, though guardedly and in severely restricted conditions. The Address[1] is remarkable (1) for the assurance with which it urged upon midwives the performance of their 'apostolic' function in the course of their professional duty, and (2) for the extent of the Pope's trust in their medical and scientific competence in matters beyond routine obstetric duty. 'Your advice and help are expected to be based, not on simple, popular publications, but on scientific facts and the authoritative judgment of conscientious specialists in medicine and biology. It is your office, and not that of the priest, to instruct married people . . . on the medical and biological aspect of the theory . . . But in this field, too, your apostolate demands of you as women and as Christians that you know and defend the moral law to which this theory is subordinated. And here the Church is competent to speak.' It is for them to instruct married people on the distinction between enjoying coitus during the infertile periods and restricting it to the infertile periods; even on the indications for complete abstinence when 'motherhood is unthinkable'. 'Here it is a question of concrete facts, and therefore a medical, not a theological question, and so it is within your competence.'

This teaching on 'A lawful method of regulation of birth' was reiterated by Pius XII in *Nell'Ordine della Natura*, an address to Family Associations on 26 November 1951; and there he added the hope, still being expressed in *Humanae Vitae* (q.v.) in 1968, 'that science will succeed in providing this lawful method with a sufficiently secure basis'.[2]

The principle on which this moral teaching is professedly based is 'the truth' that 'marriage, as a natural institution, is not ordered by the will of the Creator towards personal perfection of the husband

and wife as its primary end, but to the procreation and education of a new life. The other ends of marriage, although part of nature's plan, are not of the same importance as the first. Still less are they superior. On the contrary they are essentially subordinate to it.'

Signs of a will in the Roman Catholic Church to redress the balance somewhat in this statement of principle appear in *Gaudium et Spes*[3], the Pastoral Constitution of the Second Vatican Council, 1965. Where marriage is first enlarged upon, in s. 48, it is described as 'this bond, which is sacred for the good of the married parties, the children and society itself'; but this new order was not consistently maintained in the sections following, and the restriction of Roman Catholics to a guarded use of the infertile periods was re-asserted in *Humanae Vitae* in 1968. The debate continues. (See *Contraception; Rhythm Method.*)

1. English tr. In: *Marriage and the moral law.* Revised edn. London: Catholic Truth Society, 1960.
2. English tr. In: *Marriage and the moral law.* Revised edn. London: Catholic Truth Society, 1960.
3. English tr. In: *Pastoral constitution on the Church in the world today.* London: Catholic Truth Society, 1966; or in *The documents of Vatican II.* Abbott WA, ed. London, Dublin, etc: Geoffrey Chapman, 1966.

G. R. Dunstan

Venereal Disease. See *Sexually Transmitted Diseases.*

Vivisection. See *Animal Experiment.*

Voluntary Work. Literally 'work undertaken of one's own free will' (*Shorter Oxford English Dictionary*). 'Voluntary' is usually understood to imply 'honorary' (without remuneration) and the work to be 'good' (morally commendable).

Two converging streams have contributed to the tradition of medical voluntary work in Britain. The sensitive response of The Good Samaritan flowered in medieval times in the work of the monasteries (see *Christianity*), with their integral hospices, and now prospers in many organizations started individually in response to suffering, to social change and to the enormous recent advances in medical treatment (see *Medical Science*). Old age, disablement, specific disease, marriage break-down, food and drug abuse, all make demands on potential volunteers who strive to help those in need by personal involvement, mutual aid, or by raising money for support and research.

The second stream arose from concern of industrialists and churchmen in the 18th century. Shocked by discrepancies between the few poor London hospitals and the flourishing religious establishments on the continent of Europe, they raised public subscriptions to build many new hospitals. Rapid growth continued in the 19th century. Support came from local communities in various ways, including visiting and provision of comforts, galas, 'hospital Sundays', and contributory pensions schemes. The Voluntary Hospitals provided teaching centres for developing medical schools, and were peculiar to the English speaking world. They were held in great esteem and the 'honorary' medical staffs and some nursing sisters gave their services free. However, for many years, patronage, rather than medical need, determined which patients were admitted.

As the health care of the whole nation passed into the hands of the State in 1948, fears were expressed about the remaining place for voluntary service. Mr. Aneurin Bevan, then Minister of Health, replied that it would be found 'wherever the shoe pinches'. Since then, with growing assurance and official recognition and support, interest in voluntary work, both in hospitals and in the community, has greatly increased. With the active encouragement of King Edward's Hospital Fund for London (q.v.) and the Nuffield Provincial Hospitals Trust (q.v.), some health authorities employ voluntary service organizers to co-ordinate the work of volunteers in hospitals. All leaders, whether paid or honorary, are in key positions to identify problems arising in the care of the sick and to guide volunteers accordingly.

Several general ethical issues arise. For instance, organizations which collect money have a moral obligation to apply it to the purposes for which it was given, and also to minimize administrative costs. For these reasons, committees should ensure that a number of 'ordinary' volunteers, as well as the financial advisers, understand balance sheets. Money must be deployed advantageously while it awaits use. Voluntary work organizers should attempt to match the capabilities of the volunteers to the demands of the intended work. They should also advise or train them as appropriate and give continuing support in stressful situations.

The volunteer must be faithful to planned schedules, and keep strictly any confidences that the patient may impart (see *Confidentiality*). If he is a recent patient himself, he must not burden the client with his own problems. If a commitment becomes too onerous, the organizer should find, or even create, other work for the volunteer. No sense of failure should be generated.

The organizer may usefully provide a job description agreed with the unions, although compassion naturally leads many paid and unpaid workers to extend their prescribed duties. Agreements of this sort may need patience on either side, but they foster good relations and mutual understanding. Security of employment must not be jeopardized by use of extra volunteers, and indeed for the benefit of the patient the caring volunteer knows that high morale among all grades of staff is of great importance. If disagreement occurs among voluntary and paid workers, conciliation and common sense will usually restore confidence, but when difficulties persist The Volunteer Centre's* 'Guidelines' may be helpful.

In the event of industrial action a regular established voluntary organization would undertake normal work only: its volunteers should remain impartial. If the situation deteriorates, the hospital authorities may well call on those large and universally respected organizations devoted to emergency work. This is a much better solution than an emotive call to the public for volunteers, which may bring angry exchanges at the picket line and general mistrust of even the hospital's own voluntary workers. Unions have accepted other paid staff, sometimes the administrators, as volunteers. But if, in some circumstances, the general public *could* be accepted as volunteers, to undertake the hard and sometimes unpleasant duties of the striking workers, they might quickly change their attitude to the point at issue! If a strike is so effectual that an individual regular volunteer sees that patients are suffering, he may feel morally bound to go much further than his normally agreed duties. In this extreme case, the badge and uniform of the organization must be laid aside to preserve a clear distinction between his regular voluntary service and his individual emergency action. (See *Strike, the Right to*.)

In all their work volunteers face a dilemma of freedom. An individual will gain undoubted advantage from joining an organization, although this must be balanced against some loss of freedom imposed by membership. Yet all individuals and groups must cherish freedom: to identify a need, to seek fresh solutions, and to 'blaze a trail'. Voluntary work brings benefit to the giver and to the receiver, and also to the community, but when an enterprise is successful, freedom may be inhibited by the trappings of achievement. This is the time for critical re-examination of original aims, and for a listening ear.

Harris J. Caring for the sick: a look back at the voluntary tradition. *New Society*, 9th Aug. 1979, 287–90.

Ives AGL. *British hospitals*. London: Collins, 1948.

Merrison A. Royal Commission on the National Health Service. *Report*. London: HMSO, 1979, Cmnd 7615.

Moore S. *Working for free*. London: Pan Books, 1977.

Titmuss RM. *The gift relationship: from human blood to social policy*. London: Allen and Unwin, 1971.

Wolfenden J. *The future of voluntary organizations*: a report of the Wolfenden Committee. London: Croom Helm, 1978.

Woodham-Smith C. *Florence Nightingale 1820–1910*. London: Constable, 1950.

Involve, Journal of the Volunteer Centre and *The Hospital Friend*, Journal of the National Association of Leagues of Hospital

* The Volunteer Centre. 29, Lower King's Road, Berkhamsted, Herts, HP4 2AB.

Friends (both published quarterly) regularly contain important articles about voluntary work in the medical field.

Rachel Welbourn

W

Warning on Self-Medication. Self-medication is an individual's own choice and use of a medicine for himself, as distinct from one that is prescribed for a patient or client by a doctor, pharmacist or other health professional. Medication chosen by a parent for a child, or by one untrained adult for another, is intermediate between self-medication and prescribed medication. Another intermediate situation is a person's own idiosyncratic use of medication prescribed for him professionally.

Responsible and informed self-medication may be advantageous for the individual and society in that it helps to preserve the autonomy of the individual, making him independent of scarce, expensive and relatively inaccessible professional help. On the other hand, irresponsible or ill-informed self-medication may be needlessly dangerous and damaging on the grounds of (1) toxicity from inappropriate use of a reasonably chosen drug; (2) mistaken self-diagnosis leading to doubtful or ineffective treatment (e.g. tiredness self-diagnosed as anaemia when it is actually due to depression); and (3) the development of dependence, as with certain analgesics, laxatives and alcohol (when taken in a medicine).

Which medicines should be available for self-medication in a particular society, and which should be available only through some health professional (e.g. on prescription), depends on (1) the knowledge and skills required for their proper use, (2) the dangers of improper use (which include on the one hand avoidable toxicity and on the other hand continuance or progress of an illness through ineffective medication), (3) the availability of health professionals as providers. In some societies it may be desirable to permit self-medication with important medicines that elsewhere are better restricted, and universal rules cannot be made.

For an individual to choose for himself and use a medicine effectively and safely, certain minimum information about it must be available, including (1) the name of the medicine; (2) a brief description of its nature, the purpose for which it is suitable, and if appropriate the purposes for which it should not be used; (3) details of dosage and manner of use for each of the purposes stated; (4) unwanted effects with some indication of their seriousness and frequency, and what the user should do if an adverse effect occurs or is suspected;

(5) the expiry date if necessary. This information should be available as easily as the medicine itself, and preferably from the same source at the same time, whether this be shopkeeper, pharmacist or manufacturer. Since shopkeepers and manufacturers usually wish to maximize their sales, they may tend to advocate wide use of their medicines, with minimal restraints or warnings. This would introduce bias into the information supplied which would need to be compensated by countervailing biases from professional and consumer sources. The provision of objective and balanced information is a responsibility of society. It can be delegated to a Government agency or a professional body (e.g. in the UK to the Committee on Safety of Medicines, Health Education Council, Pharmaceutical Society). However, if ordinary users of medicines are to understand such information they must have grasped a few basic ideas about medicines, which would need to have been taught in schools or elsewhere.

Dunnell K, Cartwright A. *Medicine takers, prescribers and hoarders.* London: Routledge and Kegan Paul, 1972.
Graham-Smith DG. Self-medication with mood-changing drugs. *J Med Ethics* 1975; 1: 132–7.
Hodes B. Nonprescription drugs: an overview. *International Journal of Health Services* 1974; 4: 125.
Price TE, ed. Advertising over-the-counter drugs: a symposium. *Journal of Drug Issues* 1974; 4: 208.
Smith M, Kane P. *The pill off prescription.* London: Birth Control Trust, 1975.

Andrew Herxheimer

World Health Organization. The World Health Organization is a specialized agency of the United Nations constituted with the general objective of promoting 'the attainment by all peoples of the highest possible level of health'. Among its basic functions it is charged to undertake and support research activities, and the number and variety of such programmes administered both within Headquarters in Geneva and the various Regional Offices has increased in accordance with the emphasis now placed upon direct technical cooperation with Member States.

Much of this effort, which is directed particularly toward tropical disease and human reproduction, is undertaken in the developing world where prevailing socio-economic conditions and cultural influences are liable to evoke important ethical implications. Ethical assessment of all proposed studies involving human subjects is consequently undertaken by an independent secretariat committee of the Organization. However, in order to ensure that local factors receive adequate consideration, each prospective investigator must obtain formal governmental clearance of his proposal and also ensure, as a condition of funding, that the protocol satisfies a locally-based ethical review committee, either at institutional or national level.

The address of the Headquarters is: 1211 Geneva 27, Switzerland.

J. F. Dunne

World Medical Association. The World Medical Association is an association of national medical associations (though individual doctors can be Associate Members). It was founded in 1947. Great Britain is represented by the British Medical Association, which was host to the 3rd (1949) and 19th (1965) General Assemblies in London, The WMA is governed by its General Assembly, in which all the national member associations are represented, and by its Council, on which the main regions or continents of the world are represented. The Secretary-General is Dr André Wynen (of Belgium) and the central office is situated near Geneva, at 13 Chemin du Levant, 02120 Fernay-Voltaire, France.

The national medical associations of most of the world's leading countries are members of WMA. Its main function is to represent the collective conscience and views of the practising doctors of the world in relation to international organizations (such as the United Nations and the World Health Organization), to national governments (in cases where doctors are oppressed or their work unreasonably interfered with), and to the people of the world (e.g. in the Declaration of Tokyo (1975) in which the WMA set out Guidelines for doctors concerning torture and other cruel, inhuman or degrading treatment or punishment in relation to detention and imprisonment). The WMA has been active mainly in the fields of medical ethics and medical education. It sponsored the First World Conference on Medical Education in London in 1953. (See *British Medical Association; Declarations; World Health Organization*.)

E. Grey-Turner